Contents

Acknowledgements

Many thanks to the Marr family and the Pinder family with whom I gained my experience of working with children as a nanny.

Thanks also to the children and staff at the Badger's Sett Playscheme and the St. Thomas Rainbow Guides with whom I gained my experience of providing play opportunities for children in informal settings.

Thanks also to the pupils and staff at Rood End Primary School and Withymoor Primary School where I gained much of my experience of working with children in education settings.

Thanks to the students and staff at Birmingham College of Food, Tourism & Creative Studies and Sandwell College of Further & Higher Education where I first learned to devise and implement NVQ Level 3 Child Care and Education assessment materials.

Special thanks to Rebecca Brown, Karl Doughty, Chris Helm, Terry James and Pauline White for their technical support and invaluable contributions during the writing of this book.

The author and the publishers would like to thank the following for permission to reproduce material in this book:

Figure 1.1 Sally & Richard Greenhill © Sally Greenhill; Figure 3.4 © The Image Works / TopFoto; Figure 5.2 Sally & Richard Greenhill © Sally Greenhill; Figure 6.1 Sally & Richard Greenhill © Sally Greenhill; Figure 7.2 Maggie Murray/ Photofusion; Figure 8.1 Sarah Flanagan / Photofusion; Figure 10.1 Jennie Hart / Alamy; Figure 11.1 Rachel Torres / Alamy; Figure 11.3 Kevin Hatt/Photonica/Getty Images; Figure 13.1 Jacky Chapman / Photofusion; Figure 13.2 www.JohnBirdsall.co.uk; Figure 14.1 Paula Solloway / Photofusion; Figure 16.1 Jennie Hart / Alamy; Figure 16.2 Sally & Richard Greenhill © Sally Greenhill; Figure 18.1 educationphotos.co.uk/walmsley

CHILDREN'S CARE, LEARNING AND DEVELOPMENT

for NVQ & SVQ Level 3

Teena Kamen

HODDER EDUCATION
PART OF HACHETTE LIVRE UK

To my son Tom Jennings, with love and affection

Orders: please contact Bookpoint Ltd, 130 Milton Park, Abingdon, Oxon OX14 4SB. Telephone: (44) 01235 827720, Fax: (44) 01235 400454. Lines are open from 9.00 to 5.00, Monday to Saturday, with a 24-hour message answering service. You can also order through our website at www.hoddereducation.co.uk

British Library Cataloguing in Publication Data
A catalogue record for this title is available from The British Library

ISBN: 978 0 340 92939 1

First published 2007
Impression number   10 9 8 7 6 5 4 3 2
Year   2010 2009 2008
Copyright © 2007 Teena Kamen

Cover image © Digital Vision/Getty Images

Typeset by Fakenham Photosetting Ltd, Fakenham Norfolk
Printed in Malaysia for Hodder Education, part of Hachette Livre UK, 338 Euston Road, London NW1 3BH.

How to use this book

This book contains the knowledge requirements for a range of topics related to childcare. It includes practical ideas for linking knowledge and understanding with meeting the National Occupational Standards in Children's Care, Learning and Development for Level 3, and is suitable for students on a wide range of childcare courses, especially the NVQ/SVQ Level 3 in Children's Care, Learning and Development. The book may also be of interest to experienced childcare practitioners who want to update their current practice as part of their continuing professional development.

Read the relevant chapters for the Units you are currently studying and do the activities as specified. For ease of reference all chapter and section headings correspond to the Unit titles and Elements of the National Occupational Standards in Children's Care, Learning and Development for Level 3. Check the **exact specifications** for each Unit at: www.cwdcouncil.org.uk/qualifications/CCLD_level_3.asp.

Due to the holistic nature of children's care, learning and development some information is relevant to more than one Unit; to avoid repetition, detailed information on a particular topic appears only once in the book. Where this occurs you will find a **cross-reference** to the Element that includes this detailed information marked by 'see section ...' or 'Unit Links'.

You will only need to know and understand the information in the Mandatory Units and the particular Optional Units you are studying, but you may find the information in the other units useful as well. The **portfolio activities** include NVQ LINKS which also indicate cross-references. You will also find references to **websites** for key documents which can be downloaded for free by using your browser's search bar or the website's search function to find the title.

The portfolio activities can be done in any order, as appropriate to your college and/or childcare setting's requirements, and can contribute to your formal assessment, for example as part of your portfolio of evidence. However, *before* you start planning and implementing care routines, learning activities and play opportunities, it is suggested that you read **Chapter 3: Promoting children's development**. *Do* remember to follow your childcare setting or college guidelines.

Principles and values

All work within the childcare setting should be underpinned by the principles and values as stated in the National Occupational Standards in Children's Care, Learning and Development.

Principles:

1 The welfare of the child is paramount.
2 Practitioners contribute to children's care, education and learning, and this is reflected in every aspect of practice and service provision.
3 Practitioners work with parents and families who are partners in the care, development and learning of their children and are the child's first and most enduring educators.

Values:

1 The needs, rights and views of the child are the centre of all practice and provision.
2 Individuality, difference and diversity are equally valued and celebrated.
3 Equality of opportunity and anti-discriminatory practice are actively promoted.
4 Children's health and well-being are actively promoted.
5 Children's personal and physical safety is safeguarded whilst allowing for risk and challenge as appropriate to the capabilities of the child.
6 Self-esteem, resilience and positive self-image are recognised as essential to every child's development.
7 Confidentiality and agreements about confidential information are respected as appropriate unless a child's protection and well-being are at stake.
8 Professional knowledge, skills and values are shared appropriately in order to enrich the experience of children more widely.
9 Best practice requires reflection and a continuous search for improvement.

(NDNA, 2004)

Introduction: So you want to be a childcarer?

What is a childcarer?

A childcarer plans, organises and supervises a wide variety of routines and activities for children and young people within the age range of 0 to 16 years. A childcarer aims to encourage children and young people to: learn and understand about themselves and others; experiment with a variety of play and learning resources; explore the world around them; express themselves through play; develop co-operative and team building skills; develop their imaginative and creative skills.

Childcarers are involved in planning and supporting appropriate care routines, learning activities and play opportunities to promote all aspects of the development of the children they work with. A childcarer is also responsible for supervising the children at all times, ensuring that correct safety procedures are followed, encouraging positive behaviour and dealing with any challenging behaviour. A qualified childcarer will have gained a recognised childcare qualification relating to children and young people from birth to 16 years. He or she will have a detailed knowledge and understanding of: developing and promoting positive relationships in childcare settings; developing and maintaining a healthy, safe and secure environment for children; promoting children's development and learning; protecting and promoting children's rights; reflecting and developing professional practice.

Types of childcarer

Most childcarers work directly with children and/or young people by promoting and supporting children's care, learning and development through activities ranging from physical care routines to play and learning opportunities. A professional childcare practitioner may have one of these job roles: nursery nurse in a day nursery, children's centre, nursery unit, school or primary school, family support worker, childminder, home childcarer, nanny, crèche supervisor, pre-school supervisor, support worker in the health care or social care sector. Some childcarers, like an officer in charge of a day nursery, have less direct contact with children and young people; their work may involve planning, supervising, dealing with paperwork and organising childcare projects.

Childcarers may work in a wide range of childcare environments, for example: children's centres, community projects, crèches, day nurseries, extended schools, holiday playschemes, hospital children's wards, out-of-school clubs, playbuses, play centres, playgroups, pre-schools, schools and Sure Start programmes. Some childcare provision is needed during the day, for example working with the under-fives or on a children's ward in a hospital. Some childcare provision is available all year round, whereas other work is during term-time only, like in college crèches, playgroups and schools. Some childcare provision is required out of school hours (evenings, weekends and school holidays), in out-of-school clubs and on holiday playschemes. Some childcarers work with a specific group of children and/or young people, such as children with special needs, children from refugee families or children in women's refuges. Some childcarers may work away from home, e.g. at a summer camp. Childcarers may work full-time (about 35–39 hours per week) or part-time (less than 16 hours per week).

For more information contact your local council, local education department or the National Day Nurseries Association (www.ndna.org.uk). There are several recognised childcare qualifications, which can be studied full or part-time or at (see section on professional development and training opportunities in Chapter 4).

The role of the childcarer

The role of the childcarer includes planning routines and activities for each day, involving the children in planning what they are going to do. The childcarer supervises the children, at all times ensuring that all appropriate safety procedures are followed and giving first aid if required. He or she should encourage children's positive behaviour and deal with any challenging behaviour. A childcarer's role also involves setting up and putting away equipment, as well as encouraging the children to help with these tasks as appropriate to their ages and levels of development. At the end of each day, he or she evaluates the day's activities and keeps any necessary records. A childcarer may talk to parents or carers, colleagues and other professionals about the children, remembering to follow the setting's confidentiality policy. He or she must follow the correct child protection procedures if there is a suspicion that a child is being abused. A childcarer's exact duties and responsibilities will depend on the type of childcare provision, the location of the childcare setting and the age of the children or young people.

Finding employment

As a result of the National Childcare Strategy, the number of job opportunities for childcarers is growing rapidly. Employment opportunities for childcarers are available with local authorities, NHS hospital trusts, voluntary organisations and private companies like holiday operators and the leisure industry. There are many places you can look for employment, including recruitment agencies, advertisements in newspapers or specialist magazines like *Nursery World*, childcare colleges, local networks and the Internet, e.g. at www.greatcare.co.uk or www.jobs.nursery-world.com.

You can find more detailed information on finding and applying for a job in *The Nanny Handbook* by Teena Kamen (see the Bibliography at the end of this book).

Check it out

Have a look at the childcare jobs available in your area. For example: local childcare recruitment agencies in the *Yellow Pages*; local newspaper or specialist magazines; your college notice board or contact the local college; childcare vacancies on the Internet.

1

Developing and promoting positive relationships

CCLD 301
Develop and promote positive relationships

In order to develop and promote positive relationships within the childcare setting you must know and understand the principles and values for the childcare sector. This will enable you to:

◎ Ensure that children are at the centre of the childcare setting
◎ Empower children through play and learning
◎ Provide a stimulating and challenging childcare environment
◎ Ensure children's physical and personal safety within the childcare environment
◎ Respect every child as an individual
◎ Demonstrate a considerate and caring attitude towards children and their families
◎ Provide a childcare environment which is accessible to all children
◎ Provide learning activities and play opportunities to extend children's understanding of themselves, other people and the world around them
◎ Encourage co-operation between children, parents and colleagues.

You need also to know and understand: your exact role and responsibilities in the childcare setting; the roles and responsibilities of your colleagues and other professionals; the nature of your relationship with the children's parents, for example working in partnership; the childcare setting's behaviour policy, including strategies for promoting positive behaviour and dealing with negative behaviour; the childcare setting's equal opportunities policy; the childcare setting's special needs and/or inclusion policy; the childcare setting's child protection policy and the procedures to follow if you have concerns

about a child's welfare; and the childcare setting's confidentiality policy.

CCLD 301.1
Develop relationships with children

Knowledge Base

K3C154	K3C155	K3M156	K3D157	K3P159
K3C160	K3D161	K3D162	K3D163	K3D164
K3D166	K3D167	K3C171		

It is important to develop positive working relationships with children in the childcare setting because this helps to promote a positive environment in which children may participate fully and also helps to prevent or reduce disruptive behaviour. In addition it will result in a positive work environment for you and your colleagues.

You can help to develop and promote positive working relationships with children by: learning and using children's preferred names; using effective communication skills and encouraging these in the children; identifying their needs and preferences in order to provide appropriate care routines, play opportunities and learning activities; helping to organise and maintain a caring and stimulating environment; having well prepared play and learning resources; encouraging the children to take appropriate responsibilities, such as tidying up; and helping to encourage parental involvement where appropriate.

Childcarers work closely with individuals and groups of children. Your relationships with them are central to your role and must be professional without being too distant. When working with groups of children, give individual attention to each child and ensure that they all feel welcome and valued within the childcare setting. This includes encouraging them to answer questions, ask questions, make suggestions and contribute ideas that are appropriate to their ages, needs and abilities.

Code of conduct for positive interactions with children

As a childcarer you should know and understand what is meant by the terms 'appropriate' and 'inappropriate' behaviour when interacting with children, including the relevant legal requirements (see below). When working as a childcarer it is impossible to be emotionally detached – if you were, you would not be good at your job. To work well professionally you need to genuinely care about children. In addition to meeting children's physical and intellectual needs you need to provide emotional security by showing a genuine interest in everything the children say and do, as well as providing comfort when they are upset or unwell. Children can sense when they are with someone who really cares about them.

You should be able to share in the different aspects of children's lives (such as birthdays and other special occasions) without compromising your professionalism. Though you may share the highs and lows of their lives, you must maintain some detachment to be an effective childcarer. Personal friendships with children or their parents are best avoided as they can complicate your professional relationships within the childcare setting. However, if you are working in your local community this may not always be possible. If you are friends with children and/or their families outside the childcare setting, try to keep your personal and professional

lives separate. For example, do not give the child preferential treatment within the childcare setting or gossip with parents about anything that occurs there. (See section on confidentiality matters on page 19.)

Article 19 of The UN Convention on the Rights of the Child states that 'children have the right to be protected from all forms of physical and mental violence and deliberate humiliation'. (There is detailed information on the rights of children in Chapter 5.) Where there is conflict between the expectations of parents about the issue of punishment and those of the childcare setting, staff should point out to parents the setting's legal requirements under The Children Act 1989. Physical or corporal punishment is not allowed in maintained schools, day nurseries and play settings:

> 'Corporal punishment (smacking, slapping or shaking) is illegal in maintained schools and should not be used by any other parties within the scope of this guidance. It is permissible to take necessary physical action to prevent personal injury either to the child, other children or an adult or serious damage to property.'
> (Department for Health, 1991, The Children Act 1989; Volume 2, Section 6.22.)

In addition, using physical punishment is never acceptable because it teaches children that violence is an acceptable means for getting your own way. Shouting and verbal abuse are also totally unacceptable. Smacking and shouting do not work; they usually result in adults having to smack harder and shout louder to get the desired behaviour. As a consequence, children do not learn how to behave in more positive ways; they are just hurt and humiliated, which can have lasting damage on their self-esteem (see Chapters 9 and 10).

As a childcarer, you should have a strong

commitment to children, parents, colleagues and the local community. You should behave at all times in a manner that shows personal courtesy and integrity and actively seek to develop your personal skills and professional expertise. When working with children you should:

◎ Remember that their social, intellectual, physical welfare and emotional well-being is the prime purpose and first concern of the childcare setting
◎ Act with compassion and impartiality
◎ Express any criticism of children in a sensitive manner and avoid hurtful comments of a personal nature
◎ Never abuse, exploit or undermine the adult/child relationship
◎ Respect the confidentiality of information relating to children unless the disclosure of such information is either required by law or is in the best interests of that particular child (see section on confidentiality matters on page 19)
◎ Ensure that any necessary records on the children are based on factual, objective and up-to-date information.

Valuing children's individuality, ideas and feelings

Valuing children's individuality, ideas and feelings is an important aspect of developing and promoting positive relationships with children, which involves being sensitive to their needs. Children's *universal needs* (those required by *all* children) include physical or biological needs such as food, drink and shelter that are essential to *survival*. Then there are psychological needs such as love, affection, secure and stable relationships, friendships, intellectual stimulation, independence; these needs are essential to maintaining the individual's *quality of life*.

Remember that children's individual needs vary. Meeting the needs of children in childcare settings, especially where children are grouped according to age, can be difficult. Some children will have developmental needs which are in line with the expected *norm* for their chronological age, while others will have needs which are characteristic of much younger or older children. In recognising and attempting to meet children's needs, you should consider each child's age, physical maturity, intellectual abilities, emotional development, social skills, past experiences and relationships. Giving children respect and helping them to develop a positive self-image and identity will foster a caring, nurturing and responsive childcare environment.

Activity

List four ways in which you have shown you value children's individuality, ideas and feelings. Include practical examples of working with: boys and girls; children with special needs; children from different social or cultural backgrounds.

Involving children in decision-making

As a childcarer you must know and understand the importance of encouraging children to make choices and involving them in decision-making. This includes encouraging children to take responsibility for everyday tasks within the childcare setting. Young children are capable of making their own decisions and this helps to develop their independence and extends their communication skills even further. For example, children as young as 4-years-old can: be responsible for tidying up their own activities, getting equipment out (under adult supervision for safety reasons, of course); choose their own activities; and select and follow written and/or pictorial instructions for tasks/activities to be done that session.

Children have the right to be consulted and involved in decision-making about matters that affect them (UN Convention on the Rights of the Child, Article 12). They should have opportunities to be involved in the planning, implementation and evaluation of policies that affect them or the services they use (Children and Young People's Unit, 2001). Involving children in decision-making within your setting will help you to provide better childcare, based on the children's real needs rather than adult assumptions about children's needs. It will also help you to promote social inclusion by encouraging the children to participate as active citizens in their local community. Involve children in decision-making in the following ways:

◎ *Provide a suggestion box* for their comments and complaints about the childcare provision and play opportunities.
◎ *Use questionnaires and surveys* to find out their opinions about the setting's policies and procedures including any gaps in the childcare provision.
◎ *Use consultation exercises,* such as discussion groups, drama and role play activities, and music and games to provide opportunities for children to express ideas.
◎ *Direct involvement,* for example taking part in staff development and recruitment activities, assessing new initiatives, mentoring other children, providing information via leaflets, posters and IT for other children.

(Children and Young People's Unit, 2001)

Think About

How does your childcare setting involve children in decision-making?

Apply inclusive and anti-discriminatory practice in your relationships with children

Discrimination can be defined as biased and unfair treatment based on inaccurate judgements (for example prejudice) about an individual or group of people due to their age, gender, race, culture or disability. *Prejudice* is an opinion formed prematurely or without consideration of all the relevant information. It can arise as a result of ignorance about the differences (and similarities) between individuals and a lack of understanding or intolerance of other people's individual needs and preferences.

Anti-discriminatory practice in the childcare setting can be defined as words and actions that prevent discrimination and prejudice towards any individual or group of people and actively promote equal opportunities. This means ensuring that all children, parents, colleagues and other professionals are treated in an unbiased, fair and non-prejudiced way. You should check that all the childcare setting's policies, procedures and strategies demonstrate a positive and inclusive attitude towards all individuals regardless of age, gender, race, culture or disability.

Inclusive practice in the childcare setting can be defined as words and actions which encourage the participation of all children (including those with disabilities or from other minority groups) within a mainstream setting. This means ensuring that all children are valued as individuals and are given appropriate support to enable them to participate fully in the play and learning activities provided by the childcare setting.

Ten ways to develop positive relationships with children

Develop positive relationships with children by:

1 Remembering children's names and pronouncing them correctly.

2 Being approachable and willing to listen to children.

3 Listening and responding to children in ways which let children feel they are understood.

4 Giving time to children as individuals within the childcare setting.

5 Avoiding stereotyped judgements about individual children concerning race, gender, ability, religion.

6 Getting the child's own explanation of behaviour before criticising them; do not jump to conclusions.

7 Communicating with children in a sensitive way, for example do not interrupt them rudely or talk over them.

8 Showing children that they are valued and important people.

9 Being alert to children's feelings.

10 Looking at the world from a child's point of view!

PORTFOLIO ACTIVITY

1 Outline how you develop and promote positive relationships with children in your childcare setting.

2 Describe how you apply inclusive and anti-discriminatory practice in your relationships with children.

NVQ LINKS: CCLD 301.1 CCLD 305.2 CCLD 321.1

CCLD 301.2 Communicate with children

Knowledge Base

| K3C168 | K3C169 | K3C170 | K3C171 | K3C172 |

It is important to communicate with children in a manner that is clear and concise and appropriate to their ages, needs and abilities. This involves: using words and phrases that children will understand; actively listening to children; responding positively to children's views and feelings; and clarifying and confirming points to reinforce children's knowledge and understanding.

When communicating with children: ask and answer questions to prompt appropriate responses from them and to check their understanding; encourage

Unit Links

For this Unit you also need to understand the following sections:
CCLD 305.2 Implement strategies, policies, procedures and practice for inclusion (see Chapter 5)

them to ask questions and contribute their own ideas; adapt communication methods to suit their individual language needs, if, for example, they have special needs such as a hearing impairment or they are bilingual.

Effective communication with children

You should establish effective communication with children (and adults, too, of course). This involves being able to listen attentively to what they have to say. Nearly all breakdowns in communication are due to people not listening to each other. Effective communication requires *good interpersonal skills* such as:

◎ Being available; make time to listen to children
◎ Listening attentively; concentrate on what children are saying
◎ Using appropriate non-verbal skills, such as facing the child, leaning slightly towards them, smiling, nodding, open-handed gestures not clenched fists
◎ Following the rules of turn-taking in language exchanges; every person needs to have their say while others listen
◎ Being polite and courteous, no shouting, no talking over other people, avoiding sarcasm (especially with younger children, who do not understand it and can be frightened by your strange tone of voice)
◎ Being relaxed, confident and articulate
◎ Using appropriate vocabulary for your listener(s)
◎ Encouraging others to talk by asking 'open' questions (see below)
◎ Responding positively *to what is said*
◎ Being receptive to new ideas
◎ Being sympathetic to other viewpoints (even if you totally disagree with them!)
◎ Providing opportunities for meaningful communication to take place.

Listening to children

Communication is a two-way process that depends on the sender (talker) and the receiver (listener). Research has shown that adults tend to be poor listeners. You can be an active listener by: listening carefully to children's talk; considering the mood of the children during activities; and knowing how, if and when to intervene to encourage children's communication skills.

Childcarers need to spend time listening carefully to individual children and to what children have to say in small- or large-group situations, such as news time or story sessions. In order to do this effectively, childcare settings should be well-staffed with a high adult-to-child ratio. Many communications in childcare settings, especially in early education settings, relate to giving information or instructions, for example setting children on to activities and discussions in preparation for tasks. However, informal 'conversations' are an important part of communicating with children. When adults are not actively involved in the children's activities, perhaps because they are putting up displays or preparing materials for later activities, they should always be willing to listen to the children who will undoubtedly approach them to start up a conversation. Children can learn a great deal about language and the world around them from the spontaneous communications that occur during everyday activities such as break/playtime, milk/juice time, meal times, setting up/clearing away, play opportunities and learning activities.

Think About

Think of examples of effective communication including active listening from your own experiences of working with children.

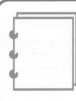

PORTFOLIO ACTIVITY

1 Listen to adults talking with children in a variety of situations within your setting both indoors and outdoors, such as circle or news time, story time, break/playtime, milk/juice time, meal times, play and learning activities.

2 Pay particular attention to the questions asked by the adults *and* the children, and *how* they are answered.

3 Consider these points:
   ◎ How effective was the communication?
   ◎ Was the adult an active listener?
   ◎ What did the children learn about communication skills, the activity and/or the environment?

NVQ LINKS: CCLD 301.2   CCLD 345.3

Recognising communication difficulties with children

All children and young people have individual language needs, but some may have additional or special needs that affect their ability to communicate effectively with others. Examples include:
◎ Autistic spectrum disorders
◎ Behavioural and/or emotional difficulties
◎ Cognitive difficulties affecting the ability to process language
◎ Hearing impairment; and physical disabilities affecting articulation of sounds.

When there are communication difficulties with children: keep information short and to the point; avoid complex instructions; speak clearly and not too quickly; be a good speech role model; build up the child's confidence gradually (for example

Unit Links

For this Unit you also need to understand the following sections:

CCLD 321.2 Help children with disabilities or special educational needs to participate in the full range of activities and experiences (see Chapter 14)

speaking one-to-one, then in a small group); encourage reluctant children to speak, but do not insist they talk; and use stories, cassettes and taped radio programmes to improve listening skills.

Communication in bilingual and multilingual settings

We live in a multicultural society in which a huge variety of languages are used to communicate. People use different accents, dialects and other ways of communicating such as sign language. All children should have an awareness and understanding of other people's languages, while still feeling proud of their own *community language* and being able to share this with others. Children in childcare settings where only English (or Welsh) is spoken still need an awareness of other languages to appreciate fully the multicultural society they live in.

Being *bilingual* may affect a child's language development and communication skills. Bilingual means 'speaking two languages' which applies to some children (and staff) in childcare settings in the United Kingdom. 'Multilingual' is used to describe someone who uses more than two languages. However, the term 'bilingual' is widely used for all children (and adults) who speak two or more languages. Children who are bilingual do not see their use of different languages as a difficulty.

Adults working in a childcare setting need to maintain this attitude and to encourage young bilinguals to see their linguistic ability as the asset it really is in our multicultural society.

It is important that you respect the languages of all the children in your setting by providing an environment which promotes language diversity through: welcoming signs in community languages; learning essential greetings in these languages; displaying photographs and pictures reflecting multicultural images; using labels with different languages/writing styles; sharing books, stories and songs in other languages; providing multicultural equipment, such as ethnic dolls, dressing-up clothes, cooking utensils; celebrating festivals; and preparing and sharing food from different cultures.

While promoting language diversity we need to remember that we live in a society in which English is the dominant language; it is essential for all children to develop language and literacy skills in

English if they are to become effective communicators both in and outside the childcare setting. Most children on starting nursery or school will speak English even if they have a different cultural background. However, there are some children who do start nursery or school with little or no ability to speak English because they are new to this country or English is not used much at home. You can support the communication skills of bilingual children by:

◎ Encouraging them to use their community languages some of the time; this promotes security and social acceptance which will make learning English easier
◎ Inviting parents/grandparents to read or tell stories in community languages or to be involved with small groups for cooking, sewing or art and design activities
◎ Using songs and rhymes to help to introduce new vocabulary
◎ Using play opportunities to develop language skills in a meaningful context, for example, focus on words used when playing in the home corner or sand pit
◎ Using games to encourage language and communication skills.

Figure 1.1 Promoting language diversity

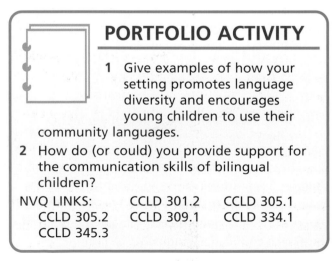

PORTFOLIO ACTIVITY

1   Give examples of how your setting promotes language diversity and encourages young children to use their community languages.
2   How do (or could) you provide support for the communication skills of bilingual children?

NVQ LINKS: CCLD 301.2   CCLD 305.1
CCLD 305.2   CCLD 309.1   CCLD 334.1
CCLD 345.3

CCLD 301.3
Support children in developing relationships

Knowledge Base

| K3C165 | K3C173 | K3D174 | K3D175 | K3D176 |
| K3D177 | K3D178 | K3D179 | K3C180 | |

Unit Links

For this Unit you also need to understand the following sections:

CCLD 321.2 Help children with disabilities or special educational needs to participate in the full range of activities and experiences (see Chapter 14)

CCLD 337.2 Promote positive aspects of behaviour (see Chapter 9)

In your role as a childcarer you will support children in developing positive relationships with other children and adults. Observing the behaviour of parents and other significant adults (childcarers, playworkers, teaching assistants, and so on) affects how children behave, how they deal with their own and other people's feelings and how they relate to others.

This is why it is so important for adults to provide positive role models for children. Good interactions with adults (and other children) in various settings encourages children to demonstrate positive ways of relating to others and using appropriate social skills. To develop positive relationships every child needs: **Security**; **Praise**; **Encouragement**; **Communication**; **Interaction**; **Acceptance**; and **Love**.

You should set limits and firm boundaries as agreed with children, families, colleagues and other professionals. To do this you will need to communicate effectively and exchange information with children according to their ages, needs and abilities. This includes understanding the possible effects of communication difficulties and attention deficit disorders. You will also need to be able to implement agreed behaviour procedures and strategies when dealing with children who continue to demonstrate challenging behaviour.

Supporting children in developing agreements about behaviour

Adults need not use aggressive or bullying tactics when trying to encourage appropriate behaviour in children. Firm discipline should include warmth and affection to show children they are cared for and accepted for who they are, regardless of any inappropriate behaviour they may demonstrate. The childcare setting should provide an appropriate framework for socially acceptable behaviour with rules to be followed by all. Language plays an important part in encouraging children to behave in acceptable ways as it enables them to: understand verbal explanations of what is and is not acceptable behaviour; understand verbal explanations of why certain behaviour is not acceptable; express their needs and feelings more clearly; avoid conflicts when handled by sensitive adults; reach compromises more easily; and have a positive outlet for feelings through discussion and imaginative play.

By about the age of 4 years, most young children will be able to demonstrate the following aspects of acceptable and positive behaviour: be fairly independent; be realistically self-controlled; have some understanding of the needs and rights of others; participate in group activities; make friends with other children; and meet the challenge of new experiences without too much anxiety.

As part of your role as a childcarer you will promote the childcare setting's policy, procedures and strategies regarding children's behaviour by consistently and effectively implementing agreements about ways to behave, such as ground rules and/or a children's code of conduct. Support children in developing agreements about ways of behaving that are appropriate to the requirements of the setting *and* their ages and levels of development.

Agreements about ways of behaving should be introduced following consultation with colleagues, children and parents. A copy of the agreement should be sent to the child's home and parents (and if appropriate, children) asked to sign as an indication of their consent and support. The agreement, which should be displayed throughout the setting as appropriate, should be brief and easy

to learn and should include rules that the setting will enforce. The reason for each rule should be obvious, but staff should also explain these to the children they work with in a manner that is appropriate to their age and level of development. The agreement may be applied to a variety of situations and should be designed to encourage children to develop responsibility for their behaviour. For example, an early education setting might set out its expectations for children's behaviour in a *home-school agreement* in the section on what the school expects of its pupils including the school's expectations for pupil behaviour and discipline, for example a children's code of conduct.

Example of a Children's Code of Conduct

1 Treat everyone and everything with respect.
2 Try to understand other people's points of view.
3 Make it as easy as possible for children to learn and for adults to teach by:
   ◎ Arriving on time with everything you need for the day
   ◎ Listening carefully, following instructions, not interrupting when an adult is talking
   ◎ Helping each other when you can
   ◎ Working quietly and sensibly without distracting or annoying your classmates.
4 Move sensibly and quietly around the school. This means:
   ◎ Never running, barging or shouting
   ◎ Opening doors or standing back to let people pass
   ◎ Helping to carry things.
5 Always speak politely to everyone, children and adults alike. Never shout.
6 Be silent whenever you are required to be. If the class is asked a question, put up your hand and answer. Do not call out.
7 Take pride in your personal appearance, attending school clean and dressed appropriately.

8 Keep the school clean and tidy so that it is a welcoming place we can all be proud of by:
   ◎ Putting all litter in bins
   ◎ Keeping walls and furniture clean and unmarked
   ◎ Taking great care of displays, particularly of other people's work.
9 Leave toys, jewellery, etc. at home as these can get lost or damaged or can cause arguments.
10 Always remember when out of school, walking locally or with a school group that the school's reputation depends on the way you behave.

Negotiating goals and boundaries

Developing agreements about ways of behaving should include negotiating appropriate goals and boundaries for behaviour. Goals are the *expectations* for behaviour, usually starting with 'Do'. Boundaries are the *limitations* to behaviour, often starting with 'Don't'. Negotiating goals and boundaries involves teaching children to develop self-control and to respect other people and their possessions. Negotiation should take into account: the ages and levels of development of the children; their individual needs and abilities; the social context, for example the type of childcare setting, the activity or the group size. Negotiating goals and boundaries involves adults: seeing things from a child's point of view; respecting their needs and ideas; realising they will test boundaries from time to time; having realistic expectations for their behaviour; and

Figure 1.2 Negotiating goals and boundaries

recognising the limitations of some children's level of understanding and memory skills.

Children are more likely to keep to goals and boundaries if they have some say about them. They need to be active participants, not only in following ground rules but also in establishing them. Having a feeling of ownership makes rules more real and gives children a sense of control.

Some children may not recognise or accept ground rules or share the same views about what is acceptable behaviour. Remember that some children from different social or cultural backgrounds may have varying expectations of behaviour. Where they are given clear guidelines for behaviour at home, they are much more likely to understand and keep to rules, goals and boundaries in the childcare setting. Your use of interpersonal skills with children, parents and colleagues should provide a good role model for children's behaviour and effective working relationships.

> **Think About**
>
> What are the goals and boundaries that might be appropriate to the children you work with in your childcare setting?

Encouraging children to recognise and deal with feelings

An essential aspect of supporting children in developing relationships is helping them to recognise and deal with their own feelings and those of other people. Feelings can be defined as: an awareness of pleasure or pain; physical and/or psychological impressions; experience of personal emotions such as anger, joy, fear or sorrow, and interpersonal emotions such as affection, kindness, malice or jealousy.

In British society we are often encouraged to keep our feelings to ourselves. Males may be discouraged from showing the more sensitive emotions, while females may be discouraged from demonstrating the more aggressive ones. Babies and very young children naturally express clearly how they feel by crying, shouting and rejecting objects. They will openly show affection and other emotions such as jealousy or anger. Young children do not understand that others can be physically or emotionally hurt by what they say or do. Gradually, children become conditioned to accept that the feelings and needs of others *do* matter.

We need to ensure that children do not forget their own feelings and emotional needs by becoming too concerned about the feelings of others or trying to please them. Children need to know that it is natural to experience a wide range of emotions and that it is acceptable to openly express strong feelings such as love and anger as long as they do so in positive and appropriate ways.

Help children to recognise and express their feelings through:

◎ Books, stories and poems about feelings and common events experienced by other children to help them recognise and deal with these in their own lives
◎ Creative activities to provide positive outlets for feelings, including: pummelling clay to express anger; and painting/drawing pictures or writing stories and poems which reflect their feelings about particular events and experiences
◎ Physical play or sports involving vigorous physical activity that allow a positive outlet for anger or frustration
◎ Drama or role play activities to act out feelings,

for example: jealousy concerning siblings; worries over past experiences; and fears about future events such as a visit to the dentist.

Babies and very young children are naturally egocentric; their belief that the world revolves around them and their wishes often makes them appear selfish and possessive. As children develop they begin to think and care about others as well as themselves. We have all experienced jealousy in our relationships with others, for example with siblings, friends, neighbours, colleagues and employers. Unchecked jealousy can be a very destructive and hurtful emotion that prevents children (and adults) from developing respect and care for others. Help children to cope with any feelings of jealousy they may have towards others by:

◎ Avoiding comparisons between children (especially siblings). For example, do not make comments like 'You're not as quiet as your brother' or 'Why can't you behave more like that group of children?'
◎ Encouraging children to focus on their own abilities. Emphasise co-operation and sharing rather than competition. Comparisons should be related to improving their individual skills.
◎ Understanding the reasons for a child's jealousy. Children feel better when adults acknowledge their feelings. Do not make children feel guilty about being jealous.
◎ Treating all children with respect and fairness. Take children's individual needs into account. Children may require varying amounts of adult attention at different times. Equality of opportunity does not mean treating everyone exactly the same, as this would mean ignoring individual needs; it means treating individuals fairly and providing the same *chances*.
◎ Reassuring children they are accepted for who they are regardless of what they do. Try to spend a few minutes with each child in your group. Give

regular individual attention to help to reduce jealousy and increase children's emotional security.

Activity

Describe an activity which supports children in understanding other people's feelings, such as sharing a story or poem about feelings and common events experienced by other children. Give an example from your own experiences of working with children.

Helping children to deal with conflict themselves

Be aware of the childcare setting's policy for dealing with conflicts and be clear about your own responsibilities, for example when and how to intervene, remembering the children's and your own safety, procedures for reporting incidents, use of sanctions, and so on. Many young children may find it difficult to co-operate with other children in group activities. Disputes are frequent, especially among young children. Often these quarrels are short-lived; early friendships are easily broken but just as quickly mended. Learning to deal with these disputes is an important part of children's social and emotional development. Very young children will use physical force to maintain ownership of a toy, but by 3 to 4 years of age they begin to use language to resolve disputes; for example 'That's mine!' By 5 to 6 years of age children continue to use language to resolve disputes and co-operate with others; for example 'After Shafiq's turn, it's my go.' Older children will use language to negotiate and compromise when there are disagreements; for example 'Let me borrow your blue felt-tip and you can use my red gel pen.' However, even some older children, such as those who have behavioural or emotional difficulties, may sometimes find it difficult to share with others. In childcare settings it is inevitable that arguments and fights will occur between children. All children will experience situations in which they feel that life is not fair. They will have disputes and disagreements with others. Initially children rely on adults to help resolve these disputes, but gradually they learn how to deal with these for themselves. Children need to learn how to use language to reach agreements so that as far as possible their needs and other people's can be met fairly.

There are only three possible ways to resolve conflicts:

1 To fight or bully: being aggressive, '*I win so you lose*'

2 To submit or retreat: being submissive or passive, '*I lose because you win*'

3 To discuss and negotiate: being assertive, '*I win and you win*'.

Children need to learn that the best way to resolve conflicts does not mean getting your own way all the time (being aggressive) or allowing others to get their own way all the time (being submissive or passive). The best way to resolve conflicts is to reach a satisfactory compromise by being assertive. Point out to children that neither shouting nor using physical violence resolve conflicts; they usually make matters worse and only demonstrate who is the loudest or strongest or has more power. Conflicts need to be discussed in a calm manner so that a mutually agreed compromise can be reached. Use books, stories and videos that depict potential conflict situations such as: sharing play equipment or borrowing toys; deciding on rules for a game or choosing a game; choosing partners or teams fairly; knocking over models or spoiling activities *accidentally*; or disrupting other children's play activities *deliberately*.

You could discuss the following with the children afterwards:

◎ What was the cause of the conflict?
◎ How was the conflict resolved?
◎ What were the best solutions?
◎ How would *they* resolve a similar conflict?

Younger children can do this type of activity with appropriate situations and guidance from sensitive adults. Using puppets and play people can also help. Where children are used to doing role play activities or drama, adults can get them to act out how to resolve conflicts in fair and peaceful ways.

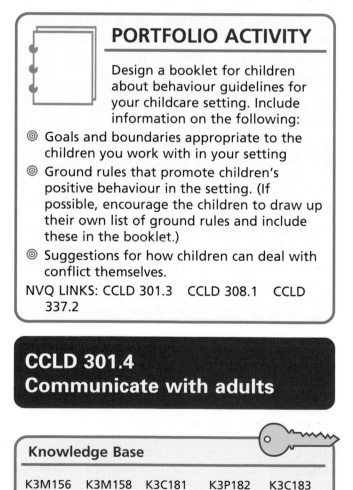

PORTFOLIO ACTIVITY

Design a booklet for children about behaviour guidelines for your childcare setting. Include information on the following:

◎ Goals and boundaries appropriate to the children you work with in your setting
◎ Ground rules that promote children's positive behaviour in the setting. (If possible, encourage the children to draw up their own list of ground rules and include these in the booklet.)
◎ Suggestions for how children can deal with conflict themselves.

NVQ LINKS: CCLD 301.3   CCLD 308.1   CCLD 337.2

CCLD 301.4
Communicate with adults

Knowledge Base

K3M156	K3M158	K3C181	K3P182	K3C183
K3C184	K3C185	K3C186		

Establishing and developing good working relationships with colleagues is important because this helps to maintain a positive childcare environment that benefits children, parents and staff. Good working relationships will also reflect the childcare setting's aims such as: providing a caring environment that fosters co-operation and respect; encouraging children's all-round development; delivering play and learning opportunities in stimulating and appropriate ways; and working in partnership with parents and the local community.

As a childcarer you should have a strong commitment to children, colleagues, parents and the local community and behave at all times in a manner that demonstrates personal courtesy and integrity. Additionally, actively seek to develop your personal skills and professional expertise.

With regard to colleagues in the childcare setting, you should:

◎ Have a duty of care towards your colleagues
◎ Demonstrate an awareness of the work-related needs of others
◎ Remember confidentiality in discussions with colleagues concerning problems associated with their work
◎ Respect the status of colleagues, particularly when making any assessment or observations on their work
◎ Never denigrate a colleague in the presence of others
◎ If relevant to your role, be frank and act in good faith in all matters relating to appointments at work and provide references that are fair and truthful.

(For more information see Chapter 18.)

With regard to parents and carers in the childcare setting, you should:

◎ Help parents and carers to feel welcome and valued in the setting

◎ Seek to establish a friendly and co-operative relationship with parents and carers
◎ Never distort or misrepresent the facts concerning any aspect of their children's care, learning and development
◎ Respect the joint responsibility that exists between the setting and parents/carers for the development and well-being of their children
◎ Respect parental rights to enquiry, consultation and information with regard to the development of their children.

(For more information see Chapter 16.)

Ensure that you use language that other adults (including parents/carers, colleagues, parent helpers, volunteers and students) are likely to understand. Try to avoid 'jargon' or technical language unless you are sure that your listener understands its meaning. Any requests for information from colleagues or parents which are beyond your knowledge and expertise, or any difficulties in communicating with colleagues or parents, should be referred to the appropriate person, such as the senior practitioner or setting manager. You may need guidance on how to handle sensitive situations regarding your interactions with some colleagues or parents, especially when a derogatory remark is made about another colleague/parent or when the childcare setting policies are disregarded (see section on handling disagreements below).

Sharing information with colleagues

You will be working as part of a team with other childcarers including the senior practitioner or setting manager. Your colleagues will need regular information about your work, for example feedback about play and learning activities, as well as updates about children's participation and/or developmental progress. Some of this information may be given orally, for example outlining a child's participation and developmental progress during a particular play opportunity or commenting on a child's behaviour. Even spoken information needs to be given in a professional manner; that is to the appropriate person (the senior practitioner), in the right place (not in a corridor where confidential information could be overheard) and at the right time (urgent matters need to be discussed with the senior practitioner immediately while others may wait until a team meeting). Some information, such as activity plans, notice boards, newsletters, staff bulletins and records, will be in written form.

Sharing information with parents and carers

As parents usually know more than anyone else about their children and their needs, it is important to listen to what they have to say. Actively encourage positive relationships between parents (or designated carers) and the childcare setting. When communicating with them use their preferred names and modes of address; for example make sure that you use the correct surname, especially when a woman has changed her name following divorce or remarriage. Only give information to a parent that is consistent with your role and responsibilities within the childcare setting. Any information shared with parents must comply with the confidentiality requirements of the setting and you should ensure that it is relevant, accurate and up to date.

Confidentiality matters

It is important that you observe confidentiality when sharing information. Only the appropriate people should have access to confidential records. Except where a child is potentially at risk, information should not be given to other adults or agencies unless previously agreed. Where it is acceptable to pass confidential information then it should be given in the agreed format. Always follow the childcare setting's policy and procedures on confidentiality and sharing information. Check with the senior practitioner or setting manager if you have any concerns about these matters. You also need to be aware of any legal requirements with regard to record keeping and accessing information in your childcare setting, such as the Data Protection Act 1998.

The basic provisions of the Data Protection Act relevant to childcarers

Under the *Data Protection Act 1998* all settings that process personal information must comply with the eight enforceable principles of good practice. Personal data must be:

- Fairly and lawfully processed
- Processed for limited purposes
- Adequate, relevant and not excessive
- Accurate
- Not kept longer than necessary
- Processed in accordance with the data subject's rights
- Secure
- Not transferred to countries without adequate protection.

The Data Protection Act also safeguards the storage of data kept on computers including hard drives and floppy disks. All records relating to personal information must be kept securely within the childcare setting and the person to whom the records refer should have access to them. Under the Data Protection Act 1998:

'... an individual is entitled:

(a) to be informed by any data controller whether personal data of which that individual is the data subject are being processed by or on behalf of that data controller,

(b) if that is the case, to be given by the data controller a description of ~
  (i) the personal data of which that individual is the data subject,
  (ii) the purposes for which they are being or are to be processed, and
  (iii) the recipients or classes of recipients to whom they are or may be disclosed,

(c) to have communicated to him in an intelligible form ~
  (i) the information constituting any personal data of which that individual is the data subject, and
  (ii) any information available to the data controller as to the source of those data ...'

(Section 7(1) Data Protection Act, 1998)

Under the Data Protection Act 1998 certain information is exempt from disclosure and should not be shared with other service providers. This includes:

◎ Material that would be likely to cause serious harm to the physical or mental health or emotional condition of the child or someone else
◎ Information about whether the child is, or has been subjected to, or may be at risk of suspected child abuse
◎ Information that may form part of a court report
◎ References about pupils supplied to another school, any other place of education or training, any national body concerned with student admissions.

The childcare setting's requirements regarding confidentiality

You may find that the parents or carers of the children you work with will talk to you about their problems or give you details about their family. Senior staff at your childcare setting may also tell you confidential information to help you understand the needs of particular children and so enable you to provide more effective support. Whenever a parent or colleague gives you confidential information you must not gossip about it.

However, you may decide to pass on information to colleagues on a 'need to know' basis; for example, to enable other members of staff to support the child's care, learning and development more effectively or where the child might be in danger. If you think that a child is at risk then you must pass on confidential information to an appropriate person, such as the senior practitioner or the member of staff responsible for child protection issues in your childcare setting. If you decide to pass on confidential information then you should tell the person who gave you the information that you are going to do this and explain that you have to put the needs of the child first. Remember that every family has a right to privacy and you should only pass on information in the genuine interests of the child or to safeguard their welfare.

Recognising communication difficulties with adults

Some adults, such as those with a hearing impairment or physical disabilities that affect their ability to articulate sounds, may find it difficult to communicate effectively with others. In addition,

Unit Links

For this Unit you also need to understand the following sections:
CCLD 305.3 Maintain and follow policies and procedures for protecting and safeguarding children (see Chapter 5)

you may meet parents who speak little or no English. Childcarers who have additional communication skills may be very useful in the childcare setting; for example the ability to use sign language to communicate with an adult who has a hearing impairment or bilingual childcarers who can liaise with parents whose community language is not English. Through sharing local community languages childcarers may help parents and carers to feel more welcome in the setting and help to avoid possible misinterpretations concerning cultural differences.

Requests for information that are beyond your role and responsibilities or any difficulties in communicating with other adults should be referred to the appropriate person, for example the senior childcare practitioner. You may need guidance on how to handle sensitive situations that may arise in your interactions with some adults, especially when they make derogatory remarks about another adult or disregard setting policies.

Handling disagreements with other adults

As a professional childcarer you need to be able to recognise and respond to any problems that affect your ability to work effectively. This includes dealing appropriately with disagreements and conflict situations that affect your working relationships with other adults. Conflicts and disagreements are a part of everyone's working life. If communication and working relationships break down, then conflict situations may arise that seriously damage the atmosphere in the childcare setting. Conflicts and disagreements can occur between you: and the children; the children's parents or carers; your colleagues; and other professionals. Most conflicts in the workplace arise due to: concerns about duties and responsibilities; disagreements about children's behaviour; disagreements about management issues; clashes concerning different lifestyle choices; and clashes between personalities.

Conflicts can also arise due to prejudice or discrimination. Incidents of such attitudes or behaviour must be challenged, as they are not only undesirable but also unlawful. However, it is essential to follow the childcare setting's policy and procedures together with any relevant legal requirements when dealing with these issues.

Many disagreements and conflicts can be resolved through open and honest discussion. This will involve arranging a mutually convenient time to talk to the other adult about the problem and may include the senior practitioner or setting manager. Sometimes another person can act as a mediator to help those involved to reach a satisfactory agreement or compromise. When handling disagreements with other adults you should remember the following important points:

◎ Focus on the facts by stating the exact nature of the problem
◎ Avoid making personal comments – be tactful!
◎ Suggest a possible and practical solution
◎ Be prepared to compromise if at all possible.

The best way to resolve conflicts or disagreements is to be assertive by discussing and negotiating a compromise that suits everyone to bring about a win/win solution to the problem. Remember, compromise equals wise! Always follow your setting's procedures for dealing with conflicts with (including complaints from) parents and carers. This may mean taking direct action and/or reporting your concerns to someone who has the authority to deal with these difficulties, such as the senior practitioner or setting manager, if you cannot resolve them or they are outside your role/beyond your capabilities.

For more information on how to deal with serious disagreements or conflict situations, see grievance and disciplinary procedures in Chapter 18.

Unit Link

For this Unit you also need to understand the following sections:
CCLD 338 Develop productive working relationships with colleagues (see Chapter 18)

PORTFOLIO ACTIVITY

1 List examples of how you communicate and share information with other adults in your childcare setting.
2 Describe how you handled any communication difficulties with adults in your setting. Remember confidentiality.
3 Outline your childcare setting's procedures for dealing with conflict.
4 Describe how you handled a disagreement with another adult in your setting. Remember confidentiality.

NVQ LINKS: CCLD 301.4   CCLD 305.3   CCLD 326.1   CCLD 328.2   CCLD 330.3   CCLD 338

2 Developing and maintaining a healthy, safe and secure environment for children

CCLD 302
Develop and maintain a healthy, safe and secure environment for children

As a professional childcarer you are responsible for developing and maintaining a healthy, safe and secure environment for children. This includes establishing and maintaining safe working procedures among colleagues and children. You also need to plan effective procedures for use in case of fire and for evacuating the setting, in addition to knowing the procedures to be followed in case of accidents, injuries and illnesses.

CCLD 302.1
Establish a healthy, safe and secure environment for children

Knowledge Base

| K3S187 | K3P189 | K3S190 | K3S191 | K3S192 |
| K3S194 | | | | |

You will need to know, understand and follow the legal and organisational requirements of the childcare setting for establishing and maintaining the health, safety and security of yourself and others at all times, as well as the procedures for reporting any concerns or problems to the appropriate person. As part of your role you need to contribute to reviewing and revising your setting's health and safety procedures in order to meet new requirements and changes in circumstances and to make improvements.

It is important that you use safe working practices in all that you do, which includes ensuring that someone in authority (for example a senior practitioner and/or your line manager) knows where you are at all times in case of an emergency. You should also know the local and national requirements regarding health, hygiene, safety and supervision in the childcare setting, including: access to premises; storerooms and storage areas; and the health and safety requirements for the materials and equipment being used.

Statutory and regulatory health and safety requirements

Professional childcarers need to be aware of the statutory and regulatory health and safety requirements for children, workers, families and visitors in the childcare setting. Health and safety legislation places overall responsibility for health and safety with the employer. However, as an employee working within a childcare setting you also have responsibilities with regard to maintaining health and safety. All employees have a responsibility under the Health and Safety at Work Act 1974 to:

◎ Take reasonable care for the health and safety of themselves and of any person who might be affected by their acts or omissions at work
◎ Co-operate with the relevant authorities (for example Ofsted) in meeting statutory requirements
◎ Not interfere with or misuse anything provided in the interests of health, safety and welfare
◎ Make themselves aware of all safety rules, procedures and safe working practices applicable

to their posts. (When in doubt they must seek immediate clarification from the delegated person responsible for health and safety in the setting)

◎ Ensure that tools and equipment are in good condition and report any defects to the delegated person

◎ Use protective clothing and safety equipment provided and ensure that these are kept in good condition

◎ Ensure that any accidents, whether or not an injury occurs, are reported to the delegated person

◎ Report potential hazards or any possible deficiencies in health and safety arrangements to the delegated person.

The Workplace (Health, Safety and Welfare) Regulations 1992 clarify and consolidate existing legislation. They also establish a consistent set of standards for the majority of workplaces. The regulations expand on the responsibilities placed on employers (and others in control of premises) by the Health and Safety at Work Act 1974 including: health and safety in the workplace; welfare facilities for people at work; and maintenance of the workplace.

The workplace and equipment need to be maintained in an efficient state, in working order and in good repair. Buildings, including mobile or temporary rooms, should be in a good state of repair and services should be in efficient working order. In general, indoor workplaces should be reasonably comfortable, reasonably clean, properly illuminated and adequately spacious.

The environmental requirements of the regulations apply to the workplace, but existing education standards for children's working space, temperature and ventilation and so on, may be more appropriate for some childcare and education settings, for example nursery units, schools and after-school

clubs. The Education (School Premises) Regulations 1999 provide the statutory requirements for the minimum standards of both new and existing schools. The regulations include a general requirement that all parts of the school's premises must be reasonably maintained to ensure the health, safety and welfare of all users. These regulations also include the specific requirements for: acoustics, ancillary facilities, drainage, heating, lighting, medical accommodation, playing fields, washrooms, staff accommodation, structural matters, ventilation, water supply and weather protection.

The Management of Health and Safety at Work Regulations 1999 require a risk assessment of facilities, a safety policy regarding these risks and appropriate health and safety training. You should be able to recognise any risks within the childcare environment and take the appropriate action to minimise them, for example report potential health and safety hazards to the relevant person. (See section on risk assessment below.)

The Day Care National Standards

Depending on the type of childcare provision and the age of the children using the setting the Day care and childminding (National Standards) (England) Regulations 2003 may apply to your childcare setting. There are 14 National Standards that are accompanied by supporting criteria for the five categories of day care and childminding provision, that is full day care, sessional day care, crèches, out-of-school care and childminding. Regulations under the Children Act 1989 require providers to meet the 14 standards and the relevant supporting criteria. Some criteria have been amended – see the *Day care and childminding: guidance to the National Standards* revisions to certain criteria October 2005. The National Standards do not supersede other relevant legislation such as health and safety, food hygiene, fire and planning requirements.

Regulations for manual handling

The Manual Handling Operations Regulations 1992, as amended in 2002, apply to manual handling activities such as lifting, lowering, pushing, pulling and carrying. The load being handled may be a box, trolley, person or animal. The Regulations require employers to:

◎ Avoid the need for hazardous manual handling, so far as is reasonably practicable
◎ Assess the risk of injury from any hazardous manual handling that cannot be avoided
◎ Reduce the risk of injury from hazardous manual handling, so far as is reasonably practicable.

The Regulations require employees to:

◎ Follow appropriate systems of work laid down for their safety
◎ Make proper use of equipment provided for their safety
◎ Co-operate with their employer on health and safety matters
◎ Inform the employer if they identify hazardous handling activities
◎ Take care to ensure their activities do not put others at risk.

(HSE, 2004)

You should be aware of the risks associated with lifting and carrying children, for example possible back injuries. Ensure that you follow your setting's procedures for lifting and carrying children.

The Health and Safety Executive (HSE) provides guidance on manual handling (see Further reading). (See section on risk assessment applicable to the childcare setting.)

Safety checks of the children's indoor and outdoor environment

It is important that you know the location of safety equipment in the different areas of the childcare environment. You must be clear about the safety arrangements for the areas and children you work with including: the position of fire exits, extinguishers, blanket, first aid boxes; your role during fire drill; what to do in case of fire or other emergency, especially the procedures for children with physical disabilities or sensory impairments, escape routes and alternatives if blocked by fire, and so on.

Facilities and equipment

Storage areas should be kept tidy with sufficient space for the materials and/or equipment being stored there. They should be easily accessible and lockable; any potentially hazardous materials must be stored away from children and locked away. Storage space should be organised so that heavy equipment is stored at a low level. Lightweight equipment may be stored above head level if space is limited. One of your responsibilities may be to ensure that all equipment and surfaces are safe, hygienic and usable. If working with children who have been using messy materials such as glue or paint, you will need to wipe tables or easels after they have finished and clean any brushes so that they are ready for use again.

All equipment should be safe and approved for safety, for example displaying the BSI Kitemark, European standards markings or BEAB mark of safety. You should know the operating procedures and safety requirements of your setting before using any equipment. Operating instructions should be available and in many cases an experienced/ knowledgeable member of staff may show you how to use the equipment beforehand. If not, it is essential to ask, especially when dealing with electrical equipment because of safety or the possibility of damaging expensive equipment – you do not want to cause hundreds or even thousands of pounds worth of damage to a computer or photocopier. Follow any instructions carefully. Allow yourself plenty of time to do this thoroughly. Do not start learning how to use the setting's video player for the first time five minutes before you need to show a group or class a video; it is not the time to do so and is also unprofessional. As for any activity, you need to plan ahead. Make sure you understand the specific requirements for equipment used by you and/or the children for activities such as: art and design; indoor and outdoor play; cooking; information and communication technology; physical education; and science.

Toy safety

Every year in the UK over 35,000 children under the age of 15 years are treated in hospital following an accident involving a toy (Child Accident Prevention Trust, 2004b). It is essential to provide children with toys that are appropriate for their ages and levels of development. Most toys will have a suggested age range. It is a legal requirement for all toys sold in the European Union to carry a CE mark but this does not necessarily guarantee safety or quality. When selecting toys for children, always look for one of the following safety marks: European Standard BS EN 71 (to show that the toy has been tested to the agreed safety standards); or the Lion Mark (to show that the toy has been made to the highest standards of safety and quality).

Play areas and playgrounds

There is a duty under Sections 3 and 4 of the Health and Safety at Work Act 1974 to ensure the health and safety of users of playground equipment as far as is reasonably practicable (RoSPA, 2004a). Evidence of good practice includes compliance with the relevant safety standards, for example EN 1176 for children's playground equipment and EN 1177 for playground surfaces. Safety checks for indoor play areas and outdoor play areas/playgrounds include:

◎ Inspecting the play area/playground equipment on a regular basis
◎ Reporting any faults to the appropriate person promptly
◎ Ensuring that children do not use the faulty equipment until mended or replaced
◎ Getting the necessary repairs done as quickly as possible
◎ Having an annual inspection by an independent specialist.

(See section on maintaining children's safety during play and learning activities.)

Activity

1 List the main play equipment used in your childcare setting.
2 How did/could you find out how to use each piece of play equipment?
3 What are the setting's safety arrangements regarding the use of indoor and outdoor play equipment?
4 What are the setting's procedures for reporting faulty or broken play equipment?

Toilet and wash areas

It is important that toilet and wash facilities are maintained in a clean and orderly condition with adequate lighting and ventilation. In childcare settings, there should be a separate base room for children under the age of 2 years with hygienic nappy changing facilities. For children over the age of 2 years there should be one toilet and hand basin for every ten children. An adequate supply of easily accessible drinking water should be made available to children. There should be separate toilet facilities for children and staff and the setting should ensure there are regular and thorough cleaning routines for toilets and washbasins to ensure the facilities are maintained to high standards of hygiene. Adequate supplies of toilet paper, soap, warm water and disposable paper towels and/or access to hot air driers should be provided. To minimise the spread of infection, the setting should advise parents whose children have diarrhoea that the children should stay away from the setting until they no longer have symptoms.

Your role may involve checking children's toilet areas to see that they are used correctly and that children wash their hands after using the toilet or before handling food. You may be required to assist very young children (or children with physical disabilities) with their toileting needs. It is important that you know the setting's procedures for dealing with children who wet or soil themselves, including the location of appropriate spare clothing.

You may need to provide reassurance and support for a girl who starts menstruation but does not have any sanitary protection. (Girls as young as 8 or 9 years of age can start their first period while at the setting.) Familiarise yourself with the setting's procedures for dealing with this situation, including accessing emergency supplies of sanitary protection and its disposal. If you are a male childcarer then you must know who to go to for help if this situation occurs.

If you experience any concerns or problems with children when carrying out hygiene routines, you should report these to the senior practitioner or your line manager. This includes reporting any hazard or unsafe situation you discover when using the setting's toilet or wash facilities.

Check it out

1 What are your setting's procedures for checking toilet and wash areas?
2 What are your responsibilities for checking these areas?

The movement and activity of children

Childcare settings cater for the arrival and departure of children, families, workers and visitors either as pedestrians or in vehicles, including delivery vans and taxis for children with special needs. Traffic routes should be properly organised so that both pedestrians and vehicles can move safely in and around the setting. Particular care should be taken of everyone using or having access to the premises, especially young children and people with disabilities. The setting may have to cope with large numbers of children and workers moving around during busy periods, for example the start and finish of sessions. Care should be taken to avoid accidents such as slips, trips or falls, particularly in main corridors and staircases. Floor surfaces should be appropriate for their use and free from hazards or obstructions that might cause people to trip or fall. Particular attention should be given to: holes, bumps and uneven surfaces; wear and tear on carpeted areas; procedures for dealing with spillages; snow and ice on external pathways; precautionary measures prior to repairs, for example barriers and alternative routes.

Security arrangements for children's arrival at and departure from the setting

You must know and follow your setting's policy and procedures for gaining access to the premises, for example entry systems, visitors' book and identity tags for visitors in the childcare setting. Security arrangements should include registration systems, such as a record of the time of arrival and departure of children and staff; a visitors' book to record name of visitor, who they are/who they work for, time of arrival, who they are visiting, car registration if applicable and time of departure. Anyone visiting the childcare setting for the first time should provide proof of identity. Children should never be left unattended with an adult who is not a member of staff.

A child must not be allowed to leave the childcare setting with an adult who does not usually collect the child, without prior permission. You should also know and follow your setting's policy and procedures for uncollected children or the late arrival of a parent/carer to collect children. Procedures for uncollected children may include:

◎ Set a time limit as to when to implement uncollected child procedures
◎ Inform parents/carers about the setting's uncollected child policy and, where applicable, the late collection fee
◎ Ensure a minimum of two staff members are on site to safeguard both child and staff

◎ Inform the senior practitioner or setting manager the child has not been collected
◎ Attempt to contact parent or carer
◎ Use registration form to find emergency contacts
◎ Never take the child home yourself
◎ Never allow someone else to take the child home unless authorised by the parent/carer
◎ If nobody can be contacted then the police/social services must be contacted
◎ Record the incident in the Incident Book
◎ Write up a report as soon as possible after the incident, for example fill in an incident report form.

Risk assessment applicable to the childcare setting

It is important for children to be given opportunities to play and learn within an environment that will not harm their health and safety. However, they still need to be provided with activities and experiences that have levels of challenge and risk that will help them to develop confidence and independence. You need to be able to identify potential hazards (such as activities likely to cause harm) and assess possible risks (that is, the seriousness of the hazards and their potential to cause actual harm).

You need to understand that:

◎ The purpose of risk assessment is to: undertake a systematic review of the potential for harm; evaluate the likelihood of harm occurring; decide whether the existing control measures are adequate; and decide whether more needs to be done
◎ The sequence for risk assessment is: classify the activity; identify potential hazard(s); evaluate

possible risks; evaluate control measures; and specify any further action

◎ Once the risk assessment has been carried out the hierarchy for control measures is: eliminate hazard; reduce hazard; isolate hazard; and control hazard

◎ Once the risk assessment and control measures have been completed, no further action needs to be taken unless there is a significant change in that area.

(RoSPA, 2004b)

Implications of child development for health and safety

You need to know and understand the basic stages of child development and their implications for health, safety and security arrangements. For detailed information go to the Child Accident Prevention Trust (CAPT) website: www.capt.org.uk and then click 'Downloads' to access free samples of age-related safety leaflets. Despite the setting's procedures to maintain children's safety, there may still be times when accidents or injuries occur. Always ensure that you keep emergency numbers near the telephone. Also make certain that you know at least basic first aid and that you have access to a first aid kit. (See section Supervise procedures for accidents, injuries, illnesses and other emergencies.)

PORTFOLIO ACTIVITY

1 Find out about the statutory and regulatory requirements that apply to your childcare setting.
2 Find out about your childcare setting's policy and procedures relating to health and safety.
3 Outline the procedures for risk assessment and dealing with hazards in your childcare setting.
4 What are your responsibilities for dealing with the following types of possible hazards that can occur in the setting:
◎ Unsafe buildings, fixtures and fittings
◎ Unsafe equipment including play resources
◎ Hazardous substances, such as cleaning materials
◎ Hygiene hazards in toilet or kitchen areas
◎ Security hazards, for example inadequate boundaries or unauthorised visitors.

NVQ LINKS: CCLD 302.1   CCLD 302.2   CCLD 306.1   CCLD 308.3   CCLD 314.1   CCLD 318.4
          CCLD 342.1

CCLD 302.2
Maintain a healthy, safe and secure environment for children

Knowledge Base

K3S192   K3D195

All professional childcarers are responsible for the health and safety arrangements of the children (and others) under their supervision. This includes exercising effective supervision over those for whom you are responsible including children, students and volunteer helpers. You must be aware of and implement safe working practices and set a good example. Provide written instructions, warning notices and signs as appropriate. Supply suitable protective clothing and safety equipment as necessary and ensure that these are used as required (for example safety goggles). Ensure there is adequate instruction, information and training in safe working methods and recommend suitable safety training where appropriate.

Encourage children's awareness of their own safety, other people's safety and their personal responsibilities for maintaining health and safety in the setting. The childcare setting should ensure that children (and where appropriate their parents) are aware of their responsibilities, through direct instruction, notices and the setting handbook. As appropriate to their ages and abilities, all children should be expected to: exercise personal responsibility for the safety of themselves and other children; observe standards of dress consistent with safety and/or hygiene (this precludes unsuitable footwear, knives and other items considered dangerous); observe all the safety rules of the setting, in particular the instructions of adults in the event of a fire or other emergency; and use and not wilfully misuse, neglect or interfere with items provided for safety purposes such as fire alarms and fire extinguishers.

Maintaining children's safety during play and learning activities

You need to know and follow the setting's policies and procedures for maintaining children's safety at all times, especially during play and learning activities, including outings. It is important to provide challenging and exciting play opportunities and learning activities that encourage children to develop and explore whilst maintaining their physical safety and emotional welfare. Children often have accidents because they are developing and learning rapidly and it can be difficult for adults to keep up with their changing developmental abilities. Accidents also occur because children are naturally curious and want to explore their environment and, in doing so, may expose themselves to danger. The childcare setting should provide play and learning activities that encourage children's curiosity and exploration whilst protecting them from unnecessary harm. They also need to learn how to deal with risk so that they can keep themselves safe as they grow up. Bumps, bruises, minor cuts and scrapes are all part of play and learning, but there is no need for children to suffer serious injuries. To avoid accidents the childcare setting should provide adult care and supervision as well as ensuring safe play equipment design and appropriate modifications to the childcare environment (CAPT, 2004a). The design, location and maintenance of play areas are important to ensuring children's safety during play and learning activities. For example:

◎ The layout must be designed so that activities in one area do not interfere with other areas
◎ Play areas for younger children should be separated from those for older children
◎ Paths must be safely situated away from equipment areas, especially swings
◎ Clear sight lines in the play area make it easier to supervise children
◎ Secure fencing is required if there are roads, rivers or ponds close to the play area
◎ Safe access for children with disabilities should be considered
◎ Lighting must be adequate for safety and supervision

◎ Repair and replace old or worn play equipment
◎ Ensure all play equipment is suitable for the age of the children using it
◎ Use impact-absorbing surfaces such as rubber, bark chips and other materials.

(CAPT, 2004c)

Making sure that children are aware of safe behaviour when using play equipment can also help to maintain their safety and protect them from unnecessary accidents. Examples of safe behaviour include: not walking in front of swings or other moving equipment; not pushing or shoving; being aware of younger children and those with disabilities; removing scarves or other things that could get caught in equipment; and taking extra care when using high play equipment such as climbing frames (CAPT, 2004c).

Ten Golden Rules for maintaining children's safety during outings

All outings with children should be both safe and enjoyable, so to make this possible follow these rules:

1 Check the outing or visit is suitable for the ages and levels of development of the children participating.
2 Obtain written permission from the children's parents.
3 Ensure the destination, leaving time and expected return time are written down.
4 Know how to get there, for example location, route and mode of transport.
5 Check the seasonal conditions, weather and time available.
6 Assess any potential dangers or risks, for example activities near water, suitability and safety of playground equipment.
7 Carry essential information/equipment such as identification, emergency contact numbers, mobile phone, first aid, spare clothing, food, money and any essential medication.
8 Make sure you and the children are suitably dressed for the occasion: for example sensible shoes or boots for walks; waterproof clothing for wet weather; sunhat and sun screen in hot weather; clean, tidy clothes for cinema, theatre, museum visits, and so on.
9 Ensure the correct number of children are accountable throughout the outing.
10 All participants, including staff, children and parents, should know who will take charge in an emergency during the outing and what their individual responsibilities are in the event of an emergency.

CCLD 302.3
Supervise procedures for accidents, injuries, illnesses and other emergencies

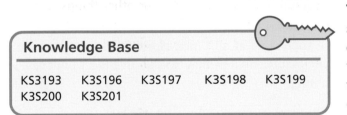

Knowledge Base

KS3193   K3S196   K3S197   K3S198   K3S199
K3S200   K3S201

An essential part of establishing and maintaining a healthy, safe and secure environment for children is the supervision of procedures for accidents, injuries, illnesses and other emergencies in the childcare setting. You can do this by: following emergency evacuation procedures in the childcare setting; following procedures for missing children; dealing with accidents and injuries; providing first aid; recognising and dealing with common childhood illnesses; following the procedures for storing and administering medicines; and supporting children with special medical needs.

Following emergency evacuation procedures in the childcare setting

It is important that you know about the fire and emergency evacuation procedures for the setting. The purpose of such procedures is to prevent panic and to ensure the safe, orderly and efficient evacuation of all occupants in the setting, using all the exit facilities available, and to help individuals to react rationally when confronted with a fire or other emergency, either at the setting or elsewhere. In the event of a fire or other emergency (such as a bomb scare) all staff should know and understand that their first consideration must be the evacuation of all the children to a place of safety. The sequence for fire and emergency evacuation procedures should be as follows: sound the fire alarm; evacuate the building; call the fire brigade; assemble at the designated assembly point; and take a roll call using registers if possible.

The fire alarm signals the need to evacuate the building. You should give calm, clear and correct instructions to the people involved in the emergency as relevant to your role in implementing emergency procedures within the setting. Make sure that any children for whom you are responsible leave the building in the appropriate manner, that is, walking, no running or talking. This will help to maintain calm and minimise panic as the children focus on following the evacuation procedures. All rooms must have instructions on how to leave the building in the event of an emergency, including exit routes, prominently displayed.

You also need to know what to do if there is a bomb scare or an intruder in the setting. Evacuation procedures would usually be the same as for a fire. Report any problems with emergency procedures to the relevant colleague, for example the senior practitioner or the setting manager. Visitors to the childcare setting should normally be asked to sign in (and out) so that the people responsible for health and safety know who is in the building (and where) in case of emergencies.

If you work with children with special needs, you need to know how to assist them in the event of an emergency; for example, a child with physical disabilities may need to leave the building via a special route or require access to a lift. Check with the senior practitioner or the setting manager about the exact procedures to follow. It is important to know where the fire alarm points and fire exits are, the location of fire extinguishers and fire blankets and their use. There may be different types of extinguishers for use with different hazardous substances; for example, in kitchens water must not

be used to put out oil or electrical fires, as this can make the situation worse. Carbon dioxide extinguishers will be located in the necessary places.

Following procedures for missing children

A register of children attending the childcare setting should be taken at the start of each session and one should also be taken for children participating in outings/visits away from the setting, with a duplicate left with the setting manager. Children should be made aware (or reminded) of the boundaries of the setting at each session and should be supervised at all times. However, despite these safeguards children may still go missing from the setting.

You need to be aware of the setting's procedures for dealing with missing children. These may include: contacting the senior practitioner or setting manager immediately; calling the register to check which child is missing; searching rooms, play areas and grounds to ensure the child has not hidden or been locked in anywhere within the setting; and the setting manager contacting the police and the parents/carers.

If a child is found to be missing while on an outing the childcarer should: contact the setting manager immediately; check the register again; keep the rest of the group together while searching the area; and contact the setting manager again (who will contact the police and the child's parents/carers).

Activity

1 Find out about your childcare setting's emergency evacuation procedures.
2 Briefly outline the setting's procedures in the event of a fire or other emergency evacuation, including your specific role.

Activity

Briefly outline your setting's procedures for dealing with missing children.

Dealing with accidents and injuries

When responding to accidents or injuries that occur within the childcare setting, you should remain calm and follow the setting's relevant procedures. Call for qualified assistance immediately (for example the designated first aider or the emergency services) and take appropriate action in line with your role and responsibilities within the setting. If you are a *designated* first aider than you can administer first aid; if not, you can comfort the injured person by your physical presence and talking to them until the arrival of a designated first aider, doctor, paramedic or ambulance staff. Help to establish and maintain the privacy and safety of the area where the accident or injury occurred and provide support for any other people involved. When qualified assistance arrives, give them clear and accurate information about what happened. Afterwards, follow the setting's procedures for recording accidents and injuries. This will normally involve recording the incident in a special book. Serious accidents are usually recorded on an official form. Accuracy in recording accidents and injuries is essential because the information may be needed for further action by senior staff or other professionals. Certain types of accidents and injuries must be reported to an official authority under the Reporting of Injuries, Diseases and Dangerous Occurrences Regulations 1985. For example, commercial and voluntary sector playgrounds must report to the local Environmental Health Office; and local authority and school playgrounds must report to the Health and Safety Executive.

All childcarers need to follow basic good hygiene procedures and take the usual precautions for avoiding cross infection. Use protective disposable gloves and be careful when dealing with spillages of blood or other body fluids, including the disposal of dressings, and so on. Be aware of issues concerning the spread of hepatitis, HIV and AIDS.

Providing first aid

It is important for you to know and understand the first aid arrangements that apply in your childcare setting, including the location of first aid equipment/facilities and the designated first aider(s). A designated first aider must complete a training course approved by the Health and Safety Executive. Remember that even if you have done first aid as part of your childcare training, your first aid certificate should be updated every 3 years.

First aid notices should be clearly displayed in all rooms; make sure you read this information. First aid information is usually included in induction programmes to ensure that new staff and children know about the setting's first aid arrangements. Detailed information on the setting's first aid policy and procedures are also given in the staff handbook.

> **Check it out**
>
> Have you got an up-to-date first aid certificate?
> If not, find out about the first aid courses available in your local area.

The aims of first aid

◎ To preserve life by: providing emergency resuscitation; controlling bleeding; treating burns; and treating shock
◎ To prevent the worsening of any injuries by: covering wounds; immobilising fractures; and placing the casualty in the correct and comfortable position
◎ To promote recovery by: providing reassurance; giving any other treatment needed; relieving pain;

ILLNESS	INCUBATION PERIOD	INFECTIOUS PERIOD	HOW TO RECOGNISE IT	WHAT TO DO
	(The time between catching an illness and becoming unwell)	(When your child can give the illness to someone else)		
CHICKENPOX	11–21 days	From the day before the rash appears until all the spots are dry.	Begins with feeling unwell, a rash and maybe a slight temperature. Spots are red and become fluid-filled blisters within a day or so. Appear first on the chest and back, then spread, and eventually dry into scabs, which drop off. Unless spots are badly infected, they don't usually leave a scar.	No need to see your GP unless you're unsure whether it's chickenpox, or your child is very unwell and/or distressed. Give plenty to drink. Paracetamol will help bring down a temperature. Baths, loose, comfortable clothes and calamine lotion can all ease the itchiness. You should also inform the school/nursery in case other children are at risk. Keep your child away from anyone who is, or who is trying to become, pregnant. If your child was with anyone pregnant just before he or she became unwell, let that woman know about the chickenpox (and tell her to see her GP). Sometimes chickenpox in pregnancy can cause miscarriage or the baby may be born with chickenpox.
MEASLES	7–12 days	From a few days before until 4 days after the appearance of the rash.	Begins like a bad cold and cough with sore, watery eyes. Child becomes gradually more unwell, with a temperature. Rash appears after third or fourth day. Spots are red and slightly raised; may be blotchy, but are not itchy. Begins behind the ears, and spreads to the face and neck and then the rest of the body. Children can become very unwell, with cough and high temperature. The illness usually lasts about a week.	See your GP. If your child is unwell give him or her rest and plenty to drink. Warm drinks will ease the cough. Paracetamol will ease discomfort and lower the temperature. Vaseline around the lips protects the skin. Wash crustiness from eyelids with warm water.
MUMPS	14–21 days	From a few days before becoming unwell until swelling goes down. Maybe 10 days in all.	At first, your child may be mildly unwell with a bit of fever, and may complain of pain around the ear or feel uncomfortable when chewing. Swelling then starts under the jaw up by the ear. Swelling often starts on one side, followed (though not always) by the other. Your child's face is back to normal size in about a week. It's rare for mumps to affect boys' testes (balls). This happens rather more often in adult men with mumps. For both boys and men, the risk of any permanent damage to the testes is very low.	Your child may not feel especially ill and may not want to be in bed. Baby or junior paracetamol will ease pain in the swollen glands. Check correct dosage on pack. Give plenty to drink, but not fruit juice. This makes the saliva flow, which can hurt. No need to see your GP unless your child has stomach ache and is being sick, or develops a rash of small red/purple spots or bruises.
PARVOVIRUS B19 (ALSO CALLED FIFTH DISEASE OR SLAPPED CHEEK DISEASE)	Variable 1–20 days	It is most infectious in the days before the rash appears.	Begins with a fever and nasal discharge. A bright red rash similar to a slap appears on the cheeks. Over the next 2–4 days, a lacy type of rash spreads to the trunk and limbs.	Although this is most common in children, it can occur in adults. In the majority of cases it has no serious consequences, but it may cause complications for people with chronic anaemic conditions (e.g. sickle cell disease). Rarely, in pregnant women who are not immune to the disease, the infection may result in stillbirth or affect the baby in the womb. Pregnant women who come into contact with the infection or develop a rash should see their GP as soon as possible.
RUBELLA (GERMAN MEASLES)	14–21 days	One week before and at least 4 days after the rash first appears.	Can be difficult to diagnose with certainty. Starts like a mild cold. The rash appears in a day or two, first on the face, then spreading. Spots are flat. On a light skin, they are pale pink. Glands in the back of the neck may be swollen. Your child won't usually feel unwell.	Give plenty to drink. Keep your child away from anybody you know who's up to 4 months pregnant (or trying to get pregnant). If your child was with anyone pregnant before you knew about the illness, let her know. If an unimmunised pregnant woman catches German measles in the first 4 months of pregnancy, there is a risk of damage to her baby. Any pregnant woman who has had contact with German measles should see her GP. The GP can check whether or not she is immune and, if not, whether there is any sign of her developing the illness.
WHOOPING COUGH	7–14 days	From the first signs of the illness until about 6 weeks after coughing starts. If an antibiotic is given, the infectious period is up to 5 days after beginning the course of treatment.	Begins like a cold and cough. The cough gradually gets worse. After about 2 weeks, coughing bouts start. These are exhausting and make it difficult to breathe. Your child may choke and vomit. Sometimes, but not always, there's a whooping noise as the child draws in breath after coughing. It takes some weeks before the coughing fits start to die down.	If your child has a cough that gets worse rather than better and starts to have longer fits of coughing more and more often, see your doctor. It's important for the sake of other children to know whether or not it's whooping cough. Talk to your GP about how best to look after your child and avoid contact with babies, who are most at risk from serious complications.

Figure 2.1 Childhood illnesses

handling gently; moving as little as possible; and protecting from the cold.

The priorities of first aid

◎ A is for Airway: establish an open airway by tilting the forehead back so that the child can breathe easily
◎ B is for Breathing: check that the child is breathing by listening, looking and feeling for breath
◎ C is for Circulation: apply simple visual checks that the child's blood is circulating adequately, by watching for improved colour, for coughing or eye movement.

First aid equipment

First aid equipment must be clearly labelled and easily accessible. All first aid containers must be marked with a white cross on a green background. There should be at least one fully stocked first aid container for each building within the childcare setting, with extra first aid containers available on split sites/levels, distant playing fields/playgrounds and any other high risk areas (such as kitchens) and for outings or educational visits. Here are some suggestions for the contents of a first aid kit:

◎ A first-aid manual or first aid leaflet
◎ Assorted bandages, including a wrapped triangular bandage, a one-inch and a two-inch strip for holding dressings and compresses in place
◎ Medium and large individually wrapped sterile un-medicated wound dressings
◎ Two sterile eye pads
◎ Safety pins
◎ Adhesive tape
◎ Sterile gauze
◎ A pair of sharp scissors
◎ Tweezers

◎ Child thermometer
◎ Disposable gloves.

Check it out

Find out about your childcare setting's policy and procedures for dealing with accidents and injuries, including methods for recording accidents/incidents and the provision of first aid.

Recognising and dealing with common childhood illnesses and allergies

Babies and young children should be vaccinated against diseases including: diphtheria, measles, meningitis, mumps, polio, rubella, tetanus and whooping cough. The first immunisations start when a baby is 2 months old. The child's parents will usually receive appointments by post to attend their local clinic or GP surgery. You need to be aware of the range of common illnesses that may affect children. These include: allergies, asthma, bronchitis, chickenpox, colds, diabetes, diarrhoea, earache, flu, glandular fever, headache, measles, meningitis, mumps, sore throat and worms.

Recognising signs and symptoms

By knowing the usual behaviour and appearance of the children you work with, you will be able to recognise any significant changes that might indicate possible illness. You need to be able to recognise the differences between children who are: pretending to be ill; feeling 'under the weather'; or experiencing a health problem. The signs of possible illness in children include:

◎ Changes in facial colour, for example becoming pale or very red

◎ Changes in temperature, for example becoming very hot or cold, or becoming clammy or shivering (A fever usually indicates that the child has an infection.)

◎ Changes in behaviour, such as not wanting to play when would usually be very keen

◎ Being upset or generally distressed

◎ Having reduced concentration levels or even falling asleep

◎ Scratching excessively (Check the setting's policy regarding head lice.)

◎ Complaining of persistent pain, including headache or stomachache

◎ Coughing or sneezing excessively

◎ Diarrhoea and/or vomiting

◎ Displaying a rash. This could indicate an infection or allergic reaction. Make sure you are aware of any children who may have severe allergic reactions.

(Watkinson, 2003)

Responding to signs and symptoms

It is important for you to know what to do if children arrive at the setting when they are unwell. The most common childhood illness is the common cold. A young child may have as many as 5-6 colds a year. Children do not need to be kept away from the setting because of a cold unless their symptoms are very bad. Make sure that a box of tissues is available for them to use and that used tissues are disposed of properly to avoid the spread of germs. Colds and flu are caused by viruses so cannot be helped by antibiotics. However, cold and flu viruses can weaken the body and lead to a secondary bacterial infection such as tonsillitis, otitis media (middle ear infection), sinusitis, bronchitis and pneumonia. These bacterial infections require

antibiotic treatment. You also need to know what to do if a child becomes ill while at the setting. Seek medical advice if you have concerns about any of the following:

◎ The child's high temperature lasts for more than 24 hours

◎ The child has a persistent cough with green or yellow catarrh (possible bronchitis or pneumonia)

◎ The child has pain above the eyes or in the face (possible sinusitis)

◎ The child has a severe sore throat (possible tonsillitis)

◎ The child has a bad earache (possible ear infection).

Seek medical advice immediately if:

◎ A baby under 6-months-old has a temperature of over 37°C

◎ You think the child may have meningitis

◎ The child has breathing difficulties

◎ The child's asthma deteriorates

◎ The child has a convulsion

◎ The child has very poor fluid intake or cannot swallow liquids

◎ A baby persistently refuses to take feeds

◎ The child has been to a country in the last 12 months where there is a risk of malaria.

Recording and reporting signs of illness

Ensure that you know what to do when children are sick; for example, where or to whom to send sick children. You may need to stay with a sick child while someone else summons assistance. If you have any concerns regarding the health of the children you work with, you should always inform the senior practitioner or setting manager. You need to be able to recognise any changes in a child's behaviour or appearance that may indicate a possible health

Unit Link

For this Unit you also need to understand the following sections:

CCLD 314.5 Recognise and respond to illness in babies and children under 3 years (see Chapter 11)

problem and report these appropriately. Whatever the illness, you should know where and when to seek assistance. It is also important that you know which types of written records are required and to whom you should report any concerns regarding any child's health. Check whether you are allowed to contact parents/carers directly regarding a sick child or whether this is the responsibility of someone else, for example the senior practitioner or setting manager.

Following procedures for storing and administering medicines

Parents are responsible for their own children's medication. Children under the age of 16 should not be given medication without their parent's written consent. The childcare setting's manager usually decides whether the setting can assist a child who needs medication during a session. The setting will have a form for the parent to sign if their child requires medication while at the setting. Many children with long-term medical needs will not require medication while at the childcare setting. If they do, children can usually administer it themselves depending on their age, level of development, medical needs and type of medication. The setting's policy should encourage self-administration where appropriate and provide

suitable facilities for children to do so in safety and privacy. (See below for information on supporting children with long-term medical needs.)

Childcare workers have no legal duty to administer medication or to supervise a child taking it. This is a voluntary role similar to that of being a first aider. The setting manager, parents and relevant health professionals should support childcare workers who volunteer to administer medication by providing information, training and reassurance about their legal liability. Arrangements should be made for when the childcarer responsible for providing assistance is absent or not available.

The health and safety of children and workers must be considered at all times. Safety procedures must be in place regarding the safe storage, handling and disposal of medicines. Some medication (for example reliever inhaler for asthma or adrenalin device for severe anaphylaxis) must be quickly available in an emergency and should not be locked away. The relevant workers and the children concerned must know where this medication is stored.

Supporting children with long-term medical needs

All settings will have children with medical needs at some time. Some medical needs are short-term, such as for example a child finishing a course of antibiotics or recovering from an accident/surgery. Some children may have long-term medical needs due to a particular medical condition or chronic illness. The majority of children with long-term medical needs will be able to attend a mainstream setting regularly and can participate in the usual setting activities with the appropriate support from the staff. The medical conditions in children that cause most concern in childcare settings are asthma, diabetes, epilepsy and severe allergic reaction (anaphylaxis).

Asthma

About 1 in 10 children in the UK have asthma. People with asthma have airways that narrow as a reaction to a variety of triggers such as animal fur, grass pollen, house dust mites and viral infections. Stress or exercise can also bring on an asthma attack in a susceptible person. A person with asthma can usually relieve the symptoms of an asthma attack with an inhaler.

It is essential that children with asthma have immediate access to their reliever inhalers in the event of an asthma attack in the setting and they should be encouraged from an early age to take charge of their own inhaler and know how to use it. Those who can use their inhalers themselves should be permitted to carry these with them at all times. When a child is too young or immature to be personally responsible for their inhaler, staff must ensure that the inhaler is kept in a safe but accessible place with the child's name clearly written on it. The symptoms of an asthma attack are: excessive coughing; wheezing; difficulty breathing, especially breathing out; possible anxiety and distress; and lips and skin turning blue (in severe attacks).

A child having an asthma attack should be prompted to use an inhaler if not using it already. It is good practice to provide comfort and reassurance (to alleviate possible anxiety and distress) while encouraging the child to breathe slowly and deeply. The child should sit rather than lie down. Medical advice must be sought and /or an ambulance called if: the medication has no effect after 5–10 minutes; the child seems very distressed; the child is unable to talk; or the child is becoming exhausted. (DfES/DH, 2005)

Diabetes

Approximately 1 in 550 children have diabetes. This is a medical condition where the person's normal hormonal mechanisms do not control blood sugar levels properly. Children with diabetes usually need to: have daily insulin injections; monitor their blood sugar glucose; and eat regularly.

Diabetes in most children is controlled by twice daily injections of insulin and it is not likely that these will need to be administered during school hours. If children do need insulin while at the setting then an appropriate, private area should be provided for this. Most children with diabetes can administer their own insulin injections but younger children will require adult supervision.

Children with diabetes need to check that their blood sugar levels remain stable by using a testing machine at regular intervals. They may need to check their levels during lunch time or more frequently if their insulin requires adjustment. The majority of children are able to do this for themselves and just need an appropriate place to carry out the checks.

Children with diabetes must be allowed to eat regularly throughout the day. This might include eating snacks during lesson time or before physical play activities or PE lessons. Blood sugar levels may fall to too low a level if a child misses a snack or meal or after strenuous physical activity resulting in a hypoglycaemia episode (hypo), which if left untreated can lead to a diabetic coma. The symptoms of a hypo include: drowsiness; glazed eyes; hunger; irritability; lack of concentration; pallor; shaking; and sweating. If a child experiences a hypo it is important that a fast acting sugar is given immediately, such as glucose tablets, glucose rich gel, sugary drink or chocolate bar. A slower acting starchy food should be given once the child has recovered, for example a sandwich or two biscuits and a glass of milk. If the child's recovery takes longer than 10–15 minutes, or if there are any concerns about the child's condition, an ambulance should be called. (DfES/DH, 2005)

Epilepsy

Approximately 1 in 200 children have epilepsy and about 80 per cent of those attend mainstream settings. People with epilepsy have recurrent seizures (commonly called fits). The nature, frequency and severity of seizures will vary between individuals, though the majority of seizures can be controlled by medication. Seizures may be *partial* when the person's consciousness is affected but not necessarily lost, or *generalised* where the person does lose consciousness.

Most children with epilepsy have symptoms that are well controlled by medication and seizures are therefore unlikely to occur in the setting. The vast majority of children with epilepsy experience seizures for no apparent reason. However, susceptible children may have seizures that are triggered by: tiredness and/or stress; flashing or flickering lights; computer games and graphics; or some geometric shapes or patterns. The symptoms of epileptic seizures include: having convulsions; losing consciousness; experiencing strange sensations; or exhibiting unusual behaviour (for example plucking at clothes or repetitive movements).

Once a seizure has started nothing should be done to stop or change its course except when medication is given by appropriately trained staff. The child should not be moved unless situated in a dangerous place, but something soft may be placed under the head. No attempt should be made to restrain the child or to put anything into the mouth. The child's airway must be maintained at all times. When the convulsion has finished the child should be put in the recovery position and someone should

stay until the child has recovered and become re-orientated. If the seizure lasts longer than usual or one seizure follows another without the child regaining consciousness or where there are any concerns about the pupil's condition, then an ambulance should be called. (DfES/DH, 2005)

Severe allergic reaction (anaphylaxis)

Children with severe allergies learn from an early age what they can and cannot eat or drink. The most common cause for severe allergies is food, especially nuts, fish or dairy products. Wasp and bee stings can also cause severe allergic reaction. Anaphylaxis is a very severe allergic reaction that requires urgent medical treatment. In its most severe form (anaphylactic shock) the condition is potentially life-threatening, but can be treated with medication. This may include antihistamine, adrenaline inhaler or adrenaline injection depending on the severity of the allergic reaction. Anaphylactic shock is rare in children under 13 years of age.

People with severe allergic reactions usually have a device for injecting adrenaline that looks like a fountain pen and is pre-loaded with the exact dose of adrenaline required. The needle is not exposed and the injection is easy to administer, usually into the fleshy part of the thigh.

A child may be responsible for keeping the necessary medication with them at all times. The safety of all children should be taken into account and it might be more appropriate to store the medication in a

---

Activity

List the main symptoms for the following: asthma attack; diabetic hypo; epileptic seizure; severe allergic reaction.

safe but instantly accessible place, especially if working with younger children. All staff should be aware of any children with this condition and know who is responsible for administering the emergency treatment. Responsibility for giving the injection should be on a voluntary basis and should never be done by a person without appropriate training from a health professional.

An allergic reaction will usually occur within a few seconds or minutes of exposure to an allergen. The symptoms of a severe allergic reaction include: metallic taste or itching in the mouth; flushed complexion; abdominal cramps and nausea; swelling of the face, throat, tongue and lips; difficulty swallowing; wheezing or difficulty breathing; rise in heart rate; and collapse or unconsciousness. An ambulance should be called immediately, especially if there are concerns about the severity of the allergic reaction or if the pupil does not respond to the medication. (DfES/DH, 2005)

Meningitis and septicaemia

Meningitis (an inflammation of the lining of the brain) is a very serious illness but if recognised and treated early most children will make a full recovery. Septicaemia (blood poisoning caused by the same germs as meningitis) is also a very serious illness which must be treated right away. There are different types of meningitis and septicaemia; some can be prevented by immunisation (see chart on page 133). Early symptoms of both illnesses may be similar to a cold or flu e.g. fever, irritability, restlessness and vomiting. Babies and children with meningitis or septicaemia can become seriously ill within a few hours so it essential to recognise the signs and symptoms of these illnesses. (DH, 2006)

The main symptoms of meningitis in children may include:
◎ A high-pitched, moaning cry (babies)

◎ Irritability when picked up
◎ A bulging fontanelle (babies)
◎ Drowsy and less responsive/vacant; being difficult to wake
◎ Floppy and listless or stiff with jerky movements
◎ Stiff neck
◎ Aversion to bright light (photosensitivity)
◎ Refusing milk feeds and/or food; vomiting
◎ Pale, blotchy skin or turning blue
◎ Fever.

The main symptoms of septicaemia in children may include:
◎ Rapid or unusual patterns of breathing
◎ Pale, blotchy skin or turning blue
◎ Fever with cold hands and feet
◎ Shivering
◎ Refusing milk feeds and/or food; vomiting
◎ Red or purple spots that do not fade under pressure (see below about the glass test)
◎ Floppiness
◎ Severe sleepiness.

(DH, 2006)

Remember that not all children develop all the symptoms listed above. If a child develops some of the symptoms listed above, especially red or purple spots, you should seek medical attention **urgently**. The *glass test*: press the side of a clear drinking glass firmly against the rash to see if the rash fades and loses colour under pressure; if the rash does not change colour contact seek medical attention **immediately**. (DH, 2006)

Strategies for supporting children with long-term medical needs

The childcare setting will need additional procedures to maintain the health and safety of children with long-term medical needs; this may include an individual health care plan (see below). The setting has a responsibility to ensure that all relevant staff are aware of children with such medical needs and are trained to provide additional support if necessary. Staff who provide support for children with long-term medical needs must know and understand: the nature of the child's medical condition; when and where the child may need additional support; the likelihood of an emergency arising (especially if it is potentially life threatening); and what action to take if an emergency occurs.

The setting manager and other staff must treat medical information in a sensitive and confidential manner. There should be an agreement between the setting manager, the child (if appropriate) and their parents about which staff members should have access to records and other information on the child's medical needs, in order to provide a good support system. However, where medical information is not given to staff they should not usually be held responsible if they provide incorrect medical assistance in an emergency but otherwise acted in good faith.

Health care plans in childcare settings

Some children with long-term medical needs may require a health care plan to provide setting staff with the necessary information to support the child and to ensure the child's safety.

A health care plan for children with special medical needs is used to identify the level of support the child requires in the setting. It is a written agreement between the setting and parents specifying the assistance that the setting can provide for the child. The plan should be reviewed at least once a year, or more if the child's medical needs change. A written health care plan should be drawn up in consultation with the child (if appropriate), their parents and the relevant health professionals. The amount of detail contained in a health care plan will depend on the particular needs of the individual child.

The plan should include: details of the child's medical condition; any special requirements, such as dietary needs; medication and its possible side effects; how staff can support the child in school; and what to do and who to contact in an emergency. (DfES/DH, 2005)

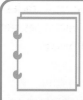

PORTFOLIO ACTIVITY

1 Find out about your childcare setting's procedures for: dealing with accidents and injuries; providing first aid; dealing with common childhood illnesses; storing and administering medicines; and supporting children with long-term medical needs.
2 Describe your role and responsibilities in the event of an accident, injury, illness and other emergencies.
NVQ LINKS: CCLD 302.3   CCLD 307.3   CCLD 314.5

3 Promoting children's development

CCLD 303 Promote children's development

Accurate observations and assessments form the foundations of all effective childcare practice. To keep precise and useful records you need to know the children you work with really well. Careful observations enable you and your colleagues to make objective assessments of children and their individual care needs, behaviour patterns, levels of development, skills/abilities, learning styles, learning needs/goals and learning achievements.

Assessing this information can help to highlight and celebrate children's strengths as well as identify any gaps in their learning. This information can form the basis for the ongoing planning of appropriate care routines, play opportunities and learning activities; it may also be a useful starting point for future learning goals/objectives.

CCLD 303.1 Observe development

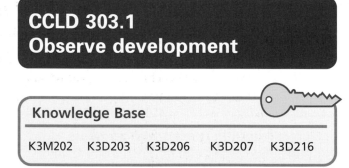

Knowledge Base

| K3M202 | K3D203 | K3D206 | K3D207 | K3D216 |

Observations should cover all relevant aspects of child development including: physical skills; communication skills and language development; intellectual abilities; and emotional development, social development and behaviour. The methods for recording observations depend on the setting policies and any legal requirements (see below). You may be involved in compiling a portfolio of relevant information about each child in the setting. This could include: child observations; examples of the child's work; photographs of the child during play and learning activities; and checklists of the child's progress.

Why do you need to observe children?

There are many reasons why it is important to observe children. For example, to:

◎ Understand the wide range of skills in all areas of their development
◎ Know and understand the sequence of children's development
◎ Use this knowledge to link theory with your own practice in the setting
◎ Assess children's development and existing skills or behaviour
◎ Plan care routines, play opportunities and learning activities appropriate to children's individual developmental needs.

Where and what should you observe?

Try to observe the child or children in a place in the setting where there is little interference or few interruptions, making sure that the situation is realistic. Children's development, learning and behaviour may be observed in a variety of situations, though you will generally observe activities which are part of the child's usual routine. For example, you might observe the following situations:

◎ A child talking with another child or adult
◎ An adult working with a small group of children
◎ A child or a small group of children playing

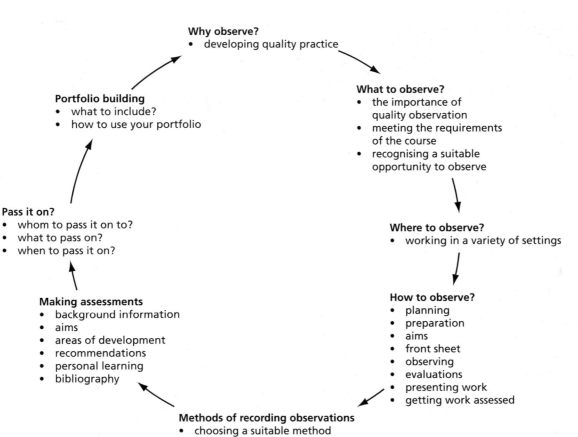

Figure 3.1 Thinking about observing by Jackie Harding and Liz Meldon-Smith

Activity

Write a short account explaining why it is important to observe and assess children's development.

indoors or outdoors, or participating in a small or large group discussion, such as circle time
◎ An adult reading/telling a story to a child or group of children
◎ A child or group of children participating in a creative, literacy, mathematics or science activity,

perhaps doing painting, writing, numeracy work or carrying out an experiment.

The basic principles of child observation

You need to consider the following:

1 Confidentiality must be kept at all times. You *must* have the senior practitioner's and/or the parents' permission before making formal observations of children.
2 Be objective. Only record what you actually see or

hear, not what you think or feel. For example, the statement *'The child cried'* is objective, but to say *'The child is sad'* is subjective, as you do not know what the child is feeling; children can cry for a variety of reasons, for example to draw attention to themselves or to show discomfort.

3 Remember equal opportunities. Consider children's cultural backgrounds. They may be very competent at communicating in their community language, but may have more difficulty in expressing themselves in English; this does *not* mean they are behind in their language development. Consider how any special needs may affect children's development, learning and/or behaviour.

4 Be positive! Focus on the children's strengths, not just on any learning or behavioural difficulties they may have. Look at what children can do in terms of their development and/or learning and use this as the foundation for providing future activities.

5 Use a holistic approach. Remember to look at the 'whole' child. You need to look at all areas of children's development in relation to the particular aspect of development or learning you are focusing on. For example, when observing children's drawing or painting skills, as well as looking at their intellectual development, you will need to consider: their physical development (fine motor skills when using a pencil or paintbrush); their language development and communication skills (vocabulary and structure of language used to describe their drawing or painting if appropriate); and their social and emotional development (interaction with others and behaviour during the drawing or painting activity).

6 Consider the children's feelings. Depending on the children's ages, needs and abilities, you should discuss the observation with the children to be observed and respond appropriately to their views.

7 Minimise distractions. Observe children without intruding or causing unnecessary stress. Try to keep your distance where possible, but be close enough to hear the children's language. Try not to interact with the children (unless it is a participant observation – see below), but if they do address you, be polite and respond positively. Explain to the children simply what you are doing and keep your answers short.

8 *Practise.* The best way to develop your skills at observing children's development, learning and behaviour is to do observations on a regular basis.

Confidentiality

The senior practitioner, setting manager or your college tutor/assessor will give you guidelines for the methods most appropriate to your role as a childcarer in your particular setting. Your observations and assessments must be in line with the setting's policy for record keeping and relevant to the routines and activities of the children you work with. You must follow the setting's policy on *confidentiality* at all times and implement data protection procedures as appropriate to your role and responsibilities (see section on confidentiality in Chapter 1). The childcare setting should obtain permission from the parents/carers of the children being observed; for example, a letter requesting permission to carry out regular observations and assessments could be sent to parents for their signature. If you are a childcare student, before doing any portfolio activities for your NVQ assessment involving observations of children you must negotiate with the senior practitioner or setting manager when it will be possible for you to carry out your observations and have written permission to do so.

Techniques of observation

When observing children you need to use an appropriate method of observation as directed by the senior practitioner. Ensure that you include all aspects of development in your observation and assessment: these are social; physical; intellectual; communication and language; and emotional. These are easily remembered using the mnemonic **SPICE**.

You will probably observe a child or group of children on several occasions on different days of the week and at different times of the day. Use developmental charts for the child's age group to identify areas of development in which the child is making progress, as well as those in which the child may be behind the norm for their age range. Remember to emphasise the positive; for example, a child with limited speech may still be developing positive social relationships with other children by using non-verbal communication during play activities.

Types of observation include:

- ◎ Naturalistic: observation of child involved in usual routines or activities, for example getting ready for lunch or playing a game
- ◎ Structured: observation of child during a particular activity set up to gain specific information about the child's development, learning or behaviour, such as a literacy activity to assess a child's comprehension skills
- ◎ Snapshot: observation of child at a specific time, perhaps recording social interaction and behaviour during play time
- ◎ Longitudinal: observations of child over a period of time, such as observing and recording a child's language and literacy skills on a weekly basis for a year.

Methods of observation include:

- ◎ Time sampling: observation of child's behaviour at regular intervals during a set period of time, perhaps every 10 minutes during a lesson. This can provide a clearer picture of behaviour changes throughout a session or day and help to identify when certain behaviour occurs during which activities and/or routines
- ◎ Event sampling: observations of particular events as they occur, for example a child's emotional outbursts. A record is made of the number of times the target behaviour occurs, when it occurs and how long it lasts
- ◎ Participant: observation where the observer is also involved in the child's activity
- ◎ Non-participant: observation involves being as unobtrusive as possible while other members of staff assist the child as necessary during the activity or routine
- ◎ Target child: observation concentrating on one particular child
- ◎ Trail or movement: observations to monitor behaviour. On a plan of a particular area of the setting (for example the classroom, indoor play area, toddler room) lines are drawn indicating the movements of the child with brief notes about the length of time spent in each area, the child's behaviour and any social interaction.

Other useful methods for observing children's development, learning and/or behaviour include checklists, coded observations and diaries. Some observations of children may not be planned; for instance, you may make a note of a child's unusual behaviour during an activity.

Tick chart: Group observation of children at snack/meal time

SELF-HELP SKILLS	CHILDRENíS NAMES			
	Shafik	Sukhi	Ruth	Tom
Goes to the toilet				
Washes hands				
Dries hands				
Chooses own snack/meal				
Uses fingers				
Uses spoon				
Uses fork				
Uses knife				
Holds cup with 2 hands				
Holds cup with 1 hand				

Key: ✓ = competent at skill/no adult assistance
\ = attempts skill/needs some adult assistance
X = no attempt/requires lots of adult assistance

Pie chart = Time sample observation of child's play activities

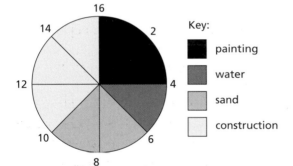

Key:
- painting
- water
- sand
- construction

Bar graph: Time sample observation of child's social play

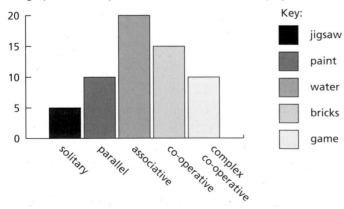

Key:
- jigsaw
- paint
- water
- bricks
- game

Figure 3.2 Observation charts

CCLD 303.2
Assess development and reflect upon implications for practice

As well as the ability to observe children's development you need to assess this development based on observational findings and other reliable information from children, parents, carers, colleagues and other appropriate adults. It is important that you can make formative and summative assessments (see below) and record your assessments as appropriate to the policies and procedures of your setting. You should share your findings with children and their parents, as appropriate, and refer any concerns about children to senior colleagues and/or relevant external agencies when required. Always remember to follow the confidentiality and record keeping requirements of your setting.

Formative assessments are initial and ongoing assessments. They identify future targets for the individual and groups as appropriate to the children's ages, developmental needs and abilities and the requirements of the setting. These assessments are continuous and inform planning provision to promote children's development and learning. Examples of formative assessments include: child observations; tick charts/lists; reading records; maths records; and daily target records for children with individual education plans.

Summative assessments are assessments that summarise findings and involve more formal monitoring of children's progress. Such assessments, which should be used appropriately, allow judgements to be made about the children's achievement. Usually in the form of criterion-based tests or tasks, examples of summative assessments include: Foundation Stage Profile; Standard Assessment Tasks (SATs); teacher assessments; annual school reports; and reviews of children with special educational needs.

(For more information see section Assess children's progress according to curriculum frameworks for early education in Chapter 12.)

Reflecting on assessments and implications for practice

Reflecting on the assessments you have made of children's development will help you to identify the implications these have for your practice. For example: evaluating assessment methods used to monitor the progress of individuals and groups; ensuring assessment opportunities are built into the planning provision to promote children's development; providing support for individual staff members as necessary; and reviewing assessment outcomes and data in order to evaluate overall standards throughout the setting.

Encouraging high, positive adult expectations of children and their abilities

Adults working with children, particularly in early education settings, have to make frequent judgements about their achievements in comparison with other children. It is important to be aware of this social context, where the emphasis is on competition and 'good' academic results, and beware of its effects on the expectations for children. Assessment, both formal and informal, creates labels for children that can affect adult expectations; such labelling may affect children adversely for many years. You can encourage high, positive adult expectations of children and their abilities by:

◎ Respecting all children as valued and important individuals
◎ Promoting children's care and development in appropriate ways
◎ Creating awareness of the effects of adult expectations, for example adults need to be aware of bias within the childcare setting (and society as a whole) and avoid stereotypical assumptions
◎ Working within the cultural and social context of the childcare setting; for example use the children's backgrounds positively; know that limitations exist, but use them to advantage even with the constraints of the National Curriculum
◎ Actively promoting equal opportunities
◎ Using the children's own perceptions of themselves, for instance by acknowledging their personal views of their individual capabilities
◎ Using friendship or temperament groups instead of ability groups
◎ Giving children more choice over their activities and involving them in decision-making.

Recording observations and assessments

You should record your observations and assessments using an agreed format. This might be a written descriptive account; structured profile (with specified headings for each section); pre-coded system of recording. Once you have recorded your observation of the child (or group of children), you need to make an assessment of this information in relation to:

◎ The aims of the observation, such as why you were doing this observation
◎ What you observed about the child's development, learning and/or behaviour in *this* particular activity
◎ How this compares to the expected level of development for a child of this age
◎ Any factors which may have affected the child's ability to learn and/or behave, for example the immediate environment, significant events, illness, child's cultural background, or special needs.

There are four stages to the assessment of children's developmental progress, skills and/or behaviour. Imagine a court case where evidence is being given by various people concerning the child's development, learning and behaviour:

1 The 'eye-witness'. This is your statement of what actually happened; what you observed during the observation. Remember to concentrate on the main focus of the observation (for example, the child's drawing or painting skills during a creative activity), but you should also include information on other related aspects of development (such as the fine motor skills used for drawing or painting).
2 The 'expert witness'. Refer to at least 2 textbooks and see what childcare, education or psychology authors have to say about children's development. State the expected levels of development, as described by the experts, for children of the same age as the child you observed.
3 The 'summing-up'. With the information from your observation and the opinions of the experts, you can now make an assessment of the child's development, learning and/or behaviour. Compare and contrast the similarities and differences between the abilities or skills demonstrated by the child during the observation with the levels of expected development (for example how this child's abilities compare to the drawing or painting skills and intellectual development as expected for children of this particular age).
4 The 'verdict'. From this comparison, draw your own conclusions regarding this child's development, learning and/or behaviour; state whether you think the child's abilities are ahead, equal to or behind the expected level of development as outlined by the experts. Remember to be tactful in your comments and also to be positive! Your conclusions should focus on what the child can do. Do not forget to mention other factors that might have affected the child's development, learning and/or behaviour in general or in this particular activity. Comment on how other aspects of the child's development affected the child's abilities in the focus area (such as poor concentration or limited motor skills).

Your assessment may include charts, diagrams and other representations of the data you collected from your observation (see examples of observation charts on page 46). Your college tutor or assessor should give you guidelines on how to present your observations. Otherwise you might find the following suggested format useful:

Suggested format for presenting observations

Date of observation:

Method:

Start time:

Finish time:

Number of children/staff:

Permission for observation:

Type of setting and age range: *e.g. children's centre, day nursery, primary school*

Immediate context/background information: *including the routine/activity and its location*

Description of child/children: *including age(s) in years and months*

Aims: *why are you doing this particular observation?*

Observation: *the observation may be a written report, a pie chart or bar graph, tick chart*

Assessment: *include the following:*
◎ *Did you achieve your aims?*
◎ *Your assessment of the child's development, learning and/or behaviour, looking at all aspects of the child's development but with particular emphasis on the focus area (e.g. drawing or painting skills)*
◎ *References to support your comments.*

Personal learning: *what you gained from doing this observation, e.g. what you have learned about this aspect of child development and using this particular method of observing children, e.g. was this the most appropriate method of observation for this type of routine or activity?*

Recommendations:
◎ *On how to encourage/extend the child's development, learning and/or behaviour in the focus area, e.g. suggestions for activities to develop the child's drawing or painting skills*
◎ *For any aspect of the child's development, learning and/or behaviour which you think requires further observation and assessment.*

References/bibliography: list details of all the books used to complete your assessment.

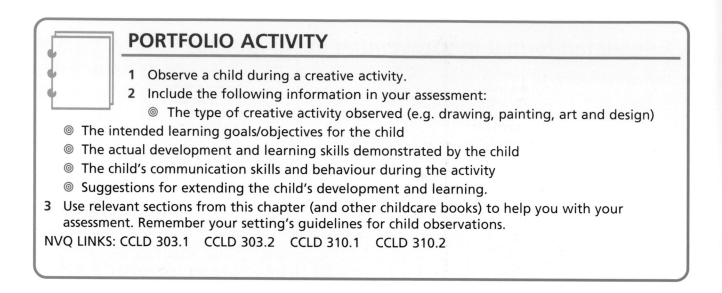

PORTFOLIO ACTIVITY

1 Observe a child during a creative activity.
2 Include the following information in your assessment:
   ◎ The type of creative activity observed (e.g. drawing, painting, art and design)
◎ The intended learning goals/objectives for the child
◎ The actual development and learning skills demonstrated by the child
◎ The child's communication skills and behaviour during the activity
◎ Suggestions for extending the child's development and learning.
3 Use relevant sections from this chapter (and other childcare books) to help you with your assessment. Remember your setting's guidelines for child observations.
NVQ LINKS: CCLD 303.1   CCLD 303.2   CCLD 310.1   CCLD 310.2

CCLD 303.3 Plan provision to promote development

Knowledge Base

K3D205   K3D209   K3D212   K3D215   K3T111

You will need to plan provision for the children you work with based on your assessment of their developmental progress. As this progress depends on each child's level of maturation and prior experiences, you should take these factors into account and have realistic expectations when planning activities and routines to promote children's development. This includes regularly reviewing and updating plans for individual children and ensuring that plans balance the needs of individual children and the group as appropriate to your setting.

Children develop at widely different rates but in broadly the same sequence. When planning provision to promote children's development you need to recognise that children's development is holistic even though it is divided into different areas. You should remember to look at the 'whole' child. You need to look at all areas of children's development in relation to the particular aspect of development or learning you are focusing on when planning provision. (See page 54 for more information on understanding children's development.)

The planning cycle

Following your observation and assessment of a child's development, learning and/or behaviour, your recommendations can provide the basis for planning appropriate routines and/or activities to encourage and extend the child's skills in specific areas. Effective planning is based on children's individual needs, abilities and interests, hence the importance of accurate and reliable child observations and assessments. Depending on the type of setting, you may also need to plan provision based on the requirements for curriculum frameworks for early education.

What is the aim of your activity for the child?

Plan the activity: What more do you need? Consider safety factors

Now evaluate this outcome. Can you identify any needs the child might have as a result of this observation?

Planning Cycle for Observations, Assessments and Activities

What is your role in this activity?

Write down the outcome of this activity. Was your aim achieved?

If possible, observe and record the child during the activity

Implement the activity. What is the child's response?

Figure 3.3 Planning children's activities by Jackie Harding and Liz Meldon-Smith

When planning care routines, play opportunities and learning activities, your overall aims should be to: support the care and development of all the children you work with; ensure every child has full access to the appropriate curriculum; meet children's individual developmental and learning needs; and build on each child's existing knowledge, understanding and skills.

Being flexible in planning activities

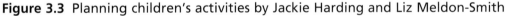

Even in settings where children are working within the National Curriculum framework or towards the 'early learning goals', your planning needs to be flexible enough to allow for children's individual interests and unplanned, spontaneous opportunities for promoting their development and learning. For example, an unexpected snowfall can provide a wonderful opportunity to talk about snow and for children to share their delight and fascination for this type of weather. Or a child might bring in their collection of postcards, prompting an unplanned discussion about other children's collections; this might be developed into a 'mini-topic' on collections if the children are really interested. It is important that children have this freedom of choice to help represent their experiences, feelings and ideas. Adults may still be involved in these activities, but in more subtle ways such as encouraging children to make their own decisions, or talking with children while they are engaged in these types of activities.

Unit Links

For this Unit you need to understand the following sections:

CCLD 309 Plan and implement curriculum frameworks for early education (see Chapter 12)

CCLD 312 Plan and implement positive environments for babies and children under 3 years (see Chapter 11)

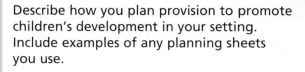

Activity

Describe how you plan provision to promote children's development in your setting. Include examples of any planning sheets you use.

Check it out

Find out what procedures and strategies are used in your setting to support children through transitions.

Think About

How have you made use of an unplanned learning opportunity?

CCLD 303.4
Implement and evaluate plans to promote development

In addition, planning activities may be based on Individual Education Plans or Behaviour Support Plans (see CCLD 339.3 in Capter 14).

You will also need to plan provision to support children through transitions, for example: from home to day care; from nursery to primary school; from Key Stage 1 to Key Stage 2; from primary to secondary school; and from secondary school to college or workplace.

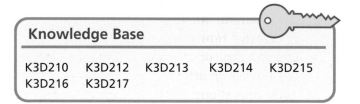

Knowledge Base

K3D210   K3D212   K3D213   K3D214   K3D215
K3D216   K3D217

Good preparation and organisation are essential when implementing plans to promote children's development, including:

◎ Having ready for the child or group of children any instructions and/or questions, such as prompt cards, worksheet, work card or written on the board
◎ Ensuring there are sufficient materials and equipment including any specialist equipment
◎ Setting out the materials and equipment on the

Unit Link

For this Unit you need to understand the following sections:

CCLD 325 Support the child or young person's successful transfer and transition in learning and development contexts (see Chapter 10)

Suggested format for routine or activity plans

◎ Title: *brief description of the routine or activity*
◎ Date: *the date of the routine or activity*
◎ Plan duration: *how long will the routine or activity last?*
◎ Aim and rationale: *the main purpose of the routine or activity including how it will encourage the child's or children's development, learning and/or behaviour. The rationale should outline why you have selected this particular routine or activity (e.g. identified particular child's need through observation; links to topics/themes within the setting). How does the routine or activity link with any early learning goals or the national curriculum?*
◎ Staff and setting: *the roles and number of staff involved in the routine or activity plus the type of setting and the age range of the child or children involved.*
◎ Details of child/children: *routine or activity plans involving an individual child or small group of children should specify first name, age in years and months plus any relevant special needs; routine or activity plans involving larger groups should specify the age range and ability levels.*
◎ Objectives/learning outcomes for the child/children: *indicate what the child/children could gain from participating in the activity in each developmental area: SPICE.*
◎ Preparation: *what do you need to prepare in advance (e.g. selecting or making appropriate materials; checking availability of equipment)? Think about the instructions and/or questions for the child/children; will these be spoken and/or written down, e.g. on a worksheet/card or on the board? Do you need prompt cards for instructions or questions?*
◎ Resources: *what materials and equipment will you need? Where will you get them from? Are there any special requirements? Remember equal opportunities including special needs. How will you set out the necessary resources (e.g. set out on the table ready or the children getting materials and equipment out for themselves)?*
◎ Organisation: *where will you implement the routine or activity? How will you organise the routine or activity? How will you give out any instructions the children need? Will you work with children one at a time or as a group? Are there any particular safety requirements? How will you organise any tidying up after the routine or activity? Will the children be encouraged to help tidy up?*
◎ Implementation: *describe what happened when you implemented the routine or activity with the child/children. Include any alterations to your original plan, e.g. changes in timing or resources.*
◎ Equal opportunities: *indicate any multicultural aspects to the routine or activity and any additional considerations for children with special needs.*
◎ Review and evaluation: *review and evaluate the following:*
  ◎ *The aims and objectives/learning outcomes*
  ◎ *The effectiveness of your preparation, organisation and implementation*
  ◎ *What you learned about children's development and learning*
  ◎ *What you learned about planning routines or activities*
  ◎ *Possible modifications for future similar routines or activities.*
◎ References and/or bibliography: *the review and evaluation may include references appropriate to children's development, learning and behaviour. Include a bibliography of any books used as references or for ideas when planning the routine or activity.*

table or let the children get the resources out for themselves, depending on their ages and abilities.

Implementing a routine or activity may involve:

◎ Giving out any instructions to the children
◎ Showing children what to do by demonstrating a new technique
◎ Keeping an individual child and/or group on task
◎ Clarifying meaning and/or ideas
◎ Explaining any difficult words to the children
◎ Assisting children with any special equipment, such as a hearing aid or a Dictaphone
◎ Providing any other appropriate assistance
◎ Encouraging the children to tidy up afterwards as appropriate to their ages and abilities; remembering to maintain the children's safety at all times.

After you have planned and implemented a care routine, play opportunity or learning activity you will need to evaluate it. Some evaluation also occurs during the routine or activity, providing continuous assessment of a child's performance. It is important to evaluate the routine or activity so that you can: assess whether the routine or activity has been successful, for example the aims and objectives or outcomes have been met; identify possible ways in which the routine or activity might be modified/adapted to meet the individual needs of the child or children; provide accurate information for the senior practitioner, setting manager or other professionals about the successfulness of a particular routine or activity. The senior practitioner, setting manager or your college tutor/assessor should give you guidelines on how to present your routine and activity plans. If not, you might find the suggested format given on the previous page useful.

PORTFOLIO ACTIVITY

Use your suggestions from your observation of a child during a creative activity (see page 50) to plan a creative activity to extend the child's skills in a specific area. After discussing your plan with the senior practitioner, implement and then evaluate the activity.

NVQ LINKS: CCLD 303.3   CCLD 303.4
CCLD 309.1   CCLD 309.2   CCLD 309.3

Understanding children's development

Knowledge Base

K3D209	K3D210	K3D212	K3D213	K3D214
K3D215	K3D216	K3D217		

K3D218 (0–3 years)   K3D219 (3–7 years)
K3D220 (7–12 years) K3D221 (12–16 years)

The most essential aspect of planning and supporting children's care and development involves your role and responsibilities for providing routines and activities that will help to meet all the children's developmental needs. To do this you need to know and understand children's development.

Nature versus nurture in children's development

Is children's development derived from nature (their genetic inheritance) or the result of nurture (their upbringing and experiences)? This is one of the major questions concerning children's development. If a person's abilities are dependent on heredity (nature) then it is possible to believe that people are born with a predetermined level of abilities which remains the same all their lives, that is they can be only as intelligent as those abilities permit. However, if a person's abilities arise as the result of their environment (nurture) it is then possible to believe that people are as capable as their learning experiences allow.

Research indicates that the development of children's abilities depends on both nature and nurture. Babies and young children have a predisposition towards learning which is activated by environmental triggers such as social interaction, language and learning opportunities. For example, research with twins, separated and raised in different environments, shows that genetics is a key factor because the twins had similar intelligence quotient (IQ) scores despite their different life experiences. Environment is also important. For example, research on children from different ethnic groups shows that where there is racial discrimination the children did less well educationally; when their families moved to areas where there was little or no discrimination these children's IQ scores were the same as those of children from the main ethnic group. Many different factors may affect children's development, for example: physical and mental health; genetic inheritance; gender; social, cultural, environmental and financial factors; family background and circumstances; disability or sensory impairment; play opportunities and learning experiences; and discrimination.

Think About

What is your own opinion regarding nature versus nurture in children's development?

The sequence of children's development

It is more accurate to think in terms of a sequence of children's development rather than stages of development. This is because *stages* refer to development that occurs at fixed ages while *sequence* indicates development that follows the same basic pattern but not necessarily at fixed ages. You should really use the term 'sequence' when referring to all aspects of children's development. However, the work of people such as Mary Sheridan provides a useful guide to the milestones of expected development, that is, the usual pattern of children's development or *norm*. As well as their chronological age, children's development is affected by many other factors, such as maturation, social interaction, play opportunities, early learning experiences and special needs. The developmental charts in this chapter do indicate specific ages, but only to provide a framework to help you understand children's development. You should always remember that all children are unique individuals and develop at their own rate.

Promoting children's social development

Promoting children's social development involves helping children to develop social skills such as: socialisation; developing independence (including self-help skills such as feeding, toileting and dressing); understanding moral concepts; developing acceptable behaviour patterns; developing positive relationships; understanding the needs and rights of others.

Socialisation

Socialisation involves how children relate socially (and emotionally) to other people. Children need to learn how to deal appropriately with a whole range of emotions, including anger and frustration, within a supportive environment. Socialisation occurs through the observation, identification, imitation and assimilation of the behaviour of other people. Children model their attitudes and actions on the behaviour of others. You need to be aware of the significant impact you make to children's social (and emotional) development and ensure that you provide a positive role model. An essential aspect of socialisation involves getting young children to behave in socially acceptable ways without damaging their self-esteem. That is, rejecting the children's unacceptable behaviour, not the children themselves. Socialisation begins from birth as babies interact with the people around them and respond to their environment.

Developing independence

Children need the freedom to develop their independence in ways that are appropriate to their overall development. Some may need more encouragement than others to become increasingly independent and less reliant on other people. Children gain independence by: developing self-help skills; making choices and decisions; and taking responsibility for their own actions. Most children start wanting to do things for themselves from about the age of 18 months to 2 years onwards. While young children want to do things for themselves (such as getting dressed and making things) they may become frustrated if they are unable to do so. Many conflicts arise between young children and other people as children increase their independence and expand the boundaries of their world. Adults caring for children should avoid inhibiting the child's need for independence, as this can lead to either emotional dependence, excessive shyness and an over-cautious nature *or* emotional detachment, anti-social behaviour and a rebellious nature. Adults should also avoid unrestricted independence as the child may be exposed to danger and physical harm (from fire, boiling water, traffic, and so on) and/or the child may become selfish and unable to recognise the needs and rights of others. It is important for adults to strike a balance between these two extremes, allowing for the individual child's need for independence and providing supervision with appropriate guidelines for socially acceptable behaviour which takes into account the needs of everyone in the childcare setting.

Developing moral concepts

As part of their social development children gradually develop moral concepts, including: knowing the difference between right and wrong, that is understanding what is and is not acceptable behaviour; developing an awareness of fairness and justice, for example understanding that goodness is not always rewarded, but that we still need to do what is right; helping others, including recognising the needs and feelings of others; sharing, including understanding the importance of turn-taking and co-operation; and developing empathy for others and their beliefs even if we disagree with them, including freedom of speech.

The sequence of children's social development: 0 to 16 years

Age 0 to 3 months

◎ Cries to communicate needs to others; stops crying to listen to others

◎ Responds to smiles from others; responds positively to others, such as family members and even friendly strangers unless very upset (when only main caregiver will do!)

◎ Considers others only in relation to satisfying own needs for food, drink, warmth, sleep, comfort and reassurance.

Age 3 to 9 months

◎ Responds positively to others, especially to familiar people such as family members; by the age of 9 months is very wary of strangers

◎ Communicates with others by making noises and participating in 'conversation-like' exchanges; responds to own name

◎ Begins to see self as separate from others.

Age 9 to 18 months

◎ Responds to simple instructions (if wants to!)

◎ Communicates using (limited) range of recognisable words

◎ Shows egocentric behaviour, for example expects to be considered first; and all toys belong to them

◎ Is unintentionally aggressive to other children.

Age 18 months to 2 years

◎ Responds positively to others, for example plays alongside other children and enjoys games with known adults

◎ Communicates more effectively with others; responds to simple instructions

◎ Wants to help adults and enjoys imitating their activities

◎ May be interested in older children and their activities; imitates these activities

◎ May unintentionally disrupt the play of others, for example takes toys away to play with by self

◎ Becomes very independent, for instance wants to do things by self

◎ Still demonstrates egocentric behaviour; wants own way and says 'No!' a lot.

Age 2 to 3 years

◎ Continues to enjoy the company of others

◎ Wants to please and seeks approval from adults

◎ Is still very egocentric and very protective of own possessions; unable to share with other children although may give toy to another child if adult requests it to please the adult

◎ May find group experiences difficult due to this egocentric behaviour
◎ Uses language more effectively to communicate with others.

Age 3 to 5 years

◎ Enjoys the company of others; learns to play *with* other children, not just alongside them
◎ Uses language to communicate more effectively with others
◎ Develops self-help skills (such as dressing self, going to the toilet) as becomes more competent and confident in own abilities
◎ Still wants to please and seeks approval from adults
◎ Observes closely how others behave and imitates them
◎ Still fairly egocentric; may get angry with other children if they disrupt play activities or snatch play items required for own play; expects adults to take their side in any dispute
◎ Gradually is able to share group possessions at playgroup or nursery.

Age 5 to 7 years

◎ Enjoys the company of other children; may have special friend(s)
◎ Uses language even more effectively to communicate, share ideas, engage in more complex play activities
◎ Appears confident and competent in own abilities
◎ Co-operates with others, takes turns and begins to follow rules in games
◎ Seeks adult approval; will even blame others for own mistakes to escape disapproval
◎ Observes how others behave and will imitate them; has a particular role model
◎ May copy unwanted behaviour, for example swearing, biting or kicking to gain adult attention.

Age 7 to 12 years

◎ Continues to enjoy the company of other children; wants to belong to a group; usually has at least one special friend
◎ Uses language to communicate very effectively, but may use in negative ways, by name-calling or telling tales, as well as positively to share ideas and participate in complex play activities, often based on television characters or computer games
◎ Is able to play on own; appreciates own space away from others on occasion
◎ Becomes less concerned with adult approval and more concerned with peer approval
◎ Is able to participate in games with rules and other co-operative activities.

Age 12 to 16 years

◎ Continues to enjoy the company of other children/young people; individual friendships are still important; belonging to group or gang becomes increasingly important but can also be a major source of anxiety or conflict
◎ The desire for peer approval can overtake the need for adult approval and may cause challenges to adult authority at home, school or in the play setting, particularly in the teenage years

◎ Participates in team games/sports or other group activities including clubs and hobbies; can follow complex rules and co-operate fully but may be very competitive

◎ Strongly influenced by a variety of role models, especially those in the media, such as sports celebrities and film/pop stars

◎ Is able to communicate very effectively and uses language much more to resolve any difficulties in social interactions

◎ Can be very supportive towards others, including people with special needs or those experiencing difficulties at home, school, in the play setting or in the wider community.

PORTFOLIO ACTIVITY

1 Observe a group of children during a play activity or playing a game. Focus on one child's social development.

2 In your assessment comment on: the child's level of social interaction; the child's use of language and communication skills; the child's behaviour during the activity; the role of the adult in promoting the child's social development; and suggestions for further activities to encourage or extend the child's social development including appropriate resources.

NVQ LINKS: CCLD 303.1   CCLD 303.2 CCLD 301.3   CCLD 308.1   CCLD 318.1   CCLD 337.1
CCLD 337.2

Five ways to promote children's social development

As a childcarer you are responsible for providing appropriate routines and activities to encourage and extend the children's social skills. You can do this by:

1 Setting goals and boundaries to encourage socially acceptable behaviour that is appropriate to the children's ages and levels of development. Using appropriate praise and rewards can help.

2 Encouraging the children's self-help skills. Be patient and provide time for the child to do things independently, for example: choosing play activities and selecting own materials; helping to tidy up; and dressing independently during dressing-up.

3 Providing opportunities for the children to participate in social play, such as encouraging children to join in team games, sports and other co-operative activities.

4 Using books, stories, puppets and play people to help the children understand ideas about fairness, jealousy and growing up and dealing with conflict situations.

5 Encouraging the children to take turns by, for example, sharing toys and other play equipment. Emphasising co-operation and sharing rather than competition.

PORTFOLIO ACTIVITY

1 Plan, implement and evaluate a play activity which encourages or extends a child's social development. Use the assessment from your observation of a child's social development from page 59 as the basis for your planning.

2 Encourage the child to use a variety of social skills. For example: positive behaviour; independence (such as using self-help skills or making choices); effective communication skills; sharing resources; and understanding the needs and feelings of others.

3 Consider how you could meet the needs of children with behavioural difficulties with this activity (see Chapter 9).

NVQ LINKS: CCLD 303.3   CCLD 303.4   CCLD 301.2   CCLD 301.3   CCLD 308.1   CCLD 318.2   CCLD 318.3   CCLD 337.1   CCLD 337.2

Promoting children's physical development

Children's physical development includes their increasing ability to perform more complex physical activities involving gross motor skills, fine motor skills and co-ordination.

Developing gross motor skills

Developing gross motor skills involves whole body movements. Examples of using these skills include walking, running, climbing stairs, hopping, jumping, skipping, cycling, swimming, climbing play apparatus, playing badminton, basketball, football, hockey, netball, rugby or tennis. Children need strength, stamina and suppleness to become proficient in activities involving gross motor skills.

Developing fine motor skills

Developing fine motor skills involves whole hand movements, wrist action or delicate procedures using the fingers, such as the palmar grasp (grabbing and holding a small brick), the pincer grip (using the thumb and index finger to pick up a pea) and the tripod grasp (holding a crayon, pencil or pen).

Examples of these skills include drawing, painting, writing, model-making, playing with wooden/plastic bricks or construction kits, cutting with scissors, doing/undoing buttons, shoelaces and other fastenings. Children need good concentration levels and hand-eye co-ordination (see below) to become proficient in activities involving fine motor skills.

Developing co-ordination

Developing co-ordination involves hand-eye co-ordination, whole body co-ordination and balance. Examples of activities that require hand-eye co-ordination include drawing, painting, using scissors, writing and threading beads. Children demonstrate whole body co-ordination when crawling, walking, cycling, swimming and playing football or netball, and they need balance for hopping and taking part in gymnastics. Co-ordination plays an important part in developing children's gross and fine motor skills, while both co-ordination and balance are needed to improve children's gross motor skills.

Provide appropriate play opportunities for children and young people to develop their physical skills. Remember that some children may be limited in their physical abilities due to physical disability, sensory impairment or other special needs.

3

The sequence of children's physical development 0 to 16 years

Age 0 to 3 months

◎ Sleeps much of the time and grows fast
◎ Tries to lift head
◎ Starts to kick legs, with movements gradually becoming smoother
◎ Starts to wave arms about
◎ Begins to hold objects when placed in hand, for example an appropriate size/shaped rattle
◎ Grasp reflex diminishes as hand and eye co-ordination begins to develop
◎ Enjoys finger play such as simple finger rhymes
◎ Becomes more alert when awake
◎ Learns to roll from side on to back
◎ Sees best at distance of 25 cm then gradually starts watching objects that are further away
◎ Needs opportunities to play and exercise, for example soft toys, cloth books and playmat with different textures and sounds.

Age 3 to 9 months

◎ Establishes head control; moves head round to follow people and objects
◎ Begins to sit with support; from about 6 months sits unsupported
◎ Rolls over
◎ May begin to crawl, stand and cruise while holding on to furniture (from about 6 months)
◎ Learns to pull self up to sitting position
◎ Begins to use palmar grasp and transfers objects from one hand to the other
◎ Develops pincer grasp using thumb and index finger from about 6 months
◎ Continues to enjoy finger rhymes
◎ Drops things deliberately and searches for hidden/dropped objects (from about 8 months)
◎ Puts objects into containers and takes them out
◎ Enjoys water play in the bath
◎ Needs opportunities for play and exercise including soft toys, board books, bricks, containers, activity centres, and so on.

Age 9 to 18 months

◎ Is now very mobile, for instance crawls, bottom-shuffles, cruises and walks
◎ Starts to go upstairs (with supervision) but has difficulty coming down
◎ Needs safe environment in which to explore as becomes increasingly mobile, so remember safety gates on stairs, and so on
◎ Throws toys deliberately
◎ Needs space, materials and opportunities to play alongside other children

◎ Watches ball rolling towards self and tries to push it back
◎ Has mature pincer grasp and can scribble with crayons
◎ Points to objects using index finger
◎ Places one (or more) bricks on top of each other to make a small tower
◎ Holds a cup and tries to feed self
◎ Continues to enjoy finger rhymes plus simple action songs.

Age 18 months to 2 years
◎ Starts using potty but has difficulty keeping dry
◎ Can feed self
◎ Walks well and tries to run but has difficulty stopping
◎ Comes downstairs on front with help
◎ Learns to push a pedal-less tricycle or sit-and-ride toy with feet
◎ Tries to throw ball but has difficulty catching
◎ Bends down to pick things up
◎ Uses several bricks to make a tower
◎ As fine motor skills improve continues to scribble and can do very simple jigsaw puzzles
◎ Enjoys action songs and rhymes
◎ Needs space, materials and opportunities to play alongside other children.

Age 2 to 3 years
◎ Uses potty and stays dry more reliably
◎ Comes downstairs in upright position one stair at a time
◎ Starts to climb well on play apparatus
◎ Kicks a ball, learns to jump and may learn to somersault
◎ Learns to pedal a tricycle
◎ Can undress self; tries to dress self but needs help, especially with socks and fastenings
◎ Fine motor skills improving: has increased control of crayons and paintbrush; tries to use scissors
◎ Enjoys construction activities and can build more complex structures
◎ Continues to enjoy action songs and rhymes
◎ Needs space, materials and opportunities to play alongside and with other children

Age 3 to 5 years
◎ Usually clean and dry but may have occasional 'accidents'
◎ Able to run well – and stop!
◎ Competent at activities involving gross motor skills such as jumping, riding a tricycle, climbing play apparatus and using a swing
◎ Throws and catches a ball but is still inaccurate

◎ Fine motor skills continue to improve, for example can use scissors
◎ Continues to enjoy action songs plus simple singing and dancing games
◎ Needs space, materials and opportunities to play co-operatively with other children.

Age 5 to 7 years
◎ Clean and dry but may still have occasional 'accidents' if absorbed in an activity or upset
◎ Can dress/undress self but may still need help with intricate fastenings and shoelaces
◎ Has improved gross motor skills and co-ordination so is more proficient at running, jumping, climbing and balancing
◎ Has some difficulty with hopping and skipping
◎ Has improved ball skills but still learning to use a bat
◎ May learn to ride a bicycle (with stabilisers)
◎ Enjoys swimming activities
◎ Fine motor skills continue to improve: has better pencil/crayon control; is more competent at handling materials and making things
◎ Continues to enjoy action songs plus singing and dancing games
◎ Needs space, materials and opportunities to play co-operatively with other children.

Age 7 to 12 years
◎ Can dress/undress self including fastenings and shoelaces
◎ Grows taller and thinner; starts losing baby teeth
◎ Improved gross motor skills and co-ordination lead to proficiency in climbing, running, jumping, balancing, hopping and skipping
◎ Can hit a ball with a bat
◎ Learns to ride a bicycle (without stabilisers)
◎ Learns to swim (if taught properly)
◎ As fine motor skills improve, handwriting becomes easier and more legible
◎ Can do more complex construction activities
◎ Continues to enjoy singing and dancing games
◎ Needs space, materials and opportunities to play co-operatively with other children.

Age 12 to 16 years
◎ Can dress/undress self including intricate fastenings and shoelaces
◎ Grows taller and thinner; continues losing baby teeth
◎ Physical changes of puberty
◎ Improved gross motor skills and co-ordination lead to proficiency in climbing, running, jumping, balancing, hopping and skipping, swimming
◎ Enjoys team games and sports

- Rides a bicycle with competence and confidence
- Improved fine motor skills make handwriting easier and more legible
- Can do more complex construction activities
- Continues to enjoy singing and dancing but often prefers performing set dance routines rather than participating in dancing games
- Needs space, materials and opportunities to play co-operatively with other children.

PORTFOLIO ACTIVITY

1 Observe a child involved in a physical activity, e.g. using play equipment. Focus on the physical skills demonstrated by the child.

2 In your assessment comment on: the child's gross motor skills; the child's fine motor skills; the child's co-ordination skills; the role of the adult in promoting the child's physical development; suggestions for further activities to encourage or extend the child's physical development.

NVQ LINKS: CCLD 303.1   CCLD 303.2   CCLD 307.1   CCLD 318.1

Five ways to promote children's physical development

As a childcarer you are responsible for promoting children's physical development and physical well-being. You can do this by:

1 Providing play opportunities for children to explore and experiment with their gross motor skills, both indoors and outdoors, with and without play apparatus or other equipment. Helping children to practise fine motor skills (by using bricks, jigsaws, play dough, sand, construction kits, drawing, and so on) and to develop body awareness through action songs such as 'Head, shoulders, knees and toes'.

2 Maintaining the children's safety by supervising them at all times and checking that any equipment used meets required safety standards and is positioned on an appropriate surface. Ensure the children know how to use the equipment correctly and safely.

3 Selecting activities, tools and materials that are appropriate to the ages and levels of development of the children to help them practise their physical skills. Encourage children to persevere with tackling new skills that are particularly difficult and praise them as they become competent in each physical skill.

4 Using everyday routines to develop the children's fine motor skills, for example getting dressed, dealing with fastenings and shoelaces, using a cup, using a spoon, fork or knife, helping prepare or serve food, setting the table, or washing up. (Remember safety.)

5 Allowing the children to be as independent as possible when developing their physical skills, including adapting activities and/or using specialist equipment for children with special needs to enable their participation in physical activities as appropriate.

PORTFOLIO ACTIVITY

1 Plan, implement and evaluate an activity which encourages or extends a child's physical skills. Use the assessment information from your observation of a child's physical development from page 64 as the basis for your planning.
2 Include examples of physical skills such as gross motor skills, fine motor skills and/or co-ordination skills.
3 Consider how you could meet the needs of children with physical disabilities with this activity (see Chapter 7).

NVQ LINKS: CCLD 303.3   CCLD 303.4   CCLD 307.1   CCLD 318.2   CCLD 318.3

Promoting children's intellectual development

Intellectual or *cognitive* development involves the processes of gaining, storing, recalling and using information. To develop as healthy, considerate and intelligent human beings, all children require intellectual stimulation as well as physical care and emotional security. Children are constantly thinking and learning, gathering new information and formulating new ideas about themselves, other people and the world around them. The interrelated components of intellectual development are: thinking; sensory perception; language and communication; reasoning and problem-solving; understanding concepts; memory; concentration; and imagination and creativity. (See Chapter 12 for detailed information on these interrelated components.)

Promoting children's communication skills and language development

Language is a key factor in all children's development as it provides them with the skills they need to communicate with others, relate to others, explore the environment, understand concepts, formulate ideas and express feelings. The word 'language' is often used to describe the process of speaking and listening, but it is much more than verbal communication.

The human ability to utilise language depends on the use of a recognised system of symbols and a common understanding of what those symbols mean. Obviously there are many different systems of symbols as indicated by the many different languages and alphabet systems used by people

The sequence of children's intellectual development: 0 to 16 years

Age 0 to 3 months
◎ Recognises parents; concentrates on familiar voices rather than unfamiliar ones
◎ Aware of different smells
◎ Explores by putting objects in mouth
◎ Observes objects that move; responds to bright colours and bold images
◎ Stores and recalls information through images
◎ Sees everything in relation to self (is egocentric).

Age 3 to 9 months
◎ Knows individuals and recognises familiar faces
◎ Recognises certain sounds and objects
◎ Shows interest in everything, especially toys and books
◎ Concentrates on well-defined objects and follows direction of moving object
◎ Anticipates familiar actions and enjoys games such as 'peep-po'
◎ Searches for hidden or dropped objects (from about 8 months)
◎ Observes what happens at home and when out and about
◎ Explores immediate environment once mobile
◎ Processes information through images
◎ Enjoys water play in the bath
◎ Sees everything in relation to self (is still egocentric).

Age 9 to 18 months
◎ Explores immediate environment using senses, especially sight and touch; has no sense of danger
◎ Concentrates more, due to curiosity and increased physical skills, but still has short attention span
◎ Follows one-step instructions and/or gestured commands
◎ Observes other people closely and tries to imitate their actions
◎ Uses 'trial and error' methods when playing with bricks, containers
◎ Searches for hidden or dropped objects (aware of object permanence)
◎ Learns that objects can be grouped together
◎ Continues to store and recall information through images
◎ Is still egocentric.

Age 18 months to 2 years
◎ Recognises objects from pictures and books
◎ Points to desired objects; selects named objects

◎ Matches basic colours; starts to match shapes
◎ Does very simple puzzles
◎ Follows 1-step instructions
◎ Concentrates for longer, perhaps searching for hidden object, but attention span still quite short
◎ Shows lots of curiosity and continues exploring using senses and 'trial and error' methods
◎ Processes information through images and increasingly through language too
◎ Shows preferences and starts to make choices
◎ Is still egocentric.

Age 2 to 3 years
◎ Identifies facial features and main body parts
◎ Continues to imitate other children and adults
◎ Follows 2-step instructions
◎ Matches more colours and shapes including puzzles and other matching activities
◎ Points to named object in pictures and books
◎ Develops understanding of big and small
◎ Begins to understand concept of time at basic level, such as before/after, today/tomorrow
◎ Enjoys imaginative play; able to use symbols in play, for example pretend a doll is a real baby
◎ Concentrates on intricate tasks such as creative activities or construction, but may still have short attention span, especially if not really interested in the activity
◎ Is very pre-occupied with own activities; still egocentric
◎ Shows some awareness of right and wrong
◎ Processes information through language rather than images.

Age 3 to 5 years
◎ Learns about basic concepts through play
◎ Experiments with colour, shape and texture
◎ Recalls a simple sequence of events
◎ Follows 2- or 3-step instructions, including positional ones, e.g. 'Please put your ball in the box under the table'
◎ Continues to enjoy imaginative and creative play
◎ Interested in more complex construction activities
◎ Concentrates on more complex activities as attention span increases
◎ Plays co-operatively with other children; able to accept and share ideas in group activities
◎ Shows some awareness of right and wrong, the needs of others
◎ Holds strong opinions about likes and dislikes
◎ Processes information using language.

Age 5 to 7 years
◎ Is very curious and asks lots of questions
◎ Continues to enjoy imaginative and creative play activities
◎ Continues to enjoy construction activities; spatial awareness increases
◎ Knows, matches and names colours and shapes
◎ Follows 3-step instructions
◎ Develops interest in reading for themselves
◎ Enjoys jigsaw puzzles and games
◎ Concentrates for longer, for example television programmes, longer stories, and can recall details
◎ Shows awareness of right and wrong, the needs of others
◎ Begins to see other people's points of view
◎ Stores and recalls more complex information using language.

Age 7 to 12 years
◎ Learns to read more complex texts and continues to develop writing skills
◎ Enjoys number work, but may still need real objects to help mathematical processes
◎ Enjoys experimenting with materials and exploring the environment
◎ Develops creative abilities as co-ordination improves, resulting in more detailed drawings
◎ Begins to know the difference between real and imaginary, but still enjoys imaginative play, such as acting out ideas, or pretending to be characters from television or films
◎ Interested in more complex construction activities
◎ Has longer attention span; does not like to be disturbed during play activities
◎ Follows increasingly more complex instructions
◎ Enjoys board games and other games with rules; also computer games
◎ Develops a competitive streak
◎ Has increased awareness of right and wrong, the needs of others
◎ Sees other people's points of view
◎ Seeks information from various sources, such as encyclopaedia, the Internet
◎ Processes expanding knowledge and information through language.

Age 12 to 16 years
◎ Reads more complex texts with improved comprehension and extends writing skills
◎ Develops understanding of abstract mathematical/scientific processes, such as algebra and physics
◎ Continues to enjoy experiments and exploration of the wider environment
◎ Develops more creative abilities, which may result in very detailed drawings and stories
◎ Knows the difference between real and imaginary
◎ Has increased concentration levels
◎ Continues to follow more complex instructions

◎ Continues to enjoy board games and computer games which require strategy skills
◎ Has a competitive streak and may have particular interests which allow them to show off their intellectual abilities, for example chess, computer clubs
◎ Has well-defined understanding of right and wrong; can consider the needs of others
◎ Sees other people's points of view
◎ Continues to seek information from various sources, such as an encyclopaedia or the Internet
◎ Continues to process increasing knowledge and information through language.

PORTFOLIO ACTIVITY

1 Observe a child during a learning activity. Focus on the child's intellectual development.

2 In your assessment comment on: the child's imaginative and creative skills; the child's level of concentration; any problem-solving skills used by the child; the child's use of language and communication skills; the role of the adult in promoting the child's intellectual development; and suggestions for further activities to encourage or extend the child's intellectual development including appropriate resources.

NVQ LINKS: CCLD 303.1   CCLD 303.2   CCLD 310.2

Five ways to promote children's intellectual development

As a childcarer you are responsible for providing play opportunities and learning to encourage and extend the children's intellectual skills. You can do this by:

1 Providing opportunities and materials to increase the children's curiosity, including books, games, posters, pictures, play equipment and toys. Encourage children to observe details in the environment, such as colours, shapes, smells and textures. Talk about weather conditions. Take the children on outings. Do gardening and/or keep pets.

2 Participating in the children's activities to extend their development and learning by asking questions, providing answers and demonstrating possible ways to use play equipment and other learning resources. Demonstrate how things work or fit together when the children are not sure what to do. Make sure your help is wanted (and necessary). Use verbal prompts where possible to encourage children to solve the problem for themselves.

3 Providing gradually more challenging play and learning activities but do not push the children too hard by introducing activities which are obviously too complex; instead of extending the children's

abilities this will only act as a deterrent as they become frustrated at being unable to do the activity. Provide repetition by encouraging the children to play with toys and games more than once; each time they play, they will discover different things about these activities. Encourage acceptable risk-taking during play opportunities.

4 Helping the children to develop their concentration and memory skills by: ensuring the children are looking and listening attentively when giving new information; explaining how new information is connected to the children's existing experiences and knowledge (for example by linking activities with a common theme); dividing complex activities into smaller tasks to make it easier for children to concentrate; using memory games to encourage and extend concentration levels; singing songs and rhymes, for example following a number sequence in songs like *Five brown teddies, Ten green bottles, When I was one I was just begun ...*

5 Encouraging the children to use their senses to experiment with different materials and to explore their environment by: doing arts and crafts; playing with sand, water, clay, dough, wood; playing with manufactured materials such as plastic construction kits; modelling with safe household junk materials; cooking activities; singing rhymes and songs; clapping games; outings to the local park; matching games, jigsaws and lotto. (See section on encouraging very young children to explore in Chapter 11.)

PORTFOLIO ACTIVITY

1 Plan, implement and evaluate a learning activity which encourages or extends a child's intellectual development. Use the assessment information from your observation of a child's intellectual development from page 69 as the basis for your planning.

2 Encourage the child to use a variety of intellectual skills. For example: imaginative and creative skills; concentration and memory skills; problem-solving skills; and language and communication skills.

3 Consider how you could meet the needs of children with learning difficulties (see Chapter 14) and children with exceptional abilities with this activity (see Chapter 5).

NVQ LINKS: CCLD 303.3   CCLD 303.4   CCLD 309.1   CCLD 309.2   CCLD 321.2

Depending on the learning activity:

CCLD 323.1   CCLD 323.2   CCCLD 323.3 (ICT activity)

CCLD 345.1   CCLD 345.2   CCLD 345.3 (literacy activity)

CCLD 346.1   CCLD 346.2 (numeracy activity)

throughout the world. At first, very young children are not able to use a complex system of symbols; it takes time to learn the system of their particular community language. People also use other ways to communicate their needs and feelings to others, for example: body language; gestures; and facial expressions.

Developing communication skills

Children (and adults) use a variety of ways to communicate. These *modes of language* are essential to being able to communicate effectively with others and to being fully involved in a wide range of social interactions. They can be described as: non-verbal communication; thinking; listening; speaking; reading; and writing. Each mode of

language involves a variety of communication skills which are interrelated; some of the skills are required in more than one mode, for instance reading and writing both involve the processing of oral language in a written form.

You should provide opportunities for children to develop the necessary communication skills to become competent at using these different modes of language. Opportunities for talk are especially helpful in promoting language development and the use of communication skills. When working with children you must be aware of and provide for appropriate play opportunities and learning activities to enable them to develop effective communication skills. Remember that some children may be limited in their ability to use some modes of language due to sensory impairment or other special needs.

The sequence of children's language development: 0 to 16 years

Age 0 to 3 months
◎ Recognises familiar voices; stops crying when hears them
◎ Aware of other sounds; turns head towards sounds
◎ Responds to smiles; moves whole body in response to sound/to attract attention
◎ Pauses to listen to others; makes noises as well as crying, such as *burbling.*

- -

Age 3 to 9 months
◎ Responds with smiles
◎ Recognises family names, but cannot say them
◎ Enjoys looking at pictures and books
◎ Even more responsive to voices and music
◎ Participates in simple games, such as 'peep-po'; tries to imitate sounds during rhymes
◎ Starts *babbling,* uses single syllable sounds, for example 'daa', 'baa' and 'maa'
◎ From about 7 months uses two syllable sounds, such as 'daada', 'baaba', 'maama'
◎ Shouts to attract attention.

Age 9 to 18 months
◎ Continues to imitate sounds; starts *jargoning,* for example joins up syllables so more like 'sentences' such as 'Maama-baaba-daa'
◎ Learns to say first real words, usually the names of animals and everyday things
◎ Uses gestures to emphasise word meanings
◎ Uses vocabulary of between 3 and 20 words
◎ Participates in simple finger rhymes; continues to enjoy books
◎ Over-extends words, that is uses same word to identify similar objects, such as all round objects are called 'ball'.

Age 18 months to 2 years
◎ Uses language to gain information, for example starts asking 'What dat?'
◎ Repeats words said by adults
◎ Acquires 1 to 3 words per month; by the age of 2 years has a vocabulary of about 200 words
◎ Participates in action songs and nursery rhymes; continues to enjoy books and stories
◎ Uses *telegraphic speech,* for example speaks in 2 to 3-word sentences such as 'Daddy go' or 'Milk all gone'.

Age 2 to 3 years
◎ Has vocabulary of about 300 words
◎ Uses more adult forms of speech, including sentences that now include words like 'that', 'this', 'here', 'there', 'then', 'but', 'and'
◎ Can name main body parts
◎ Uses adjectives like 'big', 'small', 'tall'; and words referring to relationships, such as 'I', 'my', 'you', 'yours'
◎ Asks questions to gain more information
◎ Sings songs and rhymes; continues to participate in action songs and enjoy books/stories
◎ Can deliver simple messages.

Age 3 to 5 years
◎ Has vocabulary of between 900 to 1,500 words
◎ Asks lots of questions
◎ Uses language to ask for assistance
◎ Talks constantly to people knows well
◎ Gives very simple accounts of past events
◎ Can say names of colours
◎ Begins to vocalise ideas

◎ Continues to enjoy books, stories, songs and rhymes

◎ Listens to and can follow simple instructions; can deliver verbal messages.

Age 5 to 7 years

◎ May use vocabulary of about 1,500 to 4,000 words

◎ Uses more complex sentence structures

◎ Asks even more questions using 'what', 'when', 'who', 'where', 'how' and especially 'why'!

◎ Develops early reading and writing skills

◎ Continues to enjoy books, stories and poetry; by age 7 can recall the story so far if book read a chapter at a time

◎ Shows interest in more complex books and stories; continues to enjoy songs and rhymes

◎ Gives more detailed accounts of past events

◎ Vocalises ideas and feelings

◎ Can listen to and follow more detailed instructions; can deliver more complex verbal messages.

Age 7 to 12 years

◎ Has extensive vocabulary of between 4,000 to 10,000 words

◎ Uses more complex sentence structures

◎ Develops more complex reading skills, including improved comprehension

◎ Develops more complex writing skills, including more accurate spelling, punctuation and joined-up writing

◎ Continues to enjoy books, stories and poetry

◎ Gives very detailed accounts of past events and can anticipate future events

◎ Vocalises ideas and feelings in more depth

◎ Listens to and follows more complex instructions

◎ Appreciates jokes due to more sophisticated language knowledge

◎ Uses literacy skills to communicate and to access information, for example story and letter writing, use of dictionaries, encyclopaedia, computers, the Internet, e-mail.

Age 12 to 16 years

◎ Has an extensive and varied vocabulary of between 10,000 to 20,000 words

◎ Uses appropriate language styles for different occasions, for example standard English for formal situations

◎ Has more complex reading skills, including detailed comprehension skills, and may comment on structure and themes of a book or other piece of writing

◎ Has more complex writing skills, including accurate spelling and punctuation; neat and legible joined-up writing

◎ Can use different writing styles, including word-processing on a computer

◎ Continues to enjoy more complex texts, including fiction, poetry and factual books

- Gives very detailed accounts of past events using varied expression and vocabulary
- Can anticipate future events and give detailed reasons for possible outcomes
- Vocalises ideas and feelings in greater depth, including justifying own views and opinions
- Listens to and follows complex sets of instructions
- Appreciates complex jokes and word play
- Continues to use literacy skills to communicate and to access information, such as taking notes, writing essays and letters; using dictionaries/thesaurus, encyclopaedia; computers, Internet, e-mail.

PORTFOLIO ACTIVITY

1 Observe a child involved in a conversation, discussion or circle time. Focus on the language development and communication skills demonstrated by the child.

2 In your assessment comment on: the verbal and/or non-verbal communication used by the child; the complexity of any language used by the child; the level of social interaction; the role of the adult in promoting the child's language development; suggestions for further activities to encourage or extend the child's language development.

NVQ LINKS: CCLD 303.1   CCLD 303.2   CCLD 310.2

Five ways to promote children's language development

The childcarer plays a vital role in encouraging and extending children's language development and communication skills. You can help to do this by:

1 Talking to the children about anything and everything! Show the children what you are talking about, for example use real objects/situations, pictures, books, and other visual or audio aids.

2 Using straightforward sentences with words appropriate to the children's levels of understanding and development; avoid over-simplifying language; do not use 'baby talk' – children need to hear adult speech to learn language. Use repetition to introduce or reinforce new vocabulary and ideas. Do not make the children repeat things back over and over; this is boring and frustrating.

3 Copying the children's sounds and words, including any extensions or corrections to positively reinforce and extend the children's vocabulary, sentence structures, and so on. For example: a child says 'ball', you could reply 'Yes, that is Tom's red ball'; or a child may say 'moo!', you could reply 'Yes, the cow goes "moo"!'

4 Remembering turn-taking in language exchanges. Ask questions to stimulate the children's responses and to encourage or extend their speech. Look at the children when you are talking with them. Remember to be at the children's level, for example by sitting on a low chair or even on the floor; do not tower over them.

5 Sharing books, stories and rhymes with children including babies.

Figure 3.4 Children sharing books with a childcarer

PORTFOLIO ACTIVITY

1 Plan, implement and evaluate an activity which encourages or extends a child's language and communication skills. Use the assessment information from your observation of a child's language and communication skills from page 74 as the basis for your planning.

2 Include a variety of communication techniques such as: active listening (that is listening carefully and focusing on what the child has to say); leaving time for the child to respond/talk; and careful phrasing of adult questions and responses.

3 Consider how you could meet the needs of children with communication difficulties with this activity.

4 Consider how you could meet the needs of bilingual children with this activity (see Chapters 1 and 13).

NVQ LINKS: CCLD 303.3   CCLD 303.4   CCLD 301.2   CCLD 345.3

Promoting children's emotional development

Emotional development can be defined as the development of personality and temperament. This includes how each child: develops as a unique individual; sees and feels about themselves; thinks other people see them; expresses their individual needs, desires and feelings; relates to others; and interacts with their environment.

Becoming a person

As a childcarer you need to know and understand the process of children's personality development in order to provide appropriate assistance and guidance. Research indicates that genetics plays its part in this development, for example babies only a few weeks old already have distinct personalities. Children inherit their particular temperaments, which are then influenced by the environment they are raised in. Researchers agree that personality is derived from a combination of inheritance and environment (see section on nature versus nurture in children's development).

Developing attachments to other people

Babies develop an awareness of others in relation to themselves, for instance people who fulfil their needs for food and drink, warmth and shelter, sleep, physical comfort and entertainment. They develop strong attachments to the people they see most often and who satisfy the above needs. One attachment is usually stronger than the others and this is usually the baby's mother, but the attachment can be to another family member or anyone outside the immediate family who spends a significant amount of time with the young child, such as a grandparent or nanny. The security of these early attachments is essential to babies and young children because they provide a firm foundation for promoting: emotional well-being; positive relationships with other people; and confidence in exploring the environment. These early attachments enable children to feel secure about their relationships and to develop trust in others. Security and trust are important elements in the young children's ability to separate from their parents and carers in order to develop their own independence and ideas.

The sequence of children's emotional development: 0 to 16 years

Age 0 to 3 months
- Becomes very attached to parent/carer (usually the mother)
- Experiences extreme emotions, may be very scared, very happy or very angry; these moods change in an instant
- Requires the security and reassurance of familiar routines
- May be upset by unfamiliar methods of handling and care.

- -

Age 3 to 9 months
- Has strong attachment to parent/carer (usually the mother)

◎ Develops other attachments to people sees regularly
◎ By 6 or 7 months shows clear preferences for familiar adults as can differentiate between individuals
◎ Demonstrates strong emotions through body language, gestures and facial expressions
◎ Dislikes anger in others and becomes distressed by it
◎ Has clear likes and dislikes and will push away food, drink or toys does not want

Age 9 to 18 months
◎ Likes to get own way; gets very angry when adult says 'No!'
◎ Has emotional outbursts ('temper tantrums') when does not get own way or is otherwise frustrated, for example when unable to do activity because of physical limitations
◎ Shows fear in new situations, for example attending parent/toddler group, or visiting somewhere new such as the farm or nature centre
◎ Relies on parent/carer for reassurance and support in new situations
◎ Is upset by the distress of other children (even if they caused it)
◎ Seeks reassurance and contact with familiar adults throughout waking hours.

Age 18 months to 2 years
◎ Begins to disengage from secure attachment and wants to do things by self – 'Me do it!'
◎ Still emotionally dependent on familiar adult(s) but this leads to conflict as need for independence grows
◎ Has mood swings, may be clingy one moment, then fiercely independent the next
◎ Becomes very frustrated when unable/not allowed to do a particular activity which leads to frequent but short-lived emotional outbursts ('temper tantrums')
◎ Explores environment; even new situations are less frightening as long as parent/carer is present.

Age 2 to 3 years
◎ May still rely on parent/carer for reassurance in new situations or when with strangers
◎ Still experiences emotional outbursts as independence grows and frustration at own limitations continues, for example aggressive towards toys that cannot get to work
◎ Begins to understand the feelings of others but own feelings are still the most important
◎ Has very limited understanding of other people's pain, for example when hitting another child
◎ Feels curious about their environment but has no sense of danger that they or other people can be hurt by their actions.

Age 3 to 5 years
◎ Less reliant on parent/carer for reassurance in new situations

◎ May be jealous of adult attention given to younger sibling or other children in a group
◎ Argues with other children but is quick to forgive and forget
◎ Has limited awareness of the feelings and needs of others
◎ May be quite caring towards others who are distressed
◎ Begins to use language to express feelings and wishes
◎ Still has emotional outbursts, especially when tired, stressed or frustrated.

Age 5 to 7 years
◎ Becomes more aware of the feelings and needs of others
◎ Tries to comfort others who are upset, hurt or unwell
◎ May occasionally be aggressive as still learning to deal with negative emotions
◎ Uses language to express feelings and wishes
◎ Uses imaginative play to express worries and fears over past or future experiences, such as hospital visits, family disputes, domestic upheaval
◎ Has occasional emotional outbursts when tired, stressed or frustrated
◎ Argues with other children but may take longer to forgive and forget
◎ Confidence in self can be shaken by 'failure'
◎ May have an 'imaginary friend'.

Age 7 to 12 years
◎ Becomes less egocentric as understands feelings, needs and rights of others
◎ Still wants things that belong solely to them, for example is very possessive of own toys, puts own name on everything they possess!
◎ Becomes more aware of own achievements in relation to others but this can lead to a sense of failure if feels does not measure up; hates to lose
◎ May be very competitive; rivalry may lead to aggressive behaviour
◎ Argues with other children but may take even longer to forgive and forget
◎ Has increased awareness of the wider environment, for example the weather, plants, animals, and people in other countries.

Age 12 to 16 years
◎ Sensitive to own feelings and those of others, with a growing understanding of the possible causes for why people feel and act as they do
◎ Emotional changes due to puberty
◎ Understands issues relating to fairness and justice
◎ Can anticipate people's reactions and consider the consequences of own actions
◎ Is increasingly able to see different viewpoints in order to resolve difficulties in relationships
◎ Has confidence in own skills and ideas; is more able to be assertive rather than aggressive or passive

◎ May have very strong opinions or beliefs, leading to arguments with adults and peers; may hold grudges and find it difficult to forgive or forget
◎ Has more understanding of complex issues concerning the wider environment, such as ethics, philosophy, religion, politics.

PORTFOLIO ACTIVITY

1 Observe a child during an imaginative play or creative activity. Focus on the child's emotional development.

2 In your assessment comment on: the child's imaginative and creative skills; the child's ability to make choices or decisions; the child's use of language to express needs and/or feelings; the role of the adult in promoting the child's emotional development; and make suggestions for further activities to encourage or extend the child's emotional development including appropriate resources.

NVQ LINKS: CCLD 303.1   CCLD 303.2   CCLD 310.2

Five ways to promote children's emotional development

As a childcarer you need to provide appropriate routines and activities to promote children's emotional development. You can help to do this by:

1 Using praise and encouragement to help the children focus on what they are good at. Treat every child in the childcare setting as an individual. Each one has unique abilities and needs. Help the children to maximise their individual potential.

2 Taking an interest in the children's efforts as well as achievements. Remember the way children participate in activities is more important than the end results, such as sharing resources and helping others and contributing ideas. Encourage the children to measure any achievements by comparing these to their own efforts. Foster co-operation between children rather than competition.

3 Giving the children opportunities to make decisions and choices. Letting children and young people participate in decision-making, even in a small way, helps them to feel positive and important; it also prepares them for making appropriate judgements and sensible decisions later on.

4 Promoting equal opportunities by providing positive images of children and adults through: sharing books and stories about real-life situations showing young people (and adults) the children can identify with; providing opportunities for imaginative play that encourage the children to explore different roles in positive ways, for example dressing-up clothes, cooking utensils, dolls and puppets.

5 Being consistent about rules and discipline. All children need consistency and a clearly structured framework for behaviour so that they know what is expected of them. Remember to label the behaviour, not the children, as this is less damaging to their emotional well-being, e.g. 'That was an unkind thing to say' rather than 'You are unkind'.

PORTFOLIO ACTIVITY

1 Plan, implement and evaluate an activity which encourages or extends a child's emotional development. Use the assessment information from your observation of a child's emotional development as the basis for your planning.

2 Encourage the child to use a variety of emotional abilities. For example: imaginative and/or creative skills to express feelings; ability to make choices or decisions; language and communication skills to express needs and/or feelings; and understanding the needs and feelings of others.

NVQ LINKS: CCLD 303.3   CCLD 303.4   CCLD 301.1   CCLD 301.3   CCLD 308.1   CCLD 308.2   CCLD 308.4   CCLD 312.2

4 Reflecting on and developing practice

CCLD 304 Reflect on and develop practice

In order to reflect on and develop practice you need to know and understand: effective practice; being an effective, reflective practitioner; using best practice benchmarks such as the Key Elements of Effective Practice (KEEP) and The Professional Association of Nursery Nurses Code of Practice; evaluating your personal effectiveness; developing your personal development objectives; and professional development and training opportunities.

CCLD 304.1 Reflect on practice

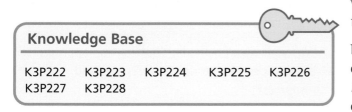

Knowledge Base

K3P222	K3P223	K3P224	K3P225	K3P226
K3P227	K3P228			

Effective practice requires committed, enthusiastic and reflective practitioners with a breadth and depth of knowledge, skills and understanding. To be an effective, reflective practitioner, you should use your own learning to improve your work with children and their families in ways that are sensitive, positive and non-judgemental. Through initial and ongoing training and development, you can develop, demonstrate and continuously improve your:

◎ Relationships with both children and adults
◎ Understanding of the individual and diverse ways that children develop and learn
◎ Knowledge and understanding in order to actively support and extend children's learning in and across all areas and aspects of learning
◎ Practice in meeting all children's needs, learning styles and interests
◎ Work with parents, carers and the wider community
◎ Work with other professionals.

(DfES, 2005a)

The Key Elements of Effective Practice (KEEP) provides a framework for early years practitioners to: reflect on their work; understand what effective practice looks like; record their qualifications; formulate their self-development plan; allow managers to understand staff experience/qualifications and training needs to support the development of the setting. KEEP supports self-appraisal, appraisal, quality assurance, self-evaluation and performance management as it links the needs of children, parents, the setting *and* practitioners. (DfES, 2005a) (See: www.standards.dfes.gov.uk/primary/publications/foundation_stage/keep/)

KEEP has been developed alongside and is consistent with *The Common Core of Skills and Knowledge for the Children's Workforce* which sets out the six areas of expertise that everyone working with children, young people and families should be able to demonstrate. (For details see: www.everychildmatters.gov.uk/deliveringservices/commoncore/)

The Professional Association of Nursery Nurses (PANN) has a Code of Practice for its members. This provides guidance for all practising professional childcarers in carrying out their duties and responsibilities. You will find it useful to bear these guidelines in mind when working with children and their families. To download the full text, visit www.pat.org.uk and use the site's search function to find 'PANN Code of Practice'.

PORTFOLIO ACTIVITY

Outline the standards of professional childcare practice expected from you and your colleagues. (This information may be included in a code of practice for staff which may be in the staff handbook and/or set out in best practice benchmarks such as KEEP.)

NVQ LINKS: CCLD 304.1   CCLD 301.1   CCLD 301.4   CCLDCCLD 340.1   CCLD 341.1

Evaluating your personal effectiveness

You need to know and understand clearly the exact role and responsibilities of your work as a childcarer. Review your professional practice by making regular and realistic assessments of how well your working practices match your role and responsibilities. Share your self-assessments with those responsible for managing and reviewing your work performance, for example during your regular discussions/meetings with your colleagues or with your line manager. Also ask other people for feedback about how well you fulfil the requirements and expectations of your role. Reflect on your own professional practice by making comparisons with appropriate models of good practice, such as the work of more experienced practitioners within the childcare setting.

Techniques of reflective analysis

As a childcarer you need to know and understand the techniques of reflective analysis:

◎ Questioning 'what?', 'why?' and 'how?'
◎ Seeking alternatives
◎ Keeping an open mind
◎ Viewing from different perspectives
◎ Thinking about consequences

◎ Testing ideas through comparing and contrasting
◎ Asking 'what if?'
◎ Synthesising ideas
◎ Seeking, identifying and resolving problems.

(NDNA, 2004)

Self-evaluation

Self-evaluation is needed to improve your own professional childcare practice and to develop your ability to reflect upon routines/activities and modify plans to meet the individual needs of the children you work with. When evaluating your own childcare practice, consider:

◎ Was your own particular contribution appropriate?
◎ Did you choose the right time, place and resources?
◎ Did you intervene enough or too much?
◎ Did you achieve your goals? (For example, objectives/outcomes for the child or children and yourself.) If not, why not? Were the goals too ambitious or unrealistic?
◎ What other strategies/methods could have been used? Suggest possible modifications.
◎ Who to ask for further advice? (For example, senior practitioner, setting manager or other professional.)

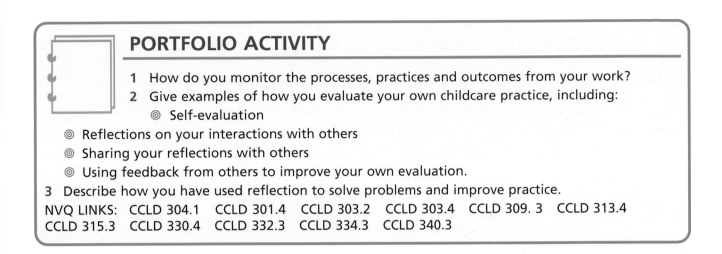

PORTFOLIO ACTIVITY

1 How do you monitor the processes, practices and outcomes from your work?
2 Give examples of how you evaluate your own childcare practice, including:
   ◎ Self-evaluation
◎ Reflections on your interactions with others
◎ Sharing your reflections with others
◎ Using feedback from others to improve your own evaluation.
3 Describe how you have used reflection to solve problems and improve practice.
NVQ LINKS: CCLD 304.1   CCLD 301.4   CCLD 303.2   CCLD 303.4   CCLD 309. 3   CCLD 313.4
CCLD 315.3   CCLD 330.4   CCLD 332.3   CCLD 334.3   CCLD 340.3

CCLD 304.2
Take part in continuing professional development

Knowledge Base

K3P223   K3P229   K3P230   K3P231   K3M232

Take part in continuing professional development by identifying areas in your knowledge, understanding and skills where you could develop further. Formulate and negotiate a plan to develop your knowledge, skills and understanding further. Seek out and access opportunities as part of this plan for continuing professional development and to improve your professional practice. (NDNA, 2004)

Developing your personal development objectives

To develop your effectiveness as a professional childcare practitioner, you should be able to

identify your own SMART personal development objectives:

◎ **S**pecific: identify exactly what you want to develop, such as the particular skills you need to update or new skills you need to acquire, for example first aid or ICT skills
◎ **M**easurable: define criteria that can be used to measure whether or not your objectives have been achieved, such as best practice benchmarks, course certificate of attendance or qualification
◎ **A**chievable: avoid being too ambitious; set objectives which you know are attainable
◎ **R**ealistic: be realistic about what you want to develop
◎ **T**ime-bound: plan a realistic time frame within which to achieve your objectives.

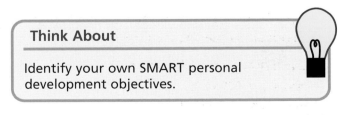

Think About

Identify your own SMART personal development objectives.

Discuss and agree these objectives with those responsible for supporting your professional development (see sections on team development and staff development in Chapter 18). This includes formulating and negotiating a plan to develop your knowledge, skills and understanding further, such as a personal development plan. For example, you may consider that some of your work tasks require modification or improvement and discuss possible changes with your line manager. Or you may feel that you lack sufficient knowledge and skills to implement particular activities and need to discuss opportunities to undertake the relevant training. To achieve your personal development objectives you should make effective use of the people, resources (such as the Internet, libraries or journals) and other professional development or training opportunities available to you (see below). When assessing your personal development and training needs you should consider:

◎ Your existing experience and skills
◎ The needs of the children you work with
◎ Any problems with how you currently work
◎ Any new or changing expectations for your role
◎ Information and/or learning needed to meet best practice, quality schemes or regulatory requirements.

PORTFOLIO ACTIVITY

1 Describe how you have identified and developed areas in your knowledge, skills and understanding. Include information on: your existing strengths and skills; skills and knowledge you need to improve; plans for improving your work; and preparing for future responsibilities.
2 Give examples of how you access opportunities for continuing professional development.
NVQ LINKS: CCLD 304.2   CCLD 304.1   CCLD 341.3   CCLD 342.4   CCLD 311   CCLD 338

A professional portfolio highlighting your existing experience and qualifications can form the basis for assessing your training needs. This portfolio will also be a tangible record of your professional development and will help to boost your self-esteem. (See *The Nanny Handbook* by Teena Kamen for information on compiling a professional portfolio.)

Activity

Compile your own professional portfolio if you do not already have one.

Professional development and training opportunities

Training courses and qualifications can have a positive influence on improving the status of childcare practitioners, as well as enabling them to share examples of good practice with others in the childcare field. It is of benefit to settings also to have childcarers who are able to improve their expertise and increase their job satisfaction. Specific training and recognised qualifications for childcarers are available; for example there are Level 2, 3 and 4 childcare qualifications and short courses for childcare practitioners.

The Department of Education's leaflet *A Guide to Qualifications: For Working in Early Years, Childcare and Playwork* (2005) contains information on all available qualifications for childcare practitioners – see: www.surestart.gov.uk/_doc/P0001400.pdf

Short courses for childcare practitioners

Possible professional development and training opportunities for childcarers include short courses in the following areas:

◎ Play and child development
◎ Supporting children's literacy and numeracy activities
◎ Developing ICT skills
◎ Strategies for dealing with challenging behaviour
◎ First aid training including paediatric first aid
◎ Child protection
◎ Equal opportunities workshops
◎ Disability and inclusion training
◎ Supporting specific special needs
◎ Conflict resolution

◎ Working with parents
◎ Arts and crafts workshops
◎ Drama and story telling workshops
◎ Children's sports or games workshops.

Other professional development and training opportunities include: NVQ assessor and verifier; staff training manager; work with local authorities or regulatory bodies as an early years advisor or quality assessor; and work with children in different sectors.

Check it out

Find out about the professional development and training opportunities for childcare practitioners in your local area.

5 Protecting and promoting children's rights

CCLD 305 Protect and promote children's rights

In the last decade there has been a major shift in attitude towards children's rights. In the past, children's rights were mainly concerned with their basic welfare needs. Now, as well as their basic rights to life, health and education, children are viewed as having a much wider range of rights including the right to engage in play activities, to express their views and to participate in making decisions that affect them directly.

Children's rights, as stated in the United Nations (UN) Convention on the Rights of the Child, are clear and universal: they apply to all children. Also, while their individual needs may differ, they all have the same rights. Children's rights are based on their needs, but emphasising rights rather than needs demonstrates a commitment to viewing and respecting children as valued citizens. (The Children's Rights Alliance for England: www.crae.org.uk/)

CCLD 305.1 Support equality of access

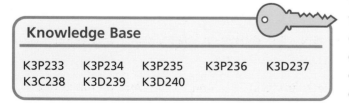

Knowledge Base

K3P233	K3P234	K3P235	K3P236	K3D237
K3C238	K3D239	K3D240		

As a childcarer you need to protect and promote children's rights by supporting equality of access to your setting. This includes providing information for children, families and communities that promotes participation and equality of access. It is important to implement transparent procedures and information about access to provision that meets the needs of all children. Welcome children from all backgrounds, ensuring that barriers to participation are identified and removed. Seek and respect the views and preferences of children, adapting your practice to their ages, needs and abilities. Involve all relevant local community groups in the setting and provide information on community resources, for example childcare services, play provision, sport and leisure activities, local libraries, support groups, multicultural resources, and specialist equipment for people with disabilities. Provide information to children about their rights and responsibilities in the context of your setting.

Providing information that promotes participation and equality of access

In your role, you will be responsible for providing information about equality of access to children and families, including representative groups and individuals, such as current and potential new users of the childcare setting and children and their families who have found services hard to access, for example those with disabilities or from different ethnic groups. You may give out information in a variety of ways including: leaflets, newsletters, newspapers, magazines; public notice boards; open days; exhibitions; and the Internet. Select the most effective way to reach your target audience; for example provide leaflets in community languages, ensure posters show positive images of people with disabilities and from different ethnic groups. Try varying styles to appeal to different target groups. Information aimed at children and/or young people, for example, will be different to that aimed at their parents/carers. (SureStart, 2003c)

PORTFOLIO ACTIVITY

Describe appropriate ways in which your setting has provided information that promotes participation and equality of access to all relevant community groups, including those who have found services hard to access, such as people with disabilities or from different ethnic groups.

NVQ LINK: CCLD 305.1

The United Nations Convention on the Rights of the Child

As a childcare practitioner it is important that you know and understand the basic requirements of the United Nations Convention on the Rights of the Child. These rights are for children and young people (up to the age of 18 years). The United Nations (UN) approved the Convention on the Rights of the Child on 20 November 1989 and the UK Government ratified (agreed to uphold) it on 16 December 1991. Countries that have ratified the Convention are legally bound to do what it states and to make all laws, policy and practice compatible with the Convention. The only two countries in the world that have not signed the Convention are the USA and Somalia. There are 54 articles in the UN Convention on the Rights of the Child, covering four different groupings of rights: survival, protection, development and participation. Each article outlines a different right. A summary of the articles most relevant to childcare is given below:

Summary of the articles most relevant to childcare settings

Article 1: Everyone under 18 years of age has all the rights in this Convention.

Article 2: The Convention applies to everyone whatever their race, religion, abilities, whatever they think or say, whatever type of family they come from.

Article 3: All organisations concerned with children should work towards what is best for each child.

Article 4: Governments should make these rights available to children.

Article 12: Children have the right to say what they think should happen when adults are making decisions that affect them, and to have their opinions taken into account.

Article 13: Children have the right to get and to share information as long as the information is not damaging to them or to others.

Article 14: Children have the right to think and believe what they want and to practise their religion, as long as they are not stopping other people from enjoying their rights. Parents should guide their children on these matters.

Article 15: Children have the right to meet together and to enjoy groups and organisations, as long as this does not stop other people from enjoying their rights.

Article 19: Governments should ensure that children are properly cared for, and protect them from violence, abuse and neglect by their parents or anyone else who looks after them.

Article 23: Children who have any kind of disability should have special care and support so that they can lead full and independent lives.

Article 28: Children have a right to an education. Discipline in schools should respect children's human dignity. Primary education should be free.

Article 29: Education should develop each child's personality and talents to the full. It should encourage children to respect their parents, and their own and other cultures.

Article 30: Children have a right to learn the language and customs of their families, whether these are shared by the majority of people in the country or not.

Article 31: All children have a right to relax and play, and to join in a wide range of activities.

Article 39: Children who have been neglected or abused should receive special help to restore their self-respect.

(From 'What Rights?' leaflet by Unicef: www.unicef.org.uk)

PORTFOLIO ACTIVITY

1 Find out more about the UN Convention on the Rights of the Child.
2 Check whether copies of the Convention and related materials are available in your setting and/or the college library.
3 Design a poster and/or leaflet outlining the Articles most relevant to childcare settings, e.g. Articles: 1 to 4, 12 to 15, 19, 23, 28 to 31 and 39. You could encourage the children in your setting to design their own posters/leaflets about these rights.

NVQ LINKS: CCLD 305.1   CCLD 305.2
CCLD 305.3

Figure 5.1 Example of child's poster about children's rights

5

National legislation relating to children's rights

To work effectively in your role you need to know and understand the basic requirements of national legislation relating to children's rights, in addition to understanding how to carry out research on children's rights and identify the implications for your setting.

The Children Act 1989 provided a step in the right direction towards implementing the articles of the UN Convention on the Rights of the Child within the UK. The Act came into force on 14 October 1991 and is concerned with families and the care of children, local authority support for children and their families, fostering, childminding and day care provision. The Children Act 1989 is particularly important because it emphasises the necessity of putting the child first. In summary, the Act states that:

◎ What is best for the child must always be the first consideration
◎ Whenever possible children should be brought up in their own family
◎ Unless the child is at risk of harm, that individual should not be taken away from their family without the family's agreement
◎ Local authorities must help families with children in need
◎ Local authorities must work with parents and children
◎ Courts must put children first when making decisions
◎ Children being looked after by local authorities have rights, as do their parents.

The Children Act 1989 provides the legislative framework for the child protection system in England and Wales. The Children (Northern Ireland) Order 1995 and The Children (Scotland) Act 1995 share the same principles as The Children Act 1989 but contain their own guidance. The Children Act 2004 introduces changes to the structure and organisation of the child protection system in England and Wales which are due to come into force between 2006 and 2008.

The Children Act 2004 also provides the legislative framework for whole-system reform to support the Government's long-term plans to improve the lives of children and their families.

For more information on the Act see http://www.everychildmatters.gov.uk/strategy/guidance/.

Part 1 of the Children Act 2004 came into force on 15 November 2004, and the first Children's Commissioner for England was appointed in March 2005, which made England's children the last in the UK to be represented by a Commissioner. The role of the Children's Commissioner is limited; its general function – 'promoting awareness of the views and interests of children in England' (Section 2.1) – is the weakest in Europe and does not comply with international standards. (Children's Rights Alliance for England, November 2004)

Children's Commissioners in the other countries of the UK are each required by law to promote and safeguard the rights of children.

The national framework for children's services

The Children Act 2004 together with *Every Child Matters: Change for Children* published in December 2004 by the Department for Education and Skills (DfES) sets out the Government's direction for 150 local programmes of change to be led by local authorities and their key partners. Many local areas have already started their local change programmes, which bring together local authority, health, criminal justice services, voluntary and community organisations and other local partners to deliver improved services for children.

Every Child Matters: Change for Children sets out the national framework of outcomes for all children, to protect them, to promote their well-being and to support the development of their full potential. The document details the action needed locally and the ways in which the Government will work with and support local authorities and their partners. (DfES, 2004b)

This national framework will enable organisations that provide services to children (including hospitals, schools, the police and voluntary groups) to access the same information and work together to protect children from harm and help them achieve what they want and need. Children will have a greater say about the issues that affect them both as individuals and collectively.

What the outcomes mean

Be healthy:
◎ Physically healthy
◎ Mentally and emotionally healthy
◎ Sexually healthy
◎ Healthy lifestyles
◎ Choose not to take illegal drugs.

Stay safe:
◎ Safe from maltreatment, neglect, violence and sexual exploitation
◎ Safe from accidental injury and death
◎ Safe from bullying and discrimination
◎ Safe from crime and antisocial behaviour in and out of school
◎ Have security, stability and are cared for.

Enjoy and achieve:
◎ Ready for school
◎ Attend and enjoy school
◎ Achieve stretching national educational standards at primary school
◎ Achieve personal and social development and enjoy recreation
◎ Achieve stretching national educational standards at secondary school.

Make a positive contribution:
◎ Engage in decision-making and support the community and environment
◎ Engage in law-abiding and positive behaviour in and out of school
◎ Develop positive relationships and choose not to bully or discriminate
◎ Develop self-confidence and successfully deal with significant life changes and challenges
◎ Develop enterprising behaviour.

Support equality of access

Achieve economic well-being:
◎ Engage in further education, employment or training on leaving school
◎ Ready for employment
◎ Live in decent homes and sustainable communities
◎ Access to transport and material goods
◎ Live in households free from low incomes.

(DfES, 2004b)

Think About

Which outcomes are most relevant to the children in your setting?

Voluntary and community organisations have a vital role to play in improving outcomes for children. As key providers of services to children, voluntary and community organisations have considerable knowledge and expertise to offer in developing strategy and planning provision. The DfES has published a strategy for working with voluntary and community organisations to improve services for children. The strategy indicates the ways the DfES will strengthen its connections with voluntary and community organisations that work with children and families. It describes what the Government is doing to support effective working with local voluntary and community organisations, through the *Every Child Matters: Change for Children* programme.

Children's trusts are the new way that local authorities are encouraging co-operation between all agencies working with children and families. By bringing together all services for children in a local area so that they can focus on improving outcomes for all children, children's trusts will provide more integrated and responsive services for children and their families. People will work in effective multi-disciplinary teams and services will be co-located in children's centres or extended schools. Local authorities will also involve voluntary and community organisations at all levels of children's trusts including the planning, commissioning and delivery of children's services.

Children's centres are excellent examples of integrated service provision for children and their families. Primary Care Trusts, local authorities, Jobcentre Plus, education and childcare providers, social services, and community and voluntary organisations work in partnership to deliver holistic services that reflect the needs of local communities. The expansion of the children's centre network means that there should be up to 2,500 centres in England by 2008. Children's centres will be established to provide services in all of the most disadvantaged areas. The *Ten Year Childcare Strategy* will recommend that more co-located and accessible children's services be established. Children's trusts will also be able to develop children's centres in response to local demand. (DfES, 2004b)

Extended schools are part of the *Five Year Strategy for Children and Learners* which plans for all primary and secondary schools to provide a core offer of services to parents. Local authorities and children's trusts will bring together local partners to plan and develop extended services that meet the needs of

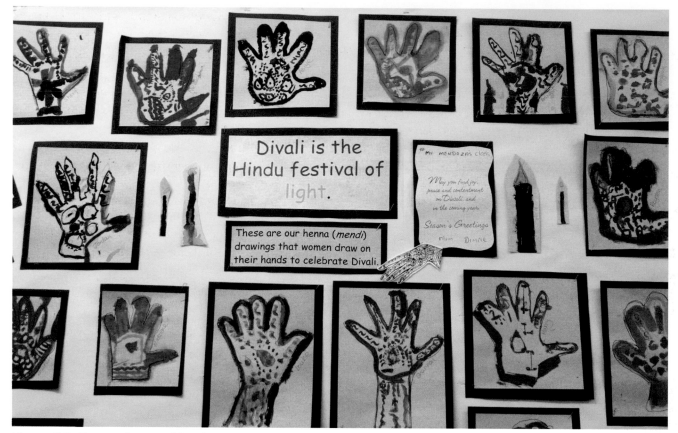

These are our henna (*mendi*) drawings that women draw on their hands to celebrate Divali.

Figure 5.2 Promoting positive images

local communities. The *Ten Year Childcare Strategy* includes a childcare offer for school-aged children that provides a guarantee of childcare provision between 8.00 am and 6.00 pm all year round. This offer builds on existing childcare provision in schools such as breakfast and after-school clubs. By 2010, all primary schools will make this offer, either on-site or in partnership with other schools and local childcare providers. By 2010 all secondary schools will offer a network of provision including out-of-school activities such as sports, arts and holiday activities. (DfES, 2004b)

The Childcare Act 2006

The Childcare Bill introduced to Parliament in November 2005 has now become The Childcare Act 2006. This new Act provides a legal entitlement to accessible high quality childcare and services for children under 5-years-old and their families. The Act will place a duty on local authorities to ensure that childcare services meet the needs of working parents, especially those with low incomes or children with special needs, and to ensure that parents have access to the full range of information they may need. The Act should simplify the current childcare and early years framework; for example the new Early Years Foundation Stage will support the delivery of integrated care and education of children

aged 0 to 5 years. For more information about the Act see:
www.surestart.gov.uk/resources/general/childcareact/

Unit Links

For this Unit you also need to understand the following section:
CCLD 309.1 Prepare curriculum plans according to requirements (see Chapter 12)

Check it out

1 Investigate the children's rights in your local community.
2 Find out what local provision is being made to meet these rights, for example: voluntary and community organisations; children's trusts; children's centres; and extended schools.

Encouraging children to understand and assert their rights

As a childcare practitioner you need to encourage children to understand and assert their rights under the UN Convention on the Rights of the Child. Ensure that they are aware of their rights under laws made in the UK such as, for example, the Children Act 1989, sex, race and disability laws.

Help children to understand their rights by:

◎ Using posters, leaflets and resource packs about children's rights, such as *Rights for Young Children* (posters from Oxfam), *What Rights?* (leaflet from Unicef), *A Right To Know* (resource pack from Article 12)

◎ Sharing books about children's rights, for example *For Every Child*; *Wise Guides: Your Rights*
◎ Providing appropriate creative activities, including designing posters/leaflets, painting pictures or making collages about children's rights
◎ Playing games promoting children's rights, for example *On the Right Track*
◎ Encouraging them to look up information about children's rights on websites aimed at children and young people, such as www.savethechildren.org.uk/rightonline/whats.html and www.therightssite.org.uk.

Help children to assert their rights by:

◎ Providing choices in activities within the setting
◎ Encouraging their participation in the day-to-day running of the setting
◎ Consulting and involving them in decision-making with regard to the setting
◎ Promoting inclusion and anti-discriminatory practice
◎ Helping to organise a children's panel or youth forum
◎ Providing accessible information
◎ Providing access to confidence/assertiveness training
◎ Providing information about play and leisure activities in the local community
◎ Providing information about local and national children's rights networks.

Think About

How do you give information to children about their rights and responsibilities within the context of your setting?

Legislation relating to equality and inclusion

It is important that you know and understand the basic requirements of legislation relating to equality and inclusion, including equal opportunities, disability discrimination and special educational needs. The Sex Discrimination Act 1975 and the Race Relations Act 1976 made it unlawful to discriminate on the grounds of sex, race, colour, or ethnic or national origin. These Acts, with subsequent amendments, established statutory requirements to: prevent discrimination; promote equality of opportunity; and provide redress against discrimination.

Amendments to these Acts and the Disability Discrimination Act 1995 have developed and extended anti-discrimination legislation. The Disability Discrimination Act (DDA) protects people with disabilities in: education; employment; access to goods, facilities and services; and the management, buying or renting of land or property. Some of the DDA became law for employers in December 1996 while other parts were introduced gradually, for example:

◎ Since December 1996 it has been unlawful to treat disabled people less favourably than other people for a reason related to their disability
◎ Since October 1999 service providers have had to make reasonable adjustments for disabled people, such as providing extra help or making changes to the way they provide their services
◎ Since October 2004 service providers have had to make reasonable adjustments to the physical features of their premises to overcome physical barriers to access.

(www.drc-gb.org)

Part IV of the DDA was amended by the Special Educational Needs and Disability Act 2001 (see below), which came into effect in September 2002, and includes new duties for education providers to ensure that they do not discriminate against people with disabilities. The Disability Discrimination Act 2005 amends the DDA 1995 and places a duty on public bodies to promote equality of opportunity for people with disabilities. The Disability Equality Duty came into force in December 2006.

The Race Relations (Amendment) Act 2000 introduced new statutory duties for the public sector including actively promoting race equality. Under a new European Union directive the grounds for discrimination go beyond the three main areas of race, gender and disability, discussed in this chapter, to include age, religious belief and sexual orientation. Individual rights are also protected by the Data Protection Act 1998, Human Rights Act 1998 and Freedom of Information Act 2000. Useful websites with summaries of equal opportunities and disability discrimination legislation include:

◎ Commission for Racial Equality: **www.cre.gov.uk**
◎ Disability Rights Commission: **www.drc-gb.org**
◎ Equal Opportunities Commission: **www.eoc.org.uk**

Check it out

Find out about the legislation covering equality and inclusion and how it relates to your setting, such as the setting's equal opportunities policy and/or inclusion policy.

CCLD 305.2
Implement strategies, policies, procedures and practice for inclusion

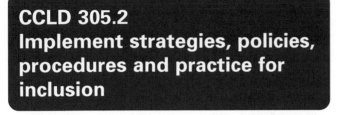

Knowledge Base

K3P241	K3D242	K3D243	K3P244	K3P245
K3P247	K3P248	K3M333		

It is important that you not only know and follow the setting's inclusion strategies, policies, procedures and practice but also understand how to develop and implement these in a manner that is consistent with your role and responsibilities in the childcare setting. Remember that to develop effective inclusion policies, procedures and practice everyone should be involved at some level including staff, children and their parents or carers.

Inclusive and anti-discriminatory practice

As a childcarer you should know how to judge whether the childcare setting is inclusive and supports diversity and be able to demonstrate that you support this through your words, actions and behaviours in the childcare setting. You need to promote the childcare setting to children who may experience barriers to participation, such as those with disabilities or those from other minority groups. Inclusion is about the child's right to: attend the local mainstream setting; be valued as an individual; and be provided with all the support needed to thrive in a mainstream setting. Inclusive provision should be seen as an extension of the childcare setting's equal opportunities policy and practice. It

requires a commitment from all staff, parents and children to include the full diversity of children in the local community. This may require planned restructuring of the whole childcare environment to ensure equality of access.

Challenging discrimination and prejudice

All childcare settings have an equal opportunities policy with procedures to ensure that it is implemented. Follow your setting's policy and procedures, together with any relevant legal requirements, when dealing with these issues. As a childcarer you need to:

◎ Challenge discrimination or prejudice when necessary. (For example, if a colleague makes a derisory comment about a person's race, culture or disability, you should tell them why it is unacceptable to express their views in this way)
◎ State that you will not condone views that discriminate against another person
◎ Provide support for children and adults who experience discrimination or prejudice by encouraging them to respond with positive action
◎ Follow the relevant setting policy and procedures.

Think About

How have you challenged (or would you challenge) discrimination or prejudice in the childcare setting?

Promoting positive attitudes towards cultural diversity, gender and disability

Children are influenced by images, ideas and attitudes that create prejudice and lead to discrimination or disadvantage. They are not born with these attitudes; they learn them. You have an important role to play in promoting children's positive attitudes towards themselves and other people. In addition, you must neither have stereotyped views about children's potential nor have low expectations of them based on culture, gender or disability. You should:

◎ Recognise and eliminate racial discrimination
◎ Have high but realistic expectations for all children

◎ Maximise each child's motivation and potential
◎ Encourage each child to feel a positive sense of identity
◎ Ensure the childcare environment reflects positive images
◎ Challenge stereotypes in the media, literature and everyday life
◎ Give all children the opportunities to play with a wide variety of toys, games and play equipment
◎ Ensure that children do not think they are superior to others
◎ Expect the same standards of behaviour from all children regardless of culture, gender or disability
◎ Recognise children with disabilities as individuals not by their condition or impairment (for example a child *with* autistic tendencies not autistic child)
◎ Encourage the 'able' world to adapt to those with disabilities, not the other way round.

Twelve ways to promote positive images of children and the wider society

Provide an environment, activities and experiences that promote positive images of children and reflect the wider society by:

1 Sharing books and stories about real-life situations with people that children can identify with.
2 Using posters, pictures, photographs, displays, jigsaws, puzzles, toys and other play materials which reflect positive images of race, culture, gender and disability.
3 Providing activities that encourage children to look at their physical appearance in a positive light, for example games looking in mirrors; self-portraits (ensuring paints are provided for all skin tones); drawing round each other to create life-size portraits.
4 Providing activities that encourage children to focus on their abilities in positive ways, such as an 'I can ...' tree with positive statements about what each child *can* do.
5 Providing activities which encourage children to express their likes and dislikes, plus confidence in their own name and who they are, for example circle games such as *The name game* where each child takes it in turn to say 'My name is ... and I like to ... because ...' or *Circle jump* where each child takes a turn at jumping into the circle, making an action that they feel expresses them and saying 'Hello, I'm ...'; then the rest of the children copy the action and reply 'Hello ... [repeating the child's name]'.

6 Sharing experiences about themselves and their families through topics like *All about me* and by inviting family members such as parents/grandparents to come into the setting to talk about themselves and their backgrounds.

7 Providing opportunities for imaginative/role play which encourages children to explore different roles in positive ways, for instance dressing-up clothes, cooking utensils, dolls and puppets that reflect different cultures.

8 Visiting local shops, businesses and community groups that reflect the cultural diversity of the setting and the local community.

9 Inviting visitors into the setting to talk positively about their roles and lives, such as a (female) police officer or fire fighter, (male) nurse, people with disabilities or from different ethnic groups. (Note: Avoid tokenism; include these visitors as part of ongoing topics.)

10 Celebrating cultural diversity through the festivals of the faiths in the local community, including Diwali (Hindu), Channuka (Jewish), Christmas (Christian) and Eid (Muslim).

11 Valuing language diversity by displaying welcome signs and other information in community languages.

12 Providing positive examples of:
   ◎ Black and Asian people and women from all ethnic groups in prominent roles in society, such as politicians, doctors, lawyers, teachers, entrepreneurs
   ◎ Black and Asian people's past contributions to politics, medicine, science, education, and so on. Look at important historical figures like Martin Luther King, Mahatma Gandhi and Mary Seacole
   ◎ People with disabilities participating fully in modern society such as Stephen Hawking, the late Christopher Reeve and Marlee Matlin as well as famous historical figures like Louis Braille, Helen Keller and Franklin D. Roosevelt.

PORTFOLIO ACTIVITY

1 Compile a resource pack that promotes positive images. You might include the following information and resources: posters, wall charts, photographs and pictures; booklets and leaflets; suggested activities to promote positive images; book list of relevant children's books and stories; and a list of useful organisations and addresses.

2 Plan, implement and evaluate at least one activity suggested in your resource pack.

NVQ LINKS: CCLD 305.2   CCLD 301.1   CCLD 321.1   CCLD 339.1

National legislation relating to children with special educational needs

The Warnock Report on Special Educational Needs 1978 was concerned with the difficulties which affect children's educational progress either temporarily or permanently. The report concluded that up to 1 in 5 children (20 per cent) required various forms of special education at some point during their school career. Warnock viewed this 20 per cent of children as part of a continuum of special needs, which is related to the child's individual need for support to participate in educational activities and *not* their particular learning difficulty or disability. Some children with serious disabilities need substantial support for learning, while at the other end of the continuum are children with moderate learning difficulties or behavioural problems who need less support. Some children may have '*only a temporary learning difficulty ... Others, however, require special help and support throughout their school lives ...*' (DES, 1978a, p. 47). Even if a child's disability is permanent, their individual learning needs may change; for example they may require more or less physical assistance as they grow older. Environmental changes may also affect the child's learning needs, such as: an increase or reduction in appropriate resources including support staff; or transition from nursery to primary school or primary to secondary school.

The Education Act 1981 put into effect many of the recommendations of the Warnock Report. The Act established that '*a child has a special educational need if he or she has a learning difficulty significantly greater than the majority of children the same age or a disability which prevents the use of educational facilities of a kind generally provided in the schools for children of that age.*' (Brennan, 1987). The Act also established the principle of *integration*: all children with special educational needs are to be educated in 'ordinary' (mainstream) schools where reasonably practicable and should participate in school activities with other children. A small percentage of children with severe or complex disabilities and/or learning difficulties still need to attend special schools.

The Education Act 1993 defines children with special educational needs as:

(a) Having a significantly greater difficulty in learning than the majority of children of the same age

(b) Having a disability which either prevents or hinders the child from making use of educational facilities of a kind provided for children of the same age in schools within the area of the local education authority

(c) An under-5 who falls within the definition at (a) or (b) above or would do if special educational provision was not made for the child.

The Special Educational Needs and Disability Act 2001 amends Part 4 of the Education Act 1996 to make further provision against discrimination, on the grounds of disability, in schools and other educational establishments. This Act strengthens the right of children with special educational needs (SEN) to be educated in mainstream schools where parents want this and the interests of other children can be protected. The Act also requires local education authorities (LEAs) to make arrangements for services to provide parents of children with SEN with advice and information. It also requires schools to inform parents where they are making special educational provision for their child and allows schools to request a statutory assessment of a pupil's SEN. (www.drc-gb.org)

The Special Educational Needs Code of Practice 2001 replaces The 1994 Code of Practice on the Identification and Assessment of Special Educational Needs and gives practical advice to LEAs, maintained schools and others concerning their statutory duties to identify, assess and provide for children's special educational needs. The new code came into effect on 1 January 2002. This incorporates a great deal of the guidance from the first code of practice but includes developments in education since 1994 and also utilises the experiences of schools and LEAs. The central aim of the Government's special needs policy is to enable all children to have the opportunities available through inclusive education. The new code re-enforces the right for children with SEN to receive education within a mainstream setting and advocates that schools and LEAs implement a graduated method for the organisation of SEN. The code provides a school-based model of intervention for children with special educational needs. The five stages of the 1994 code have been replaced with: Early Years Action or School Action (old Stages 1 and 2); Early Years Action Plus or School Action Plus (old Stage 3); and The Statementing Process (old Stages 4 and 5).

Unit Links

For this Unit you also need to understand the following section:
CCLD 339.3 Ensure that individual education plans for children are in place and regularly reviewed (see Chapter 11)

The code also includes new chapters on: Parent Partnership and Disagreement Resolution; pupil participation including The UN Convention on the Rights of the Child; early years with extra information; and the Connexions Service for young people aged 13 to 19 years. Accompanying the new code is the *Special Educational Needs Toolkit,* which expands on the guidance contained in the code. This Toolkit is not law but does provide examples of good practice that LEAs and schools can follow.

Facilitate access and participation for children with disabilities and special educational needs

You need to understand and know how to identify good inclusive provision and practice in the childcare setting. Kidsactive defines inclusive provision as: *'provision that is open and accessible to all, and takes positive steps in removing disabling barriers, so that disabled and non-disabled people can participate'* (Douch, 2004). The following inclusion indicators may help you to identify whether inclusion is being put into practice in your setting.

Inclusion indicators

Visitors can see that:

◎ Nobody makes a fuss about the presence of disabled children
◎ Activities are designed around the interests and enthusiasms of all children who attend and with regard to any dislikes or impairments they may have
◎ Each person, adult or child, is welcomed on arrival
◎ All children, including disabled children, have choices and are able to exercise those choices.

The leader/manager:

◎ Has sought out families, schools and services for disabled children and built links to promote the involvement of disabled children

◎ Runs regular staff meetings that are designed to enable staff to reflect on their practice together and develop good future practice

◎ Can identify action taken and progress made towards inclusion, and also the things they still need and plan to do to make the setting more inclusive.

The staff:

◎ Have received disability equality training and/or attitudinal training and continue to undertake other training relating to inclusion

◎ Feel that they are consulted and informed by the leader/manager.

Disabled and non-disabled children:

◎ Report being involved in making rules/policies or 'having a say in what goes on'

◎ Say they are generally happy with the setting.

Parents of disabled and non-disabled children:

◎ Feel welcome and valued

◎ Say they are consulted about how best to meet their children's needs.

Policies and paperwork indicate that:

◎ A commitment to inclusion is explicit in public and internal documentation

◎ Staff who have particular support roles with individual disabled children are full members of the team and have job descriptions which stress the inclusion of the child rather than just one-to-one support.

(Douch, 2004)

Ten ways to support children with special needs

Help children with special needs to participate in the full range of activities by:

1 Providing a stimulating language-rich childcare environment which is visually attractive, tactile and interactive.

2 Maximising the use of space in the setting to allow freedom of movement for *all* children (including those who are physically disabled or visually impaired).

3 Ensuring accessibility of resources, including any specialist equipment.

4 Providing opportunities for all children to explore different materials and activities.

5 Encouraging children to use the abilities they do have to their fullest extent.

6 Providing sufficient time for children to explore their environment and materials; some children may need extra time to complete tasks.

7 Encouraging independence, for example use computers, word processing, or tape recorders.

8 Praising all children's efforts as well as achievements.

9 Supporting families to respond to their children's special needs.

10 Accessing specialist advice and support for children with special needs.

Supporting children with special needs

Professionally you need to contribute actively to the inclusion of children with special needs, including those with hearing or visual impairment (see Chapter 14), physical disabilities (see Chapter 7), communication difficulties (see Chapter 14), learning difficulties (see Chapter 14), emotional difficulties (see Chapter 10) or behavioural difficulties (see Chapter 9).

Supporting children with exceptional abilities

Some children may have intellectual abilities which are well above the expected norm for their age group. Those with exceptional abilities (sometimes referred to as 'gifted' or 'talented' children) may have: reached developmental milestones much earlier than the expected norm; more energy than is usual for their age; a never-ending curiosity; sharp powers of observation; advanced thinking and reasoning skills; or a preference for interaction with older children and adults.

Children with exceptional abilities need additional challenges and innovative ideas to stretch their cognitive capabilities. They need access to advanced resources with plenty of opportunities for independent, original and creative thought/action. Remember the children's social and emotional needs as well as their intellectual needs; if they are made to feel different or extraordinary they may find it difficult to mix with other children in the setting.

CCLD 305.3
Maintain and follow policies and procedures for protecting and safeguarding children

Knowledge Base

K3P246	K3S249	K3S250	K3S251	K3S252
K3S253	K3D254			

All childcare settings need to establish and maintain a safe environment for children and deal with circumstances where there are child welfare concerns. Through their child protection policies and procedures for safeguarding children, childcare settings have an important role in the detection and prevention of child abuse and neglect.

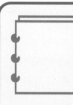

PORTFOLIO ACTIVITY

1 Find out about your setting's inclusion strategies, policies, procedures and practice.
2 Explain your role and responsibilities in developing, implementing and reviewing strategies, policies, procedures and practice for inclusion.

NVQ LINKS: CCLD 305.2   CCLD 301.1   CCLD 301.2   CCLD 321.1   CCLD 321.2   CCLD 321.3
Depending on your exact role:
CCLD 313.1   CCLD 313.2   CCLD 313.3   CCLD 313.4   CCLD 339.1   CCLD 339.2   CCLD 339.3   CCLD 339.4
Note: Unit CCLD 313 is about supporting children and families in need of early intervention. Unit CCLD 339 is about coordinating special educational needs in early education settings.

What is child abuse?

The Children Act 1989 defines child abuse as a person's actions that cause a child to suffer significant harm to their health, development or well-being. Significant harm can be caused by: punishing a child too much; hitting or shaking a child; constantly criticising, threatening or rejecting a child; sexually interfering with or assaulting a child; or neglecting a child, for example not giving them enough to eat or not ensuring their safety. The Department of Health (DH) defines child abuse as the abuse or neglect of a child by inflicting harm or by failing to prevent harm. Children may be abused by someone known to them, for example a parent, sibling, babysitter, carer or other familiar adult. It is very rare for a child to be abused by a stranger.

Types of child abuse

Physical abuse involves causing deliberate physical harm to a child and may include: burning, drowning, hitting, poisoning, scalding, shaking, suffocating or throwing. Physical abuse also includes deliberately causing, or fabricating the symptoms of, ill health in a child (such as Munchausen Syndrome by Proxy).

Emotional abuse involves the persistent psychological mistreatment of a child and may include: making the child feel inadequate, unloved or worthless; imposing inappropriate developmental expectations on the child; threatening, taunting or humiliating the child; exploiting or corrupting the child.

Sexual abuse involves coercing or encouraging a child to engage in sexual activities to which the child does not or cannot consent because of their age or level of understanding. These sexual activities may involve physical contact such as penetrative and/or oral sex or encouraging the child to watch the adult masturbate or to look at pornographic material.

Neglect involves the persistent failure to meet a child's essential basic needs for food, clothing, shelter, loving care or medical attention. Neglect may also include a situation in which a child is put at risk by being left alone without proper adult supervision. (DH, 2003a.)

Recognise indications of possible abuse

You need to be aware of the signs and indicators of possible child abuse and neglect and know to whom you should report any concerns or suspicions. As you may have contact with children on a daily basis, you have an essential role to play in recognising indications of possible abuse or neglect, such as outward signs of physical abuse, uncharacteristic behaviour patterns or failure to develop in the expected ways.

Indications of possible *physical* abuse include:

◎ Recurrent unexplained injuries or burns
◎ Refusal to discuss injuries

◎ Improbable explanations for injuries
◎ Watchful, cautious attitude towards adults
◎ Reluctance to play and be spontaneous
◎ Shrinking from physical contact
◎ Avoidance of activities involving removal of clothes, for example swimming
◎ Aggressive or bullying behaviour
◎ Being bullied
◎ Lack of concentration
◎ Difficulty in trusting people and making friends.

Indications of possible *emotional* abuse include:

◎ Delayed speech development
◎ Very passive and lacking in spontaneity
◎ Social isolation, such as finding it hard to play with other children
◎ Unable to engage in imaginative play
◎ Low self-esteem
◎ Easily distracted
◎ Fear of new situations
◎ Self-damaging behaviour, (head-banging, pulling out hair)
◎ Self-absorbing behaviour, (obsessive rocking, thumb-sucking)
◎ Eating problems (overeating or lack of appetite)
◎ Withdrawn behaviour and depression.

Indications of possible *sexual* abuse include:

◎ Sudden behaviour changes when abuse begins
◎ Low self-esteem
◎ Using sexual words in play activities uncharacteristic for age/level of development
◎ Withdrawn or secretive behaviour
◎ Starting to wet or soil themselves
◎ Demonstrating inappropriate seductive or flirtatious behaviour
◎ Frequent public masturbation
◎ Frightened of physical contact
◎ Depression resulting in self-harm (or an overdose)

◎ Bruises, scratches, burns or bite marks on the body.

Indications of possible *neglect* include:

◎ Slow physical development
◎ Constant hunger and/or tiredness
◎ Poor personal hygiene and appearance
◎ Frequent lateness or absenteeism
◎ Undiagnosed/untreated medical conditions
◎ Social isolation, for example poor social skills
◎ Compulsive stealing or begging.

(Indications of possible bullying are dealt with on page 112.)

The law regarding child protection

Information on protecting and safeguarding children can be found in the guidance document *Working Together to Safeguard Children: a guide to inter-agency working to safeguard and promote the welfare of children* (2006). This replaces *Working Together to Safeguard Children 1999. Working Together to Safeguard Children 2006* incorporates changes in safeguarding policy and practice since 1999. In response to the statutory inquiry into the death of Victoria Climbié (2003) and the first joint chief inspectors' report on safeguarding children (2002), the government produced *Every Child Matters* (see above) and set out better provisions to safeguard children in The Children Act 2004 including: the creation of children's trusts under the duty to co-operate; the setting up of Local Safeguarding Children Boards, and the duty on all agencies to make arrangements to safeguard and promote the welfare of children (HM Government 2004). This revised guidance is still informed by the requirements of the Children Act 1989, which provides a comprehensive framework for the care and protection of children. The guidance also echoes the principles covered by the United Nations Convention on the Rights of the Child, endorsed by the UK Government in 1991. It also takes on board the European Convention of Human Rights, especially Articles 6 and 8. In addition, Section 11 of the Children Act 2004 places a statutory duty on specified agencies (for example local authorities) to make arrangements to make sure that they safeguard and promote children's welfare.

Working Together to Safeguard Children 2006 sets out how agencies and professionals should work together to promote the welfare of children and to protect children from abuse and neglect. The document applies to those working in education, health and social services as well as the police and the probation service. It is relevant to those working with children and their families in the statutory, independent and voluntary sectors. The document sets out:

◎ A summary of the nature and impact of child abuse and neglect
◎ How to operate best practice in child protection procedures
◎ The roles and responsibilities of different agencies and practitioners
◎ The role of Local Safeguarding Children Boards
◎ The processes to be followed when there are concerns about a child
◎ The action to be taken to safeguard and promote the welfare of children experiencing, or at risk of, significant harm
◎ The important principles to be followed when working with children and families
◎ Training requirements for effective child protection.

Framework for the Assessment of Children in Need and their Families (2000) provides a systemic framework to help professionals identify children in need and assess the best approach to help such children and their families (see Chapter 14 for more information about early intervention for the benefit of children and families). *What to do if you're worried a child is being abused* (2003) is a guide for professionals who work with children, which explains the processes and systems contained in *Working Together to Safeguard Children* and *Framework for the Assessment of Children in Need and their Families.*

As a further safeguard to children's welfare, *The Protection of Children Act 1999* requires childcare organisations (including any organisation concerned with the supervision of children) not to offer employment involving regular contact with children, either paid or unpaid, to any person listed as unsuitable to work with children on the Department of Health list and the Department for Education and Employment's List 99. The Criminal Records Bureau acts as a central access point for criminal records checks for all those who apply to work with children and young people. (For information on enhanced disclosures see Chapter 15.)

The setting's child protection policy and procedures

The childcare setting's child protection policy should include information on the roles and responsibilities of staff members and the procedures for dealing with child protection issues. For example:

◎ All childcarers should attend child protection training
◎ The childcare setting will comply with the Local Safeguarding Children Board (LSCB) procedures
◎ If any member of staff is concerned about a child

they must inform a senior colleague and must record information regarding such concerns on the same day. This record must give a clear, precise and factual account of their observation

◎ Confidentiality is crucial and incidents should be discussed only with the relevant person, such as a senior colleague or external agency

◎ The senior practitioner or the setting manager will decide whether the concerns should be referred to external agencies, such as social services and/or the police

◎ The childcare setting should work co-operatively with parents unless this is inconsistent with the need to ensure the child's safety

◎ If a referral is made to social services, the senior practitioner or the setting manager will ensure that a report of the concerns is sent to the social worker dealing with the case within 48 hours

◎ Particular attention will be paid to the attendance and development of any child identified as 'at risk' or who has been placed on the Child Protection Register.

In your role you will have close contact with children, so need to be aware of the signs of possible abuse or neglect and know what to do if you have concerns about a child's welfare (see below). The childcare setting should have clear procedures, in line with the LSCB procedures, on the situations in which childcarers should consult senior colleagues and external agencies (for example social services and the police) when they have concerns about the welfare of a child. Local voluntary organisations can seek guidance from their national bodies (or from the LSCB) on the requirements for

staff training and how they can safeguard the children for whom they provide childcare services.

The childcarer's responsibilities for child protection

All adults who work with children have a duty to safeguard and promote their welfare. As a childcarer, you need to be aware of the signs of possible abuse, neglect and bullying and to whom you should report any concerns or suspicions. You also need to know the setting's child protection policy and procedures in general, in addition to the setting's policy against bullying, the procedures for actively preventing all forms of bullying among children and the procedure to be followed if a staff member is accused of abuse. You may be involved in child protection in a number of ways. You may:

◎ Have concerns about a child and refer those concerns to a senior colleague in the childcare setting (who will then refer matters to social services and/or the police as appropriate)

◎ Be the senior practitioner or setting manager who is responsible for referring concerns about a child's welfare to social services or the police

◎ Be approached by social services and asked to provide information about a child, be involved in an assessment or attend a child protection conference. This may happen regardless of who made the referral to social services

◎ Be asked to carry out a specific type of assessment, or provide help or a specific service to the child as part of an agreed plan and contribute to reviewing the child's progress (including attending child protection conferences).

(DH, 2003a)

Check it out

Find out about your setting's child protection policy and procedures.

Responding to suspicions of abuse

Childcarers working closely with children in childcare settings are well placed to identify the early signs of abuse, neglect or bullying. In addition, many children may view the childcare setting as neutral territory where they may feel more able to talk with an adult they trust about what is happening to them. If you have concerns that a child at your setting may be experiencing possible abuse or neglect it is essential that you report these concerns promptly to the relevant person, such as a senior colleague or external agency.

Responding to a child's disclosure of abuse

A child may make a personal disclosure to a member of staff relating to an experience in which they may have been significantly harmed. If a child makes a disclosure to you at an inappropriate place or time, you should talk again individually to the child before the end of the day. You may be able to discuss the issue with a senior colleague without giving the child's name, but if you are unable to do so, ensure that you follow the setting's confidentiality policy and child protection procedures. If a child makes a personal disclosure of abuse in some way, you should:

◎ Listen to what the child has to say
◎ Accept what the child is saying
◎ Allow the child to talk openly
◎ Listen to the child rather than ask direct questions
◎ Not criticise the alleged perpetrator of the abuse
◎ Reassure the child that what has happened is not their fault

◎ Stress to the child that it was the right thing to tell someone
◎ Reassure the child but do not make promises that you might not be able to keep
◎ Not promise the child to keep the disclosed information confidential (as it might be necessary for the matter to be referred to social services)
◎ Explain simply to the child what has to be done next and who has to be told.

After a child has made a disclosure to you:

◎ Make brief notes as soon as possible after the conversation
◎ Do not destroy the original notes, as the courts may need these
◎ Record the date, time, place and any noticeable non-verbal behaviour as well as the words used by the child. Draw a diagram to indicate the position of any bruising or other injury
◎ Record only statements and observations rather than interpretations or assumptions.

Dealing with a disclosure from a child or being involved in a child protection case can be a very distressing and stressful experience. You may need support for yourself and should discuss with a senior colleague how to access this when dealing with a case of child abuse or neglect.

Allegations of abuse against staff or volunteers

If a child, or parent, makes a complaint of abuse against a member of staff or volunteer, the person receiving the complaint must take it seriously and follow the relevant procedures in line with LSCB procedures. Professionals who are independent of the setting should investigate all allegations of abuse against staff or volunteers.

If you have reason to suspect that a child or young

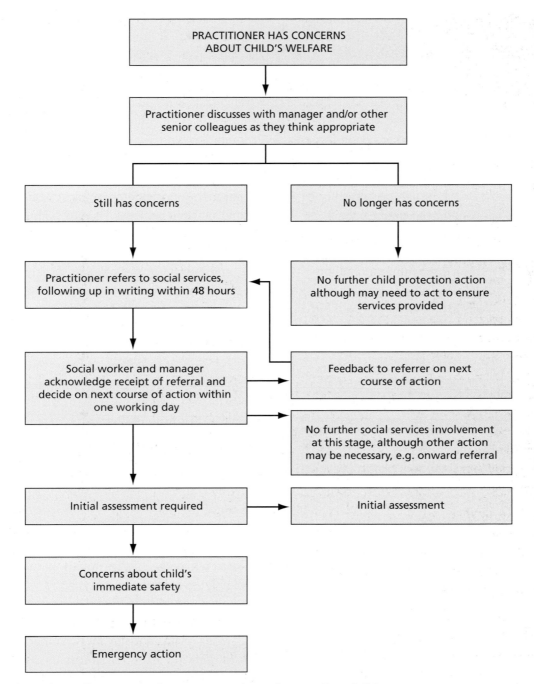

Figure 5.3 Flow chart illustrating the processes for safeguarding children
From: *What to do if you're worried a child is being abused*. Dept of Health, 2003.

person may have been abused by another member of staff, either in the setting or elsewhere, inform a senior colleague immediately. Make a record of the concerns, including a note of anyone else who witnessed the incident or allegation.

If the senior practitioner or setting manager decides that the allegation warrants further action through child protection procedures, a referral will be made direct to social services. If the allegation constitutes a serious criminal offence, it will be necessary to contact social services and the police before informing the member of staff. If it is decided that it is not necessary to refer the matter to social services, then the senior practitioner or setting manager will consider whether there needs to be an internal investigation. If the complaint is about the senior practitioner or setting manager, then the LSCB (Local Safeguarding Children Board) should be contacted for information on the necessary procedures to be followed.

> ### Check it out
>
> Find out about your setting's procedures for dealing with allegations of abuse against staff or volunteers.

The confidentiality of information relating to abuse

Child protection raises issues of confidentiality that must be clearly understood by everyone within the childcare setting. You must be absolutely clear about the boundaries of your legal and professional role and responsibilities with regard to the confidentiality of information relating to abuse. A clear and explicit confidentiality policy that staff, children and parents can all understand should ensure good practice throughout the childcare setting.

Childcare practitioners have a legal duty of confidence with regard to the personal information they hold about children and their families. Any information you receive about children (and their families) in the course of your work should be shared only within appropriate professional contexts. All information including child protection records should be kept securely. The law allows the disclosure of confidential personal information in order to safeguard a child or children. Usually personal information should be disclosed to a third party, for example social services, only after obtaining the consent of the person to whom the information relates. In some child protection matters it may not be possible or desirable to obtain such consent. The Data Protection Act 1998 allows disclosure without consent in some circumstances, for example to detect or prevent a crime, or to apprehend or prosecute an offender.

The safety and well-being of children must always be your first consideration. You cannot offer or guarantee absolute confidentiality, especially if there are concerns that a child is experiencing, or at risk of, significant harm. You have a responsibility to share relevant information about the protection of children with other professionals, particularly the investigative agencies, such as social services and the police. If a child confides in you and requests that the information is kept secret, it is important that you explain in a sensitive manner that not only is it in their interests that you refer cases of alleged abuse to the appropriate agencies but that you have a duty to do so. Within that context, the child should, however, be assured that the matter will be disclosed only to people who need to know about it.

As a childcarer you should:

◎ Be absolutely clear about your setting's child protection policy
◎ Know and understand your exact role and responsibilities with regard to confidentiality and child protection issues
◎ Tell a child who asks to speak to you in confidence that unconditional confidentiality may not always be possible if someone is in danger of abuse
◎ Tell a child if confidentiality is to be breached, who will be told, why and what the outcome is likely to be and how they will be supported
◎ Know when and who to contact if further advice, support or counselling are needed
◎ Ensure all children and their parents/carers are aware of the setting's confidentiality policy and how it works in practice
◎ Make sure children are informed of sources of confidential help, for example local advice services, Childline, and so on.

PORTFOLIO ACTIVITY

1 What are your role and responsibilities for reporting information on possible abuse to a senior colleague or external agency?

2 How and to whom should you pass on information about a child's personal disclosure of abuse? For example, your role and responsibilities for providing information on the disclosure to a senior colleague or external agency.

3 Find out about your setting's policy and procedures with regard to the confidentiality of information in child protection matters.

NVQ LINKS: CCLD 305.3 CCLD 301.4
CCLD 326.1 CCLD 326.2 CCLD 327.1

Helping children to protect themselves from abuse

An effective child protection policy will promote a caring and supportive environment in the childcare setting and create an atmosphere in which children feel that they are secure, valued, listened to and taken seriously. The setting's child protection policy should support children's development in ways that foster their security, confidence and independence. It should be regarded as central to the welfare and well-being of all children and aim to:

◎ Encourage children to have positive self-esteem and self-image
◎ Help children view themselves as part of the setting and local community
◎ Nurture children's abilities to establish and sustain relationships with families, peers, adults and the outside world
◎ Provide time, space and opportunities for children to explore, discuss and develop key ideas relating to child protection openly with peers and adults, in a safe and secure environment
◎ Equip children with the necessary skills to make reasoned, informed choices, judgements and decisions
◎ Work with parents and carers to build an understanding of the setting's responsibility to ensure the welfare and well-being of all children
◎ Establish and maintain child protection procedures so that all staff know how to act if they have concerns or need support regarding a particular child
◎ Ensure that all staff are aware of local child protection procedures so that information is passed on effectively to the relevant professional or agency
◎ Keep members of the setting well informed about child protection issues and to develop effective and supportive liaison with outside agencies

◎ Provide a model for open and effective communication between children, parents, childcarers and other adults working with children.

Child protection involves not only the detection of abuse and neglect but also the *prevention* of abuse by helping children to protect themselves. As part of this preventive role you should help children to: understand what is and is not acceptable behaviour towards them; stay safe from harm; speak up if they have worries and concerns; develop awareness and resilience; and prepare for their future responsibilities as adults, citizens and parents. Being actively involved with prevention helps children to keep safe both now and in the future. They need to know how to take responsibility for themselves and to understand the consequences of their actions. They should know and understand:

◎ That they all deserve care and respect
◎ Their rights and how to assert them
◎ How to do things safely and how to minimise risk
◎ How to deal with abusive or potentially abusive situations
◎ When and how to ask for help and support.

Helping children to develop assertiveness techniques

As a childcarer you need to help children to know and understand their rights and how to assert them. Ensure that children understand that no one should take away their right to be safe. You can help children to develop assertiveness techniques by using role play and puppets to explore the differences between being aggressive, passive and assertive. Encouraging children to develop negotiation skills is often an essential part of helping them to be assertive, which may help them to keep themselves safe. Introduce or reinforce negotiation skills by encouraging children to think about how they negotiate in everyday situations, for

example bedtimes, sharing play equipment, staying out late, using the computer/games console, visiting friends, or watching television. Encourage them to explore the idea of compromise and use role play to help them practise how to negotiate in difficult situations, such as being bullied.

Helping children to develop coping strategies

Children should be aware of a range of coping strategies for dealing with potentially risky situations. For example:

◎ Never talk to strangers. If a stranger approaches, ignore them, pretend not to hear and walk or run away
◎ Never go up to a car when someone stops to ask for directions – it could be a trick to entice children into the car. Pretend not to hear, keep at a distance and walk away
◎ Always try to stay with others, as there is safety in numbers
◎ If being followed or threatened by someone, go to a place where there are people, such as a shop or play area in a park. Go to the door of a house and pretend to ring the bell, or ring the bell if the person continues to follow or threaten
◎ Avoid anyone who is being offensive, drinking heavily, taking drugs or acting in an inappropriate way. If someone acts in an over-familiar way or gets too close, say 'no' forcefully and get help
◎ If being bullied, say 'no' without fighting, get friends to help and tell an adult. (See below for information on dealing with bullying)
◎ Do not fight to protect or retain possessions, for example if someone tries to steal your bag or mobile phone. Possessions can be replaced but people cannot. Keeping themselves safe is more important
◎ Always tell a parent or carer their intended destination and contact details. Memorise own

telephone number and address. Know how to contact parents, carers or neighbours in an emergency

◎ Communicate their limits to friends. Learn to say and mean 'no' to situations they dislike or feel uncomfortable about. If necessary they can use their parents as an excuse, for example 'I can't do that because my dad won't let me'

◎ Know and understand *The Keepsafe Code* (see www.kidscape.org.uk).

Helping children to keep themselves safe

Critical thinking and decision-making are also essential for helping children to keep themselves safe. Help them to develop these skills by encouraging them to participate in decision-making within the childcare setting and providing opportunities for co-operation. Encourage children to trust their own feelings and good judgement in difficult situations. By learning to trust their inner feelings, they can avoid many potential risky situations. Use role play to help them think about what they should do if their friends want them to do something they dislike or feel uncomfortable about, such as for example going to a party, getting drunk, having sex, shoplifting, taking drugs, and so on. Peer pressure can be very strong; encourage them to decide and set limits about what they will and will not do so that they know how to cope before the situation arises. Make sure that children understand the dangers of situations that may put their personal safety at risk such as: being left at home alone; playing in deserted or dark places; being out on their own; getting lost, for example on outings; walking home alone especially in the dark; talking to strangers; and accepting lifts from strangers, including hitchhiking.

As children get older they need opportunities to explore their environment and to develop their independence. To do this safely they will need to understand about acceptable risk-taking. This can be explored through stories (for example *Jack and the Beanstalk*) and television programmes. Children can think about and discuss the risks taken by their favourite characters. Encourage them to identify some of the risks they take in their own lives and look at ways they can minimise risk. Puppets and role play can be used to help them deal with potentially risky situations.

Helping children to access appropriate support when necessary

Children need to know where to go for help and support in difficult situations. They should be encouraged to identify people in the childcare setting and the local community who help them to keep safe: for example worries about bullying or problems at home may be discussed with a childcarer; if they get lost they can ask a police officer for assistance. Encourage children to think of a trusted adult (such as parents, other relative, best friend, teacher, or childcarer) they could talk to about a difficult situation, including abuse, bullying, negative peer pressure, and so on. Ensure that they understand that if they go to an adult for help, especially within the childcare setting, they will be believed and supported. Give them information about other sources of help and support, such as that provided by Childline and The Samaritans, for example.

Think About

Think about the ways your setting helps children to protect themselves.

Dealing with bullying

Research suggests that 85 per cent of children aged 5 to 11 years have experienced bullying in some form, including name-calling and being hit or kicked. In 2000 a survey of 11 to 16 year olds found that '*36% of children said they had been bullied in the last 12 months; 26% had been threatened with violence and 13% had been physically attacked*' (ATL, 2000). As bullying occurs both inside and *outside* of schools, childcare settings should have an anti-bullying policy that clearly sets out the ways in which they try to prevent or reduce bullying and deal with bullying behaviour when it happens.

What is bullying?

Bullying can be defined as behaviour that is deliberately hurtful or aggressive, repeated over a period of time and difficult for victims to defend themselves against. There are three main types of bullying:

1 *Physical*: hitting, kicking, taking belongings
2 *Verbal*: name-calling, insulting, making offensive remarks
3 *Indirect*: spreading nasty stories about someone, exclusion from social groups, being made the subject of malicious rumours, and sending malicious e-mails or text messages on mobile phones.

Name-calling is the most common type of bullying. Children may be called nasty names because of their individual characteristics, ethnic origin, nationality, skin colour, sexual orientation or disability. Verbal bullying is common among boys and girls. Boys experience more physical violence and threats when being bullied than girls. However, physical attacks on girls by other girls are becoming more common. Girls tend to use more indirect types of bullying,

which can be more difficult to detect and deal with. (DfES, 2000)

Any child can experience bullying but certain factors may make it more likely. While there is never an acceptable excuse for bullying behaviour, children are more likely to experience bullying if they: are shy or have an over-protective family environment; are from a different racial or ethnic group to the majority of children; appear different in some obvious respect, for example they stammer; have special needs such as a disability or learning difficulties; behave inappropriately in that they are a 'nuisance' or intrude on others' activities; or possess expensive accessories, such as mobile phones or computer games.

Recognising when a child is being bullied

Children who are experiencing bullying may be reluctant to attend the childcare setting and are often absent. They may be more anxious and insecure than others, have fewer friends and often feel unhappy and lonely. They can suffer from low self-esteem and negative self-image; they may see themselves as failures and feel stupid, ashamed and unattractive. Possible signs that a child is being bullied include: suddenly not wanting to go to the setting when they usually enjoy it; unexplained cuts and bruises; possessions have unexplained damage or are persistently 'lost'; or becoming withdrawn or depressed but will not say what is the matter. While the above signs may indicate that a child is being bullied, they may also be symptomatic of other problems such as child abuse.

Helping children who are being bullied

The behaviour of some children can lead to their experiencing bullying, though this does not justify

the behaviour of the bullies. For example, some children may: find it difficult to play with other children; be hyperactive; behave in ways that irritate others; bully weaker children; be easily roused to anger; fight back when attacked or even slightly provoked; or be actively disliked by the majority of children who use the setting. Childcarers and the child's parents should work together to identify any such behaviour. The child needs help to improve personal and social skills, including assertiveness techniques and conflict resolution. You may be able to provide support for a child who is being bullied by:

◎ Encouraging the child to talk
◎ Listening to the child's problems
◎ Believing the child if they say they are being bullied
◎ Providing reassurance that it is not their fault; no one deserves to be bullied
◎ Discussing the matter with a senior colleague
◎ Taking appropriate action, following the setting's policy on anti-bullying.

Dealing with persistent and violent bullying

Where a child does not respond to the strategies to combat bullying, the childcare setting should take tough action to deal with persistent and violent bullying and should have a range of sanctions to deal with this. Everyone within the setting should know what sanctions will be taken. These should be fair and applied consistently. Help to deal with bullying behaviour by:

◎ Knowing the setting's policy and strategies for dealing with bullying behaviour
◎ Using appropriate sanctions for such behaviour, such as exclusion from certain activities
◎ Providing help for the bully so they can recognise that this behaviour is unacceptable, for example discussion, mediation, or peer counselling
◎ Working with childcarers and parents to establish community awareness of bullying
◎ Making sure all children know that bullying will *not* be tolerated
◎ Understanding that the setting can permanently exclude children who demonstrate persistent bullying behaviour, especially physical violence.

STOP the bullies now!
LOOK out for your friends.
LISTEN to your friends who are sad or upset.
TALK to your playworkers or parents.

Figure 5.4 Example of child's anti-bullying poster

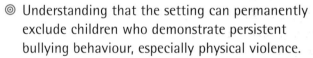

PORTFOLIO ACTIVITY

1 Outline your setting's anti-bullying policy and main strategies for dealing with bullying behaviour.
2 Give a reflective account of how you have handled concerns about bullying. Remember confidentiality.
3 Devise an activity to encourage children to speak up about bullying, for example a story, discussion, role play, drama or poster making.

NVQ LINKS: CCLD 305.3   CCLD 301.3
CCLD 308.1   CCLD 337.1

Optional Unit

CCLD 306
Plan and organise environments for children and families

CCLD 306
Plan and organise environments for children and families

CCLD 306.1
Plan and provide an enabling physical environment for children

Knowledge base

K3D255   K3S256   K3S257   K3D265   K3D266
K3D267

It is important to plan and organise a childcare environment for children and families that is welcoming and user-friendly. This involves creating an enabling physical environment for children that meets their needs, including adapting the environment (according to their ages, abilities and any special needs) and ensuring that any barriers to participation are addressed. It also involves organising space and resources to meet children's needs within an accessible, comfortable and stimulating environment. You should provide a caring, nurturing and responsive environment in which children and their families feel valued and respected. Also encourage children to care for themselves in a manner that is appropriate to their ages, needs and abilities.

You must ensure that the setting meets regulatory health and safety requirements and maintain procedures for risk assessment and health and safety including maintaining children's safety during play and learning activities.

Adapt the environment to meet children's needs, according to their ages, abilities and any additional requirements. For example: furniture should be the correct size and height for the children; play equipment and other learning resources must be appropriate to the developmental needs of the children and meet safety standards; there should be access for wheelchair users; and safety gates should be provided to prevent children accessing potentially hazardous areas. The childcare environment should be free from clutter and easily accessible to all children including those with physical disabilities or sensory impairment. Ensure that barriers to participation are addressed: for example ramps and/or lifts should be provided for those unable to use stairs.

Organising visual and tactile displays

Part of your role will be to organise visual and tactile displays to stimulate children's curiosity and involvement. When organising displays you need to consider these points:

◎ *The purpose of the display,* for example to stimulate discussion and to consolidate learning

◎ *The choice of materials,* such as the colour and texture of backing paper; using drapes or boxes to create 3D effects; different ways to frame/mount 2D work to make it more eye-catching

◎ *The vocabulary and size of lettering,* for instance use words and lettering appropriate to the children's ages and levels of development; remember to use the setting's preferred handwriting style or word process captions using an appropriate font

◎ *Use appropriate equipment,* including, paper trimmers, scissors, glue and staple gun.

Display children's work in ways that encourage creativity and positive self-esteem, giving them lots of praise for their attempts to create pictures, models or written work. Focus on the creative process of children's pictures and writing, not the end product. Do not worry that the finished results do not look neat, especially in the early years; it is 'having a go' that is important. Where appropriate, encourage the children to use their ICT skills to word process their written work and/or to create captions for their pictures and models.

Ensure that displays are appropriate to the work of the setting and the children's play and learning needs and check they are updated or renewed on a regular basis. Displays in the setting should reflect its linguistic and cultural diversity and local community. They should portray positive images of race, culture, gender and disability. Examples of displays include:

◎ *Wall displays* to provide a stimulus for discussions and to consolidate learning, including diagrams, maps, posters, pictures and children's work with appropriate labels or captions; alphabet and key words lists; number line and 100 square

◎ *Tabletop displays* to stimulate discussion and further learning, including interest tables with artefacts to talk about, look at and explore linked to topics and themes such as colour, shape, sound, musical instruments, texture

◎ *Displays of models made by the children* with captions in the form of questions to stimulate discussion; for example 'How many ...?', 'What will happen if ...?'

◎ *Book displays,* including books relating to topics and themes, to promote children's interest in books, to develop their literacy skills and to extend learning.

Your tutor/assessor should be able to give you guidance and practical tips on what to do when organising displays. You can also develop your display skills by looking at other people's displays, such as those of senior colleagues, and books about displays.

The importance of labelling

Young children respond to labels even before they can read them; they will ask adults what labels say. Using pictures or objects as well as written words helps children to make sense of labels and to develop their literacy skills. Labelling introduces young children to one of the important purposes of written language: providing information or directions. Labels encourage children's independence in reading and writing. Providing a special place for children to keep their belongings (whether on a hook, in a drawer, tray or basket), clearly labelled

Figure 6.1 Interactive display in an early years setting

CCLD 306.2
Organise space and resources to meet children's needs

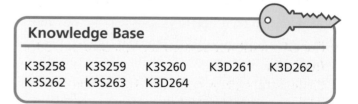

Knowledge Base

K3S258	K3S259	K3S260	K3D261	K3D262
K3S262	K3S263	K3D264		

with each child's name, is an essential part of the enabling environment. With very young children, a picture on the left-hand side of the label helps them to remember to work from left to right in reading and writing activities. Labels on important everyday objects in the setting assist children's early literacy skills and help to extend their vocabulary within a meaningful context. Where possible you should use sentences rather than single words. Clearly labelled areas and storage can help to extend children's language as well as aid the development of their social skills and independence.

Central to planning and organising a supportive childcare environment is the provision of space, time and resources appropriate to the needs of all the children who use the setting. As well as providing for learning activities and play opportunities, there should be regular times for routines such as breaks, lunchtime and so on. A regular daily routine provides stability and security for children. A timetable should be clearly displayed in a manner appropriate to the ages of the children; older children could have their own copy of their weekly timetable. Flexibility is also important to allow for special events such as educational visits/outings, swimming lessons, special visitors to the setting such as a theatre or dance group. Working as a team, childcare practitioners should decide how best to use the resources allocated to their setting; this includes adult resources such as childcarers and any parent helpers as well as equipment and materials. The senior practitioner or setting manager should ensure that these adults are used to their full potential in order to respond appropriately to the needs of all children, stimulate their learning through play, supervise their activities and safeguard their welfare.

Activity

1 Outline the daily and/or weekly routine for the children you work with.
2 Provide a copy of your personal timetable.

Here are some general guidelines about organising room space:

◎ Fire exits must not be obstructed, locked or hidden from view
◎ Chairs, tables and play equipment must be the correct size and height for the ages/levels of development of the children
◎ Books, jigsaws, computers, art and design materials need to be used in areas with a good source of light, if possible near a natural source of light
◎ Water, sand, art and design activities need to be provided in areas with appropriate floor surfaces with washing facilities nearby
◎ Any large or heavy equipment that has to be

moved for use should be close to where it is stored.

The precise way the childcare environment is organised depends on:

◎ The type of childcare setting and the age range of the children
◎ The requirements of the Day Care National Standards (see page 23)
◎ Any specific curriculum requirements (such as The Foundation Stage or The National Curriculum)
◎ The resources for particular activities
◎ The developmental needs of the children
◎ The play and/or learning objectives for the children
◎ Behaviour management strategies
◎ The inclusion of children with special needs.

Effective organisation is also influenced by the space available and the general quality of areas and staffing in the childcare environment. The childcare environment should have:

1 *Adequate staffing ratios.* For example the Daycare Trust recommends a staffing ratio of no greater than 1:10 for children aged over 7 years. The minimum staffing ratios under the Day Care National Standards in England are:
  ◎ 1:3 children under 2 years
  ◎ 1:4 children aged 2 to 3 years
  ◎ 1:8 children aged 3 to 7 years.
2 *Appropriate qualified staff.* At least 50 per cent of staff in the childcare setting should be qualified to NVQ Level 2 or equivalent. The person in charge must be qualified to at least NVQ Level 3 or equivalent. (See Chapter 4.)
3 *Adequate floor space* for the age, size and needs of the children, including space for childcarers to work with individuals or groups of children, as needed. Children with physical disabilities may require additional floor space for wheelchairs and

other specialised equipment or furniture. Children with emotional difficulties or behavioural problems may also benefit from adequate personal space. For example, the indoor space requirements under the Day Care National Standards in England are: $3.5m^2$ for children under 2 years; $2.5m^2$ for children aged 2 years; $2.3m^2$ for children aged 3 to 7 years.

4 *Appropriate areas for activities and routines* such as: arts and crafts area; home corner; dressing up; quiet activities (for example a book corner); sand and water play; large and small construction activities; computer workstations with access to mains power and any computer accessories; storage areas with adequate space for the materials and equipment needed for learning activities and play opportunities; food preparation and eating areas. Where applicable, there should be a separate base room for children under 2 years of age.

5 *Appropriate sources of heating, lighting and ventilation.* Children should be able to play and learn in an environment that is neither too hot nor too cold. The heating source must be safe and fitted/maintained to the required legal standards. There should be good sources of both natural and artificial light.

6 *Appropriate acoustic conditions* to enable children to listen during essential discussions and to help reduce noise levels. Carpeted floor areas, sound absorbent screens, displays, drapes and curtains all help to absorb reverberation.

7 *Access to outdoor play area* which is appropriate to the children's ages, such as secure area with age appropriate equipment for young children. With appropriate adult supervision children should also visit local parks and playgrounds (see Chapter 2).

8 *Appropriate access to the childcare setting,* e.g. suitable access for children, parents and staff including wheelchair access and adequate space for parking.

As part of your daily or weekly routine you should check that you are not running out of any materials or equipment, following your setting's procedure for doing this. There will be an inventory or stock list which is checked on a regular basis. Clearing away and storing equipment and materials provides you with a good opportunity to check whether supplies are running low.

> **Think About**
>
> 1 How did you find out how to use the main equipment in your setting?
> 2 What are the setting's safety arrangements regarding the use of such equipment?
> 3 What are the setting's procedures for reporting equipment breakdown or damage and any shortages of materials/equipment?

The childcare setting should be equipped with a basic set of resources and books, appropriate to the ages and developmental needs of the children. You should organise resources so that they are equally accessible to all children in the setting and enable choice and independence. Use ICT to support children's play and learning and encourage them to be actively involved in decisions about their environment, for example in selecting play and learning resources. Children should be taught how to use all resources correctly and safely, with care and respect and with regard for health and safety and waste. Remember that resources should reflect the cultural and linguistic diversity of our society. General resources may include:

◎ *Visual aids:* wall displays including children's work, maps, posters, pictures and posters; interest tables with objects related to topic work; 3D displays of children's work including construction models; videos; computer graphics and books

◎ *Indoor and outdoor play equipment* appropriate for the children's ages and levels of development and suitable for children of all abilities including those with special needs

◎ *Groups of tables for group work* including literacy and numeracy activities

◎ *Groups of tables for 'messy' practical activities* (for example arts and crafts, design technology) including storage for art/design materials and equipment, such as paint, paint pots, drying rack; sink for washing paint pots and brushes; basin for washing hands

◎ *Computers and printers* with a selection of appropriate software

◎ *CD players with headphones* and a selection of CDs

◎ *Book/story corner* with appropriate range of fiction and non-fiction books including some dual language books

◎ *Quiet area* where children can go for privacy, rest or sleep depending on their individual needs, including cushions, mats or cots appropriate to the ages of the children

◎ *Whiteboard, overhead projector and teaching base* in settings supporting children's literacy and numeracy skills, including marker pens, transparencies, textbooks, teaching manuals and other resources needed by staff on a regular basis

◎ *Writing and drawing materials,* including a variety of writing tools (crayons, pencils, pens, pastels, chalks); different shapes, sizes and types of paper (such as plain, coloured, graph)

◎ *Specialist resources for specific curriculum areas* stored in the appropriate curriculum resource cupboard/area, and regularly audited by the curriculum subject co-ordinator. Staff should contact curriculum subject co-ordinators with

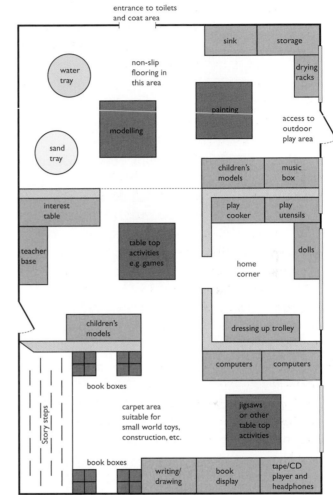

Figure 6.2 Example of a childcare setting layout

suggestions for specialist materials that may need ordering

◎ *Children's work trays* to store individual workbooks; individual folders for topic work; individual reading books and reading logs; personal named pencils; and individual crayon tins

◎ *Area with individual coat pegs* for children's coats and PE bags.

PORTFOLIO ACTIVITY

1 Draw your own plan of a childcare setting. Include the following: age range of children; heating and lighting; ventilation, including windows; layout of furniture/equipment; play areas; fire doors/safety equipment; and storage areas.

2 Highlight any specific features of the childcare environment that make it suitable for all children including those with special needs (including physical disability or sensory impairment) or those from different cultural backgrounds.

3 List ways in which you think your childcare setting maximises sensory experiences and a variety of play and learning opportunities.

NVQ LINKS: CCLD 306.1   CCLD 306.2   CCLD 302.1   CCLD 305.1   CCLD 305.2   CCLD 321.1

Encouraging children to help maintain their childcare environment

The routine of getting out and putting away equipment can seem like a chore, but it is part of the learning experience for children. Most children like to be involved in sorting and putting things away. As well as helping to develop mathematical concepts such as sorting and matching sets of objects and judging space, capacity and volume, children develop a sense of responsibility for caring for their childcare environment. They can also gain confidence and independence if they are involved in setting out and clearing away learning materials, as appropriate to their ages/levels of development and safety requirements. You should store and display materials and equipment in ways which will enable children to choose, use and return them easily. Ensure that children help in ways that are in line with the setting's health and safety policies. They must never have access to dangerous materials, such as bleach, or use very hot water for cleaning and they should not carry large, heavy or awkward objects due to the potential risks of serious injury. Remember that children have the right to be protected from harm. As a childcare practitioner, you

must ensure their physical health and safety as well as their emotional well-being.

Unit Links

For this Unit you also need to understand the following section:

CCLD 302 Develop and maintain a healthy, safe and secure environment for children (see Chapter 2)

CCLD 306.3
Provide a caring, nurturing and responsive environment

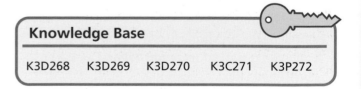

Knowledge Base

K3D268   K3D269   K3D270   K3C271   K3P272

As a childcare practitioner, you will be responsible for providing a caring, nurturing and responsive environment. All childcare settings should have a written statement outlining their expectations for both children and staff, including aims such as: providing a caring, nurturing and responsive environment that fosters respect; encouraging all children to fulfil their full potential and prepare for adult life; delivering any curriculum requirements in a stimulating and appropriate way; ensuring continuity and progression of learning appropriate to children's developmental needs through carefully planned monitoring and evaluation; and working in partnership with parents and the local community. This statement should be available in various documents throughout the childcare setting, for example in the setting's brochure and the staff handbook.

You can provide a caring, nurturing and responsive environment by showing that you value children and families, including respecting their culture, ethnicity, faith, language and background and helping children to be positive about their cultural backgrounds. Deal positively with any conflicts that may arise between children, families or colleagues and ensure that you are available to children and families who wish to communicate with you.

Unit Link

For this Unit you also need to understand the following section:

CCLD 301 Develop and promote positive relationships (see Chapter 1)

Praise and acknowledge children's efforts and achievements (see page 177) and ensure that you are consistent and fair when dealing with their behaviour. Create a stable environment for children which is suitable for their ages, needs and abilities and check that it is caring and responsive by: providing flexible routines to support children's well-being; explaining any foreseeable changes to the child's environment clearly and honestly;

providing reassurance, explanations and comfort for any unforeseen changes; being flexible and responsive to children's changing needs and circumstances. You need to meet children's attachment needs through the provision of keyworkers or key persons, especially for children aged 0 to 3 years. Allow children to take responsibility for themselves and others by providing opportunities which encourage them to become more independent, according to their age, needs and abilities.

Unit Links

For this Unit you also need to understand the following sections:

CCLD 308 Promote children's well-being and resilience (see Chapter 10)

CCLD 314.4 Provide an emotionally secure and consistent environment (see Chapter 11)

CCLD 325.2 Support the child or young person to prepare for transfer or transition (see Chapter 10)

Think About

How do you provide a caring, nurturing and responsive environment? For example: show that you value and respect children and their needs; promote children's positive self-image and well being; be flexible and responsive to children's changing needs and circumstances.

CCLD 306.4
Facilitate children's personal care

Activity

Working with a group of children, design a poster that illustrates the importance of personal hygiene. For example: hand washing after using the toilet or before handling food.

There will usually be separate toilet and wash facilities for children and staff. It is important to ensure there is adequate lighting and ventilation and that the cleaning routines for toilets and wash-basins are regular and thorough to maintain high standards of hygiene. There should be a supply of easily accessible drinking water, in addition to adequate supplies of toilet paper, soap, warm water and disposable paper towels and/or access to hot air driers. To minimise the spread of infection, parents should be advised that if their children have diarrhoea they should stay away from the setting until they no longer have any symptoms.

You may be involved in checking children's toilet areas to see that they are used correctly and that children wash their hands after using the toilet or before handling food. Teach children, especially young children, about the importance of personal hygiene and about the need for proper hand washing after using the toilet or before handling food. Education settings may teach personal hygiene through their health education programme, science lessons and as part of general school/class routines, for example washing their hands before lunch.

Encourage children to care for themselves in a manner that is appropriate to their age, needs and abilities. You may be required to assist very young children (or children with physical disabilities) with their toileting needs. It is important that you know the setting's procedures for dealing with children who wet or soil themselves, including the location of appropriate spare clothing. Ensure that personal care routines support children's protection and that of adults who work with them, for example always follow your setting's procedures for nappy changing, toilet training and toileting accidents. You should know the systems for dealing with waste (such as nappies) and follow the setting's procedures and any regulatory requirements. If you experience any concerns or problems with children when carrying out hygiene routines, you should report these to the senior practitioner or your line manager. This includes reporting any hazard or unsafe situation you discover when using the setting's facilities.

You may need to provide reassurance and support for a female pupil who starts menstruation but does not have any sanitary protection. (Girls as young as 8 or 9 years of age can start their first period while at school.) It is important that you know the setting's procedures for dealing with this situation, including accessing emergency supplies of sanitary protection and its disposal. If you are a male childcarer then you must know who to go to for help if this situation occurs.

It is important to meet children's physical care needs in ways that reflect the needs of individual children and their cultural or religious practices, as long as this does not compromise the welfare of the children. This includes understanding appropriate skin and hair care and the need for sensitivity to the diverse needs of children with a range of skin colours and types or hair texture, for example by using appropriate toiletries. You should also be aware of the damage that can be done to children's skin by sun exposure and take appropriate action to avoid this; for example check that children wear appropriate clothing, including hats, and use sun protection. Teach children about the importance of dental care through the use of posters and stories, as well as encouraging them to brush their teeth. Provide for children's nutritional needs while they are at the setting (depending on the type of setting) and deal with children's medicines or other specific medical requirements, according to your setting's procedures.

Unit Link

For this Unit you also need to understand the following section:

CCLD 302.3 Supervise procedures for accidents, injuries, illnesses and other emergencies (see Chapter 2)

PORTFOLIO ACTIVITY

Plan, implement and evaluate a care routine or activity that facilitates children's personal care. For example: washing hands; nappy changing; dental care; hair or skin care. NVQ LINKS: CCLD 306.4   CCLD 307.1   CCLD 314.3

CCLD 307
Promote the health and physical development of children

Childhood is a critical period for establishing lifestyle habits that will affect children's health and development and in their adult lives. Promoting children's health and physical development within a supportive environment encourages them to: access appropriate advice and support for health-related issues; attain good physical and mental health; make healthy lifestyle choices; understand and manage risk; develop responsible behaviour patterns; and participate in physical activity and sport in school and the local community. (DH, 2004a)

CCLD 307.1
Plan and implement physical activities and routines for children to meet their physical development needs

Knowledge Base

K3D287	K3D288	K3D289	K3S290	K3D291
K3D292	K3D293	K3S294		

You need to plan and implement physical activities and routines to meet children's physical development needs. Plan indoor and outdoor activities that provide opportunities for children to: practise physical skills and develop competence; acquire balance, skills and co-ordination of large muscles; support fine motor skills; and develop hand–eye co-ordination (for more detail about promoting children's physical development see Chapter 3).

Physical activities that can help children to develop their gross motor skills, fine motor skills and co-ordination include: indoor play opportunities such as sand/water play, drawing and painting, playdough, pretend play; action songs and movement sessions; jigsaw puzzles and construction materials; outdoor play opportunities including larger play apparatus; ball games; swimming; and outings to local parks and playgrounds. (See Chapter 8 for more information about physical play.)

Routines that help children to develop their fine motor skills and hand–eye co-ordination include: dealing with fastenings and shoelaces; using a cup; using a spoon, fork or knife; helping to prepare or serve food; and helping to set out and/or clear away play and learning equipment. These activities and routines should also encourage children to co-operate, share and take turns (see Chapter 10 for more information about encouraging children to share and co-operate). Ensure that the activities and routines provided are in line with the overall plan for the setting, for example linked to a common theme or topic and appropriate to the ages and developmental needs of the children you work with.

Check that children are wearing appropriate clothing that is comfortable and keeps them safe when involved in physical activities including: comfortable, loose clothing; appropriate footwear (pumps or trainers for ball games, bare feet for movement sessions); no belts, ties or scarves when using play apparatus (such as climbing equipment); and waterproof aprons for sand, water or painting activities. Ensure that children are given 'warm up' opportunities and include appropriate stretching exercises such as 'Pretend you are waking up in the morning, yawn and stretch your arms out as high as you can'. Remember 'wind down' opportunities afterwards, for example ask children to make a big stretch then curl up as small as a mouse, or lay down with their eyes closed and imagine they are on the beach listening to the sea. During physical activities and routines, encourage children to extend their range and level of skills and reward their efforts and achievements. Check that planned activities are inclusive and available to all children, adapting plans as necessary to meet individual needs. Make an adequate risk assessment, in line with organisational policy, without limiting opportunities to extend and challenge children's

skills and experience (see Chapter 2 for more deail on risk assessment and maintaining children's safety during play and learning activities).

As well as space to move freely (and safely) while playing both indoors and outdoors, children need space to rest and recover from physical exercise, including quiet corners to look at attractive books or engage in imaginative play. Very young children will also need an appropriate area to have a nap, especially if they are in full day care (see Chapter 11). You should plan and implement routines that allow children to rest and recover from physical exercise. Plan for and ensure there is a balance of activities and routines that include physical play and quieter rest periods.

Ensuring healthy eating and food safety within the setting enables children to maintain their health and well-being by: developing and growing properly; maintaining a healthy weight; protecting skeleton and nervous system; improving their immune system to fight off illness and infection;

Unit Link

For this Unit you also need to understand the following section:
CCLD 308.1 Enable children to relate to others (see Chapter 10))

PORTFOLIO ACTIVITY

1 Observe a child involved in a physical activity, for example indoor movement session or outdoor play. Focus on the physical skills demonstrated by the child.

2 In your assessment comment on: the child's gross motor skills; the child's fine motor skills; the child's co-ordination skills; the child's ability to co-operate and/or take turns; the role of the adult in promoting the child's physical development; and make suggestions for further activities to encourage or extend the child's physical development.

NVQ LINKS: CCLD 307.1   CCLD 303.1   CCLD 303.2   CCLD 308.1   CCLD 318.2

Unit Links

For this Unit you also need to understand the following sections:
CCLD 302.1 Establish a healthy, safe and secure environment for children (see Chapter 2)
CCLD 302.2 Maintain a healthy, safe and secure environment for children (see Chapter 2)

PORTFOLIO ACTIVITY

1 Plan, implement and evaluate a physical activity to meet a child's physical development needs. Use the assessment information from your observation of a child involved in a physical activity from page 125 as the basis for your planning.

2 Include the following:
   ◎ How the activity encourages physical skills such as gross motor skills, fine motor skills and/or co-ordination skills
   ◎ How the activity encourages co-operation, sharing and turn-taking
   ◎ Equipment and organisation, for example any play apparatus required; appropriate clothing for the children; 'warm up' and 'wind down' opportunities
   ◎ The role of the adult, for example how the adult encourages the child to extend their range and level of skills; how the adult rewards the child's efforts and achievements.

3 Consider how you could meet the needs of children with physical disabilities with this activity.
NVQ LINKS: CCLD 307.1   CCLD 307.3   CCLD 303.3   CCLD 303.4   CCLD 308.1   CCLD 318.2   CCLD 318.3

preventing dental decay; keeping fit and healthy through a balanced diet and exercise; and avoiding unnecessary illness, for example food poisoning due to poor hygiene.

PORTFOLIO ACTIVITY

Give examples of how you plan and implement routines that allow the children you work with to rest and recover from physical exercise.
NVQ LINKS: CCLD 307.1   CCLD 306.3   CCLD 314.3

CCLD 307.2
Plan and provide food and drink to meet the nutritional needs of children

Knowledge Base

K3S295	K3S296	K3S297	K3S298	K3S299
K3S300	K3S301	K3S302		

Basic knowledge of food hygiene

The Chartered Institute of Environmental Health Foundation Certificate in Food Hygiene (formerly Basic Food Hygiene Certificate) is an essential qualification for all food and beverage handlers (including childcare practitioners) and covers the basic principles of safe food handling. Many colleges include this certificate as part of their childcare courses. If you do not have this certificate already you will find that the course is available at most local colleges and includes: food poisoning trends and reasons; bacteria and micro-organisms; personal hygiene; food safety legislation; pest control; and cleaning and disinfecting.

The setting's procedures for storing and preparing food

Follow your setting's procedures for storing and preparing food. If you are responsible for the preparation and handling of food you should be aware of, and comply with, regulations relating to food safety and hygiene. For example, if the childcare setting provides meals for children, then the kitchen facility must comply with the Food Safety Act 1990 and the Food Safety Regulations 2002. Children should not have access to the kitchen unless it is being used solely for a supervised children's activity. (DfES, 2003b)

Storing food

You can help to maintain food safety by following correct food storage procedures such as:

◎ Storing the most perishable foods in the coldest part of the fridge

◎ Reading and following directions on food package labels about storage, temperature, 'use by' and 'best before' dates
◎ Avoiding any possibility of foods dripping onto other food in the fridge (always store raw meat on a shelf *below* cooked meat and dairy products)
◎ Keeping eggs in the fridge, as warmth will cause deterioration
◎ Never keeping or using damaged eggs, as eggshells harbour bacteria
◎ Maintaining a sufficiently low temperature by avoiding overfilling the fridge
◎ Removing unused food from tins, putting in a covered dish, storing in the fridge and using within 48 hours
◎ Cooling food quickly before storing in the fridge
◎ Storing bread in a bread bin with a tight fitting lid to retain freshness; bread goes stale quickly in the fridge but can be frozen for up to three months
◎ Keeping food covered, free from flies and other insects and away from any pets.

(Childs, 2001; p. 222)

You should know the relevant areas for eating and drinking in the childcare setting for both yourself and the children you work with, for example: the canteen or school hall; or designated classroom in a school or room in a community centre. Childcarers may eat with the children or eat their own packed lunches in the staffroom.

Providing a satisfying, varied and balanced diet

Depending on the type of childcare setting, you may need to provide regular drinks and food for the children. Those who attend the setting for a full day should be offered a midday meal or packed lunch that can be provided by parents. Fresh drinking water should be available to children at all times.

Any food and drink provided by the childcare setting should be properly prepared, nutritious and comply with any special dietary requirements. (DfES, 2003b)

Healthy eating involves getting the right nutrients from a satisfying, varied and balanced diet. Children and adults need these nutrients to enable their bodies to work efficiently: that is carbohydrates, proteins, fats, vitamins and minerals. People also need fibre and water to remove waste products and avoid dehydration.

A balanced diet includes a wide variety of food so that sufficient quantities of the different nutrients are consumed. Ensure that children understand that healthy eating does not have to be boring, as a balanced diet can include foods they enjoy eating. For example, eating biscuits, cakes or crisps is all right in small amounts, as long as they also eat plenty of the foods with the nutrients they need the most of; these include bread, cereals and potatoes; meat, fish and vegetarian alternatives; milk and dairy products; fruit and vegetables. (For more information on the nutritional needs of babies and children under 3 years see Chapter 11.)

Help children to learn about the guidelines for a healthy, balanced diet, which include: enjoy eating food; eat a variety of foods; eat the right amount to be a healthy weight; eat plenty of foods rich in starch and fibre; eat plenty of fruit and vegetables; do not eat too many foods that contain lots of fat; do not have sugary foods or drinks too often; and drink plenty of water (British Nutrition Foundation, 2003). You may encourage children to learn about a healthy, balanced diet through activities such as drawing their own pictures, designing posters or leaflets about a balanced diet

Figure 7.1 A balanced diet

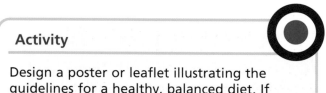

Activity

Design a poster or leaflet illustrating the guidelines for a healthy, balanced diet. If possible, encourage a child or small group of children to design their own posters or leaflets.

Special dietary requirements

If your childcare setting provides meals and/or snacks and drinks for children then their parents should be requested to give information on any special dietary requirements, preferences or food allergies the child may have. A record should be made of this information during the registration process and the relevant staff should be aware of, and follow, these requirements.

Remember that children from some families may follow strict rules about religious dietary requirements. For example: Jews do not eat pork or shellfish and many eat only *kosher* foods; Muslims do not eat pork and many will eat only *halal* foods; Hindus and Sikhs do not eat beef or are vegetarians/vegans; some Buddhists are also vegetarians. Find out if the children in your care are required to follow a certain diet during specific religious festivals, for example Muslims who have reached puberty (or 15 years of age) are required to fast from sunrise to sunset during Ramadan. If you are celebrating the cultural diversity of the childcare setting by preparing and sharing foods from different cultures, check whether the children are allowed to do this.

Children from some families are vegetarian or vegan not for religious reasons but as part of their lifestyle choices. Be aware also of the special dietary requirements of children with food allergies, especially those that can be potentially life threatening, such as a peanut allergy. Consider, too, the children's individual food preferences and any food their parents do not wish them to eat.

Consulting children on the selection and preparation of food and drink

Discussing the selection and preparation of food with children encourages their independence and decision-making skills. Involving them in helping to serve meals or snacks and clear away afterwards also encourages their independence as well as taking responsibility for looking after their childcare environment. Always follow any health and safety regulations as well as your childcare setting's procedures for these activities.

Encourage children to try a variety of foods but be careful not to force them to eat. Remember that some eat more than others and the same child may eat varying amounts at different times; for example they may eat less if tired, ill or upset and eat more after energetic play or during a growth spurt. Many children prefer plain and familiar food they can eat with their fingers, but they also need opportunities to develop skills in using a spoon, fork and then a knife. You should encourage children to use safe, child-sized versions of these, as appropriate to their age, level of development and culture.

If possible, eat with the children and use the time to share the events of the day so far. Mealtimes should be pleasant and social occasions. Eating with adults provides children with a positive role model, such as when they see you enjoying and trying new foods, observing table manners, and so on.

PORTFOLIO ACTIVITY

1 What are your childcare setting's procedures for the preparation and storage of food?
2 Plan and prepare a meal or snack for a group of children in your childcare setting. Remember the following: healthy and balanced diet; specific dietary requirements including food allergies; individual preferences.
3 Include the children in the planning and preparation of the meal or snack as appropriate to their ages and levels of development and the procedures of the setting.

NVQ LINKS: CCLD 307.2   CCLD 306.4
CCLD 314.2

Figure 7.2 Healthy eating in a childcare setting

CCLD 307.3
Promote children's healthy physical development

Knowledge Base

K3S303   K3S304   K3S305

Create opportunities to discuss healthy physical development with children. The setting will have policies and procedures relating to children's healthy physical development. In education settings these will be included in the school's curriculum for Personal, Social and Health Education (PSHE) and Science. These may cover aspects such as:

◎ Health and safety: health and safety in the setting; first aid; risk-taking; stranger danger; road safety; cycling; medicines; and sunburn
◎ Physical health: how bodies work and health needs
◎ Emotional health and well-being: self-esteem; teasing; and bullying
◎ Physical activity: sport and fitness; leisure activities; and swimming

◎ Healthy eating: a healthy breakfast; a balanced diet; and weight problems
◎ Personal hygiene: taking care of personal hygiene; and dental care
◎ Sex education: human life cycle; puberty; and emotional aspects of sexual relationships
◎ Drug education: drug facts; alcohol; tobacco; illegal substances; and peer pressure.

In addition, the setting may encourage children to become involved in national projects that promote better health, for example: Walk to School Week; Heart Week; Bike Week; World Health Day; and Allergy UK.

Check it out

Find out about your setting's policies and procedures relating to healthy physical development. If you work in an education setting, look at the relevant sections of the curriculum for PSHE and Science.

Supporting children in making positive health decisions and choices

The Internet can provide access to a wide range of information on health issues relevant to children including:

◎ Healthy eating, nutrition, food safety, weight problems and eating disorders
◎ Dentists and oral hygiene
◎ First aid and medicines
◎ Personal safety and bullying
◎ Common illnesses and medical conditions, such as asthma, epilepsy, diabetes
◎ Drugs, alcohol and smoking
◎ Sports, fitness and health

◎ Emotional well-being, mental health and counselling

◎ Stress at home and at school including exam stress

◎ Sexual health, HIV and Aids.

(See for example: www.support4learning.org.uk or www.wiredforhealth.gov.uk)

There is a series of Department of Health and Department for Education and Employment interactive websites for children that explores a wide range of health issues:

◎ **Welltown** for 5 to 7 year olds: www.welltown.gov.uk

◎ **Galaxy-H** for 7 to 11 year olds: www.galaxy-h.gov.uk

◎ **LifeBytes** for 11 to 14 year olds: www.lifebytes.gov.uk

◎ **Mind, Body and Soul** for 14 to 16 year olds: www.mindbodysoul.gov.uk

Information on healthy lifestyle choices is also available from national and local organisations including the voluntary sector, community and neighbourhood resources.

The National Healthy School Programme is organised by the Department of Health and Department for Education and Skills. The programme provides the foundation for the Government's aim for all schools to be healthy schools and is central to improving the quality of life for pupils. It provides a framework of support for a whole-school approach to dealing with health issues which might affect children's education and achievement through a healthy school team or task force including pupils, parents, staff, governors, local agencies and school nurses.

The National Healthy School Programme consists of: *The National Healthy School Standard*: a framework of quality standards for local health and education partnerships to be measured against; *Wired for Health*: clear and accessible information for teachers and pupils; *The Young People's Health Network*: information to encourage young people in

Unit Link

For this Unit you also need to understand the following section:

CCLD 319.1 Enable children and families to identify their healthy living options (see below)

PORTFOLIO ACTIVITY

Outline how you promote the healthy physical development of children in your setting. Include information on: providing opportunities for children to learn about how their bodies work and their health needs; discussions with children about healthy physical development; resources about positive health decisions and choices (including books, leaflets, the Internet and other sources); health reviews and immunisation programmes appropriate to the ages of the children you work with.

NVQ LINKS: CCLD 307.3   CCLD 307.2   CCLD 319.1   CCLD 319.2

out-of-school settings to participate in improving health and education services.

Child Health Promotion Programme

The Child Surveillance Programme has been replaced by the Child Health Promotion Programme. The Child Health Promotion Programme includes: childhood screening; immunisations; a holistic and systematic process to assess the individual needs of children and their families; early interventions to address those needs; delivering universal health promoting activities. Summary of the Child Health Promotion Programme:

◎ **Antenatal care:** prevention, detection and treatment of pregnancy complications; antenatal screening and preliminary assessment of family needs; advice on healthy eating, alcohol, drugs and smoking cessation; promotion of parent craft classes; advice on breastfeeding.

◎ **Postnatal care:** physical examination of newborn including heart, hips, eyes (cataracts) and hearing test; check weight, head circumference, spine, genitals, femoral pulse and palate; look for hernias, jaundice, large organs or dysmorphic features; review any pregnancy or birth complications; advice on breastfeeding; advice on sleeping position, sudden infant death syndrome and dangers of passive smoking; Guthrie 'heel prick' screening test for congenital hypothyroidism and phenylketonuria; administration of Vitamin K.

◎ **The 6 to 8 week review:** physical examination of heart, hips and eyes (cataracts); check weight, head circumference, spine, genitals, femoral pulse and palate; look for hernias, jaundice, large organs or dysmorphic features; review general progress; identify postnatal depression or other maternal health needs; health promotion including advice

on breastfeeding, sleeping position, sudden infant death syndrome and dangers of passive smoking, dental health, home and car safety.

◎ **Age 2, 3 and 4 months:** immunisations (see table below); check weight; health promotion as for 6 to 8 week review.

◎ **About 12 months:** immunisation (see table below); systematic assessment, by the health visiting team, of the child's physical, emotional and social development as well as family needs.

◎ **Age 12 to 15 months:** immunisation – first MMR (see table below); discussion of accident prevention e.g. stairgates, fireguards, toy safety, etc.

◎ **Age 3 to 4 years:** immunisation – second MMR (see table below).

◎ **Age 4 to 5 years:** review on school entry including check that immunisations or up-to-date and child has access to GP and dental care; assessment and interventions for any developmental problems; provision of information about specific health issues; check child's height and weight; administer 'sweep' hearing test and orthoptist pre-school vision screening.

◎ **Foundation Stage Profile:** assessment by the teacher including the child's physical social, emotional and creative development and communication, language and literacy.

◎ **Age 5 years:** school nurse to check height and weight; 'sweep' hearing test; review immunisation status.

◎ **Ongoing support for primary and secondary school pupils:** access to drop-in sessions with school nurse; referrals to specialists for children causing concern; access to nursing care within school environment for children with special medical needs; booster immunisation age 13 to 18 years (see table below).

(Tidy, 2006)

When to immunise	What is given	How it is given
Two months old	1. Diphtheria, tetanus, pertussis, polio and *Haemophilus influenzae type b* 2. Pneumococcal	One injection One injection
Three months old	1. Diphtheria, tetanus, pertussis, polio and *Haemophilus influcnzae type b* 2. Meningitis C	One injection One injection
Four months old	1. Diphtheria, tetanus, pertussis, polio and *Haemophilus influenzae type b* 2. Pneumococcal 3. Meningitis C	One injection One injection One injection
Around 12 months old	*Haemophilus influenzae type b,* Meningitis C	One injection
Around 13 months old	1. Measles, mumps and rubella (MMR) 2. Pneumococcal	One injection One injection
Three years four months to five years old	1. Diphtheria, tetanus, pertussis and polio 2. Measles, mumps and rubella (MMR)	One injection One injection
13 years to 18 years old	Tetanus, pertussis and polio	One injection

Figure 7.3 *Child immunisation programme*

Supporting children with physical disabilities

About 15 per cent of children have some kind of physical disability. Some are severely disabled by physical difficulties due to damage to the neurological system which controls motor functions, for example cerebral palsy and spina bifida. There are also children who have relatively minor difficulties such as dyspraxia. Others have multiple disabilities, affecting several physical functions, such as hearing or visual impairment combined with motor disorders.

Strategies for supporting children with physical disabilities

Develop skills and strategies to enable children with physical disabilities to participate in play opportunities and learning activities. Remember that children with physical disabilities may: not be able to make full use of materials and equipment; not be able to participate fully in some activities with other children; need the understanding and sensitive support of other children and adults; and need specially adapted toys and other learning equipment.

Working with your colleagues, you need to ensure that the childcare setting, play opportunities, learning activities and equipment are adapted where necessary to enable children with physical disabilities to participate as fully as possible. If you are involved in planning how to adapt the setting for a child with physical disability, consider the space needed for a wheelchair, frame or other walking aids, and also where ramps will be required instead of steps. Provide sufficient space between tables and chairs to allow a child with mobility aids to move freely without obstacles. If you work in a mainstream setting you will need to consider the needs of *all* the children.

Children should be encouraged to participate in a wide range of play opportunities and learning activities as appropriate to their needs, including their level of development and physical abilities/limitations. Modified or specialised equipment and learning materials should be used to meet the children's needs, allowing for maximum participation in play opportunities and learning activities. You should provide appropriate challenges for the children, whilst maintaining their health and safety. You can support children with physical disabilities by:

◎ Using learning activities that are self-correcting
◎ Encouraging children to make choices, such as selecting materials for creative activities
◎ Praising children for effort and small achievements
◎ Having high but realistic expectations for their learning
◎ Ensuring children are not ridiculed or bullied
◎ Informing colleagues and parents about the children's progress.

There are a number of agencies which offer specialist advice and support for children with physical disabilities. Examples include: advisory teacher; charities such as SCOPE; health visitor; nursery provision for children with special needs; occupational therapist; physiotherapist; special needs assistant; and speech and language therapist. (See Chapter 14.)

Unit Links

For this Unit you also need to understand the following section:

CCLD 321 Support children with disabilities or special educational needs and their families (see Chapter 14)

PORTFOLIO ACTIVITY

Describe how you have encouraged a child with a chronic illness or physical disability to positively participate in discussions and activities in your childcare setting, for example by adapting play opportunities or using specialist equipment to enable the child's full participation.

NVQ LINKS: CCLD 307.3   CCLD 305.2
CCLD 321.1   CCLD 321.2

CCLD 319
Promote healthy living for children and families

Depending on the type of setting and your particular responsibilities, you may be involved in promoting healthy living for children and families within a programme such as Sure Start or by assisting health professionals in an integrated setting such as children's centre or family centre. Promoting healthy living involves working with children and families to help them identify healthy living options and to help families to access the information, advice and practical support they need to implement lifestyle changes.

CCLD 319.1
Enable children and families to identify healthy living options

Knowledge Base

K3S504	K3S505	K3S506	K3S507	K3S508
K3S509	K3S510	K3S511		

To promote healthy living you should provide information and opportunities to enable children and families to identify healthy living options. Discuss with families the long- and short-term health implications of different lifestyles for adults and children and the benefits of healthy living.

Short-term implications include:

◎ Alcohol misuse (binge drinking) is related to absenteeism, domestic violence and violent crime
◎ Under-age drinking is associated with truancy and antisocial behaviour; it can make young people more susceptible to pressure to take drugs and/or have unprotected sex
◎ Risk-taking sexual behaviour leads to sexually transmitted infections, for example Chlamydia, genital warts, HIV and syphilis; delay in diagnosis and treatment can lead to more people being infected
◎ Smoking during pregnancy can lead to premature birth, low birth weight and increased infant mortality
◎ Drinking alcohol and smoking restricts the intake of essential vitamins and minerals
◎ Alcoholic drinks contribute to a person's energy (calorie) intake and can lead to obesity
◎ Physical inactivity and unhealthy diets lead to obesity in both adults and children
◎ Stress is the most common cause of sickness absence and a major cause of incapacity.

Long-term implications include:

◎ Alcohol misuse is associated with deaths from cancer, injury, liver disease, stroke and suicide
◎ Smoking leads to respiratory disease, heart disease, stroke and cancer
◎ Inactive and unfit people have double the risk of dying from coronary heart disease
◎ Obesity leads to cardiovascular disease, cancer, adult-onset diabetes, stroke, high blood pressure and other major chronic diseases; obesity reduces life expectancy on average by nine years

◎ Childhood obesity increases the risk of early onset of preventable disease in adulthood including diabetes, stroke and cardiovascular disease; obesity in children may mean they have a lower life expectancy than their parents
◎ Poverty and deprivation can result in lower life expectancy and poor mental health
◎ Sexually transmitted infections can lead to AIDS, cancer, infertility and death
◎ Mental ill-health can lead to suicide.

The benefits of healthy living include:

◎ Reducing alcohol consumption can reduce the problems caused by alcohol misuse
◎ Increased exercise reduces the risk of major chronic diseases and premature death
◎ Physical activity can prevent and manage conditions and diseases such as coronary heart disease, diabetes, cancer and obesity
◎ Physical activity also reduces the risk of osteoporosis, back pain and osteoarthritis
◎ Regular physical activity reduces the risk of depression and has positive benefits for mental health such as reduced anxiety, improved mood and positive self-esteem
◎ A healthy, balanced diet leads to improved physical health and emotional well-being
◎ Emotional well-being is crucial to good physical health and making healthy choices
◎ Using condoms can avoid the risk of sexually transmitted infections and unplanned pregnancies
◎ Reducing frequency and amount of sugar consumption can help to prevent dental caries.

Raising awareness of healthy living choices

Childcare settings can help children and young people to make informed choices about their diets, now and in later life, and provide them with access to healthier foods, for example by offering healthy options at meal times, such as pasta or rice instead of chips, as well as healthy snacks, such as fruit, at break time instead of crisps and biscuits. As well as promoting opportunities for healthy eating within the setting, you need to encourage children and young people to eat healthy foods at home and in the wider community.

The National Curriculum provides opportunities for children and young people to learn about healthy living. Science helps pupils to learn about the different food groups, a balanced diet, nutrition, and safety and hygiene. Food Technology introduces pupils to practical food preparation, cooking skills, using kitchen equipment and tools as well as simple food hygiene. PSHE provides opportunities for pupils to learn about the benefits of good nutrition and a healthy lifestyle. Extended schools can offer accessible, year-round activities that promote healthy eating, physical activity and well-being to children, their parents and the wider community including: breakfast clubs; sport and outdoor activities; and innovative programmes such as 'cooking nutritious meals on a budget'. (DH, 2005a)

Identify and select opportunities to discuss healthy changes to lifestyle with individual children and their families. Examples include: regular health reviews for children with their parents; well-being sessions for families; and drop-in sessions for young people and/or their parents. Health visitors and school nurses can provide individual children, young people and families with access to individual support and confidential advice to prevent obesity and promote healthier eating.

> ### Think About
>
> What opportunities do you use to raise awareness of healthy living choices and to discuss healthy changes to lifestyles with children and their families?

You should plan and implement programmes and activities that demonstrate aspects of healthy living. This includes providing opportunities for children and young people to participate in physical activities such as indoor and outdoor play in the childcare setting; physical education in school; cycling or walking to school with friends/family; and sports clubs and play projects in the local community.

You can also use government programmes and other schemes that demonstrate aspects of healthy living. As part of the '5 A DAY programme', the School Fruit and Vegetable Scheme (SFVS) provides 4 to 6 year olds in participating infant, primary and special schools in England with a free piece of fruit or vegetable (apple, banana, pear, citrus fruit, tomato or carrot) (www.5aday.nhs.uk/sfvs).

The World Cancer Research Fund UK (WCRF UK) provides an interactive newsletter with activities and competitions to promote the healthy eating and active lifestyle message to children aged 4 to 8 years who have joined the *Great Grub Club* (www.wcrf-uk.org/publications/grubclub.lasso).

> ### Activity
>
> List examples of programmes and activities you use to demonstrate aspects of healthy living.

Provide information to families that raises awareness and facilitates change. Useful publications relating to healthy living include *Choosing health: a booklet about plans for improving people's health – easy read summary* and *Choosing Health Magazine* (see the Department of Health website: www.dh.gov.uk). Put up posters and displays relating to national campaigns, such as the 5 A DAY programme (www.5aday.nhs.uk). Salt Awareness Campaign is a public health campaign to reduce high salt consumption which uses television and print advertising (www.salt.gov.uk/campaign_support.shtml). You may be involved in raising awareness in the early years through Sure Start, including the promotion of breastfeeding.

Your setting should provide responsive, accessible services and advice. For example information and advice should be tailored to the individual needs of children and families; and services should be provided within the setting, such as drop-in sessions where children, young people and parents can access health advice from a health visitor or school nurse. Integrated services for children such as Children's Trusts, Children's Centres and Extended Schools should help to make health services more accessible to children, young people and their parents.

Unit Links

For this Unit you also need to understand the following sections:

CCLD 305.1 Support equality of access (see Chapter 5)

CCLD 307.3 Promote children's healthy physical development (see above)

CCLD 314.2 Provide for the nutritional needs of babies and children under 3 years (see Chapter 11)

Check it out

Find out about the information available in your local area to raise awareness of healthy living options and to help families to facilitate changes to their lifestyle.

CCLD 319.2 Encourage and support children and families to implement healthy lifestyles

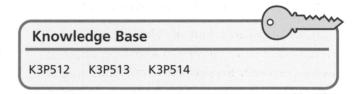

Knowledge Base

K3P512   K3P513   K3P514

Encourage and support children and families to begin living healthily by helping them to identify realistic changes to their lifestyles. For example provide dietary and health guidelines such as: choose a diet rich in a variety of plant-based foods; eat plenty of fruit and vegetables; maintain a healthy weight; be physically active; select foods low in fat and salt; prepare and store foods safely; drink alcohol in moderation, if at all [adults only]; and do not smoke or use tobacco in any form. (WCRF UK, 2004)

Encourage families to improve the nutritional balance of their diet by: eating at least five portions of fruit and vegetables per day; including 18 grams of dietary fibre per day; restricting salt intake to 6 grams per day (less for children); reducing intake of saturated fat to 11 per cent of food energy; ensuring intake of fat is no more than 35 per cent of food energy; and reducing intake of added sugar to 11 per cent of food energy. (DH, 2005a)

Offer children choice and a range of options to encourage them to be active on a daily basis; for example provide opportunities for both indoor and outdoor physical play. Encourage children and families to build everyday activity into daily routines, such as walking to the shops and cycling to school, in addition to participating in sport and leisure activities within the setting and in the wider community (aerobics, badminton, basketball, cricket, cycling, dancing, football, gymnastics, tennis and swimming). The Chief Medical Officer recommends:

◎ Children and young people should do a minimum of 60 minutes at least of moderate-intensity physical activity every day, including activities that produce high physical stresses on the bones at least twice a week to improve bone health, muscle strength and flexibility

◎ Adults should do a minimum of 30 minutes at least of moderate-intensity physical activity on five or more days a week to maintain general health; 45 to 60 minutes of moderate-intensity physical activity a day is necessary to prevent obesity; activities that produce high physical stresses on the bones are necessary for bone health

◎ The recommended amount of physical activity can be done in one session or in several shorter bouts of 10 minutes or more

◎ Physical activities include lifestyle activities (walking or cycling to school/work; vigorous housework such as vacuuming) and structured exercise or sport.

(DH, 2005b)

Encouraging and supporting children and families to take up healthy living involves supporting families' efforts to make changes to their lifestyle. This includes promoting healthier choices by: participating in national health campaigns; using children's health guides; providing vouchers for milk, fresh food; improving youth work to support young people's choices, including sex and relationships, drugs, alcohol and opportunities for physical activity; and taking action to improve emotional well-being. (DH, 2005c)

Acknowledge and reward families' efforts to make changes to their lifestyles and help them to recognise and monitor the benefits of such changes, for example assist families to record their efforts and the benefits of changes in a diary or personal health organiser. Star charts, stickers and other rewards can be used to reward children for taking part in physical activities. After-school clubs or sports clubs may encourage children to participate in schemes which offer certificates for achievement; for example British Gymnastics (www.baga.co.uk) has a structured physical play programme for children from the time they begin walking to 6 years of age, which includes badges, certificates and medals (www.earlyyearsfundamentals.co.uk/reward.php); the Amateur Swimming Association (www.britishswimming.org) provides certificates and badges through ASA Award Scheme sponsored by Kellogg's (www.awards.sportcentric.com/). Your setting could encourage families to participate in incentive schemes such as a Family Health Challenge supported by the local authority and/or local businesses. A Family Health Challenge could include: free fitness assessment at a local gym; help with drawing up a family fitness plan including healthy meal planner; healthy eating sessions involving preparing nutritious meals and snacks; free swimming sessions; prizes for the families who have made the most improvements to their lifestyles (for example mountain bikes and free swimming lessons); and free membership to health or sports club.

Activity

Give examples of how you: acknowledge, support and reward families' efforts to make changes to their lifestyles; assist families to recognise and monitor the benefits to their health and well-being or lifestyle changes.

Encourage and support children and families to implement healthy lifestyles

You should direct families towards additional help and assistance, when required, to help them to make lifestyle changes. Sources of information, guidance and practical support for children, young people and parents include:

◎ Children's Health Guides, as part of the new Child Health Promotion Programme, will be introduced which will encourage children to take responsibility for developing their own health goals with help from their parents/carers, school staff, health visitors and school nurses. These plans will form the basis for personal health guides for life

◎ Support for parents and carers including access to information on all aspects of their children's development, for example programmes to support parents in understanding their children's social, emotional and physical development in the early years through services such as Sure Start and Home Start (see Chapter 16)

◎ Healthy Start provides disadvantaged pregnant women and mothers of young children with vouchers for fresh food and vegetables, milk and infant formula (www.healthystart.nhs.uk)

◎ New guidance for carers to encourage looked-after children to improve their self-esteem, social skills and emotional well-being (see Chapter 15)

◎ Support for young people including a new *youth offer* with guidance on improving health and providing alternatives to risk-taking behaviour; and services aimed at reducing teenage pregnancies (www.dfes.gov.uk/publications/youth)

◎ Health Direct will be set up from 2007. This service will provide easily accessible and confidential information on health choices. Health Direct will include links to existing services such as support to parents provided by Sure Start and information on diet and nutrition provided by the Food Standards Agency.

(DH, 2004b)

Families on low income may experience difficulties in accessing a healthy diet. Food poverty can be defined as the inability to afford, or to have access to, food to make up a healthy diet. You can help to support families that are experiencing food poverty by participating in initiatives such as '5 A DAY' (see above) and ensuring that children whose parents receive qualifying benefits are getting the free school meals they are entitled to. In addition, school milk is available to nursery and primary schools through an EU subsidy topped up by a national subsidy; where milk is provided it must be given free to children whose families are in receipt of certain benefits. (DH, 2005a)

PORTFOLIO ACTIVITY

Compile a booklet for children and families to promote healthy living. Include the following: the long- and short-term implications of different lifestyles on adults and children; the benefits of healthy living; basic diet and health guidelines; examples of programmes and activities that demonstrate healthy living; sample family fitness plan; and sources of information, advice and practical support to help families implement lifestyle changes, including leaflets and posters, workshops at community centres, drop-in sessions at health centres, suggested reading from books available at local libraries, Internet resources, local healthy living initiatives.

NVQ LINKS: CCLD 319.1   CCLD 319.2   CCLD 307.1   CCLD 307.2   CCLD 307.3

Play is an essential part of children's development and learning. It is the central way in which children explore and develop an understanding of their environment. Children learn through play. As the term 'play' is often used to refer to children's activities that are considered unimportant and frivolous by many people, especially parents, childcarers need to stress the importance of play to those who are sceptical about its benefits. Play helps children's development and learning by providing opportunities for:

◎ Self-chosen and well-motivated learning
◎ Challenging and interesting experiences
◎ Taking responsibility for their own learning
◎ Gaining confidence and independence
◎ Co-operative work between children
◎ Developing a wide range of physical skills
◎ Developing problem-solving skills
◎ Encouraging imagination and creativity.

The role of play in children's learning and development

Early learning involves learning through stimulating play activities with appropriate adult support to provide young children with the essential foundations for later learning. Young children who are pushed too hard by being forced to do formal learning activities before they are ready may actually be harmed in terms of their development and they may also be put off literacy, numeracy and other related activities. A combination of real and imaginary experiences is needed to encourage young children to learn. This is why play is an important aspect of their development and learning. They need to handle objects and materials to understand basic concepts; for example, in mathematics using objects for counting and addition such as buttons, cones, plastic cubes. Once children have plenty of practical experiences they can cope more easily with abstract concepts, such as written sums or mental arithmetic. Children use play opportunities to encourage and extend the problem-solving abilities that are essential to developing their intellectual processes.

Play activities provide informal opportunities for children to create ideas and to understand concepts through active learning and communication in a safe and non-threatening environment, while helping to promote all aspects of their development. Language is a key component in children's thinking and learning and play is an invaluable way to provide opportunities for language and to make learning more meaningful, especially for young children.

Children's social play

Children go through a recognised sequence of social play. Younger children tend to engage in more solitary or parallel play activities because they are more egocentric, while older children are capable of more co-operative play activities as they can take turns, share play equipment and follow rules more easily. There will be times, however, when quite young children can be engaged happily in play activities with some interaction with other children (associative play) such as dressing-up, home corner, doing jigsaws, simple construction or painting. There will be occasions when older children become engrossed in solitary or parallel play activities without interacting with other children, such as doing detailed drawings and paintings, or building intricate constructions that require complete concentration to the exclusion of everyone else.

A child's level of social interaction during play activities depends on: the individual child; the child's previous experiences of play; the play activity itself; the social context, such as the setting and other people present. Play also helps to develop children's social and emotional skills by providing opportunities for: learning and developing new social skills; practising and improving existing social skills; experimenting with new situations, for example anticipating what they *might* do in new situations; preparing for new experiences; acting out past experiences; and expressing emotions in positive ways.

The sequence of social play

◎ *Solitary play:* playing alone
◎ *Parallel play:* playing alongside other children without interaction
◎ *Associative play:* playing alongside other children with limited interaction
◎ *Co-operative play:* playing together
◎ *Complex co-operative play:* playing together including following agreed rules.

Seven ways to promote children's learning and development through play

1 Plan play carefully and think about what the children will learn from the activities.
2 Provide challenging and interesting play opportunities, appropriate to the children's ages, needs, interests and abilities.
3 Provide varied play resources and encourage the children to use them.
4 Participate in the children's play to stimulate language and extend learning.
5 Encourage the children's imagination and creative ideas.
6 Encourage social interaction during play, for example the children may need coaxing to join in or guidance on taking turns and sharing.
7 Link play activities to real life situations, such as link shop play with real shopping trips.

Activity

1 Give an example of a play opportunity you have used (or could use) to promote children's learning and development.
2 Suggest other play opportunities which might encourage the children's learning and development.

Identifying children's play needs and preferences

Play is not an extra – something to be done to keep children quiet or occupied while adults are busy or as a reward for children when other tasks have been done. It is an essential part of children's (and young people's) development and learning. Children's play needs include opportunities to:

◎ Access safe play spaces
◎ Engage in a wide range of play activities and use a variety of play resources
◎ Learn about and understand the physical world
◎ Develop individual skills and personal resources
◎ Communicate and co-operate with others
◎ Develop empathy for others
◎ Make sense of the world in relation to themselves
◎ Do their own learning, in their own time and in their own way.

You should be able to identify each individual child's play needs and preferences. Play needs are the individual needs of children for play. Preferences are children's choices with regard to play. You can help to identify these by: researching playwork theory and practice to find out about children's play and development; observing children playing; and interacting with children. Find out about children's play needs and preferences by talking with them and asking for their suggestions about play spaces and resources.

Using indicators and objectives to evaluate play provision

When working in a childcare setting or play setting, you need to know and understand the indicators and objectives that can be used to evaluate play provision. Knowledge and understanding of the play objectives in *Best Play: What Play Provision Should do for Children* (see Further reading) will help you to research and identify a range of play spaces and resources that will meet children's play needs and preferences.

The play objectives

The play provision:

◎ Extends the choice and control that children have over their play, the freedom they enjoy and the satisfaction they gain from it
◎ Recognises children's need to test boundaries and responds positively to that need
◎ Balances the need to offer risk and the need to keep children safe from harm
◎ Maximises the range of play opportunities
◎ Fosters children's independence and self-esteem
◎ Fosters children's respect for others and offers opportunities for social interaction
◎ Fosters the child's well-being, healthy growth and development, knowledge and understanding, creativity and capacity to learn.

(NPFA et al, 2000; p. 18)

Use these play objectives to evaluate play needs and preferences in the setting in the following ways: observe and record the types of play demonstrated by the children and the relationships; listen to the children about their views on play spaces and the resources available; monitor the policies and procedures and how these work in practice; evaluate and review activity plans, play opportunities and resources as well as the policies and procedures. (NPFA et al, 2000)

In addition to the play objectives in *Best Play*, you can evaluate play provision by using the *characteristics of VITAL play opportunities* from *Getting Serious About Play: A review of children's play* (see Bibliography). For example, you should consider the following key elements of successful play opportunities: Value-based; In the right place; Top quality; Appropriate; and Long-term. See below.

Characteristics of VITAL play opportunities are:

1 Value-based
◎ Children and young people's interests and rights are respected
◎ All children and young people are welcomed, whatever their ability or background, especially those from disadvantaged groups
◎ Children and young people's skills and abilities are respected.

2 In the right place
◎ Close to children's/young people's homes and schools or on well-used travel routes
◎ In safe locations
◎ Located in places that children, young people and the wider community are happy with.

3 Top quality
◎ Safe, welcoming and providing choice and variety
◎ Well-designed in relation to surrounding area and local community
◎ Has balanced approach to managing risk
◎ Well-managed and maintained.

4 Appropriate
◎ Shaped by local needs and circumstances
◎ Complementing other local opportunities
◎ Taking account of all sectors of the local community
◎ Well-planned.

5 Long-term
◎ Sustainable beyond the lifetime of immediate funding
◎ Set up to be valued and respected parts of the social fabric of the neighbourhood.

(DCMS, 2004; p. 19)

PORTFOLIO ACTIVITY

1   Collect information on the play needs and preferences of the children and/or young people in your setting using these methods: research playwork theory and practice; observe the children and/or young people playing; consult them about their play needs and preferences.

2   Use this information to identify their play needs and preferences, for example make suggestions for possible play opportunities and resources.

3   You could present this information in a booklet or information pack on children's play for parent helpers, volunteers and students.

NVQ LINKS: CCLD 318.1   CCLD 301.1   CCLD 303.1   CCLD 303.3

CCLD 318.2
Plan and prepare play spaces

Knowledge Base

318K04	318K06	318K11	318K14	318K15
318K16	318K17	318K18	318K19	318K20

In order to plan and prepare play spaces it is essential for you to know about the range of different types of play spaces that support and enrich the potential for children's play. *Play spaces are areas that support and enrich the potential for children to play* (SkillsActive, 2004).

Types of play spaces include:

1   *Childcare settings,* run by professional childcarers and/or playworkers, providing play opportunities including private and local authority day nurseries and out-of-school clubs.

2   *'Formal' play provision* run by professional play staff and parent helpers/volunteers, for example playgroups and holiday playschemes.

3   *'Open access' play facilities* operated by professional playworkers but where children and young people come and go as they please, such as adventure playgrounds, some holiday playschemes and playbuses.

4   *'Informal' play facilities* that are not staffed, including public parks, play areas and playgrounds, skate parks, basketball courts, football pitches and playing fields.

5   *Non-designated play spaces* used by children and young people, especially when there are no other play spaces available, for example local streets, outside shops, abandoned buildings and open spaces.

(DCMS, 2004)

Check it out

1   Find out about the existing play spaces available in your local area.

2   What additional play spaces and resources do you think should be made available to meet the play needs and preferences of the children in your local area?

Planning play spaces that meet children's play needs

When planning play spaces you should remember that: the play environment should be welcoming and provide maximum opportunities for children to make choices; play resources should be varied, with sufficient quantities so that children do not have to wait too long to play with materials or equipment; there should also be lots of opportunities for children to interact socially with each other and adults. (Lindon, 2002b)

You will need to plan how the setting will be organised, both indoors and outdoors, and what play opportunities and resources will be available. However, your planning must take account of children's play needs and be flexible enough to allow them to enjoy play in their own way and to make their own choices and decisions about play. This includes being able to adapt play opportunities according to the ages, abilities and needs of the children and/or young people in your setting.

> **Think About**
>
> Think about the planning and creation of play spaces in your setting.

When planning and creating play spaces you should remember these important points:

1 Plan them based on children's play needs and preferences, for example find out about children's play and development and observe their play activities.
2 Involve children in the creation of play spaces, for example consult them about the play opportunities and play resources they would like in the setting.
3 Create play spaces that children can adapt to their own needs, such as flexible play areas to allow them to spread out during their play.
4 Allow children to choose and explore play spaces for themselves, such as selecting their own play activities and play resources.
5 Allow children to develop through play in their own ways, for example freedom to explore and

Figure 8.1 Child engaged in exploratory play

enjoy their chosen play activities in their own way and in their own time.
6 Allow children's play to continue uninterrupted, for example participate in their play as and when invited to do so; intervene in children's play only in order to maintain their physical safety or emotional security.
7 Address the possible barriers to accessing play spaces that some children may experience, for example ensure the play setting is inclusive and encourages participation by all the children including those from ethnic minority backgrounds and those with disabilities.

Providing for a range of play types

You should know and understand how to provide opportunities for a wide range of play types including:

◎ *Communication play* – using words, nuances or gestures (telling jokes, play acting, singing, story-telling)
◎ *Creative play* – allowing new responses, transformation of information, awareness of connections, with an element of surprise (enjoying creative activities, arts and crafts, using a variety of materials and tools)
◎ *Deep play* – allowing the child to encounter risky experiences, to develop survival skills and conquer fears (balancing on a high beam, performing skateboarding stunts)
◎ *Dramatic play* – dramatising events in which the child is not a direct participator (presenting a television show, religious or festive celebrations)
◎ *Exploratory play* – involving manipulating objects or materials to discover their properties and possibilities (playing with bricks, sand, water, clay, playdough)
◎ *Fantasy play* – rearranging the world in the child's way, in a manner unlikely to occur in real life (playing at being an astronaut or king/queen)
◎ *Imaginative play* – where conventional rules of the real world are not applicable (pretending to be a dog or a superhero)
◎ *Locomotor play* – involving movement in all directions for its own sake (playing chase, tag, hide and seek)
◎ *Mastery play* – involving control of physical aspects of the environment (digging holes, building dens)
◎ *Object play* – involving hand–eye co-ordination to manipulate objects in an infinite variety of ways (examining novel uses for a paintbrush, brick)
◎ *Role play* – exploring human activities on a basic level (doing simple domestic chores such as sweeping with a broom, making telephone calls, driving a car, with or without play equipment)
◎ *Rough and tumble play* – involving discovering physical flexibility and demonstrating physical skills (play fighting, chasing)
◎ *Social play* – involving social interaction that requires following certain rules or protocols (games with rules, conversations)
◎ *Socio-dramatic play* – involving enacting real life experiences of an intense personal or interpersonal nature (playing house, shops, hospital, dentist)
◎ *Symbolic play* – allowing controlled, gradual exploration and increased understanding, without risk (using piece of wood to symbolise a person).

(NPFA et al, 2000; pp. 33-34)

These play types can be grouped into three main areas:

1 *Physical play*: activities that provide opportunities for children to develop their physical skills. For example: locomotor play, mastery play and rough and tumble play.
2 *Exploratory play*: activities that provide opportunities for children to understand the world around them by exploring their environment and experimenting with materials. For example: exploratory play, creative play and object play.
3 *Imaginative play*: activities that provide opportunities for children to express feelings and to develop social skills. For example: communication play, deep play, dramatic play, fantasy play, imaginative play, role play, social play (see page 141 for details of the sequence of children's social play) and symbolic play.

Physical play

Children should have plenty of opportunities for physical play, such as play apparatus, outdoor play, ball games and swimming. By using their whole

Think About

Give examples of physical play opportunities from your own experiences of working with children.

with stacking toys and jigsaws. Physical play enables children to: develop body awareness and awareness of spatial relationships; understand positional relationships, for instance in and out, over and under; develop gross motor skills; and develop fine motor skills.

bodies, children learn to control and manage them. The more practice children get to develop gross motor skills, the more agile, co-ordinated and safe they will be as they get older. Using lots of energy in physical play is also fun and relaxing. Children also need opportunities to develop their fine motor skills and hand–eye co-ordination, such as playing

Exploratory play

Exploratory play encourages and extends children's discovery skills. Play is an important way to motivate children and to assist their thinking and learning in a wide variety of settings. Children learn from play situations that give them 'hands-on' experience.

Examples of play opportunities to meet children's physical play needs

1 *Outdoor play opportunities* should be provided for children every day, such as playing in the outdoor play area, going for walks, going to the park or visiting an adventure playground. As well as the benefits of fresh air, outdoor play offers children more space to develop gross motor skills such as running, hopping, jumping, skipping, throwing and catching a ball, playing football, doing somersaults and cartwheels.

2 *Play apparatus* can be used indoors or outdoors depending on the size of the equipment and the space available. Larger play equipment that cannot be easily (or safely) accommodated inside the setting, such as climbing apparatus, can be used in outdoor play. When using play equipment, whether in the play setting or at a playground, you must ensure that it is safe to use as well as appropriate for the children's ages and sizes. Always check play apparatus *before* use.

3 *Jigsaw puzzles* help children with shape recognition as well as developing fine motor skills and hand–eye co-ordination. Children can tackle standard jigsaws with a few large pieces, increasing the number of pieces as they grow and improve their physical skills.

4 *Ball games* provide children with opportunities to develop ball skills such as throwing, kicking and catching a ball. Younger children need large, lightweight balls to practise their throwing and catching skills. As they get older smaller balls, beanbags and quoits can be used to develop their skills of throwing with more accuracy. Older children can be encouraged to participate in team sports such as five-a-side football or basketball.

5 *Swimming* is an excellent all-round physical activity. Children are usually ready to learn to swim by the age of 4 or 5 years. If the setting does not have its own swimming pool, it may be possible to arrange regular outings to a local swimming pool. If not, try to encourage the children in your setting to use their local pool with their families or friends depending on their ages/swimming abilities.

Examples of play opportunities to meet children's exploratory play needs

1 *Painting* with brushes, sponges, string; finger painting, bubble painting, 'butterfly' or 'blob' painting, marble painting, wax resist painting; printing (with leaves, potatoes, cotton reels) and pattern-making (with rollers, stamps).

2 *Drawing* using pencils, crayons, felt tips or chalks on a variety of materials including different kinds of paper, card, fabric and wood. Include colouring activities linked to the children's interests by drawing your own colouring sheets, buying ready made colouring books or using free printable colouring pages from the Internet.

3 **Model making** using commercial construction kits (*Lego Explore, Mega Bloks, Stickle Bricks*), wooden blocks or clean and safe 'junk' materials to enable children to create their own designs.

4 *Collage* using glue and interesting materials to create pictures involving different textures, colours and shapes, and provide an enjoyable **sensory** experience too.

5 *Clay, playdough and plasticine* can be used creatively; they are tactile too.

6 *Cooking* provides a similar experience to working with playdough or clay except that the end product is (usually) edible. Remember to include 'no cook' activities such as icing biscuits, making sandwiches or peppermint creams.

7 *Making music* can provide opportunities for children to explore different sounds and to experiment freely with the musical instruments. Provide a portable box/trolley with a range of percussion instruments including: drum, tambourine, castanets, wood blocks, shakers, bell stick, Indian bells, triangle, xylophone and chime bars.

8 *Water play* with plain, bubbly, coloured, warm or cold water helps children to learn about the properties of water, for instance it pours, splashes, runs and soaks. Provide small containers to fill and empty, as well as a sieve and funnel.

9 *Sand play* provides opportunities for exploring the properties of sand, for example wet sand sticks together and can be moulded, while dry sand does not stick and can be poured. Use 'washed' or 'silver' sand (not builder's sand which might contain cement). Provide small containers, buckets, sieves and funnels.

Exploratory play encourages them to use their senses to discover the properties of different materials in pleasurable and meaningful ways. For example, playing with sand encourages children to consider textures and the functions of sand – getting the right consistency of sand to build sand castles, too wet or too dry and the sand will not stick together. Exploratory play enables children to: understand concepts such as shape and colour; explore the properties of materials, such as different textures; understand volume/capacity and physical forces through sand and water play; develop problem-solving skills; and devise and use their own creative ideas.

Think About

Give examples of exploratory play opportunities from your own experiences of working with children.

Imaginative play

Imaginative play provides opportunities for children to release emotional tension and frustration or express feelings such as anger or jealousy in positive ways. It also encourages children to look and feel things from another person's viewpoint, as well as developing communication skills to interact more effectively with others. Activities such as role play and dressing-up enable children to overcome fears and worries about new experiences or people, to feel more important and powerful, and to feel more secure by being able to temporarily regress to earlier levels of development. Imaginative play enables children to: develop language and communication skills; practise and rehearse real-life situations; improve self-help skills such as getting dressed; express feelings in positive ways; share ideas and co-operate with other children.

Think About

Give examples of imaginative play opportunities from your own experiences of working with children.

Examples of play opportunities to meet children's imaginative play needs

1 *Role play* includes *domestic play, shop play and drama activities.* Examples of domestic play include playing/imitating 'mum' or 'dad'; pretending to be a baby while other children act as parents; later imitating other role models such as carers, playworkers, teachers and characters from television or books. *Shop play* may be focused on the post office, hairdressers or café, where they can explore other roles. Pretending to visit the dentist, clinic, optician or hospital, setting up a home corner, a health centre or hospital can provide for this type of play. Also include *drama* activities.

2 *Dressing-up activities* include pretending to be parents, carers, playworkers, teachers, film/television super-heroes, characters from games consoles, kings and queens. It allows children to experiment with being powerful and in control. Pretending to be someone else can also help children to understand what it is like to be that person and encourages empathy and consideration for others.

3 *Dolls and puppets* can help children to deal with their feelings. For example, jealousy over a new baby can be expressed by shouting at a teddy or doll. Puppets are also a useful way of providing children with a 'voice' and may encourage shy or withdrawn children to express themselves more easily.

4 *Miniature worlds* includes play with small-scale toys such as dolls' houses, toy farms and toy zoos as well as vehicle play where children can act out previous experiences or situations while sharing ideas and equipment with other children; this can also help them establish friendships.

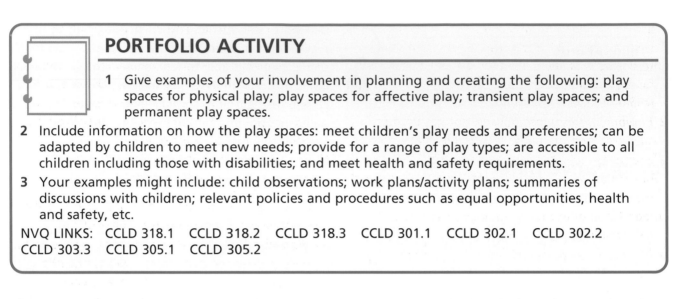

Obtaining resources for play spaces

Every setting should be equipped with play resources appropriate to the age range of the children. You should know how to obtain and/or create the resources needed for these, perhaps working within the budget available for resources and if necessary finding alternative ways to obtain or create these. Children benefit from a wide range of play resources, not just those that are commercially produced. Depending on the setting, you should be able to provide a wide selection of play resources. For example:

◎ *Recycled materials* to provide opportunities for children to construct models, and so on
◎ *The outdoor environment* to provide opportunities for exploring the natural world, for example gardening, visiting local parks and playgrounds
◎ *Natural materials* to provide opportunities for exploring different materials and their properties (sand, water, cooking ingredients)
◎ *Homemade materials* for creative activities, such as homemade playdough (encouraging children

to make the playdough themselves enriches their play and learning experience)
◎ *Clean unwanted clothing* for dressing-up activities (recycling again!), not just commercially produced outfits
◎ *Space* for children's imaginary games that require little or no props
◎ *Commercially produced resources* which are well-made, durable and safe for children's use as well as being good value for money, for instance construction kits and tools, climbing equipment and child-size domestic play equipment. Remember, quality not quantity is more important.

Remember to make use of any community resource facilities such as book loans from local libraries (usually free to non-profit organisations) and borrowing play equipment from toy libraries. Contact the local authority or disability charities for information on schemes they may operate for hiring or purchasing specialist play equipment for children with disabilities.

Resources for the setting should include:

1 *Consumables* (resources that get used up) such as paint, glue, paper; ingredients for cooking

activities; food and drinks for meals/snacks; cleaning materials. Keep track of these resources to ensure that there is always an adequate supply by regular stocktaking and reporting to the person responsible for reordering.

2 *Equipment* (resources that do not get used up) such as furniture, books, computers and play equipment (climbing frames, construction kits, board games). Check these resources for wear and tear to ensure they are safe for continued use and report any problems or damage to the person responsible for resources.

3 *Finance* for the play setting, such as the money needed to buy consumables and new equipment, pay staff wages, pay for the rent and/or maintenance of the building.

4 *Adults* who run and organise the setting. They may be paid staff, parent helpers or volunteers.

Adults are one of the most important resources in the setting. Ensure that your setting is making the best use of the adult resources (childcarers, playworkers, parent helpers and volunteers) in order to: respond to children's play needs and preferences; stimulate children's play and development; encourage children's ideas, opinions and active participation; provide appropriate support for children's self-directed play; and safeguard children's health and well-being.

It is essential that all resources within the setting are used efficiently and appropriately without undue waste, especially if the setting has a limited budget. Remember to:

◎ Discuss the efficient use of resources at team meetings
◎ Pay attention to other play provision in the local area
◎ Consult children about the play resources *they* would like
◎ Plan ahead, including long-term plans for the setting, also funding

◎ Monitor the quality and value for money of the resources in the setting
◎ Be aware of the environmental impact of the resources used by the setting. For example, use recycled materials such as paper; recycle clean household junk for use in creative activities; use and promote Fair Trade products
◎ Allocate responsibility for different areas of resources to spread the workload.

A designated member of staff should have specific responsibility for replenishing supplies of consumables (pencils, paper and card, paint, cooking ingredients) as necessary. Stock levels should be monitored on a regular basis. Staff and children should know how to use all play resources correctly and safely, with care and respect; and with regard for health and safety and waste. Care should be taken to ensure that play resources reflect the cultural and linguistic diversity of the local community, and that all children have equality of access. Visual aids should also be available. For example: videos; maps; posters; pictures; interesting objects or artefacts related to topics or themes; computer software. Display materials for use in play areas and around the setting should also be available.

As part of your role you may need to make regular checks to ensure there are adequate supplies of essential materials or equipment. You may need to keep a weekly check on consumable materials such as art and craft materials, cooking ingredients, and so on. Clearing away equipment and materials provides you with a regular opportunity to check whether any supplies are running low. Items such as soap, paper towels and so on may need to be checked every day. There will be an inventory or stock list that is checked on a regular basis. Larger items such as furniture may be included on an inventory checked annually. There should be a procedure within the setting for doing this.

PORTFOLIO ACTIVITY

1 List the main play resources available in your setting under these headings: consumables; equipment; finance; and adult resources.
2 What are your responsibilities for obtaining and/or creating the necessary resources for your setting?

NVQ LINKS: CCLD 318.2   CCLD 306.2   CCLD 328.3   CCLD 328.4

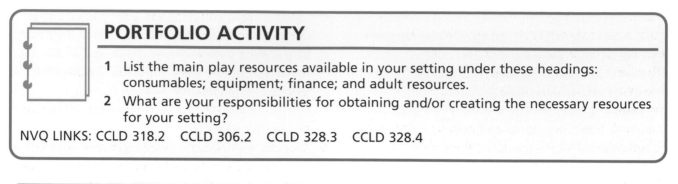

CCLD 318.3
Support self-directed play

Knowledge Base

318K02	318K05	318K07	318K21	318K22
318K23	318K24	318K25	318K26	318K27
318K28	318K29			

You should aim to provide minimum intervention in children's play activities while keeping them safe from harm and support rather than direct their play. Help to create a play environment that will stimulate children's self-directed play and provide maximum opportunities for them to experience a wide variety of play types. You can enrich children's play experiences in the following ways: planning and creating play spaces that meet their play needs and preferences; obtaining and/or creating resources for a range of play spaces; fostering positive attitudes; providing new materials and tools to stimulate their exploration and learning; and participating in their play if and when invited.

It is best to use information on children's play needs and preferences to plan appropriate play opportunities. Write down your plans for these opportunities on a planning sheet or in an activity file. Your plans may be brief or detailed, depending on the requirements of your setting. Some activities may require more detailed preparation and organisation than others (arts and crafts, cooking, outings, and so on).

A plan for a play activity could include the following:

Title: *A brief description of the activity.*

When? *Date and time of the activity.*

Where? *Where the activity will take place, e.g. indoor play area, outdoor play area, local park or playground.*

Why? *Outline why you have selected this particular activity; you may for instance have identified children's play needs and preferences through research, observation or consultation.*

What? *What you need to prepare in advance; this may include selecting or making appropriate resources and buying ingredients, materials or equipment.*

How? *How you will organise the activity. Consider any safety requirements. Think about tidying up after the activity and encouraging the children to help tidy up.*

Evaluate the activity afterwards; for example the children's response to the activity, the skills and/or learning demonstrated by them and the effectiveness of your preparation, organisation and implementation. Make a note of your evaluation on the planning sheet or in the activity file. These notes will prove helpful when planning future play opportunities and for providing information to colleagues at regular meetings. While careful planning of appropriate play opportunities is important, your planning should be flexible enough to allow for each child's individual interests and for unplanned, spontaneous opportunities for play. For example, an unexpected snowfall can provide a wonderful opportunity to explore and talk about snow as well as enabling the children to express delight and fascination for this type of weather.

Think About

How do you plan for children's self-directed play in your setting?

Providing appropriate support for children's self-directed play

Provide appropriate support for children's self-directed play in the following ways:

◎ Provide flexible planning and minimal adult supervision
◎ Enable them to choose from a broad range of play opportunities and resources
◎ Enable them to choose whether or not they wish to be involved in play activities
◎ Give them freedom to choose how they use the available materials

◎ Provide them with access to a wide range of materials and allow them to determine their own play in their own way
◎ Provide plenty of space, especially for physical games and imaginative play
◎ Encourage them to sort out fair ways to take turns on play equipment
◎ Keep the numbers of children in group activities to a reasonable size to enable everyone to enjoy play
◎ Create a stimulating and enjoyable play environment that also maintains their physical safety and emotional well-being
◎ Provide challenging play opportunities to avoid boredom; risk-taking is part of the enjoyment of play.

(Lindon, 2002b)

Identifying and responding to play cues

You need to know and understand the main stages of the *play cycle*; this is the course of play from start to finish, for example from the first play cue to completion of play. You need to be able to identify when and how to respond to play cues as part of the play cycle.

Play cues are *'facial expressions, language or body language that communicate the child or young person's wish to play or invite others to play'* (SkillsActive, 2004). Observe children's play and respond appropriately to their play cues. See brief example on page 154.

Defining a play frame

A play frame is *'a material or non-material boundary that keeps the play intact'* (SkillsActive, 2004). For example, a material boundary could be an actual physical boundary such as a specific play area, for

Child's Play Cue	Adult's Response
First play cue: child smiles and uses eye contact (facial expression) to indicate wish to play.	Adult asks the child which particular play activity they want to do. Child chooses an activity and selects own resources.
Second play cue: child makes specific verbal request (language) for adult to join in with play activity.	Adult joins in as per the child's request e.g. having a 'cup of tea' in the home corner.
Final play cue: child points (body language) to another play activity indicating wish to play something else.	Adult checks there is space for the child to do the desired play activity. Child selects resources for this activity and a new play cycle begins

Figure 8.2 *Child's play cue/adult's response*

example a play shop; a non-material boundary may be something imaginary such as a 'magic circle'. In a play setting, you must be able to hold children's play frames as necessary, for instance maintaining a play frame by adopting an appropriate role during children's play such as a customer during shop play.

PORTFOLIO ACTIVITY

1 Describe how you have supported self-directed play using the following types of play spaces: play spaces for physical play; play spaces for effective play; transient play spaces; and permanent play spaces.
2 How have you observed and responded to a child's play cues?
3 Give two examples of how you have held children's play frames.
NVQ LINKS: CCLD 318.3   CCLD 318.2

Behavioural modes associated with play

It is important to know and understand the behavioural modes associated with play. For example:

◎ *Personally directed*: child initiated
◎ *Intrinsically motivated*: play for play itself
◎ *In secure context*: freedom to explore feelings or imagination in safe environment
◎ Spontaneous: unplanned play opportunities
◎ *Without a goal*: play as a process not an end product
◎ *Controlled by children*: choosing own activities, open-ended play opportunities.

Recognising the mood descriptors associated with play

You will need to be able to recognise the mood descriptors associated with play. These are:

◎ *Active:* enthusiastic, full participation in play
◎ *Altruistic:* playing with consideration for others
◎ *At ease:* relaxed and comfortable during play
◎ *Balanced:* in harmony with others and/or the play activity
◎ *Confident:* positive and bold approach to play
◎ *Happy:* displaying enjoyment and delight during play
◎ *Immersed:* involved deeply, totally absorbed in play
◎ *Independent:* playing without influence of others
◎ *Trusting:* confidence in others involved in play.

PORTFOLIO ACTIVITY

1 Observe a child involved in a play opportunity.

2 In your assessment comment on the following: the play opportunity; the age and level of development of the child; their play needs and preferences; the play space and play type; and behavioural modes and mood descriptors.

3 Think about how you could provide future play opportunities to extend the child's development within this type of play space and/or play type.

NVQ LINKS: CCLD 318.1   CCLD 318.2
CCLD 318.3   CCLD 303.1   CCLD 303.2

CCLD 318.4
Help children and young people to manage risk during play

Knowledge Base

318K30   318K31   318K32   318K33   318K34
318K35

When working with children and/or young people, you should help them to manage risk during play as appropriate to their ages and levels of development. Children need opportunities to explore and experiment through play and to try out new, exciting play activities. Many play activities have risks, especially physical activities such as climbing, exploring and swimming. *'Risky activity, and risk taking itself, is recognised as an essential part of growing up.'* (Child Accident Prevention Trust, 2002) Always follow the relevant setting policies and procedures, for example health and safety policy, risk assessment and risk management procedures.

As children play, they will make mistakes and accidents will happen. By exploring their environment and experimenting with their physical skills and intellectual abilities, children develop confidence and competence in their own abilities. Play spaces and play opportunities should be sufficiently challenging and have different levels of difficulty to enable children to fully explore these challenges. Without these challenges and opportunities to assess risks, children will not develop the survival skills they need later in life. (ILAM, 1999)

Seven ways to help children to manage risk during play

You can help children to manage risk during play by:

1 Assessing and managing the levels of risk in play areas either through supervision or design.
2 Helping individual children to make a realistic assessment of their abilities to avoid them being under- or over-confident.
3 Taking precautions to reduce the severity of injuries if children make inaccurate judgements, for example provide appropriate safety surfaces in outdoor play areas to reduce impact of falls.
4 Informing children of the potential dangers of play activities so that they can make their own decisions.
5 Providing opportunities for children to take calculated risks, for example challenging climbing frames, adventure playgrounds.
6 Providing appropriate safety information.
7 Consulting and involving the children in developing play activities that are challenging and interesting to them.

PORTFOLIO ACTIVITY

1 Outline your setting's policies and procedures that are relevant to managing risk during play activities, for example health and safety policy; risk assessment and risk management procedures.
2 List examples of how you help children to manage risk during play according to these policies and procedures and the ages/levels of development of the children you work with.

NVQ LINKS: Level 3: CCLD 318.4   CCLD 302.1   CCLD 302.2   CCLD 308.3

CCLD 337
Create environments that promote positive behaviour

Creating an environment that promotes positive behaviour helps to shape the childcare setting ethos and reflect the setting's values. Positive behaviour is an essential building block for creating a welcoming and pleasant childcare environment in which all members of the setting feel respected, safe and secure. Identifying and implementing appropriate behaviour policies, procedures and strategies helps to establish children's and parents' confidence in the childcare setting. An effective behaviour policy also helps to attract and retain good quality and well-motivated staff. When creating an environment that promotes positive behaviour, remember that children are more likely to behave in positive ways if they are: in a welcoming and stimulating environment; engaged in interesting and challenging play opportunities and learning activities that are appropriate to their ages and levels of development; given clear and realistic guidelines on behaviour; and work with adults who have positive expectations for children's behaviour.

CCLD 337.1
Implement behaviour policies, procedures and strategies

Knowledge Base

K3D692   K3D693   K3D694   K3D695   K3D696

To promote positive behaviour in children you need to know and understand the setting's behaviour policies, procedures and strategies. You will need to recognise and respond promptly and appropriately to children's unacceptable or challenging behaviour, remembering to always follow the setting's agreed policies, procedures and strategies relating to this. Identify and remember to report any child's uncharacteristic behaviour patterns to the appropriate person, such as a senior childcare practitioner or setting manager. Liaise with colleagues, professionals and parents to plan and implement agreed approaches or programmes for responding to children's challenging behaviour. When agreeing an approach, listen to children's points of view and negotiate with them, taking into account their age, needs, abilities and level of understanding. Monitor and provide constructive feedback on the effectiveness of behaviour policies, strategies and programmes of individual children. You may also need to adapt or modify the planned approach (if necessary) in consultation with colleagues, professionals and parents. As a childcarer you should have an awareness and understanding of:

◎ The setting's behaviour policies, procedures and strategies including the setting's expectations for children's behaviour such as ground rules or code of conduct for children

◎ Your role and responsibilities for implementing behaviour policies, procedures and strategies

◎ The roles and responsibilities of other staff members in implementing behaviour policies, procedures and strategies

◎ The skills you need to implement behaviour policies, procedures and strategies

◎ A range of strategies for responding to children's unacceptable or challenging behaviour including supporting children with behavioural difficulties (see below).

Identifying appropriate behaviour policies and procedures

All childcare settings have behaviour policies, procedures and strategies. Depending on the type of setting these policies relate to the statutory requirements of the Children Act 1989 and the Education Act 2002. Ensure that you have copies of the policies, procedures and strategies most relevant to your work as a childcarer. You may not need your own copy of every setting policy but you will need to know where they are kept for future reference. The childcare setting's behaviour policy should include:

◎ The setting's aims and underlying principles for behaviour

◎ The roles and responsibilities of childcarers

◎ Ground rules for children

◎ How positive behaviour will be promoted

◎ Strategies for dealing with unacceptable behaviour, including bullying

◎ How the policy will be implemented

◎ The use of rewards and sanctions

◎ Monitoring and reviewing procedures for the policy.

The policy should ensure consistency by providing clear guidelines for childcarers on how to implement it as well as practical advice to parents and carers on how they can help. This information could be included in documents such as the staff handbook and the setting's brochure. The policy must be based on clear values (for example respect, fairness and inclusion) that are also reflected in the setting's aims and equal opportunities policy.

Unit Links

For this Unit you also need to understand the following sections:

CCLD 301.3 Support children in developing relationships. (see Chapter 1)

CCLD 305.2 Implement strategies, policies, procedures and practice for inclusion. (see Chapter 5)

PORTFOLIO ACTIVITY

1 Find out about the behaviour policies and procedures for your setting.

2 List the key points of the behaviour policies and procedures.

NVQ LINKS: CCLD 337.1   CCLD 301.3
CCLD 305.2   CCLD 305.3   CCLD 308.1

Recognising uncharacteristic behaviour patterns

You should also be able to identify and report any child's uncharacteristic behaviour patterns to the appropriate person, for instance senior childcare practitioner or setting manager. It is important to remember that some uncharacteristic behaviour patterns may indicate possible child abuse or bullying.

Uncharacteristic behaviour patterns in younger children may include:

◎ Unusually aggressive behaviour towards people and/or property
◎ Regression to earlier level of development (emotional outbursts, wetting or soiling)
◎ Defiance, for example refusing to comply with adult requests
◎ Unco-operativeness during play opportunities or learning activities
◎ Attention-seeking behaviour such as excessive swearing
◎ Being very passive or withdrawn
◎ Wandering around the setting aimlessly or staring into space
◎ Repetitive or self-damaging behaviour, such as rocking, thumb-sucking, frequent masturbation, picking own skin, pulling out own hair, head-banging
◎ Appearing very nervous and anxious
◎ Inability to concentrate at usual level
◎ Refusing to eat and/or drink while at the setting.

Uncharacteristic behaviour patterns in older children may include:

◎ Deterioration in the child's academic work
◎ Gradual changes in their appearance or behaviour over a period of time
◎ Rapid or acute increase in behavioural or emotional changes
◎ Emotional instability and mood swings; irritability
◎ Loss of confidence and heightened levels of anxiety
◎ Unexplained, persistent lateness and absenteeism
◎ Tiredness due to disturbed sleep
◎ Signs of substance abuse
◎ Withdrawal from social contact

◎ Inappropriate responses to normal situations
◎ Noticeable changes in eating habits.

Monitoring children's behaviour

It is essential to observe and assess children not only to evaluate each child's learning needs but also to monitor their behaviour. As children develop, their needs and behaviour patterns change. Regular observations can help to identify *pronounced* changes in a child's usual behaviour patterns. Through accurate observation and assessment adults can: identify the child's main areas of difficulty; respond to the child's behaviour in appropriate ways; devise strategies to encourage the child to demonstrate more positive behaviour; or seek professional advice for a child with more persistent behavioural difficulties.

When observing and monitoring a child's behaviour, remember it is not possible or helpful to record everything the child says and does at all the times. Areas of behaviour to observe and monitor may include the child's: response to the setting's organisation and routines; participation in play opportunities and learning activities; completion of tasks; responsibility; self-confidence and assertiveness; playground or outdoor play behaviour; relationships with other children; relationships with staff; verbal and social interaction; unacceptable or challenging behaviour; need for adult supervision; and personal care and presentation. By identifying and assessing inappropriate behaviour in a child staff are able to find the best means of responding to it. Keeping factual, up-to-date records on a child's behaviour enables staff (and the child) to review the behaviour and to assess the progress made. Records are also useful for keeping parents, colleagues and other professionals accurately informed. Parents and the children themselves can also be involved in record keeping.

Unit Links

For this Unit you also need to understand the following sections:

CCLD 303.1 Observe development (see Chapter 3)

CCLD 328.2 Collect and store information (see Chapter 17)

PORTFOLIO ACTIVITY

1 Observe a child's behaviour during a group activity.

2 In your assessment include information on: the child's behaviour during the activity; the child's communication skills; how the adult responds; and how the other children respond to the child's behaviour.

3 Suggest ways to monitor the child's future behaviour.

4 Suggest ways to promote the child's positive behaviour.

NVQ LINKS: CCLD 337.1   CCLD 337.2
CCLD 301.3   CCLD 303.1   CCLD 303.2
CCLD 308.1

Liaising with colleagues or other professionals about children's challenging behaviour

You need to liaise with colleagues and/or other professionals to plan and implement agreed approaches or programmes for responding to children's challenging behaviour. Discuss any serious concerns you may have about a child's uncharacteristic behaviour patterns with colleagues and perhaps other professionals, but remember confidentiality. However, childcarers have a legal duty to report serious concerns about a child's welfare, for example possible signs and symptoms of child abuse; each setting has guidelines about this. You may need specialist advice, guidance or support to provide the best possible approaches to responding to these behavioural difficulties (see below).

You need to know where to seek support if you have difficulty with a particular group of children. This may include the advice or support of senior colleagues in addition to training in behaviour management. Where a child has been referred to a colleague about their inappropriate or challenging behaviour, an assessment should be made as to whether the child's behaviour was:

◎ *Straightforward misconduct* such as breaking ground rules. Staff should be supported in applying an appropriate sanction and agreeing with all parties on how a recurrence can be avoided

◎ *A symptom of significant underlying problems,* for example behavioural difficulties, communication difficulties, learning difficulties or emotional difficulties. The setting's behaviour policy should outline the role of specific staff in the process of diagnosing and supporting children with these difficulties. This should include staff roles and responsibilities for gaining the support of other professionals or external agencies (Child and Adolescent Mental Health Service, Behaviour Support Team, Connexions Service, Educational Psychologist, Education Welfare Officer, Social Services)

◎ *The result of provocation through bullying or racist harassment.* Where racist harassment is the cause, the setting should have clear procedures for recording the behaviour and for reporting incidents to parents/carers. The setting should also have strategies for supporting the victim and working with the instigator. There should also be clear procedures to record incidents of homophobic bullying or bullying of children with special needs.

(DfES, 2003a)

Liaising with parents about their children's challenging behaviour

The setting should involve parents (and carers) in all areas of their child's care, learning and development and in particular gain parents' support for implementing effective behaviour policies, procedures and strategies; this parental support should not be taken for granted. The setting's expectations for behaviour should be clearly explained to parents so that they understand and are able to participate as fully as possible. Parents may also benefit from opportunities to share some of the training for staff in promoting positive behaviour and dealing with challenging behaviour. The behaviour policy may also include reference to how the setting will support the development of parenting skills, perhaps by offering voluntary parenting courses. (DfES, 2003a)

As a childcarer you may need to liaise with parents about their children's challenging behaviour. It is easier to discuss concerns about a child's behaviour with their parents if the sharing of information with parents and parental involvement are established practices within the setting. As appropriate to your role and responsibilities in the childcare setting:

◎ Be welcoming and create an environment that provides opportunities to talk with parents. If face-to-face contact is difficult, use a home-setting diary to share information

◎ Be clear about which aspects of the child's behaviour are causing difficulties within the

setting. Ask the parents about any similar difficulties in the child's behaviour at home and how they respond to it

◎ Be sensitive when talking with parents; be willing to share positive information about the child's behaviour, not just the negative

◎ Be tactful when asking the parents if they think their child may be worried or upset about anything

◎ Be attentive and listen carefully to the parents' views and any particular concerns *they* may have about their child's behaviour. Show parents that their involvement in their child's care, learning and development is respected and valued.

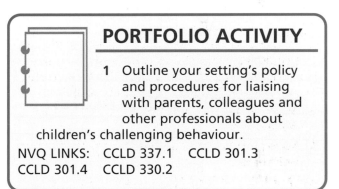

PORTFOLIO ACTIVITY

1 Outline your setting's policy and procedures for liaising with parents, colleagues and other professionals about children's challenging behaviour.

NVQ LINKS: CCLD 337.1   CCLD 301.3
CCLD 301.4   CCLD 330.2

Implementing behaviour strategies

The childcare setting should have a range of strategies for both promoting children's positive behaviour (see page 164) and dealing with children's challenging behaviour. Some children may find it difficult to settle in the childcare setting; they may have difficulties in interacting positively with other children (and adults) or be unable to concentrate on organised activities because of behavioural difficulties (see below). These children may challenge the authority of the adults working in the setting as well as their parents.

The setting should have a range of strategies for responding to children who demonstrate challenging or inappropriate behaviour including:

◎ Regular reviews to identify children most at risk
◎ Contact with parents in the early stages of any difficulties
◎ Referrals for specialist advice from agencies linked to the setting (Child and Adolescent Mental Health Service, LEA Behaviour Support Team, Educational Psychology Service or Social Services)
◎ Parent/carer consultations and family sessions
◎ One-to-one counselling with a trained specialist
◎ Support from learning mentors or trained teaching assistants
◎ Strategies for responding to children with persistent challenging behaviour.

(DfES, 2003a)

PORTFOLIO ACTIVITY

1 Outline your setting's strategies for dealing with children's challenging behaviour.
2 Give an example of how you have implemented one of these strategies when dealing with a child's challenging behaviour. Remember confidentiality.

NVQ LINKS: CCLD 337.1   CCLD 301.3
CCLD 308.1

CCLD 337.2
Promote positive aspects of behaviour

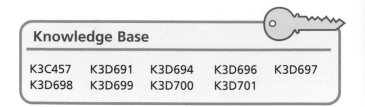

Knowledge Base

K3C457	K3D691	K3D694	K3D696	K3D697
K3D698	K3D699	K3D700	K3D701	

Behaviour can be defined as a person's actions and reactions as well as their treatment of others. It involves children *learning to conform* to their parents', the setting's and the wider society's expectations for behaviour.

The setting's expectations for children's behaviour

Children who are not prepared (or are unable) to conform have to accept the consequences such as sanctions for inappropriate behaviour. Learning about behaviour always takes place within a social context. Certain behaviour may be appropriate in one context but inappropriate in another; for example parents may make allowances for their child's behaviour, but different rules apply in the childcare setting because adults must consider the needs of *all* children and have rules to reflect this.

Think About

What are *your* expectations regarding what is appropriate behaviour for:

◎ Yourself?
◎ The children in your setting?
◎ The individual in society?

Parental expectations for behaviour

Parents have expectations for their children's behaviour based on: the media; cultural or religious beliefs; individual variations in child-rearing practices; adherence to traditional child-rearing practices; comparisons to other children (of relatives, friends and neighbours); and perceptions of their own childhood and *their* parents' attitudes to behaviour.

Many parents may have idealised or unrealistic expectations concerning their children's behaviour because some childcare/education books and the media promote unrealistic age-related expectations so that many children do not seem to 'measure up' to what the experts say. The fact that many families are now smaller (often with few or no relatives nearby) means many parents lack first-hand experience of caring for children *before* they have any of their own and may feel less confident about their parenting skills. Parents of children with special needs may be unsure of what to expect from their children in terms of behaviour; they may over-compensate for their child's special needs by being over-protective or by letting the child get away with behaviour that would not be appropriate in a child of similar age/level of development.

In the past, children did not dare challenge parental authority for fear of physical punishment. Today some parents still feel that if they were brought up this way, then this is how they expect their children to behave. In the 21st century, society recognises the rights of the child and has the expectation that all parents should be more caring and responsive to their children's needs by using positive methods such as praise, encouragement, negotiation and rewards to achieve appropriate behaviour.

Children learn what their parents consider to be appropriate behaviour and will bring these expectations to the childcare setting. Children also observe their parents' behaviour that may be:

◎ *Assertive*: sensitive to their own *and* other people's needs
◎ *Passive*: too sensitive to other people's needs so *ignores own needs*
◎ *Aggressive*: obsessed with own needs so *ignores other people's needs.*

Other influences on children's behaviour

As a childcarer you should be aware of negative or traumatic family situations (such as bereavement, serious illness, divorce, domestic violence or abuse) that may be experienced by the children with whom you work and the impact these might have on their behaviour and emotional responsiveness. Transitions such as moving house, changing carer and/or setting can also affect children's behaviour.

Childcarers may have little or no control over these situations but they *do* have control over additional factors that can lead to unwanted behaviour, such as: inappropriate responses to children's unwanted behaviour; insensitivity or inflexibility towards individual needs; inappropriate play opportunities and learning activities; unwarranted disapproval from staff or other children in the setting; failing to identify and/or support children who are being bullied.

Unit Links

For this Unit you also need to understand the following sections:

CCLD 305.3 Maintain and follow policies and procedures for protecting and safeguarding children (see Chapter 5)

CCLD 325 Support the child or young person's successful transfer and transition in learning and development contexts (see Chapter 10)

CCLD 327.1 Recognise the needs of children who have experienced trauma (see Chapter 15)

Peer pressure may have a negative influence on children's behaviour as some children may: persuade them to participate in dangerous activities including 'dares'; pressure them into socially unacceptable behaviour such as lying, stealing or bullying; exclude or threaten them if they do not conform; encourage them to act in ways they never would as an individual, for example 'mob rule'. However, you can sometimes use peer pressure to encourage positive behaviour by highlighting the positive benefits of certain behaviour for the group or the childcare setting.

The media (television, magazines and comics) and computer games can have positive or negative influences on children's behaviour, depending on what the children see and how they are affected by it. Children who are exposed to violent images may see aggressive behaviour as an acceptable way to deal with others. Those who observe more assertive behaviour (with its emphasis on negotiation and compromise) are likely to demonstrate similar positive behaviour. Television programmes, characters and personalities provide powerful role models for children's behaviour. Just consider the effectiveness of advertising!

Providing positive role models

Children model their attitudes and actions on the behaviour of others. They imitate the actions and speech of those they are closest to including acting at being 'mum', 'dad', 'nursery nurse', 'playworker' or 'teacher'; copying the actions and mannerisms of adults around the home, childcare setting or school. All adults working with children need to be aware of the significant impact they make to children's social (and emotional) development by providing positive *role models*. When working with children you should strike a balance between allowing for the child's increasing need for independence and providing adequate supervision with appropriate guidelines for socially acceptable behaviour. Observing the behaviour of parents and other significant adults (such as childcarers) affects children's own behaviour, how they deal with their own feelings and how they relate to others. This is why it is so important for adults to provide positive role models for children's behaviour.

Think About

1. Who were your role models when you were younger?
2. How do you think these early role models influenced your own behaviour?

Encouraging children's positive behaviour

What is considered to be positive or acceptable behaviour in children is determined by each adult's tolerance levels, which may depend on: their expectations for children's behaviour in relation to age/level of development; the social context in which the behaviour is demonstrated; and how the adult feels at that particular time. See also CCLD 301.3 Support children in developing relationships in Chapter 1.

Seven ways to promote positive behaviour

You can help to promote children's positive behaviour by:

1 *Keeping rules to a minimum.* Children will often keep to a few rules if they have some freedom. Explain why certain rules are necessary, for example for safety. All children should learn to understand the need for rules, but they also need to develop self-control and to make their own decisions regarding behaviour.

2 *Being proactive.* This means preparing things in advance including having the correct materials and equipment ready for play and learning activities. You should also be clear about the behaviour guidelines for the children you work with and what your responsibilities are for dealing with any problems that might occur.

3 *Being positive.* Once ground rules have been set, encourage children to keep them through rewards. Reward positive behaviour using verbal praise and other positive incentives. Keep smiling! A sense of humour goes a long way.

4 *Ignoring certain behaviour.* It may be appropriate to ignore some unwanted behaviour, especially attention-seeking or behaviour that is not dangerous or life-threatening. Sometimes it is not possible or appropriate to ignore unwanted behaviour, for instance if a child is in danger. With younger children it may be more effective to distract the child (by playing a game) or to divert their attention to another activity.

5 *Being consistent.* Once rules, goals and boundaries have been negotiated and set, stick to them. Children need to know where they stand; they feel very insecure if rules and boundaries keep changing for no apparent reason. Children need to understand that 'no' always means 'no', especially where safety is concerned.

6 *Knowing the children you work with.* An awareness of a child's home background, previous behaviour in another childcare setting or school including any special needs influences the way you respond to potentially disruptive children. Use a variety of techniques; different children respond differently to different methods, for example a reminder of a ground rule may be sufficient or give a specific warning.

7 *Keeping calm!* Be calm, quiet, firm and in control; shouting only makes matters worse. If you feel you are losing control, count to five and then proceed calmly. You may need to use strategies like **time out** to give the child a chance to calm down, but keep it short, possibly only a few seconds, until the child is a little calmer.

Rewards and sanctions

Praise and encouragement are essential components when promoting positive behaviour. All children need immediate and positive affirmations or rewards to show that their behaviour is progressing in accordance with expectations. Emphasise the *positive* aspects of each child's attempts at demonstrating positive behaviour. Rewards can provide positive incentives for positive behaviour. Children can be motivated by rewards such as: being given verbal praise; choosing a favourite activity; having a special responsibility; receiving smiley faces, stars or stamps; or receiving stickers or badges.

Rewards are most effective when they:

◎ Provide positive feedback about a specific behaviour, effort or achievement
◎ Are sincere and given with maximum attention
◎ Recognise effort not just achievement, especially with difficult activities or goals
◎ Encourage children to focus on their *own* individual behaviour or achievement
◎ Show the adult's positive expectations for the child's behaviour.

While the emphasis should be on promoting positive behaviour through encouragement, praise and rewards, there may be times when these do not work. Sometimes it is necessary to impose sanctions for children whose behaviour goes beyond acceptable boundaries or who break the ground rules of the childcare setting. It is important that there is a scale of sanctions for inappropriate behaviour within the setting and the behaviour policy should explain why these sanctions are necessary. Effective sanctions should be designed to discourage inappropriate behaviour rather than to punish children who break the rules. Staff need to be consistent when applying these sanctions and should use reprimands sparingly and fairly. Sanctions are more likely to discourage inappropriate behaviour if children see them as being fair. Sanctions for inappropriate behaviour may include: staff warnings to children that their behaviour is unacceptable; 'time out' involving isolation of the child for a short period; child making a formal apology to those affected by their unacceptable behaviour; or parents being invited into the childcare setting to discuss a serious incident. Physical or corporal punishment is not an acceptable sanction (see page 4).

Sanctions are most effective when they:

◎ Balance against appropriate rewards
◎ Are reasonable and appropriate to the child's action so that major sanctions do not apply to minor lapses in acceptable behaviour
◎ Apply only to the child or children responsible and not the whole group
◎ Discourage unwanted/unacceptable behaviour without damaging child's self-esteem
◎ Are used as a last resort; every effort should be made to be positive and to encourage acceptable behaviour through *positive* rather than negative reinforcement.

PORTFOLIO ACTIVITY

1 What methods do you use to provide praise and encouragement for children's behaviour in your childcare setting? Give examples from your own experiences of promoting positive behaviour.
2 Find out about your setting's policy for rewards and sanctions relating to children's behaviour.
3 Describe why and how you have intervened when children have demonstrated unwanted behaviour within the childcare setting.

NVQ LINKS: CCLD 337.2   CCLD 301.3
CCLD 308.2

Supporting children with behavioural difficulties

The adult's response to a child's behaviour is as important as the behaviour itself. People have differing attitudes to what is or is not acceptable behaviour. The social context also affects adult attitudes towards children's behaviour (see above). All adults should consider certain types of behaviour unacceptable. These include behaviour which causes: physical harm to others; self-harm; emotional/psychological harm to others; and destruction to property.

Identifying children with behavioural difficulties

It is usually children whose unwanted behaviour is demonstrated through aggressive or disruptive behaviour who attract the most adult attention, as they are easily identified and hard to ignore. Those who demonstrate unwanted behaviour in a withdrawn manner may be overlooked, especially by inexperienced adults or in very busy childcare settings.

Key indicators of unwanted behaviour include having: limited attention-span and concentration levels; restricted range of communication skills; hostile, uncaring or indifferent attitude towards others; negative self-image and low self-esteem; or behaviour patterns that are inconsistent with expected development (see section on recognising uncharacteristic behaviour patterns).

Contributing factors that can affect children's behaviour include environmental, social or emotional factors such as: bereavement or prolonged illness; divorce or separation; domestic violence or child abuse; moving house; changing school; and negative experiences in previous

settings. Adults working in childcare settings may have little or no control over these contributing factors but they *do* have control over *additional factors* such as: their response to children's unwanted behaviour; insensitivity or inflexibility towards individual needs; inappropriate play opportunities and learning activities; unwarranted disapproval from staff or other children in the setting; and children who are being bullied.

Other factors that may cause unwanted behaviour include:

◎ *Psychosis:* a serious psychological disorder characterised by mental confusion, hallucination and delusions; in younger children, symptoms include: regression, speech loss and extreme hyperactivity
◎ *Autistic spectrum disorders:* a rare and complex condition usually present from birth (although identification may not be made until 3 years +) ; autistic tendencies include speech loss or unusual speech patterns, isolation and withdrawal, intense dislike of environmental changes (see below)
◎ *Attention deficit disorders:* a biological condition affecting children's behaviour and concentration (see below).

Autistic spectrum disorders

Autistic spectrum disorders (ASD) cover a wide range of communication difficulties from severe mental impairment to slight problems with social interaction. Recent research suggests that as many as 1 in 100 children may have ASD, including those with high functioning autism and Asperger Syndrome. It is not known if the current apparent increase in the numbers of children with ASD is real or due to the increased awareness of ASD and the increase in professionals able to give a competent diagnosis. ASD affects four times as many boys as girls. The causes are not known, but autistic tendencies are usually present from birth, although they may not be formally identified until the child attends nursery or school. Children with Asperger Syndrome are at the more able end of the autistic spectrum; they are very intelligent, but they may have communication difficulties which may be disguised as emotional and behavioural problems.

Children with ASD have difficulty in relating to other people; they do not understand the thoughts, feelings and needs of others. In addition, they are usually unable to express their own thoughts, feelings and needs effectively to others. This presents difficulties in acquiring communication skills and being able to understand the social world. Children with ASD may appear indifferent to others or undemonstrative and often do not like physical contact. They may have difficulties with: using verbal and/or non-verbal communication; being aware of other people, which affects their ability to communicate effectively; paying attention to other people (often more interested in objects) which affects their listening and comprehension skills; socialising with other children. Children with severe ASD may not develop language at all. (See Further reading at the end of this book.)

Attention deficit disorders

Attention deficit disorder can occur with or without hyperactivity. If hyperactivity is *not present* then the disorder is usually called Attention Deficit Disorder (ADD). The term used when hyperactivity *is* present is Attention Deficit Hyperactivity Disorder (ADHD). ADD or ADHD affects about 5 per cent of school-aged children and it is possible that about 10 per cent of children have a milder form of the disorder. Some children with ADD or ADHD may also have other difficulties such as specific learning difficulties, for example dyslexia. Boys are more likely to be affected than girls. ADD and ADHD are rarely

diagnosed before the age of 6 years because many young children demonstrate the behaviours characteristic of this disorder as part of the usual sequence of development. From about 6 years old it is easier to assess whether the child's behaviour is *significantly* different from the expected norm. Most children with ADD or ADHD are formally identified between 5 to 9 years of age.

Children with ADD are usually:

◎ *Inattentive* with a short attention-span; unable to concentrate on tasks, easily distracted; forget instructions due to poor short-term memory; and may seem distant or be prone to 'day dreaming'

◎ *Lacking in co-ordination skills* and may have poor hand–eye co-ordination resulting in untidy written work; they may be accident prone

◎ *Disorganised* and unable to structure their own time; unable to motivate themselves unless directed on a one-to-one basis; and may be very untidy.

In addition children with ADHD are usually:

◎ *Over-active* with high levels of activity and movement; restless and fiddle with objects

◎ *Extremely impulsive* which may lead to accidents as they have no sense of danger; they often speak and act without thinking

◎ *Lacking in social skills* as they do not know how to behave with others; very bossy and domineering; unable to make or keep friends; and may demonstrate inappropriate behaviour or misread social cues, for example treating complete strangers as close friends

◎ *Changeable and unpredictable* with severe, unexplained mood swings; short-tempered and with frequent emotional or extremely aggressive outbursts.

The National Institute for Clinical Excellence recommends that 1 per cent of children with severe

ADHD (around 100,000) should receive medication such as methylphenidate (Ritalin). Methylphenidate is a stimulant that enhances brain function, which has been very effective in children with severe ADHD. Such medication helps to focus the child's attention, keeps them on task and allows the child to think before they act. Once the child's concentration and behaviour improve, the dose can be decreased. With or without medication, it is important to have a consistent system for managing the child's behaviour within the childcare setting and at home.

In the childcare setting staff need to provide the following for children with ADD or ADHD: a quiet group/class with one or two adults who are firm but fair and can provide consistent care and education throughout the year; calmness and a clear routine; seating near a known adult away from distracting children; step-by-step instructions; and constant feedback, praise and encouragement. (For more information see Further Reading).

PORTFOLIO ACTIVITY

1   Observe a child who regularly demonstrates challenging behaviour during group activities.

2   In your assessment include information on: the child's behaviour during the activity; the child's communication skills; how the adult responds; and how the other children respond to the child's behaviour.

3   Suggest ways to monitor the child's future behaviour.

4   Suggest ways to encourage the child to behave more appropriately.

NVQ LINKS: CCLD 337.1   CCLD 337.2   CCLD 301.2   CCLD 301.3   CCLD 303.1   CCLD 303.2
CCLD 308.1   CCLD 308.2   CCLD 321.1   CCLD 321.2

Strategies for supporting children with behavioural difficulties

Children with persistent behavioural difficulties are recognised as having special needs and such children will require additional support in the childcare setting. Providing support for these children is one of the most challenging roles that childcarers may have to undertake. When supporting such children you may sometimes feel hopeless, annoyed or helpless. However, working with them can also be very rewarding, as by providing appropriate support, you are helping them to develop the life skills and coping strategies they need.

Depending on the type of setting (nursery class or primary school) children with persistent behavioural difficulties usually have an individual education plan (IEP) and/or an individual behaviour support plan (BSP) or a pastoral support plan (PSP) if they are at risk of being excluded from school. These plans will give you information about the support being provided to help the child and will often include details of your role and responsibilities in providing behaviour support. You may sometimes be involved in drawing up these plans, along with the teacher, the child and their parents or carers.

Behaviour modification

The American psychologist B. F. Skinner believed that positive reinforcement (rewards) and negative reinforcement (sanctions) both contribute towards an individual's motivation for learning and behaviour. Behaviour modification involves using positive reinforcement to encourage acceptable behaviour; ignoring all but harmful, unwanted behaviour. Work on one aspect of behaviour at a time and reward the child for any progress no matter how small. The basic principles of behaviour modification are:

◎ Praise and reward acceptable behaviour
◎ Reduce the opportunities for unwanted behaviour
◎ Avoid confrontations
◎ Ignore minor unwanted behaviour
◎ Structure appropriate sanctions
◎ Establish clear rules, boundaries and routines.

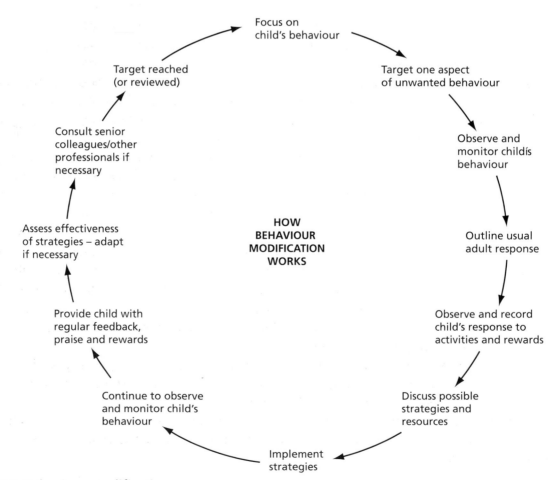

Figure 9.1 Behaviour modification

Fifteen ways to support children with behavioural difficulties

You can provide support for children with behavioural difficulties in the following ways:

1 Consider past experiences. Children learn about behaviour through their early relationships and experiences. No one's behaviour is static; everyone can acquire new behaviour patterns and discard behaviour that is ineffective or inappropriate.

2 Remember adult influences on children's behaviour. Adults working with children have a major influence on their behaviour. Their responses to children's behaviour can make things better or worse. You may need to modify your own behaviour and responses.

3 Be patient. Changing children's behaviour takes time, so do not expect too much all at once. Take things one step at a time. Remember that behaviour may get worse before it gets better because some children will demonstrate even more challenging behaviour, especially if minor irritations are being ignored.

4 Establish clear rules, boundaries and routines. Children need to understand rules and the consequences if they do not follow the rules. They need clear boundaries as to what is or is not acceptable behaviour, with frequent reminders about these.

5 Be consistent. Adults should be consistent when responding to children with persistent unwanted behaviour or the children become confused. Adults need to discuss and agree on responses to the child's behaviour. Childcarers should, where possible, work with the child's parents so the child sees that everyone is working together to provide a consistent framework for behaviour.

6 Use diversionary tactics. You can sometimes divert the child from an aggressive (or emotional) outburst or self-damaging behaviour. Be aware of possible triggers to unwanted behaviour and intervene or divert the child's attention *before* difficulties begin. Being offered alternative choices or being involved in decision-making can also divert children.

7 Encourage positive social interaction. Help children to develop their social skills so they can join in play and learning activities with other children. Start off with one to one, then small groups and then larger groups. Play tutoring can help, such as using adult involvement to develop and extend social play.

8 Help children find more positive ways to gain attention. Most children want adult attention; it is the *way* they behave to gain attention that may need changing. Instead of being disruptive, children need to be encouraged to use more positive ways to get adult attention by asking or showing the adult that they have something to share.

9 Help children to express their feelings. Encourage children to express strong feelings such as anger, frustration or fear in positive ways such as through play and communication. Older children need opportunities to express their grievances.

10 Look at the childcare environment. Identify and, where possible, change aspects of the childcare environment and routines within the setting which may be contributing towards the child's unwanted behaviour.

11 Label the behaviour, not the child. Make sure any response to unwanted behaviour allows the child to still feel valued without any loss of self-esteem. For example *'I like you, Tom, but I don't like it when you ...'*

12 Be positive. Emphasise the positive and encourage children to be positive too. Phrase ground rules in positive ways such as 'do' rather than 'don't'. Encourage children to focus on the positive aspects of setting such as playing with friends, or favourite activities.

13 Use praise more than punishments. Use regular positive feedback to encourage children to behave in acceptable ways and raise their self-esteem. Find out which kinds of rewards matter to the children and use them. Rewarding positive behaviour is more effective than punishing unacceptable behaviour. Quiet reprimands are more effective than a public 'telling off' which only causes humiliation in front of others and increases the child's resentment towards the adult.

14 Avoid confrontation if at all possible. Use eye contact and the child's name to gain/hold their attention. Keep calm, sound confident and in control. If the child is too wound up to listen, give them a chance to calm down, for example *time out*.

15 Give individual attention and support. This encourages children to share their worries or concerns with a trusted adult. *Time in* involves giving children special individual attention to reinforce positive behaviour and decreases the need for them to gain adult attention through unwanted behaviour. It involves children talking with an adult about their day including reviewing positive aspects of the day.

PORTFOLIO ACTIVITY

1 Think about how you support children with behavioural difficulties.

2 Look back at your behaviour observation above and focus on one aspect of that child's behaviour.

3 Outline a step-by-step approach (behaviour modification) to encourage the child to behave in more acceptable ways. Remember to include appropriate rewards (and sanctions).

NVQ LINKS: CCLD 337.1   CCLD 337.2   CCLD 301.2   CCLD 301.3   CCLD 303.3   CCLD 303.4
CCLD 308.1   CCLD 308.2   CCLD 321.1   CCLD 321.2

Specialist help for children with behavioural difficulties

Serious concerns about a child's persistent unwanted or challenging behaviour should be discussed with senior colleagues and when appropriate with other professionals. Remember confidentiality. However, adults working with children have a legal duty to report serious concerns about a child's welfare, such as possible child abuse (see Chapter 5). Depending on your setting, colleagues may include: the child's keyworker; senior practitioner; setting manager; the child's class teacher; key stage co-ordinator; special educational needs co-ordinator; and headteacher. Every childcare setting should have clear structures for reporting concerns about children's behaviour to colleagues and appropriate ways to deal with these concerns. Be aware of your own role and responsibilities within this structure. You may need specialist advice, guidance or support from other professionals to provide the best possible approaches to responding to some children's behavioural and/or emotional difficulties. Other professionals may include: health visitor; paediatrician; child psychologist; educational psychologist; social worker; education welfare officer; play therapist; and music therapist.

Think About

How have you provided support for a child with behavioural difficulties including accessing specialist help where appropriate?

Optional Units

CCLD 308
Promote children's well-being and resilience
CCLD 325
Support the child or young person's successful transfer and transition in learning and development contexts

Knowledge Base

K3D309   K3D310   K3D311   K3D312   K3C317

CCLD 308
Promote children's well-being and resilience

Promoting children's well-being and resilience involves helping them to: develop and sustain healthy lifestyles; keep safe and maintain the safety of others; develop and maintain positive self-esteem; take responsibility for their own actions; have confidence in themselves and their own abilities; make and keep meaningful and rewarding relationships; be aware of their own feelings and those of others; consider and respect the differences of other people; and be active participants as citizens of a democratic society. Children who are experiencing negative social or environmental factors may find your attempts to promote their well-being and resilience particularly helpful; for example, by doing so, you may help to reduce the number of young people involved in teenage pregnancies, alcohol/drug misuse, truancy and crime. (Goleman, 1996)

CCLD 308.1
Enable children to relate to others

Encouraging positive social interactions

Having at least one secure and personal relationship with a parent or carer enables children to form other relationships. Consistent, loving care from a parent/carer who is sensitive to their particular needs enables children to feel secure and to develop self-worth. Observing the behaviour of parents and other significant adults (childcarers, playworkers, teachers and teaching assistants) affects children's own behaviour, including how they relate to others. Other factors that may also affect a child's ability to relate to others include: their special needs, such as communication and/or social interaction difficulties; family circumstances such as separation or divorce; death, abandonment or other permanent separation from parent or main carer. All children need affection, security, acceptance, encouragement, patience and a stimulating environment. Children who have been deprived of these in the first 5 to 6 years of life may find it difficult to relate to other people throughout childhood (and even adulthood). However, children are amazingly resilient and subsequent sustained relationships with caring adults in a supportive environment can help them to overcome early parental separation, rejection or neglect.

Adults who provide inconsistent or inappropriate care may unwittingly encourage difficult behaviour in children, which can lead to adults spending less time interacting with the child, resulting in the child having poor communication skills as well as difficulties in establishing and maintaining positive relationships with other people. Positive social interactions with adults (and other children) in various settings will lead to children being able to demonstrate positive ways of relating to others and using appropriate social skills. There is a spiralling interaction between child and adult.

Encouraging children to share and co-operate

Encouraging children to take turns is also an essential element of helping them to interact positively with other children. From about the age of 3 years young children begin to co-operate with other children in play activities. By about 5 years of age they should be quite adept at playing co-operatively with other children. Gradually children should be able to participate in more complex co-operative play, including games with rules, as their understanding of abstract ideas increases.

We live in a highly competitive society; we all want to be the best, fastest, strongest or cleverest. The media (television, magazines and newspapers) focuses our attention on being the best. Most sports and games have only one *winner*, which means all the other participants are *losers*. To win is the aim of all contestants. *Winning* makes the individual feel good, confident and successful; *losing* makes the individual feel bad, inadequate and unsuccessful. Competitive games can prepare children for the competitiveness of real life. However, competition can also contribute to children's: negative self-image and low self-esteem; aggressive behaviour; lack of compassion for others; and an overwhelming desire to win at *any* cost.

Competitive sports and games can be beneficial to children's social development as long as they emphasise: co-operation and working as a team; mutual respect; agreeing on rules and following them; participation and the pleasure of taking part as being more important than winning; and doing their *personal* best.

As well as being competitive, people can be sociable and co-operative; we like to be part of a group or groups. Co-operative activities encourage children to: be self-confident; have high self-esteem; relate positively to others; work together and help others; make joint decisions; participate fully (no one is left out or eliminated); and have a sense of belonging.

Unit Links

For this Unit you also need to understand the following sections:
CCLD 301.1 Develop relationships with children (see Chapter 1)
CCLD 301.3 Support children in developing relationships (see Chapter 1)

Ten ways to enable children to relate positively to others

Encourage children to:

1 Celebrate individual differences. We are all important, valued and unique individuals.
2 Listen and be attentive to what others have to communicate.
3 Regard and value the needs and rights of others.
4 Recognise and respect the culture and beliefs of others.
5 Be considerate and courteous towards others.
6 Help and care for each other as much as we are able.
7 Co-operate and work together to reach the best solutions.
8 Share and take turns; remember, compromise equals wise.
9 Praise and encourage others to raise their self-esteem.
10 Inspire respect in others through our own kindness, fairness and honesty.

PORTFOLIO ACTIVITY

1 Plan and implement an activity that encourages children to relate to other children, for example play together in a positive way.

NVQ LINKS: CCLD 308.1   CCLD 301.3   CCLD 303.3   CCLD 303.4   CCLD 318.3   CCLD 337.2

CCLD 308.2
Provide a supportive and challenging environment

Knowledge Base

K3D313   K3D314   K3C317

You should help children to predict, recognise and accept the consequences of their actions. Also help children to support each other through challenging activities and achievements (see above). Show acceptance and respect for children's individuality (there is more about valuing children's individuality,

ideas and feelings in Chapter 1) and demonstrate honesty and openness yourself in interactions with children (see the code of conduct for positive interactions with children in Chapter 1).

Unit Links

For this Unit you also need to understand the following sections:

CCLD 301.1 Develop relationships with children (see Chapter 1)

CCLD 301.3 Support children in developing relationships (see Chapter 1)

CCLD 337.2 Promote positive aspects of behaviour (see Chapter 9)

The importance of praise and encouragement

It is essential that you offer children praise and encouragement when communicating with them. All children (especially young ones) need immediate and positive affirmations or rewards to show that their learning and development are progressing in accordance with the adult's (and child's) expectations. Adults should emphasise the positive aspects of children's learning and development. You can support children in managing failure and disappointment by emphasising the importance of taking part, trying their personal best and praising and/or rewarding children for their *efforts,* not just their achievements. Children gain confidence and increased positive self-esteem when they receive praise/rewards for their efforts and achievements, including encouragement to try new activities and experiences.

There are four main methods used to praise and encourage children:

1 *Verbal:* 'praise' assemblies; positive comments about the child's behaviour or activities such as 'Well done, Tom! This is a lovely story! Tell me what happened next.'
2 *Non-verbal:* body language such as: leaning forward or turning towards a child to show interest in what the child is communicating; facial expressions: smiling; sign language: 'good boy/girl!'
3 *Symbolic:* 'smiley faces' for carefully done work or positive behaviour; stickers for being a good listener or for reading well; or stars or merit points for attempting and/or completing tasks.
4 *Written:* merit certificates; written comments in headteacher's book; newsletter recording

achievements; or comments written (or stamped) on the child's work such as 'Well done!' or 'Good work!'

> **Think About**
>
> What methods do you use to provide praise and encouragement for the children's efforts and achievements in your setting?

Dealing with children's emotional outbursts

It is best to provide a calm and accepting environment that allows children to experience and express their feelings safely (see Chapter 1 for more information about how to encourage children to recognise and deal with feelings). Sometimes children (especially when young) are overwhelmed by their emotions and will act inappropriately or regress to previous patterns of behaviour. When children are unable to use language to express their feelings (because they lack the appropriate words, are too worked up, have behavioural/emotional difficulties or other special needs) they are more prone to demonstrate their emotional responses in physical ways, such as biting, scratching, kicking, shouting, screaming, throwing things, throwing themselves on the floor, and so on. These emotional outbursts or 'temper tantrums' can be very frightening to the child and others in the group/class. Adults, too, can find children's emotional outbursts difficult to deal with. When dealing with such outbursts it is essential that you:

◎ Remain calm yourself; speak quietly but confidently: shouting only make things worse
◎ Ignore the emotional outburst as much as possible while maintaining child safety

◎ Avoid direct confrontations

◎ Give the child time and space to calm down

◎ Reassure the child afterwards but do not reward them

◎ Wait until the child has calmed down, then talk in a quiet manner about what upset them

◎ Suggest to the child what they could do instead if they feel this way again.

The best way to deal with emotional outbursts is to minimise the likelihood of them happening in the first place:

◎ Avoid setting up situations where emotional outbursts are likely to happen, such as making unrealistic demands or doing complex activities when a child is tired

◎ Give advance warning, for example prepare the child for new experiences; give a five minute warning that an activity is coming to an end and that you want them to do something else

◎ Provide reasonable choices and alternatives to give the child a sense of responsibility and control, for instance a choice of activity to do next; or choice of materials

◎ Encourage the child to express feelings in a more positive way.

Unit Link

For this Unit you also need to understand the following sections:

CCLD 301.3 Support children in developing relationships (see Chapter 1)

PORTFOLIO ACTIVITY

1   Outline your setting's policy for dealing with children's emotional outbursts.

2   Describe how you have dealt with a child's emotional outburst.

3   Give examples of opportunities in your setting which allow children to experience and express their feelings safely.

NVQ LINKS: CCLD 308.1   CCLD 308.2
CCLD 301.1   CCLD 301.3   CCLD 337.1
CCLD 337.2

CCLD 308.3
Enable children to take risks safely

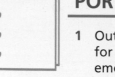

Knowledge Base

K3D306   K3D313   K3D314   K3P319

As a childcarer you should enable children to take risks safely by carrying out risk assessment in line with organisational policy, without limiting opportunities to extend and challenge children's skills.

Allow children to set their own limits within the framework of risk assessment, encouraging them to assess risks for themselves and others from their activity and behaviour.

Encourage children's self-reliance, self-esteem and resilience

Unit Links

For this Unit you also need to understand the following sections:

CCLD 301.3 Support children in developing relationships (see Chapter 1)
CCLD 302.1 Establish a healthy, safe and secure environment for children (see Chapter 2)
CCLD 302.2 Maintain a healthy, safe and secure environment for children (see Chapter 2)
CCLD 303.2 Assess development and reflect upon implications for practice (see Chapter 3)
CCLD 318.4 Help children and young people to manage risk during play (see Chapter 8)
CCLD 337.2 Promote positive aspects of behaviour (see Chapter 9)

Supervise children according to legislation (see 'Staffing ratios' on page 117) and accepted policy and practice in the setting, including intervening in situations where children are at risk of harm.

Clearly agree boundaries and limits with children and the reasons for these. Help children to manage and monitor their own behaviour and that of others.

You should demonstrate awareness of the capabilities and competence of individual children.

Check it out

What are your childcare setting's policies and procedures that are relevant to enabling children to take risk safely? (For example: health and safety policy; risk assessment and risk management procedures; and staffing ratios.)

CCLD 308.4
Encourage children's self-reliance, self-esteem and resilience

Knowledge Base

K3D307	K3D308	K3D309	K3D310	K3D313
K3D314	K3D315	K3D316	K3P318	

A childcarer should encourage children's self-reliance, self-esteem and resilience by: engaging with and providing focused attention to individual children; treating children with respect and consideration as individual people in their own right; showing empathy to children by demonstrating understanding of their feelings and points of view (see Chapter 1). You should encourage children to take decisions and make choices. Communicate with children openly and honestly in ways that are not judgemental. Help children to choose realistic goals that are challenging but achievable.

Praise specific behaviour that you wish to encourage as well as directing any comments, whether positive or negative, towards the demonstrated behaviour, not the child. (See Chapter 9 for more information on rewards and sanctions and fifteen ways to support children with behavioural difficulties.)

Work with colleagues and other professionals, as required, to encourage children's self-esteem and resilience by providing opportunities to encourage children's self-reliance, positive self-esteem and self-image (see below). You may need to work with other professionals such as counsellors, psychologists or social workers to promote the well-being and resilience of children with special needs (see Chapter 14) or children in need (Chapter 15).

Unit Links

For this Unit you also need to understand the following sections:

CCLD 301.1 Develop relationships with children (see Chapter 1)

CCLD 301.2 Communicate with children (see Chapter 1)

CCLD 313.3 Work with families and other agencies to access specialist support (see Chapter 15)

CCLD 339.1 Liaise with parents and other professionals in respect of children with special educational needs (see Chapter 14)

Figure 10.1 Child demonstrating self-help skills

Encouraging children's self-reliance

Encouraging children to become self-reliant is an important part of helping them to develop their independence and resilience, which will enable them to face life's demands and challenges in preparation for their adult lives. It involves helping children to develop: *independence* (or autonomy), for instance the ability to think and act for themselves; *dependence* on their own capabilities and personal resources; *competence* in looking after themselves; *trust* in their own judgement and actions; and *confidence* in their own abilities and actions.

Encouraging children's positive self-esteem

A person's self-esteem is changeable; sometimes we feel more positive about ourselves than at other times. Even if we have had past experiences that resulted in negative or poor self-esteem, we can overcome this and learn to feel more positive about ourselves. Self-esteem involves: feelings and thoughts about oneself (positive or negative); respect or regard for self (or lack of it); consideration of self; self-worth (value of self); self-image (perception of self). How we feel about

Eight ways to encourage children's self-reliance

You can encourage children's self-reliance in the following ways:

1   Provide *freedom* for children to become more independent.
2   Be *patient* and provide *time* for children to do things for themselves. For instance, let younger children dress themselves. Although it takes longer, it is an essential self-help skill. Children with physical disabilities may need sensitive support in this area.
3   *Praise* and *encourage* the children's efforts at becoming more independent.
4   Be aware of children's *individual needs* for independence; every child is different and will require encouragement relevant to their particular level of development. Do not insist children be more independent in a particular area until they are ready.
5   Be sensitive to children's *changing needs* for independence. Remember, a child who is tired, distressed or unwell may require more adult assistance than usual.
6   Offer *choices* to make children feel more in control. As they develop and mature, increase the scope of choices. Involve the children in *decision-making* within the childcare setting.
7   Provide *play opportunities* that encourage independence. For example dressing-up is a fun way to help younger children learn to dress independently.
8   Use *technology* to encourage independence such as specialist play equipment; voice-activated word processing; or motorised wheelchairs.

ourselves depends on a number of factors: w*ho* we are with at the time; the social context, for instance *where* we are; current and past *relationships*; and past *experiences* (especially in early childhood).

We cannot *see* self-esteem, but we can assess children's (and adults') levels of self-esteem by their emotional responses, attitudes and actions. People with positive or high self-esteem are usually: calm

and relaxed; energetic, enthusiastic and well-motivated; open and expressive; positive and optimistic; self-reliant and self-confident; assertive; reflective (aware of own strengths and weaknesses); sociable, co-operative, friendly and trusting.

People with negative or low self-esteem tend to be: anxious and tense; lacking in enthusiasm, poorly motivated and easily frustrated; secretive and/or

PORTFOLIO ACTIVITY

1   Observe a child demonstrating self-help skills such as: feeding self; washing hands; getting dressed/undressed (for PE); tidying up.
2   Assess the child's ability to perform the skill independently. Outline the adult's role in developing the child's self-reliance in this area.

NVQ LINKS: CCLD 308.4   CCLD 303.1   CCLD 303.2   CCLD 301.1   CCLD 301.2   CCLD 337.2

pretentious; negative and pessimistic; over-dependent, lacking in confidence and constantly seeking the approval of others *or* over-confident, arrogant and attention-seeking; aggressive *or* passive; self-destructive *or* abusive towards others; or resentful and distrustful of others.

Possible reasons for low self-esteem

All children begin with the potential for high self-esteem, but their interactions with others contribute to whether positive self-esteem is encouraged or diminished. Experiences in early childhood have the most significant effect on children's self-esteem, which sometimes may not become apparent until adolescence or adulthood when serious psychological and social problems may result due to very low self-esteem. Helping children to develop positive self-esteem can be a major preventive strategy (Moon, 1992). Children (and adults) are very resilient and can learn to have greater self-esteem even if their earlier experiences were detrimental to their esteem. Factors which lead to low self-esteem include: being deprived of basic needs or having these needs inadequately met; having feelings denied or ignored; being put down, ridiculed or humiliated; participating in inappropriate activities; feeling that their ideas and opinions are unimportant; being over-protected, under-disciplined or excessively disciplined; or being physically or sexually abused (Lindenfield, 1995).

Encouraging children's positive self-image and identity

The development of self-image is strongly linked to self-esteem. Self-image can be defined as the

Think About

1 Think of as many positive words to describe yourself using the same initial as your first name, for example caring, creative, Carlton; magnificent, marvellous, Miriam; sensitive, sharing, Shazia; terrific, tremendous Tom.
2 You could also try this with friends, colleagues or a group of children.

individual's view of their own personality and abilities including the individual's *perception* of how other people view them and their abilities. This involves recognising ourselves as separate and unique individuals with characteristics which make us different from others.

Self-image also involves a number of factors which influence how we *identify with* other people. For example: gender, culture, race, nationality, religion, language, social status/occupation, disability/special needs, or early experiences and relationships.

As a childcarer you need to be aware of your own self-image and the importance of having positive self-esteem. This may mean that you need to deal with issues regarding your own self-image and to raise your own self-esteem before you can encourage children's positive self-image.

Possible reasons for poor self-image

Children develop their self-image through interactions with others, starting with family members and gradually including childcarers, teachers, friends, classmates. Through positive interactions, children learn to value themselves and their abilities if they receive approval, respect and empathy. Children's early experiences and

Activity

1 Think about the factors which influence your own self-image (male or female; full or part-time student; employment status; nationality, and so on).

2 How do you think these factors influence your self-image and the ways you think other people see you? (For example, some people may consider a female doing a childcare course is appropriate for a woman, but a male studying the same course may be regarded differently.)

relationships may have positive or negative influences on their self-image.

Research shows that intelligence or physical attractiveness are not factors in children's self-image or self-esteem; very intelligent or attractive children may still have poor self-esteem and self-image. The main reason for poor self-image and low self-esteem is the treatment that children receive from their parents (Fontana, 1984). Children with positive self-image: tend to come from homes where they are regarded as significant and interesting people; have their views invited and listened to; have parents with high but reasonable and consistent expectations; and receive firm discipline based on rewards and sanctions, not physical punishment. Children with negative self-image: tend to come from homes where no one takes any real interest in them; have parents with limited, negative or unreasonable expectations; are given little consistent guidance and/or care; or receive too little or overly strict discipline or a confusing mixture of the two.

However, it is not just parents who influence children's self-image and self-esteem. Adults who work with children (such as childcarers, playworkers, teachers and teaching assistants) also influence children's self-image and self-esteem through their attitudes, words and actions. In childcare settings, children may soon become aware that certain levels of performance are expected by adults and begin to compare their own achievements with that of other children. If children regularly feel that their achievements do not compare favourably with those of other children, then they begin to experience a sense of failure and inferiority. Children may react to this feeling by either passively accepting that they are a failure and being reluctant to attempt new activities or rebelling against and rejecting all activities that remind them of failure.

Adults have important roles to play in children's development of self-image and identity. Children are able to see and feel not only the way adults interact with them personally, but also the way adults interact with other children and adults, either in the early years setting or at home. Young children are very capable and accurate at assessing what the adult expectations of them are and of behaving accordingly! The constraints of class size, time and resources mean that many classrooms group children according to ability. Nursery and primary education are now more curriculum and assessment orientated, for example early learning goals, baseline assessment, the National Curriculum including the literacy and numeracy hours, and SATs.

Some children may experience particular difficulties in developing a positive self-image; for example, those with special needs, from ethnic minorities, or who are/have been abused. These children may be experiencing prejudice and/or discrimination on a regular basis, which affects their ability to maintain a positive self-image. By praising all children and encouraging them to feel good about themselves and their achievements, adults can help them to establish and maintain a positive self-image. Developing and implementing inclusive policies, procedures and strategies will also help.

Figure 10.2 Example of child's personal flag

Ten ways to encourage children's positive self-esteem and self-image

1 Treat every child as an individual; every child has unique abilities and needs.
2 Be positive by using praise and encouragement to help children and young people to focus on what they are good at.
3 Help children and young people to maximise their individual potential.
4 Encourage children to measure their achievements by comparing them to *own* efforts.
5 Have high but realistic expectations of *all* children and young people.
6 Take an interest in each child's efforts as well as achievements.
7 Encourage positive participation during play activities, for instance sharing resources, helping others and contributing ideas.
8 Give children and young people opportunities to make decisions and choices.
9 Promote equality of opportunity by providing positive images of children, young people and adults through books, stories and songs.
10 Remember to label the behaviour not the child as this is less damaging to their self-esteem, for example 'That was an unkind thing to say' rather than 'You are unkind'.

1 Design your own 'personal flag'. Use words and pictures to describe the following: my happiest memory; my best qualities; my significant achievements; my current goal.
2 Try this activity with a child or small group of children.

Encouraging children's resilience

The pressures of modern living affect the emotional well-being and resilience of children and adults. For example:

1 Parents in the UK work longer hours than in any other country in Europe; consequently working parents have less time to spend with their children.
2 National Curriculum demands have led to a return to more formal methods of teaching with increased emphasis on academic achievement for all children, for example baseline assessment, literacy and numeracy hours, end of key stage tests.
3 Technological advances and concerns about personal safety mean many children and young people spend more time in front of televisions, computers and games consoles than playing out with friends.

Academic intelligence or achievement has very little to do with emotional well-being. According to research, IQ contributes 20 per cent to the factors that lead to success in life while other factors contribute to the other 80 per cent. These other factors include: environmental and social factors; luck, such as being in the right place at the right time or wrong place at the wrong time; emotional intelligence or competence. (Goleman, 1996)

In Britain we tend to place great importance on people's qualifications and job status. We need to put more emphasis on people's emotional intelligence or well-being as this would lead to people having better life skills, for example making better use of leisure time, maintaining positive relationships, being able to pass exams, getting satisfying and challenging jobs, and being better parents.

Emotional intelligence or emotional well-being involves developing: positive self-esteem and self-image; emotional strength to deal with life's highs and lows; confidence to face the world with optimism; and awareness of own feelings and those of other people.

We all need to feel valued – that who we are and where we come from are respected; that our ideas and abilities are important. On this solid emotional platform the building blocks for a stimulating and fulfilling life can be successfully constructed. Even if these building blocks are damaged by life experiences, personal difficulties, tragedy or trauma, they can be rebuilt in childhood, adolescence and even adulthood.

Factors that affect resilience in children

Children vary in their responses to a set of circumstances. Some children may do well even in extremely adverse circumstances while others may not be able to cope with small amounts of stress. Rutter describes resilience as *'the phenomenon of overcoming stress or adversity'*. (DH, 2000) Resilience or protective factors cushion children from the worst effects of adversity and may help a

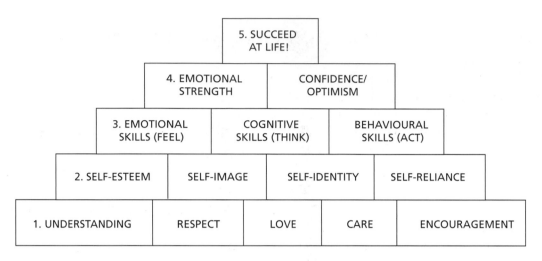

Key:

1. These **foundation stones** are established by parents, grandparents and carers in childhood; as adults we can regain them through partners/spouses, close friends, etc.
2. These **self-building blocks** are influenced by others including family, carers, teachers, friends, peers, colleagues, etc. throughout life.
3. These **skills** can be developed as a child and/or as an adult.
4. These **qualities** can be demonstrated as a child and/or as an adult.
5. **Individual achievements** in different areas of life as a child and as an adult.

Figure 10.3 Emotional building blocks

'child or young person to cope, survive and even thrive in the face of great hurt and disadvantage'. (Bostock, 2004) Resilience factors are things which help children and young people withstand adversity and cope in unfavourable circumstances or times of difficulty. Resilience factors include:

1 Positive attachment experiences, such as caring, concerned and sincere relationships with parents and/or carers, childcarers and teachers.
2 Positive early years/school experiences like participation in activities they enjoy to build positive self-esteem.
3 Recognition, respect and rewards for special skills and talents that everyone has as unique individuals, such as nurturing academic, artistic, musical, sporting and vocational abilities through activities both in the setting and in spare time.

4 Opportunities to take responsibility or contribute to decisions which affect one's life, like involvement in discussions or reviews to develop services for children and young people.
5 A sense of direction that provides stability and control by building up a picture of what the future might hold, such as helping to develop goals and how to reach these goals.

(Bostock, 2004)

Promoting children's emotional well-being and resilience

As a childcarer you can promote children's emotional well-being and resilience by providing opportunities for children to: learn about their

Five ways to promote children's emotional well-being and resilience

Help children to develop emotional well-being and resilience by:

1 Developing their self-awareness, including helping children to establish a positive self-image and to recognise their own feelings.

2 Helping them to handle and express feelings in appropriate ways, such as through creative, imaginative and physical play.

3 Encouraging their self-motivation by helping children to establish personal goals, such as developing self-control and self-reliance.

4 Developing their empathy for other people by encouraging children to recognise the feelings, needs and rights of others.

5 Encouraging positive social interaction by helping children to develop effective interpersonal skills through play and other co-operative group activities in the childcare setting and in the local community.

feelings; understand the feelings of others; develop their creative abilities (for example art and craft, drama, musical activities); participate in physical activities, games and sport; interact with other children and make friends, play together; develop emotional intelligence.

PORTFOLIO ACTIVITY

1 Describe how you have helped to promote children's emotional well-being and resilience.

NVQ LINKS: CCLD 308.4   CCLD 301.1
CCLD 301.3   CCLD 337.2

CCLD 325
Support the child or young person's successful transfer and transition in learning and development contexts

The process of adjusting to a new situation is known as a **transition**. Transitions involve the experiences of change, separation and loss. A transition may involve the **transfer** from one setting to another or changes within the same setting. For example: home to childminder's home, nursery, playgroup or school; one year group or Key Stage to another e.g. Reception to Year 1, Key Stage 1 to 2; mainstream to or from special school; secondary school to college or work; staff changes due to illness, maternity leave, promotion, retirement, etc.

A transition may also involve other significant transfers or changes in the child's life such as: death or serious illness of a family member or close friend; parental separation or divorce; moving house; going into hospital; death of a favourite pet; arrival of a new baby or step-brothers and sisters; going on holiday (especially visiting another country).

CCLD 325.1
Plan for transfer and transition

Knowledge Base

325K01	325K02	325K03	325K04	325K05
325K06	325K07	325K08		

To cope with, prepare for and accept transfers and transitions, children need: reassurance from adults to maintain their feelings of stability, security and trust; adult assistance to adjust to different social rules and social expectations; help in adapting to different group situations.

Factors that may affect children's transfers and transitions in learning and development contexts include: the child's age and level of maturity; previous experiences in other settings which may have been positive or negative; special needs (e.g. physical disability, sensory impairment, communication difficulties, behavioural and/or emotional difficulties); moving to a new area, county or even country; special family circumstances (e.g. parental separation or divorce, bereavement, serious illness, etc.); returning to the childcare setting after a prolonged illness or accident.

Children's responses to transfers and transitions often depend on the way they are prepared for the new setting, childcarer or situation. The need for preparation was not recognised in the past; for example, young children started school or went into hospital and were left to cope with the situation with little or no preparation beforehand and parental involvement was positively discouraged.

Think About

Can you remember your first day at school? What was it like? How were you prepared for this new situation?

Many children (especially when young) experience anxiety and stress when they first attend a new setting or have a new childcarer due to:

- Separation from their parent or previous childcarer
- Encountering unfamiliar children who may have already established friendships
- The length of time spent in the setting, for example 8.00am to 6.00pm in a day nursery, or 9.00am to 3.30pm in school
- Differences in culture and language of the setting to the child's previous experiences
- Unfamiliar routines and rules
- Worry about doing the wrong thing
- Unfamiliar activities such as sports/PE, playtime, lunch time or even story time
- The unfamiliar physical environment, which may seem overwhelming and scary
- Difficulties in following more structured activities and adult directions
- Concentrating on activities for longer than previously used to.

The transition from primary to secondary school may cause additional concerns due to:

- Lack of sufficient information about individual children on transfer
- Discontinuity of Year 6 and 7 curriculum in spite of the National Curriculum
- Having several subject teachers instead of one class teacher
- Decrease in pupil performance after transfer.

As a childcarer you need to plan for children's successful transfer and transition by: assessing the family situation of each child or young person; identifying the changes in expectations and activities required of the children; gathering and reviewing relevant information with an individual child or young person; working with parents and carers to ensure a full understanding of the process; identifying the support the child or young person will need to make a successful transfer or transition, including any special requirements; preparing a transition plan that assists others to develop a full understanding of the experiences and achievements of the child or young person; assisting others to develop an effective induction programme for children and young people that helps them to understand the new expectations and activities; assisting others to assess the child's or young person's current levels of achievement and learning experience and to provide a programme that will give continuity in learning; and contributing to the prompt transfer of information as an aid to effective planning, following agreed confidentiality protocols and legislative requirements. (NDNA, 2004)

CCLD 325.2
Support the child or young person to prepare for transfer or transition

Knowledge Base

| 325K09 | 325K10 | 325K11 | 325K12 | 325K13 |
| 325K14 | 325K15 | | | |

To alleviate some of this anxiety and stress, preparation is now seen as an essential part of successful transfers and transitions including nurseries, schools, foster care and hospitals. Most settings have established procedures for preparing children for such change.

You can help prepare children aged 0 to 3 years of age for transfer or transition by:

◎ In the first week arrange for one of the child's parents to stay at home before you have sole charge of the child
◎ You and/or the parents should talk to the child about what is going to happen
◎ Obtain detailed information from the parents so that the child's individual needs can be identified. This includes: the baby's or young child's existing daily routine, eating and sleeping patterns; special dietary requirements; and the child's likes and dislikes regarding food, clothes, toys and activities
◎ Provide parents with information about how you will help the child to settle in
◎ Plan appropriate activities for the first few days/ weeks that provide reassurance to both child and parents
◎ Make sure the baby or young child has easy access to a particular comfort object or favourite toy if they have one.

Unit Links

For this Unit you also need to understand the following sections:

CCLD 312.2 Communicate with babies and children under 3 years (see Chapter 11)

CCLD 312.4 Exchange information and respond to parents' needs and preferences for their babies and children under 3 years (see Chapter 11)

CCLD 314.4 Provide an emotionally secure and consistent environment (see Chapter 11)

You can help prepare children aged 3 to 11 years for transitions by:

◎ Talking to the children and explaining what is going to happen
◎ Listening to the children and reassuring them that it will be fine

◎ Reading relevant books, stories and poems about transitions, such as starting nursery or primary school; moving to secondary school; visiting the dentist; or going into hospital

◎ Watching appropriate videos or television programmes which demonstrate the positive features of the new setting or situation

◎ Providing opportunities for imaginative play to let children express their feelings and fears about the transition

◎ Visiting the children's current setting or going on home visits to meet the children in a familiar setting, particularly if working with children with special needs

◎ Organising introductory visits for the children and their parents/carers so that the children can become familiar with the setting and the adults who will care for and support them

◎ Providing information appropriate to both children and parents, for instance an information pack or brochure plus an activity pack for each child

◎ Obtaining relevant information from parents about their child, such as correct name and address, contact details, medical information, dietary requirements and food preferences

◎ Planning activities for an induction programme (the children's first day/week in the new setting).

You can help prepare children aged 11 to 16 years for transitions by:

◎ Encouraging children and parents to attend open days and evenings at the setting

◎ Visiting the children's current setting to meet the children in familiar surroundings, particularly if working with children with special needs

◎ Arranging taster days for children to experience the layout and routine of the setting, for example in secondary schools moving to various classrooms for lessons with different subject teachers and fun activities in science, IT and sport

◎ Discussing individual children's performance with relevant members of staff

◎ Exchanging relevant documentation, such as child observations and assessments, SATs test results, any special educational needs information including individual education plans, behaviour support plans, statements, and so on

◎ Looking at children's records of achievement including their interests and hobbies

◎ Encouraging children with behaviour problems to look at this as a fresh start

◎ Providing the setting's information pack or brochure for children and parents including information on bullying as this is often a key area of concern

◎ Obtaining relevant information from parents about their child, for example correct name and address, contact details, medical information, dietary requirements and food preferences

◎ Providing opportunities for work experience to help children with the transition from the learning environment to the world of work

◎ Providing opportunities for careers advice and information on further education or training, for example using the Connexions service for 13 to 19 year olds

◎ Encouraging children and parents to attend open days and evenings for local colleges.

Transition Plans

The transition of leaving school and moving onto college or employment can be a daunting experience for all teenagers but may be especially challenging for young people with special needs and their families who may need continued advice and support. A Transition Plan should be drawn up in Year 9 when the young person is aged 13/14 years.

'The Transition Plan should draw together information from a range of individuals within and

Unit Links

For this Unit you also need to understand the following sections:

CCLD 301.2 Communicate with children (see Chapter 1)

CCLD 301.4 Communicate with adults (see Chapter 1)

CCLD 303.3 Plan provision to promote development (see Chapter 3)

CCLD 306.3 Provide a caring, nurturing and responsive environment (see Chapter 6)

CCLD 330.1 Identify and negotiate requirements with children and their families (see Chapter 16)

CCLD 332.1 Provide information and establish relationships with families (see Chapter 16)

CCLD 339.1 Liaise with parents and other professionals in respect of children with special educational needs (see Chapter 14)

beyond the school in order to plan coherently for the young person's transition to adult life. Transition plans when they are first drawn up in Year 9 are not simply about post-school arrangements, they should plan for on-going school provision, under the Statement of SEN as overseen by the LEA.' (DfES, 2001c; Section 9:51)

The transition plan should address questions relating to the young person, their family, the school and the professionals supporting them. Questions should include:

◎ *What are the young person's hopes and aspirations for the future and how can these be met?*

◎ *Will parents experience new care needs and require practical help?*

◎ *How can the curriculum help young people play their role in the community?*

◎ *Does the young person have any special health or welfare needs that will require planning and support from health and social services now or in the future?*

(DfES, 2001c; Chapter 9)

PORTFOLIO ACTIVITY

1   How does your setting plan for children's transfers and transitions? For example, planning for a child or young person: transferring to or from a new childcare/education setting; transferring to different group within the same setting (moving to a new year group or Key Stage in a school); meeting a new childcarer (new keyworker, childminder or nanny); starting college or work; going into hospital for a planned operation or treatment.

2   Describe the procedures in your setting for preparing children for transitions. Include possible strategies for supporting children's preparation for transfer or transition. Consider these points: the child's level of social interaction (age and ability to communicate); the child's potential behaviour based on your existing knowledge of the child (are they likely to be cooperative or disruptive?); the child's possible emotional responses and how to deal with them.

NVQ LINKS: CCLD 325.1   CCLD 325.2   CCLD 301.2   CCLD 301.4   CCLD 303.3   CCLD 306.3
CCLD 308.1   CCLD 308.2   CCLD 314.4   CCLD 330.1   CCLD 332.1

CCLD 325.3
Monitor the success of transfer and transition and identify continued support needs

Knowledge Base

325K04   325K07   325K08   325K15

As a childcarer you need to monitor the success of transfer/transition and identify continued support

needs by: reviewing progress with the child or young person, their parents or carers and other professionals after an appropriate period of familiarisation and agreeing continuing support; ensuring that the child or young person knows how to make use of support systems within the new learning environment; and reviewing transfer arrangements with other agencies and identifying any improved ways of working together. (NDNA, 2004)

The first days (or even weeks) that children spend in a new setting require a sensitive approach from childcarers to enable the children to cope with separation from their parents and/or their adjustment to new staff and new routines.

Twelve ways to help children adjust to the childcare setting

Help children to adjust to a new childcare setting by:

1 Following a clear, daily routine to provide stability and security for the children.
2 Providing opportunities for children to express their feelings and concerns over separating from their parents and/or starting in a new setting.
3 Ensuring babies and very young children have easy access to their transition/comfort objects.
4 Working with other childcarers to identify children's individual needs during the transition period.
5 Providing activities and experiences appropriate to these needs.
6 Showing an active interest in the children's activities.
7 Giving particular praise and encouragement for participation, not just achievement.
8 Working with children to establish clear boundaries and rules.
9 Encouraging parental involvement as far as is practical and appropriate to the setting.
10 Reassuring younger children about their parents' eventual return.
11 Preparing parents for possible *temporary* effects of the transition, for example children may demonstrate their feelings of anxiety by: being clingy, hostile or aggressive; or regressing to a previous developmental level.
12 Encouraging parents to be relaxed, calm and confident so that their children do not sense their parents' anxiety. Settling in is often a more stressful experience for the parents than for their children.

PORTFOLIO ACTIVITY

1 How does your setting monitor the success of transfer and transition?
2 How do you identify children's continued support needs?
NVQ LINKS: CCLD 325.3   CCLD 303.4   CCLD 306.3   CCLD 312.3   CCLD 314.4

Optional Units

CCLD 312
Plan and implement positive environments for babies and children under 3 years

CCLD 314
Provide physical care that promotes the health and development of babies and children under 3 years

CCLD 312
Plan and implement positive environments for babies and children under 3 years

Depending on the age range of children in the childcare setting you may be involved in working with babies and children under 3 years of age. This involves observing, assessing and recording the results of observations and using these to plan positive environments, routines and activities that will enhance very young children's development.

CCLD 312.1
Observe, assess and record developmental progress of babies and children under 3 years

Knowledge Base

K3D386	K3D387	K3D388	K3D389	K3D390
K3D391	K3D392	K3D393	K3D394	K3D395

Birth to Three Matters: A framework to support children in their earliest years, published in November 2002, provides a framework for adults to support the development of very young children (see website: www.surestart.gov.uk/resources/childcareworkers/birthtothreematters). This framework includes the *Birth to Three Matters* pack which is divided into four sections: a strong child; a skilful communicator; a competent learner; and a healthy child (see below). The sections include information on these different aspects of development for the following ages:

◎ 0–8 months: Heads up, Lookers and Communicators
◎ 8–18 months: Sitters, Standers and Explorers
◎ 18–24 months: Movers, Shakers and Players
◎ 24–36 months: Walkers, Talkers and Pretenders.

Each of the four sections in the pack contains four double-sided cards which are available to download as PDF files from the Sure Start website (see above). This website also provides further information and access to supplementary resources, such as CD-ROM and video excerpts, to be used alongside the *Birth to Three Matters* pack. Please note that the *Birth to Three Matters* framework is due to be replaced with the Early Years Foundation Stage (EYFS) in 2008 (see Chapter 12 for more information). In Scotland the framework for under-3s, launched in January 2005, is *Birth to three: supporting our youngest children* (www.ltscotland.org.uk/earlyyears/sharingpractice/birthtothree/index.asp). In Northern Ireland there is currently no framework for babies and children under 3.

Check it out

What is the curriculum framework for the children you work with in your setting?

Observing and assessing babies and children under 3 years

The Component cards in *Birth to Three Matters* use the heading 'Look, listen and note' rather than 'observation' because '… *what practitioners "notice" about babies and toddlers is often much more detailed and exciting than what actually gets recorded as an observation record'* (Elfer, 2005; p.118). What you 'notice' about what a child is able to do should form part of the record of the child's developmental progress.

Suggested method for observing the under-3s:

1 Observe for 10–20 minutes, focusing on one child and their interactions with adult(s) and other children and toys and objects.
2 Observe without a notebook, concentrating as far as possible on the chosen child and being as receptive as possible to the smallest of details as well as emotional atmospheres and responses.
3 After the observation, make a written record of what you observed; write in as free-flowing a way as possible, following the main sequence of events and recording details as they come to mind.
4 Share and discuss the written observation with your supervisor/colleagues; consider and examine differing interpretations and connections.
5 Continue further observations and bring your write-ups to the group to be discussed and compared.

(Miller, 2002)

Observations and assessments (whatever methods you use in your setting) should be used not only to record developmental progress but also to inform practice, such as planning for young children's future developmental needs. For detailed information see Unit CCLD 303 in Chapter 3.

PORTFOLIO ACTIVITY

Outline how you observe, assess and record the developmental progress of babies and children under 3 years. Include information on:

◎ The relevant framework applicable to children in your setting
◎ Your setting's policy and procedures for observing and assessing children's development, including agreed formats for observation and assessment
◎ Sharing information about children's development with their parents, colleagues and other professionals in line with the setting's policies and procedures and any legal requirements, such as confidentiality and data protection.

NVQ LINKS: CCLD 312.1   CCLD 312.4
CCLD 301.4   CCLD 303.1   CCLD 303.2
CCLD 317.3   CCLD 328.2   CCLD 330.3

CCLD 312.2
Communicate with babies and children under 3 years

Knowledge Base

K3C396   K3D398   K3D399   K3C400   K3C401
K3D402   K3C404   K3D406

Babies begin to communicate from birth by interacting with self, other people and the environment. From birth, babies need many and varied opportunities for positive interactions and appropriate responses to their attempts to express themselves. The first three years of life are critical for a child's language development as important connections are being made within the child's brain. Even very young children are tuned into language and are able to take turns during conversations, for example mirroring the mouth movements of adults. (There is more information about promoting children's communication skills and language development in Chapter 3.)

Communication and positive relationships

Very young children need to be given time, attention and affection. They are social beings and need to develop affectionate social relationships because they learn through having a safe and secure base with a predictable, familiar daily routine. They also need plenty of opportunities for early communication, including physical contact and touch. Very young children learn through positive relationships with adults who relate fully and appropriately with them and this communication is essential to children's emotional and social development. Parents and childcarers who relate poorly to very young children may leave them insecure or without affection, making it more difficult for these children to establish and/or maintain future relationships. (Lindon, 2002)

Language is important as it enables children to express their needs, feelings, ideas and thoughts in a way that others can understand. It does not just include speech but also pictorial representation, sign language and Braille. (See Chapter 14 for information on supporting children with hearing and visual impairment.)

A shared language is essential to provide children with opportunities to communicate and share cultural experiences. You need to ensure that children's community language(s) are equally valued and that you support the language development of children with bilingual home backgrounds by, for example, including community languages in displays, notices, books, magazines, and so on. (See Chapter 1 for information on communication in bilingual and multilingual settings.)

To become skilful communicators, babies and children under 3 years of age need to develop close, positive and responsive relationships with adults who recognise and acknowledge their attempts to communicate and interact with others. Babies and children under 3 years need opportunities, within a stimulating environment, to practise and experiment with language by communicating with significant adults (parents and childcarers) who respond when very young children communicate either non-verbally or verbally.

Communication forms the basis for developing early literacy skills and very young children need plenty of opportunities to experience a range of communication methods including singing, talking, stories, sounds, rhymes, games and language activities. They also need opportunities to communicate through different media such as touch, mark making, pretend play and painting.

Twelve ways to communicate with very young children

You can communicate with babies and children under 3 years to develop positive relationships in the following ways:

1 Interact responsively with very young children using a warm and respectful approach by using appropriate praise and positive language during routines and activities.

2 Allow babies to take the lead in communication and respond appropriately, positively and genuinely by allowing them to initiate and engage in communication at their own pace, making eye contact only when the baby or child is comfortable with communication initiatives.

3 Model turn-taking through timing, body language and expression; encourage turn-taking through interactive games and rhymes such as '*Pat-a-cake*' and '*Round and round the garden*'.

4 Explore the baby or child's range of interests, sharing activities and using these as topics of communication in order to develop relationships.

5 Accept all attempts at communication by very young children, both non-verbal (body language and facial expressions) and verbal (babbling, jargoning, one or two word phrases). Recognise when very young children do not wish to communicate, or wish to disengage from communication, and respect their wishes.

6 Ensure that non-mobile babies have opportunities to lie and/or sit next to other babies to enable them to interact by observing each other and visually exploring early communications.

7 Observe and respond to a very young child by providing an appropriate running commentary during routines and activities (along with appropriate adult assistance). For instance, 'You're going up the slide. Now you're at the top. Well done! Now you're going down the slide . . . wheee! Now you're at the bottom. Wasn't that fun?!'

8 Involve them through non-verbal and verbal language when carrying out all routines and activities, ensuring your body language, facial expression and tone of voice support your spoken words.

9 Engage the interest and attention of very young children using methods appropriate to their ages and developmental levels, that is provide a wide range of opportunities for them to listen to and use language and sound patterns, such as stories, rhymes, songs, music, and so on.

10 Communicate clearly and effectively with them at a level and pace suited to their development and understanding. For example adapt your language level to that of the child by using short sentences.

11 Encourage very young children to communicate respectfully with adults and with each other. You should also recognise and respect the efforts of very young children to be independent and model behaviour that demonstrates respect for others.

12 Monitor when, how, why and with whom language is used by very young children. For instance observe, identify and record non-verbal and verbal interactions between the children (including their developing friendships with each other) and provide opportunities to encourage these interactions.

PORTFOLIO ACTIVITY

Outline the methods you use to communicate with babies and young children to develop positive relationships.

NVQ LINKS: CCLD 312.2   CCLD 301.1   CCLD 301.2   CCLD 301.3

CCLD 312.3
Plan and implement activities to enhance development

Knowledge Base

K3D403   K3D407   K3D408   K3S409

Planning and implementing activities to enhance very young children's development should be based on your observations of each child (see above), your relationship with each child and your understanding of holistic learning. Effective planning for very young children involves: viewing children as powerful and competent learners; using your knowledge of them as active learners (see page 246) to inform your planning; observing children closely and respecting them as individuals in order to plan rich, meaningful experiences; recognising that an experience must be holistic to be meaningful and potentially rich in learning; planning a rich learning experience around the whole child, not around a specific area or component; taking a holistic approach to the planning process by recognising

and building on the child's needs, skills, interests and earlier experiences; and making your planning flexible and flow with the child. (Abbott and Langston, 2005)

Activity

Describe how you plan and implement activities to enhance very young children's development in your setting. Include examples of any planning sheets you use.

How very young children learn

Very young children do not split their lives into different sections so neither should you – look at a baby's or young child's day as a whole rather than as a list of separate activities. Look ahead to see how you can use all the learning opportunities available for them. They are primed to learn but it is important to tune into their understanding, their current abilities and the flow of their interests. It is also important to praise and reward very young children for their *efforts* as well as achievements.

(See CCLD 308.2 in Chapter 10 for information on the importance of feedback and encouragement and CCLD 309.1 in Chapter 12 for details of theoretical approaches to how children learn and develop) When planning and implementing activities to enhance development remember that very young children:

◎ Learn best at their own pace and by following their own absorbing current interests

◎ Learn through developmentally appropriate experiences which allow them time to explore, find out, practise and learn (see below)

◎ Can have their confidence and flow of learning disrupted by adults trying to make them learn something earlier or quicker

◎ Do not need to be rushed on to the next stage and such adult pressure may block rather than enhance their learning

◎ Learn through doing and need plenty of opportunities to use their physical abilities and to apply their ideas

◎ Learn best from play resources that can be used in many different ways, not just commercially produced toys

◎ Need a safe, stimulating and challenging environment (see CCLD 314.1).

(Lindon, 2002a)

Think About

How can you use all the learning opportunities available for very young children in your setting? Focus on one child and remember to tune into their understanding, their current abilities and the flow of their interests.

Encouraging very young children to explore

Babies and young children use their senses to: explore their environment; investigate and participate in new experiences; develop new skills and abilities; and discover how things work in the world around them. Research shows that babies are born with a wide range of sensory skills and perceptual abilities which enable them to explore their environment through sight, hearing, touch, taste and smell.

Babies' responses initially consist of automatic reflexes such as grasping and sucking; within a few months they are able to explore objects in more purposeful ways. Babies and young children use various strategies for exploring their environment as they mature, gain more experience and develop their physical skills. The more opportunities they have to explore, the more they will develop their sensory skills and perceptual abilities. As their senses develop, they begin to make sense of the world around them as they perceive and process information in their environment. To begin with babies focus on human faces and brightly coloured

Figure 11.1 Very young child using senses to explore

199

objects. Later they are able to perceive more detailed information and begin to make sense of that information. For example, being able to reach for and grasp a desired object; or telling the difference between two bricks, and so on.

As well as developing their *visual perception*, babies gradually develop their *auditory perception* from merely reacting to noise to being able to concentrate on and make sense of specific sounds such as listening to an adult's voice without being distracted by other sounds during a story or rhyme. The young child's visual and auditory experiences are supplemented by tactile exploration of their environment. Intellectual development is closely linked with young children's physical development. For example, increasing mobility (from rolling to crawling to walking) enables further exploration of the environment. Developing hand–eye co-ordination and manipulative skills enables young children to participate in a wide range of creative and construction activities, jigsaws, games, and so on. These activities assist children's powers of observation, perception and imagination. (There is more on developing imagination and creativity in Chapter 12, Unit CCLD 309.1.)

Activity

Give examples of activities you have used to encourage very young children to explore using their physical and/or sensory skills.

The chart below outlines the general sequence of very young children's sensory and perceptual development. Remember that the ages referred to in the chart are only guidelines to *expected* development. Some children will acquire these sensory skills and perceptual abilities earlier than indicated, some children later.

The sequence of young children's sensory development: 0 to 3 years

Age 0 to 3 months

◎ In first month, babies' responses are reflexes, for example sucking, grasping
◎ Learns to modify reflex responses
◎ Alert to voices when awake
◎ Blinks when surprised or alarmed
◎ Can focus 18 to 23 centimetres
◎ Can distinguish between light and dark
◎ Responds to bright light and bold colours (not pastels)
◎ From about 2 months, can discriminate between shades and colours
◎ Can focus further and images become clearer as eye muscles become trained
◎ Recognises faces of well-known adults and responds with smiles and arm movements
◎ Looks around purposefully and responds to visual stimulation by smiling and/or reaching out towards objects, e.g. mobiles.

◎ Repeats basic actions such as thumb/fist sucking, wiggling fingers
◎ Reacts to prolonged noises such as washing machines or vacuum cleaners.

Age 3 to 9 months

◎ Can focus more accurately; taking in more visual detail
◎ Follows the progress of moving objects
◎ Enjoys bright, bold patterns; starts to notice different patterns
◎ From about 5 months begins to perceive differences between objects such as size, shapes and colours
◎ Can discriminate between different facial expressions
◎ Quietens or smiles in response to parent's/carer's voice; turns head towards voice
◎ Developing curiosity encourages adjusting own position to look at objects
◎ Still puts things in mouth, but fingers used increasingly to explore objects
◎ Responds to visual stimuli by touching, for example activity centre, hitting mobile
◎ Reaches out and grasps objects; may shake rattle to make a noise for example
◎ Rolls towards desired object; once can crawl will do this to reach object
◎ Enjoys putting things in containers and taking them out again
◎ From about 8 months, begins to understand object permanence; if a toy is dropped will look in appropriate direction for it
◎ By about 9 months, listens attentively to everyday sounds and reacts to quiet sounds out of sight.

Age 9 to 18 months

◎ Can focus like an adult, but still learning how to interpret visual information
◎ Can follow objects moving quickly with eyes and see them clearly
◎ Will physically follow a moving object if mobile and reach for it; if not yet mobile will point to an object out of reach
◎ Experiments with toys and everyday objects to see what will happen; still puts things in mouth, but uses fingers more to explore objects and what can be done with them
◎ Enjoys stacking, posting and/or pulling toys
◎ Enjoys finger rhymes and clapping games such as pat-a-cake
◎ As becomes more mobile, physically explores environment – watch out!
◎ Responds to own name and other familiar words such as 'no' and 'bye-bye'
◎ From about 12 months, scribbles with crayons; enjoys sensation of finger painting.

Age 18 months to 2 years

◎ May be able to concentrate on short stories with clear pictures
◎ Enjoys pop-up/novelty books with flaps (needs supervision)

- Continues to develop visual perception and hand–eye co-ordination through activities which involve sorting and matching, such as simple in-set jigsaws, 3–4 piece jigsaws, building towers, sorting bricks, and so on
- Continues to scribble with crayons and enjoys tactile/visual qualities of paint
- Able to use symbols in play activities, for instance a doll represents a real baby
- Increased mobility/co-ordination allows further exploration of their environment
- Visual memory increases, for example can remember where favourite things are kept (and has physical ability to go and get them!).

Age 2 to 3 years

- Desire to explore continues
- Enjoys 'hide and seek' games such as hiding toys to find
- Continues to develop visual perception and hand–eye co-ordination through doing more complex jigsaws, sorting/matching activities, modelling, construction
- More confident with crayons; using paintbrush as well as finger/sponge painting
- Enjoys looking at books with clear illustrations
- Can identify different letters of the alphabet and match some letters when asked
- Increasingly uses language to discover what is going on by asking questions and listening to conversations of others and listening to stories.

PORTFOLIO ACTIVITY

1 Observe a very young child engaged in a creative and/or imaginative activity.
2 In your assessment focus on: the child's responses, including any language used; the child's concentration level; the child's creativity and imagination; the physical skills and sensory skills demonstrated by the child.
3 Suggest how you could encourage or extend the child's development.
NVQ LINKS: CCLD 312.3   CCLD 303.1   CCLD 303.2

Twelve ways to enhance very young children's development

You can enhance very young children's development in the following ways:
1 Provide opportunities and materials to increase curiosity. Examples include mobiles, posters, pictures, toys, games and books.
2 Encourage them to be observant by pointing out details in the environment such as colours, shapes, smells, textures; interesting objects such as animals, birds and vehicles; talking about weather conditions; taking them on outings.

3   Provide opportunities and materials for exploratory play, such as sand and water play; simple construction activities; modelling with playdough.

4   Participate in children's play to extend their learning by asking questions, providing answers and demonstrating possible ways to use equipment.

5   Demonstrate how things work or fit together when the child is not sure what to do. For example, a child can become very frustrated when struggling to do a jigsaw, but make sure your help is wanted (and necessary); use verbal prompts where possible to encourage children to solve the problem themselves.

6   Provide repetition by encouraging children to play with toys and games more than once; each time they play, they will discover different things about these activities.

7   Provide gradually more challenging activities but do not push children too hard by providing activities which are obviously too complex; instead of extending children's abilities this will only put them off due to the frustration at not being able to complete the task.

8   Remember safety. It is important to allow all children the freedom to explore their environment and to experiment with the properties of various materials. Make sure that these materials are suitable for very young children. Objects which can pose a choking hazard or glass objects which could be broken causing cuts must be kept well out of their reach.

9   Encourage auditory perception through activities such as: singing rhymes and songs; clapping games; awareness of animal noises/environmental sounds; taped songs, rhymes, music, everyday sounds and stories; sharing books and stories; sound lotto; identifying musical instruments; speaking and listening activities.

10 Encourage visual perception through activities involving exploration of the environment including outings to the park, farm; looking at books, pictures, displays, photographs; matching games, jigsaws, lotto; activities requiring basic letter and/or number recognition including simple board games and card games such as Snap and matching pairs.

11 Encourage tactile exploration through activities which involve exploratory play such as handling sand, water, clay, dough; using manufactured materials, including wooden blocks and plastic construction kits (Duplo and Stickle Bricks); making collages using various textures; 'feely' box or bag; treasure baskets.

12 Encourage use of taste and smell senses through simple cooking activities; finding out about tastes: sweet, sour, bitter, salty; and various smells: sweet and savoury, flowers, fruit and vegetables. Remember to maintain children's safety.

PORTFOLIO ACTIVITY

1 Plan two experiences to enhance the development of a very young child. You could use your suggestions from the observation on page 202 as a starting point. Suitable experiences might be: providing a creative activity such as drawing or painting; providing an imaginative activity such as dressing up, home corner or shop play; providing a visual stimulus for a baby such as a mobile or activity toy/centre; devising a musical activity or sound game to encourage auditory perception; designing a tactile activity such as a 'feely' box/bag or treasure basket; implementing a cooking or tasting session (remember safety, food allergies and dietary restrictions); organising an outing where the focus is on exploring the environment using the senses, for example visit to local park or nature centre/trail; going on a 'bug hunt'.

2 Include suggestions for enhancing the development of: a child with a hearing or visual impairment; a child with a community language other than English.

3 Review and evaluate the activity afterwards.

NVQ LINKS: CCLD 312.3   CCLD 303.3   CCLD 303.4

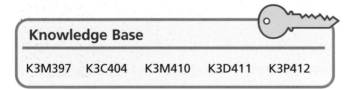

CCLD 312.4
Exchange information and respond to parents' needs and preferences for their babies and children under 3 years

Knowledge Base

K3M397   K3C404   K3M410   K3D411   K3P412

Positive working relationships with parents are essential to provide continuity of care for very young children. Partnership between parents and childcarers depends on regular and open communication where contributions from both parties are acknowledged and valued. Friendly communication on a regular basis ensures continuity and consistency in providing shared routines and timing any necessary changes. Parents and childcarers can keep up to date with what a very young child has learned or is nearly ready to do through regular conversation when they can exchange information and share delight about the child's discoveries and interests. (Lindon, 2002a)

Ensure that you take the time each day to chat briefly with parents when you hand their child back into their care. Keep it short so that the child can interact with the parents as soon as possible. Sort out how you will share more detailed information about the child with the parents, such as keeping a diary or daily log of the child's day including food/drink intake, hours slept, play and early learning activities done and any developmental progress made. You could also make a brief note of any specific plans for the next day, such as reminders about outings (going swimming or to the library). The parents can also use the diary/daily log to share information with you, such as if the child did not sleep well the night before, reminders about immunisations, dental check ups or returning library books. (More detailed information about this is given in Chapter 16.)

Unit Links

For this Unit you also need to understand the following sections:

CCLD 317.1 Liaise with families about their expectations of their child (see Chapter 16)

CCLD 320.1 Implement the requirements of parents in line with current best practice guidance (see Chapter 16)

CCLD 330.3 Establish and maintain systems for the exchange of information with children and families (see Chapter 16)

PORTFOLIO ACTIVITY

Outline the methods you use to exchange information and respond to parents' needs and preferences for their babies and children under 3 years. Include information on: how you discuss preferred care routines; how you document particular requirements; how you share this information with all those involved in a child's care; how you resolve issues relating to parental preferences which are not in line with current best practice.

NVQ LINKS: CCLD 312.4   CCLD 301.4   CCLD 317.1   CCLD 317.2   CCLD 317.3   CCLD 330.3   CCLD 332.1

CCLD 314
Provide physical care that promotes the health and development of babies and children under 3 years

Working in partnership with their parents you should provide physical care that promotes the health and development of babies and children under 3 years. This includes: providing a safe and secure environment for babies and young children; providing for their nutritional needs; supervising and using physical care routines to promote their development; and recognising and responding to illness in babies and young children.

CCLD 314.1
Provide a safe and secure environment for babies and children under 3 years

Knowledge Base

K3S413   K3S414   K3D440   K3S447

It is important that you know, understand and follow the relevant guidelines for ensuring the safety and security of the under-3s set out in *Day care and childminding (National Standards) (England)*

Regulations 2003 and the criteria applicable to your setting (see page 23).

Babies and children under 3 years must never be left unsupervised at any time. Do not leave a baby unattended while changing a nappy, especially if using a changing table as the baby could fall off; and do not leave a young child unattended when playing on large apparatus either indoors or outdoors.

Safety equipment, such as fireguards and radiator guards, should be securely installed to prevent accidental burns. Safety gates should be fitted to restrict very young children's unsupervised access to potentially hazardous areas, including stairs, kitchen, exit to the garden and/or outdoor play area, or external doors. Ensure that safety catches are fitted to doors, windows and cupboards to prevent falls, trapped fingers or access to medicines and hazardous materials. Handles on doors should be at adult height to prevent unsupervised entry or exit; some doors may be fitted with key code pads. Secure arrangements for entry and exit to the childcare premises must also be in place. This could be by entry phone (see below).

Furniture should be the right height and size for very young children; chairs should be low enough for the child to have their feet on the floor with a corresponding table size, that is a height difference of 20cm from seat to tabletop. Ensure that storage is safe, with resources placed near to where they will be used. Have accessible storage, clearly labelled using words and simple pictures with materials that are within easy reach of children. Some storage should be out of children's reach, for example items for adult use only, such as cleaning materials, or to be used under adult direction such as glue or paint.

Only use toys and equipment that are safe and hygienic as well as appropriate for the ages, needs and abilities of the children you work with. Avoid potential slips and falls by ensuring that meal areas and creative/messy play areas have non-slip, easily cleaned floor surfaces with a sink close by. Children should be provided with protective clothing to avoid soiling their clothes during these activities. Examples of suitable clothing include: bibs for babies and toddlers during meal times; aprons during painting, playdough or cooking activities; and waterproof aprons during sand/water play.

Make sure that some play areas are carpeted, especially if you are working with babies who are 'crawlers', as many activities for very young children take place on the floor. Provide boundaries to increase a young child's sense of security. For instance carpets and furniture such as low-level cupboards and shelves can act as room dividers as well as storage. Include boundaries, such as those with handholds for 'cruisers' and toddlers, which will support children's movement around the setting. Ensure boundaries do not interfere with adult supervision; adults must be able to see all the children at all times. Choose moveable room dividers for flexibility so that you can meet very young children's changing needs, preferences and interests.

PORTFOLIO ACTIVITY

Outline your setting's procedures and practices that provide a safe and secure environment for babies and children under 3 years. Include information on: safety checks, including hazard and risk assessment; installation of safety equipment (fireguards, stair gates, safety catches for doors, windows and cupboards and so on); toy safety; staff ratios and adult supervision.

NVQ LINKS: CCLD 314.1 CCLD 302.1
CCLD 302.2 CCLD 306.2

Best practice to prevent cross-infection

Following strict hygiene procedures is essential to prevent cross-infection and potentially very serious illness in the under-3s. Very young children have immature immune systems and so are vulnerable to catching infections. Your setting should have clear procedures for dealing with contagious diseases (chickenpox and measles), throat infections, diarrhoea and vomiting; and include clear guidelines on how to advise parents, for example asking parents to keep children with symptoms away from the setting for at least 24 hours. (See Figure 2.1 *Childhood illnesses* in Chapter 2.) Best practice to prevent cross-infection includes following strict hygiene procedures such as:

◎ Ensure all staff and children always wash their hands carefully with soap and water after nose wiping, after going to the toilet and before handling or eating food
◎ Ensure staff always wash their hands carefully before and after changing a nappy
◎ In group settings, wear a new pair of disposable gloves for each nappy change as well as following the usual hand-washing procedures
◎ Handle children who have diarrhoea carefully and keep them separate from well children; all nappies and soiled clothing should also be kept separate
◎ Do not allow children to attend the setting if they are ill with diarrhoea and vomiting
◎ Take care when children visit farms or come into contact with livestock; staff and children should wear gloves as well as regularly washing their hands, especially before eating; advise children to keep their hands away from their faces
◎ Avoid spreading bacteria in the setting's kitchen by: keeping raw meat and ready-to-eat food separate; never putting cooked meat on a surface or plate that has had raw meat on it; washing hands, surfaces and utensils with hot soapy water after touching raw meat
◎ Ensure that meat is thoroughly cooked before eating
◎ Check that raw fruit and vegetables have been washed thoroughly before consumption.

(Rawstrone, 2006)

Unit Links

For this Unit you also need to understand the following sections:

CCLD 302.3 Supervise procedures for accidents, injuries, illnesses and other emergencies (see Chapter 2)

CCLD 307.2 Plan and provide food and drink to meet the nutritional needs of children (see Chapter 7)

CCLD 314.2 Provide for the nutritional needs of babies and children under 3 years (see below)

Activity

1 Describe the waste disposal systems in your setting.
2 List examples of best practice to prevent cross-infection.

Protecting and safeguarding very young children

Always follow the setting's procedures for handing babies and children under 3 years back to their parents or approved carers, including ensuring the family members concerned are capable of caring for them. Take necessary precautions to safeguard and protect babies and children under 3 years from harm by following the relevant child protection procedures. (There is more information on children's arrival at and departure from the setting in Chapter 2. Detailed information on child protection procedures is given in Chapter 5.)

Unit Links

For this Unit you also need to understand the following sections:

CCLD 302.1 Establish a healthy, safe and secure environment for children (see Chapter 2)

CCLD 305.3 Maintain and follow policies and procedures for protecting and safeguarding children (see Chapter 5)

Check it out

1 What are your setting's procedures for handing young children back to their parents or approved carers?
2 Find out about the child protection procedures applicable to your setting.

CCLD 314.2
Provide for the nutritional needs of babies and children under 3 years

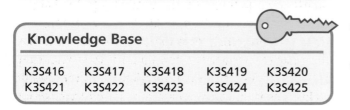

Knowledge Base

K3S416	K3S417	K3S418	K3S419	K3S420
K3S421	K3S422	K3S423	K3S424	K3S425

The parents' decision to breast or bottle-feed their baby may be based on cultural, medical, personal or social factors. Remember that regardless of your personal feelings about breast or formula feeding (see below), the choice must always be the parents' own.

Providing support for breastfeeding mothers

Breastfeeding is excellent for babies. Breast milk contains the perfect balance of nutrients for a baby and also transmits the mother's immunity to certain diseases. Breastfed babies have a lower tendency to develop food allergies, respiratory and gastrointestinal illnesses than formula-fed babies and are less likely to become obese as adults. Depending on your role and the type of setting, you may need to provide support for breastfeeding mothers in line with current best practice, parents' wishes and organisational policy. For example: providing a comfortable, private area for mothers to breastfeed or express milk in a crèche or family centre; or storing and using expressed breast milk to feed babies in a home or nursery setting. When storing and using expressed breast milk remember these important points:

◎ All equipment must be sterilised (see below)
◎ Expressed breast milk must be refrigerated immediately
◎ Bottles should be labelled with the date and the baby's name
◎ Bottles should be stored upright in a refrigerator for up to 24 hours
◎ After 24 hours empty any unused bottles and throw the milk away
◎ Always throw away any milk left over from a feed immediately
◎ Take the bottle from the fridge and warm in jug of hot water just before feeding

◎ Give the baby the bottle (see section on bottle-feeding a baby).

Preparing formula feeds

Preparing formula feeds must be done very carefully to ensure high standards of accuracy and cleanliness. You must make up formula feeds by following the manufacturer's instructions and measuring the formula exactly using the scoop designed for that formula only. **Formula milk which is too strong is very dangerous** as too much formula mix can put a strain on a baby's kidneys, leading to kidney failure and excessive, unhealthy weight gain. Too weak a formula mix may also be dangerous as it can lead to a hungry, distressed baby, poor weight gain, constipation and failure to thrive. The standard method of calculating the amount of formula feed a baby needs is for every 500 g of body weight give 75 ml of made-up formula in 24 hours (or for every lb of body weight give 2.5 fl. oz $\times$ 24 hours). This total quantity is then divided into the number of bottles the baby is likely to be given over the 24-hour period. A newborn or light-for-dates baby usually needs more, smaller feeds per day (often eight bottles) than an older or larger baby (about six bottles). (Childs, 2001; pp. 103–4)

Check it out

Find out which types of formula milk are used for babies in your childcare setting.

Sterilising bottle-feeding equipment

When using bottle-feeding equipment strict hygiene procedures must be followed to prevent any contamination that would endanger babies' health. Bottle-feeding equipment includes: bottles and bottle caps; teats; measuring spoons; plastic knife; plastic jug; bottle brush and teat cleaner; and chemical or steam sterilising unit. Sterilising bottle-feeding equipment involves washing, rinsing, sterilising and storing. Remember the following important points:

◎ Cloths or brushes used must be clean, washed, disinfected and kept solely for this purpose
◎ Work surfaces and utensils must be cleaned with very hot, soapy water
◎ Bottles, teats and other equipment must be thoroughly cleaned in hot water with detergent
◎ A bottle brush, used only for this purpose, must be used for the inside of bottles
◎ Teats must be rubbed inside and out [using a teat cleaner] and water squeezed through the feeding hole; never use salt to clean teats
◎ All equipment must be rinsed thoroughly under a running tap
◎ All traces of detergent must be removed.

(Childs, 2001; p. 105)

Bottle-feeding babies

While bottle-feeding a baby with either breast or formula milk, you need to listen and observe the baby carefully. If the baby makes a lot of noisy sucking sounds while drinking, they may be taking in too much air. To help the baby swallow less air, hold them at a 45 degree angle and tilt the bottle so that the teat and neck are always filled with formula (or breast milk). You must *never* leave a baby to feed unattended by propping the bottle up as the baby could choke. In addition, holding a baby during bottle-feeding provides invaluable opportunities for the baby to interact and form a positive relationship with the childcarer. In consultation with parents (and colleagues if you work in a group setting) you should have an agreed routine for bottle-feeding so that all individuals who feed a baby follow the same pattern to ensure continuity and security for the baby. When bottle-feeding a baby ensure that you follow a routine. See below

Procedure for sterilising and storing equipment

1 Fill the steriliser with cold water.
2 Following the manufacturers' instructions and dosage, add the chemical sterilising solution (tablets or liquid). If it is in tablet form ensure that it dissolves completely before continuing.
3 Place the bottles, teats and other equipment into the steriliser.
4 Check everything is well submerged, all bottles and containers are fully filled and there are no bubbles trapped.
5 Leave in the liquid for the time specified in the manufacturers' instructions.
6 Remove items from the solution and rinse carefully with boiled water to remove all traces of the chemicals.
7 Sterilised bottles and equipment can be stored in the emptied steriliser after it has been rinsed with boiled water.
8 Bottles and teats should be drained but not dried inside with a cloth.
9 The length of time sterilised equipment may be stored varies according to the method used; read and follow the manufacturers' guidance.
10 Note: instead of a chemical steriliser your setting may use a commercial steam steriliser; ensure that you follow the manufacturers' instructions carefully.

(Childs, 2001; pp. 105–6)

Routine for bottle-feeding a baby

1 Wash your hands thoroughly.
2 Prepare all the items you need for the baby and the feed before picking them up, for example collect the bib and tissues; cover the bottle with a cloth; stand the bottle in a jug of hot water to keep it warm; and place all items in the feeding area so they are accessible.
3 Change the baby's nappy and make them comfortable. Wash your hands.
4 Settle yourself comfortably, making sure your lower back, shoulders and the arm holding the baby are well supported.
5 Hold the baby securely in a cuddle. Spend time talking and responding to the baby. Engage and keep eye contact with the baby. Make this time relaxing, calm and enjoyable.
6 Talk to and smile at the baby as you proceed with the feeding.
7 Lift the bottle from the jug and wipe the outside to prevent drips.

8 Check the teat size by inverting the bottle. The milk should freely drip out, a few drops every second.

9 Test the milk temperature by dropping a little milk onto the inside of your wrist.

10 Touch the baby's lips to stimulate the rooting reflex and as baby seeks it place the teat into the baby's mouth over the tongue.

11 Keep a gentle tension on the teat to keep the baby sucking.

12 During feeding check there is always milk in the teat. An empty teat causes the baby to suck air and become frustrated and tired.

13 After about 10 minutes remove the teat and make the baby upright. Gently rub her/his back or apply very gentle pressure to the stomach. This will help to release any wind trapped there.

14 Finish feeding and let her/his wind come up again at the end.

15 If necessary change the nappy again and settle baby comfortably when you are both ready.

16 Clear the feeding area. Wash equipment carefully and sterilise it again so it will be ready for giving more formula or cooled boiled water.

(Childs, 2001; pp. 108–9)

Weaning

Weaning means 'to accustom a baby to take food other than milk'. It is the process of expanding a baby's diet to include foods and drinks in addition to breast or formula milk. In 2001 the World Health Organisation (WHO) recommended exclusive breastfeeding for the first six months of a baby's life. Following this recommendation the Department of Health reviewed its guidance on the introduction of solid food. The DH recommendations on feeding babies include:

◎ Breast milk is the best form of nutrition for babies as it provides all the nutrients a baby needs for healthy growth and development

◎ Exclusive breastfeeding is recommended for the first six months of a baby's life

◎ Six months is the recommended age for introducing solid foods to babies

◎ Breastfeeding (and/or breast milk substitutes, if used) should continue beyond the first six months along with appropriate types and amounts of solid foods

◎ Introducing solids before sufficient development of the neuro-muscular co-ordination or before the guts and kidneys have matured can increase the risk of infections and development of allergies such as asthma and eczema

◎ All babies are individuals and require a flexible approach to optimise their nutritional needs; mothers should be supported in their choice of infant feeding

◎ Parents should be advised of the risks associated with weaning before the neuro-muscular co-ordination has developed sufficiently to allow the infant to eat solids

◎ If a baby shows signs of being ready to start solid foods before six months (sitting up, taking an interest in what the family is eating, picking up and tasting finger foods) then they should be encouraged, but not before four months.

(DH, 2003b)

The Committee on Medical Aspects of Food Policy (COMA) Report *Weaning and the Weaning Diet* (1994) which provides advice about the types of solid foods to introduce from the age of six months still applies: fruit; vegetables; potatoes (including sweet potatoes); cereals such as rice, oats, semolina, cornmeal; finger foods such as bread, toast and pasta; meat (beef, pork, lamb); poultry (chicken, turkey); fish (cod, salmon, tuna); eggs; and pulses (beans, peas, lentils, dahl); full fat custard, fromage frais and yogurt. The following foods should be given only in limited amounts from six months: salty foods such as cheese, bacon, sausages; highly processed foods such as breakfast cereals or pasta sauces. Mild spices such as cinnamon, coriander and cumin may be used sparingly in the preparation of meals. Cow's milk can be used to make custard or cheese/white sauce.

The following foods should be avoided from six months: added salt (do not cook with salt or serve with food); added sugar; honey (safe to introduce after 12 months); soft cheese including blue cheese (safe after 12 months); hot spices such as black pepper and chilli powder may be gradually introduced after 12 months. Parents who choose to introduce solid foods from four months should avoid giving their babies wheat-based foods and foods containing gluten such as bread, flour, breakfast cereals and rusks. (SNDRI, 2006)

Providing a healthy, nutritious and varied diet for young children

Childhood is a time of rapid growth, development and activity so it is essential to provide children with a healthy, nutritious and varied diet. Healthy tooth development and the prevention of tooth decay are also important. Eating habits are formed during the first few years of life so it is important to establish healthy eating patterns for children, in both the home and childcare settings. (See CCLD 307.2 in Chapter 7 for more information on healthy eating including special dietary requirements.)

When providing food for young children remember that:

◎ Their appetites may vary on a daily basis and from one meal to the next
◎ They are very active and have high energy (calorie) and nutrient needs in proportion to their small body size
◎ They have small stomachs and may be physically unable to eat large meals
◎ Each day children need three meals plus snacks based on nutritious foods
◎ They also need adequate quantities of fluids throughout the day
◎ They need fat as a concentrated source of calories so full fat spreads and whole milk dairy products are recommended
◎ Low fat 'healthy eating' advice (and products) are not suitable for young children
◎ Children do not need sugar and sugary foods (sweets, chocolate, soft drinks, honey or jam) for energy. Remember sugar may also appear on food labels as sucrose, glucose, fructose, dextrose, syrup
◎ Starchy foods (bread, breakfast cereals, potatoes, pasta and rice) are better sources of energy as they contain other important nutrients
◎ Snacks and drinks taken between meals should be sugar-free to prevent tooth decay
◎ Frequent consumption of sugar and sugary foods between meals causes tooth decay
◎ If taken, sugary foods and drinks should be kept to main mealtimes
◎ A nutrient-rich pudding should be offered each day, preferably based on milk and fruit (fresh, stewed or tinned)

◎ Young children should be given some fibre-rich foods but a mixture of both white and wholemeal varieties of bread, pasta and breakfast cereals is more suitable for the under-5s

◎ Between 2–5 years of age children can be gradually encouraged to move towards a diet that is lower in fat and higher in fibre

◎ Dry, unprocessed bran should never be used as it can cause bloating, wind, loss of appetite and reduce absorption of important nutrients

◎ There is no need to add salt to food either in cooking or at the table as there is enough present in the food we eat; salty snacks such as crisps should be limited

◎ It is recommended that peanuts and peanut products (peanut butter) are not provided in childcare settings to protect children who may be at risk of peanut allergy.

(HPA, 2001)

PORTFOLIO ACTIVITY

Give examples of how you provide for the nutritional needs of babies and children under 3 years in your setting. Include information on: supporting breastfeeding mothers; preparing formula feeds; sterilising bottle-feeding equipment; bottle-feeding babies; weaning; providing a healthy, nutritious and varied diet for young children; special dietary requirements.

NVQ LINKS: CCLD 314.2   CCLD 307.2

CCLD 314.3
Supervise and use physical care routines to promote development

Knowledge Base

K3D426	K3D427	K3S428	K3S429	K3D430
K3D431	K3D432	K3D438	K3D439	

Providing physical care during routines is central to a well-rounded day for the under-3s. Very young children are ready to learn from any part of their day including daily routines. Physical care routines should not be hurried through in order to get on with other activities that are considered to be 'early learning'. Use these routines to promote very young children's development and learning by valuing physical care routines and resisting the temptation to rush through routines or pay them scant attention. Through affectionate and respectful touch you can demonstrate to very young children that you care *about* them as well as care *for* them. They feel secure and cherished by respectful physical care. As they grow, they begin to develop independence by sharing in their own care including dressing, feeding, toileting and looking after their environment. Routines also help children to develop: physical skills; communication skills; simple forward planning; understanding a sequence; simple time management; practising numbers when laying the table; and sharing and co-operating. (Lindon, 2002a)

Routines make up an essential part of the day for all children. It is important that routines (mealtimes, nap times, nappy changing or toileting, and so on) provide valuable opportunities for very young children to develop and learn as well as to interact positively with others. Establishing routines involves providing physical care to help maintain children's safety and security. You need to establish carefully structured routines based on a sound knowledge of the children as individuals, the requirements of the setting and the wishes of the children's parents. When establishing routines, consider the children's ages and levels of development as well as their individual needs, interests and preferences. When supervising and using physical care routines to promote development remember to:

◎ Talk, sing, smile and make eye contact with the children during care routines

◎ Use an affectionate, respectful and unhurried approach to care routines

◎ Use your knowledge of the children's personal preferences, such as how a baby likes to be held when being given a bottle, a child's favourite cup and cutlery, and so on

◎ Allow the children to be independent and practise new skills as appropriate to their ages and levels of development, such as putting on their own coat or doing up buttons

◎ Involve the children in everyday tasks, for example making a snack or setting and clearing the table (remember safety)

◎ Identify learning and development opportunities within daily routines

◎ Provide opportunities for sensory exploration during care routines

◎ Use finger rhymes, songs and simple games to make routines interesting and fun

◎ Encourage very young children to exercise, develop mobility and explore their surroundings safely.

Remember to talk to and communicate with parents to update them on their child's development, progress and achievements.

For the first week(s) in a new setting (or with a new childcarer) it is essential to maintain the very young child's usual daily routine as far as possible, in order to provide the child with the consistency and security of having a recognised pattern to the day. Very young children dislike changes or disruption to

their routines so it is especially important to maintain these during transitional periods. Try to keep to the child's regular routines including feeding/mealtimes, nappy changing/toileting, bath-time, naps and/or bedtime if applicable. You should get some idea of the child's usual daily routine on the first day (if not before) and make sure that you adhere to it; try not to establish any new routines during the settling in period – the child has enough to cope with in getting used to a new setting, or childcarer, without changes to the routine as well. Do not worry if the child is reluctant to spend time with you or to participate in routines and activities. Remember, it takes time for very young children to adjust to having someone new looking after them. (See CCLD 314.4 for more information on transitions and very young children.)

Before or during the first week of caring for a very young child the parent can provide you with essential information about the child's usual routine including mealtimes, sleeping patterns, and so on, as well as the child's likes and dislikes regarding food, clothes, toys and activities. Check that during the first week you: make a list of contact numbers for emergencies (the parents' home, work and mobile telephone numbers, the child's GP address and telephone number); make sure you know about any special medical needs and/or special dietary requirements the child may have; make a note of the child's usual daily routine (mealtimes, nap times, and so on); and ensure you know and understand what your exact duties and responsibilities are in respect of providing physical care for this particular child.

Routines are especially important during periods of change (or transitions) such as: getting used to a new member of staff; moving to a different group within the same setting; moving to a different setting; dealing with the arrival of a new brother or sister; visiting the doctor, dentist or hospital; and experiencing family separation, bereavement or serious illness. You may need to adapt the children's routines or establish new ones as the children grow and develop. For example, a nappy changing routine will eventually become a toileting routine (see below). Be consistent in your introduction of any new routines, as this will help the children to adjust to any changes more easily.

Mealtimes

You will need to follow any parental instructions regarding a baby's feeding times or a young child's mealtime routine. If the child already has an established routine then you should follow that. Sometimes the parents of a baby or young child may want you to help establish a regular bottle-feeding or mealtime routine. Remember that not everyone has the same diet. You need to talk to the family about which foods are appropriate and which are not. Most young children prefer plain and familiar food they can eat with their fingers, but they also need opportunities to develop the skills of using a spoon, fork and then knife. Encourage children to use safe, child-sized versions of these as appropriate to their age, level of development and culture.

Nappy changing

Changing a very young child's nappies frequently is essential. Expect to change a nappy before or after each feed and when the child has had a bowel movement. This will usually be several times daily as babies urinate as often as every one to three hours. Make sure you use the correct size nappies for the age and weight of the child. Before you change the baby ensure that you have everything you need nearby: a clean nappy; nappy wipes or cotton balls and warm water; safety pins, if you are using cloth

nappies; nappy cream if the baby has nappy rash; a change of clothing in case the old nappy has leaked; a diversion, for example change the baby under a mobile or give them a soft toy to play with. *Never* leave the baby unattended to fetch something you have forgotten. You must follow your setting's procedures for waste disposal to prevent cross-infection.

Toilet training

Toilet training is a huge milestone in the very young child's development and most parents cannot wait for the time their child is ready to start this. However, few parents are prepared for how long the process can take. Some very young children get the hang of it within a few days but for most children it

PORTFOLIO ACTIVITY

1 Observe a child during a mealtime or snack time routine within your setting.

2 Include the following information in your assessment: the type of routine observed; the intended learning goals/objectives for the child; the actual development and learning skills demonstrated by the child; the child's behaviour during the routine; the child's language and communication skills; and suggestions for extending the child's development and learning in this area.

3 Use relevant sections from this chapter (and childcare, education or psychology books) to help you with your assessment.

4 Remember to follow your setting's guidelines for child observation.

NVQ LINKS: CCLD 314.3   CCLD 314.2
CCLD 307.2   CCLD 303.1   CCLD 303.2

takes several months. You can help the process of toilet training run more smoothly for the child (and the parents) if you know the basics of toilet training and can make this process clear to the child.

Potty training

Start by getting the child to sit fully clothed on a potty once a day, for example after breakfast, before a bath or whenever they are likely to have a bowel movement. This helps the child to get used to the potty and to accept it as part of their daily routine. Do not worry if the child does not want to sit on the potty. You should never physically restrain the child or physically force them to sit on the potty, especially if the child appears frightened. Put the potty away and try again in a few weeks' time.

Encourage the child to use the potty whenever they feel the urge to go. Ensure the child knows that they can tell you when they want to use the potty and that you will take them to the setting's toilet area or bathroom when necessary. Remind the child at regular intervals through the day that the potty is there if they need it. If you work in a family setting and have the family's permission, let the child play without a nappy, say in the garden, with the potty nearby. Ensure the potty is always in a convenient place; as a potty is portable, it can be used not just in the bathroom but also in the garden or playroom.

In accordance with the parents' wishes, the child could wear training pants, especially when travelling or away from the setting on outings, for example. Some children like wearing training pants and they may help with potty training. However, others treat training pants as a nappy, which defeats the objective of potty training. Wearing real underwear instead encourages some young children to use the potty. Dress the child in clothing with elastic waistbands that the child can remove independently.

All young children will have several toileting 'accidents' before they are completely potty trained during the day and at night. Never get angry or punish children when they have 'accidents'; instead, calmly clean it up and suggest that next time the child tries using the potty instead. Always have spare clothes for children in case of such 'accidents' and remember to take extra clothes when taking the children on outings. Most children will have 'accidents' for up to six months after they are potty trained. If the child has more 'accidents' than successful experiences of using the potty, they are probably not ready for potty training. Try again in a few weeks. If the child is experiencing a major transition, such as getting used to a new setting or childcarer, moving to a new home or getting used to a new baby in the family, you should wait until the situation has settled before resuming (or starting) potty training. If you are concerned that something else may be causing the child to have difficulties with potty training, talk to the child's parents and suggest they discuss this with the child's health visitor or GP. If you suspect that the child's difficulties may be related to abuse then you must follow your setting's child protection procedures.

Unit Links

For this Unit you also need to understand the following section:

CCLD 305.3 Maintain and follow policies and procedures for protecting and safeguarding children (see Chapter 5)

Using an adult-sized toilet

Using an adult-sized toilet is a necessary social skill that most children develop some time around their third year. While playgroups, nurseries and schools have child-sized toilets, those in family homes have been designed for adults. If you work in a family setting (as a childminder, home-based carer or nanny) then you will need to assist young children in making the transition from using a potty to an adult-sized. You can make this easier by using a child seat fitted securely over the adult toilet and a box or step for the child to use to get onto the toilet and to rest their feet on once sitting on the toilet. As with potty training, learning to use an adult-sized toilet takes time, understanding and patience. The most important thing to remember is not to rush children into using the toilet. Remember to: teach the child good personal hygiene procedures (washing their hands after going to the toilet); continue dressing the child in clothing with elastic waistbands that the child can remove independently; keep the toilet experience positive and relaxed and praise the child when they are successful; handle any toileting 'accidents' in a calm and sensitive manner; reassure the child that they have done nothing wrong; and have extra clothes available in the setting and when going on outings.

Rest and sleep

Most babies and young children need lots of sleep. However, every child is different so some children will need more or less sleep than others.

Nap times

Nap time can present some challenging moments. The routine can either convey warmth and security or stress and turmoil to very young children. You cannot make a child sleep during the day, but you can create a relaxed and quiet rest time. Most under-3s need to lie down and relax during the day. However, some children may have trouble settling down at nap time for a variety of reasons, including a transition or crisis in their lives, excitement about a special event or they may simply have outgrown the need for a daytime sleep. For these children you should still aim to create a restful mood at nap time by reading quietly, playing soothing music or doing quiet activities such as completing a jigsaw.

Bedtime routines

If you work as a nanny or home childcarer and depending on the hours you work, you may well be involved in young children's bedtime routines. For example, as a live-in nanny caring for a young child whose usual bedtime is 7.00 pm but whose parents do not get back from work until 8.00 pm on some nights, you may be responsible for carrying out the whole of the bedtime routine. Some parents may want you to bathe the child and get them ready for bed, but prefer to put the child to bed themselves so that they can share a special time with their child to talk about the child's day, read stories and/or sing songs. Even if you work as a daily nanny, you will still have some babysitting duties and this will often include bathing and putting the child to bed.

You will need to follow any parental instructions regarding the child's bedtime routine. If the child already has established one, then you should follow that. Sometimes the parents of a baby or young child may want you to help to establish a regular bedtime routine.

Bedtime routines are an important part of a child's sleeping habits. A consistent and short routine lets the child know that bedtime is approaching and it also helps to relax them for bed. The bedtime routine needs to be carried out at the same time each evening and should be similar each night. Ensure it is a pleasurable experience by giving the child plenty of time and attention. A typical bedtime routine could be:

◎ Play a quiet game
◎ Bathe or wash, put on pyjamas and brush teeth
◎ Use the potty or toilet (whichever is appropriate)
◎ Say goodnight to everyone and get into bed
◎ Have a chat about the day's events
◎ Adult reads a short story
◎ Tuck the child in and say goodnight
◎ Adult leaves the room and the child settles to sleep.

(See important information about sudden infant death syndrome on page 225.)

Bath time

Although some parents like their babies to have a bath every day, until the baby is crawling around and getting into things a bath is really necessary only once or twice a week. (Just wash their face/hands frequently and thoroughly clean the genital area after each nappy change.) Most babies and young children find bath time very soothing and relaxing. If the baby or child really enjoys this routine (and the parents wish it) you can give them a daily bath. This can be fun for you and the child, but you must always remember safety.

Bath time safety

Always remember these important bath time safety tips:

1 *Never* leave the child unsupervised, even for a minute. Children can drown in less than an inch of water in less than 60 seconds. If someone knocks at the door or the phone rings, ignore it – if it is important they will call back.
2 *Never* put the child into a bath when the water is still running as the water temperature could change or the depth could become too high.

3 Make the bath safe by putting in a rubber bathmat and covering the taps.
4 Make sure the bath water is comfortably warm (about 32–35°C). Children generally prefer a much cooler bath than adults do.
5 Fill the bath with only 5–7.5 centimetres (2–3 inches) of water for babies up to 6 months old, and never more than waist-high (in a sitting position) for older children.
6 Teach the child to sit in the bath at all times.
7 Do not allow the child to touch the taps. Even if they cannot turn them on now, they will be strong enough to do so soon and that could lead to serious injury.

PORTFOLIO ACTIVITY

Describe how you have provided physical care for a baby or young child, for example outline the daily routines for the baby or young child. Include the following: consulting the child's parents about the child's usual routines including special dietary requirements, special medical needs (allergies), likes and dislikes; a plan or timetable of the child's routines and activities; feeding or mealtime routine including menus; nappy changing or toilet training routine; bath time and/or bedtime routine if applicable; and your role and responsibilities (as the key person) for providing physical care to promote the health and development of the child.

NVQ LINKS:　CCLD 314.1　CCLD 314.2
CCLD 314.3　CCLD 314.4　CCLD 302.2
CCLD 303.3　CCLD 306.4　CCLD 307.1
CCLD 307.2　CCLD 308.4　CCLD 312.2
CCLD 312.3　CCLD 312.4　CCLD 330.1

CCLD 314.4
Provide an emotionally secure and consistent environment

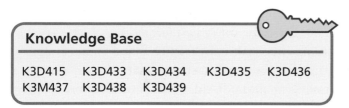

Knowledge Base

| K3D415 | K3D433 | K3D434 | K3D435 | K3D436 |
| K3M437 | K3D438 | K3D439 | | |

Attachment theory and the effects of separation

John Bowlby's theory was that to ensure a child's mental health the child required a continuous relationship with *one* mother or mother-substitute. If not, the child would be psychologically damaged by the deprivation experienced. Bowlby believed there was a parallel between the animal instinct for *imprinting* and the human need for *attachment* between mother and child. This belief was a firm foundation of Bowlby's theory of maternal deprivation. An important concept in this theory is attachment theory which suggests that the mother-baby attachment is unique and unlike any other relationship the child may have with another person. This instinctive attachment which a child has to one mother figure is described as monotropism.

Bowlby's theories have been strongly criticised, as children are able to form many attachments and distinct relationships with other family members and day care staff. The term maternal deprivation has been described as unsatisfactory. Michael Rutter disagrees with the term maternal deprivation as stated by Bowlby because children can experience deprivation in other ways, not just through separation from their mothers; children can also experience maternal deprivation within the family setting even if the mother is actually present. (Rutter, 1991) Instead Rutter prefers these definitions of deprivation:

◎ *Privation*: the child has no opportunity to form secure attachments/relationships

◎ *Disruption*: the child experiences broken attachments/relationships due to death or other separation
◎ *Distortion*: the child experiences distorted family relationships due to marital discord, inconsistent treatment or any form of abuse.

According to Bowlby, separation from their mothers causes intense distress in very young children, particularly in the critical period between the ages of 7 months and 3 years. This distress sets up a cycle of events. Following reunion with their mothers, detachment may continue, leading to babies experiencing contradictory feelings towards their mothers, alternating between being clingy and hostile. Bowlby believed that continued and persistent periods of this sort of separation caused permanent psychological damage.

Although young children do experience distress when first separating from their mother when starting nursery or school, it is short-lived and has no lasting effect on children's psychological development. Long-term effects *have* been found in children in residential care; teachers' reports indicate behavioural problems in such children with effects including extreme need for adult attention and difficulties in making friendships with peers. (Tizard, 1991)

These effects can also be apparent in young children who have been mothered at home where they are used to one-to-one with their mother and so sometimes find it difficult to be a part of a group, for example in nursery or school. Research shows that children who have attended nursery/playgroup or been cared for by a relative/childminder before they start school are often: more independent; better able to interact with their peers; more willing to share and co-operate with other children; more sociable towards unfamiliar people; and less timid or shy. However, there was no difference in the percentage of behavioural difficulties between children cared for by their mothers and children who have attended day care prior to nursery or school. (Tizard, 1991)

Bowlby's theory suggests that any family, no matter how 'bad', provides children with the care they need so that they do not experience maternal deprivation; children in 'good' residential care do less well than children in 'bad' homes. Rutter suggests that children in 'bad' families are suffering distortion; the children are still experiencing deprivation even though they remain in the family setting. Children can experience violence, cruelty or neglect at the hands of their mothers (and fathers); many children can and do receive better care away from their biological parents in foster homes, small residential homes or with adoptive parents.

The social and cultural context

The theory of maternal deprivation is related to social, cultural and even political ideas. Bowlby's theory of maternal deprivation was established in the 1950s following post-World War 2 anxieties concerning the care of children in residential nurseries. His theory may also have been politically motivated by the fact that when men returned from the war they wanted the jobs back that had been done by women during the war. Many women had enjoyed being part of the workforce and were reluctant to give up their freedom and status. Women were made to feel guilty about going out to work; the theory of maternal deprivation effectively blackmailed them into staying at home for the sake of their children's psychological well-being.

In the UK today, women are still viewed as children's primary caregivers. Mothers who work are seen by some as not being maternal, especially if their children are under 5 years old (Stoppard, 1990). Some people still feel that mothers should stay at

home and not go out to work. Children do not have to be cared for solely by their mothers; there is strong cross-cultural evidence that a child can make strong and secure attachments with five or more 'caretakers' (Woodhead, 1991). Bowlby himself recognised that the *amount* of time children spend with their mothers is not the crucial factor; it is the *quality* of the time spent together, not the *quantity*. *Quality* is also the key factor in children's other attachments. There is no evidence that quality day care has a detrimental effect on young children and it is unlikely that young children will suffer psychological damage because their mothers work (Tizard, 1991). Recent research suggests that mothers should stay at home or work only part-time until their children are 18 months old as employment started after a child is 18 months, or part-time work at any time, has no negative effects; also, young children have better cognitive outcomes when cared for by paid, qualified childcarers rather than by unpaid carers (such as a friend, relative or neighbour), especially if their mothers work full-time. (Gregg et al., 2005)

Transitions and very young children

The first days (or even weeks) that young children spend in a new setting, situation or with a new carer require a sensitive approach from the adult(s) caring for them. This enables young children to cope with the separation from their parents and to adjust to any new routines and/or people. (For more information on preparing children for transfer or transition and twelve ways to help children adjust to the childcare setting see Unit CCLD 325 in Chapter 10.)

Transition objects

A transition object is a comfort object that a baby or young child uses to provide reassurance and security when separated from a parent. The child feels connected to the parent by holding, cuddling, stroking or sucking the object. Transition objects are usually something soft like a small blanket, muslin cloth or cuddly toy such as a teddy bear.

Transition objects provide a link between the very young child and the absent parent that enables the child to feel more secure in new situations without the parent or with a new carer. Reliance on a comfort object does not mean the child is insecure or too dependent on the parent. It may actually enable the child to become more independent and secure, as they have the object to reassure them in their parent's absence. A young child *without* a comfort object may not have this reassurance or feeling of security.

Some young children have their comfort object with them at all times; some just at bedtime, during naps or to relax with when they need a break; others only when entering new situations such as visiting GP, clinic or hospital, starting nursery or playgroup. A strong attachment to a comfort object usually begins in a child's first year and often increases between the ages of 1 to 2 years. By the time a child is 3 to 4 years old the need for their comfort object usually lessens. Many children are less attached to their comfort object by the time they start school. A child may continue to need a comfort object for the occasional snuggle when they are very tired or distressed until they are teenagers. There is no set age for giving up a comfort object.

Bottles should not be used as comfort objects because they are unhygienic (bacteria in milk kept for too long), prolonged contact with teeth can lead to dental decay and can contribute to problems with the child's bite. Dummies can be acceptable as comfort objects if well-kept (they are no less hygienic than thumb sucking) but you should discourage prolonged use as this can restrict the child's communication. Comfort habits include thumb sucking and twiddling/sucking hair. These can be difficult to stop as the comfort 'object' is with the child for ever!

One of your first priorities is to meet the individual needs of the child, so if the child feels more emotionally secure, reassured and relaxed due to the presence of a comfort object then you should accommodate it. Attitudes towards transition/comfort objects or habits vary between individuals, so discuss the parents' wishes regarding the child's comfort object. Remember:

◎ Allow a baby or young child to have free access to their comfort object at all times as this can assist their sense of security, especially during transitional periods
◎ Separation from a comfort object (to participate in messy activities or mealtimes) must be done gently; it is the most precious thing the child has
◎ Comfort objects are usually irreplaceable so check with parents that a replacement or substitute is available if the worst happens
◎ Let the child decide when a comfort object is no longer necessary
◎ An older child may need access to a comfort object while experiencing exceptional distress on separating from parents or where other factors make this necessary, for example special needs such as emotional or behavioural difficulties
◎ With an older child (as their confidence in being with you increases) set time limits as to when they can have their comfort object, for example they can have it at bedtime or when the child is ill, distressed or has an accident
◎ Anything that makes transitions (such as comfort objects) easier for young children should be regarded in a positive way.

The role of the key person

Quality childcare provision for very young children can be delivered only through a caring, personal relationship between the baby or young child and the childcarer. In group settings such as a crèche or day nursery a key person (or keyworker) system is essential to provide links between individual childcare practitioners and individual children. The key features of an effective key person system are:

◎ The same practitioner is responsible for the physical needs of a very small number of individual babies and toddlers as very young children need to be able to recognise the face of the person who changes them, feeds them or to whom they wake from a nap

◎ The key person responds sensitively to individual babies and toddlers, knows their preferences and develops personal rituals of songs, smiles and enjoyable 'jokes'

◎ The key person develops a friendly relationship with the child's parent(s), sharing ideas about the very young child and communicating important information about the day or the child's state of health

◎ The key person observes, assesses and records the learning and development of their key children.

(Lindon, 2002a)

A meaningful relationship with a key person enables very young children to form a secure attachment to the adult. This relationship and attachment to a key person provides an excellent context in which the

child can feel safe to express and make sense of their emotions (Gillespie Edwards, 2002; p. 12). *The Early Years Foundation Stage,* the proposed new framework for 0 to 5 year olds, also emphasises the importance of a key person as one of its underpinning principles: 'the importance of a key person for each child in each setting, to ensure their well-being, so that they develop independence by having someone they can depend upon.' (DfES, 2006a; p. 3)

Behaviour guidelines for babies

Babies have limited comprehension and communication skills so negotiating goals and boundaries for behaviour is not possible because they cannot understand what is required or be reasoned with. You can demonstrate what behaviour is required by providing a positive role model for behaviour. Babies are not deliberately 'naughty' so sanctions or punishments for unwanted behaviour are not appropriate. Babies may display 'difficult' behaviour such as persistent crying, being irritable or unco-operative because these are the only ways they have to communicate they are feeling hungry, tired, ill, anxious or frustrated. You can establish the foundations of future rules for behaviour by:

◎ Being calm; do not get annoyed with babies' behaviour

◎ Praising and rewarding desired behaviour; ignore unwanted behaviour

◎ Giving the baby appropriate care and adult assistance

PORTFOLIO ACTIVITY

Describe how you provide an emotionally secure and consistent environment for very young children. Include information on: recognising and responding promptly to signs of emotional distress; using different techniques to calm, reassure and distract individual babies and children who are distressed; acknowledging and communicating respect for the very young children's feelings; encouraging parents to share information that may affect children's emotional security; and reassuring parents of the confidentiality of any personal information they share.

NVQ LINKS: CCLD 314.1   CCLD 314.3   CCLD 314.4   CCLD 301.1   CCLD 301.4   CCLD 306.3
CCLD 308.2   CCLD 308.4   CCLD 312.2   CCLD 312.4   CCLD 325.1   CCLD 325.2

◎ Making potentially difficult situations more fun by using games and rhymes during routines such as mealtimes, nappy changing, dressing, and so on

◎ Being positive! Try not to say 'Don't ...' or 'No' too often

◎ Using diversionary tactics such as removing the baby from the situation or removing the object from the baby's reach

◎ Not forcing the baby to behave in certain ways. For example, aggressive adult behaviour such as shouting only frightens babies and does not change their behaviour

◎ Never using physical punishment such as smacking, shaking, and so on as this can cause serious or even fatal injuries to a baby. In any case such punishment does not work; babies have no understanding of what they are being 'punished' for.

As babies develop they become more independent. But because they still lack the communication skills to express their needs effectively and are often frustrated by their lack of physical skills to do what they want, they demonstrate this through challenging behaviour such as refusing adult's choices of food, clothing and activities; asserting their likes and dislikes; or starting to have frequent emotional outbursts or 'temper tantrums'.

Behaviour guidelines for toddlers

Adults need to have realistic expectations for very young children and accept that certain types of behaviour are characteristic of the under-3s. For example, toddlers may be: attention-seeking as they dislike being ignored so will interrupt adults; very sensitive to changes and become upset if separated from parent or carer; very active and keen to explore their environment; unaware of potential dangers; unable to respect the possessions of others; stubborn and insist on having their own way; easily frustrated and prone to emotional outbursts; or unpredictable and contrary, with changeable behaviour.

The behaviour guidelines for babies also apply to toddlers, but 1-2 year olds also need a positive framework for behaviour. You can encourage a toddler to behave in socially acceptable ways through: positive interaction with adults (and older children); opportunities for channelling their frustration through play; diversions to distract the child from unwanted behaviour; and clear and consistent guidelines about what is and is not acceptable behaviour.

(See Chapter 1 for information on recognising and dealing with feelings; there is more information

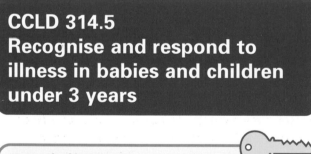

Unit Links

For this Unit you also need to understand the following sections:

CCLD 301.1 Develop relationships with children (see Chapter 1)

CCLD 308.1 Enable children to relate to others (see Chapter 10)

CCLD 337.2 Promote positive aspects of behaviour (see Chapter 9)

PORTFOLIO ACTIVITY

Describe how you communicate boundaries and limits of acceptable behaviour to very young children. Include information on: dealing with feelings and children's emotional outbursts; encouraging children to express their feelings in ways that help them manage their emotions; and praising and rewarding children's efforts and achievements.

NVQ LINKS: CCLD 314.4 CCLD 301.1 CCLD 301.3 CCLD 308.1 CCLD 308.2 CCLD 308.4 CCLD 337.1 CCLD 337.2

about promoting positive behaviour in Chapter 9; and dealing with emotional outbursts is covered in Chapter 10.)

CCLD 314.5
Recognise and respond to illness in babies and children under 3 years

Knowledge Base

K3S441 K3S442 K3S444 K3S445 K3S446 K3S448

To provide physical care that promotes the health and development of very young children you must be able to recognise and respond to illness in babies and children under 3 years of age.

It can be difficult to work out what is wrong with very young children, especially if they cannot tell you about their symptoms. Sometimes illness may appear as changes in the child's usual behaviour, perhaps by not eating as usual, being quiet or not as lively as usual. A child's normal temperature may fluctuate between 36°C and 37.5°C (97.5°F and 99.5°F). You will usually be able to tell if a child is feverish by looking at them but you should still take the child's temperature with a thermometer. However, do not rely on the temperature reading as the only sign of a child's possible ill health, as children can be very ill with no fever or quite well with a high temperature. Physical warning signs of illness in babies and children under 3 years include:

◎ The child is obviously ill and has a temperature above 38°C (100°F)

◎ There are no apparent signs of illness but the temperature rises above 39.4°C (103°F)

◎ A high fever that drops then rises again

- High temperature accompanied by infantile convulsions
- A stiff neck and headache as well as a fever
- A temperature of more than 38°C (100°F) for three days
- Skin feels cold and the child is drowsy, unusually quiet and limp, though face, hands and feet are pink (possible hypothermia)
- Feels sick and dizzy and complains of headaches
- Complains of blurred vision, especially after being hit on the head
- Has severe griping pains at regular intervals
- A pain on right side of stomach and feels sick
- Breathing becomes laboured and you notice that the child's ribs are being drawn sharply inwards with each breath
- Loss of appetite if the child usually eats well or is under 6 months
- Diarrhoea and/or violent, prolonged or excessive vomiting; very young babies can rapidly become dehydrated
- Diarrhoea accompanied by abdominal pain, temperature or any obvious illness.

(Stoppard, 1990)

As well as recognising the behaviour changes and physical signs of illness in the under-3s you must fully understand and follow the policy and procedures of your setting for the care and treatment of very young children who are ill, including: managing the symptoms of illness in the under-3s calmly and effectively whilst they are in your care; informing parents of their child's illness sensitively and at the earliest opportunity, giving details of any care or treatment given; and seeking medical assistance for those who become acutely ill whilst in your care. Make sure that you have up-to-date training in first aid for babies and children as emergency resuscitation is different for very young children. (For detailed information on dealing with common childhood illnesses and allergies see CCLD 302.3 in Chapter 2.)

Figure 11.3 Caring for a sick child

Sudden infant death syndrome

You need to know and understand information about effective practice and risk factors relating to sudden infant death syndrome (SIDS), also known as 'cot death'. The Department of Health has produced a leaflet for parents, *Reduce the risk of cot death: An easy guide (2005 edition),* available online: www.dh.gov.uk/publications. This leaflet includes guidelines to help reduce the risk of SIDS which are applicable to both home and nursery settings. Remember:

- Place the baby on the back to sleep as this will reduce the risk of SIDS
- Do not let anyone smoke in the same room as the baby as exposure to smoking increases the risk of SIDS (all childcare settings should have a firm no

smoking policy. This means no smoking anywhere on the premises)

◎ Do not let baby get too hot (or too cold) as overheating can increase the risk of SIDS

◎ Use sheets and lightweight blankets but not duvets, quilts, baby nests, wedges, bedding rolls or pillows

◎ Keep the baby's head uncovered – place the baby with its feet to the foot of the cot, to prevent wriggling down under the covers

◎ Immunisation also reduces the risk of SIDS – check with the baby's parents that these are up to date

◎ If the baby is unwell, seek medical advice promptly.

(DH, 2005)

Seek urgent medical attention if the baby:

◎ Stops breathing or goes blue

◎ Is unresponsive and shows no awareness of what is going on

◎ Has glazed eyes and does not focus on anything

◎ Cannot be woken

◎ Has a fit.

Dial 999 and ask for an ambulance.

Check it out

Find out about your childcare setting's policy and procedures relating to the care and treatment of babies and children under 3 years of age who are ill.

Optional Units

CCLD 309
Plan and implement curriculum frameworks for early education

CCLD 310
Assess children's progress according to curriculum frameworks for early education

CCLD 323
Use Information and Communication Technology to support children's early learning

Knowledge Base

K3D319	K3P320	K3D321	K3D322	K3D323
K3D324	K3D325	K3D326	K3D327	K3D328
K3D329				

CCLD 309
Plan and implement curriculum frameworks for early education

As appropriate to your particular role, you will need to plan, implement, monitor and evaluate curriculum plans, according to the relevant curriculum framework(s) for the ages, needs and abilities of the children you work with and the requirements of your setting. This includes preparing, implementing and monitoring curriculum plans according to the curriculum frameworks for early education for your home country: England, Northern Ireland, Scotland or Wales.

CCLD 309.1
Prepare curriculum plans according to requirements

Your overall aims should be to: support all the children you work with; ensure each child has full access to the relevant curriculum; encourage all children to participate; meet their individual learning and development needs; build on their existing knowledge and skills; and help all children to achieve their full potential.

Effective planning for children's early learning is based on each child's individual needs, abilities and interests; this is why accurate observations and assessments are so important. These needs have to be integrated into the curriculum requirements for your particular setting and the age group(s) of the children you work with. Depending on these, learning activities will be related to aspects of *Birth to Three Matters*, the early learning goals in the Foundation Stage or the attainment targets in the National Curriculum at Key Stage 1 (see below).

Curriculum frameworks for early education

If appropriate to your particular role, you will need to prepare curriculum plans according to the curriculum frameworks for early education for your home country: England, Northern Ireland, Scotland or Wales. For example in England the curriculum frameworks for early education are:

◎ Birth to Three Matters (0 to 3 years)
◎ The Foundation Stage (3 to 5 years)
◎ The proposed Early Years Foundation Stage (0 to 5 years)
◎ The National Curriculum Key Stage 1 (5 to 7 years).

Birth to Three Matters

Birth to Three Matters: A framework to support children in their earliest years provides a framework for adults to support the development of very young children. The framework includes the 'Birth to Three Matters' pack which is divided into four sections: a strong child; a skilful communicator; a competent learner; and a healthy child. (See CCLD 312.1 in Chapter 11.)

The Foundation Stage

Since September 2000, early education settings in England and Wales have followed the *Curriculum guidance for the foundation stage*. This sets out the *early learning goals* for children aged 3 to 5 years within six areas of learning, each of which includes several aspects of learning. These are:

1 **Personal, social and emotional development:** dispositions and attitudes; self-confidence and self-esteem; making relationships; behaviour and self-control; self-care; and sense of community.
2 **Communication, language and literacy:** language for communication; language for thinking; linking sounds and letters; reading; writing; and handwriting.
3 **Mathematical development:** numbers as labels and for counting; calculating; and shape, space and measures.
4 **Knowledge and understanding of the world:** exploration and investigation; designing and making skills; information and communication technology; a sense of time; a sense of place; and cultures and beliefs.
5 **Physical development:** movement; a sense of space; health and bodily awareness; using equipment; and using tools and materials.
6 **Creative development:** exploring media and materials; music; imagination; responding to experiences; and expressing and communicating ideas.

(QCA, 2001)

These six areas of learning form the statutory curriculum for children aged 3 to 5 years (in nursery and reception classes) since The Education Act 2002 extended the National Curriculum to include the Foundation Stage. The early learning goals for the Foundation Stage provide guidelines to help early years practitioners (and parents) understand informal approaches to learning, including the importance of play in encouraging and extending all aspects of young children's development. The guidance also outlines **stepping stones** towards the early learning goals to help practitioners understand the knowledge, skills and attitudes young children should achieve throughout the Foundation Stage. The stepping stones show progression using yellow, blue and then green bands. For more information see the curriculum guidance for the foundation stage document available in early education settings or online: www.qca.org.uk. In Scotland there is no legally established national curriculum but the Scottish Executive Education Department (SEED) provides guidelines for schools, for example A Curriculum Framework for Children 3 to 5 (2001) – see Learning and Teaching Scotland Online Service: www.ltscotland.org.uk. In Northern Ireland the relevant curriculum framework is Curricular Guidance for Pre-School Education (1997) which is currently under review – see Department of Education, Northern Ireland website: www.deni.gov.uk.

The Early Years Foundation Stage

Orders and regulations under section 39 of the Childcare Act 2006 will bring the *Early Years*

Foundation Stage into force in September 2008. This EYFS sets out clear and universal requirements for all early years providers who must register with Ofsted, as well as independent, maintained, non-maintained and special schools with provision for children from birth to the August after their fifth birthday. If these requirements are followed, settings will make a substantial contribution to enabling the youngest children to be healthy, stay safe, enjoy and achieve, make a positive contribution and achieve economic well-being in the future. (See the *Every Child Matters* outcomes on page 90 in Chapter 5.)

The principles underpinning the Early Years Foundation Stage

The EYFS brings together the *Birth to three matters* framework, the *Curriculum guidance for the foundation stage* and elements of the *National Standards for under 8s day care and childminding* into a single framework, 'the requirements for care, learning and development for children aged 0 to 5 years'. The bulk of the content of the EYFS will be familiar to practitioners who are currently using these existing frameworks. The principles underpinning the EYFS remain the same, including:

◎ The central importance of parents and families for each child's well-being and as their first educator
◎ The importance of a *key person* for each child in each setting, to ensure their well-being, so that they develop independence by having someone they can depend upon
◎ The recognition that babies and young children are competent learners from birth, and the importance to their development of relationships both with other children and with adults
◎ The need to plan for the individual child using sensitive observations and assessments –

schedules, routines and teaching must flow with the child's needs
◎ The central role of play, both indoors and outdoors, in supporting learning – very young children learn by doing rather than through being told, and when they are given appropriate responsibility, allowed to make errors, decisions and choices
◎ The recognition that learning through play and the development of imagination and creativity is a shared endeavour, some of it led by the child and some by an effective practitioner
◎ The importance of involving key partners, like health visitors and social workers, in children's successful development and learning
◎ The value to be placed on diversity, welcoming and genuinely including all children
◎ What children can already do (rather than what they cannot do) as the starting point of a child's development and learning
◎ The central importance of competent, committed practitioners to children's outcomes.
(DfES, 2006a; pp. 3–4)

New sections in the EYFS are based on these additional principles:

◎ Only when high-quality care, development and learning work together will early years provision have the maximum impact on children's development
◎ Settings should develop effective partnerships not only with parents but also with other carers, settings and practitioners important to the child; the experience of the child must be coherent and joined-up
◎ The importance of joined-up planning and delivery to provide continuity for children who attend more than one setting, for example those who are cared for by a childminder and also attend a playgroup or nursery class
◎ The importance of planning for children who attend for different parts of the day, including the

need for rest and relaxation for those attending for long periods

◎ The need to support effective practice for all children, including those following atypical development patterns.

(DfES, 2006a; p. 4)

Detailed information on the EYFS can be found in *The Early Years Foundation Stage: Consultation on a single quality framework for services to children from birth to five* available from: www.teachernet.gov.uk/publications.

The National Curriculum

The National Curriculum applies to children of compulsory school age in schools in England and Wales. It sets out what pupils should study, what they should be taught and the standards that they should achieve. It is divided into four Key Stages:

◎ Key Stage 1: Years 1–2 (5 to 7 year olds)
◎ Key Stage 2: Years 3–6 (7 to 11 year olds)
◎ Key Stage 3: Years 7–9 (11 to 14 year olds)
◎ Key Stage 4: Years 10–11 (14 to 16 year olds)

The National Curriculum is divided into three core subjects: English; mathematics; and science; plus seven *foundation subjects*: information and communication technology; design and technology; history; geography; art and design; music; and physical education. In addition to these subjects the National Curriculum in secondary schools includes: citizenship; and modern foreign languages. In both primary and secondary schools there is also a non-statutory framework for personal, social and health education (PSHE). Religious education (RE) is outside the National Curriculum framework but all schools must make provision for RE using an agreed religious education syllabus.

You can find out more about programmes of study, attainment targets and level descriptions at the National Curriculum online website (www.nc.uk.net) and also in the National Curriculum documents available in schools.

Check it out

What is the curriculum framework for the children you work with?

Drawing up short-, medium- and long-term plans

Prepare curriculum plans for early education according to requirements by basing your planning on information from the relevant curriculum documents (see above) and consulting with relevant colleagues. You should include children, parents and other professionals in the planning process as appropriate to your setting. Ensure that your plans reflect inclusion and anti-discriminatory practice.

Draw up short-, medium- and long-term plans according to the requirements of the curriculum framework in your home country. This involves planning play and learning activities that will provide all children with appropriate opportunities to learn which reflect their range of needs, interests, abilities and past achievements. Depending on your role and the setting, you will be involved in the planning and preparation of schemes of work and teaching plans by having regular planning meetings with colleagues, which may be weekly, monthly, once a term or half-term. You will need to prepare plans which take into account the pattern of children's attendance (part-time or full-time) and their need for a balanced programme of activities.

Long-term plans

Long-term plans are usually drawn up in preparation for the year ahead. A long-term plan should provide an overview of the range of learning opportunities for children and should include the content and skills in each curriculum area or subject. For example: the aspects of learning within the six areas of learning in The Foundation Stage or the programmes of study for every subject at each key stage of the National Curriculum.

Long-term plans may include an *overall curriculum plan* (usually linked to a topic or theme) demonstrating how the setting intends to encourage and extend children's learning within a curriculum framework such as Birth to Three Matters; The Foundation Stage; the National Curriculum Key Stage 1 including the National Literacy and Numeracy Strategies.

Long-term plans should include links between subjects/areas of learning as well as progression, consolidation and diversification for children (such as between units in the DfES/QCA schemes of work). Long-term plans should show progression for children's learning and development from year group to year group within each key stage.

Many early education settings use a central topic or theme to link teaching and learning across the curriculum. A topic web can be a useful starting point for schemes of work and activity/lesson plans. Using a topic web can help ensure that you cover each area of the curriculum and emphasises an integrated approach to curriculum planning with play at the heart of children's learning and development.

An effective long-term plan for the Foundation Stage will usually include an indication of:

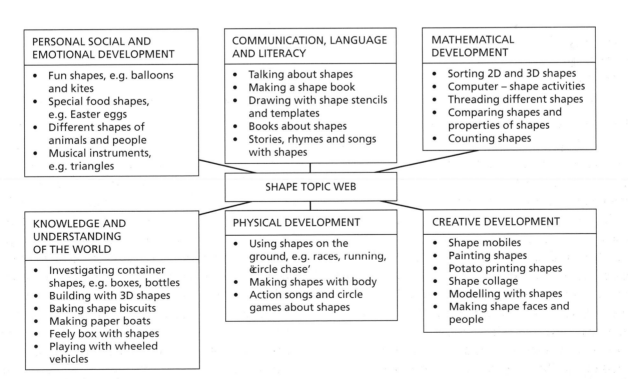

Figure 12.1 Topic web

◎ When you plan to teach areas/aspects of learning

◎ How regularly you plan to teach areas/aspects of learning

◎ How you will link areas/aspects of learning in a relevant and interesting way for children [through themes or topics]

◎ Special events and activities that provide a meaningful context and enhance learning (for example a visit to a city farm, a cultural or religious festival).

(QCA, 2001)

Medium-term plans

Some settings may only have long-term and short-plans with the content of medium-term plans included as part of their long-term plans. Other settings may use medium-term plans to bridge the gap between the outline of the long-term plan and detailed short-term plans. Medium-term plans define the intended learning outcomes for areas of learning or units of work including information on learning activities, recording and assessment methods. For example: the intentions for learning for each school term for each year group in a key stage. Medium-term plans involve the detailed planning and preparation of *schemes of work* that are central to the effective delivery of the curriculum (especially in schools) and to the provision of appropriate support for children's learning. These plans enable staff to devise and implement learning activities in their short-term planning that promote progress and achievement for all children. Staff may need to adjust the balance in the curriculum to focus on particular areas of learning so that their planning takes account of group or individual education plans. Medium-term plans also include:

◎ A group/class timetable outlining: when and where the play and learning activities will take place; periods such as story time when children can rest and restore energy; routines that must be done at specific times, for example registration, break/playtime, lunchtime, tidying-up time, or home time

◎ Practical guidelines for staff to assist with the delivery of each curriculum subject or area of learning (such as general information about resources and important teaching points)

◎ Structured learning programmes for individual children, including particular activities to encourage the development of pupils with special educational needs, for example Individual Education Plans and Behaviour Support Plans.

Short-term plans

Short-term plans should be based on the long-term plan *and* ongoing observations and assessments of children as well as discussions with colleagues and parents. Use this information to plan appropriate activities and experiences for children. Short-term plans set out detailed information about play and learning activities for each class, group or individual child on a weekly and daily basis, including lesson or activity plans with details of specific learning objectives or intentions for the children based on the stepping stones or early learning goals, as appropriate to each child's level of development. These plans should also incorporate details of the proposed implementation of each activity including: organisation and staff required; resources needed, including any specialist equipment; and strategies to be used to support children's learning and development.

To plan appropriate play and learning activities you need to: identify the intended learning outcomes that promote inclusion, participation and achievement for all children; use information about children's interests, skills and prior achievements to structure the content and progress of activities/lessons; take into account children's individual learning needs, including their individual learning styles (see page 245); include targets from individual education plans for children with special educational needs; define the roles and responsibilities of those involved; ensure that adequate and appropriate resources are available; and use ICT to support children's learning and development. (Examples of planning are in the booklet *Planning for learning in the foundation stage* – see Further reading.)

An effective short-term plan for the Foundation Stage will usually include:

◎ Clear learning intentions for individual or groups of children informed by observations and based on the stepping stones/early learning goals
◎ A brief description of the range of activities and experiences including: adult-directed and child-initiated; using indoors and outdoors
◎ How activities and experiences can be adapted for individuals or groups of children
◎ How the children will be organised
◎ The resources and equipment required
◎ The role of the adult(s) including parents
◎ Questions and/or vocabulary that the adult(s) will use during the activity
◎ Opportunities for observation and informal assessments of individuals or groups of children.
(QCA, 2001)

Theoretical approaches to how children learn and develop

There are three theoretical approaches to how children think and learn which are relevant to the study of child development: psycho-dynamic approach; behaviourist approach; and cognitive approach.

PORTFOLIO ACTIVITY

Provide examples of the planning you and your colleagues use within the curriculum framework applicable to the children in your setting. Include information on:
◎ **Long-term plans**, for example **overall curriculum plan, topic web**
◎ **Medium-term plans**, for example **schemes of work, timetables**
◎ **Short-term plans**, for example **activity plans, lesson plans**.
NVQ LINKS: CCLD 309.1 CCLD 301.1 CCLD 303.2 CCLD 305.2 CCLD 306.2 CCLD 312.3 CCLD 318.1 CCLD 318.2 CCLD 321.2 CCLD 323.1 CCLD 339.3

The psycho-dynamic approach

The Austrian physician Sigmund Freud believed that very early childhood experiences are responsible for how people think and feel in later life. Depending on these experiences, people are either well or poorly adjusted to their everyday lives. Freud considered that most of our thinking is done on a *sub-conscious* level and is therefore beyond our control. More recently psychologists, such as Carl Rogers, have suggested that most of our thinking is *conscious* and that individuals *are* in control of their own lives.

The behaviourist approach

These psychologists focus on *behaviour* which can be observed rather than thoughts and feelings which cannot be observed. Behaviourists are concerned with how external forces can be used to control behaviour; for example, B F Skinner considered that all thinking and learning is based on responses to rewards and punishments received within our environment. (See CCLD 337.2 in Chapter 9.)

The cognitive approach

These psychologists believe that human behaviour *can* be understood by studying how people think and learn. This includes the work of Piaget, Vygotsky and Bruner (see below).

Cognitive approaches to how children think and learn

This section concentrates on cognitive approaches to how children think and learn as these are the most relevant to understanding children's learning and development. The other approaches *do* contribute to our knowledge of child development, but are of more significance to understanding children's behaviour.

Early education pioneers

Friedrich Wilhelm Froebel was a German educator and the founder of the *kindergarten* (meaning 'children's garden') system, who devised activities for young children that encouraged learning through play. He thought young women had a special rapport with young children; prior to this, teachers were usually men or older women. Froebel trained many young women to become kindergarten teachers; some of these went to America where they established private kindergartens. The first year of compulsory schooling in the USA and Canada is still called kindergarten today.

Froebel had been a student of Heinrich Pestalozzi, a Swiss teacher and writer. Pestalozzi established many schools for young children and also wrote books demonstrating how basic concepts could be introduced to them. Froebel was the first educator to really see the importance of play in developing children's thinking and learning. He believed that play was central to children's learning and their understanding of concepts. He devised a set of specially designed play materials to encourage children's thinking and learning. Froebel pioneered the idea of *hands-on experience,* which forms the basis of learning through play and active learning. He also believed that childhood was a state in its own right and not just a preparation for adulthood. It was his work that moved early education away from young children sitting in rows and learning by rote.

Maria Montessori was an Italian educator and physician who became one of the best known and most influential early childhood educators. She began by working with children with special needs. She designed carefully graded self-teaching materials which stimulated children's learning through use of their senses. Montessori believed that children learn best by doing things independently without adult interference and that they concentrate better when engaged in a self-chosen activity. Adults working with young children need to be specially trained to give the appropriate support to children's independent learning. The learning environment was considered to be especially important. Montessori believed the equipment should be specifically designed for children (such as small, child-sized furniture, kitchen utensils, tools) and that children should have freedom to move and explore their environment. (See Unit CCLD 318 in Chapter 8.)

Piaget

A Swiss biologist, Jean Piaget used observations of his own children, plus a wider sample of children, to develop his theories of cognitive development. Piaget's theories of cognitive development have had a major influence on early education for over 40 years. Piaget believed that children went through different *stages* of cognitive development based on fixed ages. Within these stages the children's patterns of learning, or *schemas* as he called them, were very different from adult ways of problem-solving. He also believed in the importance of young children learning through action and exploration of their environment using their sensory motor skills. According to Piaget children are *actively* involved in structuring their own cognitive development through exploration of their environment. Children need real objects and 'concrete experiences' to discover things for themselves. The adult's role is to provide children with appropriate experiences in a suitable environment to facilitate the children's instinctive ability to think and learn. Cognitive development occurs in four set stages which are universal – they apply to all forms of learning and across all cultures.

Piaget viewed children as thinking and learning in a different way to adults. Not only do children have less experience of the world, but their understanding of it is shaped by this entirely different way of looking at their environment. Children will learn only when they are 'ready' for different experiences as determined by their current stage of cognitive development.

Piaget did not see language and communication as central to children's cognitive development because this development begins at birth *before* children can comprehend or use words. Young children's use of language demonstrates their cognitive achievements, but does not control them. He did see the

Piaget's four stages of cognitive development

Stage 1: Sensori-motor – 0 to 2 years
Babies and very young children:
◎ Learn through their senses, physical activity and interaction with their immediate environment
◎ Understand their world in terms of actions.

Stage 2: Pre-operations – 2 to 7 years
Young children:
◎ Learn through their experiences with real objects in their immediate environment
◎ Use symbols (for example words and images) to make sense of their world.

Stage 3: Concrete operations – 7 to 11 years
Children:
◎ Continue to learn through their experiences with real objects
◎ Access information (using language) to make sense of their environment.

Stage 4: Formal operations – 11 years to adult
Older children and adults:
◎ Learn to make use of abstract thinking (for example algebra, physics).

importance of language at later stages. Young children are *egocentric*. They are unable to see or understand another person's viewpoint. This also means they are unable to convey information accurately or effectively to others.

Piaget believed that children interact with their environment to actively construct their knowledge and understanding of the world. They do this by relating new information to existing information. Piaget called this interaction: *assimilation* (the need for further information); *accommodation* (the need for organised information); and *adaptation* (the need for revised/updated information). All new information has to be built on existing information; there needs to be some connection between them.

Similar information can be stored as it relates to existing information. *Discrepant* information cannot be stored because it is not related to existing information. Piaget described internal mental processes as schemas and the ways in which they are used when thinking as operations. Mental processes or schemas do not remain static; they continually develop as we acquire new information and extend our understanding of the world.

Activity

Outline the main points of Piaget's theories of cognitive development.

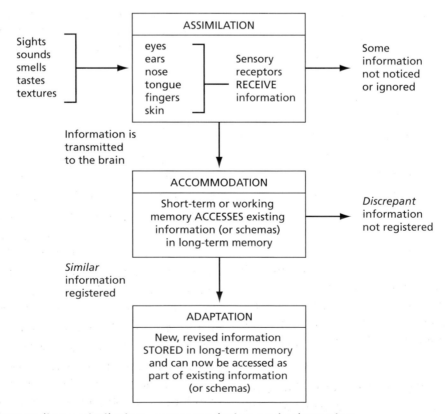

Figure 12.2 Understanding assimilation, accommodation and adaptation

Vygotsky

The Russian psychologist Lev Semonovich Vygotsky argued that the social interaction between children and other people enables children to develop the intellectual skills necessary for thinking and logical reasoning. Language is the key to this social interaction. Through language and communication children learn to think about their world and modify their actions accordingly.

Vygotsky considered adults as having an active role in fostering children's cognitive development. So while children are active in constructing their own intellectual processes, they are not lone explorers; children need and receive knowledge through interaction with other children and adults. Vygotsky (and later Bruner) viewed the adult as supporting children's cognitive development within an appropriate framework. (See *scaffolding* below.)

Adults support children's learning by assisting the children's own efforts and thus enabling children to acquire the necessary skills, knowledge and understanding. As children develop competent skills through this *assisted learning*, the adults gradually decrease their support until the children are able to work independently. With adult assistance young children are able to complete tasks and to solve problems which they would not be able to do on their own. It is important that adults recognise when to provide support towards each child's next step of development and when this support is no longer required. Vygotsky used the idea of the *zone of proximal development* or area of next development to describe this framework of support for learning. The zone of proximal development can be represented in four stages (Tharp and Gallimore, 1991).

Children can be in different zones for different skills or tasks. Each activity has its own zone of proximal

development. For example, children who are learning to read may progress in the following way:

◎ Step 1: learning phonic, decoding and comprehension skills with assistance of childcarers, parents, teachers, teaching assistants (assistance from others).

◎ Step 2: sounding out difficult/unfamiliar words, reading aloud to self, lips moving during silent reading, etc. (self-help).

◎ Step 3: reading competently using internal prompts (auto-pilot).

◎ Step 4: new words, complicated texts, learning to read in a different language, etc. require further assistance (relapses to previous steps).

Activity

Give an example of how the four stages of the zone of proximal development could apply to a young child's learning and development.

Bruner

The American psychologist Jerome S. Bruner emphasises the importance of the adult in supporting children's thinking and learning. Bruner uses the term *scaffolding* to describe this adult support. Picture a builder using scaffolding to support a house while it is being built. Without the scaffold the house could not be built; but once the house is finished, the scaffolding can be removed. The adult supports the child's learning until they are ready to stand alone. Bruner also emphasises the adult's skills of recognising where and when this support is needed and when it should be removed. The structuring of children's learning should be flexible; the adult support or scaffold should not be rigid; it needs to change as the needs of the child change, that is as the child gains knowledge and understanding and/or acquires new skills. The adult supports children's learning and development by: providing learning experiences within a meaningful context; adapting tasks and learning experiences; selecting appropriate materials for each child's needs and abilities; and encouraging children to make choices about what they want to do and when.

Bruner believed that any subject can be taught to any child at any age as long as it is presented in an appropriate way. Learning does not occur in pre-determined *stages*, but is dependent on linking knowledge to children's existing knowledge in a holistic way. Bruner's sequence of cognitive development is divided into three areas:

1 *Enactive:* understanding the world through action (relates to Piaget's sensori-motor stage).
2 *Iconic:* manipulation of images or 'icons' in child's thinking about the world (corresponds to Piaget's pre-operational stage)
3 *Symbolic:* use of language and symbols to make sense of the world (similar to Piaget's operational stage).

Bruner views language as central to children's thinking and learning and stresses how language is used to represent experiences and how past experience or knowledge is organised through language in ways that make information more accessible. Language connects a person's understanding of one situation to another. The adult has a particular role in establishing effective

Figure 12.3 Scaffolding: supporting a child's thinking and learning

communication to encourage and extend children's thinking and learning. Adults use language to: capture children's interest and direct their attention; develop children's problem-solving abilities; assist children's understanding of concepts; encourage and extend children's own ideas; and negotiate choices with children.

Intellectual development: a social constructivist view

The social constructivist view of intellectual development takes into account more recent research concerning how children think and learn within the context of home, school and the wider environment. Social constructivism integrates children's intellectual and social development within a useful framework. It moves away from the idea that the development of children's intellectual abilities occurs in stages at particular ages and that adults simply provide the means for this natural process. Instead, adults assist children's intellectual development as part of the *social process* of childhood. Age is not the critical factor in intellectual development; and assisted learning can and does occur at *any age*. The *key factor* is the learner's *existing* knowledge and/or experience in connection with the *current* problem or learning situation.

How theoretical approaches to how children learn and develop may influence practice

Understanding theoretical approaches to how children learn and develop may influence practice by improving: the quality of early education provision;

the structure of the learning environment; the provision of materials and equipment; the communication between adults and children during learning experiences; and the adult expectations of children's development. Theoretical approaches to how children learn and develop increase adults' awareness and understanding of the importance of: observing and assessing children's development very carefully; listening to children and the way they express ideas; and taking account of children's interests and experiences when planning learning opportunities.

CCLD 309.2 Implement curriculum plans

Knowledge Base

K3D319	K3P320	K3D321	K3D322	K3D326
K3D328	K3D329	K3D330	K3D331	K3D332

Implementing curriculum plans involves working with other people (parents, colleagues and other professionals) to deliver the appropriate curriculum for the children in your setting.

You should regularly check and discuss the progress of children with parents and colleagues. For instance, seek additional support if children are not progressing as expected, consulting other professionals as appropriate. You must keep relevant records about children's learning according to the requirements of your setting.

Implement planned curriculum activities and experiences that meet the needs of the children in your setting by:

◎ Providing a stimulating, enjoyable and carefully planned learning environment including using indoor and outdoor spaces (see CCLD 306.1 in Chapter 6)

◎ Using everyday routines to enhance learning (see CCLD 307.1 in Chapter 7 and CCLD 314.1 in Chapter 11)

◎ Ensuring a balance between structured and freely chosen play (see Unit CCLD 318 in Chapter 8)

◎ Supporting and extending play to encourage learning by using your knowledge of individual children (see CCLD 303.1 in Chapter 3) and their preferred learning styles (see below)

◎ Using appropriate materials and support strategies for each child's needs and abilities

◎ Encouraging children's participation and providing assistance at an appropriate level for each child, including supporting children with special needs (see CCLD 321.2 in Chapter 14)

◎ Having high expectations of children and commitment to raising their achievement based on a realistic appraisal of their capabilities and what they might achieve

◎ Encouraging children to make choices about their own learning

◎ Changing and adapting plans as required to meet the needs of all the children.

The interrelated components of intellectual development

The interrelated components of intellectual development are: thinking; sensory perception; language and communication; reasoning and problem-solving; understanding concepts; memory; concentration; and imagination and creativity.

Developing thinking skills

We cannot see a person's thoughts because the thinking process is internal. We can *see* the process and progress of a person's thinking through their *actions* and *communications*. Thinking involves: cognitive processes originating in the mind; using or processing information; and working towards finding solutions.

Developing sensory perception

Sensory perception involves the ability to use our senses to identify the differences between objects or sounds. It involves: *auditory perception* (differentiating between sounds); and *visual perception* (differentiating between objects or the distance between objects).

Research shows that babies are born with a wide range of sensory skills and perceptual abilities which enable them to explore their environment in a variety of ways. Children use their senses (hearing, sight, touch, sound, taste and smell) to: explore objects and the environment; investigate and participate in new experiences; develop new skills and abilities; and discover how things work in the world around them (see CCLD 308.4 in Chapter 10).

Babies' responses initially consist of automatic reflexes such as grasping and sucking. Within a few months babies are able to explore objects in more purposeful and controlled ways. Gradually children use different strategies for exploring their environment as they mature, gain more experience and develop their physical skills. The more opportunities children have to explore, the more they will develop their sensory perception. As their senses develop, children begin to *make sense* of the world around them as they perceive and process information in their environment.

Developing language and communication skills

Language and communication skills involve making sense of the world around us by processing information in a more accessible form. Before language, information is stored/recalled through images. Language enables us to: store more information and to make better connections between existing information and new information such as, for example, understanding concepts (see below); communicate more effectively with others, for instance by asking questions and understanding the answers; and interact with others to gain new experiences and information. Language and communication skills enable us to verbalise our thoughts and feelings as well as express our opinions and ideas.

Developing reasoning and problem-solving skills

Reasoning involves: using intellectual processes to make personal judgements; making connections between existing information and new information; problem-solving and the ability to think logically. People use their existing knowledge and past experiences to solve problems. Children (and adults) often supplement their lack of knowledge or experience by experimenting using a process of *trial and error*. Making mistakes is part of the learning process. By using logic, people can make reasonable assumptions or predictions about what might happen in a particular situation or to a particular object. Logical thinking and problem-solving are essential to the ability to make mathematical calculations and to develop scientific skills. Children need lots of opportunities to develop these scientific skills (observation; investigation; prediction; hypothesising; and recording data).

As a childcarer you need to ensure that children are provided with activities at the appropriate level for their intellectual development. There should be a balance between encouraging younger children to develop their own problem-solving skills through play with minimal adult intervention *and* complying with the early learning goals for knowledge and understanding of the world and mathematics or the objectives of the National Curriculum (for example the daily maths lesson).

Developing an understanding of concepts

Concepts are the ways in which people make sense of and organise the information in the world around them. Concepts can be divided into two categories: *concrete* and *abstract*.

Mathematics and science rely on the ability to understand abstract ideas. For young children this means developing a sound knowledge and understanding of concrete concepts first, such as: number; weighing and measuring; volume and capacity; shape; colour; space; textures; growth; and physical forces. Experiences with real objects enable young children to develop problem-solving skills and to acquire an understanding of these concepts. Some concepts require the understanding of other concepts beforehand. For example, understanding *number* and *counting* comes before *addition*; understanding *addition* comes before *multiplication*. Young children take longer to understand abstract concepts such as time and mental arithmetic, but this depends on their individual learning experiences. For example, many children *do* understand some moral concepts such as ideas concerning fairness and the rights of people (and animals) to live in freedom if these concepts are linked with *real* events.

Developing memory skills

The other components of intellectual development would be of little use to individuals without memory. Memory involves the ability to recall or retrieve information stored in the mind. Memory skills involve: *recalling information* on past experiences, events, actions or feelings; *recognising information* and making connections with previous experiences; *predicting* – using past information to anticipate future events. Many of the other components of intellectual development involve all three memory skills, for example problem-solving activities in mathematics and science or the decoding and comprehension skills needed for reading.

A person's mind is like a computer which stores information using a system of files to link different pieces of information together. Relating new information to existing information through this system makes it easier to access and use information. Information is stored in the short-term (or working) memory for about 10 to 20 seconds; from there the information is either forgotten or is passed on to the long-term memory where it is linked to existing stored information and 'filed' for future reference. Information is more likely to be stored and remembered if it is repeated several times and is linked effectively to existing information (through personal experiences, for example).

Young children have a limited number of experiences so their 'filing' system is quite basic. Gradually children create new files and have more complex filing systems to store the ever-increasing amount of information they receive through their own experiences, interaction with others and by developing knowledge and understanding of their environment. There is no limit to the amount of information that can be stored in the long-term memory. The difficulty lies in accessing this stored information. As children get older the process of remembering relies more and more on being able to use language to organise and retrieve information effectively.

Developing concentration

Concentration involves the ability to pay attention to the situation or task in hand. A person's concentration level or attention span is the length of time they are able to focus on a particular activity. Some children can concentrate for quite a long time, while other children (and adults!) find their attention starts to wander after just a few minutes. This may be due to a mismatch of activities to the individual's needs, interests and abilities which can lead to boredom and a lack of concentration. Attention Deficit Disorder or Attention Deficit Hyperactive Disorder may also be responsible for poor concentration in certain people (see CCLD 337.2 in Chapter 9).

Concentration is a key intellectual skill, which is necessary for the development of other intellectual components such as language and understanding concepts.

Being able to concentrate is an important part of the learning process. Children with short attention spans find it more difficult to take in new information; they may also need extra time to complete activities. Children need to be able to focus on one activity at a time without being distracted by other things. This is an essential skill for learning, particularly within schools. Concentrating enables children to get the most out of learning opportunities. Activities within the setting may require different kinds of concentration, for example: *passive concentration* (listening to instructions, listening to stories, watching television, assemblies); *active concentration* (creative activities, construction, puzzles, sand/water play, imaginative play, literacy activities, and problem-solving activities including mathematics and science).

Developing imagination and creativity

Imagination involves the individual's ability to invent ideas or to form images. Children express their imagination through imitative play to begin with and then gradually through imaginative play, such as pretend or role play. As children explore their environment and find out what objects and materials can do, they use their imagination to increase their understanding of the world and their role within it. For example, through imaginative play children can become other people by dressing-up and behaving like them. Imaginative play assists the development of children's imagination through activities such as dressing-up, small scale toys, doll play, shop play and hospital play.

Creativity is the *use* of the imagination in a wide variety of activities including play, art, design technology, music, dance, drama, stories and poetry. Children can express their creativity through activities such as painting, drawing, collage, playdough, clay, cooking, design and model making. Creativity involves a process rather than an end product; it cannot be measured by the end result of an activity, but is based upon *how* the child worked and *why*. Creativity involves: exploring and experimenting with a wide range of materials; learning about the properties of materials (colour, shape, size and texture); developing fine motor skills to manipulate materials; developing problem-solving techniques; and developing an understanding of the world and our personal contribution to it.

PORTFOLIO ACTIVITY

1 Observe a child involved in a learning activity.
2 In your assessment you should:

◎ Specify the learning objectives for the activity
◎ Identify the intellectual skills demonstrated by the child during the activity (for example concentration, memory skills, imagination and creativity, mathematical or scientific skills, language and communication skills)
◎ Comment on the level of adult support provided during the activity
◎ Suggest ways to encourage and extend the child's learning in this area.

NVQ LINKS: CCLD 309.1 CCLD 309.2 CCLD 301.2 CCLD 303.1 CCLD 303.2 CCLD 303.3 CCLD 303.4 CCLD 312.3 CCLD 318.2 CCLD 318.3

Providing a stimulating learning environment

It is vital that *all* children have access to a stimulating environment which enables learning to take place in exciting and challenging ways. To develop into healthy, considerate and intelligent adults, all children require intellectual stimulation as well as physical care and emotional security. Intellectual stimulation through play and other learning opportunities allows children to develop their cognitive abilities and fulfil their potential as individuals.

The children you work with will be constantly thinking and learning, gathering new information and formulating new ideas about themselves, other people and the world around them. When implementing curriculum plans, you should provide children with opportunities to:

◎ Explore their environment and/or investigate new information/ideas
◎ Discover things for themselves through a wide variety of experiences
◎ Feel free to make mistakes in a safe and secure environment using 'trial and error'
◎ Develop autonomy through increased responsibility and working independently
◎ Encourage and extend their knowledge and skills with appropriate support from adults (and other children)
◎ Learn to make sense of new information within an appropriate curriculum framework.

The possible effects of inadequate or inappropriate intellectual stimulation include:

◎ *Low self-esteem*: the lack of opportunities to explore, experiment and create within a stimulating, language-rich environment can result in children having no sense of purpose or achievement. A person's emotional well-being is based on positive interactions with others *and* the world around them (see CCLD 308.4 in Chapter 10)
◎ *Poor concentration*: a lack of opportunities to discover things for themselves can lead to an inability to concentrate and poor attention span. Poor concentration leads to weak listening skills and difficulty in following instructions. Play opportunities are a good way to motivate children's learning; children are more likely to concentrate on self-chosen activities they enjoy. If they have not had play opportunities they will find it especially difficult to concentrate in more formal learning situations (see Unit CCLD 318.1 in Chapter 8)
◎ *Boredom*: if children have not had discovery opportunities they will often lack interest in others and the world around them. This can lead to disruptive and/or attention-seeking behaviour (see Unit CCLD 337.2 in Chapter 9)

◎ *Lack of confidence*: children who have lacked appropriate play opportunities have missed out on learning in safe, non-threatening situations. This can lead to a reluctance to participate and a tendency to withdraw from activities (especially those involving problem-solving skills) due to fear of 'failing'
◎ *Over-dependency on adult support*: some children may be reluctant to do things for themselves if they have not had opportunities to engage in play and independent learning activities. Dependency on adults can also be linked to children's lack of confidence or fear of 'failing'
◎ *Learning difficulties*: the inability to concentrate, to work independently or to use investigative skills may make it very difficult for some children to participate fully in early learning situations. This may lead to subsequent difficulties in curriculum areas such as English, mathematics, science, technology, and so on. Some children are inaccurately thought to have learning difficulties when they are really suffering from a severe lack of intellectual stimulation. Children with little or no intellectual stimulation find it very difficult (or even impossible) to develop their own thinking skills or formulate new ideas (see Unit CCLD 321.2 in Chapter 14).

Learning pathways

Every learning experience can be viewed as a journey, travelling along different pathways to reach our destination or learning goal. (Drummond, 1994) At different points of a learning experience the learning may be:

◎ Very easy – speeding along a clear motorway
◎ Interesting but uncertain in parts – taking the scenic route
◎ Very difficult and complicated – stuck in a traffic jam on Spaghetti Junction

◎ Totally confusing – trying to find the correct exit off a big road traffic island

◎ Completely beyond us – entering a no through road or going the wrong way down a one-way street.

Patterns of learning

The experience of learning is a never-ending cycle; learning new skills continues indefinitely. Once one skill is gained in a particular area, further skills can be learned. For example, once children have learned basic reading skills, they continue to develop their literacy skills even as adults by: increasing their vocabulary; improving spelling; decoding unfamiliar words; and reading and understanding more complex texts.

As well as the circular nature of learning experiences, you may have noticed the importance of *active participation* in all learning experiences. Watching someone else use a computer or read a book can help only so much; to develop the relevant skills, children and adults need hands-on experience of using the computer or handling books. (See page 246 for more information about active learning.)

Learning styles

Visual learners gather information through observation and reading. Children with this learning style may find it difficult to concentrate on spoken instructions, but respond well to visual aids such as pictures, diagrams and charts. They tend to visualise ideas and remember the visual details of places and objects they have seen. According to research about 65 per cent of people have this learning style.

Auditory learners process information by listening carefully and then repeating instructions either out loud or mentally in order to remember what they have learned. Children with this learning style tend to be the talkers as well as the listeners in group or class situations and benefit from being able to discuss ideas. Auditory learners can be easily distracted by noise and may concentrate better with background music to disguise potentially disruptive noises. Research suggests that about 30 per cent of people use this style of learning.

Kinesthetic learners process information through touch and movement. All young children rely on this learning style to a large extent, hence the importance of active learning, especially in the early years. Children with this learning style benefit from physical interaction with their environment, with plenty of emphasis on *learning by doing*. About 5 per cent of people continue to use this style even as adults.

People are not restricted to learning in only one way; for example children can learn to use different learning styles for different activities within the curriculum. However, research shows that working outside their preferred learning style for extensive periods can be stressful. Providing opportunities for children to use their preferred learning style, wherever practical, increases their chances of educational success. (Tobias, 1996)

As well as relying on one particular style of learning, people tend to use one of two styles of processing information: either analytic or global. *Analytic learners* process information by dividing it into pieces and organising it in a logical manner, such as making lists, putting things in order, following clear instructions or rules, completing/handing in work on time. Analytic learners prefer order and a planned, predictable sequence of events or ideas. *Global learners* process information by grouping large pieces of information together and focusing on the main ideas rather than details, for example drawing spidergrams, using pictures or key words, and ignoring or bending rules including missing deadlines. Global learners prefer spontaneity and activities which allow them creative freedom.

> **Think About**
>
> 1 Think about a group of children that you work with. Are they visual, auditory or kinesthetic learners?
> 2 Think about how the children you work with gather information. Do they prefer to:
>   ◎ Work as an individual or in a group?
>   ◎ Follow step-by-step instructions or have open-ended projects? Read and talk about work?
>   ◎ Engage in practical activities and experiment for themselves?
> 3 Think about how the children you work with process information. Are they analytic or global learners?

Active learning

An essential part of all learning experiences is active learning, not just for children but for adults as well. For example, at college you may find that learning situations take the form of workshops, group activities and discussions rather than formal lectures. Children (and adults) learn by *doing*. Lectures would be a waste of time for children. Indeed, traditional lectures *are* a waste of time even for adults! This is because the average attention span of an adult is 20 minutes! (This is probably why commercials are shown about every 15 to 20 minutes on television.) The average attention span of a child is considerably less, more like 5 to 10 minutes or even as little as 2 to 3 minutes, especially very young children, some children with cognitive difficulties or behavioural difficulties.

In all learning situations it is important to provide information in small portions with plenty of discussion and activity breaks to maintain interest and concentration. It is essential that children become *actively* involved in the learning process. Learning needs to be practical not theoretical. Children need *concrete* learning experiences such as using real objects in a meaningful context. This is why providing appropriate play opportunities is so crucial to all children's learning and development. Active learning encourages children to be:

◎ Curious
◎ Handy at problem-solving
◎ Imaginative
◎ Creative.

You need to plan, in consultation with your colleagues, the strategies and resources to be used to promote children's independent learning. This includes: encouraging and supporting children in making decisions about their own learning; providing appropriate levels of assistance for individual children; using ICT to enable children to work more independently (see below); providing challenges to promote independent learning; and encouraging children to review their own learning strategies, achievements and future learning needs.

Being flexible and allowing for children's choice in planning activities helps their learning and development by promoting: discussion and effective communication skills; co-operative group work; opportunities for first-hand experiences and exploration; and information skills (including referencing skills, finding and using different resources). Some early years settings take children's involvement in planning as the central basis for structuring their learning activities. The *High/Scope* approach encourages children to make decisions about their own choice of activities; this approach encourages active and independent learning by involving children in the planning, doing and reviewing of activities. The children still participate in some adult-directed activities such as story time, PE and other larger group activities and also work to develop specific skills such as literacy and numeracy in small groups or as individuals. The 'plan-do-review' cycle of planning may incorporate the following:

1 **Plan:** in a small group with an adult, children discuss which activities they intend to do that session.
2 **Do:** the children participate in the activities of their choice and are encouraged to talk during this time with adults helping to extend the children's language and learning.
3 **Review:** at the end of the session the group come together again to look back on the session's activities.

Children's learning and development in bilingual or multilingual settings

You need to be aware of specific issues for children's learning and development in bilingual or multilingual settings or where children are learning through an additional language. Bilingual means 'speaking two languages' which applies to some children (and staff) in education settings in the United Kingdom. 'Multilingual' is used to describe someone who uses more than two languages. The term 'bilingual' is widely used for all children who speak two or more languages. However, since the introduction of The National Literacy Strategy, the preferred term for bilingual children in schools is pupils with **English as an additional language** (EAL).

There is a broad range of children with EAL including children who are:

◎ Literate in English and do not require extra provision
◎ Able to converse in English but need help to use language in learning activities
◎ Literate in languages other than English but need a little extra support with literacy
◎ Learning to speak English as well as learning to read and write it
◎ Below the levels of speech or literacy expected for their age and require adapted materials to meet their language and/or literacy needs.

PORTFOLIO ACTIVITY

1 Plan and implement a learning activity for a child or group of children. You could use the observation from page 243 as the basis for your plan. Include information on: the specific intended learning outcomes/objectives for the activity; organisation, resources and staff required; any special requirements, such as specialist equipment; and the support to be provided by adults.
2 Evaluate the activity afterwards including information on: the intellectual skills demonstrated by the child or children during the activity (such as concentration, memory skills, imagination and creativity, mathematical or scientific skills, language and communication skills); the adult support provided during the activity; and suggestions to encourage and extend the child's learning in this area.

NVQ LINKS: CCLD 309.1   CCLD 309.2   CCLD 301.1   CCLD 303.2   CCLD 306.2   CCLD 312.3
CCLD 318.2   CCLD 318.3   CCLD 321.2   CCLD 323.1

There are four important factors to consider when providing support for children with EAL:

1 *There are different and changing levels of competence involved in speaking two or more languages.* For example, some children are still learning their first language while adding words to their second language. Very young children often do 'language mixing' which involves combining words from two or more languages when involved in conversations or discussions.

2 *Different situations prompt the use of one language over another.* Children who are more fluent in English often use whichever language is appropriate to a particular situation. For example: they might speak to one grandparent using Standard English and speak to another grandparent using Mirpuri and Punjabi; conversations with parents and siblings might involve a mixture of Punjabi and English; and language at the setting might involve the use of a local dialect such as that used in the 'Black Country' in the West Midlands.

3 *The range of communication and literacy skills may be different in each language.* Children may be aware of different writing systems being used by their families and in the local community. They may be able to speak a particular language and not be able to write in that language. Children may have seen writing which went from right to left as in the Arabic or Hebrew scripts, not just from left to right as with English; or they may be used to vertical rather than horizontal writing systems such as Mandarin Chinese or Japanese. Developing literacy skills can be a confusing experience for some children with EAL who could be learning to read and write in English in school while learning the same skills in Punjabi at home or in a community school *and* also learning Arabic when studying the Koran at Saturday school.

4 *Changing circumstances can affect children's use of their community languages.* For example, moving to a different area where cultural attitudes may be different so that more or less of the children's community language is used.

(Whitehead, 1996)

As well as communication, language and literacy activities you can use other areas of the curriculum to develop language skills in a meaningful context; for example use play activities and/or games to encourage and extend language or focus on words used when working on the computer or during science experiments.

Specialist language support staff can help to ensure that EAL learners are encouraged to apply what they have learned in the literacy hour across the curriculum. Language support teachers should work with teachers and other staff (nursery nurses, teaching assistants) to select resources and texts that meet the needs of EAL learners (see Chapter 13).

It is important to distinguish between children who have additional language learning needs and those who also have special educational needs. Some children with EAL may also be assessed as having special educational needs (see Chapter 14).

Unit Links

For this Unit you also need to understand the following sections:

CCLD 345.3 Help pupils to develop their speaking and listening (see Chapter 13)

CCLD 339.3 Ensure that individual education plans for children are in place and regularly reviewed (see Chapter 14)

12

PORTFOLIO ACTIVITY

Design and make a booklet about supporting children's learning and development in bilingual or multilingual settings. Include information on the following: the community languages used by the children in your setting; the setting's activities and resources available to support children with EAL, such as dual language books; bilingual story sessions; language support staff; multilingual resources from the community centre or local education development centre, etc.

NVQ LINKS: CCLD 309.1   CCLD 301.2   CCLD 305.1   CCLD 305.2   CCLD 334.1

CCLD 309.3
Monitor and reflect on implementation of curriculum frameworks

Knowledge Base

K3D319   K3D320   K3D321   K3D322

Monitoring and reflecting on the implementation of curriculum frameworks involves developing monitoring strategies and documentation as required by the relevant curriculum framework in your home country. You should regularly communicate with parents and colleagues to support monitoring of curriculum frameworks (see Chapter 1). Check that each area of the curriculum is implemented to a consistent quality according to the requirements of your setting and the relevant inspection regime (see Chapter 17). Monitor the participation and learning of all the children in the setting (see section 'assess and record children's progress in consultation with others'). Then reflect on your practice in the light of your work in planning and implementing curriculum frameworks (see Chapter 4).

Monitoring and reflecting on implementation of curriculum frameworks is achieved through: regular discussions with staff concerning the progress of groups and individuals; ensuring that assessment opportunities are built into planning across the setting; regular observations and assessments of children's learning and development; working alongside colleagues to provide support to individual staff as necessary; and reviewing assessment outcomes and data in order to evaluate overall standards throughout the setting.

Unit Links

For this Unit you also have to understand the followng sections:
CCLD 301.4 Communicate with adults (see Chapter 1)
CCLD 304.1 Reflect on practice (see Chapter 4)
CCLD 342 Meet regulatory requirements in the childcare setting (see Chapter 17)

PORTFOLIO ACTIVITY

Outline the monitoring strategies and documentation required by the curriculum framework relevant to your setting. Include information on how you: communicate with parents/colleagues; monitor children's participation and learning; and reflect on practice.

NVQ LINKS: CCLD 309.3   CCLD 301.4   CCLD 304.1   CCLD 310.2   CCLD 340.1   CCLD 342.2
CCLD 342.3   CCLD 342.4

CCLD 310
Assess children's progress according to curriculum frameworks for early education

Assessment is an integral part of curriculum frameworks for early education. The setting should have a policy outlining the purpose and management of assessment in the setting. The implementation of the assessment policy is the responsibility of all the staff and should be based on local and/or national assessment requirements.

CCLD 310.1
Identify and plan assessment requirements of curriculum frameworks

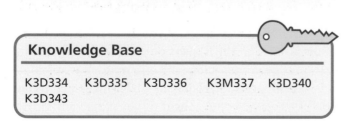

Knowledge Base

K3D334   K3D335   K3D336   K3M337   K3D340
K3D343

Identifying and planning assessment requirements of curriculum frameworks involves researching and extracting the relevant information from national or local curriculum documents on which to base your assessments. You should consult with relevant adults (parents and colleagues) when planning assessments according to local or national requirements. The aims of assessment are to:

◎ Assist and support children's learning
◎ Identify and support special needs
◎ Assist children and staff to identify strengths and weaknesses
◎ Ensure the outcomes of assessment are used in the planning of future learning
◎ Inform parents of their children's progress
◎ Promote continuity and progression between age/year groups
◎ Ensure a consistent approach to judging children's attainment
◎ Ensure that assessment opportunities are not missed
◎ Provide information to relevant inspectorates, for example Ofsted
◎ Support professional staff development
◎ Assist in evaluating the success of curriculum delivery
◎ Encourage staff reflection as to the appropriateness of provision provided.

The Foundation Stage Profile

In September 1998 statutory baseline assessment was introduced that required all primary schools to assess every pupil on entry to school using an accredited baseline assessment scheme. These schemes were based on the *desirable learning outcomes* that were previously the goals for pupils' attainment in the term after their fifth birthday. When the Foundation Stage was introduced in September 2000 children in early years settings (including nursery and reception classes in schools) began working towards the *early learning goals*. The early learning goals are the expected attainment targets for children at the end of the Foundation Stage as they start Key Stage 1. The baseline assessment arrangements and accredited baseline assessment schemes are now outdated and no longer relevant.

From September 2002, the *Foundation Stage Profile* replaced Baseline Assessment as the statutory assessment for the end of the Foundation Stage. The Foundation Stage Profile is the national assessment scheme that enables early years practitioners to record observations and summarise children's achievements towards the early learning goals at the end of the Foundation Stage. The profile consists of practitioners' notes relating to the early learning goals, maintained and reviewed in the manner specified in the *Foundation Stage Profile Handbook*. (QCA/DfES, 2003)

National Curriculum assessment

Pupils are assessed by National Curriculum tests, commonly known as Standard Assessment Tasks or SATs, at the end of each key stage:

◎ Key Stage 1 tests in English and mathematics are taken at age 7 (Year 2)
◎ Key Stage 2 tests in English, mathematics and science are taken at age 11 (Year 6)
◎ Key Stage 3 tests in English, mathematics and science are taken at age 14 (Year 9)
◎ Key Stage 4 is assessed by GCSE levels of achievement at age 16 (Year 11).

In addition to the National Curriculum tests, formal teacher assessments are used to measure each pupil's progress. Teacher assessments judge children's performance over a longer period and are an essential element of the National Curriculum assessment process. The standard assessment tasks give a 'snapshot' of each pupil's level of attainment at the end of the key stage. Teacher assessment covers the full scope of the programmes of study as demonstrated by each pupil's performance in a wide range of learning activities in the classroom. It also includes information about pupil performance and attainment gained through discussion and observation. The results from teacher assessment are reported along with the results for the standard assessment tasks. Both national and teacher assessment have equal standing and provide a balanced view of each pupil's attainment. (QCA/DfES, 2002)

In Northern Ireland, Statutory Assessment arrangements (under the 1989 Education Reform Order) support the Northern Ireland Curriculum and include a 'snapshot' of each pupil's performance at three fixed points: age 8 (Year 4 – end of Key Stage 1); age 11 (Year 7 – end of Key Stage 2) and age 14 (Year 10 – end of Key Stage 3) (see www.deni.gov.uk).

For curriculum assessment guidelines in Scotland see *Promoting Learning: Assessing Children's Progress 3 to 5* and *Curriculum and Assessment in Scotland, National Guidelines: Assessment 5–14* (see www.ltscotland.org.uk).

Check it out

What are the assessment requirements of the curriculum framework applicable to the children in your setting?

CCLD 310.2
Assess and record children's progress in consultation with others

Knowledge Base

K3M337   K3M338   K3M339   K3D341   K3P342

Assessing and recording children's progress in consultation with others involves communicating assessment requirements to all relevant people within the setting including discussing roles and responsibilities. You should involve children, families and colleagues' expertise in the assessment process as appropriate and regularly refer to available guidance to assist with assessing children's progress, such as *Curriculum guidance for the foundation stage* and *Foundation Stage Profile Handbook* (see Further reading).

Formative assessment identifies future targets for the class, group and individual as appropriate to subjects/areas of learning *and* the requirements of the setting. It is on-going and informs planning provision to promote children's development and learning. Examples of formative assessment include: child observations; tick charts/lists; reading records; maths records; and daily target records for children with individual education plans.

Summative assessment involves monitoring children's progress. It should be used appropriately and allow judgements to be made about attainment. Opportunities for summative assessment should be identified in medium-term planning. For instance, a criterion-based test or task is required at least every half-term in each of the core subjects of the National Curriculum. Examples of summative assessments include: Foundation Stage Profile; SATs; teacher assessments; annual school reports; and reviews of children with special educational needs.

Examples of statutory assessment in early education:

◎ *Foundation Stage Profiles* should be completed in accordance with advice and support from the local education authority.
◎ *Standard Assessment Tasks* in English and mathematics at Key Stage 1 must be administered in accordance with the instructions from QCA.
◎ *For each child in the final year of Key Stage 1, a teacher assessment* must be made of the level achieved in each of the attainment targets in English, mathematics and science.
◎ *Teacher assessments in all applicable attainment targets* must be made continuously throughout Key Stages 1 and 2.
◎ *Differentiation:* assessment activities should be differentiated to ensure all children have access to the task. Children may be assessed orally if they are unable to produce a piece of written work.
◎ *Annual school reports* (see below).

Examples of internal assessment in early education:

◎ *Teacher assessments:* these should be made systematically and continuously throughout each key stage. A variety of assessment techniques should be used to give all pupils the opportunity to demonstrate what they know, understand or can do. Teacher assessments should be carried out as part of normal classroom activities, using both formal and informal assessment opportunities.

Results of assessments in core subjects will be recorded on individual record sheets.

◎ *Record folders:* literacy sheets: including reading records; numeracy sheets; any on-going records; and handwritten notes, for example those made about children causing concern or needing extra challenges when measured against learning objectives.

◎ *Records of achievements:* commendations; certificates; samples of work including a piece of writing reflecting progress over half a term related to the National Literacy Strategy objectives (six pieces per year).

Assessing and recording children's progress

You should draw on everyday observations and assessments and your knowledge of individual children to inform your assessments. After you have planned and implemented play and learning activities, you will need to assess and record the children's progress. Some assessment and recording may occur during the activities, providing continuous assessment of each child's performance (child observations, checklists, and so on). Some assessment and recording may occur shortly afterwards (for example record sheets aand formal assessments). It is important to assess and record children's progress so that you can: discover if the learning activity has been successful, in that the aims and learning objectives or outcomes have been met; consider the ways in which the learning activity might be modified/adapted to meet the needs of the child or children; and inform the senior practitioner, teacher, SENCO or other professionals whether or not a particular learning activity has been successful. You can assess children's progress by asking yourself questions such as:

1 Did the children achieve the intended learning intentions/objectives? If not, why not?

2 If the children have achieved the learning intentions/objectives, what effect has it had? (For example on behaviour, learning, any special needs.)

3 Were the learning intentions/objectives too easy or too hard?

4 How did any staff involvement affect the children's achievement?

5 Was the activity/lesson plan or overall curriculum plan successful? If not, why not?

You also need to be sensitive to children's individual needs and interests. Remember to observe the children while they are involved in the learning activities and assess whether you need to change or extend these activities to meet their early learning and developmental needs more fully. The senior practitioner, setting manager or your college tutor/assessor should give you guidelines on how to record assessments according to curriculum frameworks for early education as applicable to the setting, local or national requirements.

Using children's assessments to identify areas for improving practice

Despite careful planning, you may find that a learning activity is not appropriate for all the children you are working with. You need to monitor children's responses to learning activities and take appropriate action to modify or adapt activities to achieve the intended learning goals/objectives or provide additional activities to extend their learning. You may need to provide an alternative version of the activity or you might be able to present the

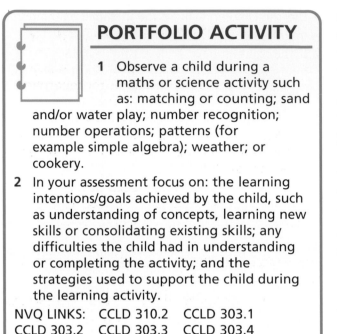

PORTFOLIO ACTIVITY

1 Observe a child during a maths or science activity such as: matching or counting; sand and/or water play; number recognition; number operations; patterns (for example simple algebra); weather; or cookery.

2 In your assessment focus on: the learning intentions/goals achieved by the child, such as understanding of concepts, learning new skills or consolidating existing skills; any difficulties the child had in understanding or completing the activity; and the strategies used to support the child during the learning activity.

NVQ LINKS: CCLD 310.2 CCLD 303.1
CCLD 303.2 CCLD 303.3 CCLD 303.4
CCLD 309.3

materials in different ways or offer a greater/lesser level of assistance. The reasons for your need to modify or adapt learning activities may include: the child lacks concentration; is bored or uninterested; finds the activity too difficult or too easy; or is upset or unwell (if so, you may need to abandon or postpone the activity).

Children's responses should also be considered when providing support for learning activities. You should be sensitive to children's needs and preferences and take notice of non-verbal responses and preferences demonstrated by them. These are just as important as what they say. Remember to give the children positive encouragement and feedback to reinforce and sustain their interest and efforts in the learning process. Use children's positive or negative responses to modify or extend activities to meet each child's needs more effectively. For example, if the learning intentions prove too easy or too difficult, you may have to set new goals. By breaking down learning

activities into smaller tasks, you may help individual children to achieve success more quickly. In modifying plans you are continuing a cycle of planning and implementing activities.

After the learning activity, use all the available relevant information to evaluate the effectiveness of your planning and implementation of the activity, for instance responses and/or information from parents, colleagues and other professionals. Provide feedback about the children's learning achievements to senior colleagues as appropriate (such as the senior practitioner or the class teacher). Any suggested changes to future activity plans should be agreed with the senior practitioner (or class teacher) and other relevant staff.

When planning and implementing learning activities for children you should ensure that you make accurate and detailed records of what has been planned and/or implemented in order to: clarify the aims and learning objectives of activity plans; avoid contradictory strategies and unnecessary duplication of work; use the time available more effectively; evaluate the success of plans/activities; and provide continuity and progression for future planning.

Reporting children's progress to colleagues and other professionals

There should be very close teamwork in the setting and all staff should know all the children. Members of staff need to liaise with each other continuously and it is important for you to liaise with those who will use your assessment information to inform planning for the children concerned. Some reporting to colleagues may be verbal and all records should be passed on to the relevant member of staff, for example the child's next teacher. Working with

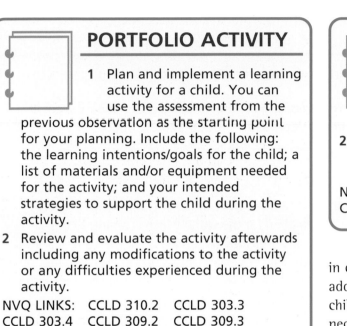

senior colleagues, you will need to ensure that full and complete records are provided for the new setting when children transfer to another nursery or primary school. You may need to share information about children's progress with other professionals, such as when working with children with special educational needs or when reporting concerns about a child's welfare. Follow your setting's policies and procedures for sharing information, including any confidentiality and data protection requirements (see CCLD 301.4 in Chapter 1 for more information about confidentiality matters).

Reporting children's progress to their parents

You should report children's progress to their parents on a regular basis depending on the requirements of your setting and provide information about their children's achievements and targets for future development and learning, as well as any difficulties they may have. This may include,

in consultation with children and parents, seeking additional support from appropriate sources if children are not progressing as expected and, where necessary, referring to external agencies.

In education settings it is a legal requirement that parents receive a written report at least once a year detailing the progress of their children in the National Curriculum subjects plus RE. General comments should also be made concerning the child's general progress and behaviour along with other achievements in the school including extra-curricular activities. All relevant personnel should be encouraged to contribute to these reports. School reports also contain teacher assessment and test level results at the end of KS1 and KS2, according to current statutory requirements. Each report must also detail the number of authorised and unauthorised absences since the last report. A pupil's annual report should:

◎ Be written clearly and concisely without too much jargon
◎ Summarise the child's performance since the last report
◎ Outline the child's level of attainment in the National Curriculum subjects. National Curriculum levels of attainment are required only in the core subjects in Years 2 and 6. However, parents are

PORTFOLIO ACTIVITY

1 Outline your setting's policy and procedures for reporting children's progress to their parents.
2 What are your responsibilities for reporting children's progress to their parents?

NVQ LINKS: CCLD 310.2   CCLD 301.4   CCLD 317.3   CCLD 330.3   CCLD 328.2   CCLD 339.1

informed if their child is working below, at or above National Curriculum levels in the remaining year groups

◎ Set out what the child has actually learned, not just what they have been taught during the school year

◎ Highlight positive achievements and progress made by the child

◎ Identify the child's weaknesses and suggest positive future action

◎ Set realistic targets to motivate the child for the coming school year.

Reports are usually given to parents in July and staff should be available to discuss children's reports by appointment at a special parents' evening arranged for this purpose. Parents should be invited to write comments about their children's reports on a separate slip that is returned to and kept by the school along with a copy of each report.

CCLD 323
Use Information and Communication Technology to support children's early learning

Children need to be able to use Information and Communication Technology (ICT) to support their learning across all areas of the relevant curriculum framework. Developing ICT skills helps prepare children for the world which is rapidly being transformed by technology. They need to learn the ICT skills necessary for work and everyday life, such as using the Internet and e-mail or computer programs for business, home and study. Using ICT can help to promote children's early learning by helping them to learn how to control a computer, including using a computer for word processing, developing pictures using 'paint' software, making tables or graphs, and accessing information via the Internet.

CCLD 323.1
Plan to use ICT in support of children's early learning

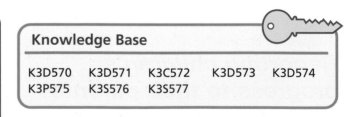

Knowledge Base

K3D570	K3D571	K3C572	K3D573	K3D574
K3P575	K3S576	K3S577		

Computers and other associated technology are now part of everyday life, so it is as important for all children to become computer-literate as it is for them to develop traditional literacy and numeracy skills (see Chapter 13). Computers can make learning more attractive and interesting by providing a different, more visual way of developing and using literacy and numeracy skills. For this reason, computers can be particularly helpful for children with language, literacy, numeracy or learning difficulties, especially as computer programs often have in-built praise or reward systems to motivate the user. Word processing can enable children to write more easily and clearly, freed from the physical constraints of pencil control, and can encourage correct spelling through the use of a spell-checker. Computers can also help referencing skills by encouraging children to access information in encyclopaedias on CD-ROM or via the Internet.

Using ICT to support children's play and learning

Use ICT to support play and learning in other curriculum subjects in ways that are stimulating and enjoyable for children, according to their ages, needs and abilities. It is important to work in partnership with families to support children's learning through ICT including creating opportunities for families to participate in ICT provision, for example ICT workshops and parent helpers for ICT activities. ICT can help to promote children's learning by enabling them to:

◎ Access, select and interpret information
◎ Recognise patterns, relationships and behaviours
◎ Observe, explore and describe patterns in number, shape and data
◎ Develop problem-solving skills including logic and reasoning
◎ Experiment and gain knowledge from feedback
◎ Model, predict and hypothesise
◎ Test reliability and accuracy
◎ Review and modify their work to improve the quality

◎ Communicate with others and present information in a variety of ways
◎ Be creative and imaginative
◎ Gain confidence and independence.

As a childcarer you need to help young children to develop their skills, competence and independence when using ICT equipment. Here is a brief outline of what you can expect from children using ICT within the Foundation Stage: show an interest in ICT, for example playing with remote-controlled cars; know how to operate simple equipment, such as playing a 'tune' on a musical keyboard; complete a simple program on the computer and/or perform simple functions on ICT apparatus by maybe using an interactive whiteboard; find out about and identify the uses of everyday technology and use ICT and programmable toys to support their learning, for instance by using a digital camera and then presentational software to make a slide show. (QCA, 2005)

Here is a brief outline of what you can expect from children using ICT within the Key Stage 1 of the National Curriculum. By age 7, most children can: use ICT to handle information in different ways including gathering, organising, storing and presenting information to others; use computer software in their everyday work (for example use a word processor to write and present their class work or use other computer packages which make use of graphics and sound); and use programmable toys, putting together computerised instructions in the right order. (DfEE, 2000)

You can support children's early learning through the use of ICT equipment such as:

◎ Computer hardware: computers; printers; scanners; modems; notebooks; adapted keyboards; computer-activated toys; concept keyboards; touch screens; interactive whiteboards; digital cameras and digital projectors

◎ Computer software: CD-ROMs; data-handling, paint, presentational and word-processing programs
◎ Computer accessories and consumables: disks; tape; paper
◎ Recording and playback equipment: tape and video recorders.

Safety issues for using ICT resources

You should find out which ICT equipment is needed and when it is required. You will need to ensure that this equipment is available and ready for use at the time required. You may need to book equipment in advance if it is shared between groups/classes or check and set up equipment already in the room where you work. You will also need to make sure that accessories and consumables (such as printer paper or spare bulbs) are the correct ones for the equipment being used. These should be stored safely but with easy access for when required. Check that ICT equipment is in safe working order and is being used correctly by yourself and the children. After use make sure that the equipment is left safe and secure. Any faults with equipment should be promptly reported to the person responsible for arranging maintenance or repair. Make sure that any faulty equipment is made safe and secure until it can be removed and/or repaired. The setting should also have guidelines for the use of ICT including information on preventing access to unsuitable material via the Internet and maintaining the safety of children who access the Internet.

PORTFOLIO ACTIVITY

1 Observe a child engaged in an ICT activity.
2 In your assessment focus on: the learning intentions/goals achieved by the child, such as learning new skills, solving problems or finding new information; the child's use of the ICT equipment; any difficulties the child had in understanding or completing the ICT activity; and the strategies used to support the child during the ICT activity.

NVQ LINKS: CCLD 323.1   CCLD 310.2   CCLD 303.1   CCLD 303.2   CCLD 309.3

Sample guidelines for staff – safe use of the Internet

1 All staff and adults in schools who will at some time be responsible for supervising pupil use of the Internet should be trained or experienced in its use and be aware of the issues surrounding use in schools.
2 All school staff must be aware that there is a considerable amount of material on the Internet that is unsuitable for pupils. This includes information that is pornographic, racist, extremist, political, drug related or deliberately misleading or incorrect.
3 Schools have a duty of care and must take all reasonable steps to protect pupils against deliberate or accidental access to such material. In practice this is likely to be through the use of

an electronic filtering mechanism supported by careful supervision of Internet use by pupils. However, staff must be aware that no filtering system will be 100 per cent secure unless it works on the basis of only giving access to previously viewed sites. Undesirable sites should be reported to the ICT co-ordinator for addition to the filtered list.

4 Supervision of pupils using the Internet by staff who are aware of the Internet and the issues surrounding its use is essential. Staff should know what they are looking at and how to trace the history of web site access during a particular lesson.

5 There are systems to monitor the use of the Internet made from individual computers. Staff and pupils need to be aware of this activity.

6 Schools may consider the use of an Intranet to store Internet information for local use while restricting live access to the Internet.

7 It may be appropriate to restrict access to the Internet from particular computers or for particular users. This is possible using a password or network access control function. Contact the ICT co-ordinator for assistance if needed.

8 Pupils should be encouraged to develop an understanding of what is and what is not appropriate material and should be encouraged to inform the teacher should such material be found.

9 Staff and pupils should sign an 'Acceptable Use Policy'.

10 Members of the community who come into school to use the ICT facilities should be aware of the school's rules and procedures when using the Internet.

(Shirley Hackett, Dudley MBC, December 2001)

PORTFOLIO ACTIVITY

1 What are your setting's procedures for the safe use and storage of ICT equipment?
2 Outline your setting's guidelines for the use of ICT including information on:
   ◎ How you prevent access to unsuitable material via the Internet
   ◎ How you maintain the safety of children who access the Internet.

NVQ LINKS: CCLD 323.1   CCLD 302.2   CCLD 305.3

CCLD 323.2
Implement ICT activities

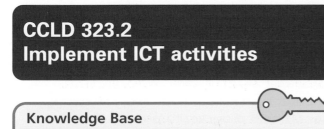

Knowledge Base

K3D570   K3D571   K3D573   K3D574

Providing required adult support during ICT activities

Your ability to provide effective support will depend on your experience of working with pupils or with the specific ICT activity. Ideally, you should be involved in the planning process and so will have a clear idea of the teaching and learning objectives for the learning activity involving ICT. Making a note of the key questions will enable you to understand the expected outcomes for pupils. Appropriate feedback at the end of a lesson can help to inform future provision. During lessons, encourage pupils, as appropriate to their age and level of development, to: think about the activities, such as why they are doing them, and what they are going to learn, practise or create; plan their own work or to speculate on 'what might happen if …'; reflect on what they know, understand and can do; and share successes and discuss any difficulties encountered. (Becta, 2004)

When supporting children during ICT activities, you need to take into account:

◎ Your competence and confidence with the hardware and software
◎ The age, ability and expertise of children; for instance, you may need to provide more support for younger children or some children with special needs; older children may be very confident users of ICT
◎ The complexity of the activity, and/or your familiarity with the appropriate software.

Twelve ways to use ICT to promote children's early learning

You can use ICT to promote children's physical, creative, social and emotional and communication development alongside their thinking and learning in the following ways:

1 Encourage children to find out about different ICT equipment (photocopier, digital camera, answer machine, scanner, walkie-talkies, and so on) and their uses.
2 Set up role play area to encourage interest in ICT, for example airport check-in, dentist reception, office or supermarket.
3 Use ICT equipment to stimulate interest and prompt discussion: display photographs taken with a digital camera; and make a slide show of photographs.
4 Encourage children to use the ICT equipment available as independently as possible by using a digital camera to take photographs, opening image on computer and printing out.
5 Demonstrate how to use a paint program and encourage children to create their own pictures using it.
6 Facilitate free play using ICT, for example use remote-controlled cars and trucks in the outside play area.
7 Encourage children to investigate moving a programmable toy including using the language of direction – forwards, backwards and turn.
8 Provide opportunities to explore the functions of an electronic musical keyboard.
9 Demonstrate how to use a cassette player or CD player so that children can listen to music or talking books by themselves.
10 Demonstrate how to use interactive books on the computer and provide opportunities for children to explore these independently.
11 Provide opportunities for children to use computer software in their everyday work, for example using a word processing or presentational program to present their work.
12 Use ICT as communication aids, such as computers and adapted keyboards or concept keyboards for children with special needs.

PORTFOLIO ACTIVITY

1 Plan and implement an ICT activity for a child. You can use the assessment from the previous observation as the starting point for your planning. Include the following: the learning intentions/goals for the child; the ICT equipment and any other resources needed for the activity; and your intended strategies to support the child during the activity.
2 Review and evaluate the activity afterwards including any modifications to the activity or any difficulties experienced during the activity.

NVQ LINKS: CCLD 323.1   CCLD 323.2   CCLD 303.3   CCLD 303.4   CCLD 309.1   CCLD 309.2
CCLD 310.2

CCLD 323.3
Evaluate children's learning through ICT

Knowledge Base

K3P578   K3P579   K3P580

It is important to develop a strategy for monitoring and evaluating children's learning of new skills and knowledge through ICT. You should also develop a strategy for monitoring and evaluating learning about ICT itself. Observe and monitor children's use of ICT including noting how they use ICT equipment and whether they are engaged and involved (see Chapter 3). In addition, ensure there is a balanced and effective approach to using ICT to support children's learning in your setting by reflecting on and improving practice (see Chapter 4). (NDNA, 2004)

The British Educational Communications and Technology Agency (Becta) has a self-review framework which sets out a structure to facilitate self-evaluation, benchmarking and action planning. This structure has eight elements: leadership and management; curriculum; learning and teaching; assessment; professional development; extending opportunities for learning; resources; and impact on pupil outcomes. (See *The self-review framework: a summary,* Becta 2006, available free from: www.becta.org.uk.)

PORTFOLIO ACTIVITY

1 Outline the strategy used in your setting to monitor and evaluate children's learning of new skills and knowledge through ICT including observations.
2 Outline the strategy used in your setting to monitor and evaluate learning about ICT itself.

NVQ LINKS: CCLD 323.2   CCLD 303.1   CCLD 303.2   CCLD 304.1   CCLD 310.2

13 Developing children's literacy and numeracy skills

Optional Units

CCLD 345
Help pupils to develop their literacy skills
CCLD 346
Help pupils to develop their numeracy skills

CCLD 345
Help pupils to develop their literacy skills

As a classroom or teaching assistant you may be involved in helping pupils to develop their literacy skills. Working under the direction of the teacher you should provide support for pupils' literacy development during whole class, group and individual learning activities including: discussing with the teacher how the learning activities will be organised and what your particular role will be. You may be required to provide the agreed support as appropriate to the different learning needs of pupils and give feedback to the teacher about the progress of pupils in developing literacy and language skills.

What is literacy?

Literacy means the ability to read and write. The word 'literacy' has only recently been applied as the definitive term for reading and writing, especially since the introduction of the National Literacy Strategy in schools. It makes sense to use the term 'literacy' as the skills of reading and writing do complement one another and are developed together. Reading and writing are forms of communication based on spoken language. Children need effective speaking and listening skills in order to develop literacy skills. Literacy unites the important skills of reading, writing, speaking and listening.

Why is literacy important?

Developing literacy skills is an essential aspect of development and learning. Without literacy skills, individuals are very restricted in their ability to: function effectively in school, college or at work; access information and new ideas; communicate their own ideas to others; or participate fully and safely in society. Education depends on individuals being able to read and write. Nearly all jobs and careers require at least basic literacy (and numeracy) skills. Our society also requires people to use literacy skills in everyday life by:

◎ Reading signs: street names, shop names, traffic signs and warning signs
◎ Reading newspapers, magazines, instructions, recipes, food labels
◎ Dealing with correspondence: reading and replying to letters; household bills; bank statements; wage slips; benefits
◎ Using computers, the Internet and e-mail
◎ Writing shopping lists, memos, notes.

At the centre of all learning are two key skills: literacy and numeracy. Literacy is probably the more important of the two as pupils need literacy to access other areas of the curriculum. For example, to tackle a mathematics problem they may need to read the question accurately before applying the appropriate numeracy skills, or they may need to record the results of a science experiment in a written form.

National frameworks and curriculum guidelines for teaching English

You should know the relevant national regulatory frameworks and curriculum guidelines for teaching English (or Welsh) relevant to the pupils you work with. In England the relevant frameworks are: *National Curriculum for English* – see the National Curriculum online website: www.nc.uk.net and also in the National Curriculum documents available in schools; *Primary National Strategy – Primary Framework for literacy and mathematics* and *Key Stage 3 National Strategy – Framework for teaching English: Years 7, 8 and 9* (see below). In Wales the relevant framework is the *National Curricula for English and Welsh in Wales* – see the Department of Education, Lifelong Learning and Skills website: http://old.accac.org.uk/index_eng.php. In Scotland there is no legally established national curriculum but the Scottish Executive Education Department provides guidelines for schools, for example the *5–14 National Guidelines* – see Learning and Teaching Scotland Online Service: www.ltscotland.org.uk. The *Northern Ireland Curriculum* (for pupils aged 4 to 16) is the relevant curriculum for those working in schools in Northern Ireland – see Department of Education, Northern Ireland website: www.deni.gov.uk.

The National Literacy Strategy for Key Stages 1 and 2

In September 1998 the National Literacy Strategy was introduced in schools to raise literacy and educational standards for all primary pupils in England. *The National Literacy Strategy Framework for Teaching YR to Y6* established the teaching objectives for literacy for pupils in primary schools.

In October 2006 the *Primary Framework for literacy and mathematics* replaced *The National Literacy Strategy Framework for Teaching YR to Y6 (1998)*. It applies to pupils aged 3 to 11 years. The renewed Framework builds on the learning that has taken place since the original Frameworks for teaching literacy and mathematics were introduced in 1998 and 1999. The changes contained in the Framework reflect national policy developments and are built upon research and evaluation undertaken since the late 1990s.

The renewed literacy Framework is different from the 1998 Framework: there exists an electronic version; and the learning objectives are simplified. The online version *Primary Framework for literacy and mathematics* can be accessed at www.standards.dfes.gov.uk/primaryframeworks. The electronic Framework provides a resource that will be added to and expanded with additional support and material as the Framework project develops. This will include any necessary revisions to the Early Years elements following the EYFS consultation. (DfES, 2006c)

Simplified learning objectives give a broad overview of the literacy curriculum in the primary phase. The learning objectives are aligned to 12 strands to demonstrate progression in each strand. These strands link directly to the Early Learning Goals and aspects of English in the National Curriculum. Covering the learning objectives will allow children to reach the Early Learning Goals for Communication, Language and Literacy and the appropriate National Curriculum levels for Key Stages 1 and 2. The learning objectives will be taught through the full range of texts described in the National Curriculum for English. (DfES, 2006c)

The twelve strands are as follows: Speak and listen for a wide range of purposes in different contexts

1 Speaking
2 Listening and responding
3 Group discussion and interaction
4 Drama

Read and write for a range of purposes on paper and on screen

5 Word recognition: decoding (reading) and encoding (spelling)
6 Word Structure and spelling
7 Understanding and interpreting texts
8 Engaging and responding to texts
9 Creating and shaping texts
10 Text structure and organisation
11 Sentence structure and punctuation
12 Presentation

(DfES, 2006c)

The literacy hour

Pupils have daily lessons for literacy where they are taught the knowledge, skills and understanding set out in the National Curriculum for English. The guidance in the renewed Framework still places emphasis on carefully planned, purposeful, well-directed teaching and learning. When the literacy framework was first published the context demanded that attention was given to the structure and organisation of the lesson. Now the challenge is about improving and refining what is in place. The literacy hour has been successful in structuring the pace of learning and planning for progression through Key Stages 1 and 2. It provides a structure for teaching in Key Stages 1 and 2 which can be adapted and revised to be sufficiently flexible to meet the learning needs of all pupils. The daily literacy hour may sometimes be planned as individual lessons. The renewed Framework promotes planning across a sequence of lessons that offers pupils continuity with a blend of approaches that sustain the challenge and maintain an interest in learning. (DfES, 2006c)

The literacy hour provides opportunities for pupils to develop their literacy skills through: high-quality oral work; the structured teaching of phonics, spelling and grammar; and guided/shared reading and writing activities.

The literacy hour includes work at word, sentence and text level:

◎ *Word level work* enables pupils to: use phonics, that is the letter sounds and blends that make words; recognise familiar letter combinations and words; learn new words to increase their vocabulary; and learn to spell words correctly.
◎ *Sentence level work* enables pupils to: learn how sentences are constructed; know, understand and use punctuation; and know and understand grammar rules.
◎ *Text level work* enables pupils to: read and understand different texts including fiction and non-fiction; develop comprehension skills by answering questions about texts; and develop composition skills by writing their own texts, including stories, poems and instructions.

The following outlines the structure of the literacy hour:

1 Whole class (15 minutes): shared text level work (both reading and writing).
2 Whole class (15 minutes): focused word or sentence level work.
3 Group and independent work (20 minutes): independent reading, writing or word work, while the teacher and teaching assistant work with at least two ability groups each day on guided text level work (reading or writing).
4 Whole class (10 minutes): reviewing, reflecting, consolidating the main teaching points and presenting work covered in the lesson.

(DfES, 1998)

13

The Key Stage 3 National Strategy

Key Stage 3 is a crucial point in a pupil's education, as evidence indicates that if pupils perform well in the National Curriculum tests at age 14, they will achieve success in their GCSEs. Equipping pupils with effective literacy skills is also the key to raising standards across all curriculum subject areas and to preparing pupils for adult life. *The Key Stage 3 National Strategy Framework for teaching English: Years 7, 8 and 9* aims to improve the achievements of 11 to 14-year-old pupils (see: www.standards.dfes.gov.uk/keystage3/). The framework is based on the programmes of study for English in the revised National Curriculum 2000. The objectives for Years 7, 8 and 9 provide a framework for progression and cover all aspects of the National Curriculum for English.

The lesson structure is similar to the literacy hour experienced by pupils in primary school.

A typical English lesson in Key Stage 3 includes:

1 A short starter activity for the whole class.
2 The main teaching activity including the teacher's contribution and pupil tasks.
3 A summary session to consolidate the pupils' learning.

Check it out

What are the national frameworks and curriculum guidelines for teaching English (and Welsh where applicable) relevant to your school?

CCLD 345.1 Help pupils to develop their reading skills

Reading is the process of turning groups of written symbols into speech sounds. In English this means being able to read from left to right, from the top of the page to the bottom and being able to recognise letter symbols plus their combinations as words. Reading is not just one skill; it involves a variety of abilities: visual and auditory discrimination; language and communication skills; word identification skills; conceptual understanding; comprehension skills; and memory and concentration.

Developing reading skills

Being able to read does not happen suddenly. Reading is a complex process involving a variety of skills, some of which (visual discrimination and communication skills) the individual has been developing since birth. Being able to use and understand spoken language forms the basis for developing reading skills. A child who has a wide variety of language experiences will have developed many of the skills needed for learning to read. (See Chapter 3 for more information about promoting children's communication skills and language development.)

Children who are pushed too hard by being forced to read and write before they are ready may actually be harmed in terms of their literacy development, as they can be put off reading, writing and other related activities. The area of learning *communication, language and literacy* included in the early learning goals for the Foundation Stage provides guidelines to help early years staff (and parents) understand the importance of informal approaches to language and literacy.

There is no set age at which children are ready to read, although most children learn to read between the ages of 4 and 6 years old. The age at which a child learns to read depends on a number of factors: physical maturity and co-ordination skills; social and emotional development; language experiences, especially access to books; interest in stories and rhymes; concentration and memory skills; and opportunities for play.

Reading skills checklist

Ask yourself the following questions to find out whether the child is ready to read:

1 Can the child see and hear properly?
2 Are the child's co-ordination skills developing within the expected norm?
3 Can the child understand and follow simple verbal instructions?
4 Can the child co-operate with an adult and concentrate on an activity for short periods?
5 Does the child show interest in the details of pictures?
6 Does the child enjoy looking at books plus joining in with rhymes and stories?
7 Can the child retell parts of a story in the right order?
8 Can the child tell a story using pictures?
9 Can the child remember letter sounds and recognise them at the beginning of words?
10 Does the child show pleasure or excitement when able to read words in school?

If the answer is 'yes' to most of these questions, the child is probably ready to read; if the answer is 'no' to any of the questions, the child may need additional support or experiences in those areas before they are ready to read.

Reading approaches

Whole-word or 'look and say' approach

Pupils are taught to recognise a small set of key words (usually related to a reading scheme) by means of individual words printed on flashcards. Pupils recognise the different words by shape and other visual differences. Once pupils have developed a satisfactory sight vocabulary, they go on to the actual reading scheme. The whole-word approach is useful for learning difficult words which do not follow the usual rules of English language. The drawback is that this approach does not help pupils to work out new words for themselves.

Phonics approach

With this approach pupils learn the sounds that letters usually make. It helps pupils to establish a much larger reading vocabulary fairly quickly, as they can 'sound out' new words for themselves. The disadvantage is that there are many irregular words in the English language; one letter may make many different sounds, for example b*ough*, r*ough*, thr*ough*. However, pupils do better with the phonics approach than with any other approach.

Apprenticeship approach

This approach, also known as the 'story' or 'real books' approach, does not formally teach pupils to read. Instead, the pupil sits with an adult and listens to the adult read; the pupil starts reading along with the adult until the pupil can read some or the entire book alone. This approach does not help a pupil with the process of decoding symbols. There has been much criticism of this approach, but it has proved effective in this country and New Zealand as part of the 'Reading Recovery' programme for older, less able readers.

Most adults helping pupils to develop reading skills use a combination of the 'look and say' approach to introduce early sight vocabulary and then move on to the more intensive phonics approach to establish the pupils' reading vocabulary. It is important for you to be flexible to meet the individual literacy needs of pupils. You should also work with parents to develop their children's reading skills.

CCLD 345.2
Help pupils to develop their writing skills

Writing is the system we use to present '*speech in a more permanent form*'. (Moyle, 1976) There are two elements to writing: the *mechanical skill of letter formation*, that is writing legibly using recognised word and sentence structures, including appropriate spaces between words and punctuation marks; the *creative skill of 'original composition'*, that is deciding what to write and working out how to write it using appropriate vocabulary to express thoughts and ideas which may be fact or fiction. (Taylor, 1973)

Developing writing skills

Children will experience written language through books and stories and learn that writing is made up

Figure 13.1 Pupils engaged in a reading activity

of symbols or patterns organised on paper in a particular way. In English this means 26 letters in the alphabet written from left to right horizontally. Children also learn, by watching adults and other children at home, in the childcare setting and/or in school, that writing can be used for:

Think About

1 How did you learn to read? How did your own children (if any) learn to read?
2 What are the approaches to teaching reading in your school?
3 Consider the similarities and differences between these approaches.

Ten ways to help pupils to develop their reading skills

You can help pupils to develop their reading skills by:

1 Providing plenty of opportunities for pupils to talk; children who are effective communicators often transfer these skills to reading.*

2 Using everyday speech, rhymes and songs to help pupils widen their vocabulary and improve their comprehension skills, for example discussions, circle time and story time.

3 Sharing books, stories, poems and rhymes to introduce pupils to different literary styles or genres. This also includes looking at other types of printed materials such as newspapers, magazines, comics and signs.

4 Using computers and other digital media to encourage and extend reading skills. These may include CD–ROMs, the Internet and television education programmes. (See Chapter 12.)

5 Encouraging pupils to participate in listening games to develop auditory discrimination like sound lotto and 'guess the sound' using sounds of everyday objects or musical instruments.

6 Encouraging pupils to participate in matching games and memory games to develop visual discrimination and memory skills such as snap, matching pairs, jigsaws and games like 'I went shopping . . .'.

7 Providing fun activities to develop letter recognition such as 'I spy . . .' using letter sounds; going on a 'letter hunt' (looking around the classroom for things beginning with a particular letter); hanging up an 'alphabet washing line'; and singing alphabet songs and rhymes.

8 Getting pupils to put sections of a jumbled poem or story into the correct order to help their comprehension and sequencing skills.

9 Using riddles to develop pupils' knowledge of rhyming. Give pupils some riddles to work out. When the pupils have worked out the answers to the riddles, they can try to make up some of their own. The pupils can write out or word process their riddles and put them together to make a group- or class-riddles book.

10 Using limericks; pupils enjoy reading limericks and can create their own. In the UK, limericks are featured in the National Literacy Strategy: in Year 3, Term 3 and in Year 6, Term 2.

* See page 271 for details of ways to help pupils to develop their speaking and listening skills.

◎ Recording past events and experiences, such as news, outings, visitors and special events

◎ Exchanging information, for example notes, memos, letters and postcards

◎ Functional purposes, composing shopping lists, recipes, menus and recording experiments or data

◎ Sharing stories and ideas by story writing and poetry.

Children do not learn to write just through exposure to a writing environment. Writing is a skill that has to be taught. Learning to write involves learning specific conventions with regard to letter shapes, the sequence of letters in words, word order in sentences, the direction of writing, and so on. It is usual to teach writing skills alongside reading. This helps children to make the connection between written letters and the sounds they make when read. Most of the activities used to develop children's reading skills will also help their writing skills. In addition, children need plenty of opportunities to develop the *co-ordination* skills necessary for writing: hand–eye co-ordination; fine manipulative skills for pencil control; and being able to sit still with the correct posture for writing.

Developing writing skills is much more difficult than reading because of the considerable physical and cognitive demands it makes, such as co-ordinating movements to write; writing legibly, that is creating letters of consistent size and shape; gaps between words; using the correct punctuation and sentence structure; following the correct spelling requirements; and writing material of the required length which also makes sense. Remember that some pupils may have special needs which require their using alternative means or specialist equipment in order to write, such as Braille, voice-activated computer or word processor. (See below.)

Think About

1 How did you learn to write?
2 Which activities for developing pupils' writing skills are used in your school?

Ten ways to help pupils to develop their writing skills

You can help pupils to develop their writing skills by:

1 Providing opportunities to write about their own experiences as appropriate to their age and level of development, such as news and recording events.
2 Providing opportunities to create their own stories and poems as a means of expressing their feelings and ideas. You can use class or group topics as well as the pupils' own interests to stimulate their ideas for stories and poems, for example weather, transport, festivals, our nursery or school, holidays, animals, spaceships, dragons, wizards, monsters, or haunted house.
3 Using storybooks as a starting point for their own creative writing. For example, read The True Story of the Three Little Pigs (by Jon Scieszka). This tells the 'Three Little Pigs'

story from the wolf's point of view. Then ask the pupils to write their own version of a traditional story from a different point of view, for example Little Red Riding Hood from the wolf's point of view or Jack and the Beanstalk from the giant's point of view.

4 Encouraging independent spelling techniques, such as word banks, key words on permanent display, topic words on the board or on paper at the pupils' tables and personal word books and dictionaries.

5 Using alternative writing methods to release younger pupils or those with co-ordination difficulties (such as dyspraxia) from their physical limitations of writing, for instance allowing them to dictate their ideas while an adult acts as scribe or to use a tape recorder or word processor.

6 Helping pupils to write their own newspaper articles. Give the pupils a selection of headlines (from a variety of newspapers) and ask them to write an article to go with a headline or give the pupils an article and ask them to make a headline for it.

7 Providing opportunities for pupils to write letters so that they experience writing for different purposes and for different audiences. Once pupils are familiar with the correct layout for letters, they can write to other pupils in their own school or at other schools.

8 Asking the pupils to write reports describing or classifying a subject area factually: information leaflet; magazine article; and topic-based group or class project.

9 Asking the pupils to write step-by-step instructions on how to do, make or fix something. Examples include: a recipe; science experiment; instructions for a game or toy; and posters, signs and notices.

10 Encouraging older pupils to write discursive texts that present all sides of an issue by making points for and against. Examples include: a leaflet or article giving a balanced account of a topical issue; newspaper editorial; a write up of a group or class debate; and practice writing essay or exam answer in secondary school.

PORTFOLIO ACTIVITY

1 List the resources available in your school to support pupils' writing skills.
2 Give examples of activities you have used to develop pupils' writing skills.
NVQ LINKS: CCLD 345.1   CCLD 345.2   CCLD 345.3   CCLD 303.3   CCLD 303.4   CCLD 306.2   CCLD 309.2   CCLD 323.2

CCLD 345.3
Help pupils to develop their speaking and listening skills

Speaking and listening are part of the National Curriculum programmes of study for English: Speaking and listening, Reading and Writing. These three areas all focus on language and how it is used in the different modes (see page 71 for information on promoting children's communication skills and language development). Each mode has its own distinct features but speaking and listening, reading and writing are interdependent. Speaking and listening skills involve:

◎ Speaking: being able to speak clearly and to develop and sustain ideas in talk
◎ Listening: developing active listening strategies and critical skills of analysis
◎ Group discussion and interaction: taking different roles in groups, making a range of contributions and working collaboratively
◎ Drama: improvising and working in role, scripting and performing, and responding to performances.

(DfES, 2003c)

Developing speaking and listening skills

All areas of the school curriculum provide opportunities for the development of children's speaking and listening skills. The skills used will vary according to the curriculum area. For example, pupils may be involved in learning activities that encourage them to: describe, interpret, predict and hypothesise in mathematics and science; express opinions and discuss design ideas in art, design and technology; discuss cause and effect in history and geography; and discuss social or moral issues in PSHE and RE.

Ten ways to help pupils to develop their speaking and listening skills

You can help pupils to develop their speaking and listening skills by:

1 Encouraging pupils to participate in appropriate opportunities, especially activities that encourage language and communication, for example role/pretend play such as dressing-up, home corner, shop play; creative and imaginative activities such as: construction kits; natural materials like water, sand, clay, cooking ingredients; and creative materials such as paint, paper, pencils, crayons, chalks, pastels.

2 Providing plenty of opportunities for discussion such as: problem-solving during activities; follow-up to activities (for example after television programmes or stories); co-operative group work; games and puzzles; television programmes for their age group; talking about key features when on outings such as visits to farms, parks and museums.

3 Using displays as a stimulus for discussions and to consolidate learning; for example wall and interactive tabletop displays with interesting objects to talk about, look at and/or play with, as well as recorded sounds to listen to including voices, music, songs, rhymes and musical instruments.

4 Encouraging pupils to participate in activities involving self-expression and self-evaluation such as: talking about their day, experiences and interests with other pupils and adults, including discussion, news time, circle time, tutorials; talking about special events, such as birthdays or a new baby; or talking while doing activities such as writing, music, art, design, drama and dance.

5 Sharing books, stories and poems with pupils, including picture books, story books, 'big' books, novels, poetry books, information books, dictionaries, encyclopaedias and

atlases. These will encourage pupils' listening skills and auditory discrimination (for example being attentive during story time, distinguishing between sounds, being aware of rhyming words) and will provide stimulus for discussion and literacy activities as well as introducing or extending their vocabulary.

6   Helping pupils to understand the rules of language. Once children start to combine words to make sentences, they progress through various stages in which the structure and organisation of language become gradually more systematic. This systematic structuring of language is called grammar. Children do not learn grammar through imitation alone; they need opportunities to discover the rules of language for themselves by experimenting and being creative with words in a variety of situations.

7   Providing opportunities for pupils to follow and give instructions, such as: introducing or extending knowledge on a specific skill; specifying tasks (verbal and/or written on a board); listening to step-by-step instructions; explaining worksheets, work cards or textbooks; verbal instructions during an activity to keep pupils on task or providing extra support for individual pupils; delivering verbal/written messages, errands.

8   Giving positive feedback, praise and encouragement to all children by commenting positively on children's efforts and achievements at communicating in various ways.

9   Considering the individual interests and abilities of children, including valuing children's home experiences/cultural backgrounds and being aware of possible developmental or psychological difficulties that may affect their speaking and listening skills by carefully observing children's development and learning.

10 Using Information and Communication Technology including television and CD-ROMs as additional stimuli for discussions and ideas. ICT can also be used to introduce or reinforce information on topics and themes within the setting. Television programmes should always be recorded to allow for possible interruptions and to provide opportunities for the adult to pause the programme while they ask or answer questions, in order to stimulate children's speaking and listening skills. Remember that ICT is not a substitute for other forms of communication, such as conversation and children's play.

PORTFOLIO ACTIVITY

1   List the resources available within your school to support the development of speaking and listening skills.

2   Describe how you have helped pupils to develop their speaking and listening skills in one of the following:

◎ Discussion during news, circle time or tutorials

◎ Playing a game with a child or small group of children

◎ Sharing a story, poem or rhyme.

NVQ LINKS: CCLD 345.1   CCLD 345.2   CCLD 345.3   CCLD 301.2   CCLD 303.3   CCLD 303.4
CCLD 306.2   CCLD 309.2

The teaching assistant's role in supporting pupils' literacy skills

The teaching assistant plays a key role in supporting the teacher and pupils during literacy activities. You will need to find out from the teacher how the literacy activities are to be organised and your specific role in supporting various learning activities, including class discussions, group activities and tasks for individuals. Ensure that you:

◎ Understand the intended learning outcomes for the pupils
◎ Agree the support strategies to be used for each pupil
◎ Obtain the resources required
◎ Implement the agreed strategies
◎ Provide feedback and encouragement during the activity (see page 177)
◎ Monitor the progress of the pupils
◎ Report any problems in providing support to the teacher.

Support strategies to help pupils to develop their literacy skills include:

◎ Using targeted prompts and feedback to encourage independent reading and writing
◎ Encouraging pupils to participate in shared reading and writing activities
◎ Developing phonic knowledge and skills to help pupils read and spell accurately
◎ Using specific reading or writing support strategies, such as paired reading and writing frames
◎ Using specific reading or writing support programmes, for example graded reading books and Additional Literacy Support (see below)
◎ Repeating instructions given by the teacher
◎ Taking notes for a pupil while the teacher is talking

◎ Explaining difficult words and phrases to a pupil
◎ Promoting the use of dictionaries
◎ Reading and clarifying textbook/worksheet activity for a pupil
◎ Reading a story to an individual pupil or small group
◎ Playing a word game with an individual pupil or small group
◎ Directing computer-assisted learning programmes
◎ Assisting pupils with special equipment, such as a hearing aid or a Dictaphone
◎ Encouraging shy or reticent pupils to participate in conversations and discussions
◎ Providing any other appropriate assistance during an activity
◎ Monitoring pupil progress during an activity
◎ Reporting problems and successes to the teacher.

Despite careful planning and organisation, you may encounter problems in providing support for pupils during learning activities. Ensure that you know and understand the sort of problems that might occur. For example: difficulties with the quantity, quality, suitability or availability of learning resources; issues relating to space, comfort, noise levels or disruptions within the learning environment; factors that may affect a pupil's ability to learn, for example social and cultural background, special educational needs, such as learning difficulties or behavioural problems (see below).

You will need to be able to deal with any problems you may have in providing support for pupils as planned. For example: modifying or adapting an activity; providing additional activities to extend their learning; providing an alternative version of the activity; presenting the materials in various ways; offering a greater or lesser level of assistance; coping with insufficient materials or equipment breakdown; and dealing with unco-operative or disruptive pupils.

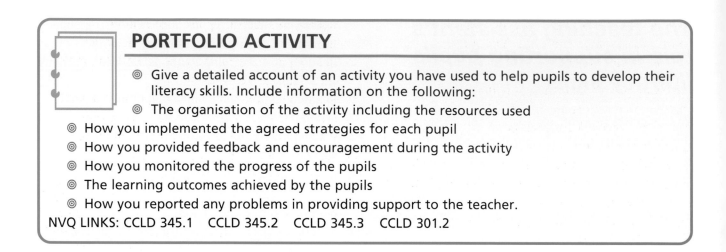

PORTFOLIO ACTIVITY

◎ Give a detailed account of an activity you have used to help pupils to develop their literacy skills. Include information on the following:

◎ The organisation of the activity including the resources used

◎ How you implemented the agreed strategies for each pupil

◎ How you provided feedback and encouragement during the activity

◎ How you monitored the progress of the pupils

◎ The learning outcomes achieved by the pupils

◎ How you reported any problems in providing support to the teacher.

NVQ LINKS: CCLD 345.1   CCLD 345.2   CCLD 345.3   CCLD 301.2

Supporting pupils with special literacy needs

Some children may have special literacy needs due to cognitive and learning difficulties or sensory impairment (see Chapter 14) or physical disabilities (see Chapter 7). Others may have special literacy needs due to behavioural difficulties (see Chapter 9) or special language needs, such as English as an additional language (see below).

Unit Links

For this Unit you also need to understand the following sections:

CCLD 307.3 Promote children's healthy physical development (see Chapter 7)

CCLD 321.2 Helping children with disabilities and special educational needs to participate in the full range of activities and experiences (see Chapter 14)

CCLD 337.2 Promote positive aspects of behaviour (see Chapter 9)

The range of pupils with special educational needs varies. Many pupils with SEN may not have special literacy needs and will not require extra or different literacy support. However, many classes will have one or more pupil with identified SEN who require a modified approach to the National Literacy Strategy.

There are two broad groups of pupils with special literacy needs:

1 The first is a larger group of pupils who experience minor difficulties in learning, which is reflected in their attainment of levels of literacy which are below those expected for pupils of their age. The structure provided by the National Literacy Strategy can benefit these pupils. They can usually overcome these difficulties through normal teaching strategies and will soon develop the essential literacy skills that will enable them to catch up and work at a comparable level to the rest of their year group.

2 The second, smaller group includes pupils with severe and complex learning difficulties that require the use of different teaching strategies. These pupils may require different levels of work from the rest of their year group. They may also need to be taught at a different pace for all or most of their school years. Some pupils with SEN

will always need access to systems such as symbols, signing, Braille or electronic communicators. (DfES, 1998)

Some pupils with identified SEN may work at earlier levels than those specified in the National Literacy Strategy Framework for their year group, while others will need to work on one term's work for several terms. With structured, intensive teaching, some of these pupils will gradually progress through the levels in the Framework and will eventually be able to work at the levels appropriate to their age. Some will require work on the development of particular literacy skills, or to work on some skills for longer than others, for example pupils with speech and language difficulties may need to work on programmes devised by a speech therapist or specialist language teacher.

Literacy support programmes

Some pupils with special literacy needs will require specific support programmes. The National Literacy Strategy has three literacy support programmes devised to provide structured, additional support for those pupils who are not making the expected progress in literacy. *Early Literacy Support Programme: materials for teachers working in partnership with teaching assistants* contains materials to support the introduction of Early Literacy Support (ELS) in Year 1. *Additional Literacy Support* (ALS) is designed to help pupils in Key Stage 2 who have already fallen behind in literacy, but who would not otherwise receive any additional support in this area. *Further Literacy Support: Resource Pack* is designed to offer structured, additional support for those pupils who are not making the expected progress in literacy.

Support staff (including specially trained teaching assistants) can provide assistance for pupils with special literacy needs by:

◎ Signing to support a pupil with hearing impairment during shared literacy activities
◎ Supporting a pupil during group work to develop specific skills such as phonics
◎ Asking questions aimed at the appropriate level
◎ Giving the pupil some extra help in a group
◎ Sitting next to the pupil to keep them on task
◎ Using a literacy support programme.

Activity

1 Describe how you could provide support for a pupil with special literacy needs.
2 Use examples from your own experience if applicable.

Supporting pupils with special language needs

All pupils have *individual* language needs, but some pupils may have *additional* or *special language needs* that affect their ability to communicate effectively with others. Being able to structure and use language is an enormous task for everyone; it takes the first 7 to 8 years of life to learn how to form all the different sounds correctly. Some sounds are more difficult to pronounce than others, for example: 's', 'sh', 'scr', 'br', 'cr', 'gr' and 'th'. Most children have problems with these sounds at first, but eventually are able to pronounce them properly.

Some pupils who have difficulties with structuring language may have problems with:

◎ *Phonology:* the articulation of sounds, syllables and words (as mentioned above)
◎ *Grammar* or *syntax:* words, phrases or sentence structure

◎ *Semantics: understanding* language (*receptive* difficulties): and/or *using* language (*expressive* difficulties).

Many of the activities already suggested in this chapter will be suitable for *all* pupils including those with special language needs. Some pupils, especially those with severely delayed or disordered language development, may need specialist help from a speech and language therapist. (For more detailed information on supporting children with communication difficulties see CCLD 321.2 in Chapter 14.)

Supporting pupils with English as an additional language

Bilingual means 'speaking two languages' which applies to some pupils (and staff) in schools in the United Kingdom. 'Multilingual' is used to describe someone who uses more than two languages. The term 'bilingual' is widely used for all children who speak two or more languages. However, since the introduction of The National Literacy Strategy, the preferred term for bilingual pupils is *pupils with English as an additional language*. There is a broad range of pupils with EAL, including pupils who are:

◎ Literate in English and do not require extra provision
◎ Able to converse in English but need help to use language in their school work
◎ Literate in languages other than English but need a little extra support with literacy
◎ Learning to speak English as well as learning to read and write it
◎ Below the levels of language or literacy expected for their age and require adapted materials to meet their language and/or literacy needs.

It is important to distinguish between pupils who have additional language learning needs and those who also have special educational needs. Some pupils with EAL may also be assessed as having SEN. You can support pupils with English as an additional language by:

◎ Encouraging the pupils to use their community languages some of the time; this promotes security and social acceptance which will make learning English easier
◎ Asking the teacher to invite parents/grandparents to read or tell stories in community languages or to be involved with small groups for cooking, sewing or craft activities
◎ Using songs and rhymes to help introduce new vocabulary
◎ Using other areas of the curriculum to develop language skills in a meaningful context, for example focus on words used when working on the computer or during science experiments
◎ Using play activities and/or games to encourage and extend language.

PORTFOLIO ACTIVITY

Describe how you have (or could have) provided support for pupils with special language needs in your setting. Include examples for pupils with:
◎ Difficulties in communicating effectively with others
◎ English (or Welsh) as an additional language.
NVQ LINKS: CCLD 345.1   CCLD 345.2
CCLD 345.3   CCLD 301.2   CCLD 305.1
CCLD 305.2   CCLD 321.2   CCLD 334.1

CCLD 346
Help pupils to develop their numeracy skills

As a classroom or teaching assistant you may be involved in helping pupils to develop their numeracy skills. Working under the direction of the teacher you should provide support for pupils' numeracy development during whole class, group and individual learning activities including: discussing with the teacher how the learning activities will be organised and what your particular role will be; providing the agreed support as appropriate to the different learning needs of pupils; and giving feedback to the teacher about the progress of pupils in developing mathematical knowledge and skills.

What is numeracy?

The term 'numeracy' was introduced in about 1982 to describe what was previously called arithmetic. Individuals who are competent at arithmetic have always been described as 'numerate'; now this competency is called 'numeracy'. Numeracy is more than an ability to do basic arithmetic. Numeracy is a proficiency that involves confidence and competence with numbers and measures. It requires an understanding of the number system, a repertoire of computational skills and an inclination and ability to solve number problems in various contexts. Numeracy also demands practical understanding of the ways in which data are gathered, by counting and measuring, and are presented in graphs, diagrams and tables.

Why is numeracy important?

Being able to do number calculations confidently is an essential life skill; it helps people function effectively in everyday life. It is also very important as a first step in learning mathematics. We use numeracy in everyday life including:

◎ Shopping: checking change; buying the right quantities; getting value for money
◎ Cooking: weighing ingredients
◎ Decorating: calculating the amount of wallpaper, paint, carpet or other materials needed for the required areas
◎ Sewing: measuring materials; using graph paper to plot designs
◎ Journeys and holidays: understanding transport timetables; planning the best route; calculating mileage or the time a journey will take; working out how much petrol is needed for a car journey.

Learning numeracy skills is the central part of mathematics, but children are also taught about geometry (for example space and shapes) and the beginnings of algebra (number patterns). Children need to develop numeracy skills that involve confidence and competence with numbers and measures, including:

◎ Knowledge and understanding of the number system
◎ Knowing by heart various number facts, such as multiplication tables
◎ Using a range of mathematical skills
◎ Making mental calculations
◎ Being able to solve number problems in a variety of contexts
◎ Presenting information about counting and measuring using graphs, diagrams, charts and tables.

National frameworks and curriculum guidelines for teaching mathematics

You should know the relevant national regulatory frameworks and curriculum guidelines for teaching mathematics relevant to the pupils you work with. In England the relevant frameworks are: *National Curriculum for Mathematics* – see the National Curriculum online website (www.nc.uk.net) and also in the National Curriculum documents available in schools; *Primary National Strategy – Primary Framework for literacy and mathematics*; *Key Stage 3 National Strategy – Framework for teaching mathematics: Years 7, 8 and 9* (see below). In Wales the relevant framework is the *National Curriculum for Mathematics in Wales* – see the Department of Education, Lifelong Learning and Skills (DELLS) website: http://old.accac.org.uk/ index_eng.php. In Scotland there is no legally established national curriculum but the Scottish Executive Education Department (SEED) provides guidelines for schools, e.g. the *5–14 National Guidelines* – see Learning and Teaching Scotland Online Service: www.ltscotland.org.uk. The *Northern Ireland Curriculum* (for pupils aged 4 to 16) is the relevant curriculum for those working in schools in Northern Ireland – see Department of Education, Northern Ireland (DENI) website: www.deni.gov.uk.

The National Numeracy Strategy for Key Stages 1 and 2

The National Numeracy Strategy was introduced into all primary schools in England and Wales in September 1999 and supported the National Curriculum for Mathematics. *The National Numeracy Strategy – Framework for teaching mathematics* from Reception to Y6 which included a systematic range of mathematics work to ensure that primary pupils develop essential numeracy skills.

In October 2006 the *Primary Framework for literacy and mathematics* replaced *The National Numeracy Strategy – Framework for teaching mathematics from Reception to Y6 (1999)* and applies to pupils aged 3 to 11 years. The renewed Framework builds on the learning that has taken place since the original Frameworks for teaching literacy and mathematics were introduced in 1998 and 1999.

The renewed literacy Framework is different from the 1999 Framework in the following ways: an electronic version; simplified learning objectives. The online version *Primary Framework for literacy and mathematics* can be accessed at www.standards.dfes.gov.uk/primaryframeworks. The *electronic Framework* provides a resource that will be added to and expanded with additional support and material as the Framework project develops. This will include any necessary revisions to the Early Years elements following the EYFS consultation. (DfES, 2006c)

Simplified *learning objectives* give a broad overview of the mathematics curriculum in the primary phase. The learning objectives are aligned to seven strands to demonstrate progression in each strand. These strands link directly to the Early Learning Goals and aspects of mathematics in the National Curriculum. Covering the learning objectives will allow children to reach the Early Learning Goals for Mathematical Development and the appropriate National Curriculum levels for Key Stages 1 and 2. The learning objectives will be taught through the full range of texts described in the National Curriculum for mathematics. (DfES, 2006c)

The seven strands are as follows.

1 Using and applying mathematics
2 Counting and understanding number

3 Knowing and using number facts
4 Calculating
5 Understanding shape
6 Measuring
7 Handling data

The daily mathematics lesson

Pupils have daily lessons for mathematics where they are taught the knowledge, skills and understanding set out in the National Curriculum for Mathematics. The guidance in the renewed Framework still places emphasis on carefully planned, purposeful, well-directed teaching and learning. When the numeracy framework was first published the context demanded that attention was given to the structure and organisation of the lesson. Now the challenge is about improving and refining what is in place. The daily mathematics lesson has been successful in structuring the pace of learning and planning for progression through Key Stages 1 and 2. The daily mathematics lesson provides a structure for teaching in Key Stages 1 and 2 which can be adapted and revised to be sufficiently flexible to meet the learning needs of all pupils. The daily mathematics lesson may sometimes be planned as individual lessons. The renewed Framework promotes planning across a sequence of lessons that offers pupils continuity with a blend of approaches that sustain the challenge and maintain an interest in learning. (DfES, 2006c)

Depending on the age of the pupils, a daily maths lesson is about 45 to 60 minutes. The main emphasis is on pupils discussing mathematics and using appropriate mathematical terminology.

The daily maths lesson is typically separated into three key sections:

1 *Oral and mental starter.* All pupils in the class are taught together for the first 10 minutes. They are encouraged to sharpen their maths skills by: counting (in ones, twos, tens, backwards and forwards, and so on) or remembering addition and/or subtraction number facts (including reciting multiplication tables for older pupils). The teacher may also ask questions or go over previous homework.

2 *Main teaching activity.* The main teaching activity lasts for about 30 to 40 minutes. The teacher may *introduce* a new maths skill, provide opportunities to *practise* previous work or *extend* their skills on more difficult problems. Pupils may work for short times in groups, pairs or individually.

3 *Plenary.* The lesson ends with a plenary (lasting about 10 minutes) when the whole class comes together for a summary of the main points of the lesson. The teacher discovers what the pupils have actually learned and repeats the key points or specific maths skills that the pupils need to remember. The teacher may also set maths homework.

The Key Stage 3 National Strategy

The Key Stage 3 National Strategy Framework for teaching mathematics: Years 7, 8 and 9 builds on the numeracy work in primary schools. This framework is aimed at teachers and trainee teachers; it will also be helpful for those who support mathematics in schools, such as teaching assistants who provide numeracy support for pupils in secondary schools. The framework provides advice on teaching strategies, inclusion and differentiation, and the assessment of pupil progress. It also sets out yearly teaching programmes illustrating how objectives for teaching mathematics can be planned from Year 7 to Year 9.

A typical mathematics lesson in Key Stage 3 involves:

1 *Oral and mental starter.* For about 5 to 10 minutes the pupils are engaged in whole class work to revise, sharpen and develop mental skills including recall skills, visualisation, thinking and communication skills.

2 *Main teaching activity.* The main teaching activity lasts for about 25 to 40 minutes. The teaching input and learning activities may involve a combination of working as a whole class, in groups, pairs or as individuals. The teacher (and teaching assistant) supports pupil activities by: *identifying and sorting out misconceptions; clarifying points; giving immediate feedback.*

3 *Plenary.* The lesson ends with a plenary (lasting about 5 to 15 minutes) when the whole class comes together for a summary of the key points or specific mathematical skills that the pupils need to remember. The teacher identifies pupil progress, makes links to other work and discusses the next steps including setting mathematics homework.

(DfES, 2001b)

Check it out

What are the national frameworks and curriculum guidelines for teaching mathematics relevant to your school?

CCLD 346.1
Help pupils to develop their understanding and use of number

To develop their understanding and use of number pupils need to learn the following mathematical skills: using and applying mathematics; counting and understanding number; knowing and using number facts; calculating; handling data.

Using and applying mathematics

Pupils learn to select an appropriate mathematical skill to tackle or solve a problem. They learn to use words, symbols and basic diagrams to record and give details about how they solved a problem. Pupils develop problem-solving skills in order to work out the best approach to finding a mathematical solution. They learn which *questions* to ask as well as developing the appropriate skills to answer mathematical problems such as: What is the problem? Which mathematical skill needs to be used? Will a graph, chart or diagram help find the solution?

Counting and understanding number

Many children learn number names and how to count before they begin school. At home or in early years settings (e.g. day nursery or playgroup) they do counting activities and sing number songs and rhymes. During the primary school years pupils develop and extend their counting skills. Younger pupils begin with numbers 0 to 20 which are the most difficult to learn as each number name is different; numbers from 20 onwards have recognisable patterns which makes learning numbers up to 100 or more much easier. Pupils begin by counting forwards and then backwards from 20; once they are confident with this they learn to count forwards and backwards in sets of 2, 5 and 10 which helps with doing sums and the early stages of learning multiplication.

Knowing and using number facts

Primary pupils should learn to recognise and use: number symbols and words for whole numbers 1 (one) to 20 (twenty) by 4 to 5 years; all the whole numbers to 100 (hundred) plus halves and quarters by 6 to 7 years; numbers to 10,000 including more fractions and decimal places by 8 to 9 years; all whole numbers, fractions, decimals plus percentages by 10 to 11 years. During the primary school years, pupils also develop knowledge and understanding of the mathematical language relevant to numbers: smaller, bigger; more/less than; even and odd numbers; factors and prime numbers, etc.

From about 4/5 years old pupils begin to learn how to make mathematical calculations using real objects to add and subtract small whole numbers. Gradually they recognise number patterns which make doing calculations easier e.g. being able to add 4 + 8 means they can also add 400 + 800. Memorising number facts also helps with calculations e.g. learning multiplication tables by heart.

Calculating

By 10 to 11 years pupils should have learned addition, subtraction, multiplication and division using whole numbers, fractions, decimals and negative numbers. As well as learning mental calculations pupils also learn the standard written methods for calculation operations.

Remember the aim for older children is to calculate mentally and to become less reliant on fingers and apparatus. Older children should be encouraged to consider mental methods first through strategies such as: 'Think first, and try to work it out in your head. Now check on your number line' (DfES, 1999). Children with special needs may need particular equipment, books and materials for mathematics activities. (See section below on supporting pupils with special numeracy needs.)

Handling data

Handling data is an essential skill in this technological age and using computers is an important aspect of mathematics today. Pupils learn to gather, arrange and convert data into useful information, e.g. working out the likelihood of rain so we know when to wear a raincoat or take an umbrella.

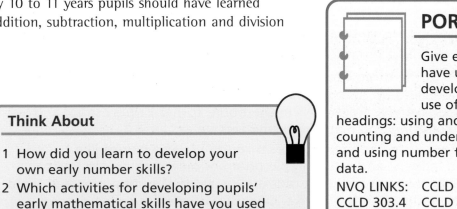

Think About

1 How did you learn to develop your own early number skills?
2 Which activities for developing pupils' early mathematical skills have you used and/or observed in school?

PORTFOLIO ACTIVITY

Give examples of activities you have used to help pupils to develop their understanding and use of number under these headings: using and applying mathematics; counting and understanding number; knowing and using number facts; calculating; handling data.

NVQ LINKS: CCLD 346.1   CCLD 303.3
CCLD 303.4   CCLD 306.2   CCLD 309.2
CCLD 323.2

Figure 13.2 Pupils engaged in a numeracy activity

Ten ways to help pupils to develop their understanding and use of number

You can help pupils to develop their understanding and use of number by:

1 Providing younger pupils with sorting and counting activities such as: stories and songs like 'Goldilocks and the three bears'; matching games (such as lotto or snap); play activities such as dressing-up (using pairs of socks, gloves and mittens) and organising sets of plates, cutlery, boxes, toys in the home corner or play shop; and using toy vehicles for counting and matching activities.

2 Encouraging younger pupils to explore numbers through playing games like dominoes, 'snakes and ladders' and other simple board games; looking for shapes/sizes and making comparisons, price tags and quantities in shop play and real shopping trips; number songs and rhymes like 'One, two, three, four, five, Once I caught a fish alive ...'.

3 Encouraging pupils to use and apply mathematics to tackle and solve everyday practical mathematical problems, such as making models, giving change in shop play and real shopping trips.

4 Providing opportunities for pupils to select, collect, organise and present appropriate data using lists, charts, graphs, diagrams, tables, surveys, questionnaires and CD-ROMs.

5 Supporting younger pupils engaged in counting, calculating and solving simple mathematical problems, for example addition and subtraction, then multiplication and division.

6 Supporting older pupils in employing standard methods to perform mental and written calculations including addition, subtraction, multiplication and division using whole numbers, fractions, decimals and percentages.

7 Prompting pupils to communicate their reasoning about problems and explaining their solutions using objects, pictures, diagrams, numbers, symbols and relevant mathematical language such as using letter symbols in algebra and setting up and using simple equations to solve problems.

8 Encouraging pupils to explore numbers and the number system, for example: positive and negative numbers; factors and prime numbers; equivalent fractions and how fractions, decimals and percentages relate to each other; and ratio and proportion.

9 Supporting pupils' use of calculator functions to complete complex calculations and understand the answers calculators give in relation to the initial mathematical problem.

10 Encouraging pupils to solve increasingly demanding mathematical problems by breaking the problem down into smaller, manageable tasks and developing deductive reasoning.

CCLD 346.2
Help pupils to understand and use shape, space and measures

To develop their understanding and use of shape, space and measures pupils need to learn these mathematical skills: understanding shape; measuring.

Understanding shape

In addition to developing competency with numbers, pupils learn to recognise and name geometrical shapes; they also learn about the properties of shapes, such as a triangle has three sides and a square has four right angles. Pupils learn about directions, angles and plotting points on a graph.

Measuring

Pupils learn to measure mass, distance, area and volume using appropriate units, including kilograms, metres, centimetres or litres. Measuring also includes learning to tell the time in hours and minutes.

Think About

1 How did you learn to understand and use shape, space and measures?
2 Which activities for helping pupils to understand and use shape, space and measures have you used and/or observed in school?

Ten ways to help pupils to understand and use shape, space and measures

Help pupils to understand and use shape, space and measures by:

1 Encouraging younger pupils to handle and describe the various features of basic shapes: for example to use the correct names for basic 2-D and 3-D shapes; and know how many sides, corners or right angles a shape has.

2 Encouraging pupils to explore shape and space through activities such as: games involving shape recognition; physical activities involving whole turns, half turns and quarter turns or right angles as well as spatial awareness when taking part in PE, movement and dance.

3 Encouraging younger pupils to explore volume and capacity during sand and water play, filling various containers to encourage understanding of full, empty, half-full, half-empty, nearly full, nearly empty, more/less than and the same amount. Use coloured water to make activities more interesting. Gradually introduce idea of standard measures, such as a litre of juice and a pint of milk.

4 Using weighing and measuring activities such as: shop play (using balance scales to compare toys and other items); real shopping (helping to weigh fruit and vegetables); sand play (heavy and light); and cooking activities (weighing ingredients to show importance of standard measures). Encourage younger pupils to develop understanding of length by comparing everyday objects/toys and using mathematical language, such as tall/taller/tallest, short/shorter/shortest, long/longer/longest, same height, same length.

5 Encouraging pupils to estimate and measure a range of everyday objects. For example measure objects using appropriate units such as centimetres, metres, kilograms or litres. Encourage them to record information. Use non-standard measures like hand spans to measure everyday objects and gradually introduce standard measures such as metre and centimetre.

6 Helping pupils to tell the time: for younger pupils using 'o'clock', 'half past' and 'quarter past the hour'; with older pupils telling the time in hours and minutes and solving problems relating to time using a 12-hour or 24-hour clock.

7   Helping older pupils to learn more about shapes and co-ordinates, constructing shapes (geometry), and measurement including using a ruler, protractor and compasses to create lines, angles and 2-D or 3-D shapes; and using the properties of straight-sided shapes, and intersecting or parallel lines to solve mathematical problems.

8   Helping pupils to know and use formulae to calculate: for example the circumference and area of a circle; the area of a straight-sided shape; and the volume of a cuboid.

9   Supporting pupils' ability to rotate, reflect, translate and enlarge 2-D shapes and understand how such changes affect the sides, angles and position of shapes.

10 Using ICT to encourage or extend pupils' knowledge and use of shape, space and measures: for example playing shape recognition games; writing instructions to create and change shapes on a computer.

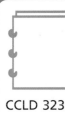

PORTFOLIO ACTIVITY

Give examples of activities you have used to help pupils to understand and use shape, space and measures under these headings: understanding shape; measuring.

NVQ LINKS: CCLD 346.2   CCLD 303.3   CCLD 303.4   CCLD 306.2   CCLD 309.2

CCLD 323.2

The teaching assistant's role in supporting pupils' numeracy skills

The teaching assistant has a key role in providing support for the teacher and pupils during numeracy activities. You need to find out from the teacher how the numeracy activities are to be organised and your specific role in supporting various learning activities, including whole class oral/mental maths activities, group work and tasks for individuals. You must be able to:

◎ Understand the intended learning outcomes for the pupils
◎ Agree the support strategies to be used for each pupil
◎ Obtain the resources required

◎ Implement the agreed strategies
◎ Provide feedback and encouragement during the activity (see page 177)
◎ Monitor the progress of the pupils
◎ Report any problems in providing support to the teacher.

Support strategies to help pupils to develop their mathematical knowledge and skills include:

◎ Using questions and prompts to encourage mathematical skills
◎ Repeating instructions given by the teacher
◎ Taking notes for a pupil while the teacher is talking
◎ Explaining and reinforcing correct mathematical vocabulary
◎ Reading and clarifying textbook/worksheet activity for a pupil

◎ Introducing follow-on tasks to reinforce and extend learning, such as problem-solving tasks and puzzles

◎ Playing a mathematical game with an individual pupil or small group

◎ Helping pupils to use computer software and learning programmes

◎ Helping pupils to select and use appropriate mathematical resources, such as number lines and measuring instruments

◎ Assisting pupils with special equipment such as a hearing aid or a Dictaphone

◎ Encouraging shy or reticent pupils to participate in conversations and discussions

◎ Providing any other appropriate assistance during an activity

◎ Monitoring pupil progress during an activity

◎ Reporting problems and successes to the teacher.

You need to know about and understand how to deal with the sorts of problems that might occur when supporting pupils during learning activities (see page 273). If a pupil is experiencing difficulties during a mathematics activity, you should consider the following:

1 Does the pupil understand the task?

2 Has the pupil learned how to do the relevant technique (for example counting, adding, learning times tables by repeating them)?

3 Does the pupil know which technique to use to solve the mathematical problem?

The pupil needs to understand the mathematical problem and decide which techniques are required to solve it. You can help the pupil to develop problem-solving skills by encouraging them to:

◎ Understand the problem by explaining the task using visual aids or equipment

◎ Plan to solve the problem by suggesting possible ways or draw diagrams

◎ Attempt the solution, for example try a technique

◎ Review the problem and its solution, that is reconsider the problem and check that the answer makes sense.

Supporting pupils with special numeracy needs

Some pupils have difficulties with numeracy because the language used in mathematics may be too

PORTFOLIO ACTIVITY

Give a detailed account of an activity you have used to help pupils to develop their mathematical knowledge and skills. Include information on the following:
◎ The organisation of the activity including the resources used
◎ How you implemented the agreed strategies for each pupil
◎ How you provided feedback and encouragement during the activity
◎ How you monitored the progress of the pupils
◎ The learning outcomes achieved by the pupils
◎ How you reported any problems in providing support to the teacher.
NVQ LINKS: CCLD 346.1   CCLD 346.2   CCLD 301.2

complex for them to understand the task. Poor memory skills can prevent some pupils from learning procedural techniques, such as their times tables. Frequent experiences of failure during numeracy activities can make some pupils anxious, discouraged and lacking in confidence so that they fall behind in their numeracy development.

Mathematical skills involve a wide range of specific capabilities, any of which can prove difficult for particular pupils and affect their mathematical development. It is important to find out what the pupil knows and where the problem lies. It is important to make sure that the pupil's problem with numeracy is not in fact a problem with literacy. For example, some pupils may: not be able to understand the written question; have handwriting or directional problems resulting in inaccurate recording and errors; or have poor motor skills causing miscalculations when using a calculator.

It is also important not to underestimate what pupils can do mathematically simply because they are learning English as an additional language (see below). They should be expected to make progress in their mathematical learning at the same rate as other pupils of the same age.

Some children may have special numeracy needs due to special educational needs such as cognitive and learning difficulties or sensory impairment (see Chapter 14) or physical disabilities (see Chapter 7). Others may have special numeracy needs due to behavioural difficulties (see Chapter 9).

The range of pupils with SEN varies from school to school. Many pupils with SEN may not have special numeracy needs and will not require extra or different numeracy support. However, many classes will have one or more pupil with identified SEN who require a modified approach to the National Numeracy Strategy. There are two broad groups of pupils with special numeracy needs:

Unit Links

For this Unit you also need to understand the following sections:

CCLD 307.3 Promote children's healthy physical development (see Chapter 7)

CCLD 321.2 Helping children with disabilities and special educational needs to participate in the full range of activities and experiences (see Chapter 14)

CCLD 337.2 Promote positive aspects of behaviour (see Chapter 9)

◎ A larger group of pupils who experience minor difficulties in learning, which is reflected in their attainment of levels of numeracy which are below those expected for pupils of their age. The structure provided by the National Numeracy Strategy can benefit these pupils. They can usually overcome these difficulties through normal teaching strategies and will soon develop the essential numeracy skills that will enable them to catch up and work at a comparable level to the rest of their year group

◎ The second smaller group includes pupils with severe and complex learning difficulties that require the use of different teaching strategies. These pupils may require different levels of work from the rest of their year group. They may also need to be taught at a different pace for all or most of their school years. Some pupils with SEN will always need access to systems such as symbols, signing, Braille or electronic communicators.

(DfES, 1999)

Some pupils with identified special educational needs may work at earlier levels than those specified in the National Numeracy Strategy Framework for their year group, while others will need to work on one term's work for several terms. With structured, intensive teaching, some of these pupils will gradually progress through the levels in the Framework and will eventually be able to work at the levels appropriate to their age.

Many pupils with special educational needs (for example those with physical disabilities or sensory impairment) will not require a separate learning programme for mathematics. For most of them access, materials, equipment and furniture may require adapting to meet their particular needs so that they can work alongside the rest of their class. They should work on the same objectives for their year group, with emphasis on access and support. Adaptations that may be necessary include: sign language; Braille and symbols; tactile materials; technological aids; and adapted measuring equipment.

Pupils with learning difficulties

Pupils with learning difficulties will usually require constant repetition and revision of previous learning in mathematics. This is especially important in terms of language and mental operations. An understanding of the language of mathematics and the ability to calculate mentally are essential to the development of numeracy skills. Pupils with learning difficulties may not have adequate language and mental strategies, which may have contributed to their problems with formal, standard methods of representing calculations. Concrete materials (real objects) are important for all pupils but especially for those with learning difficulties. Pupils need real objects and experiences to help them develop an understanding of the abstract concepts used in mathematics.

Use flash cards and illustrated wall displays to demonstrate the specific mathematical vocabulary for a particular task. Keep written instructions and explanations on worksheets to a minimum. Mathematics has a strong visual element so make frequent use of a number line, 100 square, number apparatus, pictures, diagrams, graphs and computer programs. Use games and puzzles where pupils can quickly pick up the rules after watching a demonstration.

Some pupils with specific learning difficulties (or dyslexia) may not understand key concepts in numeracy. (See CCLD 321.2 in Chapter 14 for information on supporting pupils with specific learning difficulties.)

Other pupils who are not dyslexic may also lack understanding in key mathematical concepts. The term dyscalculia, meaning difficulty in performing mathematical calculations, is given to a specific disorder in the ability to do or learn mathematics. Pupils with dyscalculia will experience difficulty with understanding number concepts and the relationships of numbers as well as using application procedures. Pupils with dyslexia or dyscalculia may need help with the following:

◎ Distinguishing between mathematics signs and symbols (1, 2, £, and so on)
◎ Distinguishing between digits that are similar in shape (such as 6 and 9, 7 and 1, 2 and 5) when reading and writing numbers
◎ Sequencing problems, like saying times tables, predicting next number in a series, use of number line, following a sequence of instructions (for example when doing a two-stage calculation)
◎ Remembering the range of alternative words and phrases for number operations (for example add, plus and sum are all addition terms)
◎ Directional difficulties which affect correct use of place value and the direction of number operations (such as subtraction starting with smallest place value, division starting with highest place value)

◎ Particular difficulties with mathematics word problems including reading and language processing difficulties or losing track of number operation mid-process, especially if this is being done mentally

◎ Organising and setting out calculations in writing

◎ Memorising and recalling maths facts (for example recalling tables, mental arithmetic).

(DfES, 2003)

Support staff (including specially trained teaching assistants) can provide assistance for pupils with special numeracy needs by:

◎ Signing to support a pupil with hearing impairment during shared numeracy activities

◎ Supporting a pupil during group work to develop specific numeracy skills

◎ Asking questions aimed at the appropriate level

◎ Giving the pupil some extra help in a group

◎ Sitting next to the pupil to keep them on task.

Pupils with English as an additional language

Whole class sessions can provide helpful adult models of spoken English and opportunities for careful listening, oral exchange and supportive, shared repetition. Group work provides opportunities for intensive, focused teaching input. You may need to repeat instructions for pupils with English as an additional language and to speak more clearly, emphasising key words, particularly when you are describing tasks that they are to do independently.

Encourage them to join in things that all pupils do in chorus: counting, reading aloud whole number sentences, chanting, finger games, songs about numbers, and so on. The structure of rhymes and the natural rhythm in songs or poems play an important part in developing number sense in any culture. Use stories and rhymes from a range of cultural backgrounds.

PORTFOLIO ACTIVITY

Describe how you have (or could have) provided support for pupils with special numeracy needs in your setting. Include examples for pupils with learning difficulties and English as an additional language.

NVQ LINKS: CCLD 346.1   CCLD 346.2   CCLD 301.2   CCLD 305.1   CCLD 305.2   CCLD 321.2
CCLD 334.1

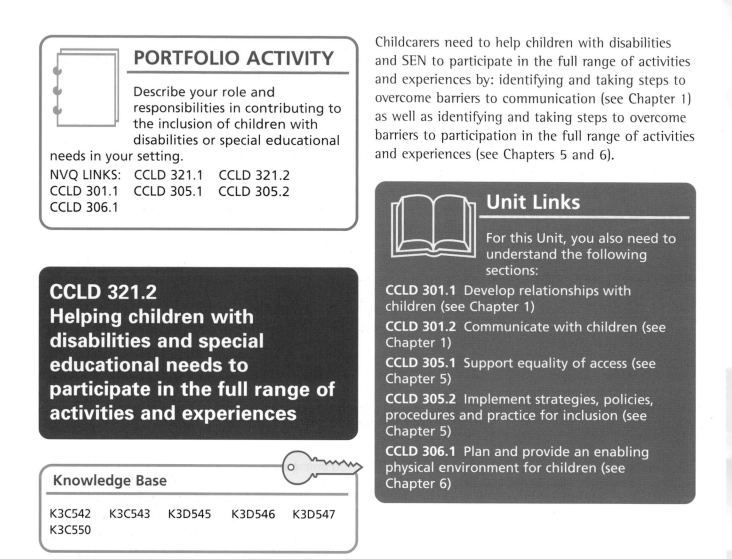

PORTFOLIO ACTIVITY

Describe your role and responsibilities in contributing to the inclusion of children with disabilities or special educational needs in your setting.

NVQ LINKS:　CCLD 321.1　CCLD 321.2
CCLD 301.1　CCLD 305.1　CCLD 305.2
CCLD 306.1

CCLD 321.2
Helping children with disabilities and special educational needs to participate in the full range of activities and experiences

Knowledge Base

K3C542　K3C543　K3D545　K3D546　K3D547
K3C550

Childcarers need to help children with disabilities and SEN to participate in the full range of activities and experiences by: identifying and taking steps to overcome barriers to communication (see Chapter 1) as well as identifying and taking steps to overcome barriers to participation in the full range of activities and experiences (see Chapters 5 and 6).

Unit Links

For this Unit, you also need to understand the following sections:

CCLD 301.1 Develop relationships with children (see Chapter 1)

CCLD 301.2 Communicate with children (see Chapter 1)

CCLD 305.1 Support equality of access (see Chapter 5)

CCLD 305.2 Implement strategies, policies, procedures and practice for inclusion (see Chapter 5)

CCLD 306.1 Plan and provide an enabling physical environment for children (see Chapter 6)

Ten ways to help children with special needs to participate in activities

You can help children with disabilities and SEN to participate in the full range of activities and experiences by:

1　Providing a stimulating, language-rich learning environment that is visually attractive, tactile and interactive.
2　Adapting the environment (such as the layout of furniture) and maximising the use of space in the setting to allow freedom of movement for *all* children (including those who have physical disabilities or visual impairment).
3　Ensuring accessibility of materials and equipment.

14

Helping children with disabilities and special educational needs to participate in the full range of activities and experiences

4 Providing opportunities for all children to explore different materials and activities as well as offering alternative activities if appropriate.
5 Encouraging children to use the senses they have to their fullest extent.
6 Providing sufficient time for children to explore their environment and materials; some children may need extra time to complete tasks.
7 Implementing adaptations that can be made without the use of special aids and equipment and/or identifying and deploying specialist aids and equipment as necessary.
8 Encouraging independence, perhaps by using computers, word processing or tape recorders.
9 Praising *all* children's *efforts* as well as achievements.
10 Ensuring adults involved are knowledgeable about children's disabilities and special educational needs and confident in their roles and responsibilities.

You need to know and understand the details about particular disabilities or SEN as they affect the children in your setting and your ability to provide a high quality service. Children with special needs may include those with physical disabilities, behavioural difficulties, emotional difficulties, hearing impairment, visual impairment, communication difficulties and learning difficulties.

Supporting children with physical difficulties

You should know how to help children with physical disabilities to participate in the full range of activities and experiences by adapting play opportunities or using specialist equipment to enable the child's full participation. (For detailed information on promoting children's physical development see CCLD 303.4 in Chapter 3; and there is more detail about supporting children with physical disabilities in CCLD 306.1 in Chapter 6 and CCLD 307.1 and 307.3 in Chapter 7.)

Supporting children with behavioural difficulties

You need to help children with behavioural difficulties to participate in the full range of activities and experiences, for example by helping the child to follow specific routines or instructions for activities; and encouraging positive social interaction with other children such as in playing together. (For detailed information about promoting children's social development see CCLD 301.3 in Chapter 3, about encouraging positive social interactions in CCLD 308.1 in Chapter 10. There is more information about supporting children with behavioural difficulties in CCLD 337.2 in Chapter 9.)

Supporting children with emotional difficulties

You need to know how to help children with emotional difficulties to participate in the full range of activities and experiences; examples of how you may do so include providing appropriate play opportunities and encouraging children to express their feelings. (For detailed information about promoting children's emotional development see CCLD 303.4 in Chapter 3; dealing with children's emotional outbursts is dealt with in CCLD 308.2 in Chapter 10; and responding to the needs of children who have experienced trauma is included in CCLD 327.2 in Chapter 15.)

Supporting children with hearing impairment

Hearing loss may range from a slight impairment to profound deafness. One in four children under the age of 7 experiences a hearing loss of some degree at some time. The loss may affect one or both ears at different levels. There are two types of hearing impairment:

1 *Conductive hearing loss*, involving the interference of the transmission of sound from the outer to the inner ear. This may be due to congestion or damage to the inner ear. The loss may be temporary or permanent; it makes sounds seem like the volume has been turned down. Hearing aids can be useful to amplify speech sounds, but unfortunately background noise is also increased. The most common form of conductive hearing loss in younger children is *'glue ear'*. This temporary condition is caused by the collection of fluid behind the ear drum triggered by congestion during an ear, nose or throat infection. Sometimes glue ear can cause language delay as it interferes with a young child's hearing at an important stage of speech development. Persistent or repetitive cases of glue ear may require a minor operation to drain the fluid and to insert a grommet or small tube into the ear drum to prevent further fluid build-up.

2 *Sensori-neural loss* is a rarer condition that is more likely to result in permanent hearing impairment. The damage to the inner ear results in distorted sounds where some sounds are heard but not others. *High frequency loss* affects the child's ability to hear consonants; *low frequency loss* is a less common condition. Hearing aids are not as effective with this type of hearing impairment as the child will still be unable to hear the missing sounds. Children with sensori-neural loss therefore find it more difficult to develop speech and have a more significant language delay.

Identifying children with hearing impairment

Children with hearing impairment, especially those with conductive hearing loss, may be difficult to identify. However, even a slight hearing loss may affect a child's language development. Look out for the following signs of possible hearing loss in children: slow reactions; delay in following instructions; constantly checking what to do; apparently day-dreaming or inattentive; over-anxiety; watching faces closely; turning head to one side to listen; asking to repeat what was said; difficulty regulating voice; poor language development; spoken work more difficult to do than written work; may have emotional or aggressive outbursts due to frustration; and problems with social interaction.

Children with hearing loss will use lip-reading and non-verbal clues such as gesture and body language to work out what is being said. Some children will wear hearing aids to improve their hearing abilities. Some settings may encourage the use of signing systems such as British Sign Language or Makaton and have specially trained staff to facilitate the use of sign language throughout the setting.

14

Helping children with disabilities and special educational needs to participate in the full range of activities and experiences

Strategies to support children with hearing impairment

The following suggestions may help when working with children with hearing impairment:

◎ Reduce background noise by using carpets on floors where possible
◎ Ensure the pupil is near to you
◎ Use facial expressions and gestures
◎ Use visual aids such as real objects, pictures, books and photos
◎ Keep your mouth visible
◎ Do not shout but speak clearly and naturally
◎ Check the child is paying attention
◎ Develop listening skills through music and games
◎ Include the child in group activities in a sensitive manner
◎ Get specialist advice and support from, for example, Royal National Institute for the Deaf (RNID); health visitor; special needs advisor; specialist teacher; or speech and language therapist.

Supporting children with visual impairment

Some children may wear glasses to correct short or long sight, but these children are not considered to be visually impaired. A child with visual impairment has partial or total lack of vision in *both* eyes. Children with normal vision in only one eye (monocular vision) are not considered to be visually impaired, because one eye enables them to see quite well for most activities. Children with monocular vision will have difficulties with 3-D perception and judging distances. Remember that children with a squint may be relying on the vision of the one 'good' eye. Some children may be 'colour blind' and have difficulty differentiating between certain colours, usually red and green. Again this is not a

visual impairment, but may cause occasional difficulties in the setting such as when doing activities involving colour recognition, colour mixing, and so on. There is also a safety implication, for example red for danger/stop may be confused with green for go.

Identifying children with visual impairment

The majority of children with visual impairment will have been identified before they start school but there may be a few children who have not, particularly in the younger age range. Be aware of the following: a child who blinks or rubs their eyes a lot; has itchy, watery or inflamed eyes; frowns, squints or peers at work; closes/covers one eye when looking at books; bumps into people or furniture; has difficulty with physical games/appears clumsy; has difficulty forming letters and numbers; omits words or sentences when reading; says they cannot see the chalkboard or worksheet; suffers from frequent headaches; or dislikes classroom/nursery lighting.

Strategies to support children with visual impairment

Vision is an essential component of learning in mainstream settings; visual impairment can affect language development in terms of written language and learning to read. It is essential to work with colleagues and parents to provide the best care and education for children with visual impairment. Specialist advice and equipment may be necessary depending on the extent of the impairment. The following strategies may help:

◎ Ensure the child is near to you
◎ Make sure the child is wearing glasses if they are required

- ◎ Keep the room tidy and free from obstacles
- ◎ Black writing on a matt white board is better than using a chalkboard
- ◎ Make worksheets clear and bold
- ◎ Allow time for writing when necessary
- ◎ Keep writing to a minimum; use oral methods, for example a tape recorder
- ◎ Use word processing where possible
- ◎ Enlarge worksheets and books
- ◎ Use other senses, for example touch and sound to reinforce learning
- ◎ Use visual aids such as a magnifier
- ◎ Be aware of possible mobility problems during physical activities
- ◎ Use talking books and story books with Braille on plastic inserts
- ◎ Get specialist advice and support from, for example, Royal National Institute for the Blind (RNIB); health visitor; special needs advisor; or specialist teacher
- ◎ Provide pre-Braille and Braille activities after consulting a specialist advisor.

PORTFOLIO ACTIVITY

Provide examples of how you have encouraged a child with hearing or visual impairment to participate in the full range of activities and experiences in your setting.

NVQ LINKS: CCLD 321.1   CCLD 321.2
CCLD 305.1   CCLD 305.2   CCLD 306.1
CCLD 313.3

Supporting children with communication difficulties

Depending on their individual language experiences, some children may not have reached the same level of language development as their peers or they may lack effective communication skills. Other children's language development may even be ahead of what is usually expected for their age.

Unit Links

For this Unit, you also need to understand the following sections:

CCLD 301.2 Communicate with children (see Chapter 1)

CCLD 303.4 Implement and evaluate plans to promote development (see Chapter 3)

Some common communication difficulties

Lisping is a common problem for many young children when they are learning to speak; it is caused by the child's inability to articulate a certain sound so the child substitutes with another similar sound. Lisping usually stops without the need for adult intervention. Sometimes lisping may be a sign of a physical problem such as hearing loss, cleft palate or faulty tongue action, in which case specialist advice is needed.

Some children may experience a period of *stammering*, usually around 3 years old. This is called *dysfluency* and is part of the normal pattern of language development. Dysfluency means that the young child cannot articulate thoughts into words quickly enough, hence the stammer. About 5 per cent of children stammer, but it can be difficult to identify them because children who stammer are often reclusive and reluctant to talk. Most children eventually conquer this communication difficulty, especially with the assistance of well-prepared and sympathetic staff and the help of speech and language therapists; only 1 per cent of children will continue to stammer as adults.

14

Helping children with disabilities and special educational needs to participate in the full range of activities and experiences

Delayed language development may be due to environmental or social factors such as poverty, race and culture, parental background or limited early language experiences. These factors may restrict some children's opportunities to explore their environment and to develop language and communication skills through positive and stimulating interactions with others. Children with delayed language development go through the same stages of language development as other children, but at a slower rate.

Disordered language development is more likely to be caused by:

◎ Minimal brain damage affecting areas relating to language
◎ Physical disabilities affecting articulation of sounds
◎ Sensory impairment affecting hearing or visual abilities
◎ Cognitive difficulties affecting the ability to process language
◎ Autistic spectrum disorders (see CCLD 337.2 in Chapter 9).

A child with a *cleft lip and/or palate* has structural damage to the top lip, palate or both, due to the failed development of these areas of the mouth during the early weeks in the womb. The impairment is clearly diagnosed at birth and a series of operations is essential to correct it; this may result in significant language delay for the child, as correct speech cannot be articulated until the gaps in lips and/or palate have been operated on successfully. Later, speech and language therapy may be necessary.

Some children choose not to speak. This is sometimes known as *elective mutism*. These children may be shy, withdrawn and uncommunicative for the following reasons: lack of confidence in group situations or lack of social skills (see Chapter 10); lack of experience in using English to communicate (see Chapter 1); emotional trauma (see Chapter 15); physical or sexual abuse (see Chapter 5). Check that there is no underlying cause for the child's reluctance or refusal to speak due to hearing loss, or a stressful event such as going into hospital or a death in the family. Most children who are uncommunicative lack confidence in themselves and their ability to relate to others, so it is important to develop their self-esteem and to improve their social skills (see Chapter 10). Do not try to make a child speak when they are reluctant to do so as this may only cause further anxiety. Give the child opportunities to speak in a welcoming and non-threatening environment; sometimes they may contribute, sometimes they will not. Even if the child does not say anything, make sure they can still observe and listen to what is going on.

Unit Links

For this Unit, you also need to understand the following sections:

CCLD 301.2 Communicate with children (see Chapter 1)

CCLD 305.3 Maintain and follow policies and procedures for protecting and safeguarding children (see Chapter 5)

CCLD 308.1 Enable children to relate to others (see Chapter 10)

CCLD 308.4 Encourage children's self-reliance, self-esteem and resilience (see Chapter 10)

CCLD 327.1 Recognise the needs of children who have experienced trauma (see Chapter 15)

Figure 14.1 Childcarer supporting child with communication difficulties

Identifying children with communication difficulties

Here are some things to look out for when identifying whether a child has a problem with communication: difficulty in understanding in one-to-one situations; difficulty understanding in group or class situations; difficulty following instructions; difficulty in pronouncing sounds (for example says 'wabbit' instead of 'rabbit'); reluctance or refusal to speak; giving one-word answers; repeating sentences; difficulty learning by rote (including rhymes, songs, alphabet and times tables); poor memory skills; and inappropriate answers.

Strategies to support children with communication difficulties

Adults in childcare settings can do a great deal to help children with communication difficulties. Many of the language activities already suggested in this book (Chapter 1 looks at effective communication with children and there is information about developing speaking and listening skills in Chapter 13) are suitable for *all* children including those with communication difficulties. Some children, especially those with disordered language development, may need specialist help from a speech and language therapist. Some possible strategies you can use when

14

Helping children with disabilities and special educational needs to participate in the full range of activities and experiences

supporting children with communication difficulties are:

◎ Keep information short and to the point
◎ Avoid complex instructions
◎ Speak clearly and not too quickly
◎ Be a good speech role model
◎ Build up the child's confidence gradually (such as speaking one-to-one, then in a small group)
◎ Develop concentration skills, for example play memory games
◎ Encourage reluctant children to speak, but *do not insist* they talk
◎ Use stories and CDs to improve listening skills
◎ Use rhythm to sound out name/phrases, music and songs
◎ Use pictorial instructions and visual cues
◎ Teach social skills as well as communication skills
◎ Provide structured play opportunities and learning activities
◎ Keep to set routines
◎ Prepare for new situations carefully
◎ Use the child's favourite activities as rewards
◎ Get specialist advice and support from, for example, AFASIC, National Autism Society; health visitors; Portage worker; special needs advisor; specialist teacher; or speech and language therapist.

Supporting children with general learning difficulties

Some children may not develop their intellectual processes in line with the expected pattern of development for their age for a variety of reasons: autistic spectrum disorders or attention deficit disorders (see Chapter 9); emotional difficulties (see Chapters 10 and 15); cognitive and learning difficulties. Cognitive and learning difficulties can be divided into two main areas: general learning difficulties and specific learning difficulties (see below). (See Chapter 3 for more informataion on promoting children's intellectual development.)

Unit Links

For this Unit, you also need to understand the following sections:

CCLD 303.4 Implement and evaluate plans to promote development (see Chapter 3)

CCLD 308.2 Provide a supportive and challenging environment (see Chapter 10)

CCLD 327.1 Recognise the needs of children who have experienced trauma (see Chapter 15)

CCLD 337.2 Promote positive aspects of behaviour (see Chapter 9)

PORTFOLIO ACTIVITY

Provide examples of how you have encouraged a child with communication difficulties to participate in the full range of activities and experiences in your setting, such as adapting play opportunities or using specialist equipment to enable the child's full participation.

NVQ LINKS: CCLD 321.1   CCLD 321.2   CCLD 339.3   CCLD 301.2   CCLD 305.1   CCLD 305.2
CCLD 308.1   CCLD 308.4   CCLD 313.3   CCLD 345.3

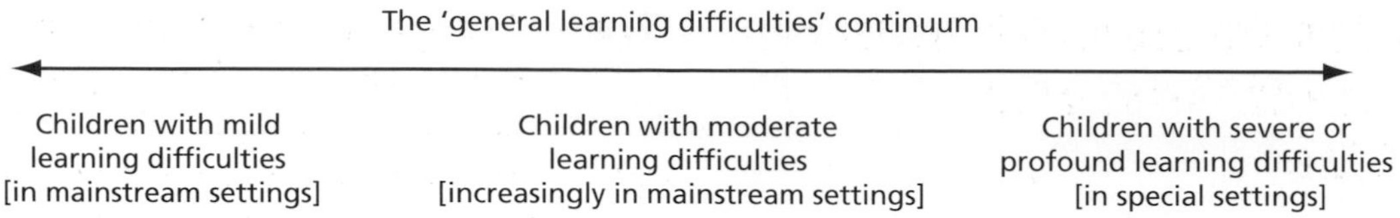

The 'general learning difficulties' continuum

| Children with mild learning difficulties [in mainstream settings] | Children with moderate learning difficulties [increasingly in mainstream settings] | Children with severe or profound learning difficulties [in special settings] |

Figure 14.2 The 'general learning difficulties' continuum

The term 'slow learners' is sometimes used to describe children with below average cognitive abilities across all areas of learning; the term *general learning difficulties* is preferable. The wide range of general learning difficulties is divided into three levels:

1 *Mild learning difficulties*: children whose learning needs can be met using resources within mainstream settings.
2 *Moderate learning difficulties*: children whose learning needs can be met using additional resources in designated classes/special units within mainstream settings or in special schools.
3 *Severe or profound learning difficulties*: children whose learning needs require the resources and staff usually available only in special schools.

Children with general learning difficulties often have delayed development in other areas; they may be socially and emotionally immature and/or have problems with gross/fine motor skills.

They need carefully structured learning opportunities where new skills are introduced step by step. Children with this type of cognitive difficulty may have problems processing information; they have difficulty linking their existing knowledge and past experiences to new learning situations which makes it difficult to reach solutions or to develop ideas.

Identifying children with general learning difficulties

These children are usually identified by the adults working with them at an early stage. Some common signs to look out for include: delay in understanding new ideas/concepts; poor concentration/shorter than usual attention span; inability to remember new skills without constant repetition and reinforcement; poor listening skills; lack of imagination and creativity; difficulty following instructions in large group situations; difficulty comprehending abstract ideas; limited vocabulary; often giving one-word answers; problems with memory skills; poor co-ordination affecting hand–eye co-ordination and pencil control; need lots of practical support and concrete materials; delayed reading skills, especially comprehension; and delayed understanding of mathematics and science concepts.

Children with general learning difficulties (especially in mainstream settings) are often aware that their progress is behind that of their peers. This can be very damaging to their self-esteem. Some may feel they are incapable of learning anything at all. Adults need to convince such children that they *can* and *will* learn as long as they keep trying and do not give up.

14

Helping children with disabilities and special educational needs to participate in the full range of activities and experiences

Strategies to support children with general learning difficulties

The following strategies may help to make learning activities more positive experiences for children with general learning difficulties:

◎ Build on what they already know
◎ Let them work at their own pace
◎ Provide activities that can be completed in the time available without their feeling under pressure
◎ Divide the learning into small steps in a logical sequence
◎ Present the same concept or idea in various ways to reinforce learning and understanding
◎ Use repetition frequently; short, daily lessons are more memorable than one long weekly session
◎ Demonstrate what to do as well as giving verbal instructions
◎ Use real examples and practical experiences/equipment wherever possible
◎ Keep activities short; work towards increasing the children's concentration
◎ Encourage active participation in discussion and group activities to extend language and communication skills
◎ Provide more stimuli for learning activities rather than expecting the children to develop new ideas entirely by themselves
◎ Help the children to develop skills in accessing information; for example use technology such as computers, the Internet; also libraries, reference books; museums
◎ Listen to the children and take on board their points of view
◎ Get specialist advice and support from, for example, MENCAP; educational psychologist; health visitor; Portage worker; special needs advisor; specialist teacher; or occupational therapist.

Praise and encouragement are essential to children's learning as they are all motivated by achieving success, regardless of ability. Make sure the learning activities you provide are appropriate by using your observations and assessments to plan activities (as appropriate to your setting) which are relevant to each child's abilities and interests. Praise and encouragement are especially important to raise the self-esteem of children who find learning difficult. (See page 177.)

Supporting children with specific learning difficulties

Children with specific learning difficulties show problems in learning in one particular area of development; they have difficulties in acquiring literacy skills and consequently other aspects of learning may be affected. The term 'dyslexia' is often used when referring to children with such problems, but the phrase *specific learning difficulties* probably more accurately describes the scope of the difficulties they experience. It is estimated that 4 per cent of children are affected by dyslexia.

Identifying children with specific learning difficulties

Look out for the following signs of possible specific learning difficulties in the **under-5s**: delay or difficulty in speech development; persistent tendency to mix up words and phrases; persistent difficulty with tasks such as dressing; unusual clumsiness and lack of co-ordination; poor concentration; or family history of similar difficulties. However, many young children make similar mistakes; specific learning difficulties are indicated only where the difficulties are severe and persistent or grouped together. (BDA, 1997)

Possible signs of specific learning difficulties in 5 to 9 year olds include: particular difficulties in learning to read, write and spell; persistent and continued reversing of letters and numerals (e.g. 'b' for 'd', '51' for '15'); difficulty telling left from right; difficulty learning the alphabet and multiplication tables; difficulty remembering sequences such as days of the week/months of the year; difficulty with tying shoelaces, ball-catching and other co-ordination skills; poor concentration; frustration, possibly leading to behavioural difficulties; and difficulty following verbal and/or written instructions. (BDA, 1997)

In assessing the possibility of specific learning disabilities in 9 to 12 year olds look out for: difficulties with reading, including poor comprehension skills; difficulties with writing and spelling including letters missing or in wrong order; problems with completing tasks in the required time; being disorganised at school (and at home); difficulties with copying from chalkboard, whiteboard or textbook; difficulties with following verbal and/or written instructions; and lack of self-confidence and frustration. (BDA, 1997)

In 12 to 16 year olds look out for the following possible signs of specific learning difficulties: reads inaccurately and/or lacks comprehension skills; inconsistency with spelling; difficulties with taking notes, planning and writing essays; confuses telephone numbers and addresses; difficulties with following verbal instructions; severe problems when learning a foreign language; and frustration and low self-esteem. (BDA, 1997)

(Note: Not all children with specific learning difficulties will display *all* these characteristics.)

Strategies to support children with specific learning difficulties

The following strategies may help when working with children with specific learning difficulties:

◎ Ensure the child is near you or at the front of the class/group
◎ Check unobtrusively that copy-writing, note-taking and so on is done efficiently
◎ Use 'buddy' system, that is another child copies for this one
◎ Give positive feedback and encouragement, without drawing undue attention to the child
◎ Use computers to help the child (for example word processing with spell-check facility)
◎ Help the child to develop effective strategies and study skills which may differ from those used by other children
◎ Get specialist advice and support from, for example, The British Dyslexia Association; educational psychologist; health visitor; special needs advisor; specialist teacher; or occupational therapist.

(BDA, 1997)

PORTFOLIO ACTIVITY

Provide examples of how you have encouraged a child with general or specific learning difficulties to participate in the full range of activities and experiences in your setting, such as by encouraging the child to participate in play and learning activities or modifying learning activities to meet the child's individual learning needs.

NVQ LINKS: CCLD 321.1   CCLD 321.2
CCLD 301.2   CCLD 305.2   CCLD 308.2
CCLD 308.4   CCLD 313.3   CCLD 345.1
CCLD 345.2

CCLD 321.3
Support families to respond to children's needs

Knowledge Base

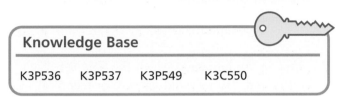

| K3P536 | K3P537 | K3P549 | K3C550 |

As a childcarer you should support families to respond to their children's needs by working in partnership with parents. Establishing such partnerships is very important as parents are the child's primary carers and may have detailed specialist knowledge about their child. Parental involvement is crucial for both parents and practitioners as it: increases parents' understanding of the learning process; enables them to reinforce tasks being undertaken by their child in the setting by engaging in similar activities with their child at home; allows two-way communication between practitioners and parents; enables shared knowledge about the individual child; and enhances the overall understanding of the child's needs in the setting and home. (Gatiss, 1991)

Most parents are usually keen to be actively involved in their children's learning. Do inform parents about the activities their child is involved in within the setting and suggest ways in which the parents can complement the work of the setting such as: encouraging family members to participate in observing and identifying the needs of children; working through an agreed programme with an understanding of its steps towards progress, for example home-school literacy and numeracy programmes (see Chapter 13) and Portage schemes (see Chapter 15); helping with individual and group activities in the setting, both indoors and outdoors;

supporting other professionals working with their child either in the setting or at home, such as physiotherapist, speech and language therapist; assisting with activities outside the setting, for example outings to the local library, park, playground or swimming pool.

PORTFOLIO ACTIVITY

Suggest practical ways to support families to respond to their children's needs.

NVQ LINKS:	CCLD 321.3	CCLD 313.2
CCLD 313.3	CCLD 315.2	CCLD317.1
CCLD 317.2	CCLD 322.3	CCLD 322.4
CCLD 324.2	CCLD331.2	CCLD 339.1

CCLD 339
Co-ordinate special educational needs in early education settings

Depending on your role and responsibilities you may be involved in co-ordinating special educational needs in an early education setting, perhaps as the special educational needs co-ordinator. The SENCO is responsible for: liaising with parents with regard to their children's special educational needs; providing appropriate advice and support for colleagues in the setting; liaising with other professionals as necessary; ensuring that individual education plans for children are implemented and reviewed; and collecting, recording and updating relevant information about the children.

CCLD 339.1
Liaise with parents and other professionals in respect of children with special educational needs

Knowledge Base

K3D709   K3P711   K3P712   K3C550

Liaising with parents and other professionals in respect of children with special educational needs involves: taking appropriate steps to clarify the scope and purpose of your role and available support systems (see CCLD 304.2 in Chapter 4); establishing positive relationships with children with such needs and their parents (see CCLD 301.1 in Chapter 1).

Liaising with parents

Parents usually know more about their children and their children's special needs than anyone else, so it is important to listen to what they have to say. Actively encourage positive relationships between parents (or designated carers) and the early education setting. Only give information to parents that is consistent with your role and responsibilities within the setting; for instance do not give recommendations concerning the child's future learning needs directly to parents if this is the responsibility of another professional. Any information shared with parents must be agreed with relevant colleagues, such as the child's keyworker. When sharing information about a child with parents ensure that it is relevant, accurate and up to date. Always follow the confidentiality requirements of the setting (find more information on confidentiality matters in CCLD 304.4 in Chapter 1 and on storing records in CCLD 328.2 in Chapter 17).

It is best to use language which the parent is likely to understand. Try to avoid 'jargon' or technical language, especially if you are not clear about its meaning. Remember to pass on information from parents about their children to the relevant member of staff. Requests for information that are beyond your role and responsibilities, or any difficulties in communicating with parents, should be referred to the appropriate person, such as the setting manager. You may need guidance on how to handle sensitive situations regarding liaising with parents, especially where a parent makes derogatory remarks about a particular staff member or setting policy. (See CCLD 301.4 in Chapter 1.) When liaising with parents about the special educational needs of their children, consider the family's home background and the expressed wishes of the parents. Ensure also that you follow the setting's policies and procedures with regard to special educational needs, such as inclusion strategies, policies, procedures and practice (see CCLD 305.2 in Chapter 5). You may need to give parents positive reassurance about their children's care and education. Any concerns or worries expressed by a child's parents should be passed immediately to the appropriate person in the setting. If a parent makes a request to see a colleague or other professional, then follow the relevant setting policy and procedures.

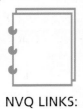

PORTFOLIO ACTIVITY

Give examples of how your setting exchanges information with parents with regard to their children with special educational needs, for example information packs, regular reviews, Individual Education Plans, home-school diaries.

NVQ LINKS: CCLD 339.1 CCLD 305.2 CCLD 317.1 CCLD 317.3 CCLD 321.3 CCLD 324.2
CCLD 328.2 CCLD 330.3 CCLD 331.1 CCLD 332.1

Liaising with other professionals

In addition to liaising with parents you will need to liaise with other professionals regarding children with SEN, as well as providing effective support for colleagues in the setting (see below). You may be involved in co-ordinating a network of relationships between staff at the setting and other professionals from external agencies such as:

◎ *Local education authority*: educational psychologist, special needs support teachers, special needs advisors, specialist teachers, education welfare officers
◎ *Health services:* paediatricians, health visitors, physiotherapists, occupational therapists, speech and language therapists, play therapists, school nurses, clinical psychologists
◎ *Social services department:* social workers; specialist social workers: sensory disabilities, physical disabilities, mental health or children and families
◎ *Charities and voluntary organisations:* AFASIC, British Dyslexia Association, Council For Disabled Children, National Autistic Society, RNIB, RNID, SCOPE.

Check it out

Find out which external agencies and other professionals are connected with the care and support of children with SEN at your setting.

Children with SEN may often have support from other professionals from external agencies. To provide the most effective care and support for such children, it is essential that the working relationships between the setting staff and other professionals run smoothly and that there are no contradictions or missed opportunities due to lack of communication. Liaising with other professionals will enable you to involve colleagues with the work of the specialists in a number of ways, for example: planning appropriate support for the child within the setting; assisting children to perform tasks set by a specialist; and reporting the child's progress on such tasks, perhaps to the child's parents.

Any interactions with other professionals should be conducted in a way that promotes trust and confidence in your working relationships. Your contributions towards the planning and implementation of joint actions must be consistent with your role and responsibilities within your setting. You should supply other professionals with the relevant information, advice and support as appropriate to your own role and expertise. If requested, you should be willing to share information, knowledge or skills with other professionals. Use any opportunities to contact or observe the practice of other professionals from external agencies to increase your knowledge and understanding of their skills/expertise in order to improve your own work (and that of your colleagues) in planning and supporting children's learning and development.

PORTFOLIO ACTIVITY

Compile an information booklet which includes the following:
1 Links with other professionals from external agencies established by your setting.
2 A diagram which illustrates how you and your colleagues work with other professionals to provide effective support for children with SEN in your setting.
3 Your role and responsibilities in liaising with other professionals to support children with SEN and their parents.
4 Where to obtain information about the roles of other professionals in the local area.

NVQ LINKS: CCLD 339.1   CCLD 339.2   CCLD 304.1   CCLD 313.3   CCLD 321.3   CCLD 324.1   CCLD 331.3

CCLD 339.2
Advise and support colleagues in the setting

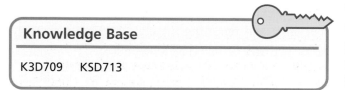

Knowledge Base

K3D709   KSD713

Advising and supporting colleagues in the setting involves: providing advice and support for colleagues who have concerns about the progress of individual children (see CCLD 303.2 in Chapter 3); advising colleagues who are providing additional interventions or a differentiated curriculum (see CCLD 310.2 in Chapter 12); supporting colleagues working with children who have emotional difficulties (see CCLD 327.2 in Chapter 15) or behavioural difficulties (see CCLD 337.2 in Chapter 9); providing support for colleagues working with children who have communication difficulties (see above); and advising colleagues on available training and occupational updating for work with children with special educational needs (see CCLD 304.2 in Chapter 4).

As part of your role of co-ordinating special educational needs in an early education setting, you will need to provide advice and support for colleagues and make sure that the necessary provision is made for any children with SEN and these needs are made known to colleagues who are likely to work with them. Ensure that your colleagues are able to provide appropriate support for children with SEN including helping these children to participate in the full range of activities (see above).

Part of your responsibility is to ensure that relevant colleagues know and understand: the setting's inclusion strategies, policies, procedures and practice; the nature of each child's special educational needs; how these needs affect the child; the special provision and learning support required; and their specific role in helping the child to access all areas of the curriculum.

PORTFOLIO ACTIVITY

Give examples of how you advise and support colleagues in your setting.

NVQ LINKS: CCLD 339.2   CCLD 328.5   CCLD 311   CCLD 335   CCLD 338

CCLD 339.3
Ensure that individual education plans for children are in place and regularly reviewed

Knowledge Base

K3P702   K3D705   K3C706   K3D707   K3D708
K3D709   K3D710

You need to know, understand and follow the relevant legislation regarding children with disabilities and SEN. This includes ensuring that the early education setting is carrying out its duties towards these children and that parents are notified of any decision that SEN provision is to be made for their child. (See CCLD 305.2 in Chapter 5 for information on national legislation relating to children with special educational needs.)

Identification, assessment and provision for children with SEN in early education settings

Some children may have been identified as having special educational needs prior to attending the early education setting, such as those with physical disabilities, sensory impairment or autism. Others may not be making sufficient progress within the early learning goals of the Foundation Stage or may have difficulties which require additional support within the setting.

This support within early education settings may be provided through Early Years Action, Early Years Action Plus or statutory assessment.

Early Years Action

Children identified as having SEN may require support in addition to the usual provision of the early years setting. Additional support through *Early Years Action* should be devised and provided if, despite participation in appropriate early learning experiences, a child is:

◎ Making little or no progress even when approaches are specifically targeted to improve the child's particular area(s) of difficulty
◎ Continuing to work at levels significantly below those expected for children of similar age
◎ Demonstrating persistent behavioural and/or emotional difficulties which are not improved by the setting's usual behaviour strategies
◎ Continuing to make little or no progress despite the provision of personal aids and equipment to assist with physical disability or sensory impairment
◎ Having communication and/or interaction

difficulties and requires specific individual interventions in order to access early learning.

(Smart, 2001)

The SENCO, in consultation with colleagues and the child's parents, will decide what additional support is needed to help the child to make progress. Additional support at *Early Years Action* may include:

◎ Devising planned intervention and monitoring its effectiveness
◎ The provision of different learning materials or special equipment
◎ Some individual or group support provided by early years practitioners
◎ Staff development and training to introduce more effective strategies
◎ Access to local education authority support services for occasional advice on strategies or equipment
◎ Staff training to provide effective intervention without the need for ongoing input from external agencies
◎ Devising and implementing an individual education plan (see below).

(Smart, 2001)

Early Years Action Plus

Children with SEN may require support which involves external support services. Additional support through *Early Years Action Plus* should be devised and provided if, despite an individual support programme, a child is:

◎ Continuing to make little or no progress in specific areas
◎ Continuing to work at levels substantially below those expected for children of similar age
◎ Demonstrating persistent behavioural and/or emotional difficulties that substantially and regularly interfere with the child's own learning or

that of the group, despite having an individualised behaviour programme
◎ Requiring additional equipment, regular visits for direct intervention or advice from a specialist service to assist with physical disability or sensory impairment
◎ Having ongoing communication and/or interaction difficulties that impede the development of social development and cause substantial barriers to early learning.

(Smart, 2001)

The SENCO, in consultation with colleagues, the child's parents and other professionals, will decide what additional support is needed to help the child to make progress. Additional support at *Early Years Action Plus* may include:

◎ Sharing information about the child's progress with other professionals to enable more specialist assessments of the child's needs
◎ Devising planned intervention and monitoring its effectiveness in consultation with other professionals
◎ The provision of specialist strategies or materials
◎ Some individual or group support provided by early years practitioners
◎ Staff development and training to introduce more effective strategies
◎ Some individual support provided by other professionals such as a physiotherapist or speech and language therapist
◎ Access to LEA support services for regular advice on strategies or equipment, such as an educational psychologist or autism outreach worker
◎ Devising and implementing an Individual Education Plan (see below).

Statutory assessment

A few children with SEN in the early education setting may still make insufficient progress through the additional support provided by *Early Years Action Plus*. When a child demonstrates significant cause for concern, the SENCO, in consultation with colleagues, the child's parents and other professionals already involved in the child's support, should consider whether to request a statutory assessment. The early years setting will need to provide the following evidence to the LEA:

◎ The setting's action through *Early Years Action* and *Early Years Action Plus*
◎ Individual Education Plans for the child
◎ Records of regular reviews and their outcomes
◎ The child's health, including medical history if relevant
◎ Educational and other assessments, for example advisory specialist support teacher, clinical psychologist, educational psychologist
◎ Views of the child and their parents
◎ Involvement of other professionals such as those working in the health service, social services or education welfare service.

(Smart, 2001)

The LEA may decide that the nature of the provision necessary to meet the child's special educational needs requires it to determine the child's special education provision through a *statement of special educational need*. The statement will include the following:

◎ The child's name, address and date of birth
◎ Details of the child's special needs
◎ The special educational provision required to meet the child's needs
◎ The type and name of the school where the provision is to be made
◎ The relevant non-educational needs of the child, such as physical or mental health needs
◎ Information on non-educational provision, for example physiotherapy and psychology services.

Individual Education Plans

As part of your responsibility for co-ordinating SEN within an early education setting you will need to ensure that Individual Education Plans for children are in place and regularly reviewed. All early education settings should differentiate their approaches to learning activities to meet the needs of individual children. The strategies used to enable individual children with SEN to make progress during learning activities should be set out in an IEP, whether they receive additional support in the early years setting as part of *Early Years Action*, *Early Years Action Plus* or *statement of special educational need*.

A child's IEP should identify three or four individual targets in specific key areas, for example communication, literacy, numeracy or behaviour and social skills. When developing Individual Educational Plans, remember to have high expectations of children and a commitment to raising their achievement, based on a realistic appraisal of children's abilities and what they can achieve. You should regularly review Individual Educational Plans in consultation with children and parents (at least three times a year). A child's IEP should include the following information:

◎ Child's strengths
◎ Priority concerns
◎ Any external agencies involved
◎ Background information including assessment details and/or medical needs
◎ Parental involvement/child participation
◎ The short-term targets for the child
◎ The provision to be put in place, for example resources, strategies, staff, or allocated support time
◎ When the plan is to be reviewed
◎ The outcome of any action taken.

PORTFOLIO ACTIVITY

Outline your setting's procedures for ensuring that Individual Education Plans for children are in place and regularly reviewed. Provide examples of the relevant forms such as an Individual Education Plan; review sheets for child's comments, parents' comments and staff comments; and a record of review. Remember confidentiality.

NVQ LINKS: CCLD 339.3   CCLD 339.1   CCLD 305.2   CCLD 321.1   CCLD 321.2

CCLD 339.4
Collect, record and update relevant background information about children with special educational needs

Knowledge Base

K3P702   K3P703   K3M156   K3M714   K3C550

PORTFOLIO ACTIVITY

Describe how you collect, record and update background information about children with special educational needs. Include examples of relevant formats and procedures, such as child observation and assessments, Individual Education Plans.

NVQ LINKS: CCLD 339.4   CCLD 301.4
CCLD 303.1   CCLD 303.2   CCLD 303.3
CCLD 303.4   CCLD 310.2   CCLD 328.2

Collect relevant background information from available sources, including children (according to their ages, needs and abilities), their families, health and social services. Record information and ensure that records are regularly updated and kept according to your setting's agreed formats and procedures, including following the confidentiality and data protection requirements. (Find more information on confidentiality matters in CCLD 304.4 in Chapter 1 and on storing records in CCLD 328.2 in Chapter 17.)

Optional Units

CCLD 313
Support early intervention for the benefit of children and families

CCLD 326
Safeguard children from harm

CCLD 327
Support children who have experienced trauma

CCLD 336
Contribute to childcare practice in group living

CCLD 313
Support early intervention for the benefit of children and families

You may be involved in working with children, families and other professionals to identify and assess the need for early intervention for the benefit of children and their families. These needs may include chronic illness, disability, sensory impairment, social interventions, literacy and/or numeracy, developmental delay as well as other circumstances. You may also be responsible for supporting them and assisting other professionals in implementing strategies and plans to meet their needs.

CCLD 313.1
Help to identify families in need of early intervention and support

Knowledge Base

K3C635   K3P636   K3P626   K3D640   K3M629
K3M642

Supporting early intervention for the benefit of children and families is essential as it can prevent or minimise potential problems escalating into crisis or abuse. Practitioners providing services for children and families, including education, health and social services as well as voluntary and private organisations, should work together to ensure that children identified as being at risk of social inclusion receive appropriate attention.

Establishing positive relationships with children and families

Your work with children and families should be underpinned by effective adult-child and adult-adult communication. You are responsible for effective communication with families to establish positive relationships based on trust and openness. Encourage families to discuss any concerns and share information likely to impact on their children's health, well-being or developmental progress. Remember these important points:

◎ Express yourself simply and clearly and use concepts that are familiar to both children and their parents

- Match your explanations of new ideas to the children's ages and levels of understanding
- Be aware of the possible impact of emotional distress on families' understanding
- Find out about the families' fears and offer them reassurances
- Give families plenty of opportunities for asking questions
- Repeat, simplify, expand and build on explanations if appropriate
- Use communication tools such as games, prompt cards, books and videos.

(DH, 2000)

The positive role of parents or carers leads to *optimal* child development from birth to adulthood. All children have biological and psychological needs (see page 5) but there is a variety of ways of meeting these needs. You must respect and accept the differences of family life which vary according to culture, class and community. There is no perfect way to raise children so you must avoid value judgements and stereotypes (see section on parenting styles in Chapter 16). Assessing children's developmental needs is a complex process which requires all relevant aspects of a child's life experience to be addressed. For children of Asian, African or Caribbean origin (including children of mixed heritage), assessments should address the impact that racism has on a particular child and family and ensure that the assessment process itself does not reinforce racism through racial or cultural stereotyping. (DH, 2000)

Children's opportunities for achieving optimal outcomes depend on their parents' abilities to respond appropriately to their children's needs at different stages of their lives. Most parents want to do the best for their children and have their best interests at heart. However, good parenting requires certain permitting circumstances such as necessary life opportunities and facilities (such as adequate

housing, satisfactory education and/or training, regular employment, reasonable income, access to affordable childcare and leisure facilities). There are many factors that may inhibit the way parents respond to their children and prevent parenting at a level necessary to promote optimal outcomes in children. These factors include: alcohol problems; drug use; mental illness; domestic violence; ignorance about child development; lack of a supportive partner; the parents' negative childhood experiences such as rejection, abandonment, neglect and feeling unloved; parents' low self-esteem; lack of resilience factors in parents' own childhood. (DH, 2000) (See sections on possible reasons for low self-esteem and factors that affect resilience in children in CCLD 308.4 in Chapter 10.)

Identifying children in need of intervention

Being a parent is hard work and many families are under stress. All families may experience difficulties at some time which may affect their children. For example: family bereavement, physical or mental health problems, marital breakdown, sudden unemployment, multiple births or having a child with special needs. Some parents are not well prepared for the ups and downs of parenthood and may find particular times in their children's lives more stressful than others, such as when their children are toddlers or teenagers. Most parents can cope with one problem at a time but not with a combination of problems all at once or in close succession. Many families under stress have adequate support from family, friends or community services and do not need or seek additional support. Others do not have such a network of support and so require additional support through paid childcare (such as a childminder or private day nursery) or from statutory or voluntary agencies such as befriending by a volunteer (e.g. Home-Start) or targeted services from health, education and social services (for example Portage, SureStart). (DH et al., 2000)

There may be problems in interpreting needs, for instance differences in the rate of development of children with similar background, disabilities, and so on. Remember, all children are unique individuals and develop at their own rate (see CCLD 303.4 in Chapter 3 for more information about understanding children's development). Some children may be 'behind' in some areas of development but may 'catch up' with support from their parents/carers and the usual early years experiences (parent and toddler group, playgroup, or nursery class) *without* the need for intervention.

However, some very young children may continue to experience difficulties even with input from skilled early years practitioners; these children and their parents may require additional or specialist support to maximise their development. It is important if early years practitioners are concerned about a child's behaviour, learning or development, to contact the relevant support service. Such action may be part of Early Years Action Plus or statutory assessment. (DfEE, 2001) (There is more about the identification, assessment and provision for children with SEN in early education settings in CCLD 339.1 in Chapter 14.)

Children may be defined as in need in many different circumstances including: disadvantaged children who would benefit from extra help from public agencies; children looked after in statutory care; children on the Child Protection Register; children with disabilities. Families referred to or seeking help will have differing levels of need ranging from advice, practical support and short-term intervention to detailed assessment and long-term intervention. (DH et al., 2000) Examples of

early interventions include: cognitive behaviour therapy; counselling; crisis intervention; family therapy; Home-Start; Portage; National Autistic Society EarlyBird Programme; the Nippers Project (Nursery Intervention for Parents and Education Related Services); special nursery provision; and SureStart.

Check it out

Find out about the early interventions available in your local area, for example counselling services, special nursery provision, Portage, Home-Start and SureStart.

Legislation and guidance relating to children in need

Families have the right to expect practical support from services such as health and education. Part III of the Children Act 1989 provides the legal basis for the provision of local services for children in need aged under 18 years. Local authorities have a duty to both safeguard and promote the welfare of vulnerable children. Safeguarding children should not be seen as separate from promoting their welfare – they are two sides of the same coin. (DH et al., 2000)

The Children Act 1989 places a specific duty on agencies to co-operate in the interest of children in need. The Act uses the following criteria to define children in need:

> *'A child shall be taken to be in need if –*
> *a   he is unlikely to achieve or maintain or to have the opportunity of achieving or maintaining, a reasonable standard of health or development without the*

provision for him of services by a local authority ...

b   *his health or development is likely to be significantly impaired, or further impaired, without the provision for him of such services; or*

c   *he is disabled.*

(Children Act 1989, section 17:10)

Working Together to Safeguard Children 2006 sets out how agencies and professionals should work together to promote the welfare of children and to protect them from abuse and neglect (for details about the law regarding child protection see CCLD 305.3 in Chapter 5).

The *Framework for the Assessment of Children in Need and their Families (2000)* provides a systemic framework to help practitioners identify children in need and assess the best approach to help them and their families – see the Department of Health website: www.dh.gov.uk and search for the title with the site's search function.

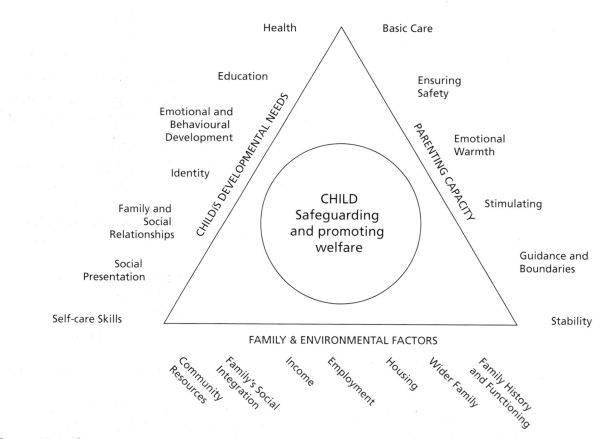

Figure 15.1 The Assessment Framework
From: *Framwork for the Assessment of Children in Need and their Families*. Dept of Health, 2000.

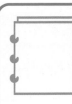

PORTFOLIO ACTIVITY

Outline the procedures you use to help identify families in need of early intervention and support. Include information on how you: communicate with children and their parents; encourage families to discuss any concerns and share information; use different sources of information to identify concerns; record information using agreed formats and confidentiality procedures; and refer concerns about children and families to the relevant agencies.

NVQ LINKS: CCLD 313.1 CCLD 301.1
CCLD 301.4 CCLD 303.1 CCLD 303.2
CCLD 305.2 CCLD 305.3 CCLD 317.1
CCLD 326.3 CCLD 328.2 CCLD 331.1
CCLD 339.1

CCLD 313.2
Negotiate and assess needs in consultation with families

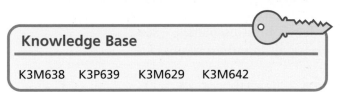

Knowledge Base

K3M638   K3P639   K3M629   K3M642

Always ensure that families are active participants in early intervention. You are working *with* families, not doing things *for* them; hence the importance of involving families in goal setting. There should be clear roles between parents and professionals (see below). You must recognise and acknowledge families' feelings about intervention and specialist help and be able to show empathy and understanding for parents' views about contact with social services and other statutory agencies. For example, parents may have worries about: being

vulnerable to child protection enquiries and losing their children; being perceived as failed or 'bad' parents; losing control once other agencies are involved, that is forfeiting parenting responsibility. Parents value family support services which include:

◎ Open, honest, timely and informative communication
◎ Social work time with someone who listens, gives feedback, information, reassurance and advice, and who is reliable
◎ Services which are practical and tailored to particular needs and accessible
◎ An approach which reinforces and does not undermine their parenting capacity.

(DH, 2000)

Knowledge and understanding of the Assessment Framework (see above) will enable you to contribute to the assessments of children in need. It is essential that you are clear about:

◎ The purpose and anticipated outputs from the assessment
◎ The legislative basis for the assessment
◎ The protocols and procedures to be followed
◎ Which agency, team or professional has lead responsibility
◎ How the child and family members will be involved in the assessment process
◎ Which professional has lead responsibility for analysing the assessment findings and constructing a plan
◎ The respective roles of each professional involved in the assessment
◎ The way in which information will be shared across professional boundaries and within agencies, and be recorded
◎ Which professional will have responsibility for taking forward the plan when it is agreed.

(DH et al., 2000; p. 7)

You should discuss and agree an assessment plan

with the child and family to ensure that they understand who is doing what, when and how the various assessments will be used to assess the child's needs and to plan intervention. To do this you need to know and understand the principles underpinning the Assessment Framework. Assessments:

◎ Are child centred
◎ Are rooted in child development
◎ Are ecological in their approach
◎ Ensure equality of opportunity
◎ Involve working with children and families
◎ Build on strengths as well as identify difficulties
◎ Are inter-agency in their approach to assessment and the provision of services
◎ Are a continuing process, not a single event
◎ Are carried out in parallel with other action and providing services
◎ Are grounded in evidence based knowledge.
                                    (DH et al., 2000; p. 10)

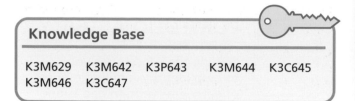

Knowledge Base

K3M629   K3M642   K3P643   K3M644   K3C645
K3M646   K3C647

Statutory services include health, education and social services. A number of services or agencies may work together to support children and their families. Support services provided by various statutory agencies should be carefully co-ordinated to meet the needs of children and families more effectively. Some areas already provide a single multi-agency service for young children and families which brings together health, education and social services, for example children's centres (see page 91).

The *Right from the Start Template* is a working document designed to help professionals to develop the policies, procedures and practice required to ensure that more families with disabled children receive a better service. The principles and good practice framework included in this document are applicable to professionals working with *all* children in need, not just children with disabilities – see www.rightfromthestart.org.uk.

PORTFOLIO ACTIVITY

Outline the methods you use to negotiate and assess needs in consultation with children and their parents.

NVQ LINKS: CCLD 313.2   CCLD 301.1
CCLD 301.4   CCLD 317.2   CCLD 324.2
CCLD 330.1   CCLD 331.2

CCLD 313.3
Work with families and other agencies to access specialist support

The role of the keyworker or lead professional

The keyworker is a named professional who assists families in accessing information and support from specialist services. Sometimes the keyworker is known as the lead professional. In *Team Around the Child* approaches (see Figure 15.2) a professional who has regular contact with the family takes on the role of keyworker or lead professional as well as their existing responsibilities for supporting the family. The core responsibilities of the keyworker are:

◎ Making sure the family has all the information it needs and, where necessary, helping families to understand and use the information received
◎ Ensuring everyone (including other agencies) has up-to-date information about the child and family
◎ Co-ordinating assessment support and intervention
◎ Ensuring a joint plan is formulated which keeps the family at the centre of decision-making and involves all the professionals and agencies in contact with the child
◎ Facilitating the regular review and updating of support plans
◎ Maintaining regular contact with the family and, where appropriate, providing emotional support.

(DfES, 2004a)

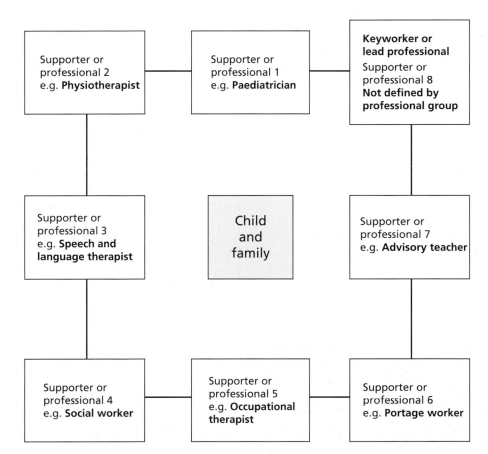

Figure 15.2 Team Around the Child approaches
From: *Early Support Professional Guidance*. DfES, 2004.

PORTFOLIO ACTIVITY

Describe how you work with other agencies to help families access specialist support. Include information on how you exchange information with families and other agencies, such as keeping records of contacts and information in line with agreed policies and procedures, such as confidentiality and data protection procedures.

NVQ LINKS: CCLD 313.3 CCLD 301.4 CCLD 321.3 CCLD 324.1 CCLD 324.2 CCLD 326.2 CCLD 328.2 CCLD 331.2 CCLD 331.3 CCLD 334.2 CCLD 339.1

CCLD 313.4
Monitor and evaluate services to ensure the needs of children and families are met

Knowledge Base

K3C645   K3M646   K3C647

Monitoring and evaluating services for children and families helps to ensure that their needs are met by:

◎ Ensuring mechanisms are in place to enable joint planning between health, education and social services
◎ Helping parents and carers to understand what is likely to happen next and how they can best encourage children's developmental progress
◎ Marking progress and celebrating achievement in children who are facing significant challenges
◎ Informing discussion between families and professionals who work with them
◎ Highlighting development that is not following an expected pattern, where additional or different intervention may be required
◎ Evaluating the impact of any early intervention and support that has been provided

◎ Including measures of consumer satisfaction/client feedback.

(DfES, 2004a)

PORTFOLIO ACTIVITY

Outline the procedures you use to monitor and evaluate services to ensure the needs of children and families are met. Include information on how you: regularly review children's individual needs; discuss services and provision with individual families; regularly liaise with colleagues and other professionals; agree and implement any changes to ensure children's needs are met; and keep accurate records of meetings and discussions.

NVQ LINKS: CCLD 313.4 CCLD 301.4 CCLD 303.1 CCLD 303.2 CCLD 310.2 CCLD 317.3 CCLD 326.3 CCLD 328.2 CCLD 330.4 CCLD 331.3 CCLD 339.1

CCLD 326
Safeguard children from harm

You may be involved in working with professionals who have statutory child protection powers, for instance social services, the police or NSPCC. To do this, you will make contributions to the processes of safeguarding children and protecting them from abuse or neglect including: referring concerns about children's welfare; participating in the assessment process; and supporting plans, interventions and reviews.

CCLD 326.1
Refer concerns about the welfare of children

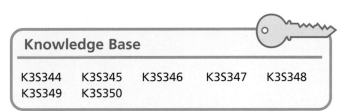

Knowledge Base

K3S344	K3S345	K3S346	K3S347	K3S348
K3S349	K3S350			

What to do if you're worried a child is being abused (2003) is a guide for professionals working with children that explains the processes and systems contained in *Working Together to Safeguard Children (1999)* and the *Framework for Assessment of Children in Need and their Families (2000)*. These documents are all available from the Department of Health website: www.dh.gov.uk. Please note that *Working Together to Safeguard Children* has been updated to take account of the *Children Act 2004* and new guidance was published in 2006.

There are four key processes that underpin work with children in need and their families. These processes are: assessment, planning, intervention and reviewing. Each process needs to be carried out effectively in order to achieve improvements in the lives of children in need. At any stage, a referral may be necessary from one agency to another or received from a member of the public. (DH, 2003a) (See page 312 for the definition of 'children in need'; the definition of 'significant harm' and detailed

information on the nature and forms of child abuse and neglect are given in CCLD 305.3 in Chapter 5.)

Practitioners who work with children and their families should know how to recognise and respond to the possible abuse and neglect of a child (see Chapter 5). All organisations providing day care and/or education must have a designated person who liaises with local child protection agencies and ofsted on child protection issues. You must know and follow your setting's policies and procedures for referring concerns about the welfare of children.

All practitioners working with children and families should:

◎ Have an understanding of the *Framework for the Assessment of Children in Need and their Families* (see page 314)

◎ Be familiar with and follow your organisation's procedures and protocols for promoting and safeguarding the welfare of children and know who to contact in your organisation to express concerns about a child's welfare

◎ Remember that an allegation of child abuse or neglect may lead to criminal investigation so do not do anything that may jeopardise a police investigation; for example do not ask a child leading questions or attempt to investigate the allegations of abuse

◎ Communicate with the child in a way that is appropriate to their age, understanding and preference

◎ If appropriate, discuss your concerns with the child's parents and seek their agreement to make a referral to social services unless you consider such a discussion would place the child at risk of significant harm

◎ Discuss your concerns with the appropriate person in your setting, such as your manager, named or designated health professional or designated teacher

◎ If you are responsible for making referrals, know who to contact regarding concerns about a child's welfare in police, health, education and social services

◎ If, after this discussion, you still have concerns then you should consider which agency to make a referral to: for example, children in need should be referred to social services; concerns about children at risk of significant harm should be referred to the police and the NSPCC as well as social services

◎ Refer any concerns about child abuse or neglect to social services or the police

◎ When referring a child to social services include any information on the child's developmental needs and their parents' ability to respond to these needs

◎ When you make your referral, agree with the recipient of the referral what the child and their parents will be told, by whom and when

◎ If you make your referral by telephone, confirm it in writing within 48 hours

◎ Record full information about the child at first point of contact including name(s), address(es), gender, date of birth, name(s) of person(s) with parental responsibility (for consent purposes) and primary carer(s), if different, and keep this information up to date

◎ Record all concerns, discussions about the child, decisions made, and the reasons for those decisions.

(DH, 2003a)

(For more detailed information about the childcare setting's child protection policy and procedures, the childcarer's responsibilities for child protection, responding to suspicions of abuse and responding to a child's disclosure of abuse see CCLD 305.3 in Chapter 5.)

PORTFOLIO ACTIVITY

Outline your setting's procedures and protocols for expressing concerns about a child's welfare. Include information on procedures for: discussing concerns with children and their parents; and referring concerns to the appropriate person in your setting or another agency.

NVQ LINKS: CCLD 326.1   CCLD 301.4
CCLD 305.3   CCLD 313.1

CCLD 326.2
Share information for the purpose of assessing children in need and their families

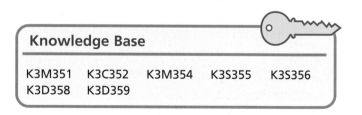

Knowledge Base

K3M351   K3C352   K3M354   K3S355   K3S356
K3D358   K3D359

The *Framework for the Assessment of Children in Need and their Families (2000)* provides a systemic framework to help professionals identify children in need and assess the best approach to help these children and their families (see CCLD 313.3 above for details of supporting early intervention for the benefit of children and families).

You must know and follow your setting's procedures and protocols for sharing information – see Chapter

1 for more information about confidentiality matters, the basic provisions of the Data Protection Act relevant to childcarers, and the childcare setting's requirements regarding confidentiality; Chapter 5 includes a section on the confidentiality of information relating to abuse; storing records is covered in Chapter 17.

Unit Links

For this Unit, you also need to understand the following sections:

CCLD 301.4 Communicate with adults (see Chapter 1)

CCLD 305.3 Maintain and follow policies and procedures for protecting and safeguarding children (see Chapter 5)

CCLD 328.2 Collect and store information (see Chapter 17)

Check it out

Find out about your setting's procedures and protocols for sharing information, including requirements regarding the confidentiality of information relating to abuse.

An *initial assessment* is a brief assessment of a child referred to social services to determine 'whether the child is in need, the nature of any services required, and whether a further, more detailed core assessment should be taken' (paragraph 3.9 of the Assessment Framework). Information should be gathered and analysed within the three domains of the Assessment Framework: the child's developmental needs; the parents' or caregivers' capacity to respond appropriately to those needs; and the wider family and environmental factors (see Figure 15.1). The initial assessment should be carefully planned and clearly state who is doing what, as well as when and what information is to be shared with parents. The planning process and decisions about the timing of the different assessment activities should be undertaken in collaboration with all those involved with the child and family. All practitioners should be involved in the initial assessment process according to the agreed plan, including providing further information about the child and family, and in the process of agreeing further action. (DH, 2003a)

If the initial assessment indicates that there is *no* suspected actual or likely significant harm then social services will decide whether the child is in need and whether to undertake a core assessment (see below) to determine what help may benefit the child and family, or whether to offer services to the child or family based on the findings of the initial assessment. Social services will discuss the findings of the initial assessment with other relevant professionals to inform decisions about what types of services, including a core assessment, it would be appropriate to offer. (DH, 2003a)

If the initial assessment indicates that there *is* suspected actual or likely significant harm then social services will initiate a *strategy discussion* to decide whether to initiate enquiries under s47 of the Children Act 1989 and therefore to commence a core assessment as the means by which these enquiries will be undertaken. Social services will consider carefully what parents are told, when and by whom. The police, GP, health visitor, school nurse, paediatrician who knows the child, the senior ward nurse (if the child is an in-patient), teacher and other relevant professionals should be involved in making these decisions. If requested to do so, you should provide available information verified at source, in a clear and comprehensible format. If social services think that a criminal offence may have been committed against a child, they will involve the police as soon as possible. Social services and the police will then consider, together with other relevant agencies, how to proceed to safeguard the child. (DH, 2003a)

A *core assessment* is the means by which a s47 enquiry is carried out. It is an in-depth assessment that addresses the most important aspects of the child's needs and the capacity of the child's parents or caregivers to respond appropriately to them within the family and community context. The core assessment begins by focusing on the information identified during the initial assessment to consider whether the child is suffering or is likely to suffer significant harm. It should also cover all the relevant dimensions in the Assessment Framework. (DH, 2003a)

As a childcare practitioner, you should contribute to the core assessment and the analysis of the findings as requested by social services. This includes providing information you have about the child or parents, contributing specialist knowledge or advice to social services or undertaking specialist assessments. Keep careful and detailed contemporary notes, as these are very important for any subsequent police investigation or court action. Also record any unusual events and distinguish between events reported by the carer and those witnessed by others, including professionals. Notes should be timed, dated and signed legibly and kept in a secure place so that they cannot be accessed by unauthorised persons. (DH, 2003a)

CCLD 326.3
Support plans, interventions and reviews that safeguard children and promote their welfare

Knowledge Base			
K3S353	K3S357	K3S360	K3S361

If, after the s47 enquiries, concerns about the child are *not* substantiated then social services will discuss with the parents and other professionals what further help or support the family may require, such as help with parenting difficulties, or support for the child's health or development. If the concerns *are* substantiated but the child is not judged to be at continuing risk of significant harm, then social services will discuss the findings of the s47 enquiry and agree with the other agencies involved with the child and family that a plan for ensuring the child's future safety and welfare can be developed and implemented without the need for a child protection conference or child protection plan. The child's health and development may require careful monitoring over time, with milestones for progress clearly set out in the plan.

You will be required to participate in these

PORTFOLIO ACTIVITY

Outline your setting's procedures and protocols for sharing information. Include information on your role and responsibilities for providing it as requested by those carrying out initial or core assessments and strategy discussions.

NVQ LINKS: CCLD 326.1   CCLD 301.4   CCLD 305.3   CCLD 313.1   CCLD 313.3

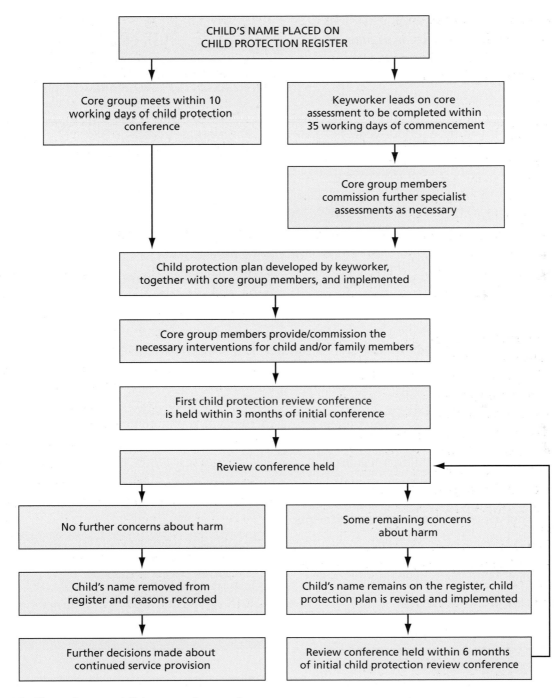

Figure 15.3 Flow chart – child protection review process

discussions and considerations when requested. Provide interventions, services or monitoring of the child's development as specified in the plan for the child. You should be fully involved in discussions about whether to convene a *child protection conference* and request that social services convene such a conference if you have serious concerns that a child may not otherwise be adequately protected. If a child protection conference is convened then you should contribute to your setting's written report prior to the conference. Discuss and agree with the conference chairperson whether your report can be shared with the parents, and if so, when. Where invited, you should attend the conference and participate in the decision-making process. (DH, 2003a)

If the child's name is placed on the *Child Protection Register* then the conference will make recommendations on how agencies, professionals and the family should work together to ensure that the child will be safeguarded from harm in the future. This will form the basis for a *child protection plan*. As a childcare practitioner you will need to discuss the development of a child protection plan with the named keyworker (a member of staff from the lead agency, such as the local authority or the NSPCC) and agree its content and any commitments for your setting. Ensure that your setting is able to deliver these commitments, or if this is not possible that these commitments are renegotiated. Provide services according to the agreed plan and where necessary undertake specialist assessments to inform the review of the plan. You will need to produce reports for the *child protection review conference*. These will provide an overview of your work with the child and an evaluation of the impact on the child's welfare in relation to the objectives set out in the child protection plan. You should attend the review meeting where appropriate.

PORTFOLIO ACTIVITY

Describe your role and responsibilities for supporting plans, interventions and reviews that safeguard children and promote their welfare.

NVQ LINKS: CCLD 326.1   CCLD 301.4
CCLD 305.3   CCLD 313.3   CCLD 313.4

CCLD 327
Support children who have experienced trauma

You may be involved in working with children who have had traumatic experiences, such as being exposed to domestic or criminal violence, being abused, being in an armed conflict or fleeing from violence and terror and coming to a new country as a refugee. It is important that you develop the skills necessary to provide appropriate support for these children's care, learning and development, including working alongside other professionals who may be supporting them.

CCLD 327.1
Recognise the needs of children who have experienced trauma

Knowledge Base

K3P362	K3P363	K3P364	K3P365	K3S366
K3D367	K3S368	K3D369	K3D370	K3D371
K3D372	K3D373	K3D591	K3C592	

Children may experience emotional difficulties for a variety of reasons. Some of these are part of the usual pattern of children's emotional development and are only temporary. For example: emotional outbursts (see CCLD 308.2 in Chapter 10); common childhood fears; reactions to family or friend's accident/illness, child's own accident/illness or pet illness/death; adjusting to transitions such as starting nursery/school or the arrival of new baby or step-sibling(s) (see CCLD 325.1 in Chapter 10); pressures at home or school; concerns about tests or exams; and worries about local, national or international crises witnessed in the media.

Some children may experience emotional difficulties of a more lasting nature, as a result of traumatic experiences such as: child abuse or bullying (see CCLD 305.3 in Chapter 5); parental separation and divorce (especially when there are disputes about child support and/or residency); terminal illness or bereavement in a child's family; domestic violence; armed conflict; or witnessing a violent or catastrophic event, such as a shooting, stabbing, car crash or natural disaster.

What is trauma?

The word 'trauma' has both a physical and a psychological definition. Physically, 'trauma' refers to a serious or critical bodily injury, wound or shock. Psychologically, 'trauma' refers to an experience (which may or may not have resulted in physical injury) that is emotionally painful, distressful or shocking. Psychological trauma is basically a normal response to an extreme event. This response involves the creation of emotional memories about the traumatic event that are stored in structures deep in the brain. The more direct the exposure to the traumatic event, the higher the risk for emotional harm; for instance, the victim of violence will be more severely affected emotionally than the person

witnessing the violence. However, even second-hand exposure to violence can be traumatic. For this reason all children exposed to violence or a disaster, even if only through graphic media reports, should be watched for signs of emotional distress. (NIMH, 2001)

Think About

Think about your reactions (and those of the children you work with) to news reports on events such as 9/11, the Boxing Day Tsunami, 7/7, Hurricane Katrina and the conflicts in the Middle East. Even though we were not there, these events had a strong emotional impact on us all.

Children's reactions to trauma

Children (and adults) who have experienced traumatic events demonstrate a wide range of reactions. Some suffer worries and bad memories that fade with appropriate emotional support and the passage of time. Others are more deeply affected and experience more long-term problems (see section below on post-traumatic stress disorder). Reactions to trauma may appear immediately after the traumatic event or days and even weeks later. Loss of trust in adults and fear of the event occurring again are responses seen in many children who have experienced trauma. Other reactions vary according to the children's ages. They may include:

◎ *Children aged 0 to 5 years*: fear of being separated from the parent(s); crying, whimpering and screaming; immobility and/or aimless motion; trembling; frightened facial expressions; excessive clinging; affected by parents' or carers' reaction to the traumatic event; or regression to behaviours from an earlier age, such as thumb-sucking, bedwetting and fear of the dark

◎ *Children aged 6 to 11 years*: withdrawn, disruptive or aggressive behaviour; inability to pay attention; sleep problems and nightmares; irritability; irrational fears; school refusal and difficulties with school work; complaints of 'tummy ache' or other symptoms that have no medical basis; depression, anxiety and emotional numbing; feelings of guilt; or regression to behaviours from an earlier age, such as thumb-sucking and bedwetting

◎ *Children/young people aged 12 to 16 years*: flashbacks; sleep disturbances and nightmares; depression, anxiety and emotional numbing; antisocial behaviour; substance abuse; withdrawal and isolation; suicidal thoughts; school avoidance and academic decline; physical complaints; avoidance of reminders of the traumatic event; guilt that they were unable to prevent injury or loss of life; or revenge fantasies.

(NIMH, 2001)

Activity

List some of the common reactions to traumatic events that may occur in the age group of children you work with.

Post-traumatic stress disorder

Some children may have prolonged difficulties after a traumatic event, including depression or prolonged grief. Another serious and potentially long-lasting problem is post-traumatic stress disorder (PTSD). This condition is diagnosed when the following symptoms have been present for longer than one month:

◎ *Re-experiencing* the event through play or in trauma-specific nightmares or flashbacks, or distress over events that resemble or symbolise the trauma

◎ Routine *avoidance* of reminders of the event or a general lack of responsiveness, such as diminished interest or a sense of having a foreshortened future

◎ Increased sleep disturbances, irritability, poor concentration, startle reaction and regressive behaviour.

(NIMH, 2001)

The disorder may arise weeks or even months after a traumatic event. PTSD may resolve without treatment, but some form of therapy by a mental health professional is usually required to help the healing process. People with PTSD are treated with specialised forms of psychotherapy and sometimes with medication or both. One form of psychotherapy that has been found to be effective is cognitive behaviour therapy (CBT). Children who undergo CBT are taught to avoid 'catastrophising'; for example, they are reassured that the fact that someone is angry does not necessarily mean that another shooting is imminent. Art therapy and play therapy can also help younger children to remember a traumatic event safely and express their feelings about it. Treatment of PTSD lasts for about 6 to 12 weeks with occasional follow-up sessions but may take longer depending on the particular circumstances of the individual. PTSD is often accompanied by depression which should also be treated. The support of family and friends is an important part of the individual's recovery. (NIMH, 2001)

Assessing the needs of children who have experienced trauma

You should consult with parents, family members, other members of the child's community or other professionals to find out information about the child's traumatic experiences and their present circumstances (see Chapter 1) and work with others, as appropriate, to assess the needs of the child (see above). Share information with colleagues, parents or carers, if appropriate, in order to promote the welfare and meet the needs of the child (see Chapters 1 and 5). This includes recording information about the child's needs accurately and securely (see Chapters 1 and 17).

Actively listen to what the child can tell you about their experience and communicate with them in a manner appropriate to their age, understanding and preference (see Chapter 1). Check that the child is able to access their rights and has access to an advocate if necessary. Also, check that the child has access to medical and legal support as appropriate. (See CCLD 305.1 in Chapter 5 and Appendix.)

PORTFOLIO ACTIVITY

Outline how you assess the needs of a child who has experienced trauma. Include information on how you: communicate with the child; consult and share information with parents, carers, colleagues and other professionals; and record information about the child's needs.

NVQ LINKS: CCLD 327.1   CCLD 301.2
CCLD 301.4   CCLD 305.1   CCLD 305.3
CCLD 313.2   CCLD 313.3   CCLD 326.2
CCLD 328.2   CCLD 331.3

Unit Links

For this Unit, you also need to understand the following sections:

CCLD 301.4 Communicate with adults (see Chapter 1)

CCLD 305.3 Maintain and follow policies and procedures for protecting and safeguarding children (see Chapter 5)

CCLD 313.2 Negotiate and assess needs in consultation with families (see above)

CCLD 313.3 Work with families and other agencies to access specialist support (see above)

CCLD 326.2 Share information for the purpose of assessing children in need and their families (see above)

CCLD 328.2 Collect and store information (see Chapter 17)

CCLD 331.3 Liaise with colleagues, professionals and agencies to support families (see Chapter 16)

CCLD 327.2 Respond to the needs of children who have experienced trauma

Knowledge Base

K3D369   K3D370   K3D371   K3D372   K3D591

Early intervention and support to help children who have experienced trauma due to violence or disaster is critical. Parents, carers and others caring for children, as well as mental health professionals, can do a great deal to help children to recover from their traumatic experiences. Support should be given as soon after the event as possible. (NIMH, 2001)

Work with others to develop a plan to meet the assessed needs of the child and promote the welfare of the child (see above). You will need to provide services and commitments as agreed in the plan or renegotiate those that cannot be delivered (see above). Participate in a regular review and evaluation of the child's plan in order to assess how well the child's needs are being met (see CCLD 313.4 above). Ensure that you maintain secure records concerning the child's response and development (see CCLD 328.2 in Chapter 17).

Twelve ways to respond to the needs of children who have experienced trauma

You can respond to the needs of children who have experienced trauma by:

1 Reassuring the child that they are safe and secure in the setting (see Chapters 10 and 11).
2 Providing a consistent and familiar environment for the child; routines and boundaries help children to feel secure, especially when they are distressed (see Chapters 1 and 11).
3 Providing opportunities for the child to express their feelings about their experience through play activities (see Chapters 1 and 8).
4 Allowing the child time to talk about their feelings and listening without passing judgement. Help the child to use words to express their feelings but do not force discussion about the traumatic event (see Chapter 1).
5 Allowing the child to cry or be sad. Do not expect them to be brave or tough. Let the child know that it is normal to feel upset after something bad has happened. Reassure the child that what happened was not their fault.
6 Responding consistently and positively to challenging behaviour (see Chapter 9).
7 Not criticising regressive behaviour or shaming the child by using words such as 'babyish'.
8 Supporting the child in developing a positive self-image and self-esteem (see Chapter 10).
9 Encouraging children to feel in control by letting them make some decisions about activities, meals, and so on (see Chapter 1).
10 Encouraging the child to breathe slowly if they start to panic, then talk about a pleasant memory you share or the child's particular interest or hobby.
11 Discussing any concerns you have about a child's emotional well-being with a senior colleague, especially if the child seems very distressed for a long time (see section above on post-traumatic stress disorder).
12 Taking care of yourself so that you can take care of the child (see below).

CCLD 327.3
Seek support for your own practice and development

Knowledge Base

K3P593   K3P594   K3P595

Strong feelings can be aroused when working with children who have experienced trauma. These feelings may include: sorrow for the child's loss; anger (especially against the perpetrators of violence); and guilt over being unable to prevent the trauma to the child. Professionals who work with children who have experienced trauma may develop symptoms of 'secondary' trauma that will need to be dealt with. Supporting children who have experienced trauma may also reawaken memories of traumatic experiences from your own childhood (see Chapter 10). Deal with your own feelings by using support systems such as discussing emotional issues with an experienced colleague or a counsellor. Remember to follow your setting's requirements concerning confidentiality (see Chapter 1). Reflect on your practice with children who have experienced trauma and take opportunities to improve your practice, such as attending courses about supporting children who have experienced abuse, neglect or domestic violence or supporting child refugees (see Chapter 4).

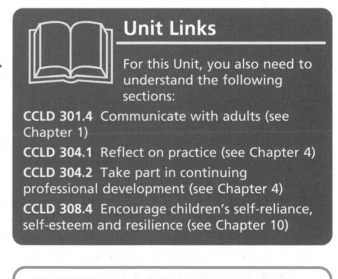

Unit Links

For this Unit, you also need to understand the following sections:

CCLD 301.4 Communicate with adults (see Chapter 1)

CCLD 304.1 Reflect on practice (see Chapter 4)

CCLD 304.2 Take part in continuing professional development (see Chapter 4)

CCLD 308.4 Encourage children's self-reliance, self-esteem and resilience (see Chapter 10)

CCLD 336
Contribute to childcare practice in group living

You should contribute to childcare practice that promotes group care as a positive experience where children and young people feel valued and safe. This includes: contributing to planning, implementing and reviewing daily living programmes for them, for example inclusive programmes set up for groups of children and young people such as residential care; working with groups of children and young people to promote their individual growth and development; and contributing to group care as a positive experience.

CCLD 336.1
Contribute to planning, implementing and reviewing daily living programmes for children and young people

Knowledge Base

336K01	336K02	336K03	336K04	336K05
336K06	336K07	336K08	336K09	336K10
336K11	336K14	336K15	336K17	336K18
336K20				

Some children and young people cannot live with their parents and so enter public care for a variety of reasons. They may be in public care due to: physical abuse, sexual abuse and/or neglect; the illness or death of a parent; family upheaval or breakdown; or inadequate care from families. Less than 2 per cent of young people are in public care because of offences they have committed. (DFEE, 2000a)

When parents are not able to look after their child, the local authority has a legal responsibility to do so. The local authority will find a place for the child or young person to live and someone to look after them. When this happens, the child is said to be 'in care' or being 'looked after'. There are two main types of being in care. Where the child's parents agree to the child being looked after, the child or young person may be voluntarily living in a home run by a local authority/charity or a foster home. When a court decides that a child could be damaged by living at home and issues a Care Order, the child can be legally removed from their family without the parents' consent and placed in care. About three out of every five children in care are under a Care Order. In the past, most children in care lived in large residential care homes. Now only 1 in 8 lives in a residential care home, which are now much smaller than before and usually house less than ten children. More than two-thirds of the UK's 78,500 looked-after children live in foster homes. (ChildLine, 2004)

Some children in care may see their families or even return home but others may not. Some do not want to see their families while some are not allowed to see their families, as the courts have ruled that it is not safe for them to do so. However, most children and young people do stay in touch with their families. Many go back to live with their own families once things have been sorted out but some will find themselves back in care again. Children and young people who do not return home stay with foster carers or live in children's homes until they are 16 or 18 years old. (ChildLine, 2004) (See above for information about identifying children in need of intervention and legislation and guidance relating to children in need.)

The effects of being in care

Most children and young people do not want to be in care even when they understand why they cannot live with their families. They often feel they are not involved in the major decisions about their lives despite the legal requirement to consider their wishes and feelings. Some children feel safer and well cared for in foster care and residential care but uncertainty about their immediate and long-term future is a major worry for most children in care. All children in care have to cope with significant losses, such as family, friends, communities and familiar neighbourhoods. Some may be separated from brothers and sisters, who may have remained with their family or be in care with a different foster family or residential care. These children have a lot of changes to cope with: new carers, new environment and new routines. In addition, children from an ethnic minority background may be placed with carers from a different ethnic background. Many children experience numerous and sometimes unplanned moves of home and each move will usually involve a change of school. (DfEE, 2000a; p. 10)

Many children in care move several times a year, which makes it almost impossible to settle down, make friends and do well at school. According to government statistics, about one in six children in care has lived in three or more different homes in the last year. Children in care often experience unexpected and prolonged absences from school and then find it difficult to catch up after having moved. They also find that most schools are not equipped to deal with their needs. Children in care say that many schools have low expectations for them and that they have difficulties forming lasting relationships with other children and adults at the school. Due to these problems many children in care experience barriers to educational achievement such as: they are 13 times more likely than other pupils

to be excluded from school; less than 1 in 12 children in care achieve five or more good GCSEs; almost 6 in 10 children in care leave school with no qualifications at all; only 1 per cent of children in care go to university. (ChildLine, 2004)

The law on children's rights and parents' rights and responsibilities

The law in England and Wales used to talk of a parent having 'rights' and 'duties', but in recent times the language has changed to one of parents having 'responsibilities' and parents' rights being balanced by children's rights.

Children now have individual rights set out in the UN Convention on the Rights of the Child (1989). The UN Convention contains three groups of children's rights:

◎ *Rights to provision:* children are entitled to education, to the best possible health care, to an adequate standard of living, to play, to family life and to alternative care if their family is unable to look after them
◎ *Rights to protection:* children are entitled to protection from abuse, neglect, sexual or economic exploitation, abduction or discrimination, and to have their best interest given primary consideration
◎ *rights to personal freedoms and to participate in decision-making:* children are entitled to have their views listened to and taken seriously, to respect for their opinions, beliefs and religion, and to privacy and information.

(NFPI, 2004)

(For more information about the United Nations Convention on the Rights of the Child see CCLD 305.1 in Chapter 5.)

The Children Act 1989 was a landmark law, redefining the relationship between parent and child. It changed the previous emphasis from one of duty and rights of the parent to one of responsibilities. This Act uses the concept of 'parental responsibility' to describe the rights, duties, powers, responsibilities and authority parents have for their child. In this Act a child is a person under the age of 18. (NFPI, 2004)

The Act also provides a comprehensive framework for the care and protection of all children and young people in need, including those living away from home. Local authorities have a specific duty to safeguard and promote the well-being of children looked after by them. (DH, 2002) (There is more information about national legislation relating to children's rights and the law regarding child protection in Chapter 5.)

Unit Links

For this Unit, you also need to understand the following sections:

CCLD 305.1 Support equality of access (see Chapter 5)

CCLD 305.3 Maintain and follow policies and procedures for protecting and safeguarding children (see Chapter 5)

Quality Protects Programme

The Quality Protects Programme is a key part of the Government's wider strategy for tackling social exclusion. It focuses on working with some of the most disadvantaged and vulnerable children in our society: children looked after by councils; in the child protection system; and other children in need – see www.dfes.gov.uk/qualityprotects/

The Government's Objectives for Children's Social Services are:

1. To ensure that children are securely attached to carers capable of providing safe and effective care for the duration of childhood.
2. To ensure that children are protected from emotional, physical and sexual abuse and neglect (significant harm).
3. To ensure that children in need gain maximum life chance benefits from educational opportunities, health care and social care.
4. To ensure that looked-after children gain maximum life chance benefits from educational opportunities, health care and social care.
5. To ensure that young people leaving care, as they enter adulthood, are not isolated and participate socially and economically as citizens.
6. To ensure that children with specific social needs arising out of disability or a health condition are living with families or other appropriate settings in the community where their assessed needs are adequately reviewed and met.
7. To ensure that referral and assessment processes discriminate effectively between different types and levels of need and produce a timely service response.
8. To actively involve service users and carers in planning services and in tailoring individual packages of care; and to ensure effective mechanisms are in place to handle complaints.
9. To ensure through regulatory powers and duties that children in regulated services are protected from harm and poor care standards.
10. To ensure that social care workers are appropriately skilled, trained and qualified, and to promote the uptake of training at all levels.
11. To maximise the benefit to services users from the resources available, and to demonstrate the effectiveness and value for money of the care

and support provided, and allow for choice and different responses for different needs and circumstances.

(DH, 2001)

Individual Care Plans

The Children Act 1989 emphasises the importance of assessment and planning, and the reviewing of plans, for children and young people who are looked after by the local authority. It is a statutory requirement that every child looked after has a *Care Plan* and a *Placement Plan* drawn up by social services as set out in the *Arrangements for Placement of Children (General) Regulations 1991.*

The Care Plan should take account of the child's educational history, the need to achieve continuity, and the need to identify any educational need which the child may have, or carry out any assessment in respect of any special educational need. The plan should take account of any existing Individual Education Plan and statement of special educational needs drawn up through the SEN Code of Practice. (For more information about national legislation relating to children with special educational needs see CCLD 305.2 in Chapter 5.) The child, his or her family, the social worker, teacher and primary carers (foster carers or residential social care workers) should all be involved in drawing up the Care Plan. The *Children (Leaving Care) Bill* (introduced in the House of Lords in November 1999) introduces a further plan, the *Pathway Plan,* for young people aged 16 to 17 in or leaving care. These, too, will need to be co-ordinated with existing plans. (DfEE, 2000a)

It is recommended good practice to amalgamate the *Looked After Children Statutory Review* with reviews of other relevant plans, as this establishes a holistic and consistent approach to planning for the child. It also encourages all the key players to be involved in

the child's long-term care, education and health. This also reduces the need for young people to be called away to too many planning and review meetings which may disrupt their education and single them out as 'different' in the eyes of their peers. A two-tier arrangement can be adopted so that the young person can express their needs and preferences with a few people they know and trust. Those few people then take on responsibility for liaison with the wider group so that the young person does not have to attend large and formal reviews. (DfEE, 2000a) (See CCLD 301.1 and 301.2 in Chapter 1 for more detail on involving children in decision-making and effective communication with children.)

Encouraging children and young people to make their views known

Children and young people have the right to have their opinions taken into account when adults are making decisions that affect them, according to Article 12 of the UN Convention on the Rights of the Child (see CCLD 301.1 in Chapter 1 for further information about involving children in decision-making and CCLD 305.1 in Chapter 5 for details of The United Nations Convention on the Rights of the Child).

A person's sense of self-efficacy (or self-direction) is about qualities of optimism, persistence and believing that one's own efforts can make a difference. There are two important ways that you can help children and young people to develop a sense of self-efficacy: by encouraging them to define their own outcomes; and involving them in the development of services. Involving children and young people in planning their care is a crucial way of promoting a sense of self-efficacy as it provides them with a sense of stability and control. Encouraging them to develop goals or outcomes can help promote a more positive sense of what the future might hold and how to reach it. They also need to participate in the development of services for looked-after children. Local authorities have a range of systems for encouraging feedback from children and young people including questionnaires, e-mail and meetings with senior managers and local councillors. Children and young people have also been involved in the design of CareZone, which is The Who Cares? Trust's secure online service for children in public care and includes an innovative package of child-centred services that aims to provide children with their own space – see website: www.thewhocarestrust.org.uk/carezone.htm. (Bostock, 2004)

Advocacy

Parents usually act as their children's advocates, recognising that certain choices and decisions (such as those relating to health, education and any special needs) affect how their children's particular needs are met as well as their life chances. The same decisions and choices also affect children and young people in public care, and the local authority as corporate parent is expected to fulfil the role of advocate. Foster carers, residential care workers, designated teachers and social workers (and in some cases parents) have a clear role in day-to-day advocacy, such as accessing appropriate services to ensure that individual children and young people in care receive the support they need when they need it. Local authorities should ensure that primary

---

Five ways to promote children and young people's self-efficacy

You can encourage children and young people to make their views known, define their own outcomes and participate in service development by:

1   Involving them in discussions about their needs and their future.
2   Helping them to contribute to care plans and reviews and ensuring that their wishes are always considered and where possible addressed.
3   Giving clear information and making sure that they know about: their reasons for entering into and remaining in care; their rights while they are in care; future plans and how they can influence these.
4   Trying to regard them as resources (not as problems) in the process of seeking solutions in their lives.
5   Encouraging them to make choices, declare preferences and define outcomes for themselves; and respecting these preferences.

(Bostock, 2004)

Activity

Give examples of how you encourage children and young people to make their views known, define their own outcomes and participate in service development.

carers, social workers and teachers have the necessary training to enable them to act as effective advocates. Local authorities may also have independent advocacy arrangements that children/young people or their carers/parents may use, for instance in order to access services to meet special needs or to challenge placement choices. (DfEE, 2000a) For more information see *Your Voice Your Choice: A guide for children and young people about the National Advocacy Standards* by Voice for the Child in Care, available from the website: www.dfes.gov.uk/qualityprotects/–then click on 'Your Voice Your Choice'.

PORTFOLIO ACTIVITY

Describe how you contribute to planning, implementing and reviewing daily living programmes for children and young people. Include information on how you contribute to: meeting their needs and preferences; planning and implementing care programmes; continuity of care provision by providing information at handover meetings; and discussions with children/young people and colleagues about the running of the care provision and quality of care provided. Include examples of any planning sheets you use.

NVQ LINKS: CCLD 336.1   CCLD 301.1
CCLD 301.2   CCLD 301.4   CCLD 303.3
CCLD 303.4   CCLD 304.1   CCLD 305.1
CCLD 306.4   CCLD 307.2   CCLD 307.3
CCLD 318.1   CCLD 327.2

CCLD 336.2
Work with groups to promote individual growth and development

Knowledge Base

336K01	336K02	336K03	336K04	336K05
336K06	336K07	336K08	336K09	336K10
336K14	336K15	336K20	336K21	336K22
336K23	336K24			

The Children Act 1989 and Regulations and Standards issued under the Care Standards Act 2000 impose clear duties on foster carers and residential workers as well as social workers and managers in improving the health of children in care. The responsibilities of foster carers, carers and residential staff for ensuring that the child's health needs are met include: understanding that achieving optimum health starts early and includes the provision of good quality care that starts in infancy and which provides a child with a positive sense of identity and self-esteem; encouraging and supporting each child in achieving optimum health and, in particular, exercising the corporate parent's responsibility as health educator; providing a home environment which actively encourages and supports a healthy lifestyle; ensuring the child attends health appointments and clinics as necessary; contributing to the child's health plan and care plan; ensuring and facilitating contact and communication with the child's parents and family in accordance with agreed plans; ensuring that the child or young person gains maximum benefit from education and broader experiences offered by leisure activities, hobbies and sport. (DH, 2002)

The Healthy Care Programme

The Healthy Care Programme provides a multi-agency framework to improve the health of looked-after children and young people in England. The framework co-ordinates the key policies and addresses the issues that affect the health and well-being of children and young people. Better outcomes depend on the integration of universal services to address the needs of the child and family. The Programme also promotes local healthy care services across agencies and makes the five outcomes of *Every Child Matters* the driving force for the development and delivery of services to looked-after children. (NCB, 2005) (See CCLD 305.1 in Chapter 5 for information on the national framework for children's services.)

The National Healthy Care Standard helps looked-after children and young people to achieve the five outcomes described in *Every Child Matters:* be healthy; stay safe; enjoy and achieve; make a positive contribution; and achieve economic well-being. A child or young person living in a healthy care environment is entitled to:

◎ Feel safe, protected and valued in a strong, sustained and committed relationship with at least one carer
◎ Live in a caring, healthy and learning environment
◎ Feel respected and supported in his/her cultural beliefs and personal identity
◎ Have access to effective healthcare, assessment, treatment and support
◎ Have opportunities to develop personal and social skills, talents and abilities and to spend time in freely chosen play, cultural and leisure activities
◎ Be prepared for leaving care by being supported in order to care and provide for him/herself in the future.

(NCB, 2005)

It is important to link the promotion of good health for children in care to their educational experiences. Access to good education has a direct impact on a child's well-being, including their sense of self-worth and self-confidence. It also enables integration within a social network and encourages a sense of being a valued member of the local community, as well as helping to establish positive peer relationships. (DH, 2002)

Personal Education Plans

As well as a Care Plan, Placement Plan and Statutory Review (see above), every child and young person in public care needs a Personal Education Plan (PEP) to: ensure access to services and support; contribute to stability; minimise disruption and broken schooling; signal particular and special needs; establish clear goals; and act as a record of progress and achievement. The PEP should be sensitive to the diverse needs of children and young people and should focus on the action that is required for them to fulfil their potential. The PEP should include: *an achievement record* (academic or otherwise); identification of *developmental and educational needs* (short- and long-term, development of skills, knowledge or subject areas and experiences); *short-term targets* (such as personal and, if appropriate, behavioural targets) including progress monitoring; *long-term plans and aspirations* (targets including progress, careers plans and aspirations) which may be broken into shorter-term, achievable goals. The PEP should also include details of who will action the plan with timescales for action and review. The PEP should be an integral part of the Care Plan, reflecting any existing education plans, such as the Individual Education Plan, Statement of Special Needs, or Careers Action Plan. (DfEE, 2000a) Information about developing a PEP can be found on the DfEE website at: www.dfee.gov.uk/incare/pep.htm.

The Government has made the education of children in care a priority – see *Guidance on the Education of Children and Young People in Public Care* – visit the website: www.dfes.gov.uk/educationprotects/ then click on 'Why Education Protects' then *Guidance on the Education of Children and Young People in Public Care.*

Out-of-school-hours learning

Out-of-school-hours learning (OSHL) describes the wide range of informal learning activities that children and young people voluntarily take part in outside normal school hours and/or during school holiday periods. These opportunities can range from sports, music, arts and drama, to revision support, homework, reading or maths clubs. Activities may be provided by schools, local authority leisure services and youth services or by community providers such as guides/scouts and Red Cross or St John Ambulance. For all children and young people taking part in activities out of school can help to raise achievement by improving pupils' self-esteem and motivation. For children and young people in care, OSHL activities can bring even greater benefits. Children and young people who have suffered damaging life experiences, including separation, loss, rejection and trauma, are highly likely to suffer from poor self-esteem, and may benefit from OSHL activities which can help to build self-confidence, self-esteem, self-advocacy and social skills. For some looked-after children, school is associated with failure. OSHL activities can offer them real

experiences of feeling motivated and provide routes to 'achievement'. OSHL can also contribute to stability by providing regular activities with a familiar group as well as a positive focus for carers and children/young people. The stimulation, diversion and enrichment provided by OSHL activities may also help to prevent some young people from engaging in risk-taking behaviours. (Fletcher and Murison, 2005)

Working with groups to promote individual growth and development

This involves supporting the positive development of children and young people (see Chapter 3 for more information about understanding children's development) and taking into account the differing needs (including cultural, emotional, social and any special needs) of both individuals and groups (see Chapter 1). Provide active support to enable children and young people to be involved in identifying and implementing group work activities that they feel would be beneficial to the group (see Chapter 10). Ensure that you take action to moderate any adverse effects on the children and young people from belonging to groups within the provision and from the whole group experience. Making the effort to show that you care about the children and young people with whom you work demonstrates that you value them, even if the relationship is short-term. This will help to bolster their self-esteem and self-image (see Chapter 10).

Unit Links

For this Unit, you also need to understand the following sections:

CCLD 301.1 Develop relationships with children (see Chapter 1)

CCLD 301.3 Support children in developing relationships (see Chapter 1)

CCLD 303.4 Implement and evaluate plans to promote development (see Chapter 3)

CCLD 308.1 Enable children to relate to others (see Chapter 10)

CCLD 308.4 Encourage children's self-reliance, self-esteem and resilience (see Chapter 10)

Twelve ways to promote individual growth and development through activities

Work with groups to promote individual growth and development through activities by:

1. Identifying activities that the child/young person is interested in and referring them to appropriate services and opportunities.
2. Helping children and young people to realise that they can take part in additional activities.
3. Discussing with foster carers how to support children in joining clubs and activities.
4. Linking with children's designated teachers and education support services to ensure they have up-to-date information about activities on offer.
5. Encouraging young people to explore what they get out of activities, and to develop their self-confidence and self-esteem.
6. Signposting young people to a range of activities provided by the youth service.
7. Facilitating the continuity of participation in OSHL activities if a child moves placement.
8. Reinforcing the importance of involvement in activities and encouraging participation to continue if young people return to their parents.
9. Ensuring children have appropriate additional support to help them catch up, prepare for exams, and address any special educational needs.
10. Thinking about what activities can be made available both in the children's home or unit (especially what the youth service can provide) and outside that allow children to meet with others of their own age.
11. Talking to young people who are not engaged in activities about what they would like to do, and taking these outcomes back to the social worker or education providers and planning how to make these happen.
12. Adding new activities and clubs to the children's home's or unit's activity file.

(Fletcher and Murison, 2005; pp. 22–23)

PORTFOLIO ACTIVITY

Describe how you work with groups to promote individual growth and development. Include information on how you: offer support to enable children and young people to be involved in identifying and implementing group work activities; contribute to identifying, planning and evaluating how individual growth and development can be met by groups within the provision; and take action to moderate any adverse effects on the children and young people from belonging to groups within the provision and from the whole group experience.

NVQ LINKS: CCLD 336.2   CCLD 301.1   CCLD 301.2   CCLD 301.3   CCLD 303.3   CCLD 303.4
CCLD 305.1   CCLD 308.1   CCLD 308.4

CCLD 336.3
Contribute to promoting group care as a positive experience

Knowledge Base

336K01	336K02	336K07	336K08	336K09
336K10	336K11	336K12	336K13	336K15
336K16	336K19	336K21	336K23	

Contributing to promoting group care as a positive experience involves working with children and young people to evaluate the outcomes from group activities (see CCLD 303.4 in Chapter 3). You will need to identify and take action to address conflict, crisis and tensions in group living (see CCLD 301.3 in Chapter 1 for information on helping children to deal with conflict themselves). Work constructively with group dynamics in order to facilitate positive interactions between individuals within the group (see CCLD 308.1 in Chapter 10 for information about enabling children to relate to others and CCLD 308.1 in Chapter 18 for details of stages in team development).

You need to ensure group members are safe and protected from danger, harm and abuse as well as working with children/young people to identify and take action where there is a risk of danger, harm and abuse (see CCLD 305.3 in Chapter 5).

It is important to contribute to maintaining a culture in which group experiences are positively valued and promoted and where children and young people are encouraged to be involved in decisions about group care experiences, including how these can be improved and promoted (for more information about involving children in decision-making see CCLD 301.1 in Chapter 1).

The process of involving children and young people includes:

◎ Informing children and young people of the issues
◎ Encouraging them to form an opinion
◎ Giving them opportunities to express their opinions to people who make decisions
◎ Giving them feedback on how their opinions have shaped service developments
◎ Making sure that appropriate and different ways are found to listen to children of various ages, with different abilities, and from diverse cultures and backgrounds.

(NCB, 2005)

Continuous planning and monitoring of plans is carried out through the Looked After Children Review, as set out in the *Review of Children's Cases Regulations 1991*. Social services have a duty to consult with all appropriate interested agencies and individuals. Statutory Reviews should act as a very important safeguard for the child or young person. It is good practice to review the Personal Education Plan (see above) at the same time or close to the time of the Review. The majority of social services departments use the Department of Health Looking After Children recording materials, which include Assessment and Action Records detailing a child or young person's educational progress and needs. Plans and records represent a very important source of continuity for the child and their carers. They are, therefore, crucial in improving outcomes. How a child's achievements and potential are recorded is especially important for children in public care. An accurate and positive educational record provides a looked-after child with a 'passport' for the future. (DfEE, 2000a)

Record and report on the effectiveness of the provision to promote group care as a positive experience within confidentiality agreements and according to legal and organisational requirements (see CCLD 301.4 in Chapter 1 for further information about confidentiality matters and the childcare setting's requirements regarding confidentiality and CCLD 305.4 in Chapter 5 for more detail of the confidentiality of information relating to abuse).

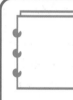

PORTFOLIO ACTIVITY

Describe how you contribute to promoting group care as a positive experience. Include information on how you: work with children and young people to evaluate the outcomes of group activities and involve them in decisions about group care experiences; ensure that group members are safe and protected from danger, harm and abuse; and record and report on the effectiveness of the care provision.

NVQ LINKS: CCLD 336.1   CCLD 336.2   CCLD 336.3   CCLD 301.1   CCLD 301.2   CCLD 301.3
               CCLD 303.4   CCLD 305.3   CCLD 308.1   CCLD 308.4   CCLD 326.3   CCLD 328.2

Optional Units

CCLD 315
Contribute to supporting parents with literacy, numeracy or language needs

CCLD 317
Work with families to enhance their children's learning and development

CCLD 320
Care for children at home

CCLD 322
Empower families through the development of parenting skills

CCLD 324
Support the delivery of community based services to children and families

CCLD 330
Establish and maintain a service for children and families

CCLD 331
Support children and families through home visiting

CCLD 332
Involve children and families in the childcare setting

CCLD 334
Deliver services to children and families whose preferred language is not English or Welsh

CCLD 315
Contribute to supporting parents with literacy, numeracy or language needs

When working in a childcare setting you may be involved in identifying parents who have language, literacy or numeracy needs and providing them with information about local learning opportunities. This may include working with parents with literacy or numeracy needs and those who require English for Speakers of Other Languages (ESOL) support.

CCLD 315.1
Identify and encourage parents with some literacy, numeracy or language needs to improve their skills

Knowledge Base

K3P449	K3P454	K3P455	K3P456	K3C457
K3P458	K3P459	K3P460		

We all use a wide range of skills to enable us to do everyday activities, to study, to do our jobs and to help our children with their school work.

Parents with lower levels of literacy, numeracy or language (ESOL) skills may be excluded in our society. It is important to encourage parents to develop and use these skills in every aspect of their lives. (DfES, 2005b) (There is more information about why literacy and numeracy are important in CCLD 345.1 and 346.1 in Chapter 13.)

'*Skills for Life*' (previously known as 'basic skills') refers to the ability to read, write and speak in English and to use mathematics at a level necessary to function and progress at work and in society in general. *Skills for Life* is also the name for the government's strategy to improve adult literacy, numeracy and language skills: *Skills for Life – the national strategy for improving adult literacy and numeracy skills* published by the DfES in 2004. For

more information see: www.dfes.gov.uk/
readwriteplus/bank/ACF35CE.pdf.

For many people, English is a second, third or even
fourth language. Some have lived in this country for
many years and find that changes in employment or
job roles mean they need to develop their spoken
and written skills. Others, more recently arrived, have
the challenge of learning a new language in order
to find work and settle into a new community.
(DfES, 2005b) (For further details on communication
in bilingual and multilingual setting and recognising
communication difficulties with adults see CCLD
301.2 and 301.4 in Chapter 1.) For more
information about ESOL see: www.direct.gov.uk/
EducationAndLearning/AdultLearning/ImprovingYour
Skills/ImprovingYourSkillsArticles/fs/en?CONTENT_ID
=10037499&chk=PdU1Gu.

You should check that your methods of
communicating with parents (and carers) do not
present barriers for those who have lower levels of
literacy or language skills. Make sure there are
opportunities for information to be shared with
parents and carers at face-to-face meetings and
social events, as well as on paper. Produce
communication materials which take into account
the fact that some parents and carers will have
lower levels of literacy, numeracy or language skills.
The booklet *Writing and design tips*, with guidelines
on making materials easier to read, is available from:
www.nala.ie/download/pdf/writing_design_tips.pdf.

Activity

List examples of how your setting
communicates with parents who have
differing levels of literacy, numeracy and
language skills.

Identifying and assessing parents with literacy, numeracy or language needs

The *National Standards for adult literacy, numeracy
and ICT* (QCA, 2005) provides the framework for all
adult literacy, numeracy and ESOL screening tests,
initial assessment, diagnostic tools, programmes of
study and qualifications – see website:
www.qca.org.uk/downloads/14130_national_standar
ds_for_adult_literacy_numeracy_ict.pdf.

There may be parents in your setting who have let
you know they do not feel confident about some of
their skills or who have perhaps asked for your help
in completing forms, for example. You may have
noticed that some parents are reluctant to
participate in certain activities within the setting or
avoid some tasks altogether. To find out about skills
for life awareness, see the resource pack *Basic Skills
Awareness Raising Pack for Wales* available from:
www.basic-skills.co.uk/downloads/
a1460_basic_skills_awareness_raising_pack_for_wale
s_bilingual.pdf.

You may observe the following clues in parents: speaks
very little English; avoids writing things down;
reluctant to communicate with others; anxious or
aggressive when faced with certain activities. These
may indicate a literacy, numeracy or language need,
but to be certain about this, you should observe
parents and talk to them to identify what they can do.
Encourage the parents to talk about the literacy,
numeracy or language tasks that they might like help
with. Screening tools, if used sensitively by staff, can
help parents to identify the skills they already have and
which skills they would like to improve. (DfES, 2005c)
To find out more about skills for life screening see:
www.dfes.gov.uk/ readwriteplus/staffpack/sitemap/.

Depending on your role and responsibilities, you may be involved in the following activities:

1 *Signposting*: giving a parent information, advice or guidance about adult learning provision, which they then follow up on their own.

2 *Referral*: giving a parent more detailed information, advice or guidance about learning provision, including agreeing to refer them to an adult learning provider and, if necessary, making the appointment for the parent to see the provider.

3 *Screening*: to find out whether a parent has a literacy, language or numeracy need, and whether they might benefit from more in-depth assessment; only practitioners trained in the use of screening tools may carry out screening.

4 *Initial assessment:* helping to place a parent in an appropriate learning programme by identifying their skills against a level or levels within the national standards; this is administered by a practitioner trained to at least Level 3, with the support of a Level 4 subject specialist teacher.

5 *Diagnostic assessment:* identifying a parent's strengths and weaknesses and highlighting any gaps they may have in their skills by using the national standards to provide a detailed profile of the parent's needs and the basis for their individual learning plan; this is carried out by a Level 4 subject specialist.

6 An *Individual Learning Plan* (ILP): setting out what a parent needs to learn, the timetable for this learning, the methods and resources required; a Level 4 specialist teacher compiles, reviews and develops the ILP, in consultation with the parent.

(DfES, 2005c)

Benefits of supporting literacy, numeracy and language skills

Improving the skills of parents (and carers) has benefits for the whole family. Family literacy, numeracy and language programmes, involving parents and children, have proved a particularly effective way of helping parents to improve their own skills and give their children a better start. Parents' own literacy, numeracy and language levels and confidence in these skills can affect the extent to which they feel able to support their children's learning. Most parents want to help their children, but those with skills gaps may find it harder or feel less confident about attempting to help their children. Parents may be particularly anxious about their children's development and learning because of their own difficulties. (DfES, 2005b)

PORTFOLIO ACTIVITY

Outline the methods used in your setting to identify and encourage parents with literacy, numeracy and language needs to improve their skills.

NVQ LINKS: CCLD 315.1   CCLD 301.2
CCLD 301.4   CCLD 305.1   CCLD 334.1

**CCLD 315.2
Provide information for parents to enable them to access support**

Think About

How do you identify parents with possible literacy, numeracy or language needs?

Knowledge Base

K3P449   K3P450   K3P451   K3P452   K3P453
K3C457

You should set up positive working relationships with providers of adult literacy, numeracy and ESOL support. For example you could form useful contacts with:

◎ Learning and Skills Council (LSC): www.lsc.gov.uk
◎ Local adult learning providers: FE colleges, local authority adult education services or private training providers (see telephone directory)
◎ Local Learning Partnerships: www.lifelonglearning.co.uk/llp/index.htm
◎ Local information and advice services: nextstep gives information and advice on learning and work to adults (see: www.nextstep.org.uk).

> **Check it out**
>
> Find out about the providers of adult literacy, numeracy and ESOL support in your local area.

You should identify appropriate local provision to meet parents' needs and provide clear accessible information for parents about this provision. Make use of any knowledge and expertise within your own organisation, such as a staff member who volunteers in a literacy programme or who already knows about working with parents who have literacy, numeracy or language needs. Remember to follow your setting's policy on confidentiality when recording personal information regarding information about parents' needs.

There are many different ways that parents can improve their literacy, numeracy or language skills, such as in groups or online, at work or in the community. The BBC Skillwise website has useful information to help adults improve their reading, writing and maths skills including resources for learners and tutors see: www.bbc.co.uk/skillwise.

Parents are eligible for free support to improve

literacy, numeracy and/or language needs up to Level 2 or a first qualification up to Level 2. For example:

◎ Developing their literacy, language or numeracy skills as part of another course or activity. For more information see: www.successforall.gov.uk.
◎ *Move On* is a national project aimed at learners who do not see themselves as needing help with their 'basic skills'. For more information see: www.move-on.org.uk
◎ *Family literacy, language and numeracy:* a mainstream programme in each LEA funded by the LSC. It offers parents and children a menu of learning opportunities including *Early Start*. For details on family literacy, language and numeracy, contact your local LEA Family Learning Officer or Local LSC (www.lsc.gov.uk).

PORTFOLIO ACTIVITY

Compile a resource file about local providers of adult literacy, numeracy and ESOL support. You could include information on: *Skills for Life*; Local Learning Partnerships; local adult learning providers, such as FE colleges; local information and advice services, for example Connexions and nextstep; family literacy, language and numeracy programmes such as Early Start. Include information about local courses and support in formats appropriate for potential learners (for example visually attractive flyers and leaflets with positive messages in English and, where applicable, community languages).

NVQ LINKS: CCLD 315.1 CCLD 315.2
CCLD 301.4 CCLD 305.1 CCLD 322.4
CCLD 324.4 CCLD 334.2

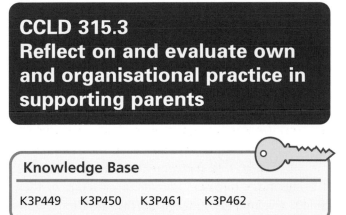

CCLD 315.3
Reflect on and evaluate own and organisational practice in supporting parents

Knowledge Base

K3P449   K3P450   K3P461   K3P462

Reflect on your own and your organisation's practice in supporting parents with literacy, numeracy or language needs. This includes discussing with parents their experiences of support received in the identification and signposting of support for their needs. You could use the following questions as a checklist to help you evaluate the effectiveness of strategies for identifying and supporting parents and to identify ways of improving the service to them:

◎ Do we know enough about how our users' or community's current levels of literacy, language or numeracy affect their ability to access our services or achieve their goals?
◎ Do we have members of staff who could benefit from improving their literacy, language or numeracy to meet the demands of a changing workplace?
◎ Would you like to improve your own skills?
◎ Do we know how to help service users, local community members or staff improve their literacy, language and numeracy? Have we checked to find out about resources that may exist in our own organisation, such as people who know about literacy, language or numeracy or who have expertise in working with particular groups?
◎ Can we help people who feel that learning is not relevant for them to get involved?

◎ Can we recognise those with very low skills and distinguish them from those who may only need to brush up their skills?
◎ Have we looked at our written materials, signs and posters to check that they are not presenting barriers to understanding? To be able to participate, people need timely access to information that is often complex. Do we provide this in a genuinely accessible way?
◎ Do we know about local literacy, language and numeracy provision?
◎ Do we know who can help us develop solutions?

(DfES, 2005b)

If you want to take advantage of professional development opportunities and enhance your skills in supporting parents and children, you could participate in training on how best to identify parents with literacy, numeracy or language needs and how to advise them. For example: *Step in to Learning* is a training and development programme for managers and staff in neighbourhood nurseries, Sure Start local programmes and children's centres. The programme enables early years and childcare staff to identify and guide parents and carers with language, literacy or numeracy needs. This programme can be run locally by your organisation in partnership with an adult learning provider. For information about the programme, including case studies and examples of good practice, see the website: www.surestart.gov.uk/stepintolearning.

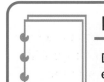

PORTFOLIO ACTIVITY

Describe how you reflect on and evaluate your own and organisational practice in supporting parents with literacy, numeracy or language needs. Include suggestions on improving the service for parents such as staff training and professional development.

NVQ LINKS: CCLD 315.3   CCLD 304.1
CCLD 304.2   CCLD 330.4   CCLD 332.3
CCLD 334.3

CCLD 317
Work with families to enhance their children's learning and development

As a childcarer you may be involved in working with families to help them develop realistic expectations of the children's development and achievements and to enhance their children's learning and development through play and other learning opportunities.

CCLD 317.1
Liaise with families about their expectations of their child

Knowledge Base

K3D474	K3P475	K3C476	K3P477	K3P478
K3P479	K3D480	K3P481	K3P481	

Parents are their children's first and most enduring educators. When childcare practitioners and parents work together in childcare settings, this has a positive impact on children's learning and development. As a childcare practitioner you should seek to develop an effective partnership with parents. A successful partnership requires a two-way flow of information, knowledge and expertise between parents and practitioners. You can develop effective practice in working in partnership with parents by: respecting and understanding the role of parents; encouraging parents' involvement in their children's learning; listening to their views on their children's development; providing flexible settling-in arrangements; ensuring all parents feel welcome and

valued by providing different opportunities for working together; using the knowledge and expertise of parents and other family adults (grandparent); keeping parents fully informed about the curriculum using a variety of methods; involving parents in discussing and recording information about the child's progress; and linking relevant play and learning activities between home and the setting. (QCA, 2000)

It is important to assess parents' knowledge of their child's development and ensure that children's views are also taken into account (see CCLD 301.1 in Chapter 1 for further information about involving children in decision-making).

Encourage parents to recognise the unique qualities, skills and capabilities of their children. When helping parents to access information about children's development and learning, ensure that they understand that all children are unique individuals who develop at their own rate. There are many books and magazines about children's development and/or learning specifically aimed at parents. Books on children's learning and development can be borrowed for free from local libraries. There are also free sources of information available via the Internet. For example:

- *Birth to Five: 2006 edition:* this Department of Health booklet is an easy-to-use guide for parents which includes information on children's development, learning, playing and behaviour: go to www.dh.gov.uk and type 'Birth to Five 2006 edition' into the website search bar
- The Parents Centre website provides information and support for parents on how to help their children's learning from 0 to 16+ years: www.parentscentre.gov.uk
- The Parentline Plus website includes information on children's development from 0 to 18+ years: www.parentlineplus.org.uk.

PORTFOLIO ACTIVITY

Give examples of how you liaise with families about their expectations for their child.

NVQ LINKS: CCLD 317.1   CCLD 301.1   CCLD 301.4   CCLD 312.4   CCLD 322.2
             CCLD 325.1   CCLD 330.1   CCLD 330.3   CCLD 332.1   CCLD 334.2

CCLD 317.2
Encourage families to be involved with their children's learning and development

Knowledge Base

K3P482   K3P483   K3D484

Encourage families to be involved with their children's learning and development by promoting the benefits of supporting children's learning through play and other learning activities. Discuss and agree developmentally appropriate learning opportunities, including books, games, toys and play activities with families. While it is important to allow children the freedom to explore their environment and to play with a wide range of materials, make sure that parents understand that these materials must be suitable for the age and level of development of their children.

Ten ways for families to be involved with their children's learning and development

Opportunities for families to be involved with children's learning and development include:

1   Talking with their children about: everyday activities; television programmes; what they did at nursery or school; and the children's hobbies and interests.
2   Involving their children in everyday activities, such as helping with food shopping, preparing meals or baking biscuits and cakes.
3   Sharing books and stories with their children, including visits to local libraries. (See websites: www.bookstart.co.uk – the national 'Books for Babies' programme; and www.readtogether.co.uk – an excellent interactive website for parents and carers that includes activities and lists of recommended books for different age groups.)
4   Providing musical activities, for example singing nursery rhymes, finger rhymes and action songs; and playing with simple musical instruments.
5   Taking their children on outings to the local park, farm, museums and art galleries.
6   Encouraging their children to look after living things, such as gardening and keeping pets.

7 Providing opportunities and materials for physical play such as: playground and/or indoor play centre; ball games; swimming; gymnastics clubs; and sports clubs.

8 Providing opportunities and materials for exploratory play such as: sand play; water play; construction kits; drawing; painting; collages; model-making; and playdough.

9 Providing opportunities and materials for imaginative play such as: dressing-up; dolls, soft toys and puppets; play house; shop play; and small-scale toys (toy cars).

10 Playing with jigsaw puzzles, card games and board games.

Homework

Families can also be involved in their children's learning and development by helping their children with homework and revision. Depending on their children's ages, homework activities may include: reading books; spelling; learning times tables; finishing off school work; doing simple science tasks; doing a project on class topic; and revising for SATs or GCSEs. Parents can find out more about helping their children to learn and helping with children's homework from: www.direct.gov.uk/ EducationAndLearning/Schools/HelpingYourChildToL earn/fs/en. Useful information and activities to support parents in helping their children with their school work is also available from: www.parentscentre.gov.uk/discover.

Out-of-school learning

Parents can also enhance their children's learning and development by encouraging their school-aged children to participate in out-of-school learning activities such as clubs where they can get help with their homework or learn new skills, for example music, cookery, dancing, sports, drama, writing, computing, photography, and so on. Out of school learning may take place in schools, libraries, museums, art galleries, football clubs, sports centres or outdoor settings. They may take place before/after school, lunchtimes, weekends or school holidays. For more information see: www.parentzonescotland.gov.uk.

Family learning programmes

You should identify any obstacles to families' involvement with their children's learning and development and discuss the options available. Examples of possible obstacles include parents who require support for their own literacy, numeracy or language needs (see Unit CCLD 315). Examples of possible options to overcome these obstacles include family learning programmes, which involve: parents and children learning together; child development courses; parent literacy and numeracy courses; and parenting courses. Family learning programmes may be available in your setting or in other community-based services.

For examples of family learning see: www.pre-school.org.uk/iacontent.php/en/59.phtml.

Check it out

Find out about the out-of-school learning activities and family learning programmes available in your local area. Information about local clubs and activities for children may be available from your library, community centre or local authority.

Parent and Child Early Learning Packs

Parent and Child Early Learning Packs can be used to encourage learning at home and foster links with the setting. These packs, which can be especially useful for parents who have limited resources for supporting their children's learning, aim to encourage children's language and communication skills as well as early reading, mathematical, scientific and technological skills. They provide information on how children learn as well as practical suggestions and materials so that the parent and child can share enjoyable activities which enhance children's learning and development. Based on themes or topics which interest young children, for example the farm, houses, gardens, picnics, space, spiders, and so on, each pack includes a book relating to the theme and sometimes an audio-cassette. Poems, rhymes, finger or glove puppets, small toys, games and puzzles all related to the theme may also be included and some packs incorporate paper, crayons and scissors or role play materials. Each pack contains: a list of contents; a theme folder with information about the pack, such as a theme sheet and notes on the learning objectives in the form of 'Why?' sheets; and an evaluation sheet for parents to comment on the pack. The materials of each pack are kept together in a clear plastic bag. (Wilcox, 1994)

The costs for compiling early learning packs can vary. If you wanted to create your own, you could keep the costs down by making some of the materials yourself or enlisting the help of willing parents (homemade finger puppets and role-play outfits); books, games, puzzles and toys in 'nearly new' condition may be obtained from car boot sales, charity shops and school fairs. (Wilcox, 1994)

CCLD 317.3
Review children's progress with families

Knowledge Base

K3C485

As part of the learning process, practitioners need to assess each child's development in relation to the relevant curriculum framework(s) applicable to their setting and the ages of the children they work with, for example Birth to Three Matters, The Foundation Stage, The National Curriculum and the proposed Early Years Foundation Stage. These assessments are made on the basis of the practitioner's accumulating observations and knowledge of the whole child. built up throughout the year by recording and reviewing children's progress periodically using the evidence from ongoing observations and assessment. Reporting a child's progress to their parents is a key requirement for all settings and reviews may be conducted with parents on a termly or even monthly basis, depending on the age and needs of the children and the requirements of the setting. (QCA, 2003)

Parents have a unique knowledge of aspects of their children's development, which is central to the assessment process. An essential feature of parental involvement is an on-going dialogue between practitioners and parents about their children's progress. Features of good practice include: practitioners using a variety of ways to keep parents fully informed about the curriculum, such as brochures, displays and videos, which are available in the home languages of the parents, and through informal discussion; parents and practitioners talking about and recording information about the child's progress and achievements, for example through meetings or making a book about the child, to which the child can contribute. Practitioners should seek parents' views on any relevant aspects of their children's development observed outside the setting. One way of gathering this information is by holding a parent conference or one-to-one conversation at a regular parents' day or evening. (QCA, 2003)

There should be an on-going sharing of information about progress, through a home/setting diary, to which the practitioner, any other staff who work with the child, the parents and the child all contribute, and/or through further meetings during the year when information is recorded following discussion. Some settings hold regular review meetings, linking ongoing assessment with suggestions about ways in which parents can support their children's development. Education settings should report progress and achievements to parents or carers at the end of the school year including an annual written report, in line with statutory requirements. (QCA, 2003)

Children should also be involved in the assessment process including: discussions about likes, dislikes

and achievements; selecting work or photographs for a child portfolio or end of Foundation Stage booklet; writing or drawing comments (such as a 'smiley face' to indicate enjoyment of a story or activity) in their home/setting diaries; recording views on tape or video. It is important to involve children in the assessment process as it enables them to develop their ability to express preferences and make choices, begin to understand that their views are respected and develop as autonomous learners. (QCA, 2003)

PORTFOLIO ACTIVITY

Describe the methods you use to review children's progress with their families. Include information on how you: agree a plan for reviewing children's progress with families and children themselves, according to their age needs and abilities; agree a timescale within which progress will be measured; agree how help, support and advice will be provided and by whom; agree how children's progress will be monitored; assess children's progress against initial information; and provide feedback and positive reinforcement to families about their children's progress. Include examples of any relevant records and review sheets. Remember confidentiality.

NVQ LINKS: CCLD 317.1   CCLD 317.2
CCLD 317.3   CCLD 301.4   CCLD 303.2
CCLD 310.2   CCLD 312.1   CCLD 328.2
CCLD 330.3   CCLD 339.3

CCLD 320
Care for children at home

Caring for children at home involves developing positive relationships with children and their parents, as well as providing positive environments, general care and stimulating activities, including outings to promote children's development. Practitioners who care for children in home-based settings include: nannies or home childcarers who care for children in the children's own homes; and childminders who care for children in the childminders' own homes.

CCLD 320.1
Implement the requirements of parents in line with current best practice guidance

Knowledge Base

| K3C515 | K3P516 | K3P517 | K3D518 |

A home-based childcarer has a very unique role compared with that of other childcare practitioners. Working in a family home is different from other childcare settings because you are: caring for child/children on a more individual basis; working more closely with the parents; working independently without the support of colleagues; being employed by the parents if you are a nanny or self-employed if you are a childminder.

Establishing a professional relationship with parents

To establish a professional relationship with the parents you need to clearly understand the roles and boundaries of everyone involved so that you can all work together to provide the best care for their child or children. Not only do children thrive when there is continuity of care from the adults who are most important in their lives, but also the parents' trust in you grows when the parent partnership is working well. A harmonious working relationship enables you to promote children's physical and emotional well-being to the fullest extent possible and gives you more job satisfaction. A professional relationship between you and the parents begins with an agreed formal contract that defines both yours and the parents' expectations about your duties, wages, hours and working conditions. (If you are working as a childminder see CCLD 316.2 in Chapter 17 for information about administering a childminding business; if you are working as a nanny see Unit CCLD 333 in Chapter 18 for information about employment rights.) To establish and maintain professional relationships with the parents you need to: work co-operatively with parents; perform your duties as agreed; communicate openly and effectively; show sensitivity to family situations; and seek constructive solutions to problems; maintain a consistent, positive attitude. Listen sympathetically if the parents wish to talk over their feelings of concern, anxiety or even guilt about leaving their child in someone else's care. You may also talk to them about current child care theories and development issues to reassure the parents that their child is getting the very best in substitute care.

Six ways to establish and maintain positive working relationships with the parents

The following guidelines may help you to foster positive working relationships with parents:

1   Exchange information with the parents: communication is the key to fostering a positive working relationship with the parents; take a few minutes each day to talk with the parents and keep a daily log; and keep the lines of communication open and deal with any problems as they occur, before they get out of hand.

2   Understand your role as a home-based childcarer: the role of the childcarer and the parent must not be confused; you are there to complement the parents, not to replace them; you may be in charge of the child's daily routines and activities but if you work in the child's own home then the parents will usually decide whether the child can invite a friend round to play or to stay for tea.

3   Respect the family's right to privacy: all matters relating to the family should be treated as private and confidential; parents need to feel that you are trustworthy and will not gossip about them; in the very rare circumstance that you are concerned about a child's welfare, you should follow the usual child protection procedures (see Chapter 5).

4   Support your employer's parenting style: recognise the ultimate authority of parents in making decisions about the welfare and care of their child/children; respect the parents' philosophy of childrearing; acknowledge the values, needs, and ideas of the parents when there is disagreement about childrearing issues; your professional expertise must not be used to impose your ideas on the parents; instead try to work *with* the parents to reach a reasonable compromise. (See page 361.)

5   Develop a partnership with parents: this helps to strengthen the childcarer/parent relationship and provides the child with consistency; children become confused when they receive contradictory messages from you and their parents; discuss and agree with parents how you will both respond to certain situations before they arise; follow the parents' rules regarding eating sweets, watching TV programmes, playing computer games; consistency over behaviour and discipline is especially important (see below).

6   Involve parents in planning the child's day: negotiate and agree a plan for the children's physical care; listen to their suggestions for outings and out-of-school activities; discuss the day's plans with parents each morning; debrief parents at the end of the day; keep a daily log of the day's activities and events; have regular meetings to discuss the decisions and choices either of you wish to make regarding the child's activities (see below).

Think About

How do you establish and maintain positive working relationships with the parents of the child or children you work with?

Insurance liability

There are three types of insurance that are relevant to your employment as a home-based childcarer:

1 Public and employer's liability insurance: check that the parents have public liability insurance to cover personal injury if you have an accident in their home; if you work in your own home then you will need to take out this insurance yourself.
2 Car insurance: if you drive the parents' car, you should check that you are included on their car insurance policy. If you use your own car to transport the children then you will need car insurance for business use. This is more expensive so make sure you agree with the parents about how the extra premiums will be paid, for instance the parents could pay the difference between your usual car insurance cover and the business car insurance.
3 Professional indemnity insurance: it is also a good idea to take out professional indemnity insurance (or nanny insurance) to provide you with cover in case a child suffers a serious injury while in your care.

Check it out

Find out about the types of insurance you need as a home-based childcarer.

Providing regular feedback

Effective communication is the key to a rewarding and positive relationship with the child and their parents. Regular feedback through daily reports, the daily log/diary and scheduled meetings will lead to better organisation of routines and activities, which will mean less stress for everyone and a smoother running household.

Daily reports

You should take the time each day to talk briefly with the parents when you hand the child back into their care. You should keep the conversation short so that the child can interact with the parents as soon as possible. Put more detailed information about the child's day in the daily log which can be read later by the parents (see below). In your daily report you should tell parents about significant events of the day, such as if the child was ill, upset or had a minor accident/injury, changes in the child's usual behaviour or any developmental progress. By keeping the lines of communication open and dealing with any problems as they occur, before they get out of hand, you will maintain a positive working relationship with the parents.

Daily log or diary

The best way to share detailed information about a child with their parents is to keep a daily log or diary of the child's day including: notes and reminders from the parents; the child's food and drink intake; nap times and hours slept; play and learning activities done; any developmental progress made; any medication and when administered; any mishaps (minor injuries, toileting 'accidents'); and notes to parents about plans for the next day (going swimming or to the library).

Regular meetings with parents

As a home-based childcarer you should have regular meetings with the parents. Perhaps hold weekly meetings during the first month and then monthly after that. If anything needs to be discussed in-between the scheduled meetings then you can mention these when giving your daily report. These meetings will enable you to make relevant contributions to provide more effective support for both the child and the parents. You may discuss specific routines and activities the parents wish you to carry out, as well as the plans you have to encourage and/or extend their child's development and learning. Prepare for such meetings carefully, making sure you have all the relevant information, such as the daily log/diary, activity file and any notes on the child's developmental progress. At the meeting express your opinions in a clear, concise manner and demonstrate respect for the contributions made by the parents. Make notes during the meeting to remind yourself of any action *you* need to take as a result of the issues discussed.

PORTFOLIO ACTIVITY

Give examples of how you implement the requirements of parents in line with current best practice including negotiating and agreeing a plan for the children's physical care. You could include copies of your contract, job description, planning sheets, daily logs and notes from meetings with parents. Remember confidentiality.

NVQ LINKS: CCLD 301.4   CCLD 303.2
CCLD 310.2   CCLD 312.4   CCLD 314.3
CCLD 316.2   CCLD 317.3   CCLD 330.3

CCLD 320.2
Create positive environments for children within the home setting

Knowledge Base

K3C519	K3D520	K3D521	K3D522	K3D523
K3D524	K3S525	K3S526	K3S527	K3S531

Your relationship with the child (or children) is the central part of your role as a home-based childcarer. This relationship involves: creating and maintaining a safe and healthy environment for the child; being sensitive to the child's individual needs; providing for the physical, emotional, intellectual, language and social needs of the child by using developmentally appropriate play/learning activities, materials and equipment (see below); providing praise and encouragement for the child's development and learning; having a warm, friendly and caring attitude; and showing an active interest in the child's activities including asking about their day at nursery/school, listening to them read, helping with homework, and so on.

Creating a positive environment for the child within the home setting involves providing routines and activities that will help to meet *all* the child's developmental needs: social, physical; intellectual; communication and language; and emotional.

Encourage and extend the child's *social skills* by: fostering self-reliance and independence through the practice of daily routines; promoting positive behaviour through appropriate behaviour management techniques; setting clear boundaries and rules in accordance with the parents' wishes; providing opportunities to meet other babies and/or young children; and providing opportunities for social play. (See Chapters 1, 3, 9, 10 and 11 for more information about children's behaviour and social skills.)

Promote the child's *physical development* by: providing routines and activities that are appropriate to their age and level of development; and serving nutritious meals and snacks. Remember to continue the parents' feeding plan (bottle feeding, weaning); see to the child's toileting needs (nappy changing, potty training); supervise rest periods, naps and sleep; provide opportunities for fresh air and exercise, including outdoor play and outings; protect the child from infection and injury, such as ensuring immunisations are up-to-date, recognising symptoms of common childhood illnesses, handling emergency situations and administering first aid; teach child appropriate standards of cleanliness, including the hygienic way to bathe and wash hands, brush hair and clean teeth; take every safety precaution when travelling with the child; and ensure the child is dressed appropriately (wearing warm clothes in cold weather, wearing a hat in sunny weather and applying sunscreen). (For more information relating to children's healthy physical development see Chapters 2, 3, 6, 7 and 11.)

Encourage and extend the child's *intellectual development* by: providing play activities and learning experiences that are appropriate to the child's age and level of development; providing toys and other play equipment that are age-appropriate to stimulate the child's thinking and learning; providing opportunities to explore and learn about their environment by taking them on shopping trips, visiting the library and going to the park; and sharing books, stories, rhymes and songs to stimulate new ideas and consolidate existing learning. (See sections on children's play and learning in Chapters 3, 8, 11 and 12.)

It is important to encourage and extend the child's *language/communication skills* by: communicating effectively at the child's level of understanding; modelling appropriate language for the child; recognising stages of language development in young children; engaging in activities that encourage the child's language development; listening carefully to the child's talk and responding appropriately; considering the mood of the child, for example sometimes will not want to talk; and providing opportunities for language including participating in everyday conversations, sharing books and stories, singing rhymes and songs. (For further information about children's language and communication skills see Chapters 1, 3, 10, 11 and 12.)

Promote the child's *emotional well-being* by: helping the child to cope with the transition of the parent(s) going to work and being cared for by a new childcarer; helping the child to cope with other transitions as they occur (starting nursery/school, moving house, arrival of new baby); respecting each child as a unique individual; creating an environment that fosters the child's trust and self-esteem; providing continuity and consistency of care by continuing the child's usual routine (as far as possible and in conjunction with the parents' wishes) to give the child emotional security and reassurance; providing stimulating play activities to promote emotional well-being; and using praise and encouragement for the child's efforts and achievements to develop the child's self-confidence and promote positive self-esteem. (There is more information about children's relationships and emotional well-being in Chapters 1, 3, 10 and 11.)

> **PORTFOLIO ACTIVITY**
>
> Give examples of how you create a positive environment for a child (or children) in a home setting. Include information on how you: communicate with and involve children in the planning of daily routines and activities; deliver stimulating and interesting activities that promote all aspects of the child's or children's development; provide healthy food and drink. You could include copies of planning sheets and menus as well as examples of routines and activities.
>
> NVQ LINKS: CCLD 301.1   CCLD 301.2   CCLD 301.3   CCLD 303.3   CCLD 303.4   CCLD 306.4   CCLD 307.1   CCLD 307.2   CCLD 307.3   CCLD 308.1   CCLD 308.4   CCLD 312.2   CCLD 312.3   CCLD 314.2   CCLD 314.3   CCLD 318.1   CCLD 318.2

Supervising and keeping children safe at all times

One of the biggest threats to children's safety and security is in their own home. Over 40 per cent of accidents involving children occur at home or in the garden. (CAPT, 2004a) It is important that when caring for children in a home-based setting you know the potential risks children face as they develop and learn new skills. Make sure you know about basic first aid, especially for babies and children (see Chapter 2). To maintain children's safety you must always keep a close watch over them in the home and garden, in the car, and when out and about (see below). Appropriate measures to help keep children safe in a home-based setting include:

◎ Never leaving a baby unattended on a changing table (or other furniture)
◎ Using safety gates fitted at the top and bottom of the stairs
◎ Encouraging children to put their toys away after use
◎ Keeping matches and lighters out of the sight and reach of children

◎ Using fireguards on all fires and heaters
◎ Keeping young children away from cookers, ovens and hobs
◎ Using short flexes with kettles and keeping them out of children's reach
◎ Keeping mugs/cups of hot drinks away from children – never hold a child while you are drinking a hot drink
◎ Never doing the ironing with the children around – do it when they are asleep or at nursery/school. Remember to turn the iron off after use
◎ Keeping all medicines out of the sight and reach of children – ideally in a locked cabinet or cupboard
◎ Keeping dangerous substances, including bleach, detergents, cleaners, paints, thinners, varnishes and glues, in their original containers and out of the reach of children
◎ Keeping perfumes, nail varnishes, essential oils and alcohol out of children's reach
◎ Supervising children in or near water at all times
◎ Never leaving a young child in the bath alone (see bath time safety in Chapter 11)
◎ Ensuring that garden ponds are either drained or securely covered

- Marking large areas of glass with large stickers, e.g. patio doors
- Ensuring safety catches are fitted on drawers containing sharp knives, and so on
- Keeping small objects such as coins and toy parts away from young children
- Keeping plastic bags and cling film out of children's reach
- Following the age recommendations on toys and outdoor play equipment.

(CAPT, 2004a)

Activity

List the measures you follow to supervise and keep children safe at all times.

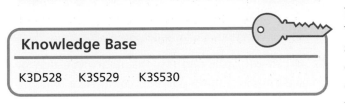

**CCLD 320.3
Take children outside the home**

Knowledge Base

K3D528   K3S529   K3S530

Safety in the car

As a home-based childcarer you may be required to transport the child (or children) in your care in the family car or your own car when taking them to playgroup, nursery, school or on outings. The main safety requirement when transporting a child in a car is that an appropriate car seat is installed and used correctly; children under 12 years who are less than 4' 5" tall must use the appropriate child car seat, booster seat or booster cushion for their height and weight. (For information see: www.childcarseats. org.uk.) Other safety issues include having child locks to prevent the child from getting out of the car should they manage to undo the child restraint. Always remember that you should never leave a child unattended in a parked car – a young child could die in hot weather or be abducted by a stranger.

Safety when out and about

It is important to always tell the parents about any planned activities or outings, so that they know where you and the children are at all times. Ensure that you have your mobile telephone with you when out and about so that you can contact someone in an emergency. Always have the telephone numbers of the parents and one of their close friends or relatives who you may contact if the parents are unavailable. Make sure the parents have your mobile telephone number so they can contact you if necessary.

You must never leave a baby or young child in a pram/pushchair outside a shop or let a toddler wander off. A five-point safety harness should always be used: to secure a young child in a pram or pushchair to prevent them falling out; and when out walking or shopping with a young child to prevent them running off, especially near busy roads or water. When visiting other people's homes, maintain the children's safety by checking that medicines and other potentially dangerous substances are out of their reach. Remember that not everyone may be as safety conscious as you and that other houses may not be organised with crawling babies or inquisitive toddlers in mind. (For more information about children's safety during outings see Chapter 2.)

There are many different places where you can take children on outings. Some outings are short, simple, cheap and easy to organise. Others take more organisation, involve a whole day and can be more exciting, but also more expensive.

The types of outings you organise will depend on the children's interests, age and level of development, as well as what is available to do in your area. Find out about activities and places of interest for children at your local library or information centre.

Activity

Find out about activities and places of interest for children's outings at your local library or information centre.

Outings provide excellent opportunities for you to encourage and extend all aspects of children's development and learning. For example providing opportunities for children to: use their senses to observe and explore details in the environment such as colours, shapes, smells, textures (going for a nature walk, visiting the local park); increase their curiosity and knowledge about the world (bug hunt, science museums); develop their gross motor skills, fine motor skills and co-ordination (outings to local parks and playgrounds, swimming, gymnastics and sports clubs); develop their language and communication skills by talking about key features when on outings (visits to farms, parks, museums); develop their reading skills by visiting the local library; and develop their maths skills by going on shopping trips.

PORTFOLIO ACTIVITY

Give two examples of outings for children, one indoors and one outdoors. Specify which age group the outings would be suitable for and outline how the activities could enhance children's learning and development. Explain how you would plan and organise the outings in consultation with the children and their parents. Include information on transport arrangements and safety measures. If possible, include examples of your own experiences of taking children on outings.

NVQ LINKS: CCLD 320.1 CCLD 320.2
CCLD 320.3 CCLD 301.2 CCLD 301.4
CCLD 302.2 CCLD 303.3 CCLD 303.4
CCLD 307.1 CCLD 312.3 CCLD 317.2
CCLD 318.1 CCLD 318.2

CCLD 322
Empower families through the development of parenting skills

As part of your role and responsibilities you may be involved in developing parents' confidence and practical parenting skills to enable them to support their children's care and development effectively. Supporting parents in this way can help to empower families.

Figure 16.1 Out and about with a toddler

CCLD 322.1
Promote parents' self-confidence in the parenting role

Knowledge Base

K3P551	K3D552	K3P553	K3P554	K3P555
K3P563	K3P568	K3P569		

Bringing up children is one of the most important things adults will ever do in their lives and for many parents it is also the most challenging. Parents often spend all their time looking after everyone else in the family and forget about themselves. Let parents know that if they want to give their children what they need from them, then they need to look after themselves too. They cannot do the best for their children if they are 'running on empty' – they may feel resentful and miserable. Encourage parents to admit to themselves that they actually have feelings and needs of their own and to recognise what these are. Most of us have had a lifetime of being told it is selfish to think about ourselves and so we may not even know what we need, let alone be able to ask for it. Let parents know that thinking about yourself does not mean not caring about other people; it means caring for yourself as well as others. Encourage parents to take time out for themselves by planning ahead to make sure they get some rest and do things they enjoy such as having a lie-in, reading a magazine or newspaper, going to the local gym, or meeting up with a friend. Remind parents that there is no such thing as the perfect parent; being a parent is about doing their best and not being afraid to ask for help when they need it.

Watching children grow up can be the greatest thing in the world, but sometimes it is not the easiest of jobs. Parents may feel every emotion when bringing children up, including love, pride, joy, despair, fear, rage, grief or confusion. Things happen in life such as birth, death, marriage, divorce, changing schools, moving house, leaving home and changing jobs. Any change to the routine or way of life can be confusing or scary and lead parents to question whether they are any good or if they are doing the right thing. Sometimes simple everyday events can become problems, for example when to eat or how to take the children to school. Parents have to give children lots of love, security and encouragement so that they grow up to be the best that they can be. A loving relationship between adult and child needs to be worked on with both sides giving and taking (www.parentlineplus.org.uk).

In order to cope with the emotional demands of parenting, parents need to: develop and maintain confidence in their own abilities; maintain or improve their self-esteem; practise assertiveness techniques; and take care of their own emotional well-being. Self-esteem is developed from childhood; some children and adults have feelings of low self-esteem that have negative effects on their confidence in their own abilities. Some parents may need to develop their own feelings of self-worth to improve their self-esteem (see below).

Developing assertiveness techniques

Assertive people gain control over their lives by expressing personal feelings and exerting their rights in such a way that other people listen. Such individuals also show respect for other people's feelings. You could help parents to demonstrate assertiveness techniques by encouraging them to: be aware of their own feelings; put their feelings into words; connect how they feel with the actions of others; be aware of the other person's feelings; arrange a specific time and place for a discussion; make a statement showing they are aware of their feelings; and listen actively to their feedback. (Houghton and McColgan, 1995) Being a parent can be very rewarding but is often challenging or even stressful. Parents need to take responsibility for their own emotional well-being and take the necessary action to tackle or reduce stress in their lives. For example: develop assertiveness techniques; take regular exercise including relaxation; have a healthy diet; and manage their time effectively.

Building self-esteem

Self-esteem affects how we feel and what we do, as well as how we treat others. It helps people to: deal with problems; get on well with others; and make the most of life. How parents talk to their children affects their self-esteem. Blaming, criticising, labelling and demanding are likely to give children negative messages about themselves that can last a lifetime. Praise and appreciation are important things that parents can give their children to build their self-esteem. Describing clearly what children have done shows that their parents have noticed and allows them to take a step back and see their own achievements so that they can value them as well. (See Chapter 10 for more information about the importance of praise and encouragement.) If parents want to help their children feel good about themselves, they need to start with themselves. Children will pick up important messages about self-esteem from how their parents act and talk about themselves. Parents can build their own self-esteem and that of their children by:

◎ Appreciating the things they do and the things their children do
◎ Understanding how they are feeling and how their children are feeling
◎ Showing their children that they love them and are interested in them
◎ Listening to their children – when they listen they show their children that their thoughts and feelings matter
◎ Encouraging their children to have a go at new things and giving them opportunities to learn through doing, without pushing them too hard
◎ Showing that they have confidence in their children, for example 'Tying laces is hard but I know you'll get there in the end!' If parents believe in them, their children are more likely to believe in themselves

◎ Taking time – spending time with their children and taking time for themselves

◎ Accepting and respecting themselves and their children as unique individuals.

(www.parentlineplus.org.uk)

It is important to encourage parents to develop skills and support networks – take a look at the National Family and Parenting Institute's booklet *Parents Together: A guide to help parents get together for support and encouragement* (2000) available from: www.nfpi.org.uk (for more information on supporting parents see below).

PORTFOLIO ACTIVITY

Describe how you promote parents' confidence in their parenting role.

NVQ LINKS: CCLD 322.1   CCLD 322.4
CCLD 301.4   CCLD 315.2   CCLD 324.2
CCLD 331.2

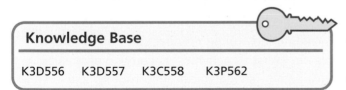

CCLD 322.2
Encourage parents to relate positively to their children

Knowledge Base

K3D556   K3D557   K3C558   K3P562

Different parenting styles and parenting skills

While all parents are individuals and have a unique relationship with their children, three general styles

of parenting have been identified: authoritative; authoritarian; and permissive. One of these three main parenting styles usually emerges during the child's pre-school years. No parent has an absolutely consistent parenting style across all situations. However, parents usually demonstrate the same tendencies in their approach to childrearing. These three parenting styles are also linked to different parenting skills and corresponding child responses and behaviour. (See below.)

Most parents show traits of all three parenting styles. How parents interact with their child will depend on a number of things including: the particular situation; the parent's mood; the child's mood; the parent's temperament; the child's temperament; the child's special needs, if any; the parent's own experiences in childhood; and other factors, such as work pressures or family crises.

Think About

1 What was your parents' parenting style(s)? How did their parenting skills affect your responses and behaviour as a child?

2 If you are a parent, what is your parenting style? How do you think your parenting skills affect your child's or children's responses and behaviour?

Some parents may need support and help to develop new parenting approaches which encourage positive behaviour. You should help parents to identify flexible strategies for promoting positive behaviour that do not involve physical punishment or humiliate and degrade the child. Strategies for parents to promote positive behaviour include:

◎ Understand that children may behave badly as a way of getting attention from parents, so try to praise your child for what he or she has done well and give hugs and attention as rewards, so they get your attention from good behaviour

◎ Try to concentrate on telling your children what you want them to do, instead of telling them what not to do. Let your children know how you see things, and explain why you are holding onto a boundary

◎ Try to be consistent about the rules and boundaries you set, so that children know that you mean what you say

◎ Do not make threats you cannot carry out, as this will just encourage them to keep pushing to find the real boundary

◎ Understand that children may push your limits but often they do this to see how firm and secure their world is – so saying no may really be what they want and need

◎ If you are feeling angry and out of control, try to get some help and support for yourself. Perhaps a friend or relative could give you a bit of a break to do something for yourself; or you might like to talk with other parents about how they cope: or ring Parentline Plus on 0808 800 2222 for someone to talk to.

(www.parentlineplus.org.uk)

PORTFOLIO ACTIVITY

Compile a booklet which provides information on how parents can promote their children's positive behaviour. Include information on: realistic expectations for children's behaviour based on their ages, needs and abilities; negotiating and setting boundaries for children's behaviour; and strategies for promoting positive behaviour.

NVQ LINKS: CCLD 322.2 CCLD 301.3 CCLD 303.4 CCLD 314.4 CCLD 317.1 CCLD 337.2

For more detailed information about children's behaviour see Chapters 1, 3, 9 and 11. Parents can find out more about children's behaviour from books available free from their local library or from booklets published by the National Family and Parenting Institute such as *From breakfast to bedtime: helping you and your children through the day!* (www.nfpi.org/data/publications/docs/nfpibedtime.pdf) and *Over the top behaviour in the under tens* (www.e-parents.org/data/behaviour/pdfs/NFPIunder10s.pdf).

CCLD 322.3
Support parents in play activities with their children

Knowledge Base

K3D559   K3P560   K3S561   K3D564

You should help parents to recognise the value and importance of play to children's development, emphasising the exploratory nature of play and its contribution to development (for more information about the role of play in children's learning and development and exploratory play see Chapter 8). Help parents and children to identify opportunities for sharing play and learning activities together, including identifying resources and opportunities for play in everyday activities. Encourage parents to include non-stereotypical opportunities and experiences, for example boys as well as girls should have opportunities to play with dolls, put on dressing-up clothes and join in cooking activities; girls as well as boys should have opportunities to play with toy cars, construction kits and join in ball games. Foster parents' involvement in their children's play activities in ways that enhance their development and reinforce positive relationships

Parenting style	Parenting skills include	Child responses and behaviour
Authoritative	Allowing their child quite a bit of freedom; setting clear standards of behaviour; reasoning with their child and listening to their views; insisting on specific behaviours; setting firm limits and sticking to them; being sensitive to their child's needs and views; praising their child's efforts and achievements; having clear expectations for their child; providing discipline with love and affection rather than power; and explaining rules and expectations to their child rather than just asserting them.	Happy, self-reliant and able to cope with stress; warm relationships with parents; tends to be popular with peers; confident with good social skills; sets own standards for behaviour; and goal and achievement orientated.
Authoritarian	Expecting child to behave at all times; enforcing rules rigidly but often not explaining these clearly; ignoring child's wishes or opinions; expecting unquestioning obedience and respect for authority; delivering harsh consequences for child's misbehaviour; relying on physical punishment and withdrawal of affection.	Tends to be obedient and orderly; may have low self-esteem and poor self-control; distant relationship with parents; may be aggressive and lose interest in school earlier (especially boys); and tends to be motivated by reward or fear of punishment rather than because it's the right thing to do.
Permissive	Allowing their child to have free expression; not enforcing clear rules on acceptable/unacceptable behaviour; accepting or ignoring bad behaviour; making few demands on their child for mature independent behaviour; setting limits by reasoning with their child rather than asserting wishes; having few expectations of their children; and imposing little discipline.	Appears happy; warm relationship with parents; does not cope with stress very well; gets angry if they don't get their own way; tends to be immature; can be aggressive and domineering with their peers; and tends not to be goal and achievement orientated.

PORTFOLIO ACTIVITY

Compile a booklet for parents about children's play. Include information on: the value and importance of play to children's development; how physical, exploratory and imaginative play contributes to their development; the sequence of social play; a chart of developmentally appropriate play opportunities and resources suitable for the children in your setting; and how parents can be involved in their children's play activities in ways that enhance their development and reinforce positive relationships with their children.

NVQ LINKS: CCLD 322.3   CCLD 322.2   CCLD 303.4   CCLD 312.3   CCLD 317.2   CCLD 318.1 CCLD 318.2

with their children. The Pre-school Learning Alliance's booklet for parents about learning through play, *Play together, playing alone,* is available free from: www.pre-school.org.uk/resources/playing.pdf.

CCLD 322.4
Support parents in accessing information and community support

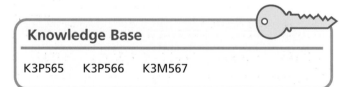

Knowledge Base

K3P565   K3P566   K3M567

Parents know their children best. As the greatest influence on their children's well-being, they are the key to fulfilling the five outcomes in *Every Child Matters* (for more information on the national framework for children's services see CCLD 305.1 in Chapter 5).

Sometimes parents struggle with family life but they may be wary of asking for help because they are worried that they will be seen as failing, not just by professionals but by society as well. Parents who

need extra help should be able to find support when and how they need it. The Just Ask campaign aims to:

◎ Reassure parents that asking for support is not a sign of failing as a parent but rather a sign of strength, demonstrating that they want to do their best for their children

◎ Encourage those working with families to involve and work with parents, acknowledging that bringing up children is a parent's most important role

◎ Promote the need for long-term, sustained investment in family support services so that parents can find information and support whenever they need it.

You can help to support parents in accessing information and community support by:

◎ Signing up to the Just Ask campaign: visit www.parentlineplus.org.uk/justask and click on the campaign button to show your support

◎ Requesting a Just Ask campaign pack which contains posters and leaflets to help spread the message to as many parents as possible

◎ Encouraging parents that it is a sign of strength to ask for support

◎ Talking to parents about what would make a difference to their family life

◎ Involving parents in shaping services in your area

◎ Encouraging parents to contact ParentlinePlus – to talk things through with another parent.

ParentlinePlus supports anyone parenting a child. Its website includes useful sections such as: *Parenting A–Z* which includes information on building children's self-esteem, bullying, truancy and teens; parenting tools; parenting tips; parents together groups; and downloadable information sheets for parents on a range of topics including family life, your life, behaviour, divorce, step-families, and so on.

Other useful sources of information for parents include:

◎ The BBC Parenting website which has information for parents of children from birth to teenage including support and information on a range of topics, such as family matters, play, learning as well as links to relevant television programmes and useful websites – see www.bbc.co.uk/parenting.
◎ The National Family and Parenting Institute which provides information and advice for parents including a Parent Services Directory – see www.nfpi.org/templates/psd/.
◎ The Parents Centre website – www.parentscentre.gov.uk.

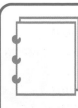

PORTFOLIO ACTIVITY

Compile a resource file to support parents in accessing information and community support. Include information on: local facilities, resources and services available to support parents and children.

NVQ LINKS: CCLD 322.1   CCLD 322.2
CCLD 322.3   CCLD 322.4   CCLD 301.4
CCLD 315.2   CCLD 317.1   CCLD 317.2
CCLD 324.2   CCLD 331.2

CCLD 324
Support the delivery of community based services to children and families

Part of your role and responsibilities as a childcare practitioner may be to support professionals in delivering a range of services to children and families within a community setting. Community based services for families may be delivered in their own homes (Home-Start) or in local centres such as health centres, clinics and community centres (SureStart centres).

CCLD 324.1
Work with other professionals to deliver community services to families

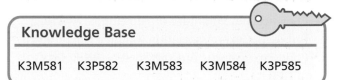

Knowledge Base

K3M581   K3P582   K3M583   K3M584   K3P585

Community based services include health, screening, treatment or support services. They may be provided as statutory, voluntary or private services. Examples of community based services include: behaviour support services; child and adolescent mental health services; children's social services; educational psychology service; extended schools; SureStart children's centres; and the voluntary and community sector. Detailed information on these and other services for children and families is available from the 'Agency A–Z' on the *Every Child Matters* website: www.everychildmatters.gov.uk/

deliveringservices/multiagencyworking/workingwith others/agencyatoz

Check it out

Find out about the community based services which have links to your setting.

As a childcare practitioner you may be involved in working with other professionals from external agencies such as:

◎ Local education authority: educational psychologist, special needs support teachers, special needs advisors, curriculum advisors, specialist teachers

◎ Health services: paediatricians, health visitors, physiotherapists, occupational therapists, speech and language therapists, play therapists, playworkers, school nurses, clinical psychologists

◎ Social services department: social workers; specialist social workers: sensory disabilities, physical disabilities, mental health or children and families

◎ Charities and voluntary organisations: AFASIC, British Dyslexia Association, Council For Disabled Children, National Autistic Society, RNIB, RNID, SCOPE.

To provide the most effective support for children and families, it is essential that working relationships with other professionals run smoothly and that there are no contradictions or missed opportunities due to lack of communication. You may be involved in working with other professionals in the following ways:

◎ Planning support for children and families with other professionals

◎ Providing information and advice to families as agreed with professionals

◎ Undertaking follow-up visits

◎ Implementing an agreed strategy, such as assisting a child to perform tasks set by a specialist

◎ Reporting progress and any concerns to the relevant professionals

◎ Evaluating and reviewing the quality of the service provided.

Interactions with other professionals should be done in ways that promote trust and confidence in your working relationships. Your contributions towards the planning and implementation of joint actions must be consistent with your role and responsibilities as a childcare practitioner in your particular setting. Ensure that you provide other professionals with the relevant information, advice and support as appropriate to your own role and expertise.

If requested, you should be willing to share information, knowledge or skills with other professionals. Use any opportunities to contact or observe the practice of professionals from external agencies to increase your knowledge and understanding of their skills/expertise, in order to improve your own work in supporting children and families.

For detailed information about working with other professionals see *Multi-agency working: Toolkit for Practitioners* published by DfES in 2005 – see: www.everychildmatters.gov.uk/deliveringservices/mult iagencyworking/practitionerstoolkit/.

Activity

1 Who are the other professionals you work with to deliver community services to families?

2 List the boundaries and limits of your responsibility with other professionals.

CCLD 324.2
Work with families to provide advice, guidance and support

Knowledge Base

K3P587   K3M588   K3P589   K3P590

You should initiate, develop and maintain a supportive relationship with families. The provision of advice, guidance and support can enable children and families who need additional services to achieve positive outcomes, thus reducing inequalities between disadvantaged children and others. These services could include additional help with learning, specialist health services, help and support to move away from criminal or antisocial behaviour, or support for parents in developing parenting skills.

As local areas move towards integrated children's services, professional and confident sharing of information is becoming more important to realising the potential of these new arrangements to deliver benefits for children and families.

Six key points on sharing information

1 Explain to children and families at the outset, openly and honestly, what and how information will or could be shared and why, and seek their agreement. The exception to this is where to do so would put that child or other people at risk of significant harm, or if it would undermine the prevention, detection or prosecution of a serious crime, including where seeking consent might lead to interference with any potential investigation.
2 Always consider the safety and welfare of the child when making decisions on whether to share information about them. Where there is concern that the child may be suffering or is at risk of suffering significant harm, the child's safety and welfare must be the overriding consideration.
3 Where possible, respect the wishes of children or families who do not consent to share confidential information. You may still share information if, in your judgement on the facts of the case, there is sufficient need to override that lack of consent.
4 Seek advice where you are in doubt, especially where your doubt relates to a concern about possible significant harm to a child or serious harm to others.
5 Ensure that the information you share is accurate and up-to-date, necessary for the purpose for which you are sharing it, shared only with those people who need to see it, and shared securely.
6 Always record the reasons for your decision – whether it is to share information or not.

(DfES, 2006b)

PORTFOLIO ACTIVITY

Give examples of how you provide information and establish relationships with families. Include information on how you: identify and target families; prepare and provide publicity information that is accessible to all; communicate with families including additional facilities such as translator or sign language interpreter; and discuss confidentiality matters with families.

NVQ LINKS: CCLD 301.1   CCLD 301.2   CCLD 301.4   CCLD 305.1   CCLD 328.1   CCLD 330.1   CCLD 332.1

families to become involved by making them feel welcome in a setting that is friendly and accessible. Creating family participation in settings is an important part of developing links with the local community.

Parents may become actively involved in the life of the setting, for example as parent helpers or volunteers, or as participants in committees, special events, outings and other activities. Remember to encourage parental involvement without putting pressure on parents who may have other commitments such as work, caring for younger children or elderly relatives. You could actively encourage parents to:

◎ Help in the setting with: play and learning opportunities; the provision of food and drinks; administration; and preparation for trips and outings

◎ Share their expertise: arts and crafts, bilingual storytelling, and so on

◎ Join in with outings: visits to parks, playgrounds and sports facilities

◎ Participate in special events: puppet shows, theatre groups

◎ Become involved in fund-raising for the setting, the local community, local and national charities

◎ Help to promote the service to other families in the local community.

Figure 16.2 Working with parents in a family centre

CCLD 332.3
Monitor provision and evaluate the involvement of families

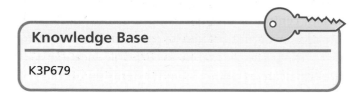

Knowledge Base

K3P679

Monitoring provision and evaluating the involvement of families involves: discussing the positive benefits of group participation with family

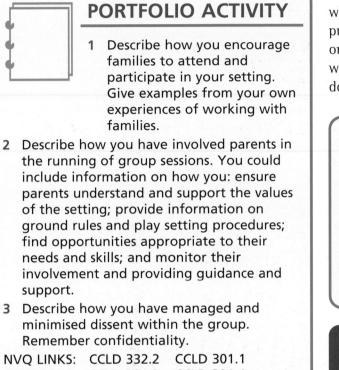

PORTFOLIO ACTIVITY

1 Describe how you encourage families to attend and participate in your setting. Give examples from your own experiences of working with families.

2 Describe how you have involved parents in the running of group sessions. You could include information on how you: ensure parents understand and support the values of the setting; provide information on ground rules and play setting procedures; find opportunities appropriate to their needs and skills; and monitor their involvement and providing guidance and support.

3 Describe how you have managed and minimised dissent within the group. Remember confidentiality.

NVQ LINKS: CCLD 332.2   CCLD 301.1
CCLD 301.2   CCLD 301.3   CCLD 301.4
CCLD 305.1   CCLD 317.2   CCLD 322.3
CCLD 328.1   CCLD 330.1

members; providing opportunities for individual discussions with participants; evaluating each session with participants and recording the outcomes and any issues arising; using the information to amend and adapt sessions to meet participants' identified needs; identifying successful and less successful strategies and activities; discussing and agreeing future activities with participants; monitoring the use of the provision by families who may find provision difficult to access; identifying the reasons for reluctance of families to participate; and making changes to encourage participation.

The Family Policy Alliance has developed a toolkit, *Parent Participation: Improving services for children and families*, an easily accessible resource which

breaks down why you should consult with parents, who to involve, and looks at the principles and practicalities of involving parents. If you want to order a copy of the toolkit see: www.parentlineplus.org.uk/fileadmin/parentline/downloads/Publications/Toolkit-flyer280905.pdf.

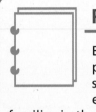

PORTFOLIO ACTIVITY

Briefly outline the policies and procedures for monitoring your setting's childcare provision and evaluating the involvement of families in the childcare setting.

NVQ LINKS: CCLD 332.3   CCLD 303.3
CCLD 303.4   CCLD 304.1   CCLD 317.2
CCLD 330.4   CCLD 334.3

CCLD 334
Deliver services to children and families whose preferred language is not English or Welsh

As a childcarer you may be involved in delivering services for children and families whose first, preferred or home language is not English or Welsh, including sign language users. In order to provide inclusive services for children and families, your setting may need to provide additional resources, facilities or access to services from other agencies, such as interpreters, translators, ESOL support, sign language interpreter.

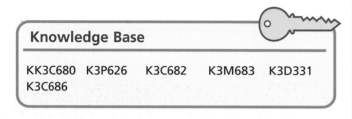

CCLD 334.1
Work with children and families to assess communication needs

Knowledge Base

KK3C680   K3P626   K3C682   K3M683   K3D331
K3C686

When working with families to assess communication needs, you should demonstrate a non-judgemental attitude that values diversity and recognises cultural, religious and ethnic differences. Establish and agree families' and children's requirements for communication support including: exploring different communication methods with families and children, to facilitate communication; identifying a range of possible options to support communication with families and between children in the setting; identifying resources to encourage and support communication and enable families and children to use these in the setting. These may include alternative communication methods, such as communication boards, voice output communication aids, sign language, facial expressions, using symbols and gestures. Provide information to families and children about local language and communication support services in a format that can be easily understood, for example leaflets in community languages. (For more information about communication in bilingual and multilingual settings and recognising communication difficulties with adults see CCLD 301.2 and 301.4 in Chapter 1; CCLD 305.1 and 305.2 in Chapter 5 give details about providing information that promotes participation and equality of access and inclusive and anti-discriminatory practice; for information on ESOL see CCLD 315 on page 341.)

Check it out

1 Find out about the languages used by the families in your setting or local area.
   ◎ How many different languages are spoken? Which languages are spoken?
   ◎ Are there any families who are bilingual? Which languages do they use? When do they use languages other than English?
   ◎ Do any of the families use sign language? Do they use British Sign Language or Makaton?
2 Check out which resources are available locally to support children and families whose preferred language is not English or Welsh, for example community resource centre, educational development centre, ESOL support; or family learning programmes.

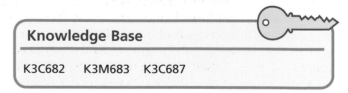

CCLD 334.2
Establish and maintain communication to support service delivery

Knowledge Base

K3C682   K3M683   K3C687

Establish and maintain communication to support service delivery by: providing detailed and accessible information about the service to families; encouraging families to express their requirements of the service, using alternative communication methods they find acceptable; communicating with families using agreed methods and adopting an open and welcoming approach that is likely to promote trust; encouraging families to share information about their child's preferences, habits and routines, using alternative communication; helping children to communicate with others in the setting, using agreed methods; recording accurately the information provided by families, and the communication methods used.

Unit Links

For this Unit you also need to understand the following sections:

CCLD 301.2 Communicate with children (see Chapter 1)

CCLD 301.4 Communicate with adults (see Chapter 1)

CCLD 305.1 Support equality of access (see Chapter 5)

CCLD 309.2 Implement curriculum plans (see Chapter 12)

CCLD 315.2 Reflect on and evaluate own and organisational practice in supporting parents (see above)

CCLD 321.2 Help children with disabilities or special educational needs to participate in the full range of activities and experiences (see Chapter 14)

CCLD 345.3 Help pupils to develop their speaking and listening skills (see Chapter 13)

PORTFOLIO ACTIVITY

Design a leaflet about the local resources and support available for families whose preferred language is not English or Welsh. Include information on: alternative communication methods (such as communication boards, voice output communication aids, sign language, facial expressions, using symbols and gestures) and how these can be used with families; resources available from the community resource centre and/or educational development centre; ESOL support; and family learning programmes. If possible, include copies of the leaflet in the main community language(s) used by the children and families in your setting; if necessary ask bilingual colleagues or parents to help you translate your leaflet.

NVQ LINKS: CCLD 334.1   CCLD 334.2   CCLD 301.2   CCLD 301.4   CCLD 305.1   CCLD 305.2   CCLD 309.2   CCLD 315.1   CCLD 315.2   CCLD 321.2   CCLD 345.3

CCLD 334.3
Monitor and evaluate communication support to ensure the needs of children and families are met

Knowledge Base

K3M685   K3C688   K3C689   K3C690

Monitor and evaluate communication and support to ensure the needs of children and families continue to be met by: monitoring children's and families' progress with communication in the setting; identifying any communication problems or issues arising as a result of communication differences; agreeing with families and colleagues how such difficulties might be solved; evaluating the effectiveness of resources and services used to support communication; discussing families' and children's views on the effectiveness of communication resources; agreeing and implementing any changes to communication services or resources; and modifying services to support communication.

PORTFOLIO ACTIVITY

Outline how you monitor and evaluate communication and support to ensure the needs of children and families continue to be met.

NVQ LINKS: CCLD 334.3   CCLD 301.2   CCLD 301.2   CCLD 303.2   CCLD 303.4
              CCLD 304.1   CCLD 310.2   CCLD 315.3   CCLD 330.4   CCLD 332.3

Optional Units

CCLD 316
Develop and maintain a childminding business

CCLD 328
Administer provision within the childcare setting

CCLD 329
Work with a Management Committee

CCLD 340
Establish, develop and promote quality systems and procedures for the delivery of childcare services

CCLD 341
Advise and mentor those implementing quality systems and procedures for the delivery of childcare services

CCLD 342
Meet regulatory requirements in the childcare setting

CCLD 316 Develop and maintain a childminding business

Childminders work in their own homes to look after children and they may also look after older children before school, after school and during the holidays. Most full-time work is with babies and children under 5. Childminding usually includes taking children to and from playgroup, nursery class or school. In order to cater for working parents, childminders are likely to work long hours. Some childminders may offer a weekend and/or overnight service. This chapter is about the business side of childminding. For more information about working in a home-based setting see CCLD 320 in Chapter 16.

CCLD 316.1 Provide information about your childminding business

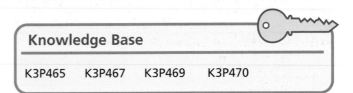

Knowledge Base

K3P465	K3P467	K3P469	K3P470

Maintaining and developing a childminding business involves: investigating the demand for childminders within your local area; identifying the types of childminding services that parents require and how you will be able to meet these needs; and working with information services to market your childminding business. Your local Children's Information Service (CIS) can provide you with information about existing childcare services in your local area. For details of your local CIS from Childcare Link, telephone: 08000 960 296 or see the website: www.childcarelink.gov.uk.

When providing information about your childminding business you will need to: investigate advertising, such as local newspapers or health clinics; review your fees regularly to make sure they are realistic in relation to your costs and fees charged by other childminders in your area; provide references from parents or other appropriate sources, where available, to support your marketing materials; provide examples of work you have done with children and information about how you have helped children to learn and develop; and ensure your home is welcoming and you are supportive when parents make an initial visit.

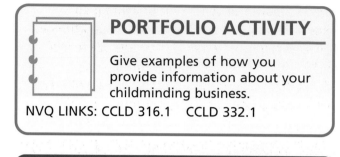

PORTFOLIO ACTIVITY

Give examples of how you provide information about your childminding business.

NVQ LINKS: CCLD 316.1   CCLD 332.1

CCLD 316.2
Administer your childminding business

Knowledge Base

K3P463	K3P464	K3P466	K3P468	K3P471
K3P472	K3P473			

An important aspect of childminding is working closely with parents (or other carers, such as foster parents) and sharing information about their children. Establish a professional relationship with families by: working with families to assess their requirements; setting up formal contracts and payment arrangements with parents; setting up financial systems, records and paperwork for your childminding business; ensuring you have all the necessary information from parents; and providing systems for record keeping in line with the requirements of the regulatory authority of your home country. (NDNA, 2004)

Registration and regulatory requirements

It is compulsory for all childminders to meet a set of National Standards and to be registered. In England Ofsted is responsible for registering and inspecting childminders. You will have to demonstrate that you meet the standards set out in *The National*

Standards for under 8s day care and childminding before Ofsted can register you. The National Standards for childminding may be obtained from your local authority or from the SureStart website: www.surestart.gov.uk/_doc/P0000409.PDF.

Guidance on the National Standards and good practice information can be found in *Childminding: guidance to the National Standards* which is available from your local authority or the Ofsted website: www.ofsted.gov.uk/childminders.

This website also contains the following useful information: how the registration process works; information sheet for childcare providers on paying fees; health declaration booklet (HDB); checklist for childminding applicants; *Are you ready for your inspection?* – a revised booklet for the new inspection framework, which explains what to expect and how to prepare for your inspection, including a self-evaluation form to complete in readiness for your next inspection; and links to useful publications such as *Birth to Three Matters* and *Curriculum guidance for the foundation stage*.

To register as a childminder in Scotland contact the Care Commission and in Wales contact the Care Standards Inspectorate for Wales – see the Appendix for contact details. In Northern Ireland contact your local Health and Social Services Trust. For detailed information about childminding contact the National Childminding Association of England and Wales, the Northern Ireland Childminding Association or the Scottish Childminding Association – see the Appendix for contact details.

Home Childcarers

Currently only registered childminders can become approved Home Childcarers, so all applicants wishing to become a Home Childcarer should be registered childminders first.

A Home Childcarer is a person approved in accordance with the criteria set out in the *Home Childcaring Code of Practice for Children Under Eight (2003)* and who is paid to look after one or more children, to whom they are not related, in the home of the children's parents. (Download the code of practice for free from: www.surestart.gov.uk/_doc/0-D06A21.pdf.)

For information on meeting the criteria see Ofsted's *Guidance to the Home Childcaring Code of Practice for Children Under Eight* available free from: www.surestart.gov.uk/_doc/0-C9B84E.pdf. See also *Being a Home Childcarer: A Workbook,* available free from www.surestart.gov.uk/_doc/P0000097.pdf.)

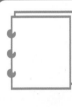

PORTFOLIO ACTIVITY

Outline how you administer your childminding business. Include information on: meeting registration and regulatory requirements; setting up formal contracts with families; setting up financial and record-keeping systems; and exchanging information with parents.

NVQ LINKS: CCLD 316.2   CCLD 320.1
CCLD 330.1   CCLD 330.2   CCLD 330.3

CCLD 328
Administer provision within the childcare setting

When administering provision within the childcare setting, it is important that you are committed to promoting an understanding of the principles and values of children's care, learning and development (see page vi). The childcare setting influences the developing attitudes of the children within it and can be a powerful vehicle for promoting an understanding and practice of equal opportunities. Every member (or potential member) of the setting should be regarded as of equal worth and importance, irrespective of his/her creed, culture, class, race, gender, sexuality and/or disability.

CCLD 328.1
Maintaining access procedures

Knowledge Base

K3P596   K3P598   K3P599   K3M600

Find out what children, parents, carers and others in the local community think about the childcare setting and the services provided. Use your knowledge of how to gain and use feedback from people in the local community about childcare provision including representative groups and individuals; this may perhaps include current and potential new users of the childcare setting; individuals who may experience barriers to access, such as those with disabilities; and relevant colleagues within the childcare setting. Feedback can be gained *informally* through discussions with individuals or small groups or *formally* using meetings or questionnaires. Ensure that you listen and respond to the views and experiences of people in the local community, especially those of children and their parents or carers. Try to include their suggestions when planning to make changes or improvements to the childcare setting. (For more information about involving children in decision-making see CCLD 301.1 in Chapter 1.)

When maintaining access procedures you should know and understand the relevant legal requirements. For example: Disability Discrimination Act 1995; Children Act 1989; UN Convention on the Rights of the Child 1989; Health and Safety at Work Act 1974; Management of Health and Safety at Work Regulations 1992; and European Standards BSEN 1176 and 1177.

The legal requirements under the Disability Discrimination Act 1995 are of particular importance to maintaining access procedures. Since 1996, the Disability Discrimination Act (DDA) has made it unlawful for service providers to treat disabled people less favourably. Since 1999, there has been a duty to make reasonable adjustments in certain circumstances. From October 2004, this was extended to cover adjustments in relation to any physical features that create a barrier for disabled people. The DDA must be taken into account when maintaining access procedures, for example by making play areas fully accessible. In addition, the *Disability Discrimination Act Code of Practice on Rights of Access to Goods, Facilities, Services and Premises* provides guidance for service providers on how the duties under the DDA might apply in practice, including recommendations for an inclusive approach to service development involving consultation with disabled people and those representing them. Another important legal requirement under the Management of Health and Safety at Work Regulations 1992 involves carrying out risk assessments of children's play facilities (see page 27.) Interpretations and understandings of risk are essential to the development and improvement of accessible play areas. (Dunn et al., 2004)

It is important for you to know and understand the organisational policies and procedures relevant to maintaining access procedures, for example health and safety (see Chapter 2), inclusion and anti-discriminatory practice (see Chapters 1 and 5). The childcare setting should keep admission records that specify any personal information required by Ofsted, DfES, the local education authority, school governors or management committee relating to children attending the setting at the time. These records should be kept up to date and amended as and when children join or leave the setting, providing that keeping such information does not contravene any law applicable at the time. (See below for information on collecting and storing information.)

Unit Links

For this Unit you also need to understand the following sections:

CCLD 301.1 Develop relationships with children (see Chapter 1)

CCLD 302 Develop and maintain a healthy, safe and secure environment for children (see Chapter 2)

CCLD 305.1 Support equality of access (see Chapter 5)

CCLD 305.2 Implement strategies, policies, procedures and practice for inclusion (see Chapter 5)

PORTFOLIO ACTIVITY

Summarise your childcare setting's access procedures. Describe how you have been involved in maintaining access procedures. Include examples of: using available research and resources; meeting legal requirements; and following the relevant organisational policies and procedures.

NVQ LINKS: CCLD 328.1   CCLD 302.1   CCLD 302.2   CCLD 302.3   CCLD 305.1   CCLD 305.2

CCLD 328.2
Collect and store information

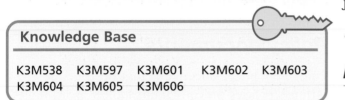

Knowledge Base

K3M538   K3M597   K3M601   K3M602   K3M603
K3M604   K3M605   K3M606

Every childcare setting keeps a variety of records, including essential personal information for each child using the facility. It will also have contact details of the person responsible for the setting, staff and volunteers. Childcare settings also have records relating to administrative duties, such as permission slips for educational visits/outings and requisition forms for equipment and materials. Records may also include: observations and assessments of the children's participation and developmental progress (see Chapters 3 and 11); activity plans with evaluations of the effectiveness of the activities provided (see Chapters 3, 8, 11 and 12); and Individual Education Plans and reviews for children with special educational needs (see Chapters 5 and 14). There will also be staff records relating to job applications and appointments (see Chapter 18).

The importance of record keeping

It is essential to keep records for the following reasons: to monitor children's participation and developmental progress; to provide accurate and detailed information regarding the children's care, learning and development; to determine the effectiveness of the play and learning activities; to determine the effectiveness of adult support or intervention; to give constructive feedback to children; to share information with parents, colleagues and sometimes other professionals; to identify and plan for new play and learning opportunities; and to facilitate effective administration in the childcare setting.

Unit Links

For this Unit you also need to understand the following sections:
CCLD 303 Promote children's development (see Chapter 3)
CCLD 305.2 Implement strategies, policies, procedures and practice for inclusion (see Chapter 5)
CCLD 318.1 Collect and analyse information on play needs and preferences (see Chapter 8)
CCLD 312 Plan and implement positive environments for babies and children under 3 years (see Chapter 11)
CCLD 309 Plan and implement curriculum frameworks for early education (see Chapter 12)
CCLD 310 Assess children's progress according to curriculum frameworks for early education (see Chapter 12)
CCLD 333 Recruit, select and keep colleagues (see Chapter 18)
CCLD 339.4 Collect, record and update relevant background information about children with special educational needs (see Chapter 14)

Types of records

The types of records you will need to keep will depend on the type of childcare setting. Where, when and how to record information should be as directed by the senior practitioner or setting manager. It is important that all records are complete, legible and updated on a regular basis. Emergency contact information must always be up to date. How often updating is necessary depends on the different types of records that you make a contribution towards.

Registration forms

Personal information about the children who use the childcare setting is usually collected from the parents/carers as part of the registration process. The registration form should include the following information for each child: home address and telephone number; emergency contact details, such as names and telephone numbers for parents/carers, GP; medical history/conditions such as allergies and dietary needs; cultural or religious practices which may have implications for the care of the child such as special diets; and who collects the child (if applicable) including the transport arrangements (such as taxi or minibus) for a child with disabilities.

Child portfolios

The childcare setting should keep and update appropriate records on children attending the setting, covering their abilities, developmental progress, academic achievements and other skills, such as a child portfolio containing relevant information about each child in the setting. A child portfolio could include: child observations and assessments; examples of the child's work; photographs of the child during play and learning activities; checklists of the child's progress; SATs results; copies of progress checks, reviews and school reports; and their Record of Achievement. Confidential reports (from Social Services, psychological reports, and so on) must be kept separately from the above general child information.

Policy documents

Curriculum policy documents that describe the setting's policies on curriculum subject areas, topics, schemes of work, and so on should be kept up to date and made available for inspection by authorised persons (including parents, advisors, inspectors and governors). The setting manager should keep a master copy of each document in their office and these should be made available for inspection by authorised and appropriate personnel upon request. The documents that describe the setting's policies on non-curricular matters as required by the governing body, Ofsted, LEA or DfES should be prepared, maintained and kept up to date and made available to authorised persons as required. A list of the required policies should also be available and updated as appropriate.

Personnel records

The setting should maintain records of personnel (staff members) relating to their qualifications, experience, length of service and salary levels. References for staff within the setting for posts outside it should be kept securely by the setting manager and should not be kept with the personnel records. Appraisal statements are the property of the appraisee and should not be stored with the above records and cannot be used in any way other than at the request of, or with the permission of, the appraisee. A single copy of appraisal statements may be kept securely in the setting's main office. Records of appraisal statements must *not* be kept on computer disc or system.

Financial records

The records of the setting's financial controls and budget will be kept in accordance with current DfES and local authority regulations and should be made available for inspection by the proper authorities under those statutes and regulations.

Other records

Examples of other records and key information include: accident/incident forms; administration of medicines; attendance registers; fire drill records; hazard and risk assessment forms; infectious, notifiable diseases forms; insurance documents; forms for outings; record of visitors; and child protection.

Storing records

You need to know the exact policy and procedures for storing records in your setting, including your role and responsibilities regarding the storage of records. Most records relating to children and staff should be stored and locked away but should be kept where staff can reach them easily. Ensure that the childcare setting's records are stored safely and securely at all times. Do not leave important documents lying around; always put them back in storage after use. As well as the physical security of records, you need to be aware of the levels of staff access to information. You should never give out the passwords to the setting's equipment (computers) unless you have permission from the member of staff responsible for the record-keeping systems. Requests for records or information from colleagues should be dealt with professionally and handed in on time. This is particularly important if the information is needed for a meeting or review, as any delay may stop others from performing their

responsibilities effectively. Remember to maintain confidentiality as appropriate to your childcare setting's requirements. (See CCLD 301.4 in Chapter 1 for information on confidentiality.)

Unit Links

For this Unit you also need to understand the following sections:

CCLD 303 Promote children's development (see Chapter 3)

CCLD 305.2 Implement strategies, policies, procedures and practice for inclusion (see Chapter 5)

CCLD 318.1 Collect and analyse information on play needs and preferences (see Chapter 8)

CCLD 312 Plan and implement positive environments for babies and children under 3 years (see Chapter 11)

CCLD 309 Plan and implement curriculum frameworks for early education (see Chapter 12)

CCLD 310 Assess children's progress according to curriculum frameworks for early education (see Chapter 12)

CCLD 333 Recruit, select and keep colleagues (see Chapter 18)

CCLD 339.4 Collect, record and update relevant background information about children with special educational needs (see Chapter 14)

CCLD 328.3
Administer budgets and financial arrangements according to the procedures of the setting

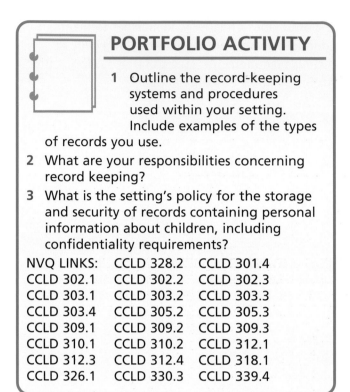

PORTFOLIO ACTIVITY

1 Outline the record-keeping systems and procedures used within your setting. Include examples of the types of records you use.

2 What are your responsibilities concerning record keeping?

3 What is the setting's policy for the storage and security of records containing personal information about children, including confidentiality requirements?

NVQ LINKS:	CCLD 328.2	CCLD 301.4
CCLD 302.1	CCLD 302.2	CCLD 302.3
CCLD 303.1	CCLD 303.2	CCLD 303.3
CCLD 303.4	CCLD 305.2	CCLD 305.3
CCLD 309.1	CCLD 309.2	CCLD 309.3
CCLD 310.1	CCLD 310.2	CCLD 312.1
CCLD 312.3	CCLD 312.4	CCLD 318.1
CCLD 326.1	CCLD 330.3	CCLD 339.4

Knowledge Base

K3P607   K3P608

As a setting manager or senior practitioner, you may be responsible for administering budgets and financial arrangements according to the procedures of your setting. To manage a budget you will need to know how to prepare, submit and agree a budget for a set period, perhaps for each month. You can do this with a monthly budget report setting out the childcare setting's expected income and expenditure. It also provides details of the childcare setting's actual income and expenditure using information from the cashbook. The monthly budget reports provide: the information for the childcare setting's profit and loss statement at the end of the year; accurate figures for the childcare setting's cash flow forecast; and they also form the basis for the next year's business forecast. Using a computer, you may be able to set up the childcare setting's budget on a spreadsheet to enable income and expenditure to be updated easily on a daily basis. By law, all businesses have to keep records of their income and expenditure. Keeping such records will also help you to manage the finances of the childcare setting more efficiently and help to prevent/detect fraud or theft. (SureStart, 2003a)

You should keep records of all the childcare setting's *income* which may come from a variety of sources, including grants, funding, donations and, where applicable, payments from parents whose children use the childcare facility. Also keep records of all the childcare setting's *expenditure* such as: receipts of anything purchased by the childcare setting for the childcare setting; details and receipts of costs, for eample rent, rates and utility bills; details of wages paid to employees; invoices for equipment repairs or replacements; invoices for travel expenses; and invoices for training expenses. (SureStart, 2003a)

Monitor the childcare setting's *actual* financial performance against the agreed budget. The most common way to do this is to update and review the budget on a monthly basis. Record all transactions in a cashbook so that you can see at a glance all the income and expenditure for the childcare setting. Use the cashbook on a daily basis to record transactions as they occur so that your records are up to date. You should also have a petty cash book for staff to record the purchase of small items such as books, crayons, ingredients for cooking activities, and so on. You or a designated member of staff should be responsible for managing the petty cash system, including keeping all receipts and keeping a locked box with the petty cash 'float'. The petty cash box should be kept in one place and locked at all times. (SureStart, 2003a)

17

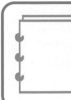

PORTFOLIO ACTIVITY

Outline the methods you use to manage a budget in your childcare setting.
NVQ LINK: CCLD 328.3

Our childcare setting – Cash flow forecast	April	May	June	July	Aug	Sept	Oct	Nov	Dec	Jan	Feb	Mar	Total
Income													
Fees													
Funding													
Fundraising													
Donations													
Total income													
Expenditure													
Wages													
National Insurance													
Premises													
Utilities													
Insurance													
Training													
Print and stationery													
Maintenance													
Materials													
Toys													
Food													
Milk													
Total expenditure													
Balance													
Cumulative cash balance													

Figure 17.1 Monthly budget sheet
From: *Managing Finance*. DfES, 2003.

CCLD 328.4
Operate systems for the supply of materials and equipment

and replacing old or damaged equipment (such as furniture, books, computer software and play equipment) as necessary. Check that stock levels are monitored on a regular basis. (For more information on resources see CCLD 306.2 in Chapters 6 and CCLD 318.2 in Chapter 8.)

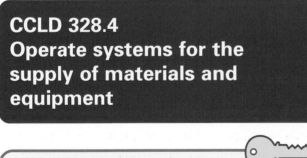

Knowledge Base

K3P609   K3P610

You may be responsible for replenishing consumables (for example pencils, paper and card, paint, cooking ingredients, exercise and textbooks)

PORTFOLIO ACTIVITY

Outline the methods you use to obtain appropriate resources for your setting.
NVQ LINKS: CCLD 328.4   CCLD 306.2
CCLD 318.2

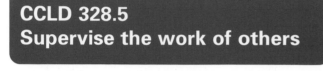

CCLD 328.5
Supervise the work of others

Knowledge Base

K3P611

Supervising the work of others involves: allocating work to colleagues to support the plans of the setting and the needs of children and families; allocating work to colleagues in ways that fairly take into account their skills, knowledge, understanding, experience and current workloads; making the best use of available resources; checking progress and quality of colleagues' work as required; and being flexible and responsive to changing circumstances and colleagues' needs. (NDNA, 2004) (See Units 311, 335 and 338 in Chapter 18.)

PORTFOLIO ACTIVITY

Outline your role and responsibilities for supervising the work of others.

NVQ LINKS: CCLD 328.5   CCLD 311
CCLD 335   CCLD 338

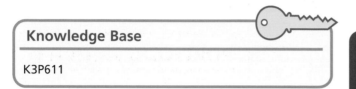

CCLD 329
Work with a management committee

Your role as a childcarer may involve working in an organisation or group that is run by a management committee (parent and toddler groups, playgroups and pre-schools). This usually involves working within community based provision whose main purpose is to support children's care, learning and development in partnership with their families.

CCLD 329.1
Prepare and present operational plans and reports to management committees

Knowledge Base

| K3P612 | K3M613 | K3P614 | K3P615 | K3P617 |
| K3M618 | K3D619 | K3P320 | K3P621 | |

The management committee is responsible for the management of the pre-school, playgroup or parent and toddler group, which includes anything from organising a fundraising event to negotiating with the landlord over terms of the lease for the setting's accommodation. The majority of its members are parents of the children who attend the setting. All decisions regarding the operation of the setting are the responsibility of the committee, although it can delegate the implementation of decisions to staff. The committee is the employer of all staff in the pre-school setting. It has overall responsibility for recruitment, wages, salaries, tax and national insurance, appraisals, contracts of employment and terms and conditions. It also has responsibility for things like developing a business plan, accounts, budgeting, funding, insurance, membership fees (for example Pre-school Learning Alliance membership), accommodation costs, staff wages and volunteer expenses, admission costs, and publicity costs. The committee, together with staff, is also responsible for health and safety, risk assessment, insurance and first aid, as well as policy-making. (PSLA, 2004)

You may be employed by a management committee to work as a playgroup or pre-school leader/supervisor in a pre-school or playgroup setting, which works with children aged between 2 and 5 years. The sessions may be full-day or part-day, for example 2-hour sessions. The emphasis in the setting is on children learning through play and parental involvement in all aspects of the pre-school or playgroup should be encouraged.

As a pre-school or playgroup supervisor, you will be responsible for the preparation of long-term, medium-term and short-term plans using the appropriate curriculum framework, such as *Birth to Three Matters, Curriculum guidance for the foundation stage* or the proposed new *Early Years Foundation Stage* (see CCLD 312.1 in Chapter 11 and CCLD 309.1 in Chapter 12). You will be responsible for organising and planning appropriate play and learning activities for the children (according to the appropriate curriculum framework); supervising staff on a day-to-day basis (see Unit CCLD 335 in Chapter 18); and reporting to the management committee on a regular basis.

Your responsibilities may also include managing the setting's petty cash system (see page 390); liaising with the management committee, local authority and other agencies as necessary to ensure that all regulatory requirements are met (see page 399); and providing the management committee with operational plans and reports as required.

As a pre-school or playgroup supervisor, you should send weekly updates of key information to the committee so that any problems can be identified quickly and action taken immediately. Regular full

committee meetings should be held, at which the supervisor should be present. A formal agenda should be used based on key information and important issues for the setting. At the conclusion of the meeting clear actions should be delegated. (SureStart, 2003b)

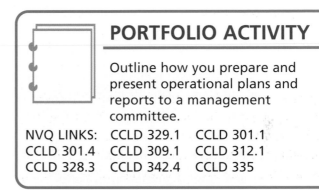

PORTFOLIO ACTIVITY

Outline how you prepare and present operational plans and reports to a management committee.

NVQ LINKS:	CCLD 329.1	CCLD 301.1
CCLD 301.4	CCLD 309.1	CCLD 312.1
CCLD 328.3	CCLD 342.4	CCLD 335

CCLD 329.2
Implement management committee policies and procedures

Knowledge Base

K3P616   K3P620

As a pre-school or playgroup supervisor, you will plan and supervise the daily programme of activities. This includes ensuring that staff and volunteers provide appropriate stimulation and support to the children, organising the key person or keyworker system (see CCLD 314.4 in Chapter 11 for more detail on the role of the key person) and supervising staff and volunteers on a daily basis (see Unit CCLD 335 in Chapter 18). You will also set up observation and record-keeping systems to regularly assess children's progress and monitor the effectiveness of assessment procedures (see CCLD 303.1 and 303.2 in Chapter 3, CCLD 312.1 in Chapter 11 and CCLD 310.2 in Chapter 12).

You may also be responsible for helping to monitor the quality of teaching, participating in staff appraisals and identifying in-service training needs, as well as attending in-service training and meetings as required (see CCLD 304.2 in Chapter 4 and Unit CCLD 338 in Chapter 18).

You need also to liaise with parents by exchanging information about their children's progress and encouraging parents' involvement (see CCLD 330.3 and 332.2 in Chapter 16).

Ensure that the setting is a safe environment for children, staff and others by ensuring hygiene standards and safety procedures are in place at all times and fire drills are practised regularly; this entails ensuring records are properly maintained, including the daily register and accident/incident book (see Chapter 2). You should help to maintain the setting's policies and procedures including those on confidentiality, equal opportunities, inclusion, special needs and child protection (see CCLD 301.1 and 301.4 in Chapter 1 and Unit CCLD 305 in Chapter 5).

PORTFOLIO ACTIVITY

Give examples of how you implement management committee policies and procedures.

NVQ LINKS:	CCLD 329.2	CCLD 301.1
CCLD 301.4	CCLD 302.1	CCLD 302.2
CCLD 302.3	CCLD 303.1	CCLD 303.2
CCLD 303.3	CCLD 303.4	CCLD 304.1
CCLD 304.2	CCLD 305.1	CCLD 305.2
CCLD 305.3	CCLD 309.2	CCLD 310.2
CCLD 312.1	CCLD 312.3	CCLD 314.4
CCLD 317.3	CCLD 330.3	CCLD 332.2
CCLD 328.2	CCLD 335	CCLD 338

CCLD 329.3
Work with management committees to identify funding streams

Knowledge Base

K3P622   K3M623   K3P624

Part of your responsibilities as a pre-school or playgroup supervisor will be to work with the management committee to identify the group's funding streams. Groups should be clear about their funding requirements. A business plan will help to clarify specific needs and should include realistic budgets. It is usually part of the application for funding, as it provides information about why the funding is required. (PSLA, 2006)

When identifying possible funding streams, the best place to start is the early years unit at your local authority, where staff will be able to provide advice about local funding. Local authorities may have revenue and capital funding available to help sessional groups move into full day care and some sustainability funding may also be available in your area. This may all come under the umbrella of SureStart funding. Local authorities also co-ordinate the Early Years Education funding provided by the DfES. This is also known as Nursery Education Grant (NEG) and it funds free early years education places for 3- and 4-year-olds. Other sources of funding include: Lloyds TSB Foundation; Futurebuilders England; Big Lottery Fund; Local Network Fund for Children and Young People (England); European Social Fund (ESF); European Regional Development Fund (ERDF); and Neighbourhood Renewal Fund. (PSLA, 2006) (For more information about Early

Years Education funding and other sources of funding download the Pre-school Learning Alliance's *Funding Factsheet,* available free at: www.pre-school.org.uk/resources/fundingfactsheet.pdf. For additional information see: *Getting Funding from Charitable Trusts* – www.pre-school.org.uk/resources/trusts.pdf and *Developing Effective Funding Applications* – www.pre-school.org.uk/resources/fundingapplications.pdf.

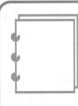

PORTFOLIO ACTIVITY

Give examples of how you: identify and suggest potential sources of funding to support the provision; investigate funding streams in partnership with others; and check that your provision is eligible for funding.
NVQ LINKS: CCLD 329.3   CCLD 328.3

CCLD 340
Establish, develop and promote quality systems and procedures for the delivery of childcare services

As part of your role you may be involved in maintaining quality systems, assessing services, monitoring and reviewing policies, procedures and practices within the childcare setting.

Monitoring and evaluation helps those working in the childcare setting: to understand how the policies and procedures are working in practice; to check the quality of work and provision of routines, play opportunities and learning activities; as well as to plan for the future. Monitoring and evaluation can also help to make day-to-day working within the childcare setting more effective.

CCLD 340.1
Establish quality systems for the delivery of childcare services

Knowledge Base

K3P716	K3P717	K3P718	K3P719	K3P720
K3P721	K3P722			

As a childcarer, you may be involved in establishing quality systems for the delivery of childcare services. Many childcare settings participate in externally validated quality schemes developed by a local authority or a national agency.

Investors in Children

Investors in Children is a government initiative designed to help childcare and early education providers find the best Quality Assurance (QA) schemes in the early education and childcare sector. QA schemes are designed to promote quality by encouraging childcare providers to be reflective practitioners (see Chapter 4). A good QA scheme will encourage providers to: look critically at the quality of their service for themselves; compare their practices with established best practice; and obtain further training to ensure they are delivering best practice.

Investors in Children endorsed QA schemes are entitled to include the Investors in Children badge within their promotional and award materials. Accreditation by an endorsed scheme demonstrates to parents that the setting is committed to delivering a high quality service for children. Investors in Children is currently under review; for further information see: www.surestart.gov.uk/improvingquality/guidance/investorsinchildren/.

Examples of endorsed QA schemes include:

◎ *Aiming for Quality* (Pre-school Learning Alliance) www.pre-school.org.uk/iacontent.php/en/11.phtml
◎ *Aiming Higher* (4children) www.4children.org.uk/whatwedo/view/node/160
◎ *Quality Counts* (National Day Nurseries Association) www.ndna.org.uk/document_tree/ViewACategory.asp?CategoryID=5
◎ *Quality First* (National Childminding Association) www.ncmaqualityfirst.co.uk.

Check it out

Find out the quality assurance systems that are available to meet the requirements of your setting.

CCLD 340.2
Maintain quality systems

Knowledge Base

K3P716	K3P717	K3P718	K3P719	K3P720
K3P721	K3P722			

Working towards recognised quality assurance systems can have a positive impact on the childcare setting and help to develop the work of the organisation. The best quality schemes encourage providers to participate in a systematic approach to on-going improvement in the standard of practice within the setting. They do not focus on administrative processes as these are covered by regulatory and inspection requirements (see Unit CCLD 342). Instead quality schemes focus on activities that have a positive impact on outcomes for children and secure real improvements in the setting. Areas that benefit from a systematic approach to quality improvement include: staff development; reflective practice: inclusion; and management and leadership. (DfES, 2006a)

Think About

How does your setting maintain quality systems?

CCLD 340.3
Evaluate and review quality systems and procedures

Knowledge Base

K3P716	K3P717	K3P718	K3P719	K3P720
K3P721	K3P722	K3P723		

An evaluation and review of quality systems and procedures helps to ensure that the childcare setting is doing what it was designed to do. Monitoring and evaluation help to make sure that the childcare setting's policies and procedures are working in practice and that the care routines, play opportunities and learning activities provided have the desired effect. Evaluation is also a way to let any providers of grants or funds know about the work of the childcare setting; it is about looking at the work of the childcare setting, how the work was done and what the results were. In addition, it provides the opportunity to review the work of the childcare setting, to make any necessary adjustments or improvements and to celebrate success.

When evaluating childcare provision you need to consider the following:

1 Does the current childcare provision:
   ◎ Meet the needs of the local community?
   ◎ Reflect mobility and access within the local community?
   ◎ Meet children's play needs and preferences?
   ◎ Help and support parents'/carers' interests?
   ◎ Contribute to sound community development objectives?
   ◎ Sustain the interest, involvement and support of children?
   ◎ Reflect differing needs: age groups, gender, ethnic/cultural, and disability acceptance?
   ◎ Meet all safety requirements, for example child protection and accident prevention?
   ◎ Have regular reviews?

2 Do the childcare setting's resources:
   ◎ Meet the needs of children and the communities in which they live?
   ◎ Reflect the principles of the UN Convention on the Rights of the Child?
   ◎ Benefit children as a first priority?
   ◎ Enable adjustment to changing circumstances?
   ◎ Receive regular reviews?

3 Do the childcare setting's training opportunities:
   ◎ Have a child-centred focus?
   ◎ Have adequate resources?
   ◎ Support parents and volunteers as well as employees?
   ◎ Include management needs?
   ◎ Meet community and voluntary sector requirements?
   ◎ Reflect the views of those seeking or needing training?
   ◎ Receive regular reviews?

(Wood, 1996)

When evaluating childcare provision, you will need to collect, record and analyse information using the agreed evaluation methods and criteria. After you have made an analysis, you will need to report your results to the relevant colleague, including any recommendations for changes or improvements to the childcare provision. Remember to follow your childcare setting's policies and procedures for collecting, recording, reporting and storing information (see CCLD 328.2).

Delivering quality services for children is a continuous process and early years providers should be involved in continuing professional development, self-reflection (see Chapter 4) and peer support (see Chapter 18 for information about mentoring and coaching) as part of the everyday operations of their settings. (DfES, 2006a)

CCLD 341
Advise and mentor those implementing quality systems and procedures for the delivery of childcare services

As part of your role and responsibilities you may be involved in providing mentoring support for those implementing formally recognised quality systems and procedures within childcare provision, such as externally validated quality assurance schemes. This includes identifying requirements, collecting and presenting evidence as well as taking appropriate action to ensure that requirements are met.

Unit Links

For this Unit you also need to understand:

CCLD 304 Reflect on and develop practice (Chapter 4)

CCLD 343.1 Plan the mentoring process (Chapter 18)

CCLD 344.1 Coach individual learners (Chapter 18)

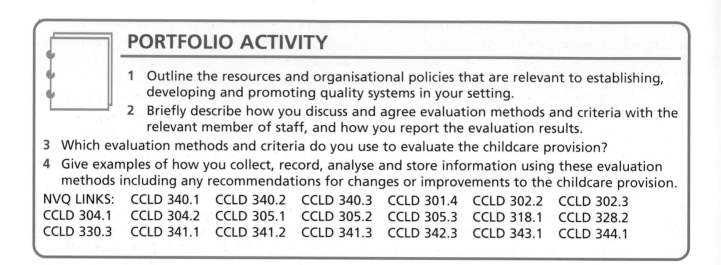

PORTFOLIO ACTIVITY

1 Outline the resources and organisational policies that are relevant to establishing, developing and promoting quality systems in your setting.

2 Briefly describe how you discuss and agree evaluation methods and criteria with the relevant member of staff, and how you report the evaluation results.

3 Which evaluation methods and criteria do you use to evaluate the childcare provision?

4 Give examples of how you collect, record, analyse and store information using these evaluation methods including any recommendations for changes or improvements to the childcare provision.

NVQ LINKS: CCLD 340.1 CCLD 340.2 CCLD 340.3 CCLD 301.4 CCLD 302.2 CCLD 302.3
CCLD 304.1 CCLD 304.2 CCLD 305.1 CCLD 305.2 CCLD 305.3 CCLD 318.1 CCLD 328.2
CCLD 330.3 CCLD 341.1 CCLD 341.2 CCLD 341.3 CCLD 342.3 CCLD 343.1 CCLD 344.1

CCLD 341.1
Identify quality assurance requirements

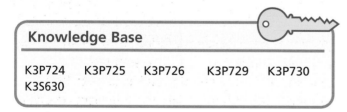

Knowledge Base

K3P724   K3P725   K3P726   K3P729   K3P730
K3S630

Identifying quality assurance requirements involves: ensuring that information on quality assurance criteria is made available to colleagues who are responsible for implementing the scheme; providing detailed information about the requirements of the quality assurance scheme to colleagues who are responsible for implementing it in ways that are easy to understand; discussing with colleagues how the quality assurance criteria relate to regulatory requirements for children's care and education; assisting colleagues to identify links between supervisory systems, colleagues' training and development, health and safety at work and quality assurance systems; and helping colleagues to clearly identify how the setting's policies and procedures relate to quality assurance. (NDNA, 2004) (For more information see CCLD 301.4 in Chapter 1; CCLD 302.1 in Chapter 2; Unit CCLD 304 in Chapter 4; Units CCLD 311, CCLD 335, CCLD 338 and CCLD 343.3 in Chapter 18; CCLD 340.1 and CCLD 342.1 in this chapter.)

CCLD 341.2
Support the collection of evidence

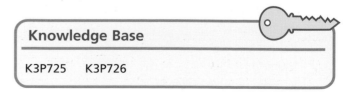

Knowledge Base

K3P725   K3P726

Supporting the collection of evidence involves: helping colleagues to identify what evidence is required to demonstrate that quality assurance procedures are being followed; assisting colleagues to identify individual documents, records and written information that meet quality assurance requirements; helping colleagues to present the information in a way that meets the stated requirements for evidence; helping colleagues to review evidence against the criteria of the quality assurance and identify any gaps; where gaps are identified in the evidence, assisting colleagues to identify and locate alternative evidence wherever possible; and where no alternative evidence is available, encouraging and supporting colleagues to report and acknowledge the gap to those reviewing the quality assurance procedures. (NDNA, 2004) (For more information see Unit CCLD 302 in Chapter 2; Unit CCLD 303 in Chapter 3; Unit CCLD 305 in Chapter 5; CCLD 337.1 in Chapter 9; Unit CCLD 312 in Chapter 11; Units CCLD 309 and CCLD 310 in Chapter 12; Units CCLD 311, CCLD 335, CCLD 338 and CCLD 343.3 in Chapter 18; CCLD 328.2, CCLD 340.2 and CCLD 342.3 in this chapter.)

CCLD 341.3
Support the development of practice to meet quality assurance requirements

Knowledge Base

| K3P727 | K3P728 | K3C732 | K3P733 | K3M734 |

Supporting the development of practice to meet quality assurance requirements involves: helping colleagues to objectively review policies and

practices and to identify changes in order to meet quality assurance criteria; supporting colleagues to give positive feedback to their colleagues on the implementation of quality assurance systems; helping colleagues to give constructive criticism to colleagues using emotionally neutral language; assisting colleagues to discuss and negotiate changes to their practice with colleagues; supporting colleagues to identify how changes will improve quality of service delivered to children and families; and helping colleagues to identify where systems may be improved. (NDNA, 2004) (For more information see CCLD 301.4 in Chapter 1; Unit CCLD 304 in Chapter 4; Unit CCLD 311, CCLD 338 and CCLD 343.3 in Chapter 18; CCLD 340.3 in this chapter.)

CCLD 342
Meet regulatory requirements in the childcare setting

As a childcare manager you will be involved in meeting regulatory requirements, such as statutory requirements for registration and inspection. This includes: identifying regulatory requirements relevant to your setting; planning for inspection in consultation with your colleagues; collecting required evidence; and taking appropriate action to meet requirements.

CCLD 342.1
Identify regulatory requirements

Knowledge Base

| K3P735 | K3M736 | K3M737 | K3D738 | K3P739 |
| K3P741 | K3P744 | | | |

To identify regulatory requirements you must know and understand the National Standards and criteria for childcare provision in your setting, such as the *Day care and childminding (National Standards) (England) Regulations 2003* and *Day care and childminding: guidance to the National Standards revisions to certain criteria October 2005* and *Guidance to the National Standards* relevant to the type of care you provide – full and/or sessional day care, holiday playscheme, out-of-school club or an open-access facility. These National Standards set out the relevant criteria for each type of childcare setting with regard to: premises and equipment (see Chapters 2 and 6); the provision of food and drink, including guidelines for healthy eating (see Chapters 7 and 11); health and safety, including first aid and fire safety (see Chapters 2, 7 and 11); staff numbers/ratios, suitability and qualifications (see Chapter 18); management of information systems and records, including confidentiality (see CCLD 328.2 above and CCLD 301.4 in Chapter 1); curriculum requirements for the under-3s, for example *Birth to Three Matters* (see Chapter 11); curriculum requirements for the under-5s, for example *Curriculum guidance for the foundation stage* or the proposed new *Early Years Foundation Stage* (see Chapter 12).

Check it out

What are the regulatory requirements for your childcare setting?

CCLD 342.2
Plan for inspection in consultation with colleagues

Knowledge Base

K3P735   K3M736   K3M737   K3D738   K3P739
K3P740   K3M743

From April 2005 Ofsted changed the way it carries out inspections of childcare and nursery education. It continues to inspect and report on: *the quality and standards of childminding and day care* offered by registered childminders and day care providers; *the quality and standards of nursery education for children aged 3 and 4 years* provided by settings included in local authorities' directory of providers entitled to receive nursery education funding. However, in April 2005 Ofsted began also to carry out an 'integrated inspection' with a single inspection report in settings that provide both care and nursery education. To assess the overall quality of the setting's care and, where applicable, nursery education, inspectors will ask *what is it like for a child here?* To answer this important question the inspectors will judge how you meet the outcomes for children set out in *Every Child Matters* (see Chapter 5). The inspectors will also judge how well you organise childcare to promote children's well-being, including: whether you

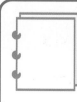

PORTFOLIO ACTIVITY

Outline how you advise and mentor those implementing quality systems and procedures for the delivery of childcare services. Include examples of how you: identify quality assurance requirements; support the collection of evidence; and support the development of practice to meet quality assurance requirements.

NVQ LINKS: CCLD 341.1   CCLD 341.2   CCLD 341.3   CCLD 340.3   CCLD 301.4   CCLD 304.1
CCLD 304.2   CCLD 343.3   CCLD 311   CCLD 338

> ### Unit Links
>
> For this Unit you also need to understand the following sections:
>
> **CCLD 301.4** Communicate with adults (see Chapter 1)
>
> **CCLD 302.1** Establish a healthy, safe and secure environment for children (see Chapter 2)
>
> **CCLD 302.3** Supervise procedures for accidents, injuries, illnesses and other emergencies (see Chapter 2)
>
> **CCLD 306.1** Plan and provide an enabling physical environment for children (see Chapter 6)
>
> **CCLD 306.2** Organise space and resources to meet children's needs (see Chapter 6)
>
> **CCLD 307.2** Plan and provide food and drink to meet the nutritional needs of children (see Chapter 7)
>
> **CCLD 314.2** Provide for the nutritional needs of babies and children under 3 years (see Chapter 11)
>
> **CCLD 312.1** Observe, assess and record developmental progress of babies and children under 3 years (see Chapter 11)
>
> **CCLD 309.1** Prepare curriculum plans according to requirements (see Chapter 12)

meet the National Standards for the type of care you provide; the quality of teaching and learning in the Foundation Stage (if you provide nursery education for 3 to 4 year olds); whether you use good practice as set out in *Birth to Three Matters* (where you care for children under 3 years). (Ofsted, 2006)

(For detailed information see: *Are you ready for your inspection? A guide to inspections of childcare and nursery education conducted by Ofsted*; it is available free from: www.ofsted.gov.uk/publications/ index.cfm?fuseaction=pubs.summary&tid=3883)

Eight ways to prepare for inspection

Prepare for inspection in the following ways:

1   Check that you and your colleagues are familiar with the relevant documents, such as the National Standards for the type of childcare you provide; and the appropriate curriculum frameworks for the children you work with (see above).

2   Make sure you have put right any weaknesses identified in your last inspection report.

3   Complete the self-evaluation form.

4   Check you have all the required records.

5   Make sure you understand the revisions to the National Standards.

6   Keep any information about how parents view your service and any improvements you have made as a result.

7   Make sure you have available the record you keep of complaints about the childcare that you provide.

8   Make sure you have notified Ofsted of any significant changes to your provision.

(Ofsted, 2006)

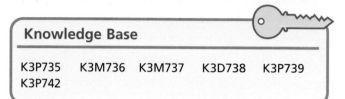

CCLD 342.3
Collect required evidence

Knowledge Base

K3P735   K3M736   K3M737   K3D738   K3P739
K3P742

It is essential that you have the following documents ready to show the inspector.

For all childminders and day-care providers:

◎ The name, home address and date of birth of each child who is looked after on the premises (not open-access schemes)

◎ The name, home address and telephone number of a parent of each child (not open-access schemes)

◎ The name, home address and telephone number of any person who will be looking after children on the premises (childminding only)

◎ A daily record of the names of the children looked after on the premises, their hours of attendance and the names of the persons who look after them (not open-access schemes)

◎ A record of accidents occurring on the premises

◎ A record of any medicinal product administered to any child on the premises, including the date and circumstances of its administration, by whom it was administered, including medicinal products which the child is permitted to administer to himself/herself, together with a record of a parent's consent

◎ A record of complaints that includes brief details of the complaint, the National Standard(s) it relates to, how it was dealt with, the outcome of any investigation including any action(s) taken and whether and when the parent was notified of the outcome.

Additional documents for day-care providers only:

◎ The name, address and telephone number of the registered person

◎ A statement of the procedure to be followed in the event of a fire or accident

◎ A statement of the procedure to be followed in the event of a child being lost or not collected (not open-access schemes)

◎ A written procedure to be followed where a parent has a complaint about the service provided by the registered person

◎ A statement of the arrangements in place for the protection of children, including arrangements to safeguard the children from abuse or neglect and procedures to be followed in the event of abuse or neglect.

(Ofsted, 2006; pp. 19–20)

Check it out

Check that you have collected the required evidence. Use the above to help you.

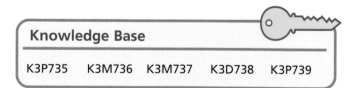

CCLD 342.4
Take appropriate action to meet requirements

Knowledge Base

K3P735   K3M736   K3M737   K3D738   K3P739

As part of your role in meeting the regulatory requirements in the childcare setting you need to be able to take appropriate action to meet these requirements. This includes: reviewing and updating policies and procedures; examining premises and making any necessary changes prior to inspection;

ensuring colleagues' personal details are correct and up to date; ensuring children's developmental records are up to date and based on observations; reviewing materials and equipment to ensure they meet health and safety requirements; reviewing curriculum plans and amending where necessary so they meet objectives; ensuring records of children's attendance, contact details and other essential information are up to date; keeping accurate and legible records of meetings and discussions; and working with colleagues to develop confidence in the inspection process to provide positive benefit for children and their families. (NDNA, 2004)

PORTFOLIO ACTIVITY

1 Outline the regulatory requirements for your setting.
2 Describe how you plan for inspection in consultation with colleagues.
3 List the different sources of evidence and records required for inspection.
4 Outline how you have taken appropriate action to meet regulatory requirements.

NVQ LINKS: CCLD 342.1 CCLD 342.2 CCLD 342.3 CCLD 342.4 CCLD 302.1 CCLD 302.3 CCLD 303.3 CCLD 305.2 CCLD 305.3 CCLD 309.1 CCLD 310.2 CCLD 312.1 CCLD 328.2 CCLD 337.1

Optional Units

CCLD 311
Provide leadership for your team

CCLD 333
Recruit, select and keep colleagues

CCLD 335
Allocate and check work in your team

CCLD 338
Develop productive working relationships with colleagues

CCLD 343
Support learners by mentoring in the workplace

CCLD 344
Enable individual learning through coaching

CCLD 311 Provide leadership for your team

This unit is not divided into individual elements.

As a childcare practitioner, you may be responsible for the management of a childcare setting either as the setting manager or senior practitioner in one of the following types of setting – children's centre, community project, crèche, day nursery, holiday playscheme, out-of-school club, playbus, play centre, playgroup, pre-school or SureStart programme. The childcare setting may be: privately owned or voluntary managed; 'not for profit' or profit making; a charity, co-operative organisation, private company or social enterprise; state funded; or any form of childcare business, such as childminding. (SureStart, 2003b)

Leadership styles and management skills

Knowledge Base

311K05   311K06   311K08   311K09

It is important to have a clear management structure in a childcare setting. The management team members usually share the management of the setting, with one person having overall responsibility. Members should know what their key responsibilities are within the management team and know and understand the legal, regulatory and ethical requirements of the childcare sector (see Chapters 1, 2, 5 and Unit CCLD 342 in Chapter 17).

Leadership styles and leadership skills

To manage a childcare setting effectively you need to know and understand leadership styles and leadership skills. *Leadership styles* affect the behaviours, beliefs and attitudes of the people working together as a team. They are also important in creating a positive atmosphere in the workplace by reducing work stress and promoting job satisfaction. There are three different leadership styles: autocratic, laissez-faire and democratic.

1 *Autocratic leadership:* involves demonstrating a lack of confidence and trust in colleagues. The team leader imposes decisions without consulting or involving other team members. There is little effective communication and few opportunities to be involved in the decision-making process within the setting. Team members feel that they are

expected to follow instructions on their working practices without being critical or reflective.

2 *Laissez-faire leadership:* involves allowing colleagues to make their own decisions but providing some support as required. The whole team is responsible for day-to-day management including budgeting and evaluating the effectiveness of the work in the setting. Team members may feel stressed and under pressure, especially if there is a lack of guidance and support.

3 *Democratic leadership:* involves encouraging team members to contribute to the development of the setting's policies, procedures and practices including the recruitment of staff. The team leader acknowledges and values the individual skills and contributions of each team member. Colleagues feel motivated and actively share their knowledge and experience for the mutual benefit and support of team members.

(Houghton and McColgan, 1995)

An effective team leader needs a range of *leadership skills* including the ability to:

◎ Respond to the individual needs of team members
◎ Promote team spirit and co-operation between colleagues
◎ Motivate the team members to carry out agreed tasks
◎ Allow team members to express their ideas and opinions
◎ Enable the team to devise action plans and effective strategies
◎ Direct the team towards making decisions
◎ Use the skills and experience of all team members effectively
◎ Be supportive to fellow team members
◎ Give positive feedback to team members.

(O'Hagan and Smith, 1994)

Think About

1 What would you say is your leadership style?
2 List your own leadership skills.

Basic management skills

Basic management skills are required to manage a childcare setting effectively. They can be divided into four main categories:

1 *Managing people:* this entails recruiting and retaining colleagues; motivating staff; providing training opportunities; managing difficult team members and dealing with personality clashes; dealing with disciplinary issues (see below); working with parents and carers (see Unit CCLD 330 in Chapter 16) and working with difficult children (see Unit CCLD 337 in Chapter 9).

2 *Managing activities:* this means effective planning and organisation, such as activity plans, work rota, holidays, etc. (see below); and monitoring children's care, learning and development (see Unit CCLD 303 in Chapter 3, Unit CCLD 312 in Chapter 11 and Units CCLD 309 and 310 in Chapter 12).

3 *Managing resources:* this includes securing funding; organising finances; managing a budget (see CCLD 328.3 in Chapter 17); and obtaining appropriate resources (see CCLD 306.2 in Chapter 6).

4 *Managing information:* for instance, registration including following legal requirements; day-to-day administration, such as daily attendance registers; and establishing, developing and evaluating quality assurance systems (see CCLD 328.2 and Unit CCLD 340 in Chapter 17).

Team development

Much of adult life involves working with other people, usually in a group or team. Individuals within a team affect each other in various ways. Within the team there will be complex interactions involving different personalities, roles and expectations as well as hidden agendas that may influence the behaviour of individual members. Teamwork is essential when working closely and regularly with other people over a period of time. Effective teamwork is important because it helps all members of the team to:

◎ Take effective action when planning and/or assigning agreed work tasks
◎ Efficiently implement the agreed work tasks
◎ Agree aims and values which set standards of good practice
◎ Motivate and support each other
◎ Welcome feedback about their work
◎ Offer additional support in times of stress
◎ Reflect on and evaluate their own working practices
◎ Know and use each person's strengths and skills.

As a manager or team leader in a childcare setting, you must know and understand: your exact role and responsibilities and that of each member of your team; how to contribute to effective team practice (see CCLD 304.1 in Chapter 4); and how to participate in team meetings (see below).

Effective communication with colleagues

You will need to communicate effectively with members of your team, as it is essential for developing effective team practice. (Look at the list of good inter-personal skills on page 8.) Effective lines of communication are also important to ensure that all members of the team receive the necessary up-to-date information to enable them to make a full contribution to the life of the childcare setting. Make sure you use any notice boards, newsletters and/or staff bulletins to advise team members of important information. You can also use informal opportunities, such as breaks or lunch-times, to share information, experiences and ideas with colleagues. You may find a communications book or file useful, as well as regular meetings with members of your team. As an experienced childcare practitioner you can make a valuable contribution to the induction or on-going training of new childcarers, possibly acting as a mentor (see below).

18

Stages in team development

As a manager or team leader, you should also know and understand how *group dynamics* affect the various stages of team development; that is, people's social interaction and their behaviour within social groups. Each individual has different personal characteristics that affect their ability to communicate effectively and work comfortably alongside others. From your experiences of working with colleagues you may have identified their differing characteristics that influence their willingness or reluctance to interact within the team. You also need to be aware of the stages in the development of a team and how these affect group dynamics. Research suggests that groups and teams grow and develop through a four-stage cycle:

1 *The forming stage.* A team starts by its members learning about each other. First impressions are important and the team leader should assist colleagues in this early stage by providing appropriate introductions, 'ice-breaking' activities and an induction programme. The team leader should also ensure participation by all team members.

2 *The storming stage.* Team members establish their positions within the team and decide on group functions. There may be arguments and personality clashes between certain members of the team. The team leader can assist by providing opportunities for group discussion that tackle these matters in an open and positive manner, helping colleagues to sort minor disagreements between themselves and acting as an impartial referee if necessary. This can be a difficult stage but it is essential to the healthy development of the team as more serious conflicts may emerge later on if the team does not work through this stage.

3 *The norming stage.* Team members reach agreement on how to work together including establishing ground rules for the team and their individual responsibilities. They plan and organise the setting's working practices, for example ground rules for the children using the childcare setting, the timetable/provision of activities and the rota for routine tasks such as tidying up, providing refreshments, and so on.

4 *The performing stage.* Group trust is established and the team works well together. At this stage the team is usually positive, enthusiastic, co-operative and energetic, with team members supporting each other. There is a positive atmosphere within the setting.

(Houghton and McColgan, 1995)

Remember that colleagues will need to work through these stages again when changes arise, for instance if a person leaves or joins the team. You also need to be aware of the possible problems that can arise within a team and how to identify any signs of tension. These include: frequent arguments about differing views and ideas; uncertainty concerning team objectives or activities; confusion over roles and responsibilities within the team; lack of participation by some team members; and lack of support for team members. (For information about handling disagreements with other adults see CCLD 301.4 in Chapter 1 and see CCLD 338 for detail on resolving conflicts.)

Team objectives

You need also to know and understand the purpose, objectives and plans of your team including: how to set and achieve team objectives which are SMART (Specific, Measurable, Achievable, Realistic and Time-bound) in consultation with team members; demonstrating to team members how their personal work objectives contribute to team objectives (see

CCLD 304.2 in Chapter 4 for further information on developing your personal development objectives). You should also be aware of the types of support and advice that team members may require (see Unit CCLD 338 on page 418).

PORTFOLIO ACTIVITY

Describe how you set and achieve team objectives in consultation with your team members.

NVQ LINKS: CCLD 311   CCLD 338
CCLD 301.4 CCLD 304.1

CCLD 333
Recruit, select and keep colleagues

This unit is not divided into individual elements.

As a childcare setting manager (or senior practitioner) you will be involved in recruiting and selecting people to undertake specific activities or job roles within your area of responsibility. The staff recruitment procedures should reflect the principles and values of childcare that include anti-discriminatory practice, inclusion and positive attitudes (see page vi). Good practice in staff recruitment involves finding the right person for the job. Any new employee should have the right skills and experience for the job, and must be a suitable person to work with children. Good practice starts with the way in which you advertise the job and the information sent to potential applicants. (SPRITO/SkillsActive Playwork Unit, 2001)

Recruitment and selection

Knowledge Base

333K08	333K09	333K10	333K11	333K12
333K13	333K14	333K15	333K17	333K19
333K20	333K21	333K23	333K25	333K26
333K27				

There are many places where you can advertise for job opportunities at your childcare setting, including newspapers or specialist magazines, local schools and colleges, local shops, libraries, community centres, leisure/sports centres and the Internet. A job advertisement should include: a brief description of what the job involves; the hours of work and rate of pay; location of the job; job-share opportunities (especially for full-time jobs); closing date for applications; contact details; phone number that potential applicants can call for more information; and the interview date. (SPRITO/SkillsActive Playwork Unit, 2001)

Application packs

It is a good idea to compile an application pack with all the relevant information, including a letter for applicants, a job description, a person specification, an application form and details about the childcare setting. You may ask applicants to send a covering letter outlining why they have applied for this particular post and their suitability for the job, together with a copy of their curriculum vitae, as well as the completed application form (see sample application form in *The Nanny Handbook* by Teena Kamen).

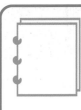

PORTFOLIO ACTIVITY

Compile an application pack for the post of childcarer at your childcare setting. Include the following: advertisement for the job; letter for applicants; job description with details of the duties and responsibilities of the job; person specification detailing the skills and qualities needed for the job; application form; and brief details about the childcare setting.

NVQ LINK: CCLD 333

Shortlists, interviews and references

After the closing date for applications, you need to decide which applicants to invite for interview. If you are not going to interview all applicants, you will need to draw up a shortlist of those who are suitable. Prepare a shortlist by identifying which applicants meet the criteria in the person specification. If the applicant meets all the essential criteria, then invite them for an interview.

The interview panel should consist of at least three people, including one person who knows about recruitment and someone who understands childcare. Select someone to chair the interview. The chair will greet the applicant, introduce the other interviewers, explain about the structure of the interview, watch the time and keep the interview on track. The interview panel should decide beforehand who will ask which questions and when. Remember to allow time for presentations (if applicable) and for applicants to ask any questions. Have a 10 to 15 minute break in-between interviews so that the panel can make notes and discuss any points about each interview. (SPRITO/SkillsActive Playwork Unit, 2001)

Questions you might ask applicants at interview could include:

- ◎ How long have you been working in childcare?
- ◎ What ages of children/young people have you worked with?
- ◎ Why do you enjoy working with children/young people?
- ◎ What are your particular strengths when working with children/young people?
- ◎ What childcare training and qualifications do you have?
- ◎ What special skills or creative talents do you have (such as arts and crafts, drama, playing a musical instrument, and sports)?
- ◎ Which aspects of this particular job do you think you will enjoy?
- ◎ What learning activities and/or play opportunities would you provide for children or young people?
- ◎ What difficulties have you experienced as a childcarer and how were they resolved?
- ◎ What would you do if a child/young person had an accident while in your care?
- ◎ How would you deal with a child's difficult behaviour, for example an emotional outburst?
- ◎ How many days have you had off sick in the last 12 months?
- ◎ Why did you leave your last job or why will you be leaving your present position?

(DfES, 2004c)

You will need to take up references for the successful applicant. The purpose of references is to validate the information given by the applicant on the application form, to find out if the applicant is of good character and to see if the referee thinks the applicant is a suitable person to work with children. It is usual to ask the applicant for at least two references. One reference should be from their current or last employer. If the applicant is a student straight from college, you should ask for a reference from their college tutor and another reference from their final work placement. You could ask referees about the applicant's work as a childcarer such as: how they rated the applicant's care of the children; why the applicant left their employment; what the applicant's strengths and weaknesses were; any difficulties they think the applicant might have if working unsupervised; and whether they would consider re-employing the applicant. (DfES, 2004c)

When you offer the job to the successful applicant remember to: allow time for a reply before rejecting the other applicants in case the chosen applicant does not accept the job; clarify that the job offer is subject to satisfactory references and disclosure (see below); explain the length of the probationary period and how it will be monitored. If no applicants meet all the essential criteria, either at the shortlisting stage or after the interviews, then you should not appoint anyone to the post. Review the recruitment procedures and start again. The completed application forms and any notes made during shortlisting and interviews are confidential (see CCLD 301.4 in Chapter 1 for more information about confidentiality and CCLD 328.1 in Chapter 17 for details about storing information). They must be kept locked away when not in use. Keep information for both the successful applicant and the unsuccessful applicants, in case they contact you about why they were not successful in gaining the post. (SPRITO/SkillsActive Playwork Unit, 2001)

Legislation affecting recruitment

You need to be aware of relevant legislation affecting recruitment, including the laws to protect children. For example:

◎ The Children Act 1989: this Act covers a number of issues regarding the care of children. The part relevant to recruitment relates to the description of a 'fit' person

◎ The Daycare and Childminding (National Standards) (England) Regulations 2003: regulations under the Children Act 1989 require providers to meet the 14 standards and the relevant supporting criteria. The relevant standard for recruitment is 'Standard 1 – Suitable person: Adults providing day care, looking after children or having unsupervised access to them are suitable to do so'

◎ The Protection of Children Act 1999: this Act reinforces the duty of care and is linked to checks by the Criminal Records Bureau (see below).

You also need to be aware of relevant legislation designed to protect people applying for jobs from being unfairly treated in the recruitment process. For example:

◎ The Sex Discrimination Act 1975 (amended 1986): this Act makes it unlawful to discriminate against a person on the grounds of sex or marital status in employment, training or the provision of goods, facilities and services

◎ The Race Relations Act 1975 (amended 2000): this Act makes it unlawful to discriminate against a person in relation to employment or training on the grounds of race, colour, ethnic origin, nationality or national origin

◎ The Disability Discrimination Act 1995: this Act makes it unlawful to discriminate against a disabled person in employment or for an employer to fail to provide the necessary reasonable adjustments for disabled employees and applicants or to offer less favourable terms to disabled employees including those with mental illness

◎ The Employment Rights Act 1996: this Act entitles the employee to a written statement of employment. (See below for more information on employment rights.)

Criminal Records Bureau and Disclosures

The Police Act 1997 (Part V) was introduced to protect certain vulnerable groups. The Act makes applicants for certain posts 'exempt' from declining to give employers details of their past criminal history. These posts include those involving access to children, young people, the elderly, disabled people, alcohol or drug users and the chronically sick. Organisations that include exempt posts are legally entitled to ask applicants for details of all convictions, whether they are 'spent' or 'unspent' under the Rehabilitation of Offenders Act 1974. Registered organisations are now authorised to obtain details of an applicant's criminal history from the Criminal Records Bureau (CRB), an executive agency of the Home Office. The details of this information are set out in a Disclosure. There are three types of Disclosure: Basic, Standard and Enhanced.

Basic Disclosures are *not* suitable for applicants intending to work with children, young people, the elderly and other vulnerable groups. A Basic Disclosure includes only information held on central police records that is unspent according to the Rehabilitation of Offenders Act 1974.

Standard Disclosures include information about spent and unspent convictions, cautions, warnings and reprimands. Standard Disclosures are available for applicants applying for posts involving regular contact with children, young people and/or other vulnerable groups. A Standard Disclosure also checks information held by the Department of Health and Department for Education and Skills (List 99). A Standard Disclosure can be obtained only through a Registered Body to the CRB and not by the individuals themselves.

Enhanced Disclosures are for posts listed in Section 115 of The Police Act 1997, such as those involving unsupervised contact with children, young people and vulnerable groups. It is the most comprehensive and appropriate check that is available to organisations and gives thorough information on all records held on: the police national computer for convictions; the Department of Health and Department for Education and Skills (List 99); the POCA list (Protection of Children Act); the POVA list (Protection of Vulnerable Adults).

These are lists of adults who are considered *not* suitable to work with children, but who may not have been prosecuted. The Chief Officer of Police may also release information for inclusion in an Enhanced Disclosure and additional information may be sent which is not released to the applicant. An Enhanced Disclosure can be obtained *only* through a Registered Body to the CRB and not by the individuals themselves.

The Protection of Children Act 1999 and the Criminal Justice and Court Services Act 2000 make it an offence for any organisation to offer employment involving regular contact with children to anyone who has been convicted of certain offences or is included on lists of people considered unsuitable for such work. It is also a criminal offence for someone who knows they are banned from working with children to apply for, accept or undertake such work.

Employment rights

By law most employees who are employed for a month or more must receive a written statement of employment within eight weeks of the start date. The written statement of employment or contract must include: the start date, the period of employment and notices, main duties, working hours, salary, holidays, sick pay and grounds for dismissal.

As well as what is required by law, it is helpful for a childcarer to have a written statement of employment that also includes more detailed information so that you and the employee are both clear about exactly what you expect from each other. You should make sure the written statement of employment covers all aspects regarding the care of children and the employee's conduct in the childcare setting. Although the law says that an employee must have a written statement of employment within eight weeks of employment, ideally you should provide a written contract after you have made an offer of employment and before the new employee starts work.

To avoid misunderstandings and possible problems make sure the written statement of employment or contract includes the following: the name and address of the employer; the employee's name and address; the hours of work; job description, with the exact duties and responsibilities in detail; details of the salary and salary review; extra pay (or time off in lieu) for extra hours; holiday entitlements and holiday pay; rules about absence, sickness and sick pay entitlements; maternity/paternity rights; pensions arrangements, if any; disciplinary and grievance procedures; notice periods; and the probationary period.

After an offer of employment has been accepted, you should agree a probationary period. This will allow you and the new employee to try out arrangements before you both commit yourselves to a more permanent agreement. Ensure that any agreed probationary period is clearly stated in the written statement of employment or contract and includes the period of notice required during this period. For example, a probationary period of four weeks or one month is quite usual, with either party being able to terminate the employment by giving one week's notice in writing. In addition to the written statement of employment, a childcarer is entitled to a number of statutory employment rights that apply to all employees as soon as they start work. These include protection against: unlawful deductions from their salary; adverse treatment on grounds of sex, race or disability; and dismissal for seeking to enforce their statutory employment rights.

Other statutory employment rights that apply to working as a childcarer include:

◎ Maximum working hours. This is covered by the *Working Time Directive*, which regulates the hours an employee can be expected to work. An employer cannot insist that an employee work more than 48 hours per week

◎ National Minimum Wage. An employer must pay employees at least £4.45 per hour if they are aged between 18 and 21 years old and £5.35 per hour if they are aged 22 years or over

◎ Statutory Sick Pay (SSP). An employer must pay employees SSP if they are sick for four days or more

◎ Paid annual holiday. An employee, whether full-time or part-time, is entitled to four weeks' annual paid leave

◎ Notice of termination of employment. A childcarer is entitled to one week's notice if their employer terminates their employment when they have been working for more than one month. When an employee has been employed for two years, they are entitled to two weeks' notice. This continues (one week for each year worked) until they have worked for the same employer for 12 years. The notice period can be over-ridden by a longer period if it is included in the contract of employment. For example, it is usual practice for an employee to give at least four weeks' notice (after the probationary period) to enable the employer to make alternative arrangements to maintain adult:child ratios.

Other statutory employment rights apply on completion of a qualifying period of service. For example:

◎ Protection against unfair dismissal. If an employee has been in continuous employment (with the same employer) for at least one year they are automatically protected against unfair dismissal

◎ Statutory Maternity Pay (SMP). If a female employee becomes pregnant and has been working for the same employer for at least nine months prior to the baby's due date, she is entitled to SMP and maternity leave

◎ Statutory Paternity Pay (SPP). As from April 2003 new fathers are entitled to two weeks' SPP, with a right to a further 13 weeks of unpaid leave. To qualify, the employee must have been in continuous employment for at least six months

◎ Redundancy pay. An employee is entitled to redundancy pay if they have been in continuous employment for a minimum of two years, as long as they are not employed on a fixed-term contract.

PORTFOLIO ACTIVITY

1 Give a reflective account of your involvement in the recruitment and selection process at your childcare setting.
2 Review your childcare setting's recruitment and selection process and suggest possible improvements.
NVQ LINK: CCLD 333

Taking action to keep colleagues

Knowledge Base

333K01	333K02	333K03	333K04	333K05
333K06	333K07	333K16	333K18	333K22
333K24				

Taking action to keep colleagues is an important challenge, especially when you need to maintain the relevant adult:child ratios (see page 117). Staff members are one of the most important resources you have and you need to know how to keep colleagues who have the knowledge, experience and skills that are the greatest assets to the childcare setting. If colleagues keep leaving, not only do you lose their knowledge, experience and skills but the setting will also incur extra recruitment costs. Long hours and low pay, particularly in day nurseries in the private sector, can lead to high staff turnover. This is detrimental to children who will miss out on continuity of care. Planning appropriate play and learning activities can also be more difficult when there are uncertainties about the staffing.

There can also be an adverse effect on the atmosphere of the setting where constant staff changes mean there is little time to develop and maintain positive working relationships with both children and adults. High staff turnover can also put pressure on the remaining staff and lead to absenteeism or low morale.

Twelve ways to keep colleagues

You can take positive action to keep colleagues by:

1 Communicating with them and ensuring they have up-to-date information.
2 Talking to them and learning what de-motivates them.
3 Talking to them and learning what motivates them.
4 Eliminating as many de-motivating factors as you can and maintaining these changes.
5 Listening to your colleagues' ideas, such as introducing a suggestion scheme.
6 Considering and implementing some of the ideas suggested by your colleagues.
7 Identifying the learning needs of your colleagues and consulting them about the learning opportunities they feel they need in order to do their work more effectively.
8 Ensuring that they have the knowledge and skills they need for work, such as providing access to appropriate training courses and qualifications.
9 Providing accessible support systems, for example a mentoring system.
10 Having an 'open door policy' so that colleagues know that you are approachable.
11 Providing consistent, supportive leadership and giving constructive feedback on performance.
12 Recognising staff achievement and celebrating success. Remember to say 'Thank you'!

PORTFOLIO ACTIVITY

Describe the methods you use to help keep colleagues.
NVQ LINK: CCLD 333

CCLD 335
Allocate and check work in your team

This unit is not divided into individual elements.

When managing routines and activities in a childcare setting you must have a clear knowledge and understanding of the following: effective planning and organisation within the childcare setting; allocating work in your team including job rotation and effective delegation; monitoring work in your team; monitoring children's care, learning and development; making the best use of the available resources. For more detailed information on planning and monitoring routines and activities for children see CCLD 303.1 and 303.2 in Chapter 3, CCLD 306.2 in Chapter 6, CCLD 309.3 and CCLD 310.2 in Chapter 12 and CCLD 312.1 and CCLD 314 in Chapter 11.

Effective planning and organisation within the childcare setting

Knowledge Base

335K01   335K22   335K30

Staff meetings are essential for effective planning and organisation within the childcare setting. Such meetings also provide regular opportunities to share day-to-day information and to solve any problems. These should be held regularly – about once every 4 to 6 weeks. Ensure that there is an agenda for the meeting and that the minutes of the meeting are recorded and can be easily accessed by staff. Encourage colleagues to share best practice, knowledge and ideas on developing appropriate play and learning activities in the childcare setting. As well as general staff meetings you should have regular team meetings for the more detailed planning of routines, play and learning activities as well as the allocation of work within your area of responsibility. (See Chapters 1, 3 and 4 for more information about effective communication with colleagues and participating effectively in team meetings.)

Allocating work in your team

Knowledge Base

335K02   335K03   335K04   335K05   335K06
335K07   335K17   335K18   335K19   335K20
335K21   335K22   335K23   335K24

You can allocate work and responsibilities in a variety of ways. For example:

◎ *Responsibility for an area.* Each childcarer (or group of childcarers) is responsible for a specific area of the childcare setting and promoting children's care, learning and development within that area, for example the baby room, toddler room, or pre-schoolers. The childcarer(s) will provide support for the individual needs of the children in that area including appropriate adult supervision or intervention as and when necessary

◎ *Responsibility for an activity.* Each childcarer is responsible for a specific activity, for example arts and crafts. The adult stays with the same activity throughout the day/week and is responsible for: selecting and setting out materials or helping the children to access these for themselves; encouraging the children's interest and participation in the activity; providing appropriate

Unit Links

For this Unit you also need to understand the following sections:
CCLD 301.4 Communicate with adults (see Chapter 1)
CCLD 303.3 Plan provision to promote development (see Chapter 3)
CCLD 304.1 Reflect on practice (see Chapter 4)

adult supervision or intervention as required; and helping children to clear away afterwards

◎ *Responsibility for a group of children.* Each childcarer is responsible for a small group of children as their key person or keyworker and helps them to settle into the setting. The childcarer is responsible for: greeting their group of children on arrival; encouraging the children's care, learning and development in the setting; and establishing and maintaining a special relationship with each child and their family. (For more information on the role of the key person see Chapter 11.)

◎ *Responsibility for an individual child.* A childcarer may have special responsibility for a child with a disability and will be responsible for: ensuring that child's particular needs are met in an inclusive way within the childcare setting; ensuring they have the necessary materials to participate in routines and activities, including any specialist equipment; and establishing and maintaining a special relationship with the child and their family. (See Chapter 15 for more detail on the role of the keyworker or lead professional.)

Job rotation

Job rotation involves giving colleagues the opportunity to experience other roles within the childcare setting. It can be an interesting and positive way for them to gain varied work experience and to develop new skills and can also be extremely useful when covering staff absences. A staff rota system ensures the fair allocation of work within the childcare setting and enables you to share out some of the more routine jobs within the setting, such as washing paint pots. If you use a rota, make sure you give adequate notice of any changes to it so that your colleagues know what areas and activities they are responsible for in any particular week.

You can use staff questionnaires to gain useful information about your colleagues' views on the planning and allocation of work. For example:

◎ Is the current staff rota system working?
◎ What difficulties (if any) do they have with balancing their work and family needs?
◎ What do they believe you could offer to give them more support?
◎ What suggestions do they have to make the childcare setting more effective?

Effective delegation

Effective delegation is another important factor in managing a childcare setting. It involves motivating your colleagues to carry out specific tasks to enable you to focus on the jobs that you need to do. Delegation also enables you to make use of the particular strengths and skills of your colleagues. Remember, developing effective delegation takes time and practice.

Eight steps to effective delegation

You can demonstrate effective delegation by:

1 *Finding the right person:* consider existing and potential abilities, attitude and personality.

2 *Consulting first:* allow your colleagues to be involved in deciding what is to be delegated.

3 *Thinking ahead:* do not wait for a crisis to occur and then delegate; try to delegate in advance.

4 *Delegating whole tasks:* where possible, delegate a complete task to a colleague, rather than just a small section of it.

5 *Specifying expected outcomes:* make it clear what outcomes are expected from your colleagues.

6 *Taking your time:* especially if you have been under-delegating or are dealing with less experienced staff. A gradual transfer of responsibility will allow both you and your colleagues to learn what is involved.

7 *Delegating the good and the bad:* if you delegate the tasks that are pleasant to do and also those that are not so pleasant, your colleagues will have the opportunity to gain valuable, realistic experience of many types of jobs.

8 *Delegating, then trusting:* when you delegate a task to a colleague, together with the responsibility for getting it done, you then need to trust that person to complete the job to your specified and mutually agreed requirements.

(Wandsworth EYDCP)

Monitoring the work of your team

Knowledge Base

335K08	335K09	335K10	335K11	335K12
335K13	335K14	335K15	335k16	335K25
335K26	335K27	335K28	335K29	

When monitoring the progress and quality of work of individuals or teams within your area of responsibility, you should encourage your colleagues to take responsibility for their own work tasks and to use existing feedback systems to keep you informed of work progress. When establishing procedures for monitoring work in the childcare setting include the following: formal procedures (reports, formal meetings, mentoring, staff appraisals, supervision); informal procedures (observations, informal meetings, conversations); the type of information required (checklists, evaluation sheets, progress reports); when the information will be delivered to you or others in the team (daily, weekly, monthly, half-termly, termly, annually); the form of the information (verbal, written, e-mail, audio-visual); where and how the information will be delivered (meeting, face-to-face, presentation, electronic); and the amount of detail required. (Wandsworth EYDCP)

Figure 18.1 Team meeting

CCLD 338
Develop productive working relationships with colleagues

This unit is not divided into individual elements.

Developing productive working relationships with colleagues involves a knowledge and understanding of the following: providing effective support for colleagues; staff induction; supervision in the setting; staff appraisals; motivating colleagues; staff development; resolving conflicts; grievance and disciplinary procedures; and mentoring in the setting (see CCLD 343 on page 423) and coaching (see CCLD 344 on page 426).

Providing effective support for colleagues

Knowledge Base

338K01	338K02	338K05	338K06	338K11
338K15	338K16	338K17	338K18	

Developing productive working relationships with colleagues is important because this helps to maintain a positive childcare environment that benefits children, parents and staff. As a member of a team, you need to develop such relationships with your colleagues by: being supportive towards them; helping to reduce sources of stress; challenging discrimination and prejudice; and improving your own performance. To provide effective support for colleagues you need to know: the setting's principles and values (see page vi); the setting's expectations for children's care, learning and development (see CCLD 303.2 in Chapter 3); the aims and objectives for children's play and learning (see Unit CCLD 318 in Chapter 8 and Unit CCLD 309 in Chapter 12); the childcare setting's expectations for children's behaviour (see CCLD 337 in Chapter 9); the inclusion policy for children with special needs (see CCLD 305.2 in Chapter 5); your role and responsibilities as a supervisor or manager (see Unit CCLD 311 above).

You can also provide effective support for colleagues by being an attentive listener. This will enable you to recognise possible signs of stress. You can then respond in the following ways: be sympathetic and understanding; offer to help directly if you can; give information on sources of help and advice, including help available within the setting, national and local advice lines, the Citizens' Advice Bureau and counselling services such as Relate. If you have concerns about a colleague with a serious problem ask a senior colleague about what to do next but *always* remember to maintain confidentiality, especially if the colleague concerned has told you something in confidence. (See CCLD 301.4 in Chapter 1 about confidentiality.)

Staff induction

Knowledge Base

338K02	338K05	338K06	338K09	338K10
338K11	338K13	338K15	338K16	338K18
338K19				

Induction provides new members of staff with the opportunity to learn about the childcare setting and what is expected of them. It can be helpful to compile an *induction pack* including: welcome letter; statement of principles and values; copies of essential policies and procedures, such as equal opportunities, health and safety, child protection, fire and emergency procedures; information about the childcare setting's administration, for example registration and consent forms, monitoring forms, risk assessment, time sheets; names of staff and their main roles and responsibilities; the management structure of the childcare setting; details of who to contact if they have any problems; general information and publicity about the childcare setting; and a floor plan of the building.

Sometimes it might be appropriate to ask the childcarer who is leaving to stay on during the new childcarer's first week. The departing childcarer can share the workload and help the new member of staff to familiarise themselves with their new working environment. This will also help the new member of staff to gain a better understanding of their exact duties and responsibilities.

Supervision in the workplace

Knowledge Base

338K02	338K06	338K07	338K08	338K10
338K12	338K13	338K18	338K20	

PORTFOLIO ACTIVITY

1   Describe how you have asked for help, information or support from your colleagues.

2   Give examples of how you have offered support to colleagues including: childcarers working at the same level as you; your line manager (the senior practitioner or setting manager); and staff for whom you are responsible (nursery assistants, playgroup assistants, volunteer workers).

NVQ LINKS: CCLD 338   CCLD 301.4

Supervision provides opportunities for your colleagues to reflect on their work performance and to review any difficulties they may have, as well as to discuss issues that may not be appropriate to raise at a team meeting. Some organisations prefer to use terms like 'keep in touch' or 'one-to-one' instead of supervision. Plan regular sessions with each member of staff. Agree and set clear ground rules about supervision and confidentiality. Keep written records of supervision sessions and ensure that they are kept in a locked file. A suggested format for a supervision session includes: discuss current feelings about the job; review of work since last supervision, including any goals set; discuss current work including successes and difficulties; and provide support or training as required. (Wandsworth EYDCP)

Staff appraisals

Knowledge Base

338K02	338K06	338K07	338K08	338K10
338K12	338K13	338K18	338K20	

Staff appraisals or reviews are a formal way for you to keep up to date with the work performance of your colleagues and to identify their ongoing training needs. Staff appraisals, which usually take place once a year, should have an agreed format, for example a form to be completed by the childcarer prior to the appraisal meeting that is used as the basis of discussion at the actual appraisal meeting.

PORTFOLIO ACTIVITY

Outline the methods you use to monitor the work of colleagues and provide feedback on their performance. For example: staff and/or team meetings; supervision sessions; and staff appraisals.

NVQ LINKS: CCLD 338   CCLD 311   CCLD 335
CCLD 328.5

Motivating colleagues

Knowledge Base

338K02	338K06	338K08	338K12	338K13
338K14	338K19	338K20		

Motivating colleagues is an essential part of your role as a manager or supervisor. Motivation is a key factor in creating a positive childcare environment and helps to maintain positive working relationships within the childcare setting. Remember that everyone is an individual and your colleagues will each respond in a different way to motivating factors. Find and use the motivating factors for the colleagues in your team.

Seven ways to motivate colleagues more effectively

You can help to motivate your colleagues more effectively by:

1 Identifying and trying to understand the individual needs and personal goals of your colleagues.
2 Remembering that higher pay is not the only way to motivate colleagues. Other rewards may be more appropriate.
3 Setting work targets that are realistic and achievable but also providing your colleagues with some challenges to prevent boredom and increase job satisfaction. Involve colleagues in setting their own targets, for example using SMART objectives (see page 83).
4 Always consulting your colleagues before changing agreed targets.
5 Using praise or other rewards to acknowledge your colleagues' achievements.
6 Using group pressure to influence motivation in positive ways, such as involving your colleagues in group decision-making to strengthen their commitment.
7 Keeping your colleagues regularly informed about what is happening in the childcare setting.

Staff development

Knowledge Base

338K02	338K06	338K07	338K08	338K09
338K10	338K12	338K13	338K15	338K18
338K19	338K20			

Good quality and appropriate staff development and training can have a huge, positive impact on workplace performance, which in turn can greatly enhance the play and learning experiences of the children using the childcare setting. To be effective, staff development should take into account the needs of individual staff members and the needs of the childcare setting as a whole.

When providing learning opportunities for your colleagues, start by identifying their learning needs; for example, what additional knowledge and skills do they need to work more effectively? Staff appraisals can help you to identify these learning needs. Once their learning needs have been identified, you need to agree with your colleague(s) on an appropriate training course or qualification that will help to meet their learning needs.

When considering staff development you will have a choice of training options including: sending staff on existing training courses (as a group or individually); inviting trainers in to the setting to run sessions for you; or running in-house training. Another aspect of staff development is to look at ways that your colleagues can pass on their knowledge, skills and experience to other childcarers, such as training as childcare trainers or childcare NVQ assessors. Training opportunities should also be offered to parents and carers as well as staff members, including meetings with speakers, discussion groups, reading materials available, such as books, factsheets and information packs.

Each member of staff should have a Personal Development Plan or Continuing Professional Development Plan that includes training and personal development goals and how these relate to the aims of the childcare setting. (For more information see CCLD 304.2 in Chapter 4 on professional development and training opportunities.)

PORTFOLIO ACTIVITY

Describe how you identify the learning needs of your colleagues and provide training opportunities to meet these needs.

NVQ LINKS: CCLD 338   CCLD 311   CCLD 333
CCLD 304.2

Resolving conflicts

Knowledge Base

338K02	338K03	338K04	338K05	338K10
338K18	338K19	338K20		

Conflicts can arise in even the best-run childcare settings. The resolution of conflict situations requires the senior practitioner to work with colleagues. Whenever possible it is better for colleagues to find their own solutions, with the senior practitioner or manager acting as a *facilitator* or *mediator*. Sometimes a colleague may not make allowances for parent/carer's particular problems or does not show respect for the needs and rights of

parents/carers. Conflicts need to be handled sensitively and resolved as quickly as possible to avoid creating a negative, unpleasant atmosphere for everyone which can have a detrimental effect on the well-being of the children. (For further information on handling disagreements with other adults see CCLD 301.4 in Chapter 1.) Personal problems may also affect a colleague's working relationships with others in the childcare setting. The senior practitioner or manager should have a one-to-one discussion and suggest where sources of help might be found. (See above for information on providing effective support for colleagues.)

Grievance and disciplinary procedures

Knowledge Base

338K02	338K03	338K04	338K05	338K09
338K10	338K18	338K19	338K20	

The Employment Rights Act 1996 requires that all employees who work for more than 16 hours a week have a contract (a formal written agreement stating their terms and conditions of employment). This statement should also include information about the setting's grievance and disciplinary procedures. The Employment Act 2002, sections 35-38, deals with changes to the rules concerning written particulars of employment including ensuring the statement complies with the Act's requirements for minimum statutory internal grievance and disciplinary procedures.

If an employee has a grievance relating to their employment, they are entitled to invoke the childcare setting's grievance procedure (which may be part of a local authority agreement) and should be included in the staff handbook. The grievance should be raised initially with their line manager (such as the senior practitioner). The grievance should be raised orally in the first instance, although the employee may be requested to put it in writing. If the grievance relates to the employee's line manager, then the grievance should be referred to their line manager's superior (for example the setting's manager).

The childcare setting will expect reasonable standards of performance and conduct from all staff members. Details of the disciplinary procedure (which may be part of a local authority agreement) should be included in the staff handbook. If an employee is dissatisfied with a disciplinary decision they should in the first instance contact the setting manager, usually within five working days of the date of the decision.

PORTFOLIO ACTIVITY

1 Describe how you have responded or would respond to a conflict situation as senior practitioner or manager in a childcare setting. (Be tactful and remember confidentiality.)
2 Outline the grievance and disciplinary procedures for childcarers in your setting.

NVQ LINKS: CCLD 338   CCLD 311   CCLD 333
CCLD 335   CCLD 301.4

CCLD 343
Support learners by mentoring in the work place

Mentoring is a structured approach to supporting a colleague by pairing an experienced member of the team with one who is less experienced, such as a trainee on a modern apprenticeship. Mentoring is a very effective way for colleagues to share knowledge, skills and experience.

CCLD 343.1
Plan the mentoring process

Knowledge Base

343K01	343K02	343K05	343K06	343K07
343K08	343K09	343K10	343K12	343K14
343K15	343K19	343K21	343K27	343K28

Mentoring involves: 'shadowing' (watching the work of a more experienced colleague); learning 'on the job' (developing new skills; and asking and answering everyday questions); introducing other people in the childcare setting; providing guidance and constructive criticism; agreeing and setting daily objectives; reviewing progress; providing feedback to managers on progress; identifying further training needs; and providing friendly and reassuring support.

Code of practice for mentoring

As a mentor you need to identify and apply an appropriate code of practice for mentoring which should include: demonstrating a commitment to best practice; recognising the limits of your own experience and competence; setting and maintaining boundaries within the mentoring relationship; being open and truthful; monitoring and evaluating your own performance throughout the mentoring process; using appropriate sources of support; answering to the trainee and their organisation for your mentoring activities; and managing differences between your own values and beliefs and the agreed ethical code. (NDNA, 2004)

The stages involved in planning the mentoring process:

1 Identify the development needs and expectations of trainees.
2 Recruit mentors and provide them with training and guidance on mentoring activities.
3 Match mentors with trainees to form mentoring pairs.
4 Mentoring pair negotiates a mentoring agreement based on development needs.
5 Devise an individual development plan based on development objectives.
6 Implement individual development plans.
7 Mentoring agreement concluded.
8 Evaluate the individual development plan and the mentoring process.

CCLD 343.2
Set up and maintain the mentoring relationship

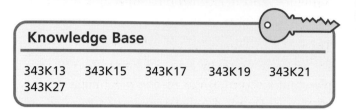

Knowledge Base

343K13   343K15   343K17   343K19   343K21
343K27

The aims of the mentoring process may include: to provide help and advice on all aspects of the practitioner's role; to support the transfer of skills, such as putting theory into practice by applying knowledge and learning to practical tasks in the workplace; to provide constructive feedback on routines and activities; to help in identifying and planning personal development; and to provide a friendly support outside the management framework.

Think About

What are the aims of the mentoring process in your workplace?

Check it out

Find out about the support for trainees in your setting:
◎ Which training programmes are available in your setting, for example NVQs, modern apprenticeships, and so on?
◎ What resources, facilities, information and support are available to help trainees?
◎ What is the code of practice for mentoring in your setting?
◎ Which documents and activities are available to help trainees in the early stages of mentoring?

The roles and responsibilities of the mentor and trainee should be agreed, including agreements about the timing and location of discussions and meetings as well as regular reviews of the trainee's progress and development. You could use a learning log or diary to monitor the mentoring relationship on a regular basis.

The role and responsibilities of the mentor include: setting up a mutually agreed mentoring contract; planning a series of one-to-one meetings with the trainee; keeping a brief record of mentoring meetings and discussions; using e-mail as well as other communications to keep in touch with the trainee; sharing knowledge and skills with the trainee; demonstrating practical skills; providing opportunities for the trainee to practise new skills while ensuring the safety of the trainee, the children and other adults at all times; reviewing the trainee's progress and revising development objectives as appropriate.

The role and responsibilities of the trainee include: being an active participant in the mentoring process; identifying their own development needs; initiating discussions and meetings with the mentor; taking responsibility for their own development; being open to constructive criticism; using e-mail as well as other communications to keep in touch with the mentor; observing the practice of experienced practitioners, including the mentor; practising new skills while ensuring the safety of the children and other adults at all times; reviewing their progress with the mentor and revising their development objectives as appropriate; and keeping their line manager informed.

You could use a 'mentoring contract' as a useful starting point for the mentoring relationship. See www.hebs.scot.nhs.uk/learningcentre/trainers/mentoringworkshop.cfm for an example of a mentoring contract.

CCLD 343.3
Give mentoring support

Knowledge Base

343K03	343K04	343K11	343K13	343K15
343K16	343K17	343K18	343K19	343K20
343K21	343K22	343K23	343K24	343K25
343K26	343K27			

To be an effective mentor you need the following important skills and personal qualities: good interpersonal skills, including being a good listener (see page 8); good coaching/counselling skills (see below); appropriate workplace experience; honesty and integrity; well informed about the work of the setting and other relevant agencies; enthusiasm; patience; reliability; reflective practitioner; and commitment to supporting trainees.

Giving effective mentoring support involves: setting aside enough time for each mentoring session; helping trainees to express and discuss ideas and any concerns affecting their experience in the workplace; giving them information and advice that will help them to be effective in the workplace; giving them the opportunities that help them to understand and adapt to the working environment; identifying ways of developing their confidence in performing activities in the workplace; helping them to take increasing responsibility for developing their skills in the workplace; giving them the opportunities to gain experience in the workplace to increase their confidence and self-development; helping them to look at issues from an unbiased point of view that helps them make informed choices; giving them honest and constructive feedback; identifying when the mentoring relationship needs to change to still be effective and agree any changes with the trainee; identifying when the mentoring relationship has reached a natural end and review the process with the trainee; agreeing what extra support and help the trainee needs or can access; and planning how to provide extra support and help. (NDNA, 2004)

PORTFOLIO ACTIVITY

Give a reflective account of how you have supported learners by mentoring in the workplace. Include detailed information on how you: planned the mentoring process; set up and maintained the mentoring relationship; and provided mentoring support.

NVQ LINKS: CCLD 343.1   CCLD 343.2
CCLD 343.3   CCLD 301.4   CCLD 304.1
CCLD 304.2   CCLD 328.5   CCLD 311
CCLD 335   CCLD 338

CCLD 344
Enable individual learning through coaching

Part of your role within the setting may involve using coaching as a way of encouraging individual learning. You may be involved in activities such as: identifying individual needs and learning styles; choosing the manner and speed of coaching; checking on the progress of learners; giving feedback; reviewing the potential of e-learning for their support; helping learners to apply their learning; and giving on-going support.

CCLD 344.1
Coach individual learners

Knowledge Base

344K01	344K02	344K03	344K04	344K06
344K07	344K08	334K09	344K10	344K11
344K12	344K13	344K14		

Coaching is … 'a process that enables learning and development to occur and thus performance to improve. To be a successful Coach requires a knowledge and understanding of process as well as the variety of styles, skills and techniques that are appropriate to the context in which the coaching takes place'
(Parsloe, 1999; p. 8)

Coaching individual learners involves helping children or adults to fulfil their potential and achieve success in their learning. It involves working with people on a one-to-one basis to help them successfully complete a course of education/training in school, college and/or the workplace. Coaching is particularly useful for individual learners who have lost their motivation or belief in their ability to succeed.

You need to know and understand how to match coaching opportunities to individual learning needs and objectives and how to identify: individual learning needs; different learning styles (visual, auditory, kinaesthetic); styles of processing information (analytic or global – see Chapter 12).

You should know how to: identify and use different learning opportunities (observation, presentations, workshops, simulation, role play, practical experience); structure learning activities and how to choose and prepare appropriate materials, including technology-based materials (see below).

You should be able to put information in order and use language that is appropriate for individual learners and put learners at their ease, for example by being approachable and communicating with learners in a sensitive way. You should also provide learners with positive feedback and encourage them to recognise their own achievements (see page 177). Check learners' understanding and progress by asking questions and by observing and assessing the skills they demonstrate during learning activities (see Chapter 3).

It is important that you know how to recognise the things that are likely to prevent learning. There may be learners who have difficulties accessing some learning activities, such as people with disabilities or from different ethnic groups. You need to know how to overcome these difficulties by providing appropriate support and resources. (For more information about inclusion and anti-discriminatory practice see CCLD 305.1 and 305.2 in Chapter 5.)

CCLD 344.2
Assist individual learners to apply their learning

Knowledge Base

344K05	344K09	344K11	344K12	344K13
344K14	344K15	344K16		

You can assist individual learners to apply their learning by: giving them the opportunities to practise skills, apply their knowledge and get experience in a structured way; considering using technology-based support for learners, including e-support; identifying opportunities for learners to achieve agreed learning objectives and giving them positive feedback on their progress; identifying ways to use different learning opportunities and agreeing action with learners; giving clear and accurate information on the resources available to help them apply their learning; giving positive feedback on the learning experience and the outcomes achieved; identifying anything that prevents learning and reviewing this with learners; and explaining to learners the on-going support that is available to them. (NDNA, 2004)

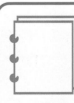

PORTFOLIO ACTIVITY

Describe a learning activity in which you have coached individual learners.

Include information on: individual learning needs and learning styles; the coaching style selected to meet the learning objectives; the structure of the learning activity, including organisation and resources; providing feedback and encouragement to learners; checking learners' understanding and progress; and any difficulties experienced by the learners and how you overcame these.

NVQ LINKS: CCLD 344.1   CCLD 344.2

When coaching you may be involved in helping individual learners to: express their problems and concerns; identify possible solutions to their problems, such as access advice and support networks; identify personal and study goals, for example complete a written assignment or practical task; develop their own ideas and how to present these; work out how to do assignments, coursework and/or portfolio activities; develop time management by prioritising tasks and planning for study time and social life; develop study skills including where to find information, for example acquire word-processing skills and using the Internet; and complete a portfolio of evidence.

You should know and understand how to identify the opportunities available for learners to apply their learning and provide information on the resources and ongoing support that is available to them. You need to know how to analyse and use developments in learning and new ways of delivery such as technology-based learning and how to choose and prepare technology-based materials (see Chapter 12). Ensure that everyone acts in line with health, safety and environmental protection legislation and best practice (see Chapter 2).

Unit Links

For this Unit you also need to understand the following sections:

CCLD 302.1 Establish a healthy, safe and secure environment for children (see Chapter 2)

CCLD 302.2 Maintain a healthy, safe and secure environment for children (see Chapter 2)

CCLD 323 Use Information and Communication Technology to promote children's early learning (see Chapter 12)

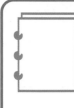

PORTFOLIO ACTIVITY

Describe how you have assisted individual learners to apply their learning. Include information on: identifying the opportunities available to enable this; using technology-based materials including e-learning support; providing them with information about resources and on-going support; providing positive feedback about their progress; and identifying anything that prevents learning and reviewing this with learners.

NVQ LINKS: CCLD 344.1   CCLD 344.2

Appendix: Useful Information

A – Z of useful contacts and information

A

Advisory Conciliation and Arbitration Service (ACAS)
Head Office: Brandon House, 180 Borough High Street, London, SE1 1LW
Tel: 020 7210 3613
Helpline: 08457 47 47 47
Website: www.acas.org.uk/

All4KidsUK Ltd
14 The Service Road, Potters Bar, Hertfordshire, EN6 1QA
Tel: 01707 659383
Website: www.all4kidsuk.com
(A comprehensive children's directory for parents and carers)

Amateur Swimming Association
Head Office: ASA, Harold Fern House, Derby Square, Loughborough, LE11 5AL
Tel: 01509 618700
Website: www.britishswimming.org

Anti-Bullying Network
Moray House School of Education, University of Edinburgh, Holyrood Road,
Edinburgh, EH8 8AQ
Tel: 0131 651 6100
Website: www.antibullying.net/

Article 12 in Scotland
Burnbank, Ogilvie Terrace, Ferryden, Montrose
Angus, DD10 9RG
Tel: 01674 674086
Website: www.article12.org
(Scottish network of young people which promotes young people's rights)

B

Barnardo's Head office: Tanners Lane, Barkingside, Ilford, Essex, IG6 1QG
Tel: 020 8550 8822
Website: www.barnardos.org.uk

Bar Pro Bono Unit
7 Gray's Inn Square, London, WC1R 5AZ
Tel: 020 7831 9711
Website: www.barprobono.org.uk/
(Provides free legal advice and representation for people in England and Wales who cannot afford legal assistance or where legal aid is not available)

British Red Cross
9 Grosvenor Crescent, London, SW1X 7EJ
Tel: 020 7235 5454
Website: www.redcross.org.uk

British Youth Council
The Mezzanine 2, 2nd Floor, Downstream Building,
1 London Bridge, London, SE1 9BG
Tel: 0845 458 1489
Website: www.byc.org.uk/
(A charity run by young people for young people)

Bully Online
9 Knox Way, Harrogate, North Yorkshire, HG1 3JL
Website: www.bullying.co.uk
(A registered charity providing information for children, parents and teachers)

C

The Care Commission
Compass House, 11 Riverside Drive, Dundee, DD1 4NY
Tel: 01382 207100
Website: www.carecommission.com

Care Standards Inspectorate for Wales
National Office: 4/5 Charnwood Court, Heol Billingsley, Parc Nantgarw, Nantgarw, CF15 7QZ
Tel: 01443 848450
Website: www.csiw.org.uk

Child Accident Prevention Trust (CAPT)
18-20 Farringdon Lane, London, EC1R 3HA
Tel: 020 7608 3828
Website: www.capt.org.uk

Children's Law Centre (for Northern Ireland)
Tel: 0808 808 5678 (for young people)
Tel: 028 9043 4242 (for adults)
Website: www.childrenslawcentre.org

Children's Legal Centre (for England and Wales)
University of Essex, Wivenhoe Park, Colchester, Essex, CO4 3SQ
Tel: 01206 873820 (general legal advice)
Website: www.childrenslegalcentre.com
(The organisation offers free legal advice and information on the law in relation to children)

Children Now
Haymarket Professional Publications, 174 Hammersmith Road, London, W6 7JP
Tel: 020 8267 4706
Website: www.childrennow.co.uk
(Weekly magazine for people working with children and their families)

Children's Play Council
National Children's Bureau, 8 Wakley Street, London, EC1V 7QE
Tel: 020 7843 6016
Website: www.ncb.org.uk

Children's Rights Alliance for England
94 White Lion Street, London, N1 9PF
Tel: 020 7278 8222
Website: www.crae.org.uk

Children's Workforce Development Unit
Albion Court, 5 Albion Place, Leeds, LS1 6JL
Tel: 0113 244 6311
Website: www.cwdcouncil.org.uk

Commission for Racial Equality (CRE)
Head Office: St. Dunstan's House, 201-211 Borough High Street, London, SE1 1GZ
Tel: 020 7939 0000 (general enquiries)
Website: www.cre.gov.uk

Criminal Records Bureau (CRB)
Information line: 0870 909 0811
Website: www.crb.gov.uk
Disclosures website: www.disclosure.gov.uk

Department for Education & Skills (DfES)
Sanctuary Buildings, Great Smith Street, London, SW1P 3BT
Tel: 0870 000 2288
Website: www.dfes.gov.uk

Disability Rights Commission (DRC)
DRC, Freepost MID 02164,
Stratford upon Avon, CV37 9BR
Helpline: 08457 622 633
Textphone: 08457 622 644
Website: www.drc-gb.org

E

Equal Opportunities Commission
Arndale House, Arndale Centre, Manchester, M4 3EQ
Tel: 0845 601 5901 (general enquiries)
Website: www.eoc.org.uk

F

4children (formerly Kids Club Network)
Bellerive House, 3 Muirfield Crescent, London, E14 9SZ
Tel: 020 7512 2112
Website: www.4children.org.uk

G

Games For Kids
Website: www.games4kids.co.uk
(Contains links to websites with educational games and fun activities for children)

H

Healthy Living
Helpline: 0845 2 78 88 78
Website: www.healthyliving.gov.uk
(Scotland's healthy living campaign website)

I

Institute of Leisure and Amenity Management (ILAM)
ILAM House, Lower Basildon, Reading, Berkshire,
RG8 9NE
Tel: 01491 874800
Website: www.ilam.co.uk

J

Justice for Children
Website: www.childline.org.uk/extra/campaigns-
childwitnesses.asp
(A coalition of more than 60 organisations campaigning
for child-centred changes to the justice system)

K

Kidscape
2 Grosvenor Gardens, London, SW1W ODH
Tel: 020 7730 3300
Website: www.kidscape.org.uk
(The national charity to help prevent bullying and child
abuse)

L

The Law Centres Federation
Duchess House, 18-19 Warren St, London, W1T 5LR
Tel: 020 7387 8570
Website: www.lawcentres.org.uk
(Free and independent professional legal advice)

Learndirect
Tel: 0800 100 900 (free advice line)
Website: www.learndirect.co.uk

Learning and Skills Council
Head Office: Cheylesmore House, Quinton Road, Coventry,
CV1 2WT
Tel: 0845 019 4170
Helpline: 0870 900 6800
Website: www.lsc.gov.uk/National/default.htm

M

Mind
Granta House, 15 – 19 Broadway, London, E15 4BQ
Tel: 020 8221 9666 (publications)
Tel: 08457 660 163 (Mind Info Line)
Website: www.mind.org.uk
(Provides mental health support and information on
mental health issues)

N

**National Childminding Association of England and
Wales**
Royal Court, 81 Tweedy Road, Bromley, Kent, BR1 1TG
Tel. 0845 880 0044
Website: www.ncma.org.uk

National Children's Bureau
8 Wakley Street, London, EC1V 7QE
Tel: 020 7843 6000
Website: www.ncb.org.uk

National Day Nurseries Association Oak House,
Woodvale Road, Brighouse, West Yorkshire, HD6 4AB
Tel: 0870 774 4244
Website: www.ndna.org.uk

**National Institute for Health and Clinical Excellence
(NICE)**
MidCity Place, 71, High Holborn, London, WC1V 6NA
Tel: 020 7067 5800
Website: www.nice.org.uk

National Playing Fields Association (NPFA)
Head Office: Stanley House, St Chad's Place, London,
WC1X 9HH
Tel: 020 7833 5360
Website: www.npfa.co.uk

**National Society for the Prevention of Cruelty to
Children (NSPCC)**
Weston House, 42 Curtain Road, London, EC2A 3NH
Tel: 020 7825 2500
NSPCC Child Protection Helpline: 0808 800 5000 (24 hour)
Website: www.nspcc.org.uk

National Youth Agency
Eastgate House, 19-23 Humberstone Road, Leicester,
LE5 3GJ
Tel: 0116 242 7350
Website: www.nya.org.uk

Northern Ireland Childminding Association
16/18 Mill Street, Newtownards, Co. Down,
BT23 4LU
Tel: 028 9181 1015
Website: www.nicma.org

Nursery World
Admiral House, 66-68 East Smithfield, London, E1W 1BX
Tel: 020 7782 3000
Website: www.nurseryworld.co.uk
(Weekly magazine for early years and childcare
practitioners)

O

Office for Standards in Education (Ofsted)
Alexandra House, 33 Kingsway, London, WC2B 6SE
Tel: 020 7421 6800
Helpline: 08456 014771
Website: www.ofsted.gov.uk

P

Pre-school Learning Alliance
London Head Office: Unit 213–216, 30 Great Guildford
Street, London, SE1 0HS
Tel.: 020 7620 0550
Website: www.pre-school.org.uk

Q

Qualifications and Curriculum Authority (QCA)
83 Piccadilly, London, W1J 8QA
Tel: 020 7509 5555
Website: www.qca.org.uk
(Useful information on the qualification and training
framework for childcare, early years and playwork)

R

Royal Society for the Prevention of Accidents (RoSPA)
Edgbaston Park, 353 Bristol Road, Birmingham, B5 7ST
Tel: 0121 248 2000 (general information)
Website: www.rospa.com

S

St. John Ambulance
27 St. John's Lane, London, EC1M 4BU
Tel: 08700 10 49 50
Website: www.sja.org.uk

Save the Children
Head Office: 1 St. John's Lane, London, EC1M 4AR
Tel: 020 7012 6400
Website: www.savethechildren.org.uk

Scottish Childminding Association
Suite 3, 7 Melville Terrace, Stirling, FK8 2ND
Tel: 01786 445377
Website: www.childminding.org

Scottish Child Law Centre
54 East Crosscauseway, Edinburgh, EH8 9HD
Tel: 0131 667 6333 (information helpline)
Tel: 0800 328 8970 (free legal advice for under 18s)
Website: www.sclc.org.uk
(Provides information on Scottish law and children's
rights)

Scottish Pre-school Play Association
14 Elliot Place, Glasgow, GC8 EP
Tel: 0141 227 3922
Website: http://www.sppa.org.uk

SkillsActive Playwork Unit
Central Office: 6th Floor, Castlewood House, 77–91 New
Oxford Street, London, WC1A 1PX
Tel: 020 7632 2000
Website: www.playwork.org.uk

SureStart Unit
Head Office: 2C, Caxton House, Tothill Street, London,
SW1H 9NF
Tel: 0870 000 2288 (Public Enquiry Unit)
Website: www.surestart.gov.uk

T

Trades Union Congress (TUC)
Tel: 020 7636 4030 (general enquiries)
Tel: 0870 600 4882 (rights line)
Website: www.tuc.org.uk
(For comprehensive information on many work-related issues)

Traveline
Public transport information
Tel: 0870 608 2 608
Website: www.traveline.org.uk
(Impartial information on planning your journey, by bus, coach or train)

U

UNICEF UK
UNICEF UK Helpdesk
Tel: 0870 606 3377
Website: www.unicef.org.uk

V

Voice
Unit 4, Pride Court, 80-82 White Lion Street, London, N1 9PF
Tel: 020 7833 5792
Tel: 0808 800 5792 (for young people)
Website: www.vcc-uk.org/ngen_public/default.asp
(Provides advocates for young people who are in care, have left care, or are involved with social services)

W

Winston's Wish
Clara Burgess Centre, Bayshill Road, Cheltenham, GL50 3AW
Tel: 0845 2030405
Website: www.winstonswish.org.uk
(Support for bereaved children, young people, families and professionals)

Women's Aid Federation of England
PO Box 391, Bristol, BS99 7WS
Helpline: 0808 2000 247 (freephone 24 hour)
website: www.womensaid.org.uk
(A national charity offering support, advice and information on domestic violence)

X

Xylophone
Website:
http://www.vocalist.org.uk/downloads/xylophone1.html
(Freeware xylophone applet)

Y

Young Minds
102-108 Clerkenwell Road, London, EC1M 5SA
Tel: 020 7336 8445
Website: www.youngminds.org.uk
(Information on children's mental health for young people, parents and professionals)

Young People Now
Haymarket Professional Publications, 174 Hammersmith Road, London, W6 7JP
Tel: 020 8267 4793
Website: www.ypnmagazine.com/home/index.cfm (Weekly magazine for those working with young people aged 11 to 25 years)

Z

Zoo directory
Website: www.ukwebstart.com/listzoos.html
(Zoos, aquariums, safari parks, wildlife parks, sea life centres, theme parks, castles, museums, art galleries and other attractions suitable for children)

Glossary

active learning: learning by doing; participation in activities in meaningful situations.

activity: learning opportunity which involves active participation and discussion.

anti-discriminatory practice: taking positive action to counter discrimination and prejudice.

behaviour: a person's actions, reactions and treatment of others.

carer: any person with responsibility for the care/education of a child during the parent's temporary or permanent absence.

cognitive: intellectual abilities involving processing information received through the senses.

community language: main language spoken in a child's home.

concepts: the way people make sense of and organise information.

conflict situation: verbal or physical disagreement, for example arguments, fighting, disputing rules.

egocentric: pre-occupied with own needs; unable to see another person's viewpoint.

emotional outburst: uncontrolled expression of intense emotion, for example rage or frustration.

ethnicities: identification with a group of people who share some or all of the same culture, geography, history, language, nationality, race and religion.

facilitator: person who makes things easier by providing the appropriate environment and resources for learning.

holistic approach: looking at the 'whole' child, such as *all* aspects of the child's development.

inclusive practice: identifying barriers to participation and taking positive action to eliminate them and encouraging participation in the full range of activities provided by the setting.

intelligence quotient: a person's mental age in comparison to their chronological age.

key factor: an essential aspect affecting learning and development.

language-rich environment: a place where opportunities for language and communication are actively and positively promoted, for example through play, conversation, books and displays.

manager: the person in day-to-day charge of the setting. The manager need not be the same person as the registered person. If not, the manager will be recruited and vetted by the registered person. A manager must have appropriate qualifications and experience.

mediator: a person who acts as an intermediary between parties in a dispute.

milestones: significant skills which children develop in and around certain ages as part of the usual

or expected pattern of development.

nature: genetic inheritance or biological factors; the characteristics a person is born with.

norm: the usual pattern or expected level of development/behaviour.

nurture: environmental/social factors which influence a person's characteristics/skills, such as early childhood relationships and experiences.

operations: the term used by Piaget to describe the way people use their cognitive abilities.

parent: any person with parental responsibility for a child.

peers: children of similar age within the setting.

personality: distinctive and individual characteristics which affect each person's view of themselves, their needs, feelings and relationships with others.

problem-solving: activities which involve finding solutions to a difficulty or question.

psychological: relating to the study of the mind and behaviour, including language, cognitive, social and emotional development.

quality: standard of care/education provided in early years setting (ideally high/excellent).

ratio: the number of adults in relation to children within a group setting, for example three adults with a group of thirty children would be shown as a ratio of 1:10.

rationale: the main reason for implementing a particular activity; the principle behind an idea or opportunity.

registered person: a person deemed qualified to care for children and whose name appears on the certificate of registration. The registered person has overall responsibility for ensuring that the requirements of the national standards are met. A company, committee or other group may be the registered person.

regression: demonstrating behaviour characteristic of previous level of development.

role model: significant person whose actions, speech or mannerisms are imitated by a child.

scaffolding: adult assistance given to support child's thinking and learning, as child develops competence the adult decreases support until child works independently.

schemas: term used mainly by Piaget and Froebel to describe internal thought processes.

sensory: relating to the senses; sensory experiences enable children to *make sense* of their environment.

sequence: development following the same basic pattern but not necessarily at fixed ages.

social context: *any* situation or environment where social interaction occurs, such as home, early years setting, local community.

social interaction: *any* contact with other people including actions and reactions, for example play, verbal and non-verbal communication.

specialist: person with specific training/additional qualifications in a particular area of development, for example speech and language therapist, educational psychologist.

special needs: all children have *individual* needs, but some children may have *additional* needs due to physical disability, sensory impairment, learning difficulty or emotional/ behavioural difficulty.

stages: development which occurs at fixed ages.

stereotype: simplistic characterisation or expectation of a person based on perceived differences or prejudices relating to their race, culture, gender, disability or age.

temperament: person's disposition or personality, especially their emotional responses.

time in: giving children special individual attention to reinforce positive behaviour, such as an adult discussing positive aspects of the day with a child.

time out: a short break or suspension of an activity which allows a cooling off period for all involved but which especially gives the child a chance to calm down.

zone of proximal development: Vygotsky's description for a child's next area of development where adult assistance is required only until the child has developed the skill and can do it independently.

Bibliography

Abbott, L. and Langston, A. (2005) *Birth to Three Matters: Supporting the framework of effective practice.* Milton Keynes: Open University Press.

ATL (2000) 'ATL guide to children's attitudes' in *Report.* June/July issue. London: Association of Teachers and Lecturers.

Bartholomew, L. and Bruce, T. (1993) *Getting to know you: a guide to record-keeping in early childhood education and care.* London: Hodder & Stoughton.

Becta (2004) *Data protection and security – a summary for schools.* British Educational Communications and Technology Agency.

Bostock, L. (2004) *Promoting resilience in fostered children and young people.* London: Social Care Institute for Excellence.

Brennan, W.K. (1987) *Changing Special Education Now.* Milton Keynes: Open University.

BDA (1997) 'Dyslexia: an introduction for parents and teachers and others with an interest in dyslexia'. London: British Dyslexia Association.

British Nutrition Foundation (2003) *The Balance of Good Health.* London: British Nutrition Foundation.

CAPT (2004a) *Factsheet: children and accidents.* London: Child Accident Prevention Trust.

CAPT (2004b) *Factsheet: home accidents.* London: Child Accident Prevention Trust.

CAPT (2004c) *Factsheet: playground accidents.* London: Child Accident Prevention Trust.

CAPT (2004d) *Taking Chances: The Lifestyles and Leisure Risks of Young People.* London: Child Accident Prevention Trust.

ChildLine (2004) Children in care. London: ChildLine.

Childs, C. (2001) *Food and Nutrition in the Early Years.* London: Hodder & Stoughton.

CYPU (2001) *Learning to Listen: Core Principles for the Involvement of Children and Young People.* Children and Young People's Unit. London: DfES.

DCMS (2004) *Getting Serious About Play: A review of children's play.* London: Department for Culture, Media & Sport.

Department of Education and Science (1978) *Special Educational Needs* (The Warnock Report). London: HMSO.

DfEE (1998a) *Guidance on first aid for schools: a good practice guide.* London: Department for Education and Employment.

DfEE (1998b) *Health and safety of pupils on educational visits: a good practice guide.* London: DfEE.

DfEE (2000a) *Guidance on the Education of Children and Young People in Public Care.* London: DfEE.

DfEE (2000b) *Learning Journey 3–7.* London: DfEE.

DfEE (2001a) *National literacy strategy: developing early writing.* London: DfEE.

DfEE (2001b) *Promoting Children's Mental Health within Early Years and School Settings.* London: DfEE.

DfES (1998) *The National Literacy Strategy – Framework for teaching YR to Y6.* London: Department for Education and Skills.

DfES (1999) *Numeracy Strategy – Framework for teaching mathematics from Reception to Year 6.* London: DfES.

DfES (2000) *Bullying: Don't Suffer in Silence – an anti-bullying pack for schools.* London: DfES.

DfES (2001a) *The Key Stage 3 National Strategy – Framework for teaching English: Years 7, 8 and 9.* London: DfES.

DfES (2001b) *The Key Stage 3 National Strategy – Framework for teaching mathematics: Years 7, 8 and 9.* London: DfES.

DfES (2001c) *The Special Educational Needs Code of Practice 2001.* London: HMSO.

DfES (2002) *Birth to Three Matters: A framework to support children in their earliest years.* London: DfES.

DfES (2003a) *Key Stage 3 National Strategy: advice on whole school behaviour and attendance policy.* London: HMSO.

DfES (2003b) The National standards for under 8s day care and childminding. London: DfES.

DfES (2003c) *Primary National Strategy – Speaking, listening, learning: working with children in Key Stages 1 and 2 Handbook.* London: DfES.

DfES (2003d) *Electronic Adult Numeracy Core Curriculum with Access for All.* London: DfES.

DfES (2004a) *Early Support Professional Guidance.* London: DfES.

DfES (2004b) *Every Child Matters: Change for Children.* London: DfES.

DfES (2004c) *Need a Nanny? A Guide for Parents.* London: DfES.

DfES (2005a) *Primary National Strategy: KEEP – Key Elements of Effective Practice.* London: DfES.

DfES (2005b) *Skills for Communities – Skills for Life: The National Strategy for improving adult literacy and numeracy skills.* London: DfES.

DfES (2005c) *Family Literacy, Language and Numeracy – a guide for children's centres.* London: DfES.

DfES (2006a) *The Early Years Foundation Stage: Consultation on a single quality framework for services to children from birth to five.* London: DfES.

DfES (2006b) *Information Sharing: Practitioners' Guide.* London: DfES.

DfES (2006c) *Primary National Strategy – Primary Framework for Literacy and Mathematics.* London: DfES.

DfES/DH (2005) *Managing Medicines in Schools and Early Years Settings.* London: DfES/Department of Health.

DH (1991) *The Children Act 1989 Guidance and regulations ~ Volume 2: Family Support, day care and educational provision for young children.* London: HMSO.

DH (2000) *Assessing Children in Need and their Families: Practice Guidance.* London: The Stationery Office.

DH (2001) *Transforming Children's Services – An Evaluation of Local Responses to the Quality Protects Programme.* London: DH.

DH (2002) *Promoting the Health of Looked After Children.* London: HMSO.

DH (2003a) *What to do if you're worried a child is being abused.* London: HMSO.

DH (2003b) *Infant Feeding Recommendation.* London: DH.

DH (2004a) *Choosing Health: making healthy choices easier.* London: TSO.

DH (2004b) *Choosing Health: making healthy choices easier – Executive Summary.* London: TSO.

DH (2005a) *Choosing a better diet: a food and health action plan.* London: DH.

DH (2005b) *Choosing activity: a physical activity action plan.* London: DH.

DH (2005c) *Delivering Choosing Health: making healthier choices easier.* London: DH.

DH (2006) *Birth to Five: 2006 Edition.* London: DH.

DH et al. (2000) *Framework for the Assessment of Children in Need and Their Families.* London: The Stationery Office.

Douch, P. (2004) 'What does inclusive play actually look like?' in *Playtoday.* Issue 42, May/June.

Drummond, M. et al. (1994) *Making Assessment Work.* Swindon: NFER Nelson.

Dunn, K. et al. (2004) *Research on developing accessible play space: final report.* London: HMSO.

Elfer, P. (2005) 'Observation Matters' (see Abbott, L. and Langston, A.)

Fletcher, B. and Murison, J. (2005) *Taking Part: Making out-of-school-hours learning happen for children in care.* London: ContinYou.

Fontana, D. (1984) 'Personality and personal development' in D. Fontana (ed.) *The education of the young child.* Oxford: Blackwell.

Gatiss, S. (1991) '5. Parents as Partners' in *Signposts to Special Needs: An information pack on meeting special educational needs in the mainstream classroom.* London: National Children's Bureau and NES Arnold.

Gillespie Edwards, A. (2002) *Relationships and Learning: caring for children from birth to three.* London: National Children's Bureau.

Goleman, D. (1996) *Emotional intelligence.* Bloomsbury.

Gregg, P. et al. (2005) 'The Effects of a Mother's Return to Work Decision on Child Development in the UK' in the *Economic Journal,* February. London: Royal Economic Society.

Harding, J. and Meldon-Smith, L. (2001) *How to make observations and assessments.* 2nd Edition. London: Hodder & Stoughton.

Hines, D. (2002) *Resolving Conflict in Marriage.* Pittsburgh, PA: Whitaker House.

HM Government (2006) *Working Together to Safeguard Children: a guide to inter-agency working to safeguard and promote the welfare of children.* London: TSO.

Home-Start International (1999) *Home-Start International Statement of Principles and Practice* (www.home-start-int.org).

Houghton, D. and McColgan, M. (1995) *Working with children.* Collins Educational.

HPA (2001) *Nutrition matters for the early years: Guidance for feeding under fives in the childcare setting.* Belfast: Health Promotion Agency.

HSE (2004) *Getting to grips with manual handling: A short guide.* Leaflet INDG143 (rev2). London: Health and Safety Executive Books.

Hutchcroft, D. (1981) *Making language work.* London: McGraw-Hill.

ILAM (1999) *Indoor Play Areas: Guidance on Safe Practice.* Reading: Institute of Leisure and Amenity Management.

Jordan, R. et al. (2001) *A Guide to Services for Children with Autistic Spectrum Disorders for Commissioners and Providers.* The Mental Health Foundation.

Kamen, T. (2000) *Psychology for childhood studies.* London: Hodder & Stoughton.

Kamen, T. (2003) *Teaching assistant's handbook.* London: Hodder & Stoughton.

Kamen, T. (2004) *The Nanny Handbook.* London: Hodder & Stoughton.

Kamen, T. (2005) *The Playworker's handbook.* London: Hodder Arnold.

Kirby, P. et al. (2003) *Building a Culture of Participation: Involving children and young people in policy, service planning, delivery and evaluation – Handbook.* London: DfES.

LGNTO (2001) *Teaching/Classroom Assistants National Occupational Standards.* London: Local Government National Training Organisation.

Lindenfield, G. (1995) *Self Esteem.* London: Thorsons.

Lindon, L. (2002a) *Good practice in working with babies, toddlers and very young children.* London: SureStart.

Lindon (2002b) *What is Play?* Children's Play Information Service factsheet. London: National Children's Bureau.

LT Scotland (2005) *Birth to three: supporting our youngest children.* Glasgow: Learning and Teaching Scotland.

Matterson, E. (1989) *Play with a purpose for the under sevens.* London: Penguin.

Miller, L. (2002) *Observation Observed: An outline of the nature and practice of infant observation.* London: Tavistock Clinic Foundation.

Moon, A. (1992) 'Take care of yourself' in *Child Education*, February. Leamington Spa: Scholastic.

Mort, L. and Morris, J. (1989) *Bright ideas for early years: getting started.* Leamington Spa: Scholastic.

Moyle, D. (1976) *The teaching of reading.* London: Ward Lock Educational.

NCB (2005) *Healthy Care Programme Handbook.* London: National Children's Bureau.

NDNA (2004) *National Occupational Standards in Children's Care, Learning and Development.* Brighouse: NDNA.

NFPI (2004) *Is it legal? A parents' guide to the law.* London: National Family and Parenting Institute.

NIMH (2001) *Helping Children and Adolescents Cope with Violence and Disasters.* Bethseda, MD: National Institute of Mental Health.

NPFA et al. (2000) *Best Play: What play provision should do for children.* London: National Playing Fields Association.

Ofsted (2003) *Guidance to the Home Childcaring Code of Practice for Children Under Eight.* London: Ofsted Publications.

Ofsted (2006) *Are you ready for your inspection? A guide to inspections of childcare and nursery education conducted by Ofsted.* London: Ofsted Publications.

O'Hagan, M. and Smith, M. (1994) *Special Issues in Child Care.* London: Baillière Tindall.

Parentzone (2005) *Making the difference: out of school learning.* Edinburgh: Scottish Executive.

Parsloe, E. (1999) *The Manager as Coach and Mentor.* London: Chartered Institute of Personnel & Development.

PSLA (2004) *Volunteering for Your Pre-school Committee.* London: Pre-school Learning Alliance.

PSLA (2006) *Funding Factsheet.* London: Pre-school Learning Alliance.

QCA (2000) *Curriculum guidance for the foundation stage.* London: Qualifications and Curriculum Authority.

QCA (2001) *Planning for learning in the Foundation Stage.* London: QCA.

QCA (2003) *Foundation Stage Profile Handbook.* London: QCA.

QCA (2005) *ICT in the foundation stage.* London: QCA.

QCA/DfES (2002) *Assessment and reporting arrangements 2003.* London: QCA.

Rawstrone, A. (2006) 'Keep it clean' in *Nursery World*, 25 May. London: TSL Education Ltd.

RoSPA (2004a) *Play Safety Information Sheet: Information Sheet Number 16 – Legal Aspects of Safety on Children's Play Areas.* Birmingham: Royal Society for the Prevention of Accidents.

RoSPA (2004b) *Play Safety Information Sheet: Information Sheet Number 25 – Risk assessment of Children's Play Areas.* Birmingham: Royal Society for the Prevention of Accidents.
Rutter, M. (1991) *Maternal deprivation reassessed.* London: Penguin.

Scottish Executive (2006) *Nutritional guidance for early years: food choices for children aged 1–5 years in early education and childcare settings.* (Query insert place) Scottish Executive.
Scottish Executive (2005) *Birth to three: supporting our youngest children.* Edinburgh: Scottish Executive.
SkillsActive (2004) *National Occupational Standards NVQ/SVQ Level 3 in Playwork.* London: SkillsActive.
Smart, C. (2001) *Special Educational Needs Policy.* Abbots Bromley: Special Needs Information Press.
SNDRI (2006) *Weaning.* Glasgow: Scottish Nutrition & Diet Resources Initiative.
SPRITO/SkillsActive Playwork Unit (2001) *Recruitment, Training and Qualifications in Playwork – an Employer's Guide.* SPRITO/SkillsActive Playwork Unit.
Stoppard, M. (1990) *The New Baby Care Book.* London: Dorling Kindersley.
Street, C. (2002) The Benefits of Play. Highlight No. 195. London: National Children's Bureau.
SureStart (2003a) *Managing finance.* London: SureStart.
SureStart (2003b) *Managing your childcare business.* London: SureStart.
SureStart (2003c) *Marketing your childcare business.* London: SureStart.

Taylor, J. (1973) *Reading and writing in the first school.* London: George Allen and Unwin.
Tharp and Gallimore (1991) 'A theory of teaching as assisted performance' in Light, P., Sheldon, S. and Woodhead, M. (eds.) (1991) *Learning to think.* London: Routledge.
Tidy, C. (2006) *Child Health Surveillance.* Leeds: Egton Medical Information Systems.
Tizard, B. (1991) 'Working mothers and the care of young children' (see Woodhead, M.).
Tobias, C. (1996) *The Way They Learn.* Colorado Springs: Focus on the Family Publishing.
Tough, J. (1984) 'How young children develop and use language' in D. Fontana (ed.)
The education of the young child. Oxford: Blackwell.

Watkinson, A. (2003) *The essential guide for competent teaching assistants.* London: David Fulton Publishers.
WCRF UK (2004) *Choosing Health? White Paper: response from World Cancer Research Fund.* London: World Cancer Research Fund UK.
Whitehead, M. (1996) *The development of language and literacy.* London: Hodder & Stoughton.
Wilcox, B. (1994) 'A Rural Initiative' in *Child Education,* June. Leamington Spa: Scholastic.
Wing, L. (2003) *The Autistic Spectrum: A Guide for Parents and Professionals.* Revised Edition. London: Constable and Robinson.
Wood, S. (1996) *Qualitative and Quantitative Assessment of Provision.* Bognor Regis: Fair Play for Children.
Woodhead, M. (1991) 'Psychology and the cultural construction of children's needs' in M. Woodhead, P. Light and R. Carr (eds.) *Growing up in a changing society.* London: Routledge.

Further reading

Introduction

Amos, J. (2003) *Writing a Winning CV: Essential CV writing skills that will get you the job you want.* How to Books.

Early Years National Training Organisation (2003) *Get that job in Early Education, Childcare and Playwork.* [Available from the Early Years NTO website: www.early-years-nto.org.uk/]

Kamen, T. (2003) *Teaching Assistant's Handbook.* Hodder & Stoughton.

Kamen, T. (2004) *The Nanny Handbook: The Essential Guide to Being a Nanny.* Hodder & Stoughton.

Kamen, T. (2005) *The Playworker's Handbook.* Hodder Arnold.

Lifetime Careers (1998) *Working with Children and Young People.* Hodder & Stoughton.

Parkinson, M. (2002) *Your Job Search Made Easy: Everything you need to know about Applications, Interviews and Tests.* Kogan Page.

Petrie, P. (19997) *Communicating with Children and Adults: Interpersonal Skills for Early Years and Play Work.* 2nd Edition. Hodder Arnold.

Chapter 1

Children and Young People's Unit (2001) *Learning to Listen: Core Principles for the Involvement of Children and Young People.* DfES. [Available online: www.dfee.gov.uk/cypu]

Lindon, J. (2006) *Equality in Early Childhood: Linking Theory and Practice.* Hodder Arnold.

Petrie, P. (1997) *Communicating with Children and Adults: Interpersonal Skills for Early Years and Playwork.* Hodder Arnold.

Chapter 2

Dare, A. and O'Donovan, M. (2000) *Good Practice in Child Safety.* Nelson Thornes.

DfES (2003) *The National standards for under 8s day care and childminding.* DfES.

HSE (2004) *Getting to grips with manual handling: A short guide.* Leaflet INDG143 (rev2). HSE Books.

HSE (2005) *COSHH: a brief guide to the regulations: What you need to know about the Control of Substances Hazardous to Health Regulations 2002.* Leaflet INDG136 (rev3). HSE Books.

HSE (2006a) *Five steps to risk assessment.* INDG163 (rev2). HSE Books.

HSE (2006b) *Health and safety law: What you should know.* Leaflet. HSE Books.

[Single copies of these HSE leaflets available free from: www.hse.gov.uk]

St. John Ambulance, St. Andrew's Ambulance Association and British Red Cross (2006) *First Aid Manual.* Dorling Kindersley.

Chapter 3

Harding, J. and Meldon-Smith, L. (2000) *Helping Young Children to Develop.* 2nd Edition. Hodder & Stoughton.

Harding, J. and Meldon-Smith, L. (2001) *How to make observations and assessments.* 2nd Edition. Hodder & Stoughton.

Hitchin, V. (1999) *Right from the Start: Effective Planning and Assessment in the Early Years.* Hodder Murray.

Hobart, C. and Frankel, J. (2005) *A Practical Guide to Activities for Young Children.* 3rd Edition. Nelson Thornes.
Kamen, T. (2000) *Psychology for Childhood Studies.* Hodder & Stoughton.
Lindon, J. (2005) *Understanding Child Development: Linking Theory and Practice.* Hodder Arnold.
Sheridan, M.D. (1997) *From Birth to Five Years: Children's Developmental Progress.* Routledge.
Wyse, D. and Hawtin, A. (1999) *Children: a multi-professional perspective.* Arnold. [Covers child development and learning from birth to 18 years.]

Chapter 4

Abbott, L. and Moylett, H. (eds.) (1997) *Working with the Under Threes: Training and Professional Development.* Open University Press.
Dryden, L. (2005) *Essential Early Years.* Hodder Arnold.
Lindenfield, G. (2000) *Self esteem: simple steps to developing self-reliance and perseverance.* HarperCollins.
Miller, L. et al. (2005) *Developing Early Years Practice.* David Fulton Publishers.
Mitchell, A. (2001) *Study Skills for Early Years Students.* Hodder & Stoughton.

Chapter 5

Alderson, P. (2000) *Young Children's Rights: Exploring Beliefs, Principles and Practice.* Jessica Kingsley Publishers.
Department for Education and Skills (2004) *Every Child Matters: Change for Children.* [Available online: www.everychildmatters.co.uk]
Department of Health (2003) *What To Do If You're Worried A Child Is Being Abused.* DH.
(Free copies of this booklet are available via the DH website: www.dh.gov.uk)
Elliott, M. and Kilpatrick, J. (2002) *How to stop bullying: a Kidscape training guide.* Kidscape.
Lindon, J. (2003) *Child Protection.* 2nd Edition. Hodder & Stoughton.
Lindon, J. (2006) *Equality in Early Childhood: Linking Theory and Practice.* Hodder Arnold.
Tassoni, P. (2003) *Supporting Special Needs: Understanding Inclusion in the Early Years.* Heinemann.
UK Committee for Unicef (2000) *The Convention on the Rights of the Child.* Unicef.

Chapter 6

Cole, J. et al. (2001) *Helping Children Learn Through Activities in the Early Years.* Hodder & Stoughton.
Harding, J. and Meldon-Smith, L. (2000) *Helping Young Children to Develop.* 2nd Edition. Hodder & Stoughton.
Lindon, J. (2005) *Understanding Child Development: Linking Theory and Practice.* Hodder Arnold.
Whiteford, R. et al. (1996) *Hands on Display.* Belair Publications.

Chapter 7

Childs, C. (2001) *Food and Nutrition in the Early Years.* Hodder & Stoughton.
Dare, A. and O'Donovan, M. (2002) *A Practical Guide to Child Nutrition.* 2nd Edition. Nelson Thornes.

Harding, J. and Meldon-Smith, L. (2000) *Helping Young Children to Develop.* 2nd Edition. Hodder & Stoughton.
HPA (2001) *Nutrition matters for the early years: Guidance for feeding under fives in the childcare setting.* Health Promotion Agency. [www.healthpromotionagency.org.uk]
Scottish Executive (2006) *Nutritional guidance for early years: food choices for children aged 1–5 years in early education and childcare settings.* Scottish Executive. [Available free online: www.scotland.gov.uk]

Chapter 8

Brown, F. (ed.) (2002) *Playwork: Theory and Practice.* Open University Press.
Children's Play Council (2002) *More than Swings and Roundabouts – Planning for Outdoor Play.* Children's Play Council.
Kamen, T. (2005) *The Playworker's Handbook.* Hodder Arnold.
Kidsactive (2000) *Side by Side: Guidelines for inclusive play.* Kidsactive.
Lindon, J. (2001) *Understanding Children's Play.* Nelson Thornes.
Tassoni, P. (2005) *Planning Play and the Early Years.* Heinemann Educational.

Chapter 9

Glenn, A. et al. (2003) *Behaviour in the Early Years.* David Fulton Publishers.
Kay, J. (2006) *Managing Behaviour in the Early Years.* Continuum International Publishing Group.
Kutscher, M. (2005) *Kids in the Syndrome Mix of ADHD, LD, Asperger's, Tourette's, Bipolar and More!: The One Stop Guide for Parents, Teachers and Other Professionals.* Jessica Kingsley Publishers.
Mortimer, H. (2002) *Behavioural and Emotional Difficulties.* Scholastic.
Train, A. (2004) *ADHD: How to Deal with Very Difficult Children.* Souvenir Press Ltd.
Wing, L. (2003) *The Autistic Spectrum: A Guide for Parents and Professionals.* Revised Edition. Constable and Robinson.

Chapter 10

Bayley, R. et al. (2003) *Smooth Transitions: Building on the Foundation Stage.* Featherstone Education Ltd.
Broadhead, P. (2003) *Early Years Play and Learning: Developing Social Skills and Co-operation.* Routledge Falmer.
Dowling, M. (2000) *Young Children's Personal, Social and Emotional Development.* Paul Chapman Publications.
Lindenfield, G. (2000) *Self esteem: simple steps to developing self-reliance and perseverance.* HarperCollins.
Newman, T. and Blackburn, S. (2002) *Transitions in the Lives of Children and Young People: Resilience Factors.* Scottish Executive.

Chapter 11

Bruce, T. (2004) *Cultivating Creativity in Babies, Toddlers & Young Children.* Hodder & Stoughton.
Childs, C. (2001) *Food and Nutrition in the Early Years.* Hodder & Stoughton.
Health Promotion Agency [www.healthpromotionagency.org.uk/Resources/nutrition/nutritionmatters.htm].

HPA (2001) *Nutrition matters for the early years: Guidance for feeding under fives in the childcare setting.*
Hughes, A. (2006) *Developing Play for the Under 3s: The Treasure Basket and Heuristic Play.* David Fulton Publishers.
Meggit, C. (1999) *Caring for Babies: A practical guide.* Hodder & Stoughton.
Parker, L. (2006) *How to Manage Accidents, Illness and Infection in the Nursery.* David Fulton Publishers.
Parlakian, R. and Seibel, N. (2002) *Building Strong Foundations: Practical Guidance for Promoting the Social-Emotional Development of Infants and Toddlers.* Zero to Three [www.zerotothree.org].
Scottish Executive (2006) *Nutritional guidance for early years: food choices for children aged 1–5 years in early education and childcare settings.* Scottish Executive.
[www.scotland.gov.uk/Publications/2006/01/18153659/15]

Chapter 12

Bruce, T. (2001) *Learn Through Play: Babies, Toddlers & The Foundation Stage.* Hodder & Stoughton.
Bruce, T. and Meggitt, C. (2002) *Child Care and Education.* 3rd Edition. Hodder & Stoughton.
DfES (2006) *Primary National Strategy – Primary Framework for literacy and mathematics.* London: DfES. [The online version can be accessed at www.standards.dfes.gov.uk/primaryframeworks]
Harding, J. and Meldon-Smith, L. (2001) *How to Make Observations and Assessments.* 2nd Edition. Hodder & Stoughton.
Hobart, C. and Frankel, J. (2005) *A Practical Guide to Activities for Young Children.* Nelson Thornes.
Hutchin, V. (2003) *Observing and Assessing for the Foundation Stage Profile.* Hodder Murray.
Learning and Teaching Scotland (2003) *Early Learning, Forward Thinking: The Policy Framework for ICT in the Early Years.* Learning and Teaching Scotland.
Pound, L. (2005) *How Children Learn: From Montessori to Vygotsky – Educational Theories and Approaches Made Easy.* Step Forward Publishing Ltd.
Siraj-Blatchford, J. and Whitebread, D. (2003) *Supporting ICT in the Early Years.* Open University Press.
QCA (2001) *Planning for learning in the Foundation Stage.* QCA.

Chapter 13

Berger, A. and Gross, J. (ed.) (1999) *Teaching the literacy hour in the inclusive classroom.* David Fulton Publishers.
Briggs, M. and Pritchard, A. (2002) *Using ICT in primary mathematics teaching.* Learning Matters.
Godwin, D. and Perkins, M. (2002) *Teaching Language and Literacy in the Early Years.* David Fulton Publishers.
Kamen, T. (2003) *Teaching Assistant's Handbook.* Hodder & Stoughton.
Palmer, S. and Bayley, R. (2004) *Foundations of Literacy: A Balanced Approach to Language, Listening and Literacy Skills in the Early Years.* Network Educational Press Ltd.
Tanner, H. et al. (2002) *Developing numeracy in the secondary school: a practical guide for students and teachers.* David Fulton Publishers.
Whitehead, M.R. (2004) *Language and Literacy in the Early Years.* Sage Publications Ltd.
Williams, S. and Goodman, S. (2000) *Helping young children with maths.* Hodder & Stoughton.

Chapter 14

Alcott, M. (2002) *An Introduction to Children with Special Needs.* Hodder & Stoughton.

Dare, A. and O'Donovan, M. (2005) *Good Practice in Caring for Young Children with Special Needs.* 2nd Edition. Nelson Thornes.

Mortimer, H. (2002) *Special Needs Handbook.* Scholastic.

Tassoni, P. (2003) *Supporting Special Needs: Understanding Inclusion in the Early Years.* Heinemann.

Wilson, R. (2003) *Special Educational Needs in the Early Years.* Routledge Falmer.

Chapter 15

Brett, T. Litz (2004) *Early intervention for trauma and loss.* Guilford Press.

Childline booklet *'I can't stop feeling sad'* at: www.childline.org.uk/BereavementReport.asp

DH (2003) *What To Do If You're Worried A Child Is Being Abused.* Department of Health.
(Free copies of this booklet are available via the DH website: www.dh.gov.uk)

Gilligan, R. (2001) *Promoting resilience: A resource guide on working with children in the care system.* British Agencies for Adoption and Fostering.

Jones, D. (2003) *Communicating with Vulnerable Children.* Gaskell.

Lindon, J. (2003) *Child Protection.* 2nd Edition. Hodder & Stoughton.

NSPCC (1997) *Turning Points: A Resource Pack for Communicating With Children.* NSPCC.

Chapter 16

Dwivedi, K.N. (ed.) (1997) *Enhancing Parenting Skills: A Guide for Professionals Working with Parents.* John Wiley and Sons Ltd.

Hobart, C. and Frankel, J. (2003) *A Practical Guide to Working with Parents.* Nelson Thornes.

Kamen, T. (2003) *The Nanny Handbook.* Hodder Arnold.

Siraj-Blatchford, J. and Clarke, P. (2000) *Supporting Identity, Diversity and Language in the Early Years.* Open University Press.

Smidt, S. (2002) *A Guide to Early Years Practice.* 2nd Edition. Routledge.

Weinburger, J. (ed.) (2005) *Learning from Sure Start: Working with Young Children and Their Families.* Open University Press.

Whalley, M. & The Pen Green Family Centre Team (1997) *Working with Parents.* Hodder & Stoughton.

Chapter 17

Harding, J. and Meldon-Smith, L. (2003) *Childminding: A Step By Step Guide.* Hodder & Stoughton.

Jameson, H. and Watson, M. (1998) *Starting and Running a Nursery: The Business of Early Years Care.* Nelson Thornes.

Ofsted (2005) *Day care: Guide to registration for day-care providers.* Ofsted Publications.
[Available free from: www.ofsted.gov.uk/publications]

PSLA (2004) *Planning a Pre-school Curriculum: Making it work for you.* Available to order from the Pre-school Learning Alliance: www.pre-school.org.uk.

SureStart (2003a) *Managing finance.* SureStart. Available free from: www.surestart.gov.uk/_doc/P0001660.pdf.

SureStart (2003b) *Marketing your childcare business.* SureStart. Available free from: www.surestart.gov.uk/_doc/P0001658.pdf.

Chapter 18

Ashman, C. and Green, S. (2004) *Self-Development for Early Years Managers.* David Fulton Publishers.

Brockbank, A. and McGill, I. (2006) *Facilitating Reflective Learning Through Mentoring and Coaching.* Kogan Page Ltd.

Department of Trade and Industry (DTI) (August 2001) *Contracts of Employment* (PL810 Rev 6) and (August 2000) *Written Statements of Employment Practice* (PL700 Rev 5). Both are available from your local Jobcentre Plus or the DTI website: www.dti.gov.uk.

DTI (July 2003) *Your Guide to the Working Time Regulations.* A free booklet is available from the DTI or the DTI website (see above).

DTI (July 2003) *Individual Rights of Employees* (PL 716 Rev 10), and (May 2003) *Redundancy Entitlement-Statutory Rights: a guide for employees* (PL808 Rev 6). These booklets can be obtained from your local Jobcentre Plus or the DTI website (see above).

Lyus, V. (1998) *Management in the early years.* Hodder & Stoughton.

SureStart (2003) *Recruitment and retention: A good practice guide for early years, childcare and playwork providers.* Available free from: www.surestart.gov.uk/_doc/P0000375.pdf.

SureStart (2003) *Managing your childcare business.* Available free from: www.surestart.gov.uk/_doc/P0001657.pdf.

Index

Index